Exploring ART

A GLOBAL, THEMATIC APPROACH

Margaret Lazzari
The School of Fine Arts, University of Southern California

Dona Schlesier
Divine Word College

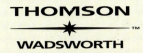
THOMSON
WADSWORTH

Australia • Canada • Mexico • Singapore • Spain
United Kingdom • United States

To Mike, "in sickness and in health," and to Julia Rose,
with thanks for walking this road with us
Margaret Lazzari

For Douglas, Kimberly, Robert,
Jackson Calder (Jake), and Luca Peter Douglas,
with gratitude and love
Dona Schlesier

Brief Contents

Contents

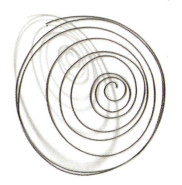

Preface

Art opens up the world: the world of many cultures, the past and present worlds, the world of the human heart and mind.

With the second edition, we believe again that the best way to learn about art is to start with essential ideas and to see them made concrete in art from around the world. *Exploring Art* remains **global** and **thematic.** It encourages critical thinking and meets the needs of today's students from diverse backgrounds. The new edition, however, has several very exciting additions that strengthen an already engaging and innovative approach to learning about art.

CONTINUING FEATURES OF THIS TEXT

GLOBAL, THEMATIC APPROACH

Art from around the world is fully integrated throughout this book. Students are enriched and challenged when studying art in the context of themes and ideas, rather than chronology or geography. The themes (*Survival and Beyond, Religion, The State,* and *Self and Society*) show art to be a meaningful endeavor that deals with basic human concerns. By studying integrated global art traditions, the students can see the similarities that connect cultures as well as their differences. *Exploring Art* reveals the universality of the human impulse to create art.

ILLUSTRATION PROGRAM

The artwork in this book represents an almost equal balance of Western and non-Western traditions. It includes a larger percentage of women and minority artists than almost any other general art text available today. Found throughout this book are examples of painting, sculpture, photography, and architecture; new multimedia forms, such as digital art and performance; and ceramics, jewelry, and film.

We examine several artworks in multiple contexts. An artwork may be used to illustrate a formal concept and then used again in discussing its content. For those images that are repeated, the caption gives the cross-reference so students can easily find the other coverage of that art in the text.

ACTIVE LEARNING

We want to encourage readers to be active and questioning as they encounter new works of art, and for that reason this book is structured around questions. The Part Openers are questions about the nature of art and art making. At the beginning of each chapter is a list of questions for students to consider while reading, to help them critically evaluate the chapter's material.

At the end of each chapter, a short *Food for Thought* section asks students to enter into the unresolved debates and moral issues associated with art in our time and in the past.

Connections are cross-references that appear throughout the book, relating works, artists, cultures, ideas, and themes. These lateral-thinking devices help students link ideas across chapters. For example, the relationship between food and art is covered in Chapter 7, Food and Shelter. One *Connection* asks students to consider whether utilitarian dishes and storage vessels can be considered art, and refers them to Chapter 1 for more discussion. Another Food and Shelter *Connection* directs them to Chapter 9 to read about deities concerned with successful crops and water supply.

NEW TO THIS EDITION

HISTORICAL MATERIAL

New to the second edition are **World History in Context boxes** that appear in Chapters 7–16, which are the thematic chapters. They contain chronological summaries of world history and important developments in religion, culture, and technology. Each is accompanied by a **map** and **timeline.** The History boxes help readers place the artworks in *Exploring Art* in their historical and geographic contexts.

NEW DESIGN

This edition of *Exploring Art* is beautifully designed with larger, higher-quality artwork and easily readable pages. It is a visual pleasure throughout!

NEW ARTWORK AND MORE CONTEMPORARY ARTWORK

We have added many new images to this edition, and the vast majority of them are from the past few years. This strengthens the contemporary content of the book, making it more relevant to today's students.

REORGANIZED STRUCTURE

The second edition of *Exploring Art: A Global, Thematic Approach* contains sixteen chapters and has been completely reorganized around two Parts. This gives a tighter focus to the entire book. The key concepts are (1) an understanding and appreciation of artworks from around the world and (2) the function of art in human societies.

In Part 1, we have brought together the information the reader needs for understanding definitions of art, exploring ways to analyze artworks, and examining art world structures.

Chapter 1, A Human Phenomenon, is completely rewritten and is a composite of two separate first-edition chapters. This provides a more cohesive presentation of the definitions of art, art vocabulary, global styles, and categories of art, such as high art versus popular culture. Now this chapter forms a solid conceptual foundation upon which the rest of the book is built.

Chapter 2, The Language of Art, and Chapter 3, The Language of Architecture, still present thorough coverage of the elements and principles of art as well as the structural systems of architecture. Both chapters have been edited for greater clarity and conciseness.

The fourth chapter, Deriving Meaning, has added new, contemporary material to the overall question of how art and architecture have meaning, and the ways by which people understand what the meanings are. Visual Culture is introduced as a twenty-first-century philosophical position from which to critique art.

Both Chapter 5 and Chapter 6, Who Makes Art? and What Do We Do with Art?, have been shortened to focus on key concepts. The Chapter 6 text has an expanded discussion of personal art collections.

In Part 2, the theme chapters are still grouped under four major headings: *Survival and Beyond, Religion, The State,* and *Self and Society.* Within those headings, however, the chapters have been reorganized for even more thought-provoking juxtapositions of ideas.

Chapter 7 combines two first-edition chapters to examine why humans have turned to art in relation to Food and Shelter: to use art to help sustain life through them, to expand the aesthetic dimension and pleasurable appreciation of both, and to understand our relationship to them. The chapter contains a new model by Iraqi-born architect Zaha Hadid and a discussion of the recent emergence of Deconstructivist architecture.

Reproduction and Sexuality are covered in Chapter 8, again combining material from two first-edition chapters. New to the second edition are works by Rogier van der Weyden, Alice Neel, and Catherine Opie. Readers see that art can be used for widely varying purposes, such as sympathetic magic or socially critical analysis, in regard to the sensitive topics of sexuality and procreation.

Deities and Places of Worship are examined in a single chapter, Chapter 9, rather than split into two. Placing sacred imagery and sacred architecture together results in a more coherent overview of religious art.

Chapter 10 is Mortality and Immortality, which deals with funerary and commemorative art. New to this chapter is *Tribute in Light,* the temporary light sculpture memorial at the site of the World Trade Center, as well as the designs for the new center and permanent memorial, *Reflecting Absence.*

Power, Politics, and Glory, Chapter 11, has been revised to show the ways that art and architecture contribute to the power of the state or of individual rulers as well as documenting or commenting on war and peace. This is a combination of two first-edition chapters that thoroughly lays out the ways that artworks become instruments of power.

Chapter 12, Social Protest/Affirmation, continues as an investigation of art that protests injustice or affirms the rights of the oppressed. Additions to this chapter include fourteenth-century Italian artist Ambrogio Lorenzetti as well as very recent pieces by Mona Hatoum, Pepón Osorio, Yinka Shonibare, and Kara Walker. These add Palestinian, Puerto Rican, and African perspectives.

As before, Chapter 13, The Body, covers the wide range of body imagery found around the world. Recent works by artists Jin Soo Kim, Mariko Mori, and Bill Viola show body imagery in relation to dolls, pop culture, industrial detritus, and historical paintings.

The topics of Race, Gender, Clan, and Class were formerly covered in two separate chapters, but here are together in Chapter 14. This thought-provoking combination makes sense, given that artists who deal with these socially sensitive issues often use similar strategies in their work.

Chapter 15, Nature, Knowledge, and Technology, has been rewritten to be more concise and clear. We have augmented the text with a recent work by Chris Ofili, an artist whose work has been made sensational by his use of elephant waste products.

Chapter 16, Entertainment, still looks at the many ways that art functions as entertainment, or the ways that art and the entertainment industries overlap. New works by Laurie Anderson, Matthew Barney, and Frank Gehry bring the material up to date.

ANCILLARY PACKAGE

FOR INSTRUCTORS

INSTRUCTOR'S GUIDE AND TEST BANK

This useful tool—presented in both print and electronic formats—includes detailed chapter outlines, discussion topics, studio and class projects, and support material. It also provides chapter tests with multiple-choice and short essay questions. Sample syllabi are also enclosed.

EXAMVIEW®

ExamView computerized testing (available on a cross-platform CD-ROM) allows you to easily customize the *Test Bank* provided in the *Instructor's Guide* or to create your own tests.

MULTIMEDIA MANAGER

This one-stop lecture tool makes it easy to assemble, edit, publish, and present custom lectures for your art appreciation course using Microsoft® PowerPoint®. Designed specifically to accompany the text, *Multimedia Manager* lets you combine high-quality, projectable digital images and lecture outlines from this CD-ROM, the Web, and your own sources—culminating in a powerful, personalized, media-enhanced presentation.

SLIDE SET

Over 120 carefully selected, high-quality, global slides will enhance your lectures. Commentary on many slides is available as a resource for instructors.

BOOK COMPANION WEB SITE

http://art.wadsworth.com/lazzari02/

This full-featured resource provides students with an online *Study Guide,* tutorial quizzing, *InfoTrac® College Edition* exercises, Internet activities, links to museum Web sites, artist flashcards with pronunciations, and more.

WEBTUTOR™ TOOLBOX ON WEBCT AND BLACKBOARD

http://webtutor.thomsonlearning.com

Available FREE with this text (if requested), *WebTutor ToolBox* is preloaded with content and available via PIN code. *WebTutor ToolBox* pairs the content of the text's Book Companion Web Site with the course management functionality of a WebCT or Blackboard product. Assign materials (including online quizzes) and have the results flow automatically to your grade book. *ToolBox* is ready to use as soon as you log on—or you can customize its preloaded content by uploading images and other resources, adding Web links, or creating your own practice materials. Students have access only to student resources, while instructors have the option to access password-protected instructor resources.

FOR STUDENTS

Free with each new copy of the text!
The *ArtExperience CD-ROM* contains studio art demonstrations, interactive exercises that explore the foundations of art, and image flashcards to enhance students' understanding of art in the world and in the classroom. In addition, an interactive timeline applies the text's themes chronologically, an expanded historical feature adds further context with animated maps and other resources, and an expanded *Food for Thought* section gives guidance to students engaged in critical thinking activities.

Packaged free with each new copy of the text!
InfoTrac® College Edition
http://www.infotrac-college.com

You and your students automatically receive four months of FREE access to ***InfoTrac College Edition,*** an online library that offers complete articles from nearly five thousand scholarly and popular publications. Updated daily and going back more than twenty years, ***InfoTrac College Edition*** is great for doing homework or for catching up on the news. **New!** Students now have instant access to critical thinking and paper writing tools through *InfoWrite.*

ARTBASICS: AN ILLUSTRATED GLOSSARY AND TIMELINE

A brief introduction to the basic terms, styles, and time periods, *ArtBasics* is a handy reference for any beginning art student. It presents full-color fine art images and high-quality line art depicting the styles and techniques discussed. A four-color world map and foldout timeline are also included. Free when bundled with any new copies of *Exploring Art: A Global, Thematic Approach,* Second Edition.

STUDENT TEST PACKET

This useful, inexpensive resource features one full-length practice test per chapter, along with answers and page references in the back. Each test contains multiple-choice and essay questions.

THE MUSEUM EXPERIENCE

This practical handbook enriches any student's understanding of art in a museum setting, providing everything from a primer on museum etiquette and preparation tips to a step-by-step guide for writing a review of an exhibition or a particular piece. *The Museum Experience* includes end-of-chapter activities, a remarkable appendix that supplies readers with an extensive listing of museums across the United States and the world, a directory of Internet sites, and a glossary of art terms.

ACKNOWLEDGMENTS

Our warmest thanks and gratitude go to John Swanson, Acquisitions Editor, whose enthusiasm and support for our book have encouraged, guided, and motivated us through much of the first edition, and the entire second edition. Sharon Adams Poore has been outstanding as our Development Editor, and it is due to her guidance and oversight that you have this beautiful book in your hands. Both John and Sharon had the vision and objectivity that we needed to help us shape the second edition.

The entire production required the expertise of many, and we are grateful for their creativity, hard work, and dedication to the project. *Exploring Art* is more than just the book, and we thank Amy McGaughey, Assistant Editor, for the ancillary package, as well as Melinda Newfarmer, Technology Project Manager, who produced the media package. Cowtown Productions produced the CD-ROM. Brianna Brinkley, Editorial Assistant, maintained our art logs, and we thank her. The production phase of any book is critical, and we feel we had a wonderful team. Kirk Bomont and Trudy Brown were the Production Project Managers, while Sheila McGill was the Project Manager. Our vigilant copyeditor was Carolyn Crabtree. Our thanks also to Mark Orr, Marketing Manager, through whose efforts our book has been widely publicized.

In addition, we continue to be thankful for the original editorial team from the first edition, Barbara Rosenberg, Acquisitions Editor, and Stacey Sims, Development Editor. Our book has taken a new approach to teaching art, and without their support, the first edition would not have been realized.

Reviewers were enormously helpful, as we began the task of reshaping *Exploring Art* for the second edition. Their comments and advice guided us throughout our work, and we are very grateful to them. They include:

Janet Oliver, University of North Carolina–Greensboro; Kelly Donahue-Wallace, University of North Texas; Barbara G. Pogue, Essex County College; Lynn Metcalf, St. Cloud State University; Jeffrey Kaller, Columbus State University; Michel S. Demanche, University of Maryland Eastern Shore; Lealan N. Swanson, Jackson State University; Lynn Galbraith, University of Arizona; Robert McColl, Saint Mary's University of Minnesota; Samantha S. Birk, Indiana University–Purdue University, Fort Wayne; Marion J. de Koning, Grossmont College; Louise Lewis, California State University–Northridge; Richard Siegesmund, University of Georgia; Daniel Powell, Salve Regina University; Jocelyn Curtis, Towson University; Malia Finnegan Serrano, Grossmont College.

We also wish to acknowledge the first edition reviewers, whose comments helped shape our book from the beginning: Alan Atkinson, University of Alabama–Birmingham; Ann Stewart Balakier, University of South Dakota; Martin W. Ball, Kent State University; Gleny Beach, Southeastern Oklahoma State University; Jasmin W. Cyril, University of Minnesota–Morris; Paula Drewek, Macomb Community College; Jaymes Dudding, University of Science and Arts of Oklahoma; William B. Folkestad, Central Washington University; Robert Hardy, Cypress College; M. L. Heivly, California State University–Bakersfield; Janette Hopper, Columbia Basin College; Joyce Howell, Virginia Wesleyan College; Jeffrey A. Hughes, Webster University; Susan Josepher, Metropolitan State College; Ellen Konowitz, Vanderbilt University; Jeff Kowalski, Northern Illinois University; Charles Licka, University of Alaska–Anchorage; Sheila Lynch, Rio Hondo College; Nancy Magner, Bakersfield College; Carol Miura, Rancho Santiago College; Johanna D. Movassat, San Jose State University; Ken Nelsen, Northwest Missouri State University; Richard Nicksic, Yakima Valley Community College; Frank Oehlschlaeger, Notre Dame College; Thomas Parker, Drury College; Brian Percival, Queens College–CUNY; Robert T. Soppelsa, Washburn University; Judy Sund, Queens College–CUNY; Dianne Taylor, University of North Texas; Joe Thomas, Clarion University of Pennsylvania; Keith Williams, Concordia College–St. Paul; Kristin Woodward, Mississippi State University.

We thank our respective teaching institutions for sabbaticals, as well as our colleagues for their support, as we worked on both the first and second editions. In particular, we acknowledge Divine Word College, its president, Fr. Michael Hutchins S.V.D, the Administration, and Brother Dan Holman S.V.D. Likewise, our thanks to the School of Fine Arts of the University of Southern California and Dean Ruth Weisberg. Both of us teach wonderful students who come from all kinds of backgrounds, and even from distant lands, who motivated us to imagine and work on a thematic art appreciation book with global coverage.

Thank you to our families and friends who have provided interesting perspectives, good advice, and moral support throughout. They are too many to name. We especially thank Dona's husband, Douglas Schlesier, and also Margaret's husband and daughter, Michael Dean and Julia Lazzari-Dean. They have been truly supportive throughout the entire process, listening to ideas, helping with technical issues, and assisting with clerical tasks. They have "been there" from the very beginning. Douglas continued to give his expertise as both an artist and educator. And we thank each other, for another great writing experience together!

Art appreciation that is global in scope can foster a greater understanding among the peoples of the world. May we live in a peaceful, tolerant world.

Margaret Lazzari
Dona Schlesier

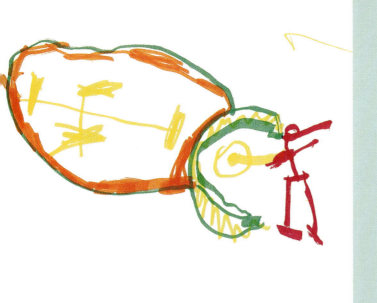

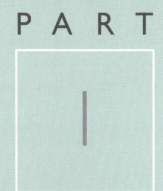

Julia Lazzari–Dean. *Dinosaur Eating a Man.* Detail of Figure 1.7. Collection of Margaret Lazzari and Mike Dean.

PART 1

WHAT IS ART, WHO MAKES IT, AND WHAT DO WE DO WITH IT?

Art has a richness and an intelligence that illuminate our lives. What are art's components, and those of architecture? Why do they have meaning? How does cultural context influence meaning?

Who are artists and what roles do they play in society? How does art become part of our lives and our history?

For the next six chapters, discussion centers on the following areas:

- The definition of art, and ways we describe and categorize it

- Art's formal qualities, and the principles for organizing them

- The structural and aesthetic systems of architecture, and architecture's relation to nature

- The ways that we come to understand meaning in art and architecture

- The training of artists, their roles within their cultures, and the means for supporting their work

- The ways people use art objects, keep them, destroy them, and study them

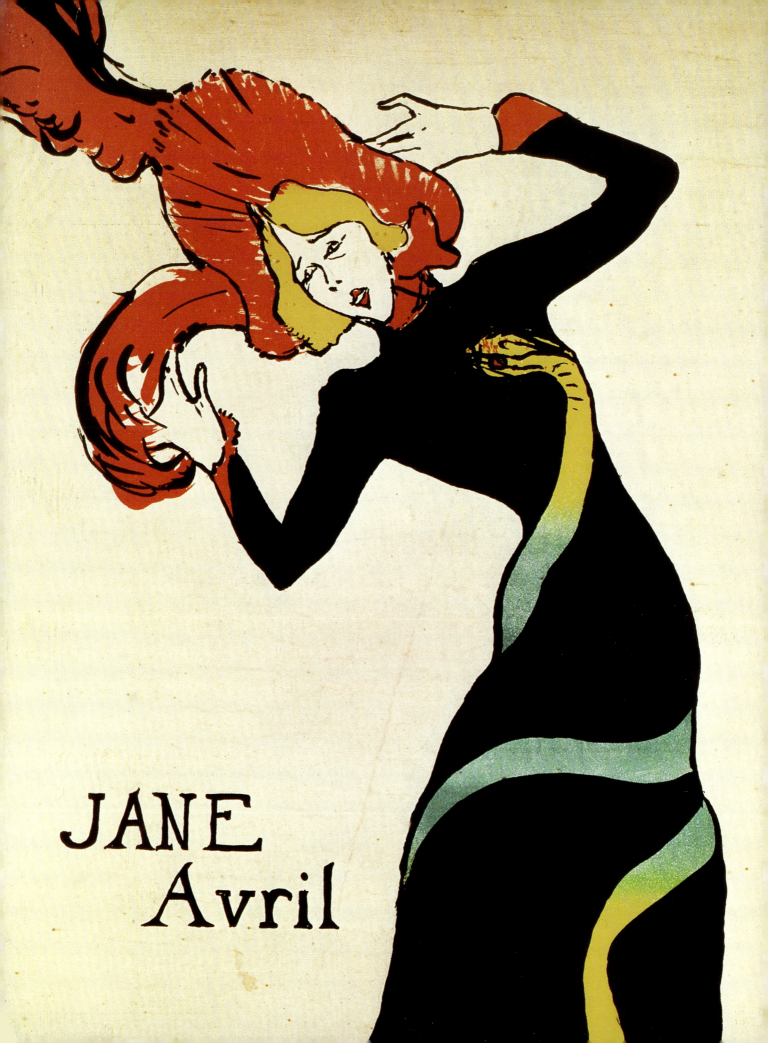

A HUMAN PHENOMENON

INTRODUCTION

What is art? Art is strictly a human phenomenon. Some animals make tools, but they do not consider the aesthetics of their tools, or attempt to carve beautiful handles for them. None except humans make art to better understand their life experience, or to communicate ideas about the world to others.

Consider the following questions as we attempt to define art:

What are some ways to approach a definition of art?

What are the components of art making?

What is creativity, and who is creative?

How does culture influence what we think about art?

How do we categorize visual arts within cultures?

Jane Avril. Detail of Figure 1.2. © Erich Lessing / Art Resource, NY.

TOWARD A
DEFINITION OF ART

No definitions are universal, timeless, and absolute. All definitions are framed within larger systems of knowledge, and these systems shift and evolve.

Therefore, to answer the question "What Is Art?" we would have to ask: What is art *for whom,* and *when?* For the United States at the beginning of the twenty-first century, a good definition of art would be this: *Art is a primarily visual medium that is used to express ideas about our human experience and the world around us.* This definition holds true for many other cultures and periods, but not for all.

To get a better idea of what art is for a specific culture, we will center our inquiry on four major areas: function, visual form, content, and aesthetics.

FUNCTION

Art functions. At the time a work of art is made, it is intended to do a job within a culture, as in the following examples:

- Art assists us in rituals that promote our spiritual or physical well-being.
- Art communicates thoughts, ideas, and emotions.
- Art gives us pictures of deities, or helps us conceive what divinity might be.
- Art serves and/or commemorates the dead.
- Art makes evident the power of the state and its rulers.
- Art celebrates war and conquest, and sometimes also peace.
- Art is a means for protesting political and social injustice.
- Art promotes cohesion within a social group.
- Art records the likenesses of individuals and the context in which the individuals exist.
- Art educates us about ourselves and the world around us.
- Art entertains.

Of course, other arts do similar things, as do other fields of human endeavor. But one way to measure whether a work of art is "good" is to determine its intended function, and then see how well it succeeds. In addition to its original purpose, art can function as an area for study. As cultural "documents," artworks can tell us volumes about existing and past cultures. For example, the study of art can reveal power structures within a culture, allude to what a people thought was the essence of human nature, tell us what the "ideal" body looked like in a culture, show attitudes toward sexuality, indicate what gender roles existed, and so on.

Here is an example. Figure 1.1 shows two sculptures called *Akuaʹmma Dolls,* from the Ashanti (Asante) people of Africa in the twentieth century. At the time they were made, such sculptures were intended to help a woman become pregnant if she was having problems conceiving. They were effective only if the woman used these sculptures in a ritually prescribed way, and they would be considered successful if the woman using them was able to have a healthy baby.

Several decades later, these dolls are in the British Museum. Their functions today are to educate users about another culture, to provide visual pleasure, and to entertain. Scholars also study these works and have gleaned considerable information about Ashanti culture from them. For example, the *Akuaʹmma Dolls* show us that the Ashanti people place a great value on children; that a woman's reproductive role is heavily emphasized; and that balanced, abstracted, simple, geometricized forms express the visual ideal within this culture.

From Chapter 7 onward, we will study the functions of hundreds of artworks in greater depth.

VISUAL FORM

Art has a visual form that has been carefully considered and manipulated to help it better fulfill its function. Visual form includes:

- the materials from which the artwork is made
- its formal elements, such as line, shape, color, texture, mass, volume, space, and so on
- its overall composition, size, internal balance, and so on.

What is the visual form of the *Akuaʹmma Dolls?* They are made from wood, which is the most common sculptural material in sub-Saharan Africa. In addition, the one on the right has beads on its head and around its neck. Their formal elements consist of generally geometric shapes, with round heads and rectangular or cylindrical bodies. Facial features are also simplified geometric shapes. Pattern is important as we see the necks are stacks of repeated disks, while the texture of the surfaces is polished smooth. In the overall composition, each doll is symmetrical and balanced, except where broken. They are small compared to the size of an average adult. In proportion, they emphasize the head, as it is oversized compared to the body.

The visual form is critically important to a work of art. It is the material embodiment of an idea. Its physicality is what allows it to be seen or touched, and the idea to be communicated. The subtleties of visual form are what make nuances of meaning possible. The visual form of the *Akuaʹmma* embodies Ashanti ideals and ritual function.

Every work of art has visual form, which we will study throughout the book. In addition, we deal with visual form in

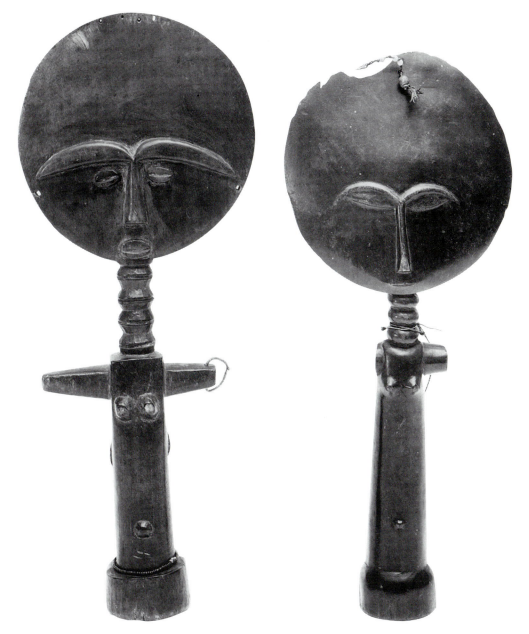

1.1 *Ashanti Akuaʹmma Dolls.* Wood, 13" high. Ghana, Africa, c. twentieth century. The British Museum, London. Photo © The British Museum, London. For more on this artwork, see also the text accompanying Figure 8.10.

depth in Chapter 2, The Language of Art, and Chapter 3, The Language of Architecture.

CONTENT

Content is the mass of ideas associated with a work of art, communicated through the following:

- the art's imagery

- its surroundings where it is used or displayed

- its symbolic meaning

- the customs, beliefs, and values of the culture that uses it

- the text incorporated with the work, or writings about the work

Content can both be immediately apparent and require considerable study. Let us return once more to the *Akuaʹmma.* If we see them for the very first time without any explanation, we could still understand some of their content. They are based on the human form, but abstracted. They are not photographic representations of any one individual, but rather generalized entities with simplified and geometric bodies. Closer observation shows them to be females.

If we spent time observing these sculptures in the surroundings in which they are used, we would see women carrying them and children playing with them, and perhaps guess that they are related to motherhood. If we first saw them in a museum, we would see them as valuable cultural artifacts or works of art. Even if you are seeing them for the first time in this art book, you know that they are considered works of art. That is part of their content.

However, some content is not readily apparent. Without studying the context or being part of Ashanti culture, we would not likely know that these sculptures represent future children or that the Ashanti consider these to be ideal forms. It would be necessary to conduct research to find out what the Ashanti people themselves say about the *Akuàmma,* or read anthropological studies that relate these works to women's roles, ritualistic practices, and play.

For more on how meaning is derived from art, read Chapter 4, Deriving Meaning.

AESTHETICS

Aesthetics is the branch of Western philosophy originating in ancient Greece that deals with art, its creative sources, its various forms, and its effects on individuals and cultures. Western philosophers as well as thinkers from India, Japan, and China have written for centuries about aesthetic issues. In several African, Oceanic, and Native American cultures, art practice demonstrated a clear aesthetic long before there was written material about it. You are thinking aesthetically when you read a book like this one.

Modern aesthetic theory in the West became a field of study in the eighteenth century, when many philosophers thought that art dealt with beauty, and that beauty could be universally defined for all times and places. Their standard of beauty was ancient Greek sculpture, which had been excavated in Europe for some time and was enormously influential on later Western art. That universalist position is discredited now, as we recognize that there is no worldwide agreement about what constitutes beauty. In addition, philosophers today consider many other qualities besides beauty as significant attributes of art.

The *Akuàmma Dolls* embody the aesthetic preferences of the Ashanti people. There is a distinct preference for geometrically round heads, with the face occupying the lower half or third of the disk. The chin is generally nonexistent, with the mouth positioned at the very bottom of the face. Eyes are half-moons or almond-shaped. Eyebrows are long arcs connected above the nose. Overall, there is a great preference for symmetry. We know that the Ashanti people consider these qualities to be aesthetically superior to others.

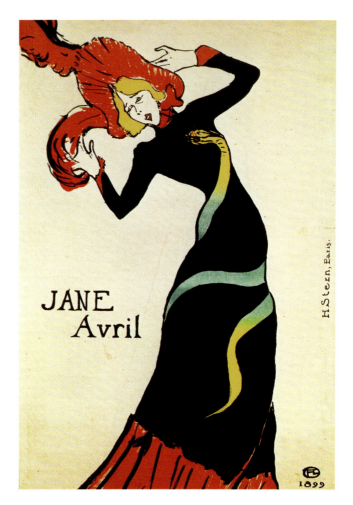

1.2   HENRI DE TOULOUSE-LAUTREC. *Jane Avril.* Lithographic poster, 22" × 14". Paris, France, 1899. The Museum of Modern Art, New York. © Erich Lessing / Art Resource, NY. See also the text accompanying Figure 16.13 for more on this artwork.

A very different aesthetic sensibility is apparent if we study the image of *Jane Avril* (Figure 1.2), an 1899 French poster by Henri de Toulouse-Lautrec. Jane Avril was a popular nightclub performer, and therefore embodied idealized, attractive, or desirable qualities. Yet, how different these are from those of the composed and balanced *Akuàmma!* We see a preference for elongated forms, serpentine lines, bright colors, and expressive gestures. The singer's pose is twisted and off balance. The promise of a sexual encounter and the potential of danger were important in *Jane Avril,* as evident in the snake image encircling her body.

CREATING ART

What is the process for creating an art object? Various components are important, including perception, response, creativity, and expression.

VISUAL PERCEPTION

Sight evolved in humans as an aid to survival: to locate food, find mates, and detect foes. As a result, our eyes are especially equipped to do two things: (1) to perceive movement; and (2) to detect edges and shapes by perceiving differences in adjoining areas of color, brightness, or texture. These abilities allowed early humans to move through their environment and identify other objects within it.

We have inherited the same eye structure that our ancestors had, and we respond to the same stimuli that they did, namely, movement, edge, color, brightness, and texture. It may seem strange, but our eyes and brain are actually set up to filter out and ignore most visual stimuli. Only by filtering are we able to focus our attention rather than be helplessly bombarded by a never-ending stream of visual information. Therefore, we generally pay less attention to things that are not moving. Because of the placement of our eyes, we focus on what is in front of us, in contrast to many creatures that have near-360-degree vision. Only a small part of what we see is sharp, while the bulk of our visual field is blurry. And finally, our brain often processes visual stimuli unconsciously. How often have you been lost in thought while driving, and later had absolutely no recollection of seeing what you passed along the way?

Looking at art is different from our everyday, ordinary seeing. Visual art is comprised of organized colors and shapes. It offers a specific set of ideas. It is not simply a copy of our everyday environment, much of which we ignore. It fulfills some function within our culture. Art is designed to be arresting, to engage our attention, to make us look and to be aware of our act of looking, and potentially be enriched as a result. That gift of engaged vision, in contrast to our everyday inattentiveness, is one of the greatest benefits of art.

THE ARTIST'S RESPONSE TO THE WORLD

Although everyone sees by means of the same process, we may interpret our perceptions differently. This difference can be seen in art. Though artists may base their work on visual perceptions of the world around them, almost every artist's work is different from any other's. Their work reflects their point of view, values, and individual experiences. They also learn from others. In Figure 1.3, we see a delicate rendering of *Apricot Blossoms* by Ma Yuan, from thirteenth-century China, which is not a direct copy from life. The artist singled out a branch and

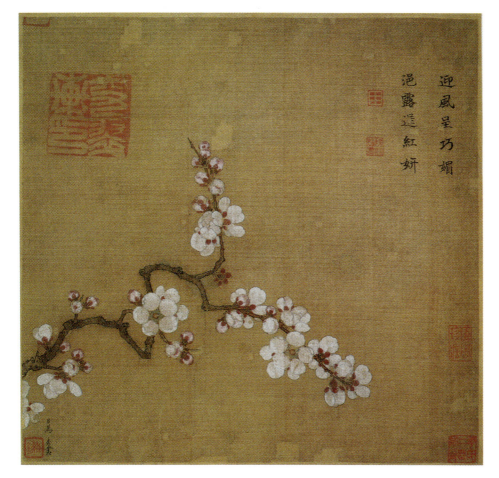

1.3 MA YUAN. *Apricot Blossoms.* Album leaf with ink and color on silk, 10" high. China, Southern Song Dynasty, early thirteenth century. National Palace Museum, Taiwan. See also Figure 15.15.

removed it from a distracting background to best present the blossoms' delicate outlines, irregular but rhythmic groupings, and the twisting shape of the nubby branch. Before making this painting, Ma Yuan certainly studied the blossoms carefully, and perhaps even sketched them from life. Yet this painting was made from memory, as the Chinese valued paintings in which memory and repeated experience allowed the artist to capture the essence of the apricot blossoms along with a feeling for their delicateness and scent.

In contrast now, think of some of the thousands of flower pictures you have seen in your life, from oil paintings to watercolors to photographs and on to calendar images, wallpaper, wrapping paper, linoleum, and fabric designs. Each has its own visual form, content, and value. Every one of those representations of flowers was based on the visual perceptions of some artist or designer. These artists and designers reinterpreted the flowers through their own perception, combined with the values of their cultures and the expectations of their audience for a certain kind of product.

Clearly, art reflects humankind's perceptions of and responses to its reality, including all aspects of life, from birth to death and the hereafter, and of everything in between. In Figure 1.4, we see Edward Hicks's *The Peaceable Kingdom,* in which he painted his response to the world as he would like it to be, as his religion had taught him. Young children and beasts rest side by side while adults sign a peace treaty in the distance. The whole composition exudes a peaceful mood. Looking at another painting, *Echo of a Scream* by David Alfaro Siqueiros (Figure 1.5), we see disturbing imagery of babies crying in despair, invoking sadness and perhaps anger. Here, the artist's response to his reality, contrary to Hicks's painting, is what he wishes the world not to be.

ARTISTIC EXPRESSION AND CREATIVITY

Creativity is the quality that allows us to originate something or to cause some object to come into being. What that means exactly can vary from culture to culture. In the United States

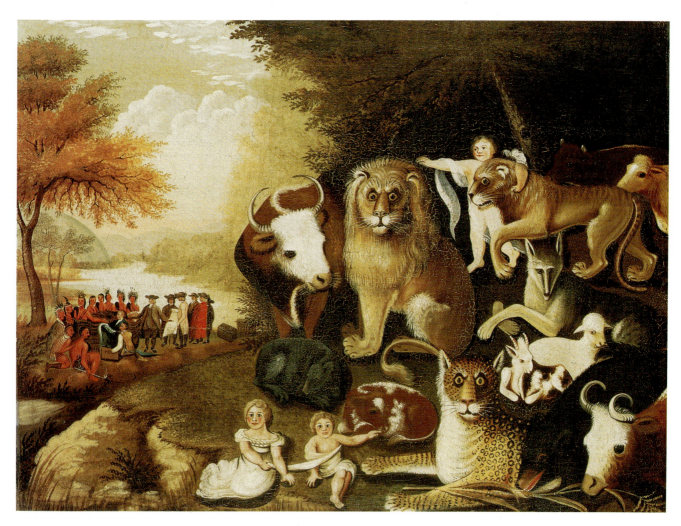

1.4 EDWARD HICKS. *The Peaceable Kingdom.* Oil painting. USA, 1830–1840. Brooklyn Museum, New York. See also Figure 11.35 for more on this painting.

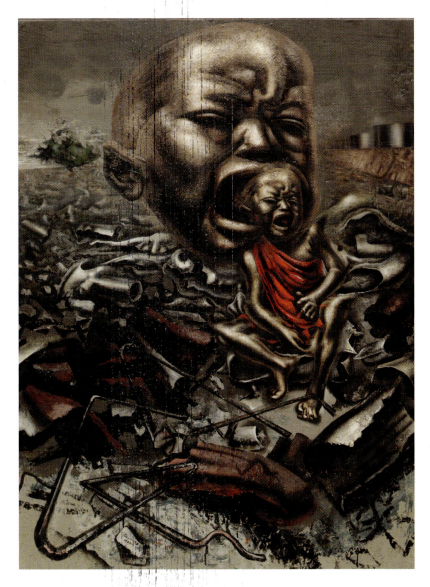

1.5   DAVID ALFARO SIQUEIROS.
Echo of a Scream. Enamel on wood,
48" × 36". Mexico, 1937. Gift of
Edward M. M. Warburg. (633.1939)
The Museum of Modern Art, New
York, NY © Estate of David Alfaro
Siqueiros/SOMAAP, Mexico City/
VAGA New York. See also Figures
2.21 and 12.5.

today, creativity is often thought to have two essential ingredients. The first is innovation, or the making of something that is new. The second is artistic self-expression. In the Hicks and Siqueiros paintings we have just seen, the artists' imagery and art styles convey different ideas about the world, and therefore are different forms of artistic self-expression. This expression refers to individual artists' own artistic styles and personal concepts of the world, all of which are embedded in their unique works of art.

However, innovation and artistic self-expression are not always necessary ingredients in creating artwork. In this book, we will see several examples of great art in which the artists followed formulas or copied other works, because their culture valued the re-creation of old forms more than innovation. Also, some artists today devote their work to critiquing existing culture, rather than creating something new.

Psychologists have not fully identified the components of the creative process in art making. However, some contemporary artists have delineated their own idea of the creative process. It begins with a formative stage, in which the artist decides to make a work in response to a problem, a vivid experience, or a commission. The artist may research intensely, read, look at other art, explore freely, and/or make sketches. This period may be long or short. Often, artists try to stay open to the possibility of unexpected results that may come from internal play or speculation, or from external sources.

The making of the artwork comes next. For some artists, the execution might be very rapid, as it was for Vincent van Gogh, who painted quickly, with creative and unexpected results happening in the process of painting. Other works may take many years or be ongoing, as was the construction of the Great Wall of China. Some may never be completed or may

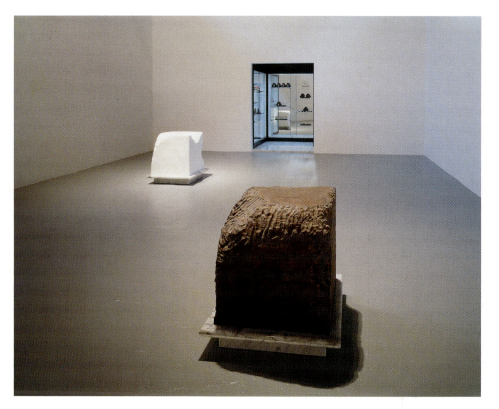

1.6 JANINE ANTONI. *Gnaw.* Three-part installation. Chocolate: 600 lbs. of chocolate gnawed by the artist; lard: 600 lbs. of lard gnawed by the artist; display: 130 lipsticks made with pigment, beeswax, and chewed lard removed from the lard cube; 27 heart-shaped packaging trays made from the chewed chocolate removed from the chocolate cube, dimensions variable. USA, 1992. Courtesy of the artist and Luhring Augustine. See also Figure 7.24.

be in a constant state of revision. In some cases, the execution of the work is the actual piece itself, as in Janine Antoni's 1992 performance/installation called *Gnaw* (Figure 1.6). What we see in our image is a partly gnawed six-hundred-pound block of chocolate, with six hundred pounds of lard in the background. But the act of eating was a primary part of this artwork. The art changed during the exhibit as Antoni ate away at the block. The artist is interested in everyday body rituals and in converting the most basic sorts of activities, such as bathing, mopping, and eating, into sculptural processes.

Another important component in the creative process is critique or review. Once the work has been completed, or even while it is in process, artists critically assess their work. Other critiques come from peers, curators, writers, academics, and the audience. All this provides a certain degree of affirmation.

Who is creative? It is easy, but inaccurate, to think that the only creative people are artists, designers, or someone in an art-related field. We all have the potential for creativity. It is not limited to art fields, but can be found among mathematicians, scientists, health care professionals, social workers, teachers, parents, gardeners, and so on. While we think of creativity as residing in the individual, it has a social dimension as well. With broad support, someone's artistic abilities can blossom. Negative social pressures can cause someone to squelch or divert creativity, or be embarrassed or ridiculed to the point of avoiding it.

Children perceive the world around them without inhibition, and express it freely in their art. Everything is new and

fresh to them. Julia Rose Lazzari-Dean, age four, drew *Dinosaur Eating a Man* (Figure 1.7) based on her dinosaur and bug books and her own observations. The "dinosaur," a composite of her perception of insects and dinosaurs, is dramatically drawn with details of menacing jaw, tongue, head, and body. The human victim is drawn smaller, making the dinosaur even more impressive. By the time children reach teenage years, peer pressure and their self-perception of non-talent may cause many to abandon art making, unless there is strong family encouragement and support from teachers, the community, and figures of authority. Creativity must be fostered.

CATEGORIES OF VISUAL ARTS

A few decades ago, a definition of art circulated in the United States, saying in effect that art is whatever the artist says is art. There is some truth in this, as artists often have taken the lead in defining new art forms long before society accepted them. However, when we view the long history of art, there is even more truth to this definition: Art is whatever a society or culture says is art. What does this mean? Basically, the definition of art is not universal and fixed in all its details, as we saw earlier. It fluctuates, because cultures are alive and changing.

Some peoples, both past and in the present, have no word that corresponds to ours for art. As we have seen with

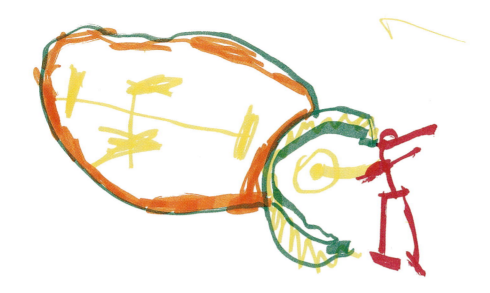

1.7 JULIA ROSE LAZZARI-DEAN. *Dinosaur Eating a Man.* Markers on paper, 8" × 6". USA, 1997. Collection of Margaret Lazzari and Mike Dean.

the *Akua'mma Dolls,* the Ashanti blur the boundaries between areas that Western cultures might consider very distinct, such as art, ritual, and play. Before the nineteenth century, the Japanese did not consider much of their painting to be a fine art, as we do. When Western Art History was exported to Japan in the late nineteenth century, the concept of painting as fine art was also exported.

In the United States today, we are inundated with images and visual objects. They surround us in galleries and museums, and are everywhere in mass media and in stores. Some are considered art, and others are called popular culture. Other categories exist. Crafts sometimes are distinguished from art. And among art objects themselves, we make groupings according to styles.

ART, POPULAR CULTURE, AND KITSCH

During the past 150 years in highly industrialized countries, art critics have made distinctions between art, popular culture, and kitsch. Prior to that time, all visual material was seen as a form of entertainment:

> "highbrow" and "lowbrow" . . . were both popular. Shakespeare appealed to lower class audiences; and the same can be said of most stage literature, of music (including grand opera), and of the visual arts. Norms now taken for granted did not exist; audiences were not demurely appreciative but highly demonstrative; there was an endless indiscriminate mixing of genres, of high art and kitsch. Relatively little was sacred. (Wallach 1998: 14)

Art (also called high art or fine art in Western cultures) is a category of refined objects considered to be among the supreme cultural achievements of the human race. Art is believed to transcend average human works and may be produced by only the best artists with unique sensibilities. Art requires sensitivity to be appreciated by its audience. One definition of high art is simply that it is what is displayed in art museums:

> Art museums sacralize their contents: the art object, shown in an appropriate formal setting, becomes high art, the repository of society's loftiest ideals. Indeed, without art museums, the category high art is practically unthinkable. (Wallach 1998: 3)

Historically, fine art has tended to be media-defined: its most traditional forms include painting, sculpture, and architecture. It has been expanded to include film, photography, prints, and, most recently, installation, performance, video, and computer art. High art also is promoted and taught in college and university art departments.

However, the category of fine art is constantly evolving and changing in real life. In the early and mid-nineteenth century, it was defined in Western industrialized nations solely in terms of classical art: Greek, Roman, and Italian Renaissance art, mostly sculpture. At the beginning of the twentieth century, contemporary painting was favored. Later, the mid-twentieth-century critic Clement Greenberg identified high art as "avant-garde," which he saw as detached from society, as "art for art's sake" and "pure poetry." "The avant-garde poet or artist tries in effect to imitate God by creating something valid solely on its own terms, in the way that nature itself is valid. . . . [A] work of art or literature cannot be reduced in whole or in part to anything not itself" (Greenberg 1939: 5–6). Definitions of art are also in flux when Western people look at art from other cultures. At the beginning of the twentieth century, *Akua'mma* sculptures would not have been displayed in art museums in the United States or Europe, but they are now.

Popular culture consists of magazines, comics, television, tourist art, advertising, folk art, tattoos, customized cars, graffiti, video games, posters, Web sites, calendars, greeting cards, dolls, toys, movies (as opposed to film or cinema), and snapshots and commercial photography (as opposed to fine photography). Popular art is often perceived as being more accessible, inexpensive, entertaining, commercial, political, naive, primitive, amateur, colorful, folksy, or touristy than fine art.

Fine arts and popular culture are part of a continuum that contains all the visual imagery that Western culture produces. The division between the two came about in part with the rise of the middle class during the Industrial Revolution, as the bourgeois sought to emulate nobility by creating art museums for the appreciation of art, and to separate themselves from lower classes who presumably appreciate only popular art. The existence of high art "proves" the merits of bourgeois culture beyond mere consumerism.

Popular culture images and objects may share many attributes of high art. The work is often highly creative, innovative, and expressive. It shares the same attributes of function, visual form, and content. It reflects the values and structures of our social systems, political hierarchies, and religious beliefs. Popular culture is studied in many academic areas, including visual culture, art history, philosophy, and anthropology. It is often

collected and may be displayed in museums. Art and popular culture often share the same images. Some objects from popular culture eventually "become" art, as with the *Jane Avril* poster we have already seen.

Some artists want to occupy the space between high art and popular culture. For example, Barbara Kruger is an artist, a social and political observer, and an agitator. Her background is in both fine arts and mass media. For a period in the 1980s, she was chief designer for the popular fashion magazine *Mademoiselle.* Like other artists interested in effecting a difference in "real life," Kruger produces unique, costly artworks for galleries and distributes her work to the larger public as inexpensive street posters, billboards, and matchbook covers. *Untitled (Your body is a battleground)* in Figure 1.8 is an artwork in a famous art collection, but it has also been reproduced as street posters, T-shirts, book covers, and postcards.

Webster's New World Dictionary defines kitsch as "art, writing, etc. of a pretentious but shallow kind, calculated to have popular appeal." Objects or images are kitsch if they display an emotional appeal that is generalized, superficial, and sentimen-

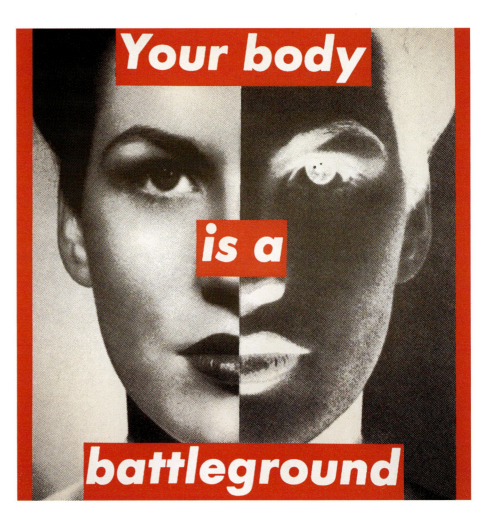

1.8   BARBARA KRUGER. *Untitled (Your body is a battleground).* Photographic silk screen on vinyl, 112" × 112". USA, 1989. Courtesy: Mary Boone Gallery, New York. Photo © Zindman / Fremont. Eli Broad Family Foundation Collection, Los Angeles. See also Figure 8.24.

tal. Kitsch is the opposite of an original experience, a uniquely felt emotion, or a thoughtful, introspective moment. Because of its broad appeal, kitsch imagery is often used in advertising and in political propaganda. We see several instances here:

> Christian kitsch—exemplified by plastic Jesus babies—combines universal elements of kitsch with symbolism relating to the articles of Christian faith. Communist kitsch—depicting smiling workers in factories, young couples on tractors cultivating a collective farm or building a hydroelectric power station—played on the mythical values of the joy of work and the enthusiasm for building a classless society. Capitalist kitsch, exemplified by advertising, on the other hand, uses class distinctions and status symbols to create artificial needs and illusions to foster the ideology of the consumer society. (Kulka 1996: 28)

The Smithsonian Institution's 150th anniversary Rose Parade float (Figure 1.9) exhibits many properties of kitsch because of its sentimentalized emotional message. The collection of images, from astronauts to the first airplane to pandas to butterflies to baseball, evokes a variety of kitsch emotions: Technology is wonderful! Come to the museum to understand the world! Wild animals are cute! All of America loves the Smithsonian! A representation of the oldest building of the Smithsonian Institution rides at the back of the float. The building has been scaled down, its windows made proportionally larger, the most exotic features—its towers—emphasized. The building is much smaller in scale than the objects in front of it, to make the museum appear diminutive, cute, and fun. In this float, it does not appear to be a site of serious research. Finally, the translation of an *Akua'ba* sculpture into a six-foot-high maquette of seaweed and flowers is kitsch (*Akua'ba* is the singular form of *Akua'mma*).

But, like all other categories of visual art, the idea of kitsch is evolving and changing. Critics such as Susan Sontag

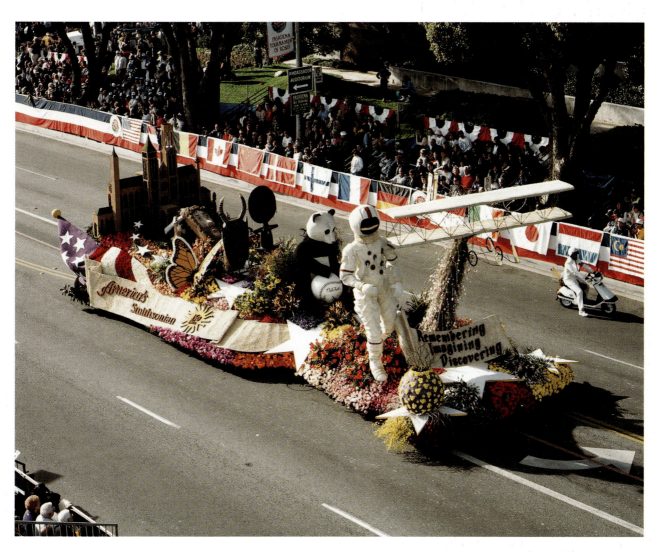

1.9   The Smithsonian Institution's 150th anniversary float in the 1996 Rose Parade in Pasadena, Calif. Photograph courtesy of the Pasadena Tournament of Roses.

have reclaimed some kitsch as "camp," which means objects and images of such extreme artifice (and often banality) as to have a perverse sophisticated and aesthetic appeal. Sontag believed that an appreciation of camp was "the sensibility of failed seriousness." It revealed "another kind of truth about the human situation" (Sontag 1966: 287).

CRAFT

Another category of art making is craft. Craft refers to specific media, including ceramics, glass, jewelry, weaving, and woodworking. Craft usually involves making objects, rather than images or image manipulation, although craft may involve surface decoration. Often, craft objects have a utilitarian purpose, or perhaps evolved from a utilitarian origin. In addition, however, there are aesthetic and/or conceptual dimensions that go beyond its mundane use. Like the categories of fine art, popular culture, and kitsch, the art/craft distinction is culturally specific and in flux.

The *Tlaloc Vessel* (Figure 1.10), c. 1470, is a good example of an art object that might be categorized as craft or art. Like other vessels, this holds water. But the face is a representation of Tlaloc, the Aztec rain deity, in whose temples such vessels were broken, allowing the water to run out, as an offering for more rain. Tlaloc's face and headdress complement and accentuate the shape of the vessel itself, as do the inscribed ovals, circles, arcs, and curves. This vessel's aesthetic qualities and ritualistic uses carry it beyond its utilitarian origin as water carrier.

STYLISTIC CATEGORIES

Style is the manner of expression that is characteristic of art either made by an individual artist or from a historic period

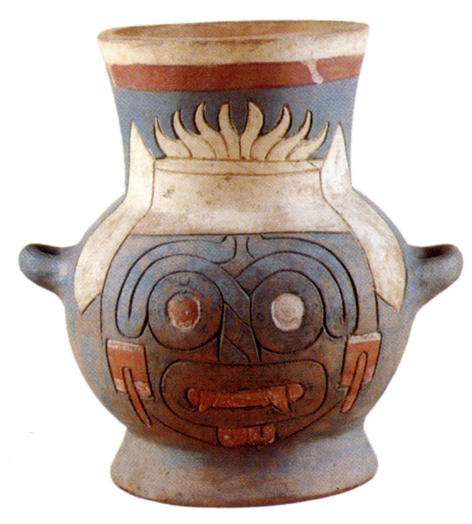

1.10 *Tlaloc Vessel.* Ceramic, 12" high. Aztec. Templo Mayor, Mexico, c. 1470. Photo © 2004, Metropolitan Museum of Art, New York. See also the text accompanying Figure 9.12.

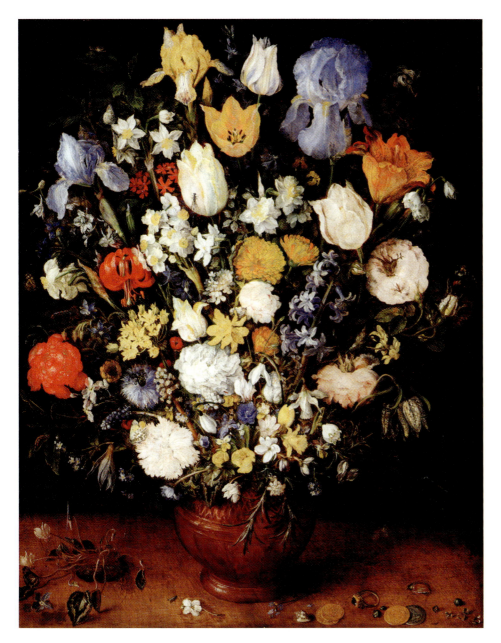

 1.11   JAN BRUEGEL. *Little Bouquet in a Clay Jar.* Oil on panel, 20" × 15.75". Flanders, c. 1599. Kunsthistorisches Museum, Vienna. © Archivo Iconographico, S.A. / Corbis. See also the text accompanying Figure 15.16.

or an entire civilization. So a rose might be a rose, but all artistic representations of it are not the same. The following is a vocabulary that helps describe style. This list is by no means complete, and some terms have more than one meaning.

STYLE VOCABULARY

Art that is **naturalistic** generally contains recognizable imagery that is depicted very much as seen in nature. Jan

Bruegel's painting of a *Little Bouquet in a Clay Jar* (c. 1599), Figure 1.11, is rendered in a naturalistic style. Close observation of each flower and leaf by the artist has been translated clearly and pristinely into imagery.

In **idealized** art, natural imagery is modified in a way that strives for perfection within the bounds of the values and aesthetics of a particular culture. Among the Baule people in nineteenth-century Africa, the ideal human form was

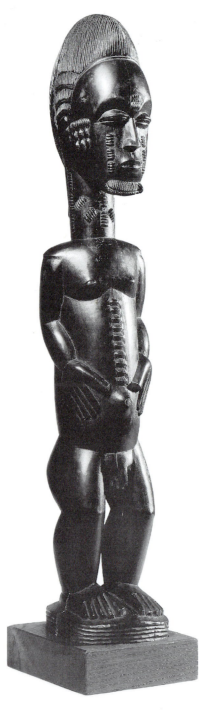

 1.12 *Male Torso (Ancestor).* Wood, 20.5" high. Baule. Africa, nineteenth–twentieth century. The British Museum, London. See also the text accompanying Figures 5.17 and 13.15.

divided roughly into thirds: one part each for the head, the torso, and the legs, as illustrated in Figure 1.12, a *Male Torso (Ancestor)* from the late nineteenth or early twentieth century. This ideal system of proportions visually expressed the importance given to each part of the body. The Baule ideal contrasts strongly with the idealized style that the fifth-century BCE Greeks developed for the "perfectly"

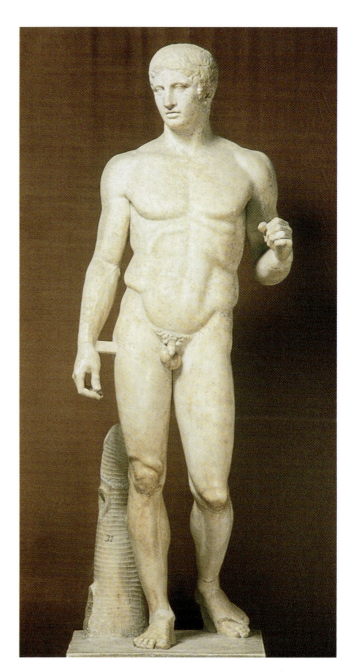

 1.13 POLYKLEITOS. *Doryphoros (Spear-bearer).* Roman marble after a bronze original of c. 450–440 BCE, 6'11" high. Museo Nazionale, Naples. Saskia Ltd. See also the text accompanying Figure 13.14.

proportioned human body, such as Polykleitos's *Doryphoros* (Figure 1.13). For Polykleitos, the head had to be a certain size in relation to the body, while width and length of various body parts were carefully adjusted to be in ideal harmony.

CONNECTION

Read about the idealized human form from ancient India in the discussion of the Yakshi (Figure 13.13, page 377).

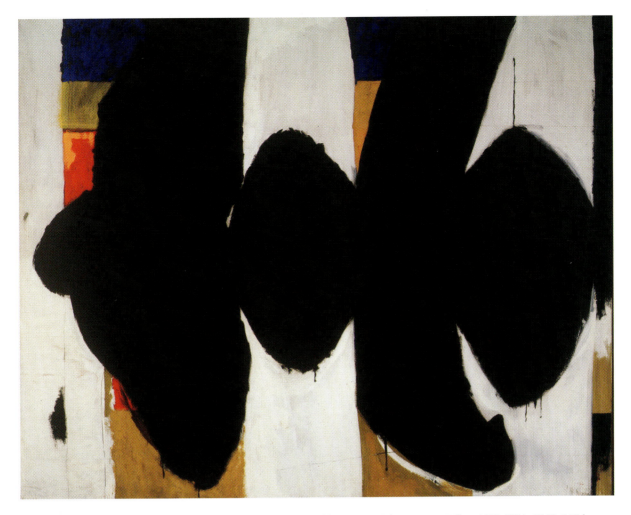

1.14 ROBERT MOTHERWELL. *Elegy to the Spanish Republic XXXIV*. Oil on canvas, 80" × 100". USA, 1953–1954. Albright-Knox Art Gallery, Buffalo, N.Y. © Dedalus Foundation / Licensed by VAGA, New York, NY. See also the text accompanying Figure 12.6.

Nonobjective (nonrepresentational) art has no recognizable imagery from the outside world. The imagery is completely generated by the artist. Robert Motherwell's imagery is nonobjective in his 1953–1954 painting, *Elegy to the Spanish Republic XXXIV* (Figure 1.14), even though it referred to actual historical events.

The term "abstract art" is often used to mean the same thing as "nonobjective," but there is an important distinction. **Abstracted** imagery may or may not be recognizable, but has been derived from reality by distorting, enlarging, and/or dissecting objects or figures from nature. We have already seen the *Tlaloc Vessel* (Figure 1.10), in which a face has been carved in an abstracted style. The facial features have been simplified and geometricized, and are therefore abstracted from the natural appearance of a human face.

When an abstracted element is **stylized,** it reoccurs almost the same in several works of art. For example, the simple, geometric facial features of the *Tlaloc Vessel* can be seen in other ceramic vessels from fifteenth-century Mexico. This repetition of the same abstractions can be called a stylization of that ele-

ment. When stylizing, artists follow established artistic conventions rather than working from observation or imagination.

Related terms are **mannered** or **mannerist;** they refer to artificial, highly stylized, or derivative styles of art. For example, the artist Michelangelo was such an overwhelmingly influential artist in sixteenth-century Italy that many artists who followed him worked in imitative, eccentric, mannered styles based on his work.

Expressive or **expressionist** styles of art are those that communicate heightened emotions and often a sense of urgency or spontaneity. Expressive styles frequently appear bold and immediate, rather than carefully considered or refined. They often feature distorted or abstracted imagery, and may appear asymmetrical or off balance. Textured surfaces and thick paint application signal an expressive style. The large, stark, expressive shapes in Motherwell's *Elegy* (Figure 1.14) have mottled paint, rough edges, and drips.

The term **classical** has several related meanings in reference to style. It can refer to art that is orderly, balanced, clear, and well proportioned vertically and horizontally, like the *Akuaìmma*. In this sense, classical is the opposite of expressive. "Classical" also describes a point in the evolution of styles: classical works represent the full development of a certain style, in contrast to its early formative stage or its late transformation into another style. When written with a capital C, "Classical" refers specifically to the art made in ancient Greece in the fifth century BCE. The related term **classic** indicates a judgment of excellence, such as a classic work of art with widely recognized outstanding qualities.

Both the first and second meanings of "classical" can be used to describe the sacred center of the Mesoamerican city of Teotihuacán, with the *Pyramid of the Sun* (Figure 1.15) and the *Avenue of the Dead,* dating from the first through sixth centuries. This sacred precinct was laid out in an orderly manner, along axes oriented north-south and east-west. Pyramids and temples were positioned at key points, and there is a sense of balance between the "positive" shapes of the enormous pyramid structures and the "negative" spaces of depressed open plazas interspersed among them. In addition, Teotihuacán represents the classical phase of Mesoamerican cultures, when great civilizations flourished in Mexico and Central America.

CULTURAL STYLES

A **cultural style** consists of recurring and distinctive features that we see in many works of art emanating from a particular place and era. For cultures, stylistic traits help us identify works from ancient Egypt, for example, and see them as distinct and coher-

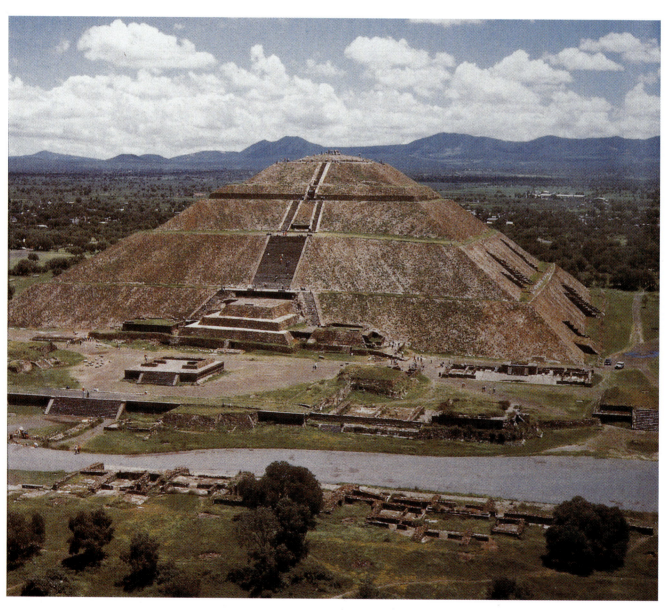

 1.15 *Pyramid of the Sun,* with the *Avenue of the Dead* in the foreground. Pyramid is 768' along one side of the base. Teotihuacán, Mexico, begun before CE 150. Photo courtesy Ester Pasztory. See also the text accompanying Figure 9.36.

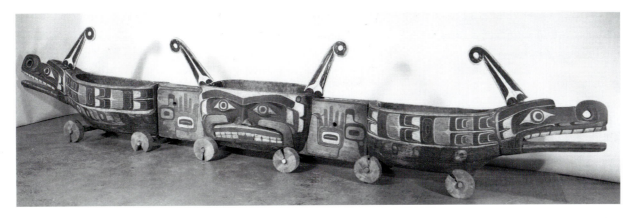

 1.16   CHARLIE JAMES. *Feast Dish.* Wood with green, black, red, and white paint, 20' long. From Turnour Island, British Columbia, 1907. Museum of Anthropology, University of British Columbia. See also the text accompanying Figure 7.20.

ent as a group. Stylistic differences make the art of ancient Egypt readily distinguishable from the art of, say, seventeenth-century France. Cultural styles reflect and express the cultures from which they come. Along with language, religion, and social customs, the styles of art and architecture form a culture's identity.

A few definitions are helpful here. **Culture** can mean the totality of ideas, customs, skills, and arts that belong to a people or group. This cultural totality is communicated or passed along to succeeding generations. A **culture** may also be a particular people or group, with their own ideas, customs, and arts. A **civilization** is a highly structured society, with a written language or a very developed system of communication, organized government, and advances in the arts and sciences. A country and a people with a high degree of social and cultural development can also be called a "civilization."

So, when referring to ancient Egypt, we may call it a civilization, as it was a structured society with government, writ-

ten language, and the arts and sciences. We may also refer to Egyptian culture, that is, its collective ideas, customs, and beliefs, and the articles of art that it produced. Most important here is our ability to distinguish the Egyptian style of art, as one representation of its cultural identity.

Cultural styles are recognizable across a broad spectrum of art objects created by a people. These art objects share content and many formal qualities. For example, the art of the Native Americans of the Northwest Coast has many distinct, identifying features, as we can see in two examples, the *Feast Dish* (Figure 1.16) by Charlie James from 1907, and the *Transformation Mask* (Figure 1.17). The *Feast Dish* is a twenty-foot-long serving bowl, while the *Transformation Mask* fits over a performer's face and is used during dance and storytelling. Despite differences, the imagery in both objects comes from the same iconographic system that standardized the representation of many animals and spirit forms. It was important in Northwest Coast art that the

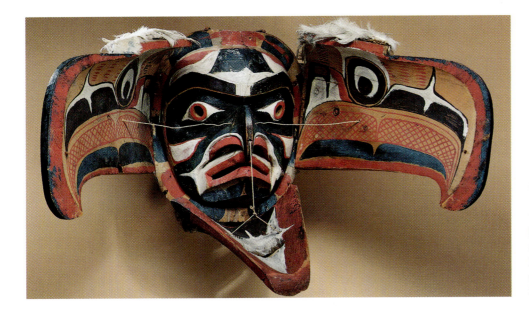

 1.17   *Transformation Mask.* Painted wood. Kwakiutl. British Columbia. American Museum of Natural History, New York. See also the text accompanying Figures 2.13 and 9.13.

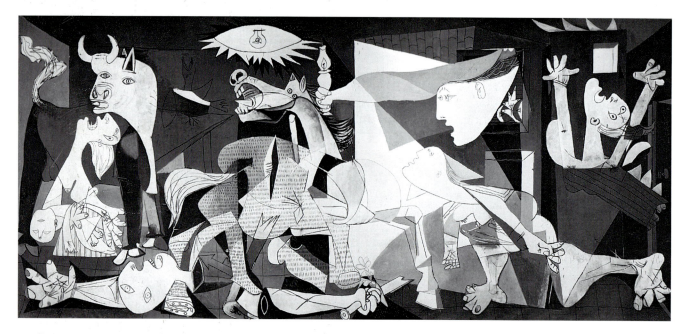

 1.18 PABLO PICASSO. *Guernica.* Oil on canvas, 11' × 28'8". Spain, 1937. The Prado Museum, Madrid. Institut Amatller D'art Hispanic © Museo del Prado. © 2004 Estate of Pablo Picasso / Artists Righs Society (ARS), New York. See also the text accompanying Figure 11.31.

animal and spirit imagery was recognizable. Both objects are wood carvings, which is the typical art form of that area. Both share many formal attributes, such as heavy black outlines that emphasize carved areas, bright colors, and shapes that are flat, flowing, and abstracted from nature. Both fulfilled similar functions, to delineate and celebrate the genealogy of a clan.

Similar examples can be found in almost every culture. For example, during the seventeenth-century reign of King Louis XIV of France, the court style, which was ornate and lavish, could be seen in everything from architecture to painting, furniture design, and clothing. Even hairstyles were affected. Men and women wore enormous, elaborate, powdered wigs; some apparently even had jeweled model ships "floating" among the curls and waves. You can see broad cultural styles around you today. Do you notice certain shared qualities among some contemporary art, popular music, and the latest ads for clothing?

 CONNECTION
The Hall of Mirrors at the Palace at Versailles (Figure 11.10, page 310) is a good example of the ornate Louis XIV style.

Cultural styles are not static, but evolve due to many circumstances, such as changes in religion, historical events such as war, and contact with other cultures through trade or colonization. For example, we see that the art of Europe changed profoundly because of African influences, especially apparent in works like *Guernica* (Figure 1.18), painted by Pablo Picasso in 1937. In European art from the fifteenth through the nineteenth

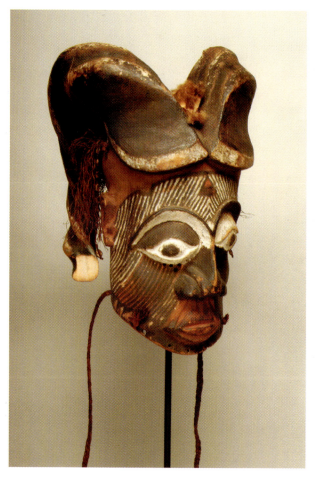

1.19 *Mask.* Wood, paint, fiber, and beads, 22" high. Zaire, Africa. African Art Collection of the Museum of Texas Tech University, Lubbock, Texas.

centuries, the human form had been rendered in a naturalistic, idealized, or Classical Greek–inspired manner, like *Doryphoros* (Figure 1.13). In contrast, Picasso's rendering of the face and his use of pattern owe much to African sculpture, such as the *Mask* from Zaire (Figure 1.19). When viewed as a whole, Picasso's lifetime output is an amalgam of styles from Africa and Europe, dating as far back as Classical Greece and Rome, and forward to the twentieth century. Conversely, African artists are influenced by the European styles to which they have been exposed.

STYLES OF ARTISTS WITHIN THEIR CULTURES

Style can also refer to the distinguishing characteristics of one artist's work. Individual artists can develop unique, personal styles. In some cases, their names would be known even without the signature on their work. Artist Vincent van Gogh is famous for his expressive paintings rendered in rich, thick paint in brilliant colors. Using a palette knife, he applied his paint quickly, allowing for a heavily textured surface throughout. His unique style, readily distinguished from other European painters, can be seen clearly in his *Portrait of Dr. Gachet* (Figure 1.20) from 1890.

Even given van Gogh's unique vision and skills, his work can still be grouped with that of other artists of his time, such as Georges Seurat's *A Sunday on La Grande Jatte* (Figure 1.21). There are differences, of course. Van Gogh put down energetic

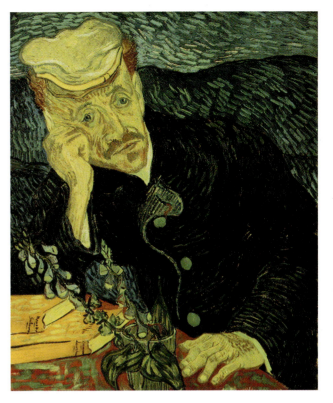

 1.20 VINCENT VAN GOGH. *Portrait of Dr. Gachet.* Oil on canvas. Netherlands, 1890. Photo courtesy Christie's. © Christie's Images, Inc. / Christies Images—All rights reserved. See also the text accompanying Figure 13.3.

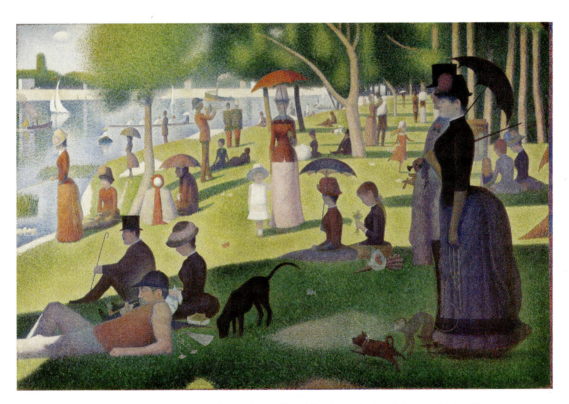

 1.21 GEORGES SEURAT. *La Grande Jatte* (also called *A Sunday on LaGrande Jatte—1884*). Oil on canvas, approx. 6'9" × 10'. France, 1884–1886. The Art Institute of Chicago, Helen Birch Bartlett Memorial Collection. Photo © The Art Institute of Chicago. All Rights Reserved. See also the text accompanying Figure 14.29.

dashes of paint, while Seurat painted painstakingly small colored dabs that blend together when seen from a distance. Van Gogh completed most works quickly, while Seurat worked for two years to complete this large canvas.

Yet we can also see what aspects of the prevailing cultural style van Gogh and Seurat share. Both are **Post-Impressionists,** a group for whom individualized paint application was important. Like the Impressionists before them, Post-Impressionists often chose subject matter that reflected everyday scenes. They painted mostly in oil and used bright-colored, thick paint (called impasto), rather than thin washes of subdued color.

Some artists seek to develop their own styles and some do not. European and U.S. artists in the early part of the twentieth century sought to develop their own distinct styles, as innovation and individuality were seen as marks of artistic value. This changed somewhat in the late twentieth century, as more artists in Europe and the United States created work in collaborations, or even incorporated copies of other images, so that a unique, individual style no longer necessarily denoted quality.

In some cultures, copying a venerable example is valued more than producing a new, unique object. For example, Egyptian artists had a distinct style of rendering figures that was so well established and effective for their culture that very little change occurred in it over hundreds of years. It was more important for the Egyptian artists to follow canons of representation than to invent new imagery or new ways to depict it. We see similar attitudes in some Chinese landscape paintings and in medieval Europe, where new religious manuscripts were carefully copied from old manuscripts. Artists from the Pacific Northwest also copied conventional forms in order to make their imagery recognizable, as we saw previously with the *Feast Dish* and *Transformation Mask.* These artists were charged with the need to copy old forms, while investing new spirit and vigor in them.

OTHER CATEGORIES

There are other ways to categorize art. Disciplines such as drawing, painting, or sculpture may be grouped as separate categories. Some cultures have art forms that do not translate directly into Western categories, such as ancient puppet theater in Japan, or the masquerade in Africa. We will see all these again in subsequent chapters.

Chronological categories follow a cultural style as it develops through the years. This approach is common in art books dealing with the history of Western art, with titles like *A History of Renaissance Art,* or *Survey of Art from the Middle Ages.* A geographic approach studies the art from a particular area, usually also in chronological order. Western writers often take a geographic approach to art of other cultures, and so we might see books on *The Art of Africa* or *The Art of India.*

Yet another approach (and that of much of this book) is thematic, in which a core idea is the basis for discussing art from many different cultures. Part 2 of this book is organized around a cluster of themes and is divided into the following four sections: Section 1, Survival and Beyond; Section 2, Religion; Section 3, The State; and Section 4, Self and Society. Each chapter expands on aspects of these themes.

Other divisions are possible. Certainly all observers of art could create their own categories for grouping artworks, and these areas can vary according to preference. You are part of a living, growing culture, and the final word has not been written about it.

SYNOPSIS

No single definition of art absolutely applies for all times and places. Generally, however, art is a primarily visual medium that expresses ideas about our human experience and the world around us. Art engages our attention in a way that our everyday environment cannot. Various cultures have developed their own aesthetic systems that identify in detail what art is for them.

Creativity is the quality that allows us to originate something or to cause some object to come into being. In some cultures, creativity is tied to artistic expression and innovation, while in others it is essential to follow precedents. The creative process is not entirely understood, but many contemporary artists have described their experience of the act of creation.

Societies may group visual arts into various categories. In the United States today, categories of visual products include art, popular culture, craft, or style. Other categories may be created, such as geographic boundaries, disciplines, or humanistic themes, as used in this book.

FOOD FOR THOUGHT

When we began this chapter, we stated that art making is strictly a human phenomenon. This brings several questions to mind.

- Could the evolutionary theory of the development of humankind include the ability to make art?
- If all humankind has the potential to be creative, can we all be artists?

Categorizing art is also a human phenomenon! As we have seen, almost all studies of art are organized in one of three ways: chronologically, geographically, or thematically.

- Any of these three methods of study has its virtues and its pitfalls. Can you think of any particular advantages of each?

YOUR CD-ROM RESOURCES

- Foundations–Interactive Modules
    Style, Form, and Content
- Flashcards
- Food for Thought
- Companion Site
    Chapter 1 Quiz
    InfoTrac® College Edition Readings
    Artist Flashcards
    Online Study Guide

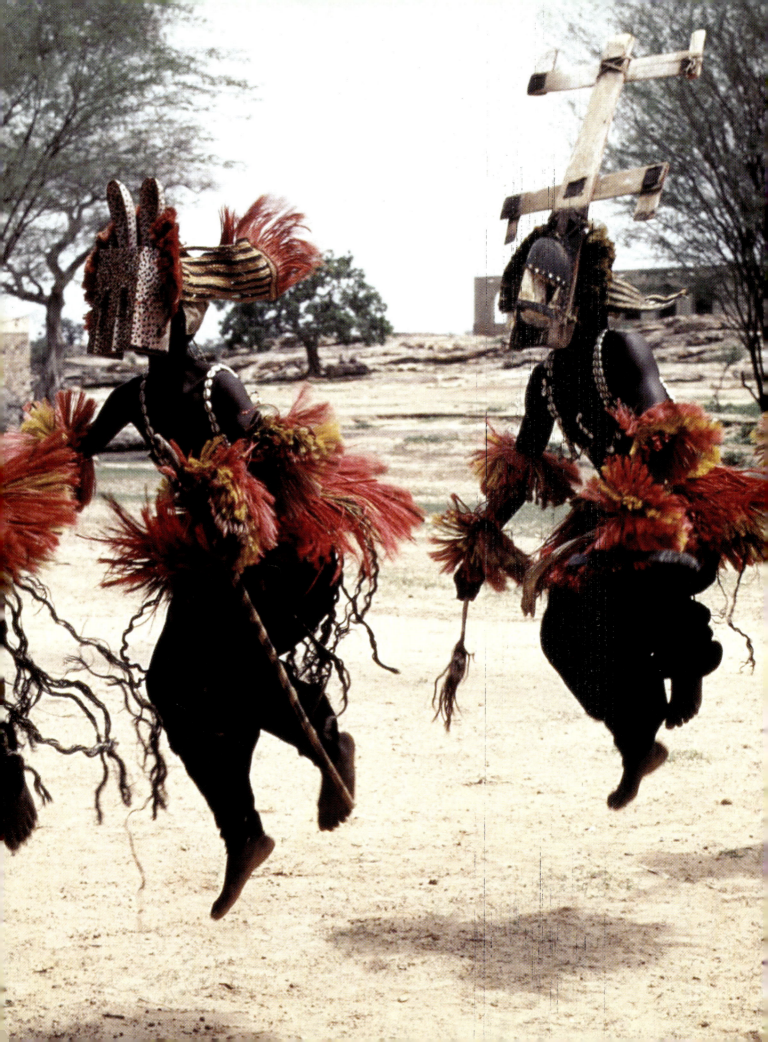

THE LANGUAGE OF ART

INTRODUCTION

Communication often means the use of oral and written language. However, people also use other languages to communicate their ideas. These include the languages of numbers and music, and, of course, the language of art. Like the others, the language of art is composed of elements arranged into a structure so it can make sense to observers. In this chapter, we will examine those elements and the principles by which they are composed, structured, or organized into a work of art.

Our discussion covers the plastic arts (art pieces that are tangible and permanent, i.e., drawing, painting, and sculpture) and the ephemeral arts (art pieces that are intangible, passing, and not permanent, i.e., ritual and performance). Architecture is discussed in the next chapter.

This chapter contains many art terms and introduces the basic vocabulary that we will use throughout this book. Terms are defined within the chapter, and definitions are repeated in the Glossary at the end of the book.

As we examine the language of art, keep in mind the following questions:

If art is a language, what is its grammar?

How can communication be visual?

How can a visual language be composed?

Instead of words, what do artists use to make their statement?

Kanaga Masked Dancers. Detail of Figure 2.23. Hutchison Library.

FORMAL ELEMENTS

Words are the basic elements of oral and written languages. Likewise, visual arts have basic units, which are the **formal elements.** They are line, light and value, color, texture and pattern, shape and volume, space, and time and motion. Other art forms might also include the elements of chance, improvisation, and spontaneity. Also, some artworks engage senses other than sight, so we will look at those elements, too.

LINE

When children first encounter crayons, the results are lines—lines on paper, on walls, on any available surface. Those first marks begin a lifelong career of making lines, whether children become artists or not. Line is a basic element of visual and written communication. Every letter, word, map, diagram, flowchart, or doodle uses lines to record an idea.

What is a line? Mathematically, a **line** is a moving point, having length and no width. In art, a line usually has both length and width, but its length is the more important dimension.

Lines made with some material are **actual lines.** They physically exist and vary widely in the way they look—some are broad, some thin, some straight, some jagged. **Implied lines** in an artwork do not physically exist, yet they seem quite real to viewers. One example is the dotted line, in which several individual, unconnected elements can be grouped into a single "line." We see examples of actual and implied lines in the Australian aboriginal painting, *Witchetty Grub Dreaming* (1980), Figure 2.1. Although some of the lines in this painting are actual lines, created by a continuous stripe of paint, others are implied lines, created by aligning discrete dots of paint that we perceive as lines. In fact, in this painting, we can see the image simultaneously as lines, dots, and areas. Lines come in great varieties, such as the jagged, stabbing lines seen in Käthe Kollwitz's *The Outbreak* (1903), Figure 2.2.

Lines have **direction.** They are horizontal, vertical, diagonal, curved, or meandering. In artwork, the direction of lines can describe spatial relationships in the world. Something is above something else; some path leads from left to right; something starts at one location, and then moves to another. Certain ideas can be conventionally associated with line direction. For example, horizontal lines may imply sleep, quiet, or inac-

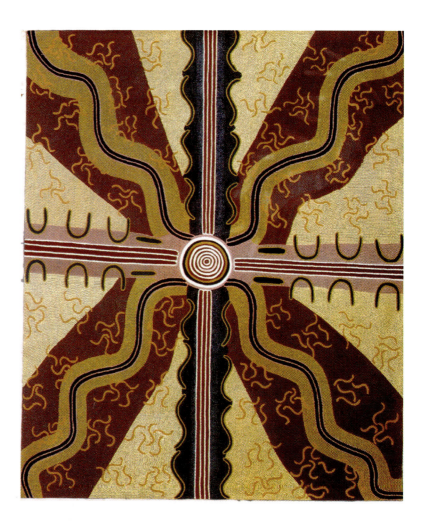

2.1   PADDY CARROLL TJUNGURRAYI. *Witchetty Grub Dreaming.* Paint on canvas. Australia, Aboriginal, from Papunya, 1980. Photo by Jennifer Steele. © Jennifer Steele / Art Resource, NY. See also the text accompanying Figure 7.2.

tivity, an association resulting from the position of the human body at rest. Vertical lines may imply aspiration and yearning, like the defiance of gravity. Diagonal lines may suggest movement, because they occur in the posture of running animals and blowing trees, while curving lines may suggest flowing movement. In Kollwitz's *The Outbreak,* diagonal lines do indeed suggest movement—the peasants to the right are charging forward in revolt. The horizontal lines at the far left, however, do not indicate rest; rather, they show people running at the greatest speed, even faster than the figures drawn with diagonals! The important point to remember is that each artwork provides the context for understanding the meaning of specific lines.

When several lines occur together, their arrangement can be significant. Lines that are all parallel or repetitive in some way may suggest structure or restfulness, while lines that collide or tangle may seem random, conflicting, or unbalanced, like the mass of lines that describe the rioters in *The Outbreak.*

Our eyes see a world full of areas of varying gray tones and shapes, yet many artworks contain nothing but lines. Outlines can show **shape,** which is a two-dimensional entity we will discuss more on page 35. Outlines mark the outer edges of an object, allowing artists to reduce internal detail but retain recognizability of the object. If artists choose to draw only the outline, they are rendering the image in a **contour** line. Artists also can use lines to describe **tones,** or different

areas of gray, some lighter and some darker. Lines put down in parallel or crisscross patterns are called **hatching.** Hatching produces tonal gradation, or the appearance of subtly varying shades of gray, as we can see in *The Outbreak.*

Lines can also express emotion, because they come in such great variety. Some are precise and controlled. Others are blunt, rough, or heavy, as if the result of a gouging, jabbing action. Others may be fine, wavering, or delicate, and still others may be sweeping, broad, and vigorous. Artists use the range of possible line qualities not only to describe the world they see, but also to express their own emotions about it. The lines in *Witchetty Grub Dreaming* are orderly, controlled, and either smoothly curving or parallel and straight. These qualities permeate the entire artwork. In contrast, *The Outbreak* has jagged and jabbing lines, appropriate for an image of a riot. These are expressive **gesture lines,** and they give a sense of the fury of a riot. The heavy, blunt, dark diagonals of the woman in the foreground, combined with her pose, communicate a sense of terrible anger. The almost horizontal woman at the far left speaks of out-of-control, breakneck speed.

Linear elements can exist in three dimensions, in architecture as well as in sculpture. Any thin string, rope, wire, chain, stick, or rod used in a sculpture can function like a line. Even substantial logs can appear linear when placed in an open space, where their thickness is less important than their height. Artist Paddy Dhatangu and his colleagues use a series of vertical

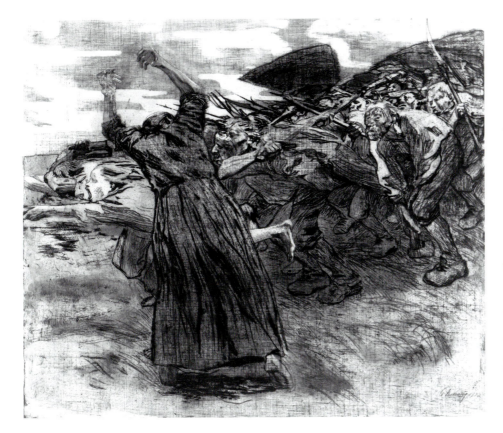

2.2 KÄTHE KOLLWITZ. *The Outbreak. ("Losbruch").* Etching, 20" × 23¼". Germany, 1903. Reproduced from the collections of the Library of Congress Washington, D.C. / © 2004 Artists Rights Society (ARS), New York / VG Bild-Kunst, Bonn. See also the text accompanying Figure 12.2.

standing logs in their piece entitled *The Aboriginal Memorial* (1988), Figure 2.3. Even though some logs are thick and are decorated with horizontal bands of paint, the upward linear emphasis remains a dominant element in the piece.

LIGHT AND VALUE

Light is the basis for vision. People need light to begin the process of perception from which we form ideas. Without light, we cannot visually define form and spatial relationships. Only with light is art possible.

What is **light?** It is electromagnetic energy. It is radiation from the sun in certain specific wavelengths that stimulate the eyes and brain. Light produces visual sensations.

There are two kinds of light, one natural and the other artificial. The sun, moon, stars, lightning, and fire are natural sources, while incandescent, fluorescent, neon, and laser lights are artificial. In art, light might be an actual element. However, more artists depend upon general illumination to make their work visible because their art reflects light. They also create lighter or darker surfaces within their artwork to make a picture of something. **Value** refers to lightness or darkness of a surface in non-light-emitting media. White is the lightest tone, black is the darkest, and all the gray tones form a continuum in between, as we see in the value scale in Figure 2.4A. This is called an **achromatic** value scale, as it deals only with grays. Value can also be associated with color: red can still be red, but it can be lighter or darker, or different values of the color, as we see in the **chromatic** value scale in Figure 2.4B. Artists can carefully manipulate gradations in values to create the appearance of natural light on objects. This is called **shading,** and it can be seen in the drawing of the ball in Figure 2.4C.

Artists use the element of value in various ways. With it, artists can depict depth and volume, or they might express an emotion, or they can create emphasis in an image. In Figure 2.5, we see Raphael's *Madonna of the Meadow* (c. 1505), where value creates the illusion of depth and volume. The figures look rounded because of the chromatic and achromatic gradations in value, but the surface of the painting is actually flat. Raphael also achieved the illusion of deep space because the background fades into light, low-contrast values. Both uses of value became popular with fifteenth-century Italian painters. They used the term **chiaroscuro** for the light–dark gradations that give the illusion of rounded form on a flat painting, and the term **atmospheric perspective** (or **aerial perspective**) for the light, bleached out, fuzzy handling of distant forms to make them seem far away.

Artists also use the element of value in their work when they want to express an emotion or an idea with emotion, or to arouse the emotion of a viewer. We already saw Käthe Kollwitz's *The Outbreak* (Figure 2.2), in which the artist used strong contrasts in value to create a disturbing scene.

Many media lend themselves easily to the creation of value. Charcoal, graphite, pastels, and oil paint are just a few

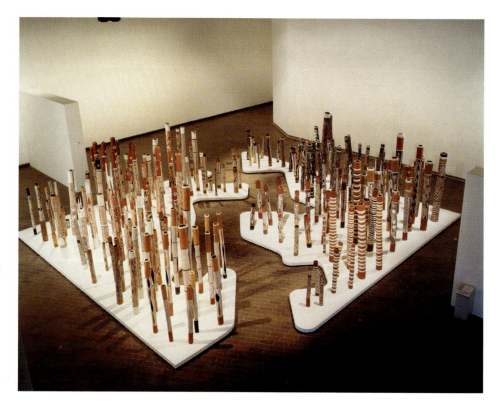

2.3 PADDY DHATANGU, DAVID MALANGI, GEORGE MILPURRURRU, JIMMY WULULU, AND OTHER ARTISTS FROM RAMINGINING. *The Aboriginal Memorial.* Natural pigments on 200 logs; heights: 16" to 128". Australia, 1988. National Gallery of Art, Canberra. © 2004 Artists Rights Society (ARS), New York / VI$COPY, Australia. See also the text accompanying Figure 12.21.

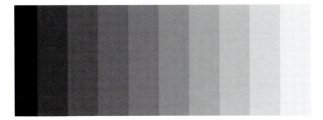

A. Achromatic value scale

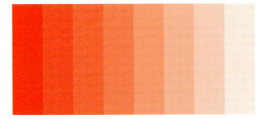

B. Chromatic value scale

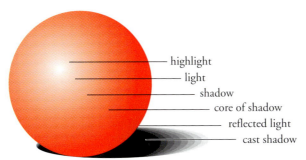

- highlight
- light
- shadow
- core of shadow
- reflected light
- cast shadow

C. Values creating the illusion of volume

2.4 Value Diagram.
A. Achromatic value scale, showing only black, white, and gray tones.
B. Chromatic value scale, showing various values of red.
C. Values can create the illusion of volume.

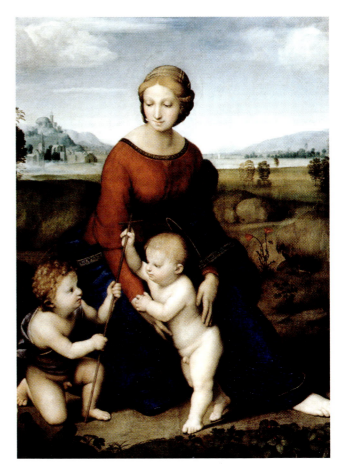

2.5 RAPHAEL. *Madonna of the Meadow.* Panel painting, 44^1/$_2$" × 34^1/$_4$". Italy, c. 1505. Kunsthistorisches Museum, Vienna. © Francis G. Mayer / Corbis. See also the text accompanying Figure 9.9.

of the traditional materials that can produce a great variety of values. Newer media, including photography and film, also create a wide range of values, especially in black-and-white formats.

COLOR

Color is a wonderful phenomenon that people are lucky to enjoy. This section is saturated with color terminology. As you read through all the terms, however, remember the intense associations that colors bring to us, including delight, pleasure, sensuality, or even revulsion.

People see color because of **ambient light,** which is the light all around us in our world. Ambient light comes directly from such sources as the sun or a lamp, or is reflected off surfaces all around us. Some of that ambient light passes

into our eyes. It has various wavelengths, which stimulate light-sensitive structures in our eyes. We call these sensations "colors."

We can see colors in two ways, either in refracted light or in the reflection of light from an object. We see color in refracted light when a prism breaks a light beam into a **spectrum** of color, or in a rainbow after a storm. We see color in reflected light when we look at the objects around us, because their surfaces reflect certain rays of ambient light while absorbing others. Those rays that are reflected to our eyes are the color of the object. For example, a green chair absorbs all the wavelengths of visible light except the "green" wavelength, which is reflected back into our eyes.

The properties of color are hue, value, and intensity. **Hue** is the pure state of color our eye sees in the color spectrum and is the name given to that color, such as red, blue, yellow, green, purple, and orange. **Value** in color is lightness and darkness within a hue, as we already saw in *Madonna of the Meadow* (Figure 2.5). When black is added to a hue, a **shade** of that color is created, while the addition of white results in a **tint** of that color. **Intensity** in color is the brightness and dullness of a hue. Another word for intensity is **chroma**. A high-intensity color is brilliant, vivid, and saturated, while a low-intensity color is faded or dull. *Madonna of the Meadow* has both high- and low-intensity colors. We see high-intensity colors in the spectrum. All colors in Figure 2.6 are high-intensity. Black and white have value, but do not have intensity among their properties.

Artists mix colors through one of two systems: additive and subtractive (Figure 2.6). The **additive color system** is the mixture of one light wavelength with another, resulting in mixed colors in a light-emitting medium. In additive color systems, absence of all light produces darkness (or black), and all light added together results in the brightest, whitest light at the center of Figure 2.6A. In our diagram, we see what happens as red, green, and blue lights are mixed. Theater lighting, performance art, light displays, and computer and video monitors use the additive color system.

In the **subtractive color system,** artists mix pigments to manipulate and control the exact light wavelengths that they want an object to reflect. Thus, the mixture of pigments subtracts (or absorbs) available light in order to let us see certain colors. *Pigment* is color matter that occurs naturally, such as melanin in our skins or chlorophyll in plants. **Pigments** are also powdered substances that can be mixed with oil, water, or other binders to create paints. In the subtractive color system, white is a pigment that reflects almost the entire spectrum of light. Our diagram shows the mixing of red, yellow, and blue. Mixing more and more pigments gives darker results, as the mixture increasingly absorbs the available light, as we see in the center of Figure 2.6B. Many artists use the subtractive color system in creating their work.

Primary colors are those colors that combine to produce the largest number of new colors. Various art media have their distinct primary colors. For example, for light-emitting media, the primary colors are red, blue, and green, as we see on our additive color system diagram. **Secondary colors** result from mixing two primary colors. Again, in light-emitting media, the secondary colors are yellow, cyan, and magenta. Paints use pigments to create colors in the subtractive system, and their primary colors are red, yellow, and blue, while the secondary colors are orange, green, and purple. Mixing one primary color with one of its neighboring secondary colors produces **tertiary colors.** Blue-green is a tertiary color in paint. **Analogous colors** are those that are similar in appearance, especially those in which we can see related hues, such as yellow, yellow-orange, and orange. Analogous colors are next to each other on the color wheel. **Complementary colors** are opposites of each other and, when mixed, give a dull result. In paint, red and green are complementary colors. The color wheel again shows us this relationship. We can see the various colors on the **color**

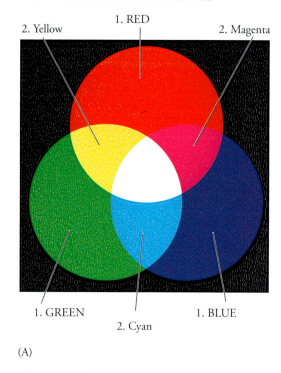

ADDITIVE COLOR SYSTEM

2. Yellow
1. RED
2. Magenta
1. GREEN
2. Cyan
1. BLUE

(A)

2.6 Diagram Showing the Additive and Subtractive Color Systems. Also included is the color wheel, which is a diagram of the subtractive color system as it applies to paint. Note that all three diagrams show the primary colors labeled with "1," secondary colors labeled with "2," and tertiary colors labeled with "3."

wheel in Figure 2.6C, which is a diagram that applies only to color mixing with paints and pigments.

Let's look at the primary and secondary colors in one more medium. Many color images we encounter in our lives are commercially printed, including the color images in this book. Commercial printers use semitransparent inks, and the color mixtures in printed images are all derived from the following primary colors: yellow, magenta (a bright pink), and cyan (a bright blue-green), plus black added for darkness and contrast. The secondary colors are blue, red, and green. You can easily see these primaries, and their resulting mixtures, if you use a strong magnifying glass while looking at a color image in a newspaper. You encounter these same inks and the same CMYK (cyan, magenta, yellow, black; black = K) primaries in your home computer printer, and your printouts of color images are made from mixtures of these colors.

The chart in Figure 2.7 sums up the primary and secondary colors in various media, plus other color attributes.

Color perception is **relative,** meaning that we see colors differently depending upon their surroundings. Low or high

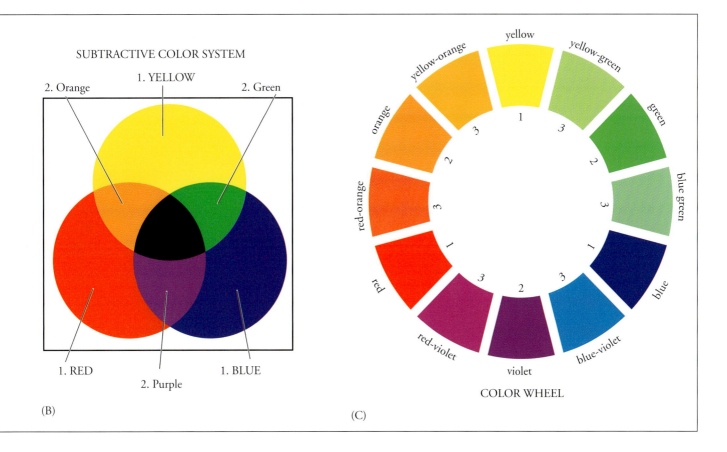

COLOR PROPERTIES IN VARIOUS MEDIA

	Paint	Light-Emitting Media (e.g., Computer Monitor)	Commercial Printing or Computer Printer
Color System	subtractive	additive	subtractive
Effects of Environmental Light Levels	more room light, the brighter the colors	less room light, the brighter the colors	more room light, the brighter the colors
Primary Colors	blue, red, yellow	red, green, blue	cyan, magenta, yellow, black (CMYK)
Secondary Colors	purple (blue + red) green (yellow + blue) orange (red + yellow)	yellow (red + green) cyan (green + blue) magenta (red + blue)	red (magenta + yellow) blue (cyan + magenta) green (yellow + cyan)
Complementaries	blue − orange red − green yellow − purple	red − cyan green − magenta blue − yellow	cyan − red magenta − green yellow − blue
Mixture of All Primaries	gray or dull neutral	white	black

2.7 Chart Showing Color Properties in Various Media.

light levels in our environment affect our perception of color. Light-emitting media are much more dramatic in a dark room. Watch TV in the dark, and you will see this effect. In a very bright room, however, you can barely see the television image. Conversely, reflective media need a lot of light in order to be seen well. A spotlight on a painting makes its colors vivid, while a dim room makes it hard to see. Because natural light is constantly changing, our visual perception is also. As more light illuminates our environment, the brighter the colors become in paintings. As the light fades, so does color. There is no single, fixed, permanent state that the painting "looks like."

We also experience **relativity of color perception** when we look at certain combinations of colors. In Figure 2.8, the colors in the center of the top row of squares appear to be dif-ferent even though they are exactly the same, while the dull pink squares in the lower row appear to be the same, but are different. Eye fatigue also affects our color perception. Stare at the white dot in the center of the "flag" printed in Figure 2.8 for one minute. You will notice as the minute wears on that you have trouble seeing the colors, which at first were so clear and bright. After the minute has passed, look at a white wall, and you will see an afterimage of the flag, but the colors have shifted and appear to be red, white, and blue, the complemen-tary colors of the colors used in the printed "flag." Because of eye fatigue, your eyes see the opposite of the printed colors.

Color can be used to depict **local colors,** which are the colors we normally find in the objects around us. Look again at the *Madonna of the Meadow* (Figure 2.5), in which the

The three small center squares above seem to be different shades of orange, but they are all the same.

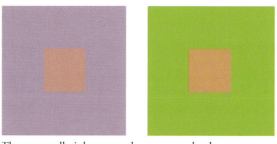

The two small pink squares above seem to be the same . . .

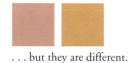

. . . but they are different.

2.8　The Relativity of Color Perception. Color perception changes, depending upon surrounding colors and eye fatigue. The inner orange squares are the same on the top row, but look different. The pink inner squares look the same on the second row, but they are different. The flag at the bottom demonstrates the relativity of color perception due to eye fatigue. Stare at the white dot in the center of the flag for 60 seconds. Then look at a blank white wall to see an afterimage of the flag in red, white, and blue.

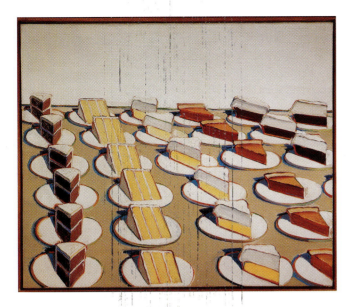

2.9   WAYNE THIEBAUD. *Pie Counter.* Oil on canvas, 30" ×
36". USA, 1963. Photo © 2004 Whitney Museum of
American Art. © Wayne Thiebaud/Licensed by VAGA,
New York, NY. See also the text accompanying Figure 7.16.

paint gives a convincing representation of the local colors of
landscape, sky, and people.

Color can identify ideas, suggest sensations, and even
evoke emotions. It can make us feel warm or cool, happy or
sad, peaceful or angry, motivated or discouraged. Some colors are considered warm while others are deemed cool. Colors associated with the sun and fire, such as yellows, reds,
and oranges, would be **warm.** Colors associated with plant
life, sky, and water, such as greens, blues, and purples, would
be **cool.** Warm and cool colors can affect an audience both
physically and emotionally. Certain colors in the surroundings can actually influence your alertness, sense of well-
being, and sense of inner peace. In Figure 2.9, we see Wayne
Thiebaud's painting, *Pie Counter* (1963). The artist expres-
sively used color to increase the visual appeal of the brightly
colored food and to allude to the modern phenomena of
artificial light, artificial food coloring, and the standardiza-
tion of food production.

Colors can be symbolic and, thus, associated with ideas
or events. The colors of a country's flag are tied to concepts of
national identity and patriotism. Certain colors might mean a
holiday or a celebration, such as red and green for Christmas-
time in Western cultures, or red for a wedding in Asian cultures.
The colors used in *The Aboriginal Memorial* (Figure 2.3) are
those used in traditional Aboriginal art, and, thus, they represent Aboriginal culture.

Different cultures may associate colors with various
attributes. For example, you might think of blue in relation to
the ethereal, to purity, or to depression. Yellow might mean
cowardice, or it might mean youth, spring, and rebirth. Asso-

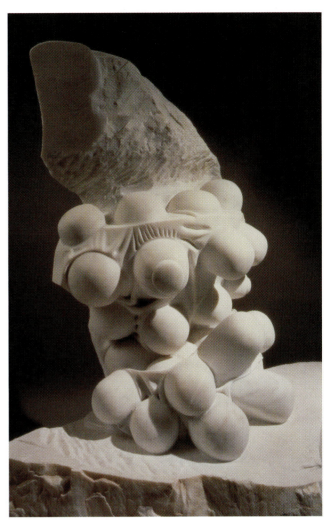

2.10   LOUISE BOURGEOIS. *Blind Man's Bluff.* Marble, 36"
× 35½" × 25". USA, 1984. Collection Cleveland Museum
of Art. Courtesy Cheim & Read, New York. Photo by Allan
Finkelman. Art © Louise Bourgeois/ Licensed by VAGA,
New York, NY. See also the text accompanying Figure 8.28.

ciations change from culture to culture (so the red for wed-
dings in Asia becomes white in Western cultures). Even within
a culture, the same color may have contradictory meanings—
as blue and yellow do.

TEXTURE AND PATTERN

Texture is a surface characteristic that is tactile or visual. **Tactile texture** consists of physical surface variations that can be
perceived by the sense of touch. Sculptures often have distinctive tactile textures, as on Louise Bourgeois's *Blind Man's Bluff*
(1984), Figure 2.10, a marble sculpture with some velvety
smooth areas and some roughly gouged areas. Even a painting
or drawing may have a tactile texture if the canvas or paper
surface is rough or if the medium produces a tactile texture.
There are thick, textured brushstrokes in Thiebaud's *Pie Counter*
(Figure 2.9). Sometimes a medium has an inherent texture.

Mosaic is an example. Mosaic is a method of creating a picture out of small, colored glass or stone pieces, which are glued to a surface, as can be seen in Figure 2.11, *Emperor Justinian and His Attendants.*

Visual texture is an illusionary texture that may be simulated, abstracted, or invented. Returning to Figure 2.11, we see that it has not only the tactile texture of the mosaic stones, but also illusionary visual textures that **simulate** the fabrics the people are wearing. Texture can be **abstracted** as well, meaning that it is based on some existing texture, but has been simplified and regularized. Look back at the first illustration in this chapter, *Witchetty Grub Dreaming* (Figure 2.1), where the curving grubs and the texture of dirt have been abstracted. The painting also has **invented** textures, which are apparently products of human imagination. The closely placed dots and strokes of paint that fill many areas are examples.

Pattern is a configuration with a repeated visual form (or forms). Texture and pattern are related, because if a pattern is reduced drastically in size, it is often perceived as a texture, and if a texture is greatly increased in size, it is likely to be perceived as a pattern. **Natural patterns** occur all around us,

in leaves and flowers, in cloud and crystal formations, in wave patterns, and so on. In natural patterns, the repeated elements may resemble each other, but not be exactly alike. The intervals between elements also may vary. **Geometric patterns** have regular elements spaced at regular intervals. They are common in math, interior design, and art.

Pattern in art is often an organizing element, and it may appear irregularly or with great regularity. In Thiebaud's *Pie Counter* (Figure 2.9), the pies repeat in an irregular pattern. The pies themselves, and the space, are not rigid. Figure 2.12 shows the exquisite wall pattern in the main portal of the *Masjid-i-Shah* (1612–1637), an Islamic mosque. Area upon area of pattern creates a striking visual impression. Some patterns are totally invented, some are geometric, some contain highly abstracted plant forms, and some are highly sophisticated writing. Pattern can also have symbolic value. In our example here, the overwhelming variety and richness of the pattern is an Islamic device to express the idea that all the wonder of creation originates in Allah.

We often see pattern used as **decoration,** for example, on wrapping paper, wallpaper, or fabric design. Pattern's function

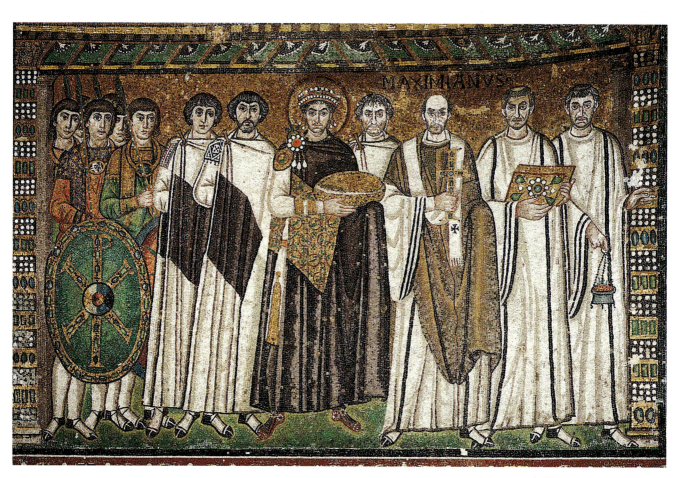

 2.11   *Emperor Justinian and His Attendants.* Mosaic on the north wall of the apse. Church of San Vitale, Ravenna, Italy, c. 547. Canali Photobank. See also the text accompanying Figure 11.2.

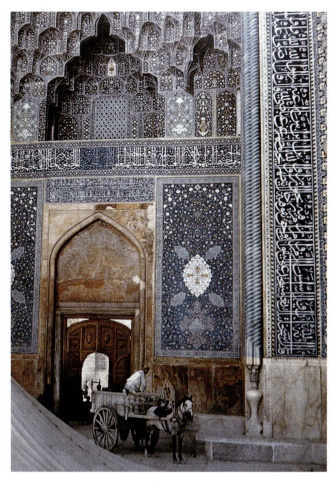

2.12 Detail of the main portal of the *Masjid-i-Shah,* or Royal Mosque. Isfahan, Iran, 1612–1637. Photo Wim Swaan, Getty Research Library. See also the text accompanying Figure 9.45.

in these instances is to give visual pleasure. Yet pattern is also an important tool for thinking visually. Pattern helps organize ideas and concepts into visual **diagrams** that make relationships clear. We see pattern as the basis of flowcharts, street maps, mechanical diagrams, and floor plans. We see patterns in the creative work of many artists, engineers, scientists, and untrained people.

SHAPE AND VOLUME

Two more elements in an artwork are shape and volume. **Shape** is a two-dimensional visual entity. **Regular shapes** are **geometric.** We have names for many regular shapes, such as *circle, square, triangle, hexagon,* and *teardrop.* **Irregular shapes** are unique and often complex, and, therefore, have no simple, defining names. Instead, they are the shapes of mysterious rug stains, color patches of a cat's fur, star clusters in space, or the outline of a human body. Irregular shapes are often **organic** or **biomorphic,** in that they resemble living beings. We can create shapes by defining their outer edges through line, or with areas of color or value changes.

Volume is a three-dimensional entity, in contrast to shape, which is two-dimensional. Like shape, volumes can be regular or irregular, geometric or biomorphic. And, like pattern and texture, shape and volume may have simulated reality, may be abstracted from reality, or may be invented. Volumes may have more or less physical bulk, or **mass.** An open or wire-frame structure, like a birdcage, can have a large volume but little mass. A large block of solid stone has both considerable mass and volume.

Let us discuss shape and volume as they appear in three works of art. The Kwakiutl *Transformation Mask* (Figure 2.13) is a three-dimensional mass of shaped wood (which can change

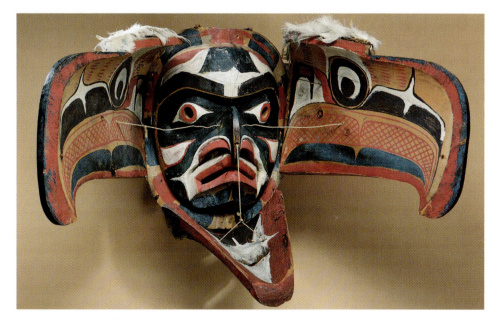

2.13 *Transformation Mask.* Painted wood. Kwakiutl. British Columbia. American Museum of Natural History, New York. See also the text accompanying Figures 1.17 and 9.13.

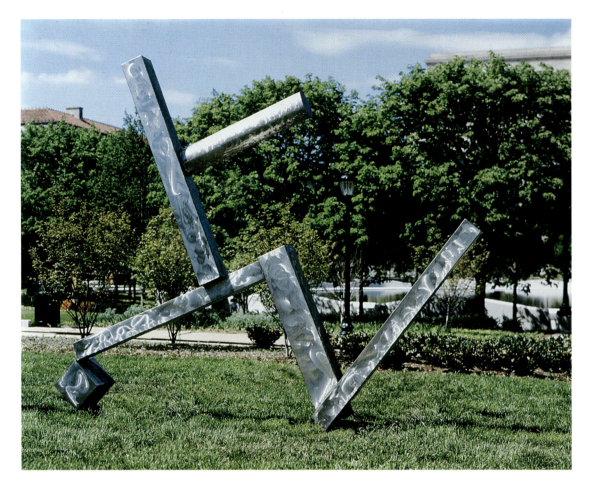

 2.14 DAVID SMITH. *Cubi XXVI*. Steel, approximately 10' × 12'6" × 2'3". USA, 1965. National Gallery of Art, Washington, D.C. Image © National Gallery of Art, Washington. Art © David Smith/Licensed by VAGA, New York, NY. See also the text accompanying Figure 15.34.

its mass when the outer mask is closed), abstracted from a bird and a person. In addition, its surface is painted with various geometric two-dimensional shapes, which in turn are abstracted from feathers, eyes, claws, beaks, and so on. Louise Bourgeois's *Blind Man's Bluff* (Figure 2.10) has different qualities. Its organic forms simulate women's breasts. The overall silhouette of the sculpture resembles a phallus, while it sits on a block that resembles a raw stone. Both the *Transformation Mask* and *Blind Man's Bluff,* however, are examples of sculpture as solid mass. In contrast, *Cubi XXVI* (Figure 2.14), by David Smith from 1965, is a volume that incorporates voids and solids. Smith's geometric shapes and volumes seem to be invented, rather than simulated or abstracted, although, in its general appearance, his sculpture does recall the machine age and industrialism.

SPACE

When one hears the word *space,* one might think of the void of outer space, or perhaps one's own personal space, or a work space. In art, space is the element that allows the object to exist. All artwork occupies space. Even "two-dimensional" works, such as paintings, are actually three-dimensional objects. In this section, we will look at three kinds of space in relation to art: (1) the kinds of space that exist on the flat picture plane; (2) the space of sculpture, which is both the area it occupies and the voids it contains; and (3) the space of performance art, installation, and inter-media work.

First, let us look at space in two-dimensional art. The first kind is **planar space,** the height and width of the picture surface. The imagery in Figure 2.15, Jacob Lawrence's *No. 36 . . . ,* exists on the surface plane. Both the images and background appear flat. In *Self-Portrait with Monkey* painted in 1938 (Figure 2.16), Frida Kahlo's imagery has the illusion of some depth. Her face and neck seem to have volume because of **shading.** Because of **overlapping,** her body appears to be in front of the monkey and plants, creating a shallow space.

To create the appearance of deeper space in pictures, artists use **perspective,** which is a group of methods for creating the

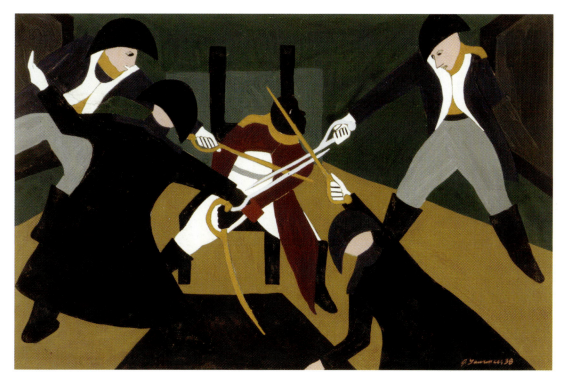

2.15   JACOB LAWRENCE. *No. 36: During the Truce Toussaint Is Deceived and Arrested by Leclerc. Leclerc Led Toussaint to Believe He Was Sincere, Believing That When Toussaint Was Out of the Way, the Blacks Would Surrender.* Tempera on paper, 11" × 19". USA, 1937–1938. Photograph courtesy of Gwendolyn Knight Lawrence / Art Resource, NY © 2004 Gwendolyn Knight Lawrence / Artists Rights Society (ARS), New York. See also the text accompanying Figure 12.12.

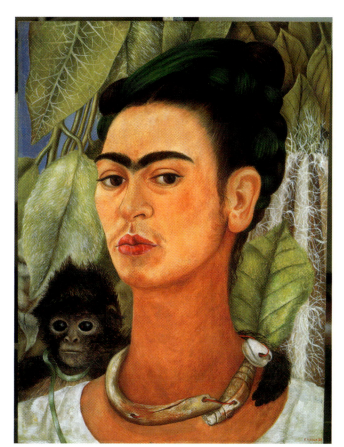

illusion of depth on a flat picture plane. We already saw one example in the section "Light and Value," where we discussed **atmospheric perspective,** or **aerial perspective,** in which distant objects appear in low contrast and faded. Another kind is **linear perspective,** which operates on the theory that parallel lines appear to converge as they recede. They seem to meet on an imaginary line called the **horizon line,** or on eye level. The horizon line is the division between objects that are above the viewer's eye level in a picture, and those that are below.

2.16   FRIDA KAHLO. *Self-Portrait with Monkey.* Oil on masonite, 16" × 12". Mexico, 1938. Albright-Knox Art Gallery, Buffalo, New York, Bequest of A. Conger Goodyear, 1966. See also the text accompanying Figure 13.9.

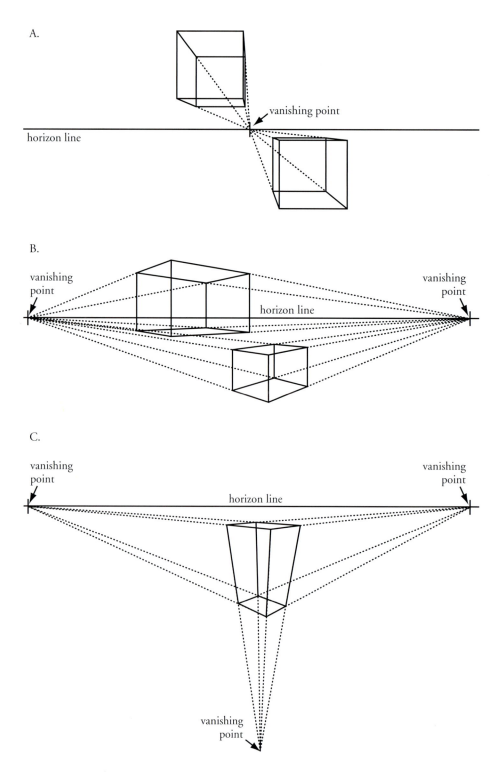

2.17   Diagram of Linear Perspective. A. One-point perspective. B. Two-point perspective. C. Three-point perspective.

The three types of linear perspective—one-, two-, and three-point—are shown in the diagram in Figure 2.17. In **one-point perspective,** the frontal plane of a volume is closest to the viewer, and all other planes appear to recede to a single vanishing point. In **two-point perspective,** a single edge (or line) of a volume is closest to the viewer, and all planes appear to recede to one of two vanishing points. In **three-point perspective,** only a single point of a volume is closest to the

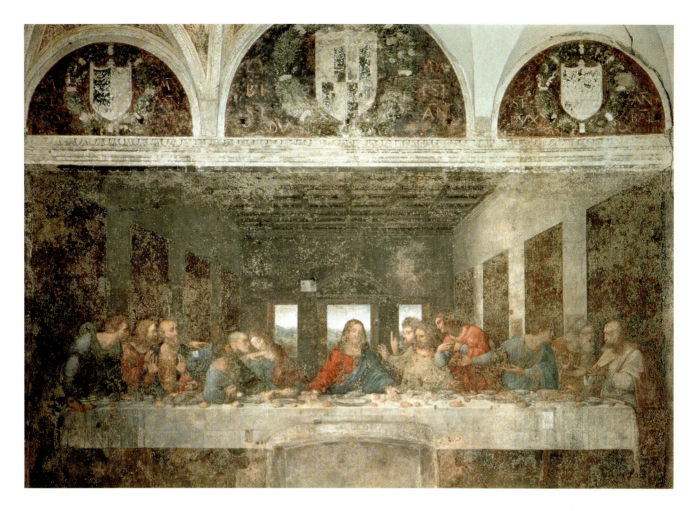

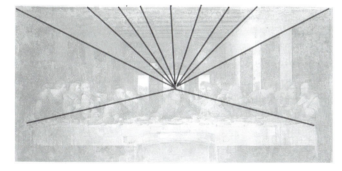

2.18A

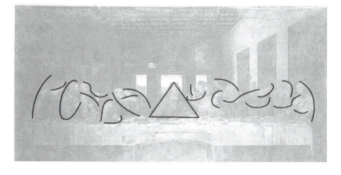

2.18B

2.18 LEONARDO DA VINCI. *Last Supper.* Experimental paint on plaster, 14'5" × 28'. Refectory of Santa Maria della Grazie, Milan, Italy, 1495–1498. Diagram 2.18A shows one-point perspective. Diagram 2.18B shows the symmetry of the composition, as well as its variety in the gestures. © Edimédia/CORBIS. See also the text accompanying Figure 7.19.

viewer, and all planes seem to recede to one of three vanishing points. In Figure 2.18, we see Leonardo da Vinci's *Last Supper* (1495–1498), a precise exercise in one-point perspective. The vanishing point is Christ's head, located exactly in the center of the pictorial space. All the parallel planes in the room con-verge to that vanishing point, which emphasizes the Christian symbolism of redemption through Christ.

Two other systems to show space in a picture are isomet-ric perspective and oblique perspective. **Isometric perspec-tive,** which is especially used in architectural drafting, renders

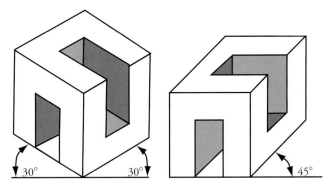

30°   30°   45°

2.19   A. An example of an ISOMETRIC projection. B. An example of an OBLIQUE projection.

planes on a diagonal that does not recede in space (Figure 2.19A). The side planes are drawn at a thirty-degree angle to the left and right. In **oblique perspective,** a three-dimensional object is rendered with the front and back parallel (Figure 2.19B). The side planes are drawn at a forty-five-degree angle from the front plane. In Figure 2.20, *Babur Supervising the Layout of the Garden of Fidelity* (c. 1590), we see the boxlike gardens painted in oblique perspective. The parallel planes of the gardens do not visually recede.

CONNECTION
Compare the deep space and use of the horizon line in the painting of The Harvesters *(Figure 7.12, page 164) with the shallow space in* Witchetty Grub Dreaming *(Figure 2.1, page 26).*

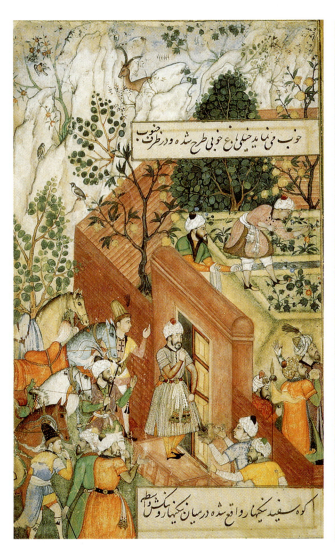

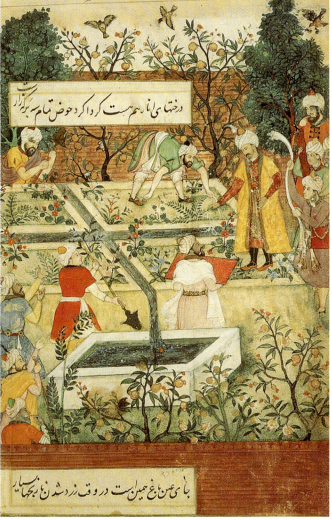

2.20   BISHNDAS, PORTRAITS BY NANHA. *Babur Supervising the Layout of the Garden of Fidelity.* Manuscript painting, gouache and gold on paper, 8³/₄" × 5³/₄". Mughal, India, c. 1590. Victoria and Albert Museum, London, IM 276–1913. See also the text accompanying Figure 15.17.

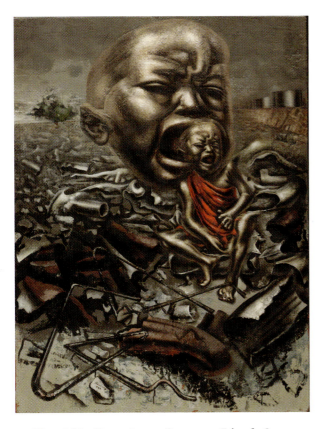

2.21 DAVID ALFARO SIQUEIROS. *Echo of a Scream.* Enamel on wood, 48" × 36". Mexico, 1937. Gift of Edward M. M. Warburg (633.1939). The Museum of Modern Art, NY © Estate of David Alfaro Siqueiros / SOMAAP, Mexico City / VAGA, New York. See also the text accompanying Figures 1.5 and 12.5.

Artists may use **multipoint perspective** in an image, where they employ many different systems for various details all in the same drawing. They also may use **amplified perspective** to give their imagery dramatic emphasis, as seen in Figure 2.21, *Echo of a Scream* (1937). The baby's face is exaggerated, achieving a harsh visual impact, which is the intent of the piece.

Now, let us turn to space in sculpture. First, that space consists of voids and solids within the sculpture itself. We have already seen David Smith's *Cubi XXVI* (Figure 2.14), where the voids within the sculpture are important parts of the overall design. They create the suggestion of other, "missing" geometric shapes. We call these voids the **negative space** in an artwork. Sculptural space includes the volume that a sculpture occupies. *Cubi XXVI* occupies a considerable amount of floor and air space, giving it a presence that is beyond just the mass of the materials alone.

Space is an essential element in installation, performance, and inter-media art. In Figure 2.22, we see Jenny Holzer's installation, *Untitled (Selected Writings),* dated 1989, which she created specifically for the interior space of the Solomon R. Guggenheim Museum in New York City. This piece can only appear as it is in this space. In any other space, the elements in the piece would have to be rearranged, thus creating a new piece, albeit a variation of the original work.

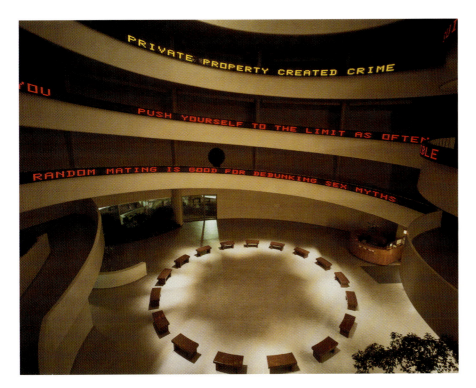

2.22 JENNY HOLZER. *Untitled (Selected Writings).* Extended helical LED electronic signboard, with selected writings; 17 Indian Red granite benches. Installation view at Solomon R. Guggenheim Museum. USA, 1989. Photo: David Heald, courtesy Solomon R. Guggenheim Museum. © 2004 Jenny Holzer / Artists Rights Society (ARS), New York. See also the text accompanying Figure 12.29.

TIME AND MOTION

Although it is invisible, time certainly impacts everyone's life. Time is an important element in all artwork. For static work, or art that does not move, **time** is the period in which audience members receive the artwork, or the period during which they view it. For artists who make non-static works of art, time is the continuum in which they present images and events. Related to time is **motion,** the act or process of something changing place. Obviously, motion cannot exist without time, and motion is one way to illustrate the passage of time.

Time and motion are important components in Jenny Holzer's installation, *Untitled (Selected Writings).* Short sentences scroll upward at a fast pace on a long, spiral, flashing display that circles the inside of the Guggenheim Museum. The words are in motion, and they move fast, so we have only limited time to try to make sense of them as they rush by. The longer we stand there, the more phrases move past us. Motion and time are important components of performance or ritual art. Figure 2.23 shows a performance by *Kanaga Masked Dancers* of the Dogon people of Mali, Africa. The human body in motion is a frequent component in performance art. Film and video are two time- and motion-based media.

Artist Umberto Boccioni used implied motion in his sculpture, *Unique Forms of Continuity in Space,* dated 1931 (Figure 2.24). The forward attitude and flowing forms of the figure suggest acceleration and speed, almost as if a race was going on. Repeated imagery also expresses motion in static art. In 1885, Eadweard Muybridge photographed *Handspring, a flying pigeon interfering* (Figure 2.25), with two sequences of images that arrest motion at specific time intervals. His work was a precursor to film.

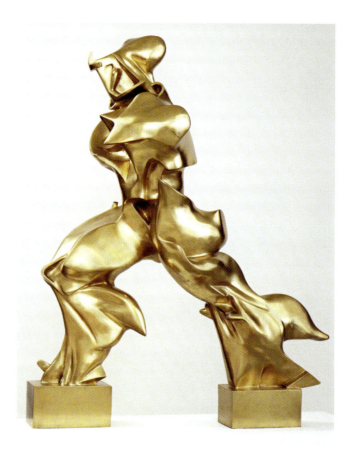

2.24   UMBERTO BOCCIONI. *Unique Forms of Continuity in Space.* Bronze (cast 1931), approx. 43.3" high. Italy, 1913. The Museum of Modern Art, New York. Acquired through the Lillie P. Bliss Bequest. © Digital Image © The Museum of Modern Art/Licensed by SCALA / Art Resource, NY. See also the text accompanying Figure 13.21.

2.23   *Kanaga Masked Dancers.* Dogon people, Mali, Africa, twentieth century. Hutchison Library. See also the text accompanying Figure 16.20.

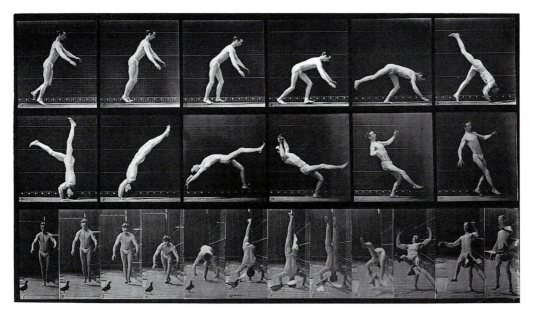

 2.25   EADWEARD MUYBRIDGE. *Handspring, a flying pigeon interfering, June 26, 1885.* Print from an original master negative, Plate 365 of "Animal Locomotion." Britain/Scotland/USA, 1887. International Museum of Photography at George Eastman House, Rochester, New York. See also the text accompanying Figure 13.19.

CHANCE/IMPROVISATION/ SPONTANEITY

Many artists purposely structure their work so that it allows for the introduction of the elements of chance, improvisation, or spontaneity. Those chance, improvised, or spontaneous occurrences strongly affect the visual organization of the artwork. It may seem strange to include the "uncontrolled" as an element

of composition. Yet, to many artists, such events are opportunities to incorporate the unexpected into a work, or to make it unique each time it is seen.

In *Household* (1964), Figure 2.26, artist Allan Kaprow carefully planned the event, but in doing so, he did not control the outcome. His role as artist was to set up certain parameters that allowed for audience improvisation. Likewise, in Jean

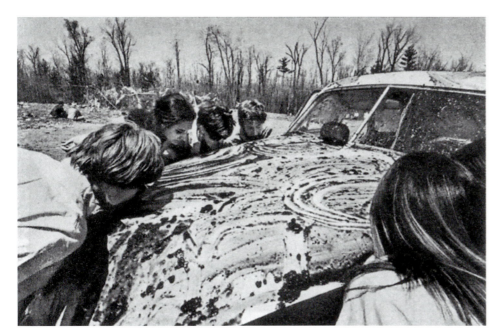

 2.26   ALLAN KAPROW. *Household,* performance "Happening." Commissioned by Cornell University, New York, May 1964. © 2004 Allan Kaprow. Used by permission of the J. Paul Getty Museum, Los Angeles. See also the text accompanying Figure 16.15.

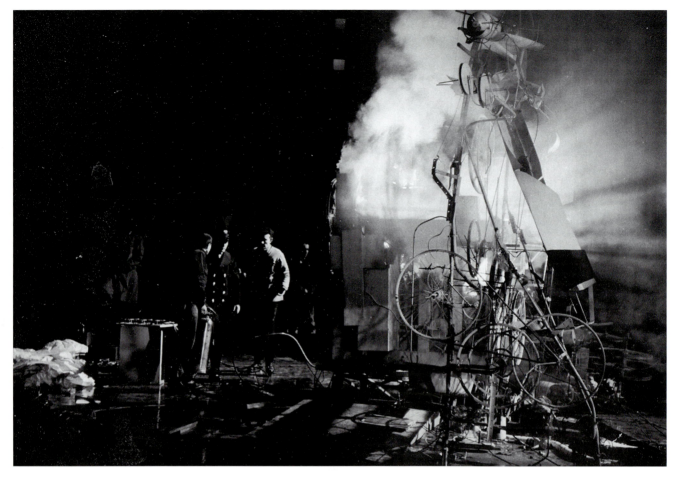

2.27   JEAN TINGUELY. *Homage to New York: A Self-Constructing, Self-Destructing Work of Art.* Mixed media sculpture. Switzerland, 1960. Photograph of the work as it self-destroyed in New York City on March 17, 1960. Photo by David Gahr. © 2004 David Gahr © 2004 Artists Rights Society (ARS), New York / ADAGP, Paris. See also the text accompanying Figure 15.36.

Tinguely's *Homage to New York* (1960), Figure 2.27, it was important that the artwork self-destruct in an uncontrolled way, even though Tinguely set it up to do so. With Lynn Hershman's *Deep Contact* (1990), Figure 2.28, the viewers/participants have unique and individual experiences of the artwork because of the choices they make as the program is running. In addition, their faces are introduced into the art piece by means of a video camera that is trained on them as they interact with *Deep Contact.*

ENGAGING ALL THE SENSES

Although we tend to think of art in visual terms, many artworks appeal to other senses as well. The *Kanaga Masked Dancers* (Figure 2.23) are one obvious example. The dancers perform to music, and that sound component is integral to the art. Many artworks appear to be strictly visual, especially when on display in an art museum. Some of them, however, have been removed from their original context in which they were not simply visual.

For the last several centuries, most Western art has emphasized the visual component, as we have seen in Leonardo's *Last Supper* and Raphael's *Madonna of the Meadow.* Recently, however, that has changed. The erotic nature of Louise Bourgeois's *Blind Man's Bluff* (Figure 2.10) invites touch, while museum protocol forbids it, creating some of the tension in the piece. Other works are more accommodating to all the senses. Film and video have entered the fine arts area, and sound again is an essential formal element, as essential to the whole as the visual. Jean Tinguely's *Homage to New York: A Self-Constructing, Self-Destructing Work of Art* (Figure 2.27) was not so much an object as a spectacular event, as an artwork/machine destroyed itself amid the sound of crashing machine parts and the smell of smoke. In some cases, viewers may experience a piece through taste, touch, and smell, in addition to sight and sound. Kaprow's *Household* (Figure 2.26) was an art event called a Happening in which all the senses were engaged by all the participants.

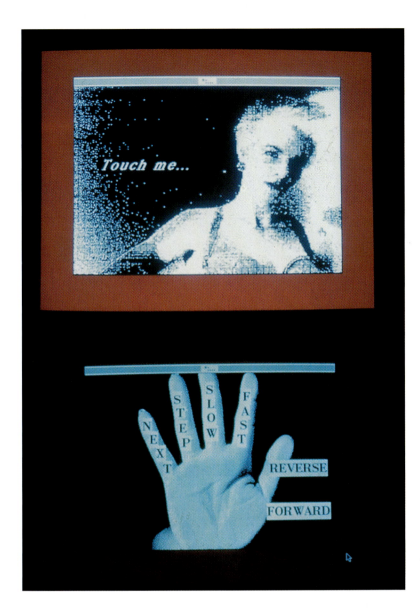

2.28 Lynn Hershman. *Deep Contact.* Interactive computer-video installation at the Museum of Modern Art, San Francisco. USA, 1990. Courtesy of the Artist. See also the text accompanying Figure 8.23.

PRINCIPLES OF COMPOSITION

Now that we have the formal elements of art, it is necessary to see how artists put them all together successfully in an artwork. The arrangement of the formal elements in a work of art is called its **composition.** Certain guides facilitate the composing of an artwork, and they are called the principles of composition. Those principles include balance, rhythm, scale, proportion, emphasis, variety, and unity. We'll look at each principle and see how it functions in art.

BALANCE

Balance in an artwork is the placement of all the elements of the composition so that their visual weights seem evenly distributed. *Weight* generally means the amount of attention an

element commands from the viewer. For example, large shapes demand more attention than small; complex forms have greater visual weight than simple ones; and vivid colors are visually weightier than faded colors. When artists compose their artwork, they arrange the visual elements to balance them in a way that helps express the work's theme. We can see several types of balance in artwork.

In **symmetrical balance,** visual weight is distributed evenly throughout the composition. If an imaginary line is drawn vertically down the center of the work, one side would mirror the other. The *Last Supper* diagram (Figure 2.18B) shows the symmetry of the painting, despite the varying lights and darks, and the animated gestures of the apostles.

In **asymmetrical balance,** visual weights are still evenly distributed, but there is no mirror image on each half of the composition. Balance is achieved by the careful distribution

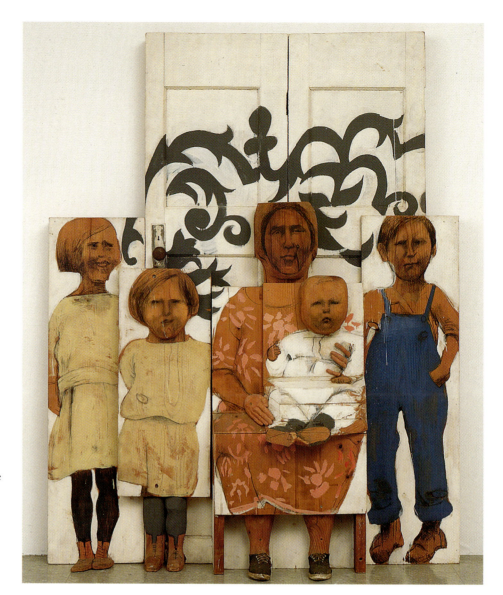

2.29 MARISOL. *The Family.* 1962. Painted wood and other materials in three sections, overall, 6'10⅝" × 65½" × 15½". Advisory Committee Fund. (231.1962.a-c) The Museum of Modern Art, New York, NY. © Museum of Modern Art, New York / Art Resource, NY. Art © Marisol Escobar/Licensed by VAGA, New York, NY. See also the text accompanying Figure 14.19.

of uneven elements. Look at Marisol's sculpture, *The Family* (1962), Figure 2.29. The work is balanced, although the mother figure is off-center, as are the doors in the background. This apparent lack of balance is compensated for by the two girls on one side versus the boy and the baby on the other. The painted decoration keeps your eye at the center of the composition.

Radial balance occurs when all the elements in the composition visually radiate outward from a central point. We have already talked about the line quality in *Witchetty Grub Dreaming* (Figure 2.1), but the radiating lines also unite the entire composition. The small, curved lines create an overall interlace pattern, while the larger lines form a bold shape. The patterns and shapes radiate out from the center, and all is in balance. Although it certainly can communicate other ideas, radial balance is often an organizing principle in spiritually

based art, featured in mandalas, church windows, temple plans, and mosque domes.

RHYTHM

Rhythm in music or poetry consists of repetitive beats, separated by intervals. In an artwork, **rhythm** is the repetition of elements carefully placed in a composition, again separated by intervals. These recurrent visual "beats" may be regular, eccentric, smooth, jerky, fast, slow, progressive, up and down, and alternating. They move the viewer's eye through the composition to give it its rhythm. Rhythm is related to pattern, as we discussed earlier; however, rhythm affects the entire composition, while pattern can be merely one element within a composition.

Regular rhythm is smooth and even, where some visual element is systematically repeated with a standard interval in

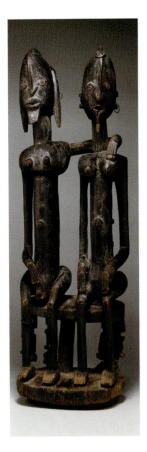

between. Closely related is **alternating rhythm,** where different elements are repeatedly placed side by side, which produces a regular and anticipated sequence. *The Dogon Primordial Couple,* c. nineteenth–twentieth centuries (Figure 2.30), from the Dogon people of Africa, is an excellent example of visual rhythm. Look at it from side to side. The dark, sculptural forms alternate with the voids, or negative spaces. The artist used a rhythmic progression to determine the placement of forms within the composition. The Dogon people associate that rhythmic placement with a sense of order and clarity.

Eccentric rhythm is irregular, but not so much so that the visual beats do not connect. Magdalena Abakanowicz's *Backs* (1976–1982), Figure 2.31, shows a group of hunched figures, slightly irregular in size, with slightly irregular intervals in between. Her work addresses the condition of people in oppressive situations. The visual rhythm seen in the placement of the backs in linear formation communicates the idea of forced conformity.

PROPORTION AND SCALE

Proportion refers to the size of one part in relation to another within a work of art, or the size of one part in relation to the whole. Let us compare the use of proportion in two works of art.

2.30 *The Dogon Primordial Couple.* Wood, 29" high. Mali, Africa, c. nineteenth–twentieth centuries. Metropolitan Museum of Art, New York, Gift of Lester Wunderman, 1977. (1977.394.15) Photograph © 1993 The Metropolitan Museum of Art. See also the text accompanying Figure 8.11.

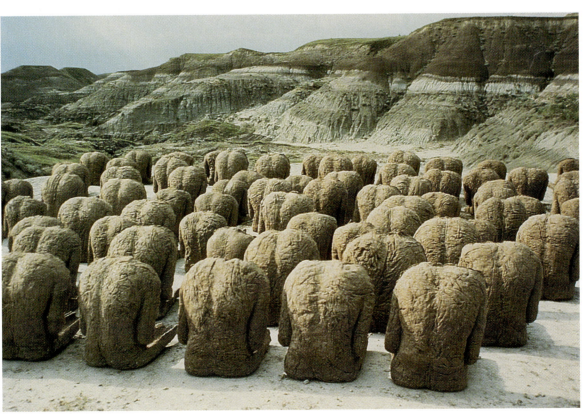

2.31 MAGDALENA ABAKANOWICZ. *Backs.* 80 pieces, burlap and glue, each over life-size. Poland, 1976–1982. Courtesy of Marlborough Gallery, New York. See also the text accompanying Figure 12.28.

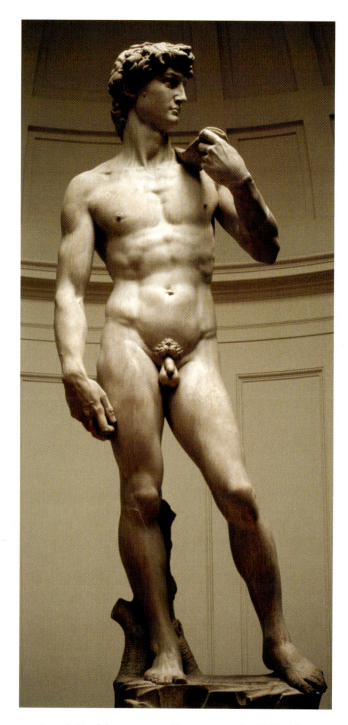

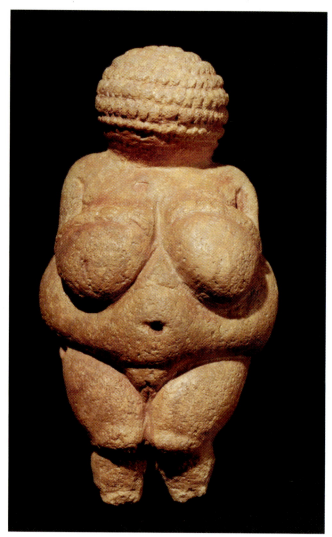

2.33 *Venus of Willendorf.* Early fertility figure. Stone, 4³/₈" high. Austria, c. 25,000–20,000 BCE. © Ali Meyer/Corbis. See also the text accompanying Figure 8.1.

2.32 MICHELANGELO BUONARROTI. *David.* Marble, 14'3" high. Italy, 1501–1504. Galleria dell'Accademia, Florence. ©Michael S. Yamashita/CORBIS. See also the text accompanying Figure 13.18.

Michelangelo's *David,* Figure 2.32, is a Renaissance sculpture in which proportion was somewhat modeled after the Greek canon of proportions developed by the sculptor, Polykleitos. According to Polykleitos, the size of the face is one-ninth the size of the whole figure. The length of the middle finger is exactly one-half that of the entire hand, the

length of the arm is proportional to that of the hand, and so on. Michelangelo added his own interpretation to the Greek proportions by making *David's* hands larger than the canon describes.

By comparison, the *Venus of Willendorf* (c. 25,000–20,000 BCE), Figure 2.33, exhibits different kinds of proportions, and for different reasons. This sculpture certainly resembles a female figure, but the proportions are exaggerated. Breasts, belly, and buttocks are bulbous and proportionally enlarged compared to the rest of the figure. Conversely, the arms are greatly shrunken, the face is deemphasized, and the feet are nonexistent. The unknown sculptor of the *Venus of Willendorf* chose these proportions to guide the composition of this sculpture. The exaggerated body parts correspond to female reproductive forms, presumably making this a fertility goddess or charm.

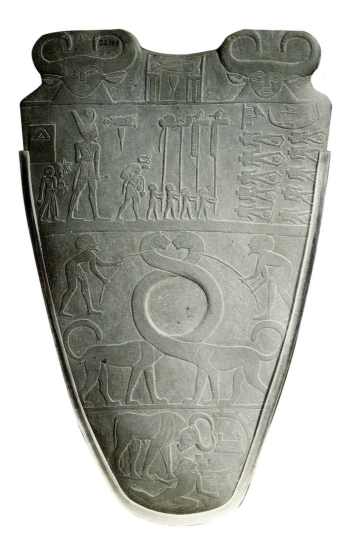
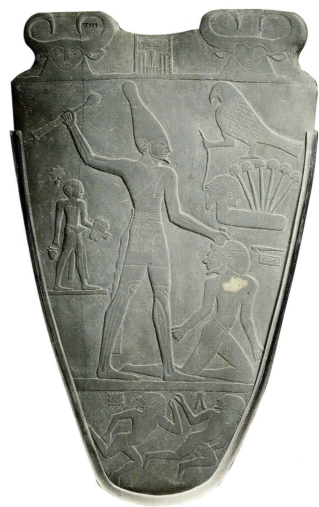

 2.34   *Palette of King Narmer.* Slate, 25" high. Egypt, c. 3000 BCE. Jurgen Liepe, Berlin. See also the text accompanying Figure 11.26.

Scale is the size of something in relation to what we assume to be "normal." *David* was sculpted on a large scale, larger than life-size. The *Venus of Willendorf,* on the other hand, is small-scale at just over four inches high.

Scale is very deceptive when you are looking at art only in books. You often have no way of knowing how large an artwork is, just by looking at its reproduction. Reading the caption gives you some information, but you have to exert your imagination to really "see" *David* standing in front of you, over fourteen feet tall, and the *Venus of Willendorf* easily fitting into your hand. Whenever possible, it is always best to see the original artwork rather than rely on the impression given in reproductions.

We saw with the *Venus of Willendorf* that proportion can be changed to express a certain idea. The same holds true with scale, including the scale relationships within a picture. On the *Palette of King Narmer* (Figure 2.34), we see the Egyptian pharaoh depicted much larger than the other peo-

ple. This is an example of **hieratic scaling,** a device that conveys the highest-ranking person in the scene.

EMPHASIS

Emphasis is the creation of one or more focal points in an artwork. When there are several focal points, the ones with lesser emphasis are called **accents.** Emphasis enables the viewers to recognize the most important element within a composition. Looking again at the *Palette of King Narmer* (Figure 2.34), the king is accentuated by the placement of the smaller characters that flank him. Behind and looking toward him is his servant; in front of and facing him is the falcon who represents Horus, god of Upper Egypt; and before him kneels the fallen enemy.

UNITY AND VARIETY

Unity is the quality of overall cohesion within an artwork. **Variety** is the element of difference within an artwork. They would seem on the surface to be mutually exclusive qualities, but in fact, they coexist in all artworks, evoking in viewers a fascination that makes them keep coming back and keep looking. The sameness of Abakanowicz's *Backs* seems to be an obvious expression of unity. The figures hunch forward, side by side, without motion. Yet even within this piece, there is subtle variety in the posture and texture that gives us a sense of individuality within an image of deadening uniformity.

In a different visual, a unifying factor in the *Palette of King Narmer* is the distinct rendering of the figures in Egyptian relief. Depicted both frontally and in profile, the figures' flat shapes and contours are the same throughout the carving. This easily allows the viewer to read without distraction an important event in Egyptian history.

ART MATERIALS AND MEDIA

We have seen the visual elements of the language of art and the principles by which they are composed. But artworks are realized through the material and media. **Material** is the physical substance that the artist uses to make a work of art. A **medium** is a mode of artistic expression and communication, such as oil painting, film, or silk-screen printing. Materials and media affect meaning as well as enable the artwork to exist. We will look at a variety of art materials and media, some traditional and some nontraditional.

NATURAL AND SYNTHETIC MATERIALS

Art can be made from an astounding array of materials. Not the least of these is the human body. People have used their bodies in performance, have had them painted and tattooed as art forms, have participated in ritual dances in costumes and masks, have practiced scarification, and so on.

Materials that are readily available in nature are commonly used for art. Sculpture and architecture often use stone, clay, and wood. We see a fine example of the use of animal materials in the *Mesquakie Bear Claw Necklace* (c. 1860), Figure 2.35, made of fur and grizzly bear claws. Natural fibers can be woven into baskets, mats, and clothing. Even lightning has been used as an art material in Walter De Maria's *The Lightning Field* (1971–1977), Figure 2.36, where four hundred stainless-steel poles over a large area in New Mexico attract lightning strikes during electrical storms. Manufactured or synthetic materials have provided artists with more art materials. Metals, glass, ferroconcrete, fiberglass, synthetic pigments, and plastics are just a few that artists have explored. Unexpected elements can become material for art. Mierle

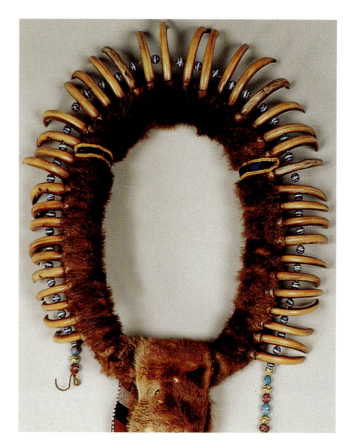

 2.35 *Mesquakie Bear Claw Necklace* (detail). Otter pelt, grizzly claws, glass beads, silk ribbon. 16¼" long. Tama, Iowa, USA, c. 1860. Photo archive of the National Museum of the American Indian. Photo by Carmelo Guadagno. See also the text accompanying Figure 11.5.

Laderman Ukeles combined glass and metal with a New York City garbage truck in *The Social Mirror* (1983), Figure 2.37. The mirrored sides of the garbage truck reflect the onlookers, dramatically showing us the individuals who together comprise the society that has created an immense waste problem on the planet. **Found objects,** such as old doors and shoes, can be incorporated into art, as happened in Marisol's *The Family* (Figure 2.29). Fragments from newspapers and magazines can be **collage** material for artists.

Art media refers to the particular techniques for making art that often use specially developed materials. Many art media have well-established histories and have been used repeatedly by artists in many cultures. We can subdivide them into painting media, printmaking media, sculptural media, and technology-based media. Figure 2.38 contains a brief explanation of the most common art media for the plastic arts. We did not include performance art or many other art forms that engage more than the visual. Their varied materials and processes cannot be easily categorized.

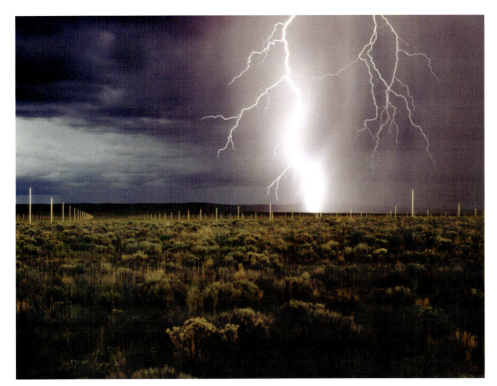

2.36 WALTER DE MARIA. *The Lightning Field.* 400 stainless-steel poles, average height 20'7"; land area 1 mile × 1 kilometer in New Mexico. USA, 1971–1977. Photograph by John Cliett. © Dia Center for the Arts. See also the text accompanying Figure 15.21.

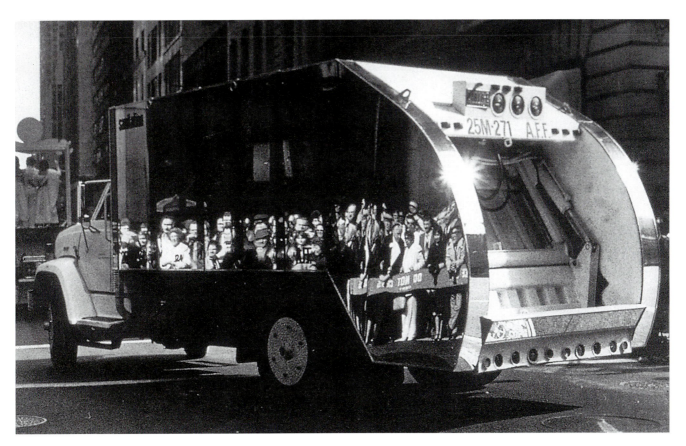

2.37 MIERLE LADERMAN UKELES. *The Social Mirror.* 20-cubic-yard New York City garbage collection truck fitted with hand-tempered glass mirror with additional strips of mirrored acrylic. USA, 1983. Courtesy Ronald Feldman Fine Arts, New York. The New York City Department of Sanitation. Photo: Michael James O'Brien, courtesy of Barbara Gladstone Gallery. See also the text accompanying Figures 5.24 and 15.23.

PAINTING

Painting media consist of three basic components: pigment, binder, and support. **PIGMENTS** are intense colors in powder form, derived from animals, plants, minerals, and synthetic chemicals. The **BINDER** is the liquid into which the pigments are ground and which holds the pigment particles together once the paint dries. The **SUPPORT** is the surface upon which the painting is made. Supports include canvas, wood panel, paper, plaster walls, and so on.

ACRYLIC: Paint made with pigment ground into a synthetic polymer liquid, which quickly dries into flexible film. A twentieth century invention, acrylics can be used thickly, or thinned with water to give thin stains. They can be applied directly to paper, canvas, or wood supports. One example is Paddy Carroll Tjungurrayi's *Witchetty Grub Dreaming* (see Figure 2.1).

ENCAUSTIC: One of the most ancient forms of paint. Pigments are mixed into hot beeswax and can be manipulated until the wax cools. Encaustic paintings thousands of years old still have brilliant colors and lustrous surfaces.

FRESCO: Fresco is often used for big murals. There are two kinds of fresco. In **buon fresco,** or true fresco, finely ground pigment suspended in water is applied to a wet plaster surface. The pigment becomes totally bonded with the drying plaster, resulting in a very durable painting. Because plaster dries quickly, the fresco painter must work quickly and in small areas rather than working over the entire painting. Colors are generally muted in buon fresco, because they are soaked into the plaster. In **fresco secco,** paint is applied to a dry plaster wall. Colors are more brilliant, but the painting is less durable and more likely to flake off the wall because the pigment has not bonded with the plaster. Diego Rivera's *Dia de Los Muertos* (Figure 10.28) is an example of fresco painting.

INK WASH/WATERCOLOR: Ink is a black or colored material used for writing and drawing. It usually comes in liquid form, but it is also available in dry sticks that must be ground in water to become liquid. Ink can be diluted with water and applied to paper with a brush to make a light-toned wash. An example of ink drawing is Sheng Maoye's *Beyond the Solitary Bamboo Grove* (Figure 15.10).

Watercolor is related to ink wash, except that watercolors are pigments suspended in a gum arabic solution (gum arabic is a natural glue). Both ink wash and watercolor are applied as thin stains to the paper, and depend upon paper quality and color for much of their effect.

OIL: Powdered pigments are mixed with oil, usually linseed, and often with varnishes and turpentine. Oil paint is applied onto a support, most often wood or canvas, which has been primed. The oil dries slowly to a hard, durable, flexible film. Artists have an extended time to mix and manipulate their colors before the paint dries. When dry, the paintings can have high-intensity color with lustrous, glowing surfaces. Oil painting was invented in Northern Europe more than five hundred years ago and is popular for easel painting. Jan Davidsz de Heem's *A Table of Desserts* is an oil painting (see Figure 7.14).

TEMPERA: Traditional tempera painting consists of pigments mixed with egg yolk as the binder. Egg tempera is a very strong, quick-drying medium that is excellent for sharp lines and fine details. Gradual tonal transitions must be created by hatching, as wet areas cannot be easily blended together because they dry so quickly. Egg tempera is usually painted on a wood panel support, because it is not flexible and cracks easily.

PRINTMAKING

Printmaking includes any medium that can create multiple copies of the same image.

INTAGLIO: Intaglio comes from the Italian verb meaning "to cut into." Artists cut into a flat surface, usually a metal plate, to make the design. Ink is applied into the cutaway areas, and then plate and paper are sent through a press to transfer the image to paper.

Intaglio prints can have fine lines, a high level of detail, and rich, dark tones. There are several intaglio processes. With **drypoint,** artists scratch a metal plate with a thin, pointed tool. **Engraving** entails cutting lines into a polished metal plate with a sharp tool. In **etching,** the metal plate is coated with a sticky protective substance called a ground, into which the artist scratches a design. The plate is then put into an acid bath, which "eats away" the exposed metal surface. These etched areas hold the ink during printing. An example of engraving is *The Fourth Plate of Muscles,* by Andreas Vesalius (Figure 15.24).

LITHOGRAPHY: A nineteenth-century invention, lithography starts with drawing with an oily crayon on a stone or metal surface. The rest of the surface is treated with water-based substances to be oil-repellent. The printing is then done with oil-based inks that print only from the oily areas of the stone or plate. Lithographs tend to look much like drawings. Our example is Henri de Toulouse-Lautrec's *Jane Avril* (see Figure 16.13). Commercial printing is an industrial version of lithography: This book was printed with that process, called **offset lithography.**

RELIEF PRINTING: Areas not to be printed are cut away from the printing surface, so that areas to be printed are left higher. Ink is applied to those higher areas, and then the printing surface is sent through the press to transfer the image to paper. One of the most common forms of relief printing is done on wood blocks, as seen in Kitagawa Utamaro's *A Pair of Lovers* (Figure 8.16).

SCREEN PRINTING (SERIGRAPHY): A stencil is attached to a piece of fabric stretched over a frame, forming a screen that supports and gives strength to the stencil. Ink is then squeezed through the open areas of the stencil and deposited on paper below. Andy Warhol's *Heinz 57 Tomato Ketchup* and *Del Monte Freestone Peach Halves* (see Figure 7.9) are examples of silk screen on wood.

SCULPTURE

Sculpture can be **free-standing** (meant to be seen from all sides), or it may be **relief,** in which forms project from a surface and are primarily visible only from the front. **Site-specific sculpture** has been designed for a particular place and cannot be moved without changing its form and meaning. **Kinetic sculpture** has moving parts.

ASSEMBLING: Sculptures can be made from various fabricated parts that are then put together. Almost any material can be assembled into sculptures, including wood or metal. Sometimes found objects or readymades are included, resulting in works called **assemblages.** Marisol's *The Family* (see Figure 2.29) is assembled from various blocks of wood, which are carved, painted and drawn, and from found objects, such as doors and shoes.

CARVING: Artists cut away unwanted material from a large block to create a carving. This is a subtractive sculptural process, because material is taken away. The most common carving materials are wood or stone. The *Yakshi,* from ancient India, was carved from a block of sandstone (see Figure 13.13).

2.38 Common Media, Processes, and Materials.

CASTING: A sculptural form is made first in an easily manipulated material, such as wax or clay. A mold is made around this form, and then removed. A more durable material, such as plaster or molten metal, is poured into the mold, resulting in a solid, durable sculpture. All except the smallest sculptures, however, are hollow cast by means of the **cire perdue,** or **lost wax casting,** method. This method produces hollow metal sculptures with thin walls. A thin layer of wax is suspended between an interior and an exterior mold. The wax is melted out and replaced with molten metal. *Crowned Head of an Oni* (see Figure 11.3) is a cast sculpture made with the lost wax process.

MODELING: Sculptural forms are created by pushing and pulling a malleable substance, such as clay or wax. Often this is considered an additive sculptural process, because material is built up to create the final sculptural form. Clay is a common modeling material used for sculpture and ceramic, and when fired becomes hard and very permanent. The Aztec *Eagle Knight* is a life-sized ceramic sculpture (see Figure 11.23).

TECHNOLOGY-BASED MEDIA

PHOTOGRAPHY: A photosensitive surface, such as film, is exposed to light through a lens, which creates an image from the environment on that surface. Multiple copies can be made of that original image on other light-sensitive surfaces. Louis Daguerre's **daguerreotype** was an early form of photography, dating from the 1830s. Platinum prints and silver prints are two black-and-white printing processes. Color photography came into common use after the 1940s. Dorothea Lange's *Migrant Mother, Nipomo Valley* (Figure 14.31) is a photograph.

FILM: A sequence of still photographs is shot in rapid succession on a strip of film. When projected onto a screen, the progression of still images gives the illusion of movement. Film has higher image resolution than video.

VIDEO: Audio and visual information are shot and stored simultaneously on magnetic videotape, and displayed on television monitors. Video cameras first became accessible to artists and the public in 1965. Video sound and image quality are generally considered to be lower than those of film.

DIGITAL IMAGING: The computer-based creation or storage of still or moving images as digital information. In addition, all kinds of existing imagery can be scanned to become digital information. Digital images can be easily manipulated. Output from digital images can be printed on hard copy, displayed on computer monitors, or projected. Nam June Paik's *Megatron* is an example of computer images displayed across two hundred stacked monitors (see Figure 15.37).

SYNOPSIS

Like every language, art has a structure made up of elements arranged in a composition according to certain organizing principles. The elements of art are line, light and value, color, shape and volume, texture and pattern, space, time and motion, and chance, improvisation, and spontaneity. The principles of composition are balance, rhythm, scale and proportion, emphasis, unity, and variety. Some artworks engage senses other than just the visual.

Artists have explored a full range of traditional and nontraditional materials, ranging from their own bodies to natural and synthetic materials. Media include painting, sculpture, printmaking, and recent technologies. Today, the artist's art box might contain anything and everything.

FOOD FOR THOUGHT

When you view any artwork, you can examine its visual elements, analyze how they were put together, evaluate the materials used, and ask the following questions:

- What are the basic visual elements in this artwork?
- Has one specific element been employed, or have more than one been incorporated?
- How do the elements of the art piece work together, or do they not work together?
- What is the most important element in the work? Are the lesser elements important?
- Does the artwork evoke thoughts or emotions? If it does, how?
- Are the media and materials appropriate for the piece?

YOUR CD-ROM RESOURCES

- Foundations–Interactive Modules
    Visual Elements
- Flashcards
- In the Studio-Videos
    Painting, Printmaking, Sculpture
- Food for Thought
- Companion Site
    Chapter 2 Quiz
    InfoTrac® College Edition Readings
    Artists Flashcards
    Online Study Guide

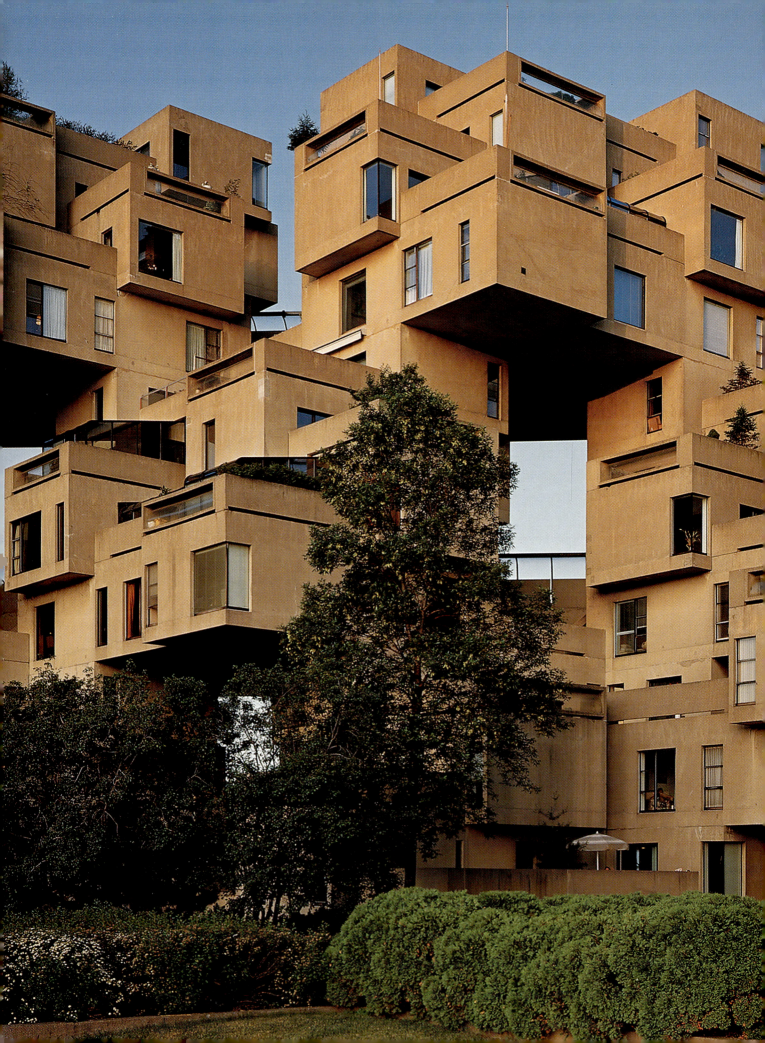

THE LANGUAGE OF ARCHITECTURE

INTRODUCTION

Architecture is the science and art of designing structures for human use. Buildings shelter us from the elements, protect our possessions, and allow us to do many different kinds of work. Buildings are practical, aesthetic, meaningful, and symbolic. They communicate a wide range of spiritual, social, and political ideas.

Like visual artists, architects use the basic art elements, but they also employ structural systems to make their buildings functional, safe, and resistant to the stresses of gravity and weather. Consider the following questions while reading this chapter:

How do architects enclose space?

What is the impact of different building materials and visual elements?

How does architecture engage all the senses?

What principles organize building design?

How do buildings relate to the natural environment?

Habitat. Detail of Figure 3.24. Photo by Russell Thompson. The Arkansas Office, Inc.

CONNECTION
In this book, the following chapters also deal with architecture in depth: Chapter 7, Food and Shelter; Chapter 9, Deities and Places of Worship; Chapter 10, Mortality and Immortality; Chapter 11, Power, Politics, and Glory; and Chapter 16, Entertainment.

STRUCTURAL SYSTEMS

Buildings have to stand up. They have to enclose space. How can inert materials, such as brick, stone, wood, steel, and concrete, be shaped and arranged to do that? The answers are found in structural systems, as explained throughout this section.

TRADITIONAL BUILDING METHODS

Some structural systems date back hundreds, even thousands, of years. These older building methods show great variety, because they represent local solutions to the problem of construction. These local solutions are frequently quite different from one another because local architects had to work within the limits of available material, existing technology, and the traditional and aesthetic preferences of their cultures.

LOAD-BEARING CONSTRUCTION

Early architecture was made of shaped earth, bones, wood, or stacked stone. Whatever materials were locally available were used. The igloo made of ice blocks is one example. Ancient houses in China were dug right out of the earth.

In many places, people began to stack or pile materials, creating solid walls that were usually thicker at the bottom and thinner at the top to provide stability. Early roofs were often lightweight, impermanent material, such as reeds or thatch. Examples of such architecture are old adobe structures in the Americas and sun-dried brick structures in the ancient Near East. The *Moche House Model* (Figure 3.1) is a small, ceramic model of a style of house made by the Moche people, who lived in coastal Peru from around 500 BCE through about CE 600. The Moche house foundations were bundled reeds or willow branches, with liquid adobe poured over them. The walls were made of mass-produced adobe brick reinforced with grass. The roofs were thatch. The hearth was a stone. The houses were brightly painted.

This kind of architecture is called "load bearing" because all areas of the walls support the roof and walls above them. With this kind of stacking construction, it is difficult to create openings in the walls, because those voids cannot support the material above them. Most such buildings have heavy, thick walls

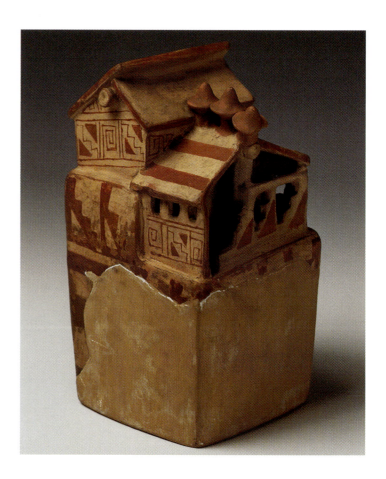

3.1 *Moche House Model.* Ceramic, red and white paint. Moche Civilization, Peru, c. 500 BCE–CE 600. Linden Stuttgart Museum.

BASIC POST-AND-LINTEL MODULE
Arrows indicate the downward distribution of weight

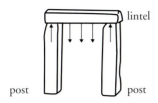

COLONNADE

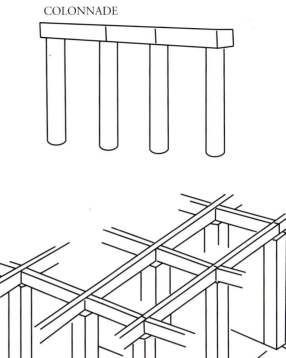

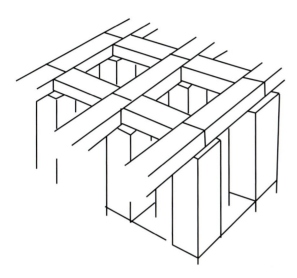

GRID OF POST-AND-LINTEL MODULES,
IN STONE
Many interior posts are needed to support
the stone lintels

GRID OF POST-AND-LINTEL
MODULES, WITH WOOD LINTELS
Fewer posts are needed, and longer
lintels are possible

3.2   Diagram Showing Post-and-Lintel Construction

with few openings. The buildings are mostly modest in size, usually enclosing only one or two small rooms. Where there are openings, as we see with the *Moche House Model,* wooden beams are used in post-and-lintel construction, which we will see next.

Solid walls let no air or light into the interior. Yet since ancient times, people have made the aesthetic decision to have air and light in their buildings. In the rest of this section, we will look at the many ways that people have devised to build walls, open up windows, and permanently cover large interior spaces.

POST-AND-LINTEL CONSTRUCTION

One ancient method of constructing walls, making openings, and supporting a roof is the **post-and-lintel system.** The basic module consists of two upright posts that support a cross beam or lintel (Figure 3.2). Posts can be either rectangular or cylindrical. When a cylindrical post is refined and deco-

rated, it is often called a **column,** which we will discuss further in just a moment. A row of post-and-lintel modules placed side by side is called a **colonnade.** A three-dimensional grid of posts and lintels can be the basic structure that supports the roof of a large interior space (see Figure 3.2). Post-and-lintel structures are marked by a strong emphasis on vertical and horizontal lines. They are rectilinear in design.

The materials used in post-and-lintel architecture are important. Stone, for example, produces a very durable building. Some of the very oldest structures are stone with post-and-lintel construction. Stone, however, is a relatively brittle material. If stone lintels are used to span large spaces, they will break from their own weight or the weight of the roof above. Stone is also heavy. Therefore, posts must be thick and closely spaced if a building has a post-and-lintel roof in stone (see Figure 3.2). The interiors of such buildings look like a forest of columns, as we can see in Figure 3.3, the *First Hypostyle Hall* at the Horus Temple at Edfu (c. 237–57 BCE) in Egypt.

If the lintels are wood, however, a very different effect is possible. Wood is a light, flexible, strong building material that can span great distances. Larger interior spaces can be opened up, and the posts can be thinned down. Both wood and stone lintels were used in the *Parthenon* (447–432 BCE), Figure 3.4. The exterior colonnade is heavy and closely spaced because it has stone lintels. Two rooms in the interior of the building were roofed in wood and, therefore, were relatively open and airy. The walls of the *Parthenon*'s inner chamber

were load bearing, with few openings. They held up the wood roof. In fact, it was common to see load-bearing walls in structures combined with post-and-lintel construction. As we saw in the *Moche House Model,* many traditional buildings are constructed with more than one structural system.

The wooden roof of the *Parthenon* is long gone, while the stones remain. In fact, the relative impermanence of wood and its ability to burn are its greatest drawbacks as a building material.

Important subcategories of post-and-lintel architecture are the Classical Greek and Roman architectural orders (Figure 3.5).

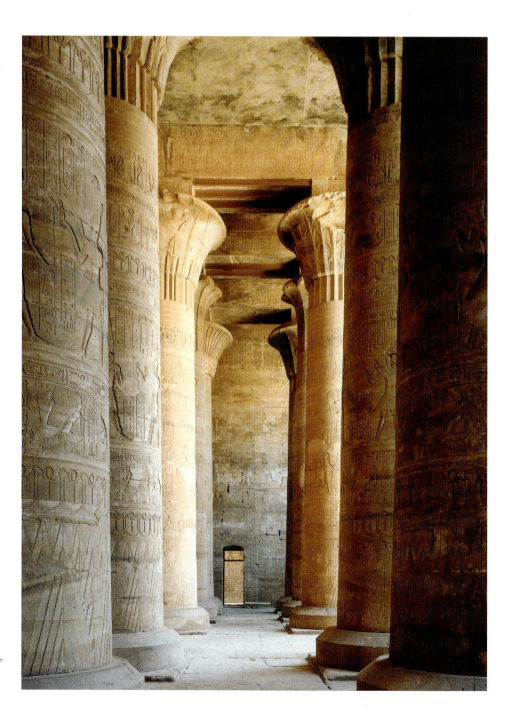

3.3 *First Hypostyle Hall.* Horus Temple at Edfu, Egypt, c. 237–57 BCE. The roof slabs are 50 feet from the floor. © Scala/Art Resource, NY. See also the text accompanying Figure 9.35.

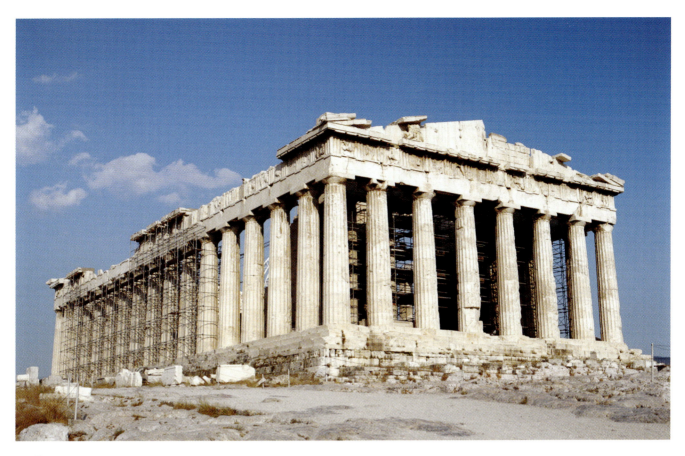

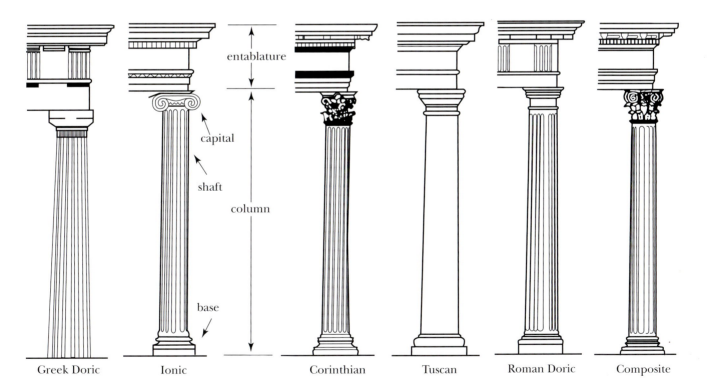

3.4   IKTINOS AND KALLIKRATES. *Parthenon*. Pentelic marble; columns: 34' high; dimensions of structure: 228' × 104'. Athens, Greece, 447–432 BCE. © Photodisc Green / Getty Images. See also the text accompanying Figure 9.32.

Greek Doric   Ionic   Corinthian   Tuscan   Roman Doric   Composite

entablature

capital

shaft

column

base

3.5   Diagram of Greek and Roman Orders

An order consists of a specifically designed column with a **base,** a **shaft,** a **capital,** and an **entablature,** all exhibiting standardized proportions and decorative ornamentation. The oldest is the **Doric Order,** originating in the Greek Archaic period (650–500 BCE). The simplest in design, the Doric Order is geometric, heavy, and relatively without ornamentation. Its column has no base, and its capital is a simple cushion. The ancient Greeks considered the Doric Order to exhibit masculine qualities. The *Parthenon* is a Doric structure. The second order to appear was the **Ionic Order,** which is taller, more slender, and more decorative than the Doric, and was considered feminine. It has a stepped base and a carved capital. It originated during the Greek Classical (Hellenic) period (500–323 BCE). Later still was the **Corinthian Order,** which is the most complex and organic,

with delicately carved acanthus leaves on its capital, dating from the Hellenistic period (323–100 BCE). Roman variations on those orders are Tuscan, Roman Doric, and Composite.

WOOD FRAME CONSTRUCTION

The Chinese developed a distinctive wood frame architecture, based in part on the simple post-and-lintel module. But the Chinese elaborated the post and lintel and added some structural innovations to create a truly distinctive building style. This building style was a **complete frame system,** which meant that the walls were totally non-load-bearing and could be eliminated. The upright posts carried all weight of the structure.

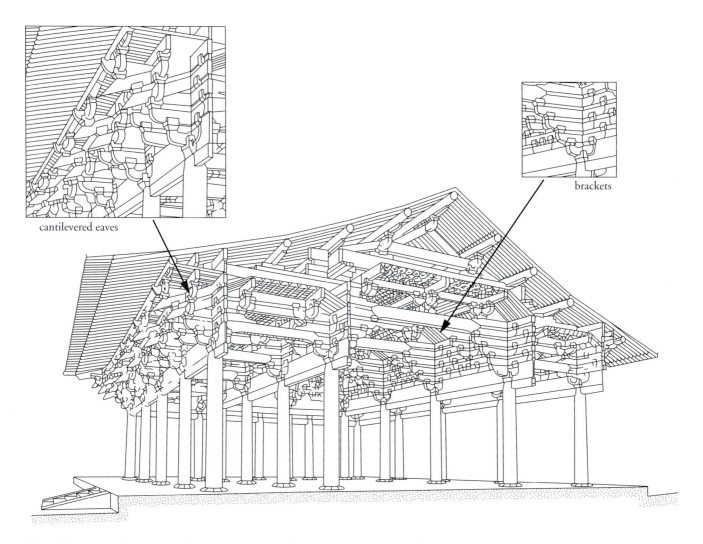

cantilevered eaves

brackets

3.6   Chinese wood frame structural system, showing brackets and cantilevers. Notice the upright posts supporting the roof, and the lack of load-bearing walls. This diagram of beam-bracketing construction is based on the Foguang Si Temple, Wutai Shan, northern China, Tang dynasty, c. 857 (after L. Liu).

To reduce the number of posts needed to hold up the roof, the Chinese developed **brackets,** which are clusters of interlocking pieces of wood shaped like inverted pyramids. Builders placed bracket clusters at the tops of upright posts, directly beneath the roof (Figure 3.6). Brackets greatly increased the amount of area each post could support. With fewer posts needed, the interior space was more open and uncluttered. Brackets date back as far as the fifth century BCE in China and were relatively simple at first. Brackets eventually became more complex, highly ornate, and very colorful, but we will cover that more in the following pages.

In the third century BCE, the Chinese developed roof tiles that overlapped each other and were half-cylinder in shape. Ceramic tile roofs were very heavy, but their weight actually added to the stability of the wood frame structure below. In Chinese structures, the roof design is, in many cases, the most important and distinct feature of the building. The roofs project away from the building, with shapes that incorporate very complex curves. In addition, roof tiles could be glazed in many different colors, adding an extra design element to the structure.

Beginning in the eighth century CE, Chinese architects incorporated the **cantilever** in their structures. The cantilever is a supporting beam that is anchored at one end to an upright post and then projects from a structure (Figure 3.6). The cantilever was used to create roofs with deep eaves that projected far beyond their supporting upright posts, as we can see in the detail from a structure in the Forbidden City (Figure 3.7). Temples from as early as the ninth century CE have fourteen-foot eaves. The cantilever also supported balconies on multi-story buildings.

Thus, the distinctive visual features of Chinese wood frame architecture are large, complex-curving roofs that dominate the structure; sturdy upright posts; and generally a symmetrical design. We can see variations on wood frame construction throughout Asia. One example is traditional Japanese domestic

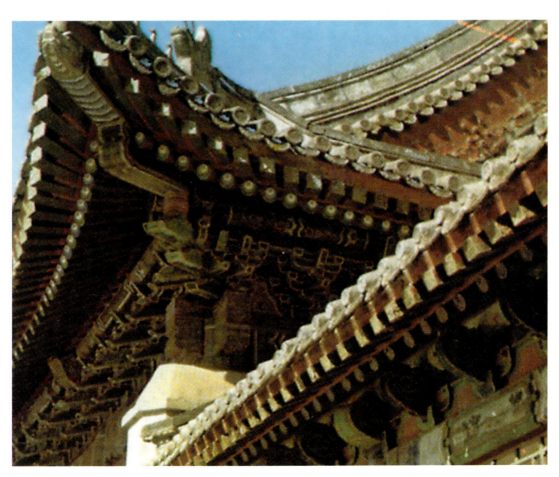

3.7   Detail showing highly ornate cantilevered eaves with brackets from a Forbidden City structure. Photo by Robert Harding Associates.

and temple architecture. Another is the design of traditional houses in Indonesia, such as the *Toba Batak House,* which we will see in Figure 3.25. The wood frame of the *Toba Batak House* is very visible in the lower floors, and the house sports a distinctive roof, this time in thatch. Wood frame architecture is also very common in the West, especially for houses and small apartment buildings. In contrast to the Chinese model, most wood frame structures in the West feature load-bearing walls.

ARCHES, VAULTING, AND DOMES

We have seen that a stone lintel cannot span much distance, so it would seem that stone is a very limited building material.

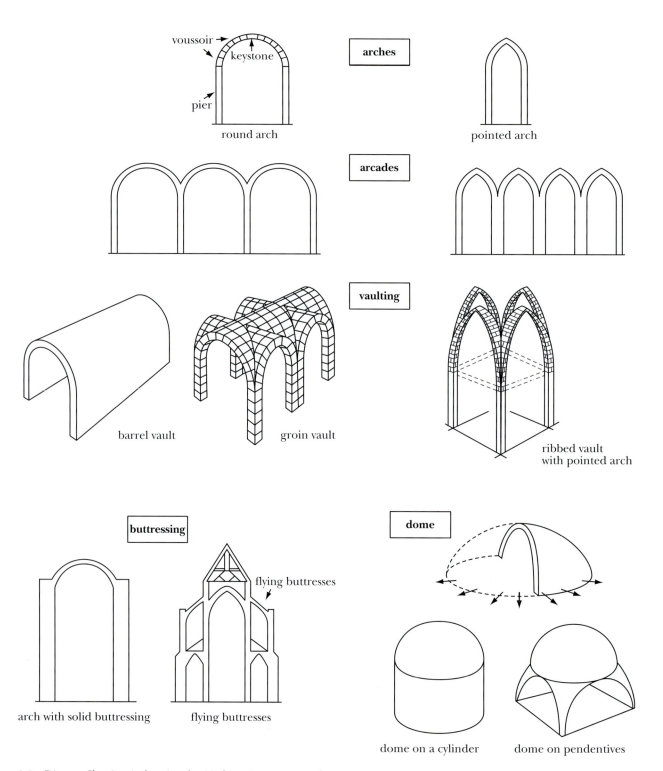

3.8   Diagram Showing Arches, Arcades, Vaulting, Buttressing, and Domes

But the round stone **arch** (Figure 3.8), a structural innovation that dates back to ancient Egypt, changed that. The arch is made of wedge-shaped stones or **voussoirs** that are constructed from bottom to top, using a wooden scaffold for support. When the final **keystone** is placed in the center, the arch can support itself and the scaffolding can be removed. Arches can rest either on cylindrical columns or on rectangular **piers.**

Arches can be either round or pointed (Figure 3.8). With a round arch, the distance between the supports determines the height of the arch, because the arch is a semicircle. A pointed arch is actually a round arch with some of the center removed. Builders can make a pointed arch as high as they wish, regardless of the distance between its supports. A straight row of arches placed side by side is called an **arcade.**

Unlike post-and-lintel structures in which the weight of the roof and lintel press down equally on all parts below, the weight of the arch is directed outward and then downward to the load-bearing columns or piers. There is no downward pres-

sure over the void of the arch, and so higher and larger spaces can be spanned without need for additional support posts. Arches can be constructed of stone, brick, or concrete. Arches, however, do have to be supported from the outside to prevent lateral movement that would cause them to collapse. That support is called **buttressing** (Figure 3.8), which is additional exterior masonry placed at key points to keep the arch stable. Buttresses can be solid masonry, or they may be opened up with their own internal arches, called **flying buttresses.**

Builders can expand and multiply the arch in a number of ways to create entire roofs made of stone. These stone roofs are called **vaults,** or **vaulting,** and are very durable and fireproof (Figure 3.8). A **barrel vault** is an arch extended in depth from front to back, forming a tunnel-like structure. Barrel vaults have the disadvantage of creating rather dark interiors, as there are no windows in the vault area. The sumptuous *Hall of Mirrors* (c. 1680) at Versailles (Figure 3.9) is an example of a barrel vault ceiling that has been highly

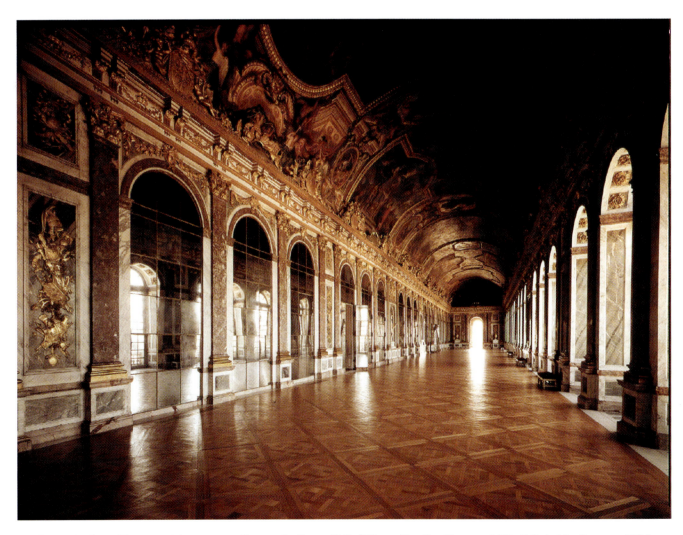

3.9   JULES HARDOUIN MANSART AND CHARLES LE BRUN. *Hall of Mirrors.* Versailles, France, c. 1680. © Scala / Art Resource, NY. See also the text accompanying Figure 11.10.

ornamented. In the *Hall of Mirrors,* unlike in earlier vaults, one side of the walls is pierced with tall windows that flood the space with light. This light is reflected in the responding line of mirrors on the opposite wall. The result is that the room is bright, while the vault is still relatively dark. **Groin vaults,** sometimes called **cross vaults,** are barrel vaults positioned at ninety-degree angles to cross or intersect one another. This innovation allowed light to enter vaulted spaces for the first time and gave variation to the interior space. The *Markets of Trajan* (100–112), Figure 3.10, provided airy and lighted space for the vendors and shoppers in ancient Rome.

A **ribbed vault** (see Figure 3.8) is a variation of the groin vaulting system in which arches diagonally cross over the groin vault, forming skeletal ribs. Pointing the arch in the ribbed vault creates a **gothic vault.** This innovation allowed builders to eliminate large wall areas under arches and to fill the resulting space with gleaming stained glass. The interior of *Chartres Cathedral* (1194–1260) in France shows the ribbed gothic vault (Figure 3.11).

A **dome** theoretically is an arch rotated on its vertical axis to form a hemispheric vault. A dome can be used several ways: It can rest on a circular drum as in the *Pantheon*

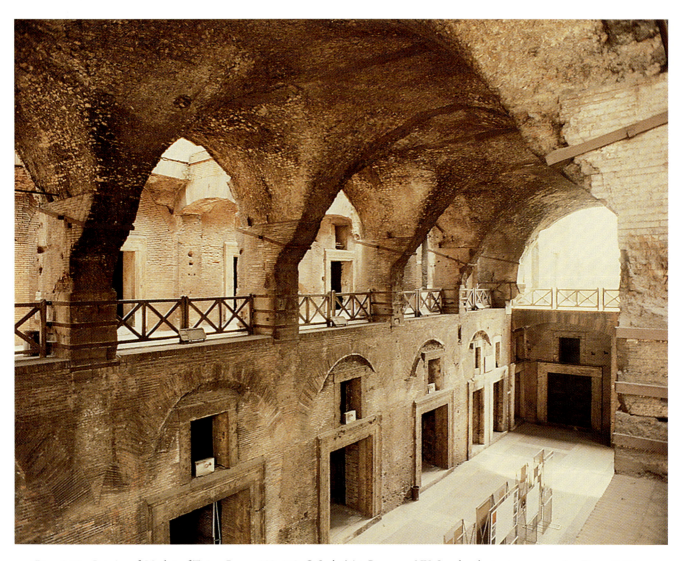

3.10   Interior of *Markets of Trajan.* Rome, 100–112. © Scala / Art Resource, NY. See also the text accompanying Figure 7.35.

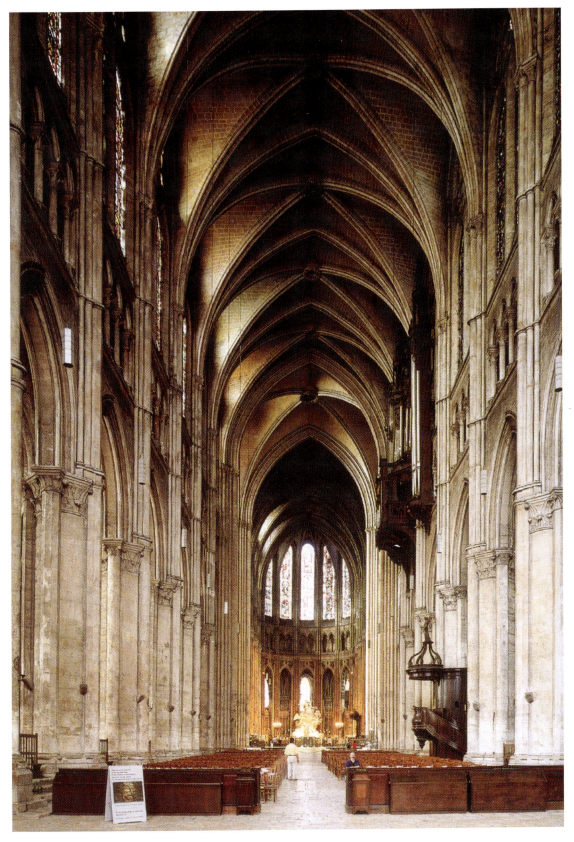

3.11   Interior of *Chartres Cathedral*. The center space, called the nave, is 130' long, 53' wide, and 122' high. Chartres, France, completed 1194–1260. Photo Francois Lauginie. See also the text accompanying Figure 9.40.

(118–125), Figure 3.12, or it can be placed on **pendentives,** which are the triangular concave sections created when a dome is placed on arches (see Figure 3.8). Domes may also be placed on a square or a polygonal base, in which case the spaces created between the dome and its base are called **squinches.**

Vaulted or domed buildings are generally quite massive, because of the material used to make them—stone, brick, or concrete. Vaults are very heavy structures and require thick supports. In many cases, architects disguise the massiveness of vaulted structures. The thick piers and heavy vaults are apparent in the *Markets of Trajan* (Figure 3.10). But originally, the *Markets of Trajan* were faced with decorative materials, such as colored brick, marble veneer, or stucco, to diminish the brute mass of the structure. The massive dome of the *Pantheon* (Figure 3.12) has square, sunken panels called **coffers** cut into it, which subdivide its vast expanse. *Chartres Cathedral* is also a massive structure, but its builders shaped the stone to emphasize verticality, so again mass is visually diminished.

It is important once again to mention that a single building can incorporate different structural systems. Builders

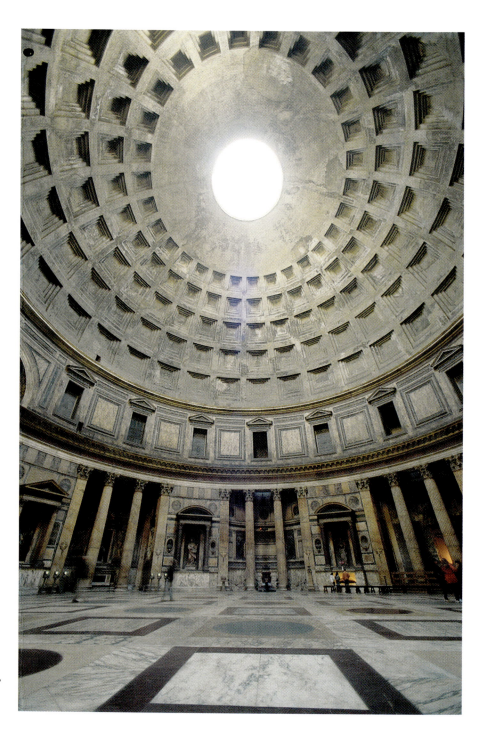

3.12 *Pantheon.* Concrete and marble; height from floor to opening in dome is 142'. Rome, Italy, 118–125. See also the text accompanying Figure 9.28.

roofed the interior of *Chartres Cathedral* with vaults. However, they placed an exterior, wood frame, pitched roof above the vaults, which protected them from the weather. You can see the wood frame roof in the flying buttress diagram in Figure 3.8. In the *Markets of Trajan,* you can see that builders used post-and-lintel systems to frame doors and windows for the individual shops.

RECENT METHODS AND MATERIALS

Modern buildings differ from older structures in many ways. New materials, such as steel and steel-reinforced concrete, have made new construction methods possible. Buildings now can be taller than anything ever built before the nineteenth century. Like the human body, many modern buildings feature an internal skeletal support system. The outer surface of the wall is like a skin stretched over the bones.

Our expectations of "basic" comforts have changed, too, so buildings are designed with a variety of operating systems, such as heating and cooling systems, electricity, plumbing, and telephone and computer wiring, as well as appliances, intercoms, and surveillance systems. Two hundred years ago, this was all unknown.

STEEL FRAME CONSTRUCTION

High-strength structural steel was developed in the late nineteenth century and, with the invention of the elevator, made very tall buildings possible for the first time. **Steel frame construction** essentially expands the post-and-lintel grid both horizontally and vertically, only using steel instead of wood or stone. Because steel is very strong both vertically and horizontally, it can function as a skeleton that will support multistoried buildings with large floors on each level (Figure 3.13). Steel framed buildings usually have floors of reinforced concrete, which is poured concrete with metal reinforcing bars embedded in it. We will see more on reinforced concrete in the next section.

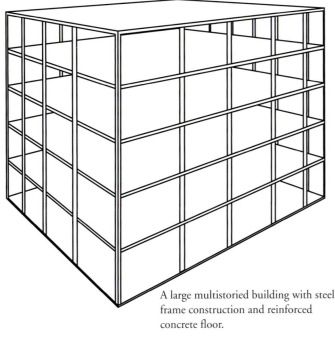

A large multistoried building with steel frame construction and reinforced concrete floor.

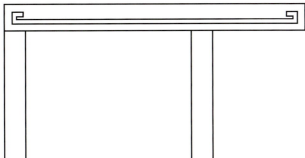

Diagram of reinforced concrete showing a metal bar embedded in concrete. This diagram shows a reinforced concrete floor with a cantilevered balcony.

3.13   Diagram of Steel Frame Construction and Reinforced Concrete

The first architects working with steel frame construction disguised the steel framework with stone facings so that their buildings had rugged exteriors, traditional appearances, and the look of durability. In contrast to that attitude was the work of Louis Sullivan, the first architect to really redefine the steel frame building. An example is his *Carson Pirie Scott* building (1904), Figure 3.14. The building looks pared down, almost insubstantial, compared to the massive stone buildings that preceded it. Sullivan's building was also higher, thanks to steel frame construction. The emphasis on height was reflected in the new name for such buildings: skyscraper. The external appearance of the *Carson Pirie Scott* building reflects the steel frame beneath its walls. The simple horizontal and vertical lines of the frame are emphasized and apparent. Windows are opened up and big, reaching from framing member to framing member. Sullivan did not neglect ornamentation, as we will see later in this chapter.

Steel frame construction has been widely used ever since for all kinds of structures, but especially the high-rise office buildings that filled the downtowns of major cities all over the world from the mid to late twentieth century. Called the **International Style,** these stripped-down, glass-covered, rec-tangular box buildings were enormously popular throughout the world. These buildings generally had no ornamentation at all. Some critics argued against the widespread use of the International Style. Many older, distinctive structures were torn down in cities all over the world so that steel-and-glass boxes could be built. The International Style's ubiquity resulted in many cities' civic centers losing much of their individuality and distinct character.

REINFORCED CONCRETE

Another building innovation that resulted from the development of high-strength structural steel was **reinforced concrete,** also known as ferroconcrete. Concrete was used by the Romans. The dome of the *Pantheon* (Figure 3.12), which we saw already, is concrete. However, concrete is relatively brittle and cracks easily, as you might notice on your own driveway. In the late nineteenth century, builders began to embed steel reinforcing bars in wet concrete, and the combination of the two had many advantages. The steel gives the concrete tensile strength, while the concrete provides a durable surface. Reinforced concrete was used for the floors of skyscrapers from their early days.

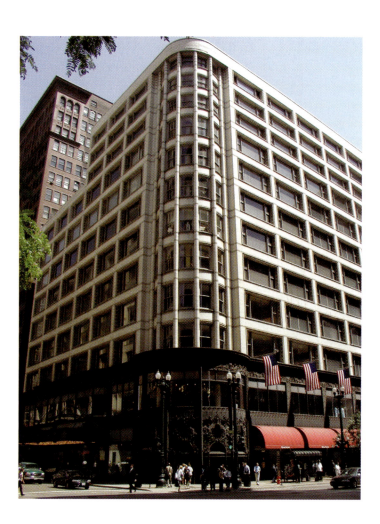

3.14   LOUIS H. SULLIVAN. *Carson Pirie Scott and Company.* Chicago, Illinois, USA, 1904. Photo courtesy of Stephen A. Edwards. See also the text accompanying Figure 7.36.

Gradually, architects began using reinforced concrete as an external building material for the finished surfaces of buildings. In *Fallingwater* (1936–1938), Figure 3.15, Frank Lloyd Wright made extensive use of ferroconcrete for the house's balconies. It contrasts with the vertical elements that are faced in stone. *Fallingwater* features cantilevered balconies. We saw the cantilever first in connection with Chinese architecture. Ferroconcrete made it possible to expand the size and projection of cantilevered structures, so that they can extend dramatically beyond their vertical support. As you can see in *Fallingwater,* the balconies extend so far beyond their vertical supports that they overhang a waterfall, adding considerably to the distinct character of the house.

Reinforced concrete is not limited to floors, balconies, or rectangular structures. Concrete can be poured over steel reinforcing rods or mesh that can be shaped into any form the architect wishes. It makes possible free-form architecture, which places no limitations on the shape and mass of a structure.

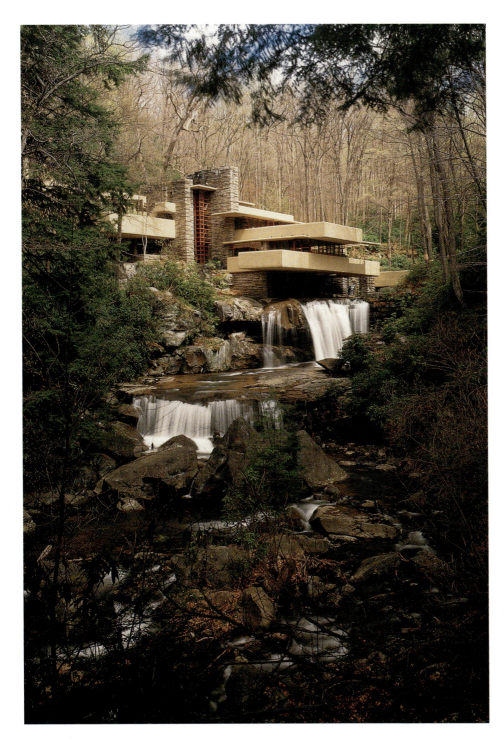

 3.15 FRANK LLOYD WRIGHT. *Fallingwater.* Kaufmann House, Connellsville vicinity, Pennsylvania, USA, 1936–1938. ESTO © Scott Frances. See also the text accompanying Figure 7.34.

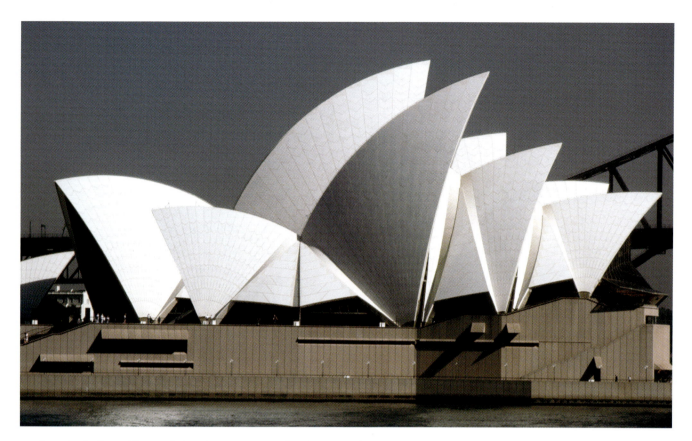

 3.16   JOERN UTZON. *Sydney Opera House.* Reinforced concrete; highest shell, 200' high. Sydney, Australia, 1959–1972. © Roger Ressmeyer / Corbis. See also the text accompanying Figure 16.4.

The *Sydney Opera House* (1959–1972) designed by Joern Utzon, is an impressive structure with cascading shells, constructed in the free-form system (Figure 3.16).

CONNECTION
Another example of free-form architecture is the spiral-shaped Solomon R. Guggenheim Museum *(Figure 16.5, page 474).*

TRUSS AND GEODESIC CONSTRUCTION

Another skeletal structure is the truss, which can be constructed in wood or steel. The truss system is based on a frame made of a series of triangles (Figure 3.17). Trusses are very rigid, because the triangle is a rigid shape, and can be used to span great spaces or to support other structures. You probably have seen steel trusses in railroad bridges, or wooden trusses in the attics of most frame homes in the United States. The *Bank of China* (1989), Figure 3.18, by I. M. Pei and Partners, in Hong Kong, features enormous triangular braces, which are like trusses on a grand scale, to stabilize the building, which is in an earthquake zone.

R. Buckminster Fuller made an innovation on the truss skeletal system in his design of a geodesic dome (Figure 3.19).

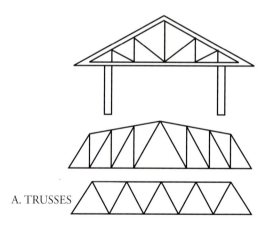
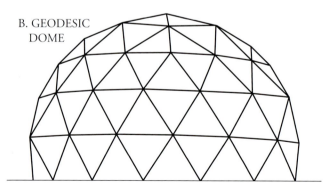

A. TRUSSES

B. GEODESIC DOME

3.17   Truss (A) and Geodesic Dome (B) Structural Systems

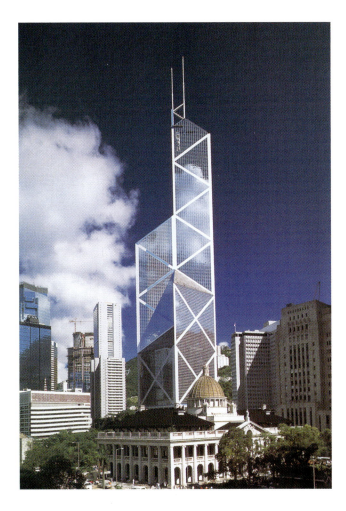

3.18   I. M. PEI AND PARTNERS.
Bank of China. Hong Kong, 1989.
Courtesy Pei Cobb Freed & Partners.
See also the text accompanying
Figure 7.38.

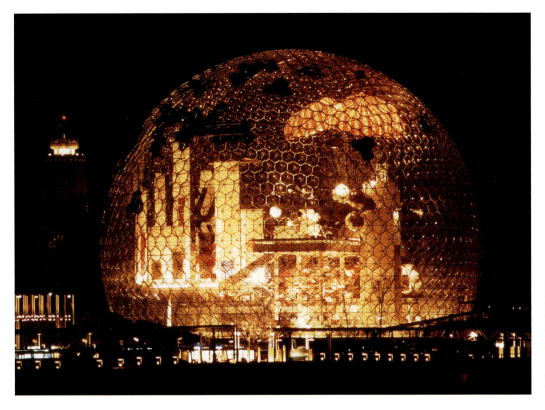

3.19   R. BUCKMINSTER
FULLER. *U.S. Pavilion.*
Geodesic Dome, diameter
250'. Expo '67, Montreal,
Canada, 1967. Comstock.
See also the text
accompanying Figure
7.37.

The geodesic dome is a skeletal frame based on triangles that are grouped into very stable, strong polyhedrons, which are solid geometric figures having many faces and are found in nature. Geodesic domes can be very large, and they require no interior supports. Builders can easily assemble the skeletal frame from prefabricated modular parts. The framework can be sheathed in glass, plastic, plywood, or a variety of other materials. Fuller's *U.S. Pavilion* (1967), Figure 3.19, at the 1967 World's Fair (Expo '67) in Montreal, was an example of a geodesic dome that was 250 feet in diameter.

The triangles of truss or geodesic structures may be left visible when buildings are finished. In these cases, the buildings have a pronounced geometric appearance. The linear network of the truss skeleton thus becomes an important visual feature.

AESTHETIC DESIGN DECISIONS

We have covered some of the most common structural systems used in architecture. But architecture is not simply a matter of engineering or of making useful spaces. An important aspect of a building is simply visual. How does it look? Is it visually appropriate, or striking and memorable? To be effective as architecture, a structure must also be visually well designed.

VISUAL ELEMENTS

As in the visual arts, architects carefully arrange and employ visual elements to create striking visual effects in their buildings. The visual elements are the same as those we saw for the visual arts: line, light and value, color, texture, pattern, shape and volume, space, time, and motion. In addition, there are nonvisual elements that include chance, improvisation, and spontaneity. And aspects of architecture engage senses other than sight. We defined and illustrated all these terms in Chapter 2, The Language of Art, as they relate to visual art. But the way the elements are employed in architecture is different. To illustrate these visual elements, we will use the *Piazza d'Italia* (1975–1980), Figure 3.20, by Charles Moore with U.I.G. (Urban Innovations Group) and Perez Associates. The *Piazza d'Italia* is a circular plaza lined with arches and colonnades, with a raised speaker's rostrum. The *Piazza* is used for open-air festivals.

Although architecture may contain few, if any, lines, it does feature a number of **linear elements.** The lines of columns we see in the *Piazza d'Italia* add an element of linearity to the

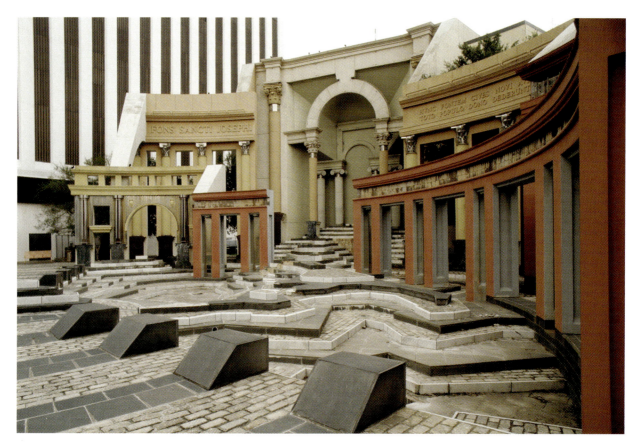

3.20   Charles Moore with U.I.G. and Perez Associates. *Piazza d'Italia.* New Orleans, USA, 1975–1980. © Robert Holmes / Corbis. See also the text accompanying Figure 7.39.

space. We can also speak of line as direction in relation to architecture. When seen from above, the lines of the *Piazza d'Italia* are mostly curving. *Chartres Cathedral* (Figure 3.11) and the *Bank of China* (Figure 3.18) feature strong vertical lines that emphasize an upward direction. The geodesic dome of the *U.S. Pavilion* (Figure 3.19) is a network of intersecting lines.

Light is an essential element in the visual design of architecture. **Light** creates areas of illumination and shadow that animate and activate a surface. A building is a totally different experience on a sunny day than on an overcast day. In the case of the *Piazza d'Italia,* sunlight creates constantly shifting lights and darks, making each trip to the plaza a unique experience. Sunlit arches are distorted and recreated in their own shadows. These shadows skim across the ground and over other walls. Elements that were lost in shadow suddenly pop out in brilliance when the light hits them. At night, the *Piazza d'Italia* is artificially illuminated, giving a very different appearance. Colored neon lights outline the *Piazza's* main arch.

Color is a vital element in architecture. Even in buildings that seem colorless, there is a range of neutral colors—grays, beiges, tans, whites, and creams—that enrich our visual appreciation of the building. Color in the *Piazza d'Italia* is very evident. The ochres, dull reds, and gleaming steel of the colonnades contrast with the gray stone floor and the blue and green neon that outlines the rostrum. As in a painting, color often sets a tone for architecture. The colorfulness of the *Piazza* contributes to the festivities that take place there.

Building materials each have their unique **textures,** and these textures again enhance our visual (and tactile) appreciation of a building. Just think of the appeal of marble, stone, wood, concrete, cloth, glass, stucco, plaster, metal, brick, or glazed tile, each with a different surface, each with its own temperature. The floor of the *Piazza d'Italia* has alternating circles of polished and rough stone. These contrasting surfaces are visually rich. And they massage our feet as we walk across them.

Pattern is an important feature in almost every building. Pattern is inherent in almost all structural systems. Look at the patterns in the diagrams of structural systems throughout this chapter. Architects may also choose to incorporate pattern as a feature beyond the patterns inherent in the structural systems. In these cases, pattern often adds visual distinction and identity, as is the case of the pattern of concentric circles in the *Piazza d'Italia.*

Shape, volume, and **space** are key elements in architecture. The *Piazza d'Italia* features curved shapes that enclose small volumes, but define the large open area of the plaza. The *Piazza* has relatively little architectural mass for its size. Look at the buildings around you. What are their predominant shapes? What volumes do they enclose? How much mass do the structures have? What spaces surround them?

In architecture, the elements of **improvisation** and **spontaneity** occur in the changes in style we see from one building to the next. Charles Moore designed the *Piazza d'Italia* at a time when plain, rectangular, glass-and-steel skyscrapers were the architectural forms of all new city-center buildings. Moore improvised on older architectural forms and translated them into a modern aesthetic. The result was a plaza that seemed fresh and spontaneous in style compared to the status quo.

In addition to the elements of improvisation and spontaneity, architecture has features that **engage all our senses.** Buildings have sounds, smells, temperature, and texture. Large, vaulted spaces, such as old stone churches, often have cool interiors with hollow and echoing sounds. They sometimes smell damp. Smaller, domestic spaces are usually warm, with the cushioning of wood floors or rugs underfoot that hush sounds. The *Piazza d'Italia* has many fountains, filling the air with cool mist and the sound of splashing water. It is a festival site, so there may be music and food.

Because architecture encloses spaces and contains various sides, we cannot grasp all its features in an instant, from a single point of view. Buildings unfold in **time** as we move through them. New vistas open up because of our **motion.** Large spaces alternate with small, and openings frame upcoming spaces. We have to take time and move around a building before we can understand all aspects of its design. If we are seeing it only in a book, we need multiple views and verbal descriptions in order to imagine what it would be like to be there. We have provided some of that for the *Piazza d'Italia.*

ORGANIZING PRINCIPLES

We also studied and defined the organizing principles of design in Chapter 2. They are balance, rhythm, proportion, scale, emphasis, unity, and variety. Let us look at them again here as they relate to architecture.

Balance is visual equilibrium, which occurs when architectural elements have been organized to achieve evenly distributed visual weight. Balance can be symmetrical, asymmetrical, and radial. Symmetry is common in many kinds of formal architecture, such as government buildings, office buildings, or places of worship. The *Parthenon* (Figure 3.4) had a symmetrical facade. Asymmetrically balanced buildings seem more casual, dynamic, or unexpected. The *Piazza d'Italia* is asymmetrically balanced in its arches and colonnades. In addition, the large open space (with less visual weight) asymmetrically balances the smaller structure, with greater visual weight. *Fallingwater* (Figure 3.15) is also asymmetrically balanced, reflecting natural order like the arrangement of trees, overhanging rocks, and waterfalls. The *U.S. Pavilion* (Figure 3.19) is an example of radial balance in architecture.

Rhythm is the repetition of alternating elements and intervals. It is related to pattern, but here we see it as an overall organizing principle, rather than simply one of the visual elements. Like pattern, rhythm is inherent in many structural systems. Rhythm is apparent in most architecture as alternating voids and solids. The *Piazza d'Italia's* regular rhythmic elements include the concentric floor circles, and the alternating columns and voids of the colonnades. Irregular rhythms are suggested by its staggered "rooflines."

Proportion is essential in architecture, as it represents the adjustment of one part relative to another, and the size of each part relative to the whole. As the architect, Charles Moore carefully considered the relative size of one part of the *Piazza d'Italia* to another, and the size of the structure relative to the plaza. Proportion was an important consideration when the architects Iktinos and Kallikrates designed the *Parthenon.* Height was determined in relationship to width, and the thickness of columns was adjusted to be proportional to the entablature and the whole structure.

Scale in architecture is its overall size in relation to the human body. Large-scale buildings tend to dwarf and overwhelm people, while smaller-scale buildings may relate to the individual. The *Bank of China* (Figure 3.18) towers over not only the individual, but all the buildings around it, and that scale gives it monumental importance. We do not even think of the building in reference to a single individual, but rather as representative of a powerful corporation. The scale of the *Piazza d'Italia* suggests its intended use for a group of people. The height of the arches and colonnades keeps them visible to all in the crowd. The *Piazza's* arches and columns make the crowd of people identify with Italian architecture and, as a community, celebrate it. The raised rostrum, framed by the arch, allows the community to identify its leaders. The implied scale of the *Moche House Model* (Figure 3.1), on the other hand, indicates its family use.

Emphasis in architecture means that one part of a building becomes a focal point. As important as the open plaza is to the *Piazza d'Italia,* the colonnades and arches are more emphasized, and the single most important focal point is the tallest arch that frames the rostrum. **Unity** is the quality that makes the disparate architectural parts coalesce. **Variety** provides for opposing or contrasting elements that add interest without disrupting the overall unity. The color, circular shape, and classical architectural elements unify the *Piazza d'Italia,* while being varied enough to hold visual interest.

ORNAMENTATION

Architectural ornamentation is the embellishment of forms or surfaces beyond structural necessity. Sometimes, however, ornamentation grows out of structural systems. Review the discussion of brackets in Chinese wood frame architecture (Figure 3.6). As we noted there, the brackets were originally developed as a device to allow each interior column to support a greater area of the roof. Because they were wood, the brackets were painted to protect them from insects and from weathering. But, as we can see in Figure 3.7, the brackets themselves and the way

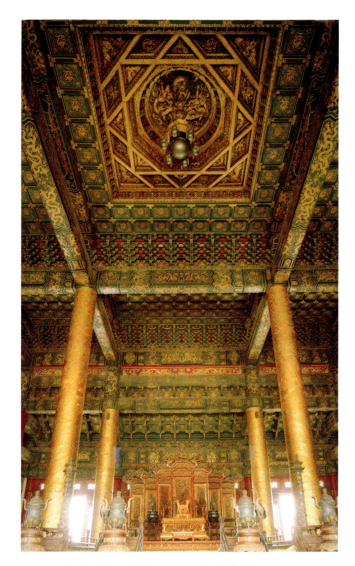

 3.21 *Imperial Throne Room* in Hall of Supreme Harmony. Forbidden City, Beijing, 1644–1911. China Photographic Publishing House, Beijing. See also the text accompanying Figure 11.9.

they were painted eventually became highly ornate. That ornate aesthetic is also visible in the interior of the Hall of Supreme Harmony around the *Imperial Throne Room* (1644–1911), Figure 3.21. The lavish proliferation of color and pattern is not a structural necessity, but it expresses visually the exalted state of the Chinese emperors who presided there as Sons of Heaven.

Architects often use ornamentation for emphasis. We saw Louis Sullivan's *Carson Pirie Scott* building in Figure 3.14. This early skyscraper is relatively plain on its upper floors, but its main entrance, on the ground floor at the center, is highly ornate (Figure 3.22) and is a focal point for the building. This grand doorway is made of cast iron according to designs by Sullivan himself. He wanted modern buildings to retain an element of nature-based ornamentation to counter their increasingly geometric appearance.

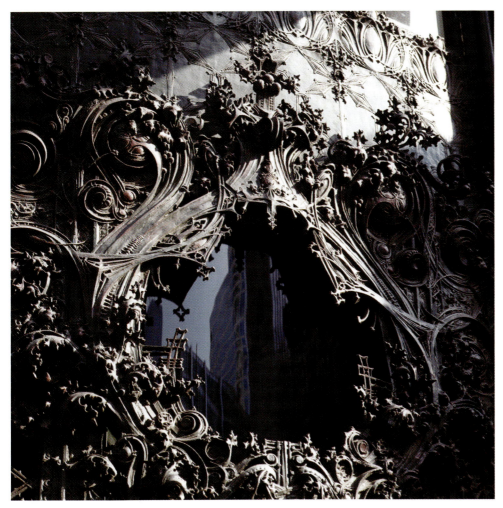

 3.22　Louis H. Sullivan. *Carson Pirie Scott and Company.* Ornate decoration. Chicago, Illinois, USA, 1904. Detail of Figures 3.14 and 7.36 © Angelo Hornak / Corbis.

During the mid-twentieth century, architects often omitted ornamentation because they felt it was not functional and, therefore, was extraneous. In fact, ornamentation is highly functional. As we just saw, it can represent imperial power, or it can highlight a certain feature of a building. Ornamentation can often carry religious or symbolic meaning. We will see more of this in Chapter 4, Deriving Meaning.

CONNECTION
One of the most popular parks in the United States is New York City's Central Park, designed by landscape architects Frederick Law Olmsted and Calvert Vaux from 1857 to 1887. Turn to Chapter 16, Entertainment (Figure 16.8, page 476), for more information.

THE NATURAL ENVIRONMENT

The natural environment is the background to all architecture. Even the densest urban center is not devoid of nature. The color of the sky, the sun, the wind, and the air temperature affect our visual impression of buildings. Throughout history, and increasingly in the present day, architects have been aware of nature and natural elements as they design buildings.

LANDSCAPE ARCHITECTURE

Landscape architects plan and alter the natural environment for some desired effect. Most landscape architects modify the natural environment so that it can be better suited for human use, as in the design of national parks or large city parks. They also design nature so that it interfaces with our constructed environment, both on the architectural and urban planning levels. The earliest landscape architects were garden designers.

The *Mortuary Temple of Hatshepsut* (Figure 3.23) from ancient Egypt is an excellent example of architecture that was well integrated with the natural environment. The temple is sited and designed to be a wonderful transition from the fertile banks of the Nile River in front of it to the barren rock cliffs behind it. The low, horizontal flood plain of the Nile was extraordinarily fertile land, where all kinds of plants grew and wildlife abounded. The *Mortuary Temple* rises from that flat land in three wide terraces, which were once gardens planted with myrrh trees, frankincense trees, and other rare plants. The continuity with the Nile is interrupted by the post-and-lintel colonnades, whose vertical stone surfaces echo the cliffs behind them. Thus, both garden and architecture work together to integrate with the landscape.

CONNECTION

We can see other examples of garden designs in this book, specifically, the vast garden and palace at Versailles (Figure 5.4, page 105), the Taj Mahal in India (Figure 10.21, page 285), and the gardens of Babur (Figure 15.17, page 448). All these gardens were associated with royalty.

Another building designed to fit within the natural environment is *Fallingwater,* which we saw in Figure 3.15. It is surrounded by nature, rather than plopped on a stretch of lawn bulldozed out of the forest. Its rock facing was quarried

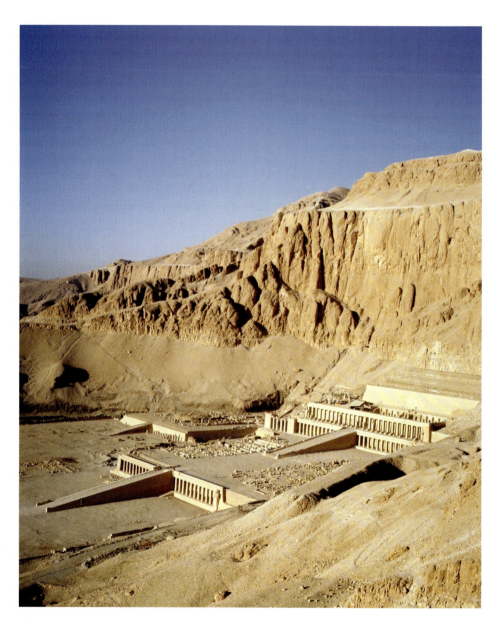

3.23 *Mortuary Temple of Hatshepsut.* Deir el-Bahri, Egypt, c. 1490–1460 BCE. © Dallas and John Heaton / Corbis. See also the text accompanying Figure 10.6.

nearby. Its wide balconies are like geometric versions of rock outcroppings. The waterfalls animate it.

INCORPORATING NATURE INTO THE CONSTRUCTED ENVIRONMENT

Today, the concern of landscape architects is not so much about building royal gardens or houses in the woods, but rather about incorporating the natural environment in an increasingly urbanized world. This is not an entirely new problem. The ancient Romans who dwelt in large cities felt the loss of nature. The wealthy had houses that incorporated open courtyards and gardens into their designs, as we will see in the *House of the Vettii* in Chapter 7.

Nature is often obliterated in downtown areas. Our image of the *Carson Pirie Scott* building (Figure 3.14) shows an entirely paved environment. Most cities have regulations to help ensure fresh air and sunlight for urbanites, a minimal encounter with nature indeed. High-rise office buildings can be built so high and so close together that the people on street level may be always in shadow, breathing stale, polluted air. To counter this effect, many large cities have regulations regarding building "setbacks," so that tall buildings are placed away from the street and are often terraced at higher levels. Most cities also have planting programs and small, open plazas to enliven downtown areas. On a much larger scale, the huge *Central Park* in New York City was planned and built in the nineteenth century to counter the loss of nature in the midst of Manhattan (see Connection on page 75).

Other architects look for ways to integrate nature thoroughly with the constructed environment. Moshe Safdie's *Habitat* (1967), Figure 3.24, is an example of high-density urban living designed to include nature throughout.

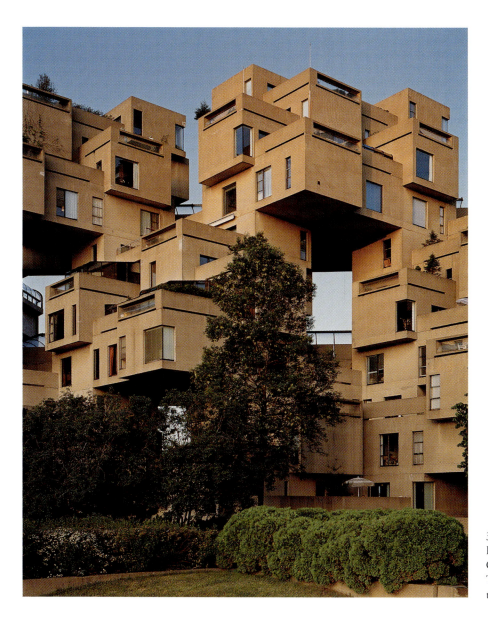

3.24 MOSHE SAFDIE. *Habitat.* Designed for Expo '67 in Montreal, Canada. Photo by Russell Thompson. The Arkansas Office, Inc. See also the text accompanying Figure 7.28.

Prefabricated modular living units are stacked in ways that allow for maximum air and sun exposure. Roofs of some structures become the gardens for others.

ECOLOGICAL CONCERNS

Indigenous people around the world have produced all kinds of unique buildings. As we saw earlier in this chapter, these traditional architectural styles made creative use of available materials. In addition, however, these buildings were designed to take advantage of desirable natural amenities and to counter those that were undesirable. All these considerations were made in response to local conditions.

In the hot, humid climate of Indonesia, for example, indigenous people built houses on stilts to raise them above the most humid air, which hovers at ground level. We see this feature in the *Toba Batak House* (Figure 3.25) from Sumatra. The middle level has no walls, while the upper level has wide windows to catch available breezes. Thick, thatched roofs, steeply pitched, shed the heavy rains common in the area. Thatch is a plentiful, lightweight material that is a renewable resource. The dual necessities of using available materials and dealing with the local climate have resulted in a house design that is distinctive and memorable.

We can find other examples from other regions. The igloos of far North America were constructed of ice blocks. They were designed to trap layers of air on the inside, which functioned as a kind of insulation. The igloos enabled people to thrive in extreme freezing conditions. Adobe construction common throughout the Southwest United States, Central America, and areas of South America featured thick walls of

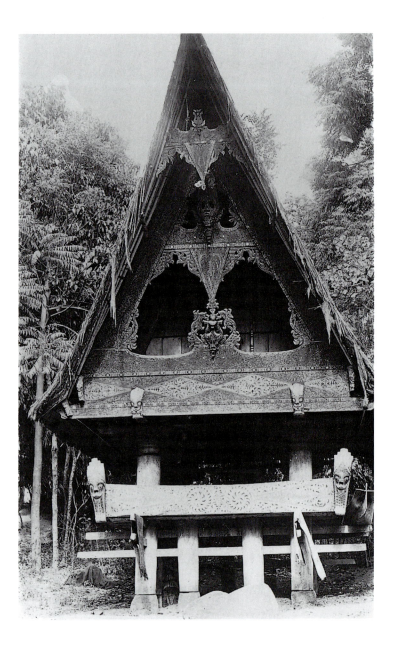

3.25   Decorated facade of *Toba Batak House*. Sumatra, Indonesia, c. nineteenth–twentieth centuries. Royal Tropical Institute, Amsterdam. See also the text accompanying Figure 7.32.

sun-dried brick. Like a cave, the thick walls insulated people from high daytime and low nighttime temperatures. The shaded interior provided relief from the sun.

Now, indigenous housing styles are being replaced with more standard houses designed after Western models. Builders often use imported materials instead of those locally available. Central air conditioning and heating mean that builders no longer have to consider local conditions. City-center areas, as we mentioned earlier, have often conformed to the International Style, with its rectilinear, glass-and-steel box buildings.

Unfortunately, all these factors require materials that are sometimes not renewable. Often, energy demands are higher, resulting in increased energy costs and greater pollution. In addition, the uniformity of style has represented a cultural loss for our world as a whole. Architects often are called now to create buildings that are more energy efficient and responsive to the local conditions in which they are placed. As a result, architects are turning to older, indigenous ideas about building as well as envisioning new forms of architecture. The future awaits us.

SYNOPSIS

We began this chapter by looking at some of the most common structural systems. The following were seen first on traditional buildings: load-bearing walls; post-and-lintel architecture; wood frame construction; and arches, vaulting, and domes. We then examined architecture made possible by recent innovations in structural systems or the introduction of new materials. These included steel frame buildings, reinforced concrete structures, and truss and geodesic construction.

Next, we considered the visual design of buildings. We looked at the basic elements of art, which include line, light and value, color, texture, pattern, shape and volume, space, time and motion, and chance/improvisation/spontaneity. Buildings also engage the other senses. The organizing principles that guide architecture include balance, rhythm, proportion, scale, emphasis, and unity and variety. Some buildings feature ornamentation, which usually functions symbolically or aesthetically.

Finally, we took a quick look at the interface between the natural environment and the constructed environment. We saw a few structures specifically designed to be in tune with their natural surroundings. We also mentioned briefly the ecological concerns that are becoming increasingly important in building design.

FOOD FOR THOUGHT

We live our lives surrounded by architecture. Only some of it is distinctive or memorable. There are many reasons why certain buildings are outstanding. Some reasons are formal: The building may be especially well designed and visually striking, it may represent a stylistic innovation, or it may feature distinctive ornamentation or a rich color scheme. Some reasons may be structural: A building may embody a structural innovation, or it may just be really big. Finally, there may be historical, religious, or symbolic reasons for the importance of a particular building.

- What are the architectural landmarks in your hometown?
- Why have they become landmarks?

YOUR CD-ROM RESOURCES

- Foundations–Interactive Modules
    Principles of Design
- Flashcards
- Food for Thought
- Companion Site
    Chapter 3 Quiz
    InfoTrac® College Edition Readings
    Artist Flashcards
    Online Study Guide

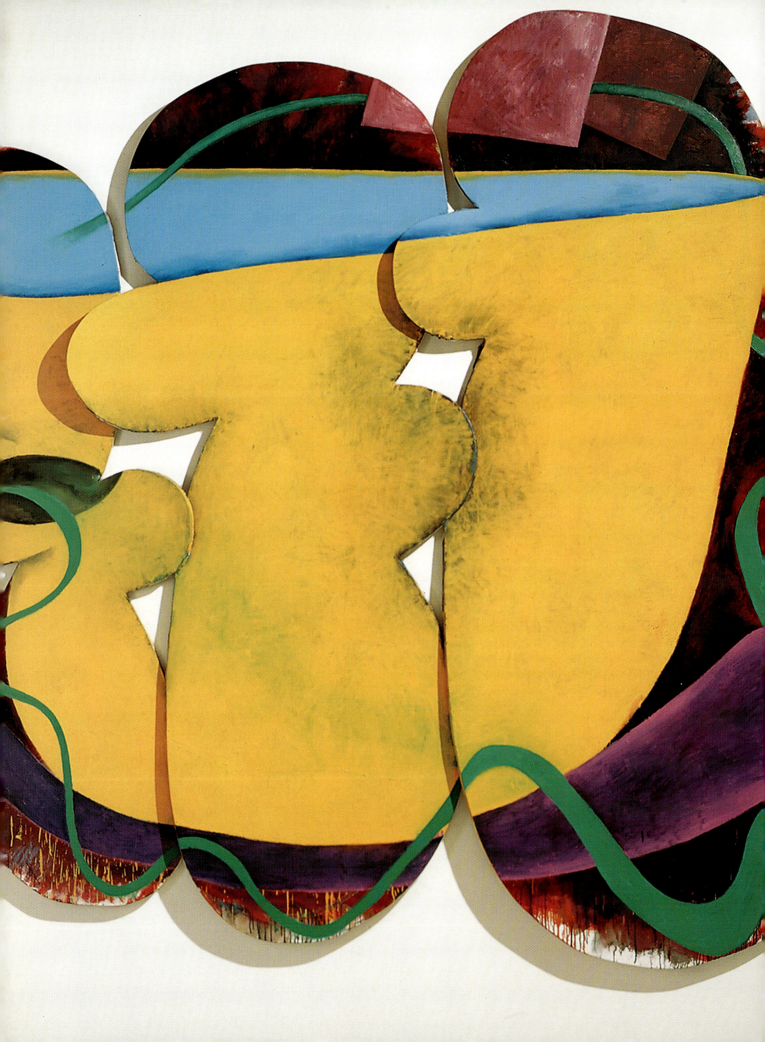

CHAPTER 4

DERIVING MEANING

INTRODUCTION

Art and architecture have meaning. They are simultaneously expression and communication. The artist "shapes" an object to visually express a complex set of ideas, and the audience receives that expression. Architects create livable or usable spaces, but their architectural structures are also significant beyond their functionality.

But how does that process work? Here are our questions for this chapter:

How do artists or architects visually present ideas in their works?

How does the audience understand the message?

In this chapter, we will see that we derive meaning in four basic ways: (1) we analyze works formally; (2) we study their content; (3) we learn about the context in which they were created; and (4) we look at the ways that we encounter them, to see how that affects their meaning.

Sail Baby. Detail of Figure 4.8. Walker Art Center, Minneapolic, MN.

FORMAL ANALYSIS

As we saw in Chapters 2 and 3, every example of art and architecture has formal qualities. These consist of visual elements arranged into a composition, using the principles of composition. What we did not discuss thoroughly in Chapters 2 and 3 was this: formal qualities add meaning to an artwork or architectural structure. **Formal analysis** is an integrated study of all the formal qualities of an art object to see how they work together. We can then see how they add to the overall meaning of that piece of art. We will formally analyze a few works now, and tie formal qualities to meaning.

Value and texture are the primary visual elements of *Migrant Mother, Nipomo Valley* (1936), Figure 4.1, by U.S. photographer Dorothea Lange. The image is composed of varying gray tones. There is no enlivening color. Texture appears primarily in the center of the photograph in clothing, skin, and hair, and is especially dense in the shirt and jacket worn by the woman.

Lange used various principles to organize the elements of value and texture into a coherent composition. The woman's face is the focal point of the picture: it occurs in the upper center of the image, and it is the most dramatically lit element. The strongest lights and darks of the entire photograph

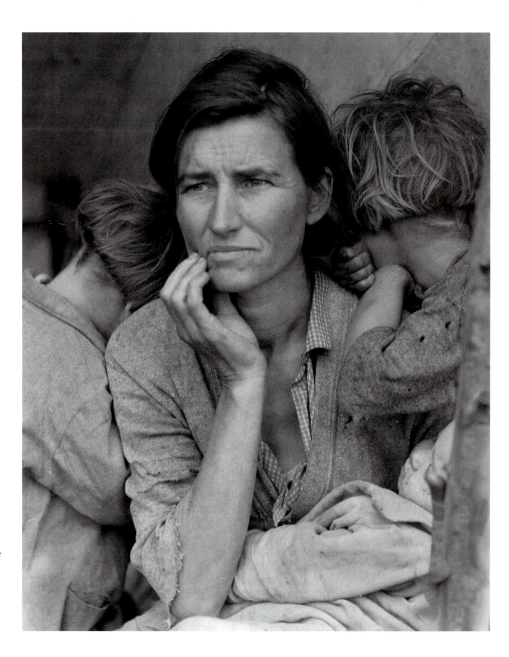

4.1 DOROTHEA LANGE. *Migrant Mother, Nipomo Valley.* Gelatin Silver Print. USA, 1936. From the Collections of the Library of Congress. See also the text accompanying Figure 14.31.

occur together in and around the woman's face. The face and arm make a vertical axis in the center of the picture. Symmetry is an important organizing principle, with children like wings at the woman's sides. The space of the picture is shallow. There is no deep space around the subjects. The woman and children are shown on a large scale, almost entirely filling the available space.

What does our formal analysis of *Migrant Mother, Nipomo Valley* contribute to the meaning of the work? Because the woman's face is the most important element, we take care to read her expression. Symmetry and verticality are often used for religious art. Here, they suggest that the woman and children share a strong, almost sacred, emotional tie. The textures are mostly rough and unkempt. Taking these formal elements together, we read the qualities of worry, fear, family devotion, and poverty in the picture.

The formal qualities of any other artwork could be similarly analyzed—for example, the *Palace Sculpture,* by Olowe of Ise, from Ikere, Nigeria (1910–1914), Figure 4.2. Without knowing anything about the work, we can still analyze it formally. The work is frontal and symmetrical, the most formal of all arrangements, often reserved for religious or royal representations. The sculptures are obviously human forms, but simplified and distorted for emphasis. Body parts are rendered almost geometrically. The necks are elongated and cylindrical, breasts are almost cylindrical, and bellies are barrel-shaped. The bodies are smooth, but the textures on clothing and jewelry add emphasis at the heads, necks, lower torsos, and wrists. The headgear is complex, decorative, and impressive. There is a greater density of smaller shapes at the bottom of the sculpture, where human legs, chair legs, and small kneeling people all crowd. Toward the top, the forms become larger, grander, and more surrounded by empty space. Verticals dominate the composition—the postures of both figures are vertical, and so is the chair. But there are also several parallel diagonal lines that knit the composition together. We see these diagonals in the implied direction of the standing woman's glance, in the upper contour of her breasts, in the direction of her lower arms, in the conical hat of the seated figure, and in the lines of the bird atop that same hat.

From our formal analysis, we can presume that the big figures represent important beings, from the formality of their arrangement and from their large size compared to the small, squatting figures below. Both figures seem important but in different ways: the large woman is more imposing, but she stands, rather than sits, at the back. The placement of her arms on the back of the chair indicates a supporting role. The seated figure in front is facing forward, as if addressing an unseen audience. Although his position and

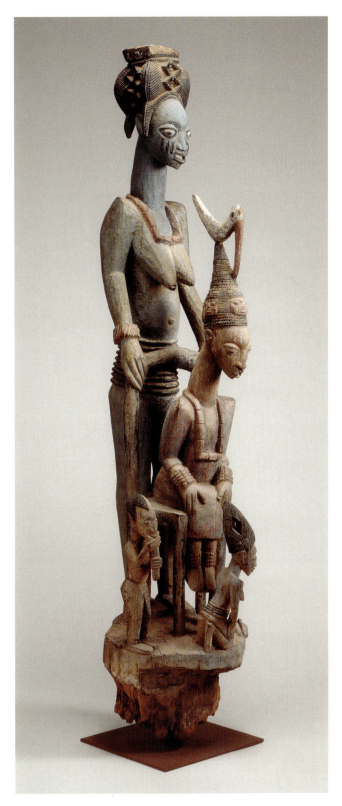

4.2 OLOWE OF ISE. *Palace Sculpture* from Ikere. Wood and pigment, 60⁷/₈" × 13¹/₄". Yoruba. Nigeria, 1910–1914. Photograph by Bob Hashimoto. Reproduction: The Art Institute of Chicago. See also the text accompanying Figure 11.12.

headgear are impressive, he seems somewhat diminutive compared to the woman.

Formal qualities add to an artwork because they are aesthetically satisfying. The arrangement of elements in the *Palace Sculpture* is balanced, hierarchical, and coherent. The thoughtful arrangement of gray tones and textures around the woman's arresting face in *Migrant Mother, Nipomo Valley* (Figure 4.1) is memorable. Looking at art is a very different experience from looking at the general environment, which is visually disjointed and disorganized. The formal qualities of artworks make them satisfying visual experiences, which adds considerably to the power of art.

The last work we will examine formally here is the 2003 *Walt Disney Concert Hall* (Figure 4.3), located in Los Angeles and designed by Frank Gehry. Its curving stainless-steel exterior has no right angles in it and looks more like a colossal piece of sculpture than a traditional building. The flowing design is an abstraction of flower petals. The shimmering surface reflects light in all directions. The exterior has no resemblance to the wood-clad, large, spacious concert space inside. The exterior is multifocal, without one single point of

supreme interest. The building's formal qualities and the materials used look very contemporary.

The hall's formal design was deliberately developed to appeal to a young and ethnically- diverse audience. Previous concert halls modeled on Greek, Roman, or Baroque art may seem dated or intimidating to such an audience. The Los Angeles Philharmonic Orchestra wanted the *Walt Disney Concert Hall* to be a vehicle for expanding its base of support. Also, city leaders wanted a concert hall with high visibility in order to increase Los Angeles's cultural profile beyond the movies and Hollywood.

READING THE CONTENT

Content is an artwork's themes or messages. Some aspects of content may be obvious just by looking at an artwork. Others must be learned. Content is conveyed primarily in three ways: (1) through the artwork's subject matter; (2) through interpreting (or reading) its symbolic or iconographic references that go beyond the subject matter; and (3) by studying the

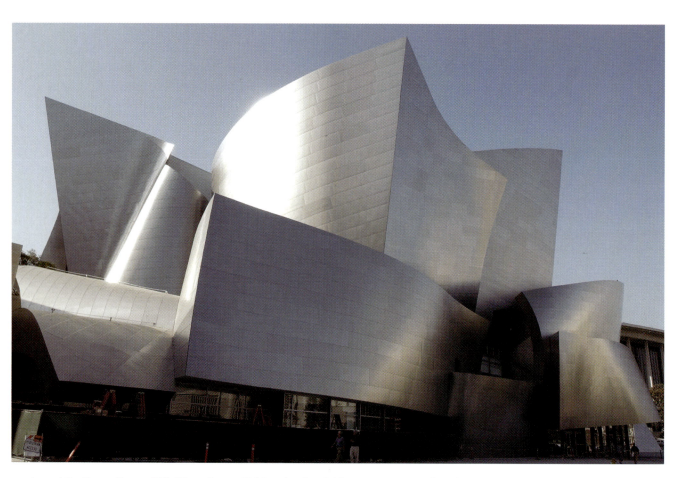

4.3 FRANK GEHRY. *Walt Disney Concert Hall,* Los Angeles, California. USA, 2003. Photo by Al Seib. © Lucy Nicholson / Reuters Newmedia Inc. / Corbis. See also the text accompanying Figure 16.6.

written materials and cultural background that explain or expand the artwork's content.

SUBJECT MATTER

The most obvious factor in the content of an artwork is its **subject matter.** What is it about? With observation, we can grasp much of the subject matter of *Migrant Mother, Nipomo Valley* (Figure 4.1). The image is not just tones and textures, but a woman surrounded by three children. Based on body language, we presume that she is the mother, as she cradles an infant in her arms, while two children cling to her shoulders. The signs of poverty and fear are evident. The title fills in more gaps and adds meaning: the woman is indeed a mother and a migrant farmworker.

We may grasp some of the subject matter of the *Palace Sculpture* (Figure 4.2) just by observation. It represents the king and queen of the palace at Ikere, a royal family portrait. This sculpture is more, however, than just a royal portrait, and more can be learned from research. The seated, frontal pose of the king shows him ceremonially enthroned. Behind him is his senior wife. She is shown larger because the women were revered for their ability to procreate. Among the Yoruba people of Nigeria, the senior wife was the one who crowned the new king. It was she who bestowed power on him, the procreative power of women and the link to all previous kings. That power relationship is reflected in the positions of the figures, in the forward position of the king and the supporting posture of the queen, and in their relative sizes. The sculpture seems balanced, direct, straightforward—all qualities cherished by the Yoruba. Also, the king's youthful figure and the queen's matronly maturity were both prized by the Yoruba.

All works of art have subject matter, even abstract works. In *Lucifer* (Figure 4.4), painted by Jackson Pollock in 1947, the subject matter is paint itself, and how it looks when dripped and splattered in layer upon layer on a very large canvas. Three kinds of paint were used—oil, aluminum paint, and enamel—each drying to a different sheen, with a different surface. Overall, *Lucifer* looks somewhat like a pattern, resembling a spread net.

Artworks also have subtexts as part of their subject matter. **Subtexts** are underlying themes or messages associated with the work of art. The subtext in *Lucifer* is the energy of the artist himself. The splattered paint marks are traces of the artist's vigorous actions as he flung, dabbed, and poured the paint. This style of art is called **Abstract Expressionism,** but Pollock's works were placed in a subcategory of that, tellingly entitled "Action Painting." Another subtext of this painting comes from its title, *Lucifer,* and the predominance of black paint in the topmost layer. The work seems to be alluding to the underworld as part of its subject matter.

ICONOGRAPHY

Artists can use metaphors or symbols to convey content. A visual **metaphor** is an image or element that is descriptive of something else. In *Lucifer,* splashes of paint are literally only splashes of paint. But the splashes are also visual metaphors for artistic energy.

A **symbol** is an image or element that stands for or represents some other entity or concept. Symbols are culturally determined and must be taught. For example, in the United States today, a dove is a symbol of peace. But people from other cultures would not know by observation alone to connect "dove" and "peace."

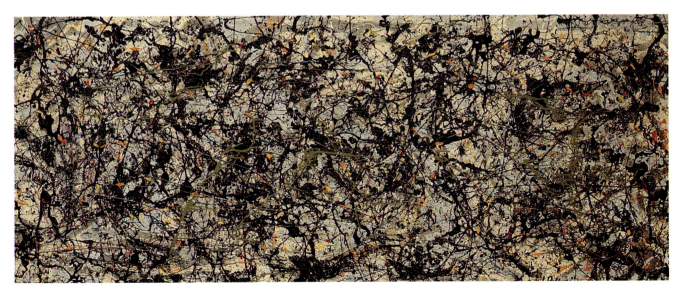

 4.4 JACKSON POLLOCK. *Lucifer.* Oil, aluminum paint, and enamel on canvas, approximately 3'5" × 8'9". USA, 1947. Collection of Harry W. and Mary Margaret Anderson. © 2004 Pollack–Krasner Foundation / Artists' Rights Society (ARS), New York. See also the text accompanying Figure 13.33.

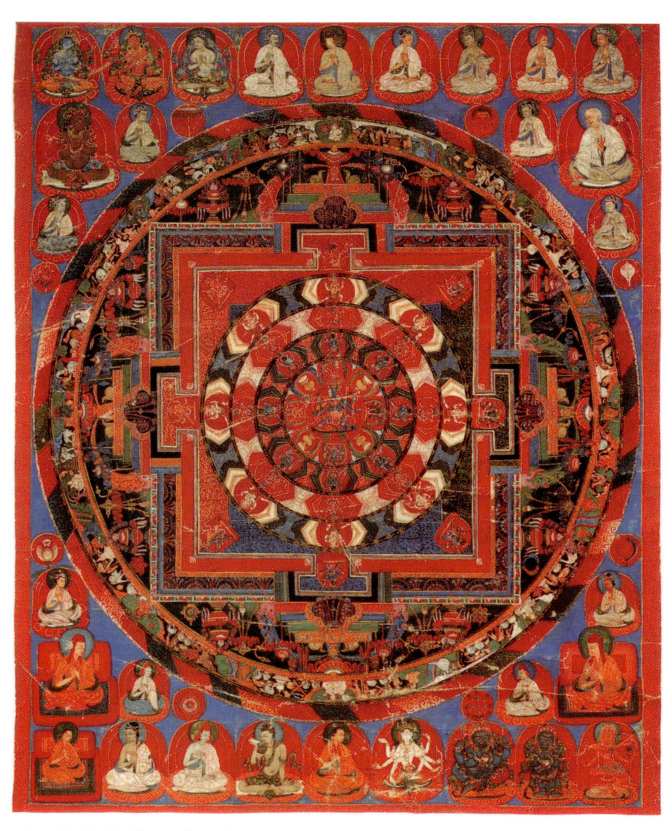

4.5 *Mandala of Samvara (Kharamukha Cakrasamvara Mandala).* Water-based pigments on cotton cloth, 23" high, 18" wide. Tibet, c. sixteenth century. The Zimmerman Family Collection. Otto Nelson. See also the text accompanying Figure 9.20.

A discussion of symbols leads to iconography, which literally means "image" (icono-) and "to write" (-graphy). **Iconography** is a kind of picture writing, with images and symbols, that allows artists to refer to complex ideas. Let us look at a few examples. In the *Palace Sculpture,* the king's crown is topped by a bird, which is a Yoruba symbol for mothers and female reproductive power. We would not necessarily know that iconographic reference, but once we have learned it, its symbolic value adds a greater depth to our understanding of that sculpture.

Some religions and cultures have developed very complex systems of iconography. The *Mandala of Samvara* (Figure 4.5), from sixteenth-century Tibet, is an example of a kind of painting used by some Hindu or Buddhist believers to help them in meditation. Almost anyone can appreciate the formal qualities of this work, its composition and colors. And, possibly, many would guess its relation to religious beliefs, due to the formal symmetry of the image and the serenity of the figures. In fact, the painting is full of iconographic symbolism. The full meaning behind the mandala is known only to those who study all the symbols and then meditate on the relationships between them. We can give a few superficial indications of the iconography in this mandala. The mandala is organized geometrically, with circles inside squares inside circles inside squares, representing fluctuating energy states and cycles of reincarnation. The circle symbolizes unbounded cosmic energy, which is transformed into physical reality (the square). The center indicates

enlightenment. The images represent Tibetan deities who each symbolize certain qualities or elements of the cosmos. Other elements symbolize either gifts from the deities or forces that are harmful to people.

CONNECTION

For more information about Hindu iconography and gods, such as Shiva, see Figure 9.4, page 228.

Other complex iconographic systems were associated with ancient Egypt, Byzantine art, medieval Europe, Buddhism, and Hinduism, to name only a few. In medieval Christian symbolism, the unicorn stood both for Jesus Christ and for a faithful husband in marriage. Mary, mother of Jesus, was often shown with flowers symbolizing purity or sorrow. A "portrait" of Mary with flowers symbolically referred to many aspects of her life. In this way, iconography adds to the content of a work of art, allowing the artist to allude to complex ideas by means of symbols and their relationship to each other. Thanks to iconography, many non-Christians recognize a painting of Jesus, just as non-Buddhists recognize an image of Buddha. This is all due to the pervasiveness and strength of iconographic representation.

Iconography can be embedded in architecture. *Te Mana O Turanga* (Figure 4.6) is a meeting house that was built by a

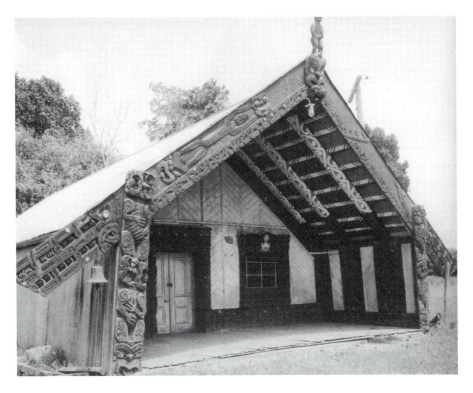

4.6 RAHARUHI RUKUPO AND OTHERS. *Te Mana O Turanga.* Exterior of Maori meeting house. Carved and painted wood. Whakato marae, Manutuke, New Zealand, opened 1883. From *Whakairo Maori Tribunal Art* by David Simmons, 1985, pp. 38–39. Reprinted by permission of Oxford University Press, New York. See also the text accompanying Figures 5.22 and 11.15

clan of the Maori people of New Zealand in 1883. Clan identity is very important among the Maori. The meeting house is essential in the creation of clan identity, because it is the site of clan meetings, and also symbolizes clan identity, through its political, religious, and genealogical iconography. Carvings symbolizing ancestry, clan history, and religious beliefs cover the house. The very structure of the meeting house is symbolic! It is seen as the body of a powerful ancestor—for example, the insides are its belly and the rafters, its ribs.

CONNECTION
For a more complete explanation of the iconography of a Maori Meeting House, see Figure 11.14, page 313, and Figure 11.15, page 314.

WRITINGS ABOUT ART

What else adds to the meaning of artworks, besides their subject matter and iconography? We all rely on the writings of art professionals to help us understand the full content of what we see. Various people write about art. Art critics describe works of art and then evaluate those works' value, their importance as art, and their success in communicating their themes. Art historians are academics who primarily research art of the past and art of other cultures, identifying styles, attributing works to certain artists, and placing them in a chronological and cultural continuum. Museum curators write catalog essays, wall labels, and didactic material in exhibitions to help us understand the full import of what we are seeing. We all rely on these materials when we go to a museum and encounter unfamiliar work.

All these writings develop the content of artworks. Content is not fixed and permanent in artworks from the moment they are made. Rather, content is formed repeatedly, as people in subsequent periods reexamine and assess work. Writers from different periods may have different interpretations of the same works of art. Let us look at *Oath of the Horatii* (Figure 4.7), painted by Jacques-Louis David in 1784. The painting shows three young Roman men, standing together at the left, vowing to their father (in the center) that they will die if they do not return victorious from a duel against warriors representing a rival state. To the right, women grieve over the upcoming battle, as two women are related by blood and marriage to warriors on both sides of the conflict.

Here are excerpts from two twentieth-century writers discussing this painting. The first, John Canaday, writing in 1959, focused on the concepts of heroic action, virtue, and duty to the state. He saw the painting as moral and revolutionary:

David invented a new style of painting . . . in order to express what amounted to a moral and philosophical revolution in art. . . . [T]he subject of "The Oath of the Horatii" is dedication and sacrifice. . . . [W]e have vigorous young males pledging their lives to the defense of their honor, their family and their country. The chaste matron and swooning girl express their grief with admirable reserve, submissive to the will of the dominant men. . . . Service to a moral and social ideal is glorified as a virtue as opposed to its parallel vice, the indulgence of personal yearnings. (Canaday 1959: 11)

Linda Nochlin agrees with Canaday's interpretation in her 1988 essay, but asserts that the picture not only reflects but also actively reinforces the status quo of social inferiority for women:

[R]epresentations of women in art are founded upon and serve to reproduce indisputably accepted assumptions held by society in general, artists in particular, and some artists more than others about men's power over, superiority to, difference from and necessary control of women, assumptions which are manifested in the visual structures as well as the thematic choices. . . . The binary division here [is] between male energy, tension and concentration as opposed to female resignation, flaccidity, and relaxation. . . . David's message [is] about the superior claims of duty to the state over personal feeling. (Nochlin 1988: 1–2, 4)

Each writer represents what the painting means to a certain group at a certain point in time. These messages may be contradictory. In fact, many works of art have the capacity to convey conflicting, complex messages. Such artworks often have the greatest staying power, holding our attention longest, because they challenge us and because they are multilayered. Such art reflects life itself, with its compromises, conflicting claims, and profound (but sometimes very mixed) emotions. Meaning for a work of art develops over time. Why else would two twentieth-century writers still be occupied with a painting that is more than two hundred years old?

Some art critics and writers base their work on their personal or subjective reactions to art. Most influential critics, however, write from particular philosophical positions. The twentieth and twenty-first centuries saw the rise of six major positions from which most critics write, and we will look very briefly at each now.

FORMALIST CRITICISM

The first philosophical position, from the mid-twentieth century, is **formalist criticism.** Formalist critics emphasized

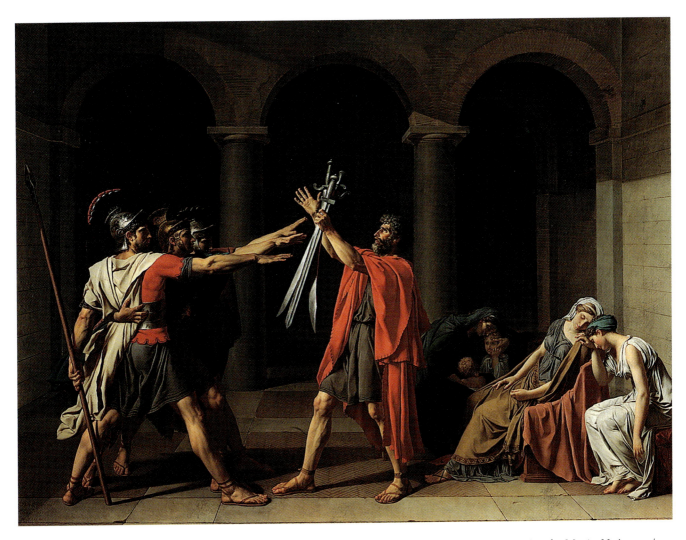

4.7   JACQUES-LOUIS DAVID. *Oath of the Horatii*. Oil on canvas. 10'10" × 14'. France, 1784. © Réunion des Musées Nationaux / Art Resource, NY. See also the text accompanying Figure 14.9.

the importance of formal qualities in art. Formalism first appeared in England in the early twentieth century as a way to appreciate works of art from other cultures. In particular, Japanese prints and African sculptures were widely circulated in Europe. Although their subject matter and iconography were unknown to the European audience, it seemed possible to appreciate them from a formalist point of view.

After World War II, formalist criticism came to be associated with Modern Art in the United States. The most famous formalist critic was Clement Greenberg, who defined the important qualities of Modern Art in terms of formalism, and who promoted the works of U.S. Abstract Expressionists. Works such as Jackson Pollock's *Lucifer* (Figure 4.4) were hailed because they were "self-critical," focusing on what was "unique to the nature of [their] medium," so that "art would

be rendered 'pure'" (Greenberg 1961: 13). *Lucifer* was "pure" painting because it was abstract and it emphasized paint quality and the flatness of the painting surface. Formal qualities were most important. Representational elements, such as recognizable imagery, symbolism, or narrative, were considered distractions. Representation was unnecessary and often detrimental. Modernism viewed art as removed from society and independent of nature.

Formalist criticism was generally discredited in the later twentieth century because it was too narrow a theory of art. It has been replaced by the five philosophical positions we will see next, which are associated with Postmodern Art. Nevertheless, formal analysis of art continues to be important, as we saw at the beginning of this chapter, for understanding the full meaning of art. Elizabeth Murray's 1983 painting, *Sail Baby* (Figure 4.8), can still be analyzed in terms of composition and the arrangement of colors and shapes on the flat canvas surface, although the deeper content of the painting is family relationships.

IDEOLOGICAL CRITICISM

Of the various late-twentieth-century philosophical positions for art criticism, we will look first at **ideological criticism.** Ideological criticism, rooted in the writings of Karl Marx, deals with the political implications of art. All art, according to this position, supports some particular political agenda, cultural structure, or economic/class hierarchy. We have just seen that Abstract Expressionist artworks were first written about in formalist terms. However, in the late twentieth century, even they were reexamined in the light of ideological criticism. In his book *How New York Stole the Idea of Modern Art*, Serge Guilbaut analyzed Abstract Expressionist art not in terms of Greenberg's formalism, but in terms of the political reasons for its amazing success after World War II. Guilbaut explained that Abstract Expressionism promoted the artists's individuality and self-expression. However, that ideology also fit with some aspects of U.S. cold war politics, as the United States positioned itself as the land of democracy and freedom versus the repressive Soviet government. In addition, Abstract Expressionism was an art style unique to the United States, emerging at a moment when the country was asserting itself as cultural leader over Europe, rather than continuing to follow European models. This strategy was aimed especially at Paris, which had been the art capital of the Western world. Guilbaut argued that Abstract Expressionism received timely support from museums and from the U.S. government, which helped ensure its great success.

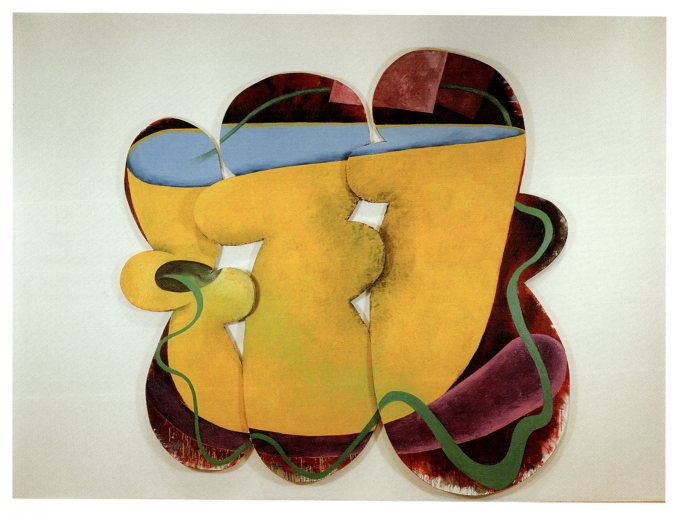

4.8   ELIZABETH MURRAY. *Sail Baby.* Oil on three canvases. 126" × 135". USA, 1983. Walker Art Center, Minneapolis, Minnesota. See also the text accompanying Figure 14.20.

Not all ideological criticism is written. Hans Haacke's 1985 piece, *MetroMobiltan* (Figure 4.9), examined the relationship between the art museum and corporate funding. Haacke used art to make the point that the Mobil Corporation was sponsoring a U.S. exhibit of African art at New York's Metropolitan Museum of Art as a public-relations strategy. Mobil had been the target of protests because it was supplying goods to the South African police who were enforcing apartheid, or forced racial segregation. In his artwork, Haacke "argued" that by sponsoring an art exhibition, Mobil apparently hoped to improve its image with liberal protestors in the United States. *MetroMobiltan* pointed out that neither art nor art institutions were free from political entanglements. Haacke's work showed that those political entanglements could be far-reaching. In this case, an art exhibit in New York City depended on the continuation of apartheid in South Africa and a U.S. corporation's profits from that system's enforcement.

STRUCTURALIST-BASED CRITICISM

Let us move on to a host of critical positions that emerge from **structuralism.** Structuralists work from the theory that the study of art (or any other system of communication) cannot focus simply on the significance of any one artwork. The study of art must be the study of the structure of art, and individual artworks are only a part of that structure. Social and cultural structures also shape the meaning in art.

Structuralism was originally applied to the study of language, as was **semiotics,** which is the study of signs in verbal or written communication. These systems of communication not only represent ideas, but they can also be used to fabricate concepts about our world. However, the signs and structure of our languages have underlying biases and limitations. Language is a system of communication that both conveys and limits knowledge. These ideas about language evolved in the first part of the twentieth century. However, in the late twentieth century, they came to be applied to any communication system, including art and mass media.

Deconstruction holds that there is a multiplicity of meanings to any text or image, and that these texts and images do not refer to any authentic, coherent world outside themselves. Rather, they grow out of the structure of society, which is a cultural, human construction that defines and limits humans and human communication. The Western view of the world is constructed, not real, and it serves a Western point of view. Such systems of knowledge limit any knowledge outside themselves, because our ability to conceive and express ideas is limited by our systems of language and representation.

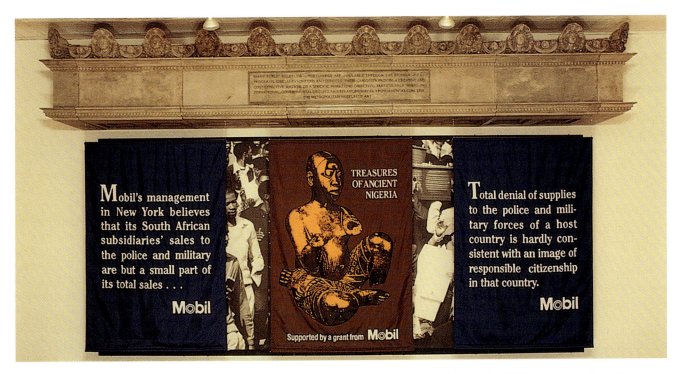

4.9   HANS HAACKE. *MetroMobiltan.* 1985. Fiberglass construction, three banners, photomural, 11' 8" × 20' × 5'. Collection Centre Georges Pompidou, Paris. © Georges Pompidou, Paris / Art Resource, NY © 2004 Artists Rights Society (ARS), New York / VG Bild-Kunst, Bonn. See also the text accompanying Figure 12.31.

Thus, from the inside, one perception of reality will come to seem universal and natural. Deconstructive artists and philosophers seek to "deconstruct" (or undermine and reveal) the myths, clichés, and stereotypes that are embedded in our language and our art and media sign systems.

A good illustration of these ideas is Cindy Sherman's *Untitled Film Still #35* (Figure 4.10), a photograph from 1979. This work is one of many such "film stills" that together constitute Sherman's self-portraits. In them, she takes on femi-

nine movie stereotypes, such as girl-next-door or vulnerable hitchhiker. She stages her work to look like film stills, which are themselves staged imagery. In her "self-portraits," there is no real Cindy Sherman. Her identity and behavior are copied. As the critic Douglas Crimp wrote,

> Sherman [as a person] is literally self-created in these works; her self is therefore understood as contingent upon the possibilities provided by the culture in which Sherman participates, not by

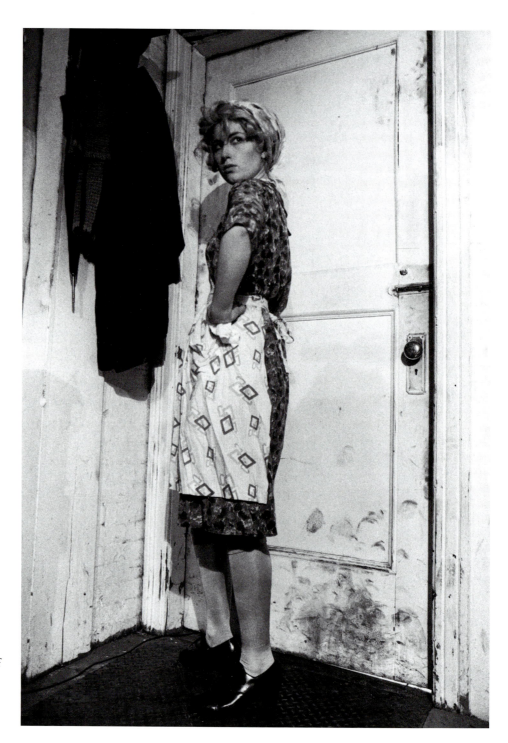

4.10 CINDY SHERMAN. *Untitled Film Still #35.* Gelatin Silver Print, 10" × 8". USA, 1979. Collection of Eli and Edythe Broad, Los Angeles. Courtesy of the artist and Metro Pictures. See also the text accompanying Figure 13.10.

some inner impulse. As such, her photographs reverse the terms of art and autobiography. They use art not to reveal the artist's true self, but to show the self as an imaginary construct. There is no real Cindy Sherman in these photographs; there is only the guises she assumes. And she does not create these guises; she simply chooses them in a way that any of us do. (Crimp 1989, reprinted in Risatti 1990: 138–39)

Thus, deconstructive critics show that our very sense of self is culturally determined and limited.

Structuralist-based critics have also examined what the category of "art" means, and how that designation is culturally determined. Modern Art placed great importance on the unique art object, which was seen as being original, one of a kind, "handmade" by an artist who was distinguished as a person of great talent, even an artistic genius. Painting was an important Modernist medium. In contrast, Postmodernists in the late twentieth century often focused on photography in the art world as a critical practice. Postmodernists question the unique quality of artwork and the idea that art has a sin-gle, universal meaning or theory to explain it. Postmodernists dispute that the artist is the author of original artworks. Photography, which easily copies existing things and allows for multiple copies as well as for the wide distribution of these copies, fits with the idea common among Postmodernists that there is no original, no "real," only copies.

PSYCHOANALYTIC CRITICISM

Psychoanalytic criticism looks at art as the product of individuals who have been influenced and shaped by their own personal pasts, their unconscious urges, and their social histories. Sigmund Freud wrote what was probably the first psychoanalytic examination of art when he looked at Leonardo da Vinci's work in light of Leonardo's presumed homosexuality and episodes from his early childhood. Psychoanalytic criticism seems appropriate to apply to work that deals with strong emotional content, dream imagery, or fantasy, such as the 1931 Surrealist painting *The Persistence of Memory* (Figure 4.11). The artist, Salvador Dali, explored his own psyche,

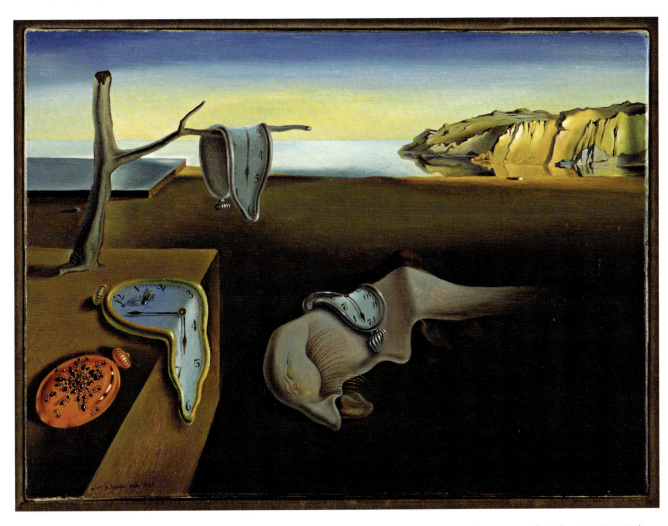

4.11   SALVADOR DALI. *The Persistence of Memory.* Oil on canvas, 9.5" × 13". Spain, 1931. The Museum of Modern Art, New York. © Digital Image © The Museum of Modern Art/Licensed by SCALA / Art Resource, NY. © 2004 Salvador Dali, Gala-Salvador Dali Foundation / Artists Rights Society (ARS), New York. See also the text accompanying Figure 15.28.

dreams, and erotic impulses as the basis of his work. The dreamscape is filled with absurd or fantastic imagery, all meticulously painted as if real. Psychoanalytic criticism helps to assign meaning to such imagery.

In addition to writing about individual artists, psychoanalytic critics have looked at the general psychological attributes of artists as a group. The critic Donald Kuspit exposes and then questions the preconceived notions about artists that psychoanalysis has given us:

> [P]sychoanalysis generally follows Plato in believing that the artist's psychopathy, or "madness," is intense and intractable, "inspiring" him or her to art yet making for a damaged life. But psychoanalysis is not alone here; many people follow Plato in this view. This preconception has led to the psychoanalytic correlation of art and madness, a correlation with profound implications yet also a great potential for shallow misuse. Psychoanalysis often seems to suggest that art does not so much overcome madness as intricately reflect it, and that the artist has a more intimate, aware experience of madness than any other human type, apart from the outright mad. (Kuspit 1987, reprinted in Risatti 1990: 291)

FEMINIST CRITICISM

Feminist criticism is another late-twentieth-century philosophical position that is concerned with the oppression of groups (especially women) in a given society along with the oppression of their belief systems. Feminism advocates equality—that is, equal social, political, and economic rights for women and men. A specific area of **feminist criticism** deals with the representation of gender in art, and how this representation can be used to support male-dominated social structures. Feminist criticism borrows from the ideas and methodologies of ideological criticism, structuralist-based criticism, and psychoanalytic criticism.

Linda Nochlin's earlier quote in reference to *Oath of the Horatii* is an example of feminist criticism. Rather than seeing the painting in terms of its heroic subject matter, Nochlin showed that the painting is based on widely held social assumptions about "[woman's] weakness and passivity, her sexual availability for men's needs, her defining domestic and nurturing function, her identity with the realm of nature, her existence as an object rather than a creator of art; the patent ridiculousness of her attempts to insert herself actively into the realm of history" (Nochlin 1988: 2). Feminist critics seek to reveal these power relationships because they can be "invisible and can be exercised only with the complicity of those who fail to recognize either that they submit to it or that they exercise it" (Nochlin 1988: 2).

The Guerrilla Girls' 1986 poster *Do Women Have to Be Naked . . .* (Figure 4.12) is an example of an artwork functioning as feminist criticism. The poster protests the small number of female artists whose works were included in the collection of New York City's Metropolitan Museum of Art. In contrast, the collection has many artworks showing female nudes, almost all done by men. Feminists point to this as a power relationship that is oppressive to women. Women make art, but their work is denied legitimacy by social and cultural structures. Images of women as sexually available for the presumed male audience are given the highest recognition in museums.

Gender issues are also explored in Chapter 14, Race, Gender, Clan, and Class.

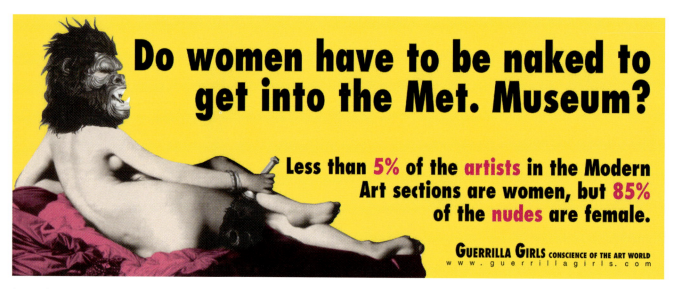

4.12   GUERRILLA GIRLS. *Do Women Have to Be Naked to Get into the Met. Museum?* Street Poster. USA, 1986. Courtesy www.guerrillagirls.com See also the text accompanying Figure 14.12.

WRITINGS ON VISUAL CULTURE

The most recently developed topic in critical writing is **visual culture,** a discipline that attempts to integrate and analyze the visual components of the whole of contemporary culture. To give you an idea of what that might encompass:

> You can buy a photograph of your house taken from an orbiting satellite or have your internal organs magnetically imaged. If that special moment didn't come out quite right in your photography, you can digitally manipulate it on your computer. At New York's Empire State Building, the queues are longer for the virtual reality New York Ride than for the lifts to the observation platforms. Alternatively, you could save yourself the trouble by catching the entire New York skyline, rendered in attractive pastel colors, at the New York, New York resort in Las Vegas. . . . Life in this alter-reality is sometimes more pleasant than the real thing, sometimes worse. . . . This is visual culture. It is not just part of your everyday life, it *is* your everyday life. (Mirzoeff 1998: 3)

People in industrialized nations consume massive numbers of images in their everyday lives, seeking information, meaning, or pleasure. To writers in visual culture, art is but one part of this intense barrage of images, and absolutely must be analyzed in relationship to all the others in order to understand what it means. Images pervade our daily lives, in film, advertisements, the Internet, television, art, and so on. People have become spectators rather than participants in their own lives, and the writers examine how we receive and use this diverse imagery.

PERSONAL INTERPRETATION

Finally, in reference to meaning, let us look at how you, an individual, may produce your own meaning for a work of art. When you look at art, its formal qualities and the subject matter outline an area of meaning for you. Your understanding can be augmented by art books like this one or by writings you find in newspapers, museums, and galleries. But there is also another dimension, and that is you—your own ideas, personal tastes, experiences, and history. The work may mean something to you that it may not mean to everyone else.

In addition, you have an emotional response to the work. You are shocked, befuddled, pleased, bored, fascinated, excited, soothed, or horrified by it. You also have an aesthetic response to it, for example, one of pleasure if the work has qualities that satisfy the eye or hand. These emotional and aesthetic reactions add to the meaning that the work has for you. Then your own background and experiences make a fertile ground for you to add meaning to the works of art that you study. That meaning often shifts as you change. A work of art may seem very different to you now than it did a few years ago.

THE INFLUENCE OF CONTEXT

Context consists of the interrelated social and political conditions that surround a work of art. Context includes a host of factors, such as historical events, economic trends, contemporary cultural developments, religious attitudes, other artworks of the time, and so on. It is important to consider how the context influenced artists while they were making their art, and how that helps us understand work as we look at it today.

Indigenous customs and historical events are important in the context surrounding the Maori meeting house, *Te Mana O Turanga* (Figure 4.6). The Maori people traditionally place great importance on genealogy, with all people tracing their heritage to powerful mythic ancestors. Therefore, the meeting house represents the body of a powerful ancestor. In addition, *Te Mana O Turanga* was built after a long period of land wars during which European settlers seized much of the land held by the native Maori people of New Zealand. Eventually, some confiscated land was returned to the Maori, but only after the clans established their tribal identity according to European standards. The meeting house was a vehicle for accomplishing this.

Let us also look at the context that surrounded *Migrant Mother, Nipomo Valley* (Figure 4.1). This work is a black-and-white photograph, and as such, other black-and-white photographs form a context in which we assess this work. *Migrant Mother, Nipomo Valley* resembles documentary or news photographs, where photography is used to record a fact. Such photographs look different from studio portrait photographs (the purpose of which is to record someone's likeness) or "fine art" photographs (the purpose of which is to create an aesthetically pleasing visual pattern). We usually consider documentary or news photographs to be objective records of fact. We believe that they show us what happened. Even though we all know that photographs can be manipulated, staged, or faked, we generally accord a high degree of truth to documentary photographs. In this case, however, the artist herself wrote that she made several exposures of this family and that they posed for her. Lange edited her prints and used her artistic skills to create the most effective image. Lange wrote that she felt a special rapport for the woman and that the woman cooperated in posing for the picture taking. Nonetheless, the context of documentary photography affects how we interpret her picture. We accept the image as real, not staged, and therefore our emotional reaction is for a real family in actual, dire circumstances.

The historical and economic context for Lange's photograph is the Great Depression in the United States, a ten-year period of economic collapse. The fierce personal hardships that many people experienced during the Depression were well known through photographs such as Lange's and through literature, such as John Steinbeck's *Grapes of Wrath*. U.S. government agencies employed Lange and other artists to make pictures such as this one. In this case, the Farm Security Administration, which aided farm families impoverished and displaced by the Depression, wanted such images to advertise its services to the public and to document the agency's work. The combined efforts of artists and government have left us a comprehensive picture of life during the Great Depression. In *Migrant Mother, Nipomo Valley,* the woman was a displaced farmer who resorted to picking other people's crops to feed her seven children. However, the crop had just frozen in the field. There was no work and, thus, no pay. This woman had just sold the tires from her car to buy what may have been their last food, as she could not seek further work unless she could travel.

Thus, context provides a wealth of additional information that adds to the total meaning of *Migrant Mother, Nipomo Valley.* Again, for any other work of art, we can similarly research the context and add immeasurably to our understanding of the work.

In some cases, context may determine whether we see an object as a work of art at all. Brazilian artist Cildo Meireles's

1970 work, *Insertions into Ideological Circuits: Coca-Cola Project* (Figure 4.13), appears at first to be plain old Coca-Cola bottles. If we happened to inspect one of the bottles closely, we might notice that some small print appears to have been added to each bottle, including "yankees, go home!" and "Projeto Coca-Cola." It is hard to know what average viewers would make of that. They might simply ignore it. However, in certain contexts, the work was quite meaningful and politically charged. Meireles targeted his work at the Brazilian population. He was protesting U.S. economic ventures in Brazil. To Meireles, U.S. companies buying Brazilian land and selling their products in Brazil were promoting a form of economic colonization that was detrimental to his country. Such practices also resulted in the clearing of rain forests and the uprooting and destruction of Brazilian indigenous populations. In addition, Meireles was protesting the military government in power in Brazil at that time, which profited from the U.S. ventures.

Meireles silk-screened the extra words on Coke bottles that were used repeatedly (sold full, returned for a deposit, refilled, and then put out again on the market shelf). He was

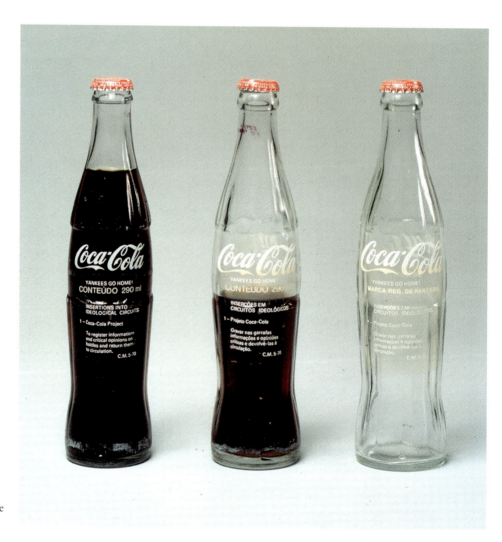

4.13 CILDO MEIRELES. *Insertions into Ideological Circuits: Coca-Cola Project.* Screen print on Coca-Cola bottles. Brazil, 1970. Courtesy of the artist and Galerie Lelong, New York. See also the text accompanying Figure 12.15.

using an existing system of distribution to distribute his own artwork. When the bottles were empty, the message was nearly invisible. When full, and in the hands of the Brazilians drinking the beverage, the message was readable.

WAYS WE ENCOUNTER ART

We encounter art in all kinds of ways, and the nature of our encounter adds meaning to the artwork.

Migrant Mother, Nipomo Valley first appeared in a San Francisco newspaper just a few days after Lange took the picture. People in the area were so moved by the image that they rushed donated food and supplies to the Nipomo Valley to feed the hungry workers. To those who saw it in the newspaper, the picture was a current event. Its immediacy caused them to act. Today, we see *Migrant Mother, Nipomo Valley* in art books or an art museum. To us, it is a work of art that refers to events in the past. We may feel sympathy, but we are not roused to rush aid and relief.

The way we encounter art even changes how the art looks. Lange's photograph has been reproduced in newspapers, reproduced in art books, and hung in a gallery. In each instance, the work of art looked very different. Newspaper-quality printing has coarse dot patterns, high contrast, and few intermediate grays. The photographic reproduction in this book is better than the one in the newspaper, but it is still small, still rendered as patterns of dots, and still crude in its tones. The actual, full-size photographic print has continuous and subtle tones, and records the textures with fine sensitivity. The newspaper image is most crude and immediate, while the photographic print in the gallery is the most aesthetically refined. A work of art is not the same if we know it only through reproductions without seeing the actual work. Even photographs, as we just saw, change with reproduction. If this is true for a photograph such as Lange's, then it is even more so for our experience of architecture, sculpture, large paintings, and performance art, where a single static image communicates only a fraction of the total experience.

Even when we are looking at the actual art, and not photographic reproductions, art changes as a result of where we encounter it. Art can appear in museums, in galleries, at family gatherings, as part of political events, in religious ceremonies, at outdoor festivals, at malls, at home shows, and so on. In each instance, the venue affects the value and meaning of the piece. Today, we can go to see the *Interior House Post* (Figure 4.14) at the Seattle Art Museum, where we would have the opportunity to examine up close the traditional carvings and painting of the Kwakiutl, a tribe of Native Americans who live along the Northwest Coast of Washington state and of Canada. The museum favors our experiencing art with our eyes. Most museums are very quiet, and we are strictly forbidden to touch anything. Because this post is preserved with great care,

we understand that it is valuable and rare. The museum setting may lead us to presume that it is an artifact from a dead and distant culture. Art displayed in museums is always more or less out of its original religious, historical, and social environment.

But the people for whom this house post was carved had a very different experience of it. The house post is one of four main supports in a large ceremonial house, called the Raven House. The house was completed and first used in 1916 for festivities celebrating the founding of a new family line. These festivities, called potlatches, were amazing, elaborate celebrations lasting several days. In addition to feasting, there were performances, singing, masquerades, and storytelling that glorified the family history. The ceremonial animals and figures carved in the Raven House were integrated into these performances, as they represent deities and ancestors important to the family. It was also a time of drinking and sexual license. At the end of the potlatch, the new leaders gave large quantities of gifts to all who attended, as giving gifts was a sign of power (and giving the most splendid gifts was the sign of the most supreme power). By accepting these gifts, the recipient acknowledged the power of the giver. After the potlatch was over, the house was subdivided, and several small families lived there.

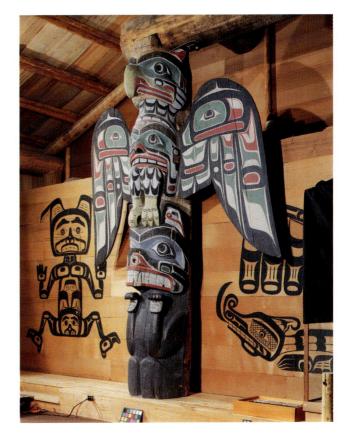

 4.14 ARTHUR SHAUGHNESSY. *Interior House Post.* Carved and painted red cedar, 180" × 132" × 34". Kwakiutl. Gilford Island, British Columbia, Canada, c. 1907. Seattle Art Museum. Gift of Mr. John H. Hauberg. See also the text accompanying Figure 14.15.

CONNECTION

Turn to Figure 7.20, page 171, to read about a feast pot used at a potlatch celebration.

This is so different from our modern museum experience of the *Interior House Post*. The potlatch was an experience for all the senses. Afterward, people lived every day with these large carvings in their houses. The house post was part of the very structure of their house and the fabric of their family lives.

Our discussion of the *Interior House Post* brings up another aspect of art and the ways we encounter it. Art is both mimetic and performative. It is **mimetic** because its appearance mimics something, resembles something, or represents something. Art is **performative** because it does something. It is used, and, in its use, it performs specific functions. The way we encounter the art greatly influences its performative aspect.

The carvings on the *Interior House Post* are mimetic. They imitate the forms of bears and thunderbirds and are readily identifiable, although they do not look like wildlife photographs. The carvings record certain external features (the bear's paws; short, upturned nose; and fearsome teeth) and certain characteristic qualities (such as fierceness) of the animals. The carvings are also iconographic, in that they are part of a large body of

symbols and images that relate to tribal histories along the Northwest Coast. The carvings are also performative. This was apparent for those who attended the potlatch in 1916, where the house post was the visual part of performances, masquerades, and storytelling. The carvings were also performative for those who later lived in the house, as the carvings recreated their history in a vivid and proud way. Visitors to the house would be awestruck by the imposing works.

But how is the *Interior House Post* performative to the people who visit the Seattle Art Museum today? The museum setting determines the performative dimension of this work. Rather than being something to live with, or to celebrate with, the *Interior House Post* in the museum becomes something to study or appreciate. The post is a record of the living history of the area, especially to the Kwakiutl people of today. We can understand from it some aspect of the underlying Kwakiutl philosophy of the physical and spiritual interrelatedness of animals and people. The carvings are still the visual component of potlatch festivities, even though we can now only mentally reconstruct them. And the museum setting encourages us to appreciate the formal qualities of the post. At nearly sixteen feet tall, it is a phenomenal visual experience, covered with strikingly bold geometric shapes, black outlines, and vivid colors. Its large scale, frontality, and symmetry are still visually impressive.

SYNOPSIS

Art communicates complex ideas and emotions through its formal qualities, its content, its context, and the ways in which we encounter it.

Formal qualities are the structure and composition of a work of art. Formal qualities organize our visual perception, emphasize certain areas of an artwork, communicate general emotional moods, and add to our aesthetic pleasure in a work.

An artwork has content, in its subject matter, in its iconography, and in the writings by art professionals. We saw six philosophical positions from which art has been analyzed for the past sixty years and even today: formalist criticism, ideological criticism, structuralist-based criticism, psychoanalytic criticism, feminist criticism, and visual culture. Finally, we shape very personal meanings for ourselves in artworks. The meaning of art is not permanent or fixed. Sometimes contradictory meanings can come from a single work of art, depending upon the viewers' backgrounds and how they use the art.

Every work of art was created in a specific historical, political, social, or religious context. Knowing about that context broadens and deepens our understanding of a work of art.

Our understanding of art is different if we know it through reproductions, or if we see it in a museum, or if we see it in its original environment. Every work of art we see is both mimetic (representative) and performative (functional). The way in which we encounter art greatly affects its performative aspect.

FOOD FOR THOUGHT

We have talked a lot about writing in relationship to art in this chapter. But what do artists think of writings about art?

Some artists have left considerable verbal or written information about their work, passed on through their own writing, through interviews they give, or through their informal conversations. Georgia O'Keeffe frequently painted details of flowers, up

close and large, as in *Grey Line with Lavender and Yellow* (1923), Figure 4.15. In private letters, the artist indicated that her art was concerned with emotional and formal arrangements of colors and shapes, inspired by landscape and plant forms. Her letters reveal over and over again her deep love of the colors and patterns of nature, especially in New Mexico, where she lived for many years. She wrote in one letter:

There has been no rain since I came out but today a little came—enough to wet the sage and moisten the top of the dry soil—and make the world smell very fresh and fine—I drove up the canyon four or five miles when the sun was low and I wish I could send you a mariposa lily—and the smell of the damp sage—the odd dark and bright look that comes over my world in the low light after a little rain . . . (Cowart 1987: 239)

Other writers, especially later feminists, have perceived a feminist content to O'Keeffe's work. In particular, they perceived her flower imagery as representing female sexuality in a positive way. Judy Chicago, a leader in the feminist art movement, wrote:

> [O'Keeffe] seemed to have made a considerable amount of work that was constructed around a center. . . . There also seemed to be an implied relationship between [her] own body and that centered image. . . . In her paintings, the flower

suggests her own femininity, through which the mysteries of life could be revealed. (Chicago 1975:142)

How important is the artist's intention versus the critical reception of the work? Which should be most important in the interpretation of the meaning behind a work? Are both important?

Georgia O'Keeffe disliked that many writers saw feminist content in her work. Yet she avoided writing artist's statements herself. As she wrote in personal letters, "Words and I—are not good friends at all except with some people," and later, "The painter using the word often seems to me like a child trying to walk. I think I'd rather let the painting work for itself than help it with the word" (Cowart 1987: 135).

Mark Rothko, whose painting we will see in Chapter 15, Nature, Knowledge, and Technology, wrote frequently about art in general and his paintings in particular in the early part of his career, but ceased doing so after 1950. In a personal letter, he wrote, "I simply cannot see myself proclaiming a series of nonsensical statements, making each vary from the other and which ultimately have no meaning whatsoever. . . . At this time I would have nothing to say in words which I would stand for. . . . This self-statement business has become a fad this season, and I cannot see myself just spreading myself with a bunch of statements everywhere, I do not wish to make." (Clearwater 1984: 67).

CONNECTION
See Figure 15.29, page 457 for more information about Mark Rothko's painting Green, Red, Blue.

Yet other artists have been very prolific with the pen, or the word processor. Judy Chicago, quoted earlier, is a prominent artist whose writings have been very influential. She led the crews of artists who produced *The Dinner Party,* a large, multimedia installation covered in Chapter 7. Donald Judd was a leading artist of the Minimalist movement in the 1960s and 1970s, and his articles and essays were widely published. Chicago and Judd are only two examples of artists who have written about art.

- Does the written word add to the public's experience of art?
- Do writings bias or limit our experience of art?

YOUR CD-ROM RESOURCES

- Foundations–Interactive Modules
     Style, Form, and Content
- Flashcards
- Food for Thought
- Companion Site
     Chapter 4 Quiz
     InfoTrac® College Edition Readings
     Artist Flashcards
     Online Study Guide

4.15   GEORGIA O'KEEFFE. *Grey Line with Lavender and Yellow.* Oil on canvas, 48" × 30". USA, 1923. The Metropolitan Museum of Art, © 2004 The Georgia O'Keefe Foundation / Artists Rights Society (ARS), New York. See also the text accompanying Figure 8.26.

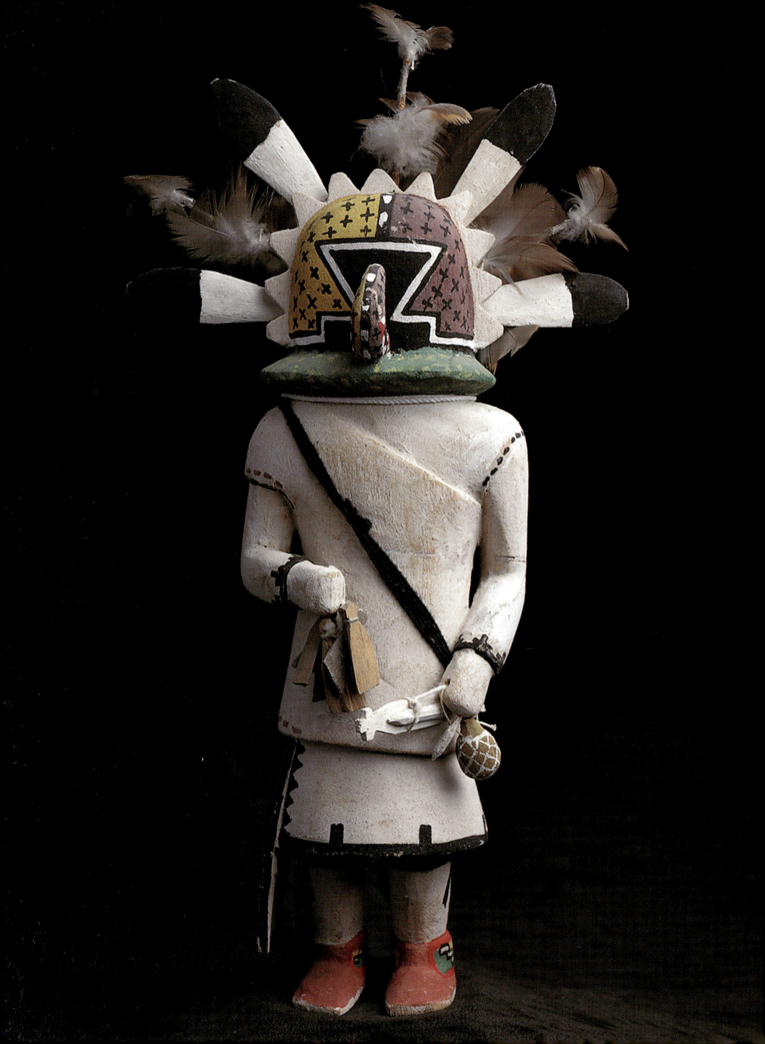

WHO MAKES ART?

INTRODUCTION

One might answer "Artists make art," in response to the title for this chapter. But art making, in reality, is much more complex than that.

Artists generate ideas for artwork, and may or may not make the actual object. But who are artists? Various cultures have different expectations of artists and their social roles and responsibilities. Imagine how differently artists functioned in medieval Europe than they do in the United States today. In addition, many people assist in the production of art. These include teachers, audiences, patrons, salespeople, taxpayers, manufacturers, critics, and curators. Their contributions are extremely important.

For this chapter, we will be asking the following questions:

How is art an individual's endeavor, and how is it a social product?

Who are artists? How are they educated?

What social role do artists have, and what functions do they fulfill?

Do artists work alone, in groups, or both?

Who supports the making of art?

Ahola Kachina. Detail of Figure 5.21. Museum of Northern Arizona.

ART PRODUCTION AS A SOCIAL ACTIVITY

We often think of art production in terms of artists who apply their skills, work a while, and then, suddenly, there is the art! But many people contribute to this process:

- The culture develops a tradition of art making and an understanding of what art is. Artists operate within that framework.

- Teachers and manufacturers supply the materials and knowledge for making art.

- Others often support artists while they make art.

- Rulers, priests, teachers, shamans, masters, publishers, art critics, merchants, connoisseurs, gallery owners, and curators are important for setting standards and determining what art is within a culture.

In every respect, the *Great Pyramids* of Egypt, dated c. 2600–2475 BCE (Figure 5.1), were social products, even though they were the tombs of individual pharaohs. Think of all the groups who contributed to them. Preceding generations of Egyptians had already developed a religion and cult of the dead, necessary conditions for the building of the pyramids. Previous pharaohs and architects had already developed funerary architecture and even a primitive form of the pyramid (see the text about Imhotep in the section "The Creative Genius" later in this chapter). Support for the pyramids came from the Egyptian economy. This required the acquiescence of the Egyptian population, whose social organization depended on the hierarchy descending from the divine pharaoh. And, of course, the actual construction of the pyramids needed the efforts of thousands—architects, engineers, priests, skilled workers, and laborers. The audience for the pyramids consists of those who lived during their construction all the way to our present age. Even today, writings and films on the pyramids increase their meaning for us. Without that accumulated body of knowledge and appreciation, the pyramids would not be seen as art, but as piles of rocks.

Other art forms—film, architecture, or any work of large scale—obviously require the active participation of many to be realized. What about small-scale work such as the painting

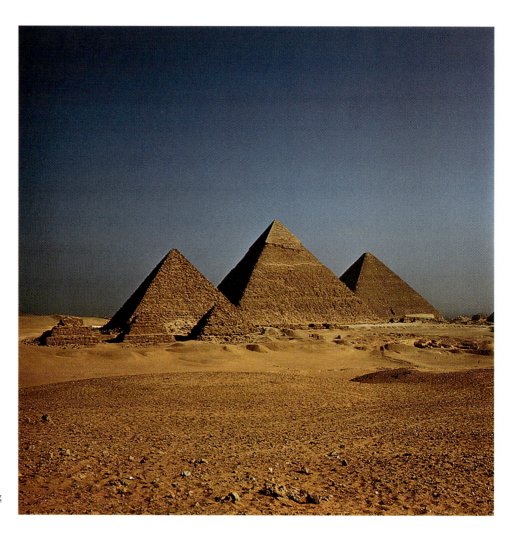

5.1 *Great Pyramids.* From left: Menkaure, c. 2525–2475 BCE; Kahfre, c. 2575–2525 BCE; Khufu, c. 2600–2550 BCE. Stone blocks. Gizeh, Egypt. © E. Strouhal / Werner Forman / Art Resource, NY. See also the text accompanying Figure 10.2.

just completed by a college art student? The teachers, past oil painters, and art critics provide the necessary background of skills and ideas. Obviously, the materials—oil paints, canvas, stretcher bars, primer, solvents, and brushes—were developed by artists and scientists, are manufactured by art supply firms, and are sold by store employees. Teachers and other college students are the audience for the work. They articulate its meaning.

The student's financial support to study oil painting probably comes from family funds, loans, or scholarships. Thus, large groups of people with means (parents, politicians, wealthy donors, university administrators, and so on) consider the study of oil painting to be important enough to pay for it. Perhaps the student is self-supporting. But that still means that extra money from some source can be devoted to art training.

CONNECTION
A few important related areas on art as a social product are discussed in other chapters. Many people develop the meaning of a work of art, as we saw in Chapter 4. What people do with art once it is made is also a social process, as covered in Chapter 6.

ABOUT ARTISTS

The fact that art is a social production does not diminish the importance of artists. Artists are creative people with exceptional skills. They are able to take meaningful ideas—social ideas, intensely personal ideas, spiritual ideas, political ideas—and embody them in a visual form that holds our attention, grips our emotions, or engages our imagination. Artists' works either are unique and innovative or are vital restatements of traditional ideas.

TRAINING OF ARTISTS

How do artists learn their profession? Almost all are trained in art techniques, skills, styles, and in some cultures, the nitty-gritty of running a small business.

Many artists have been trained by the apprentice method, in which a promising young person works directly with a practicing artist to learn materials, manual skills, and styles. Sometimes very skilled apprentices actually make part of the master's artwork, but the final product is owned by and credited to the master artist. Leonardo da Vinci was apprenticed for many years to the artist Andrea del Verrocchio, and painted parts of Verrocchio's paintings, for example, the face of an angel in one baptismal painting. Michelangelo was apprenticed to the Florentine painter Domenico Ghirlandaio and worked with the sculptor Bertoldo di Giovanni, in addition to

studying the work of previous Italian artists and the art of ancient Rome. Throughout Africa, artists traditionally were trained by the apprentice method, learning the tools and methods as well as aesthetic standards, as in *Bamana Female Figure* (Figure 5.2). Among the Yoruba artists in modern Africa, "the final sharp cutting is best done by the master" while apprentices do the "mechanical aspects of the work, and as their skill increases, more and more is entrusted to them" (Fr. Kevin Carroll, quoted in Willett 1993: 236).

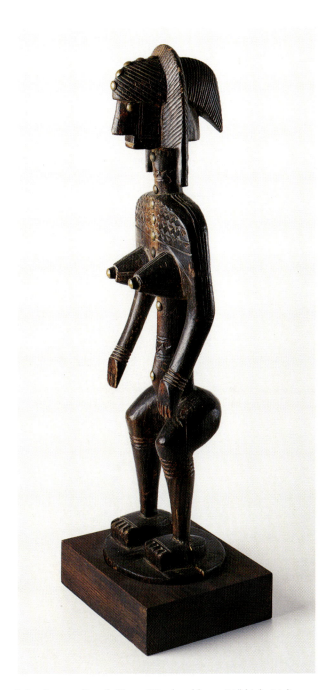

5.2   *Bamana Female Figure.* Wood and brass, 21" high. Mali, 1947. Photo courtesy Galerie Carrefore, Paris. See also the text accompanying Figure 8.7.

Specialized societies sometimes preserve technical information important in the training of artists, and regulate art making. Guilds in medieval Europe were prime examples of such organizations. Guilds were unions that protected artists' interests, just as they did for other professionals like goldsmiths, stone workers, weavers, barrel makers, and bakers. Guilds contributed many of the craftsmen who worked on medieval building projects, such as *Chartres Cathedral* (Figure 5.3). Sometimes, the guild system created unusual groupings. For example, in medieval Florence, painters belonged to the guild of "Medici e Speziali" (physicians), and sculptors belonged to the "Fabbricanti" guild (builders) or to the Goldsmiths' guild, which included jewelers.

Art academies, or schools that provide systematized art instruction, are a more recent invention for the training of artists. Among their many functions, academies generally (1) provide art training for students; (2) sponsor lectures in theory and established aesthetic standards; and (3) accept mature artists as members, which allows them to receive more commissions.

An early example of academy-like training comes from thirteenth- to seventeenth-century Persia (Iran). The *kitab-khana* were libraries that produced fine illuminated manuscripts executed by highly trained Islamic artists. The libraries were both centers of learning and studios for book production, where students were taught the fine arts of calligraphy and illumination. The kitab-khana eventually spread to India under the Mughal shahs, where this tradition of art training continued.

CONNECTION
Babur Supervising the Layout of the Garden of Fidelity *(Figure 15.17, page 448) is an example of a royal manuscript produced in Mughal India.*

The first academy in Europe appeared in fifteenth-century Italy. In part, academies helped break the power of the guilds, which to some extent were stifling innovation because their regulations imposed uniformity. Academies were usually supported by the state or by some powerful patron and often used by them. For example, in 1648, France's King Louis XIV founded the powerful Royal Academy (Académie

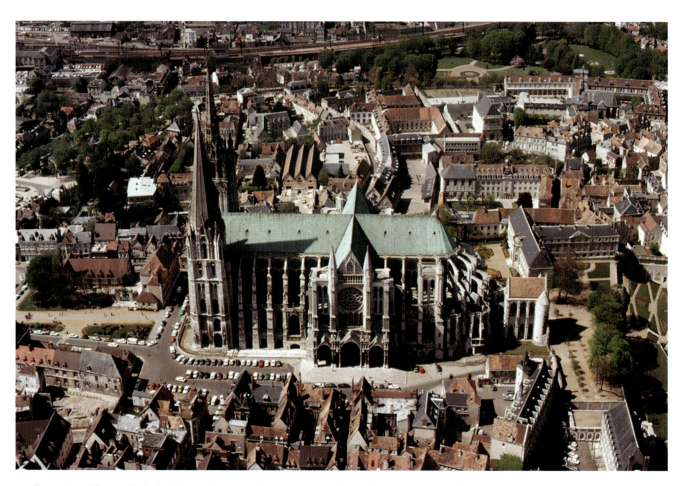

 5.3 *Chartres Cathedral.* Some older parts from 1145–1170; bulk of exterior from 1194–1220. Chartres, France. © Marc Garanger / Corbis. See also the text accompanying Figures 3.11, 9.39, 9.40, and 9.41.

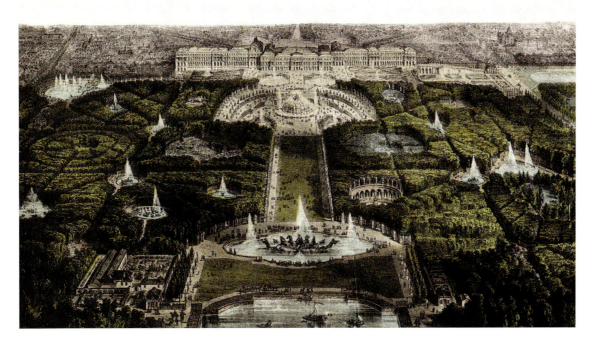

5.4 *Versailles.* Anonymous seventeenth-century painting.
© Bettmann/Corbis. See also text accompanying Figure 11.10.

Royale de Peinture et de Sculpture). Through his ministers and the academy, the king controlled high-level art production throughout France to promote his own power and fame. This included the decorative arts, architecture, painting, and landscape architecture, all of which can be seen at *Versailles* (Figure 5.4). Among mature artists, only those whose work conformed to certain standards received commissions.

Modern art education in the United States now takes place most often in a college or university. Many artists now have a Master of Fine Arts (MFA) degree from a university as their final art training, although most MFA programs date only from the 1960s. Prior to that time, most U.S. artists either were academy-trained or studied with established artists. Even in the university, however, the apprentice method persists in internships, where students receive college credit for working with art professionals.

Some artists are self-taught, meaning that they have received no formal art training. Many self-taught artists have learned from other images and works of art, and so their art reflects the current culture. Others work in isolation. Their output is generally categorized as naive art, outsider art, or folk art, since it is produced without education and outside the current aesthetic standards. Simon Rodia was an untrained artist who single-handedly built the Watts Towers (Figure 5.5).

THE CONTEXT FOR ART MAKING

Who makes the art object? Sometimes the artist, and sometimes others, as we will see.

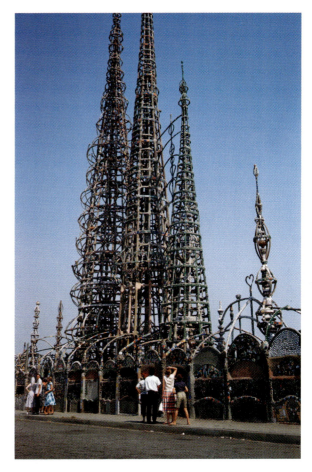

5.5 SIMON RODIA. *Watts Towers.* Reinforced concrete with mixed media and found materials; tallest tower is 100' high. Los Angeles, California, USA, 1921–1954. © Bettmann/Corbis. See also the text accompanying Figure 14.34.

WORKSHOPS

Workshops are businesses composed of apprentices, assistants, and specialists who operate under the name of a master artist. The specialists might prepare art materials, excel at certain crafts, or handle the workshop's business affairs. Workshops can produce a prodigious amount of artwork.

Workshops associated with famous artists are common among important sculptors in Africa. The Yoruban sculptor Olowe of Ise was so prominent and respected that he was responsible for carvings in a number of palaces in Nigeria (see Figure 11.12, page 311). After receiving an important commission, he and his assistants often traveled to the site, where they would be housed and fed while they completed their work.

Likewise, much European art of the last several centuries is the product of workshops. Peter Paul Rubens was an enormously successful artist credited with producing a vast number of important paintings for many of the nobles and royalty of Europe in the early seventeenth century. However, to meet the demand for his work, Rubens employed at times as many as two hundred assistants and apprentices. Rubens himself would generally develop the color scheme and composition for a painting, often as a very small oil sketch. Assistants would enlarge the sketch as a drawing, prepare a canvas, transfer the drawing to canvas, and put down underpainting. Rubens's best assistants painted much of the final work. Anthony Van Dyck, who became a well-known portrait painter after working in Rubens's workshop, painted substantial amounts of Rubens's *Abduction of the Daughters of Leucippus* (Figure 5.6), from 1617. Rubens would do important parts, such as the faces, and then finishing touches once the painting was installed in its final location.

CONNECTION
Rubens was assisted also by other established professional artists, such as Jan Bruegel, who painted background landscapes and flowers, much like his own Little Bouquet in a Clay Jar (Figure 15.16, page 447).

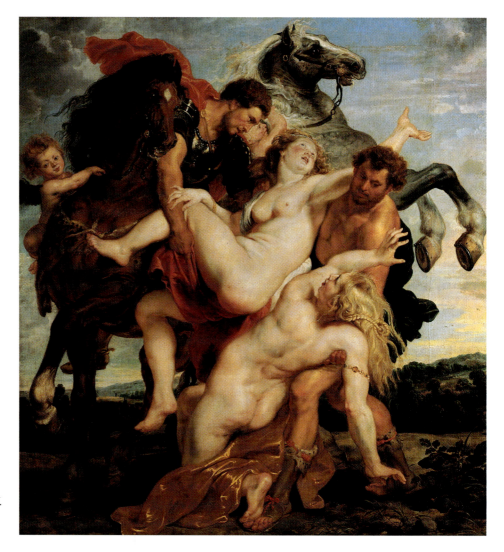

5.6   PETER PAUL RUBENS. *Abduction of the Daughters of Leucippus.* Oil on canvas, approximately 7'3" × 6'10". Flanders, 1617. Alte Pinakothek, Munich. © Scala / Art Resource, NY. This painting is also discussed in Chapter 14, Figure 14.8.

The Rent Collection Courtyard (1965; Figure 5.7) is the product of artists working in a workshop-like situation. *The Rent Collection Courtyard* is a tableau of over one hundred life-size figures made out of clay that illustrate scenes of repression from China's past, when powerful landlords grimly exploited peasant laborers, whom we see here offering their harvest to pay the landlord's excessive rent and taxes. The work was completed by a team of amateur and professional sculptors working together, under the leadership of Ye Yushan at the Sichuan Academy of Fine Arts. Almost any large-scale work of art requires the coordinated efforts of a workshop.

COMMUNITY ART MAKING

In community art making, large groups of people contribute directly to the production of a work of art. In some cases, they control to some extent what their contribution looks like. In community art making, people not normally considered specialists produce the art.

In community art making, many people collectively realize a big project. One example is *Chartres Cathedral,* dated 1194–1220 (Figure 5.3), one of the large, impressive churches built in northern Europe from the twelfth through the fourteenth centuries. These churches were almost all located in cities and were symbols of community pride. Their construction required the collective effort of an army of craftsmen, from

sculptors to stained-glass makers, stone masons, woodworkers, and more. But the people of Chartres, from the wealthy to the poor, also contributed. Not only did they substantially pay for the church, which we will discuss more on page 119, but they contributed their labor. Abbot Haimon wrote an eyewitness account in a letter that describes the townspeople dragging building materials and food to the construction site:

> Who has ever seen!—Who has ever heard tell, in times past, that powerful princes . . . nobles, men and women, have bent their proud and haughty necks to the harness of carts, and that, like beasts of burden, they have dragged to the abode of Christ these waggons, loaded with wines, grains, oil, stone, wood and all that is necessary for the wants of life, or for the construction of the church? (Holt 1947: 45)

Among the Hindu-Balinese people on the South Pacific island of Bali, almost everyone makes art, either visual art, dance, or music, although certain people are recognized as teachers or people of superior ability. Art, religion, and social institutions are completely intertwined. The visual arts alone consist of stone temples with carved reliefs, wooden pagodas, wooden statues for smaller shrines, paintings, large decorated cremation towers used in funerals, items for personal adornment, masks for performances, textiles, small sculptures made of baked dough, and food offerings for temples. An example of a temple food

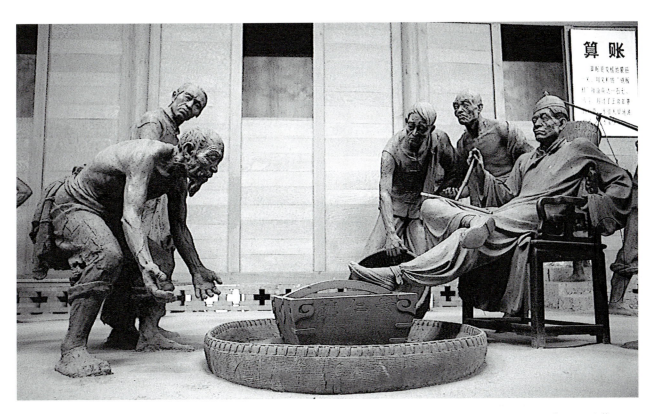

 5.7 YE YUSHAN AND A TEAM OF SCULPTORS FROM THE SICHUAN ACADEMY OF FINE ARTS, CHONGQING. *The Rent Collection Courtyard* (detail). Clay, life-size figures. China (Dayi, Sichuan), 1965. See also the text accompanying Figure 12.13.

offering is *Offering with Cili-Shaped Crown,* c. 1985 (Figure 5.8). Offerings like this exist but a short time, but the obvious care and skill that go into them indicate the significance of art in everyday life. A ceramic basin forms the base, onto which are artfully arranged flowers, colored rice cakes, and palm leaves cut and woven into intricate patterns.

The *AIDS Memorial Quilt,* begun in 1989 (Figure 5.9), provides us with another example of community art making. The *AIDS Memorial Quilt* is a composite of thousands of three-by-six-foot panels, each made by an ordinary person to memorialize someone lost to AIDS. It is a collection of individual remembrances, and each remembrance is an equal contribution to the fabric of the whole. The people who made the panels communicated their love and loss in ways that may be naive or may be sophisticated, but collectively are very moving.

The quilt is an ongoing project, ever growing in size, organized by the Names Project, begun by gay activist Cleve Jones in San Francisco in the 1980s. It is also used as a fund-raising tool for AIDS research. As an ongoing community work in progress,
it welcomes contributions from anyone who steps forward. The quilt can be found on the Internet, again a sign of accessible community-level art. It has been the subject of books and documentaries and was nominated for the 1989 Nobel Peace Prize.

FABRICATORS, CONSTRUCTION ASSISTANTS, TECHNICIANS, AND PRODUCTION STAFF

A lot of artists hire others to make their artwork, either totally or partially. Many printmakers hire other printers to make their editions of prints. Many artists hire fabricators to make part or all of their artworks, especially if the fabrication requires skills that the artists do not have. Many sculptors make their work in clay, and then have a commercial foundry cast the work in bronze.

Robert Smithson's *Spiral Jetty,* dated 1970 (Figure 5.10), is a long spiral of rock that extends outward into the Great Salt Lake in Utah. Smithson required the assistance of an engineer to plan the work, and then hired a construction crew to make this piece about the human manipulation of the earth, energy potential, and the passage of time.

Matthew Barney's *Cremaster* films require the help of many, as the still in Figure 5.11, based on one production,

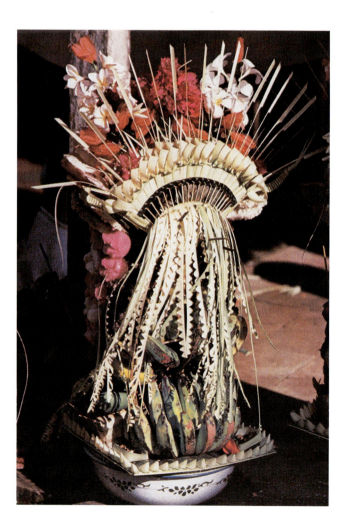

 5.8 *Offering with Cili-Shaped Crown.* Flowers, fruit, and palm leaves, approximately 24" tall. Bali, c. 1985. Photo Hans Hinz. See Figure 9.14 for more on this work and sacred offerings.

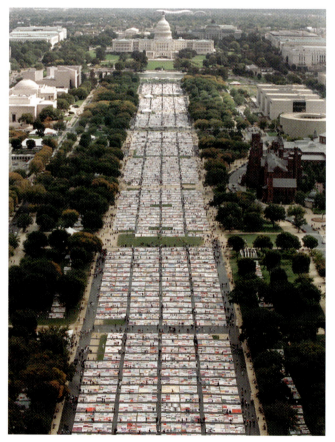

 5.9 *AIDS Memorial Quilt.* Displayed on the Mall in Washington, D.C., October 11, 1996. Organized by the Names Project, San Francisco. © AP / Wide World, Ron Edmonds. See the text accompanying Figure 10.31 for more information on the quilt.

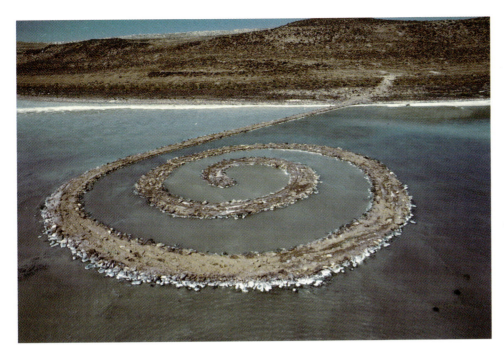

5.10   ROBERT SMITHSON. *Spiral Jetty.* Great Salt Lake, Utah, U.S.A., April 1970. Black rocks, salt crystals, earth, red water (algae), $3^1/_2' \times 15' \times 1,500'$ long. James Cohan Gallery, New York. Art © Estate of Robert Smithson/ Licensed by VAGA, New York, NY. For more on this artwork, see the text accompanying Figure 15.20.

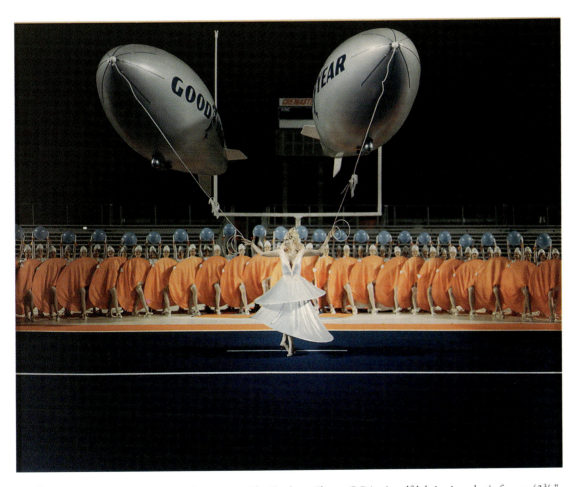

 5.11   MATTHEW BARNEY. *Cremaster 1: The Goodyear Chorus.* C-Print in self-lubricating plastic frame, $43^3/_4"$ $\times 53^3/_4"$. USA, 1995. Photo: Michael James O'Brien. Courtesy Barbara Gladstone Gallery. See also the text accompanying Figure 16.26.

shows. Films are inherently collaborative projects, and the contributions of the actors, set builders, makeup artists, costumers, choreographers, lighting technicians, and camera operators affect the results in profound ways. Most computer-intensive projects require technical support.

THE ARTIST AS OBJECT MAKER

In many cases, individual artists make their own artwork. Michelangelo Buonarroti did most of the painting on the colossal *Sistine Ceiling* because he was dissatisfied with the work that collaborators did. Peter Paul Rubens would complete a work with his own hand if an important patron insisted upon it. Vincent van Gogh painted all his own paintings, because, as he wrote to his brother Theo, "In life and in painting too I can easily do without God, but I cannot—I who suffer—do without something that is bigger than I, that is my life: the power to create" (quoted in *Gardner's Art Through the Ages* 1996: 998).

Much of Yayoi Kusama's work is incredibly labor-intensive, such as *Accumulation No. 1,* dated 1962 (Figure 5.12), in which she sewed phallic-like protrusions onto a chair, which became part of a whole environment similarly covered. Kusama applied other kinds of patterns to other surfaces in a similarly overwhelming, almost menacing way. The labor-intensive quality of her work fits its themes, which include compulsion, self-obliteration, "women's work," uncontrolled consumption, problematic sexuality, and the effects of pervasive paternalism on the individual and the human environment.

COLLABORATIONS

In many instances, art making is a collaborative activity among professionals of equal standing. The knowledge and skill of each collaborator are essential to the final art product. Let us look at a few examples now.

Ukiyo-e prints from Japan are the products of professional collaboration, although usually only the artist's name is associated with an edition of prints. *Komurasaki of the Tamaya Teahouse* (Figure 5.13) is credited to the artist Kitagawa Utamaro, who created the original drawing in black ink on thin

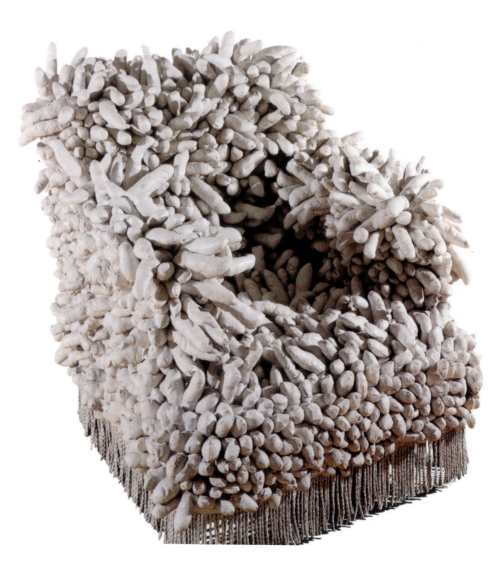

5.12 YAYOI KUSAMA. *Accumulation No. 1*. Sewn stuffed fabric, paint, fringe on chair frame, 37" × 39" × 43". Japan/USA, 1962. Beatrice Perry Family Collection. The Los Angeles County Museum of Art. See also the text accompanying Figure 12.27 for more on this sculpture.

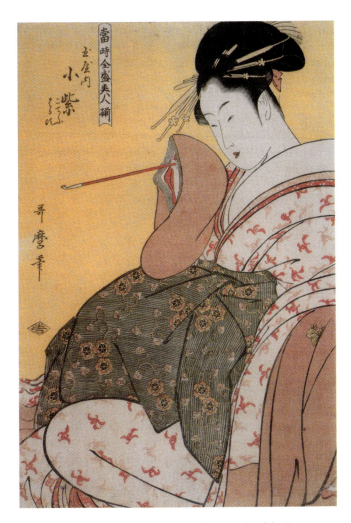

right tones, the subtle color transitions, and the correct edges. Each piece of paper had to be printed from several blocks until all colors were applied in order and the print was finished.

Two more professionals made substantial contributions to the production of an ukiyo-e print. The publisher commissioned the prints, selecting the three professionals to make an edition, paying the costs, and then distributing the final product. We know the names of many important publishers, such as Tsutaya Jusaburo and Eijudo. The papermakers were the other important contributors to this process. The mulberry-bark paper had to be tough, resilient, and beautifully textured. Colors had to print well on it. The performance and look of the paper were as essential to the final product as were any of the other processes.

Another example of artistic collaboration is John James Audubon's *Birds of America. Carolina Paroquet,* dated 1827–1838 (Figure 5.14), is one of 435 plates from the book.

 5.13 Kitagawa Utamaro. *Komurasaki of the Tamaya Teahouse.* Multicolor woodblock print from the series "A Collection of Reigning Beauties," 10" × 15". Japan, 1794. Tokyo National Museum. See also the text accompanying Figure 14.33 for more on the theme of this print and the relationship between class hierarchies and different kinds of art in seventeenth- and eighteenth-century Japan.

paper. The next step was completed by the engraver, who glued the original drawing to a plank of cherry wood and cut out the printing block right through the original drawing, destroying it. The block had to be carefully cut to retain the amazingly graceful and fluid line quality. Once the first block was completed, a proof was made, and the artist would add color to the proof. Then other blocks were cut, one each for every color to be printed. Each block had to be the same size and perfectly aligned with all the other blocks.

The printer is the one who actually made ukiyo-e prints. The printer carefully applied paint thickened with rice paste to the surface of the block, placed a piece of mulberry-bark paper on top, and hand rubbed the paper so that the paint transferred from the block to the paper. The printer really acted more as a painter, carefully mixing colors to get the

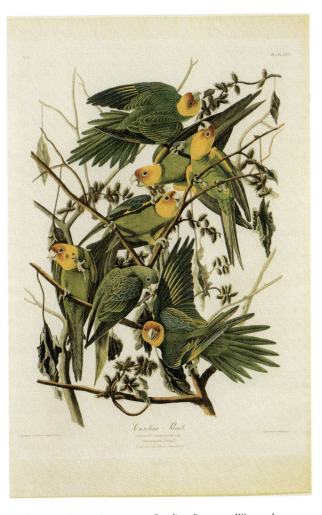

5.14 John James Audubon. *Carolina Paroquet.* Watercolor, 29½" × 21¼". Original for Plate #26 of *Birds of America.* USA, 1827–1838. North Carolina Museum of Art. See also the text accompanying Figure 15.25.

Audubon himself created the original watercolors for the book, but the work of other professionals was required to bring *Birds of America* to fruition. The naturalist William McGillivray helped write the text for this book. Robert Havell, Jr., was the professional engraver who transformed almost all of Audubon's bird paintings into engravings that could be printed. Havell's contribution was essential for a successful book. So important was engraving quality that Audubon traveled to Europe to seek out the best professionals, not trusting anyone in North America at the time to have sufficient experience and skills.

THE ROLE OF ARTISTS IN VARIOUS CULTURES

The artist's position in society reflects how that culture uses art, how it values art, and what it expects the artist to do.

ART MAKING BASED ON GENDER

In some cultures, men make certain art objects, while women make others. This usually reflects the different roles, rights, and responsibilities of males and females within their social groups. For example, the major architectural monuments and the sculpture of the ancient Greeks were all made by men. These monuments were symbols of the political power, leadership role, and achievements in the arts of the city-state of Athens.

The fact that only men were responsible for the design and building of these monuments reflects the realities of Greek society, where women were secluded in their homes and excluded from political and public life.

Among the Navajo people, men make some kinds of art, while women make others. Sand paintings are almost all made by men, because the sand paintings are part of ritual ceremonies, and men are the ceremonialists among the Navajo. During rituals, they sprinkle natural pigments directly onto the earth, creating symbols and sacred images to cure the sick, promote fertility, promote general well-being, or for successful hunting (Figure 5.15). Women produce other arts, primarily the weavings. Interestingly, this division reflects broader Navajo philosophy about the nature of men and women. For sand paintings to be effective, each must look like its traditional prototype, or the ceremony may not achieve its desired results. That strict conformity to tradition fits the Navajo concept of men, who are seen as being static in nature. Women, by contrast, are seen in Navajo philosophy as dynamic, and in their weaving designs, they are always aspiring to innovation and unique designs. Each work is new (Anderson 1990: 98, 107).

Among the various tribes of the Sepik region in Papua New Guinea, art making is men's work, and they produce a vast amount of visual art for ritual purposes. Art making and rituals create male solidarity in a tribe and protect their power from threats posed by women in general or by hostile men in

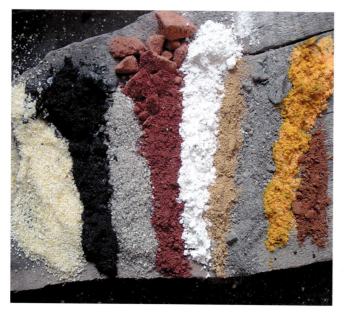
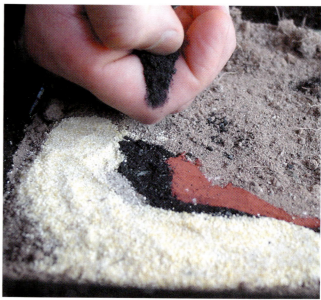

5.15   Natural pigments, similar to those used by the Navajo people, in preparation of ritual sand paintings. In the left image, from left to right, the pigments are corn meal, pulverized charcoal, brown sand, red ochre, ground gypsum, yellow ochre, gray sand, pollen, and brown clay. The image at right demonstrates one way to apply pigments to sand paintings. Photo by Margaret Lazzari.

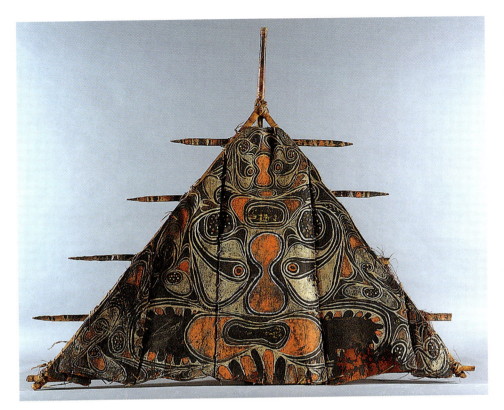

5.16 *Painting from a Cult House.* Palm leaves on a bamboo frame, painted with earth pigments, 44" × 61½". Slei, Middle Sepik region, Papua New Guinea, c. 20th century. Museum der Kulturen, Basel, Switzerland. Review the information on Sepik rituals and artworks accompanying Figures 14.6 and 14.7.

other tribes. Men collectively build large cult houses and then fill these houses with sculptures and paintings, such as the *Painting from a Cult House* at Slei (Figure 5.16). Individual men, with the help of a master artist, also produce paintings and carvings, and then through rituals invest their spirit and power in these works. The art is the vehicle by which an older man can pass his spirit to a younger man who is at an earlier stage of ritual development. That younger man, in turn, will later do the same. By these means, the collective power and knowledge of the men are preserved within their group.

THE ARTIST AS SKILLED WORKER

In some cultures, artists are skilled workers or laborers. The names of the craftsmen who worked on *Chartres Cathedral* are unknown to us today, as were almost all medieval artists. Medieval artists were not famous "personalities," but were more like union members, people of skill who were part of a new, emerging middle class.

Among the Baule people of Western Africa (Ivory Coast), artists are skilled professionals. A sculpture like the *Male Torso,* c. nineteenth to twentieth century (Figure 5.17), required considerable time to make. Very skilled carvers are accorded

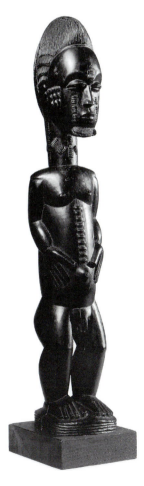

5.17 *Male Torso* (Ancestor figure). Baule sculpture, wood, 20½" high. Africa, c. nineteenth–twentieth century. The British Museum, London. See also the text accompanying Figures 1.12 and 13.15.

great honor and prestige and are paid well. However, among the Baule, the name of the owner is associated with a sculpture, not the artist who made it. This is done because the spiritual purposes for which the work was made are more important than its appearance, and it is the owner of the piece who performs rituals and develops the artwork's spiritual cult. A sculpture such as this can be equally effective ritualistically, whether it is well made or badly made. In addition, a spirit piece would be less effective the more its human maker was emphasized. For all these reasons, artists are remotely connected to the work they make. Interestingly, Baule artworks are not meant for sustained visual display, like Western art. Our example was likely hidden away in a personal shrine in the home and may not have been seen even by other family members.

The Rent Collection Courtyard (Figure 5.7) is officially credited to an anonymous team of eighteen amateur and professional sculptors, even though the names of many of the artists are known. Significantly, the posture of anonymity and collective action was important for all artworks sponsored by the Communist government of China from the 1950s until the late 1980s. Artists were not to seek personal glory, but to produce work for the common good.

THE ARTIST SCIENTIST

Art, mathematics, geometry, and architecture are all means of finding sense and order in the cosmos in many Islamic cultures, especially those of Persia and the Middle East. Islamic math, geometry, art, and architecture emphasize pattern as a means of overcoming the apparent contradiction between unity and diversity, between one Creator and the variety of life forms. The pattern on the dome of the *Masjid-i-Shah,* or Royal Mosque of Isfahan, 1612–1637 (Figure 5.18), expresses endless variety, but there is unity in its underlying geometric grid. The intricate designs have no beginning and no end, a metaphor for the infinite spirit of Allah. The three smaller diagrams to the right show how the pattern was developed through spirals superimposed on squares. Islamic philosophers from the tenth century saw the square as representing what was rigid, inert, cold, and earthbound, like rocks and crystals, whereas the circle represented heat, organic things, movement, and closeness to the Creator. The dome shape also is significant. The circular base of the dome has no beginning and no end, and so expresses infinity. The circular dome (= heaven) sits above the square structure below (= earth).

At various times, the role of scientist has been combined with that of artist, mostly for understanding, depicting, or

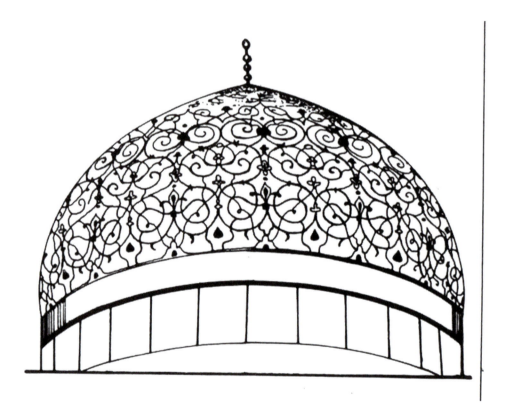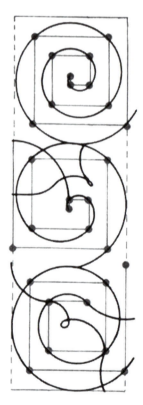

5.18 *Diagram of the Dome of the Masjid-i-Shah,* or *Royal Mosque.* Isfahan, Iran, 1612–1637. The left diagram shows the pattern design on the dome, while the three on the right show the interrelatedness of the square and circle, and the geometric basis of the patterns. Review the information on the Masjid-i-Shah mosque accompanying Figures 9.44 and 9.45.

manipulating the physical world. One of the most famous of all Western artist-scientists was Leonardo da Vinci. Although he is well known for two paintings, the *Last Supper* and the *Mona Lisa,* he also filled many notebooks with his own observations on botany, anatomy, hydraulics, zoology, geology, optics, and physics. In a letter to the Duke of Mantua asking for a position in his court, Leonardo outlined his many skills:

> I have a sort of extremely light and strong bridges, adapted to be most easily carried, and with them you may pursue, and at any time flee from the enemy. . . . And if the fight should be at sea I have kinds of many machines most efficient for offence and defence; and vessels which will resist the attack of the largest guns. . . . In case of need I will make big guns, mortars and light ordnance of fine and useful forms. . . . In times of peace I believe I can give perfect satisfaction . . . in architecture and the composition of buildings, public and private; and in guiding water from one place to another. . . . I can carry out sculpture in marble, bronze, or clay, and also I can do in painting whatever may be done, as well as any other, be he whom he may. (Holt 1947: 169–170)

To Leonardo, observation was essential to understanding the mechanics and the beauty of the world, and thus the foundation of both science and art. Careful observation held more authority for Leonardo than did the authority of religion or the art and writing of antiquity.

As we previously mentioned, John James Audubon's *Birds of America* is recognized as the outstanding work in ornithology of its day. Although Audubon is occasionally criticized for placing birds in fanciful poses, his images and notes are valuable scientific records, especially for certain species, like the passenger pigeon, which was hunted to extinction by 1900.

THE ARTIST PRIEST

Art is often a vehicle for spirituality. The artist who makes spiritual art is sometimes also a holy person, priest, or shaman.

The sculpture *God Te Rongo and His Three Sons,* c. 1800–1900 (Figure 5.19), is a representation of a deity from the Cook Islands in Polynesia and is connected to virility and human reproduction. A carving such as this was used and reused in religious rituals and passed down through generations, and only the group's most important leaders would have access to it. The sculptors who created ritual pieces such as *Te Rongo* were specialists called *Ta'unga,* a word that also means "priest." Such sculptors trained for a long time as apprentices, not only to learn the skills of carving and finishing pieces, but also to attain the spiritual knowledge to tap into and control the inherent power of their tools and the materials they used.

There is sometimes a tie between sacred writing and art making. During the early medieval period in Europe, one of the major art forms was illuminated manuscripts, which were

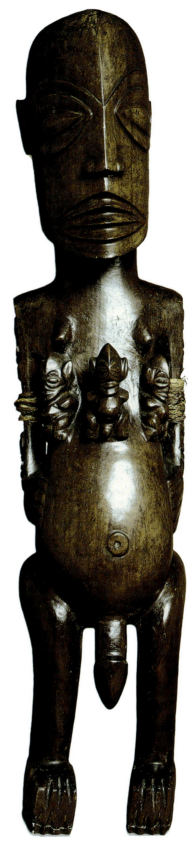

5.19   *God Te Rongo and His Three Sons.* Wood, 27³⁄₈" high. Cook Islands, Polynesia, c. 1800–1900. The British Museum, London. See also the text accompanying Figure 8.3.

handwritten and illustrated prayer books or Bibles. Monks in monasteries made them. Calligraphic renderings of twenty-two verses of the Quran adorn the *Taj Mahal* (Figure 5.20). The calligraphy was designed by the artist Amanat Khan, who also selected many of the verses. Amanat Khan's knowledge of the Quran and his skill as an artist/calligrapher were considered so significant and essential that of all the craftsmen, builders, and architects who worked on the design and construction of the Taj Mahal, only Amanat Khan is known. His signature appears on the south portal of the Taj Mahal.

As we have seen, the men who make Navajo sand paintings perform sacred ceremonies, or *sings,* at the same time. *Sings* can last as long as nine days and nights of chanting,

prayer, ritual cleansing and sand painting. The largest sand paintings can be 25 feet wide. The Navajo sand painters have both amazing skills and vast ritual knowledge. The Native Americans who made kachina dolls like the *Ahola Kachina* (Figure 5.21) also performed important spiritual ceremonies for the Hopi to ensure the welfare of their community and good crops.

THE CREATIVE GENIUS

Some cultures believe that an artist is a creative genius, with almost transcendent abilities, operating in some way differently from or on a higher plane than regular humans. Interestingly, the name of the first artist in recorded history has been associated with the concept of genius. Imhotep was an ancient

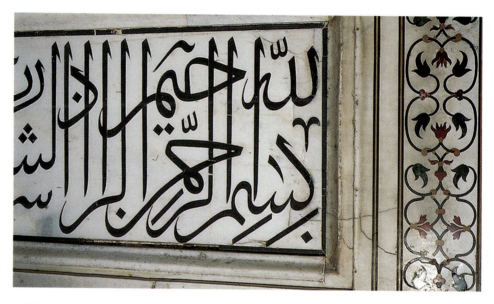

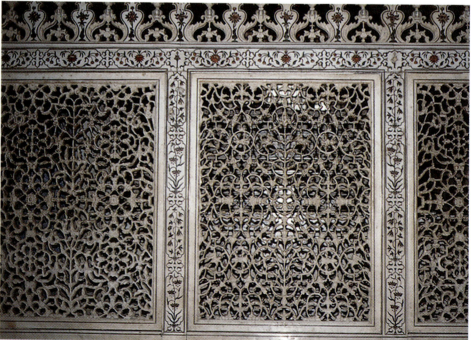

5.20   Two details from the interior of the *Taj Mahal.* Marble inlaid with colored tile and semiprecious stones. Agra, India, 1632–1654. Black Star / Dinodia. See the text accompanying Figures 10.21 and 10.22 for information on the structure of this building, its history, its decoration, and the significance of its gardens.

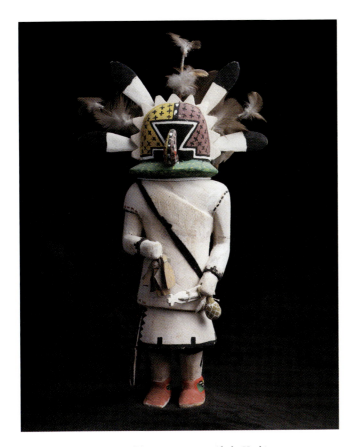

5.21   JIMMIE TEWANWYTEWA. *Ahola Kachina.* Cottonwood, paint, feathers, wool, 13" high. Hopi, Third Mesa, Oraibi, 1942. Museum of Northern Arizona. See also the text accompanying Figure 9.19.

Egyptian architect, priest, scribe, physician, and minister to the pharaoh. He was responsible for the design of the first pyramid, which predates by about twenty-five years the oldest of the *Great Pyramids* that we saw in Figure 5.1. After his death, Imhotep was worshiped as one of the Egyptian gods.

Some artists from the Yoruba culture in Africa were so great that they were referred to in heroic and grand terms. They emerged from a supporting environment, as indicated here:

> Constant suitable work is necessary for the full development of a carver's abilities. It was the group of carvers in a district—repeating the same themes and only gradually introducing new ones—which built up a cumulative genius capable of supporting the less gifted carvers. It was . . . this evolution as a group, rather than the religious intensity or emotion of the carvers, which gave much of its artistic power to the old carving. If sufficient carvers could be similarly employed—and fully employed—in modern times, the artistic level of the whole group would rise and individual geniuses would emerge. (Fr. Kevin Carroll, quoted in Willett 1993: 22–23)

In Europe, the concept of the artist as a creative genius began to emerge during the Renaissance, around the fourteenth century. Prior to that time, in medieval Europe, artists were considered skilled workers. But the rise of the philosophy of humanism changed that attitude by asserting the dignity and value of the individual. Learning was emphasized, especially in the humanities, science, and the arts. The model person was not the holy recluse who rejected the world, but the intelligent and thoughtful person of the world, like Michelangelo or Leonardo da Vinci.

During the Romantic era in Europe, roughly 1750 to 1850, the notion of the artist as creative genius was augmented. The Romantics emphasized personal creativity, uniqueness, strong feeling, individuality, and imagination, and saw these qualities exemplified in artistic freedom and expressiveness. The Romantics were also interested in the sublime and in adventure. These attitudes developed at the same time that capitalism was rising in Europe and the bourgeoisie saw themselves as self-made, unique individuals.

A final variation of the idea of creative genius is the artist as the troubled, tragic, or alienated genius, like Vincent van Gogh. Although van Gogh was devoted to painting, his life was unhappy, as he was unable to make friendships and human connections. He committed suicide at age thirty-seven. The tragic, damaged, or alienated artist has become a kind of hero in industrialized nations today. Yayoi Kusama, who made *Accumulation No. 1* (Figure 5.12), has voluntarily lived in a mental institution in Japan since 1977. She suffers from compulsive behavior and visual hallucinations. Her childhood was scarred by her early family life, the oppressive Japanese right-wing political state, and the devastation and deprivations of World War II. The following quotation is from a museum catalog:

> Daring—for better or worse—can be a by-product of true obsession, and Kusama has been daring, creating the art that she must against great odds. At another time we might have mythologized her in the manner of Vincent van Gogh and Jackson Pollock, romantic figures whose obsessive need to create was paralleled by an even stronger inclination to push the emotional and physical boundaries to the edge of self-destruction. If Kusama is heroic, it is for an opposite and arguably more prosaic reason. Rather than suffering for her art, she has used it to fight psychic disintegration. . . . Today, in the United States, much of the art world is disenchanted with movements . . . and global theories. Kusama—offbeat, relentless, and female—may be the only kind of hero that we can accept. (Zelevansky 1998: 31)

RULERS AS ARTISTS

Rulers sometimes have been responsible for the creation of important artworks. Most often, they are patrons who oversee the work, as we will discuss later in this chapter. In some cases, they actually make the work.

Among the Maori of New Zealand, sculptors were usually chiefs or members of ruling families. This was especially true for carvings in meeting houses, which were so important that the activity was seen as fitting only for a leader. The meeting house reinforced clan identity. The clan gathered there for political and social events. Children were educated in clan history, using the carvings on the walls that represented their ancestors, like those on the entrance doorway of *Te Mana O Turanga* (Figure 5.22) from 1883. Thus the meeting house consolidated the group, just as effective leadership would.

SUPPORT FOR ART MAKING

Art making can occur only when there is support and some kind of surplus—time, food, or money. Art reflects the needs, ideas, and aspirations not only of the artist, but also of those who support the artist.

There are three ways to support art making: (1) providing for the artist's living, by giving material goods or money; (2) commissioning the artist to make a particular work of art and paying for it; and (3) buying a work of art that the artist has already made.

PATRONAGE AND PRIVATE SUPPORT

Frequently, artists receive family support. Students, for example, generally receive monetary support from their families. Sepik men in Papua New Guinea work part-time as artists and rely on their wives to attend to the tasks of day-to-day living to support their families. John James Audubon's wife helped support the family while he made the paintings for *Birds of America,* in addition to his being a taxidermist, portrait painter, and drawing instructor. Later in his life, his sons assisted him in his paintings. Vincent van Gogh was dependent upon his brother Theo for emotional and financial support.

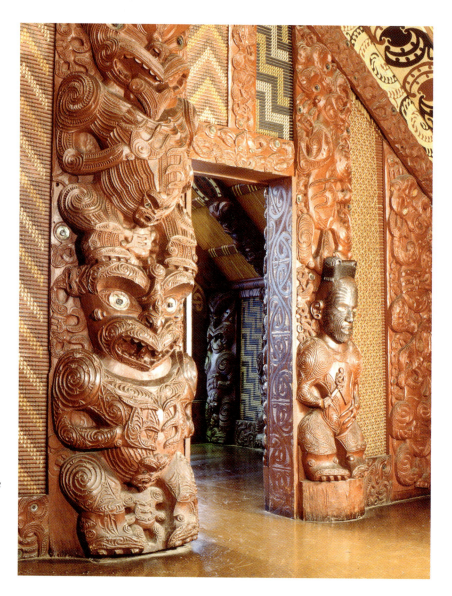

5.22   RAHARUHI RUKUPO AND OTHERS. Entrance doorway of a Maori meeting house called *Te Mana O Turanga.* Carved and painted wood. New Zealand, opened 1883. © Werner Forman / Art Resource, NY. See also Figures 4.6, 11.14, and 11.15 for more information on the meeting house.

Ordinary people, both individually and in groups, support art that is important to them, as in building *Chartres Cathedral* (Figure 5.3) as well as paying for it, along with funding from royalty, nobility, and leading churchmen from around France. In addition, people from all over Europe made pilgrimages to religious shrines at Chartres and donated money for the building of the church. Much of Baule sculpture, like *Male Torso* (Figure 5.17), is commissioned by ordinary individuals for their personal shrines. Among the Baule, all artwork is owned by individuals, who specify how they want it to look, which they have determined either through their dreams or with the help of diviners. The *AIDS Memorial Quilt* (Figure 5.9) is funded by private donations.

The university in the United States today is a major patron of the arts. Many contemporary artists make their livings as teachers in colleges and universities. Artist-teachers have a stimulating work environment, a living wage, and sufficient free time to make their art. Art making is generally seen as a form of research, and the mission of the university is to promote learning and research in all disciplines. The support of universities makes it possible for artists to make work that is not market driven; in other words, artists are not dependent upon sales to keep working. This allows them freedom to experiment with new art forms.

In Chapters 9 and 10, we will see many works of art made for religious reasons or to tend to the dead. These religious works of art may be made as part of everyday life, as is Balinese religious art. They may be financed by ordinary people, as was *Chartres Cathedral*. In some cases, they are funded by rulers through taxation, tariffs, tribute payments, or profits from war. Still others are commissioned by religious groups.

A tremendous amount of the art produced all over the world serves the purposes of rulers (see Chapter 11). This ranges from the *Great Pyramids* to the *Taj Mahal*. Other rulers are known as champions of the arts. The Medici were a famous and powerful family who produced four generations of rulers in Italy and were patrons to many fine artists during the Renaissance. One of the Medici, Cosimo, founded the Academy of Design in 1563. Peter Paul Rubens, whom we have already seen in connection with workshop activities, was a favorite of the aristocracy and certain segments of the Catholic Church. He lived like a prince. An artist of outstanding skill, he also was urbane, articulate, and intelligent. He was a courtier and diplomat, and he painted for the dukes of Mantua, King Philip III of Spain, the Spanish governors of Flanders, King Charles I of England, and Maria de' Medici, queen consort and queen mother of France.

THE MARKET

Many artists create for the open market. They work on speculation, meaning that they make a large quantity of works that

they later try to sell, either directly or through agents. This is the opposite of working on commission, when artists make specific works for clients.

THE FINE ART MARKET

In the fine art market, artists make works to sell through commercial galleries. Dealers not only sell work, but also promote the artist's career, for example, by arranging museum exhibitions. In exchange for these services, the sales price of an artwork is usually split 50/50 between artist and dealer.

The fine art market is very competitive, with more artists wanting to display their work than there are galleries to accommodate them. Artists often strategize to make their way in this environment. When Yayoi Kusama arrived in New York from Japan in 1958 at age twenty-nine, many artists were competing for attention, and the market favored male artists. Kusama created some spectacular and controversial works that got attention in the art press and in the daily newspapers. She also enlarged her previously small work, making it as big as thirty-three feet long, so that it fit the expectations of the art market at that time. In the late 1950s, easel-sized works were seen as passé, unheroic, and conservative. Works like *Accumulation No. 1* (Figure 5.12) were variations on pop art and minimalism, both important movements of the 1960s. Kusama also made friends with some of the most prominent artists in New York and in Europe.

The fine art market also consists of auction houses, where art is resold. A few works of art have brought fabulous prices in auctions, such as some van Gogh paintings that sold for tens of millions of dollars. Because auction houses resell art that was already in the hands of collectors or museums, artists are not directly benefited by auction house sales. (Interestingly, however, some artists were appalled at the lavish consumerism and elitism of high-priced art, and they turned to making public art, performance, video, and installation, art forms that may be accessible to more people or are not as easily bought and sold.)

THE TOURIST MARKET

Traditional indigenous artworks sometimes are sold in the tourist market. These artworks are made specifically for foreign collectors or tourists. The work that artists make for the tourist trade is high-quality, professional work. But it does not have the meaning or the spiritual dimension of the work they make for their own culture. Baule artists often work both for the tourist trade and for local clients. The art they make for local clients is done on a commission basis and has the spiritual and private uses that we discussed in connection with the *Male Torso* (Figure 5.17). The art made for the tourist trade is done on speculation.

The tourist market may help local art production to survive. For example, in Papua New Guinea, the making of ritual art and tourist art are mutually dependent enterprises, each supporting and invigorating the other. On other, more remote islands, where there is little tourism and therefore little tourist trade, the visual arts are falling into a general decline (Lewis 1990: 149–163).

TAX-SUPPORTED ART

Taxes have paid for a lot of art production, in one of two ways: (1) artists receive government-sponsored stipends or grants; or (2) tax monies finance specific buildings, paintings, or sculptures. Almost all public monuments, government buildings, and palaces, including Louis XIV's *Versailles,* are paid for by tax revenues. All tax monies come ultimately from ordinary people and the agriculture and commerce they generate.

The shrines of the *Acropolis* in Athens, Greece, were built with subverted tax monies. The Greek city-states formed a mutual defense league after defeating the Persians in 480 BCE,

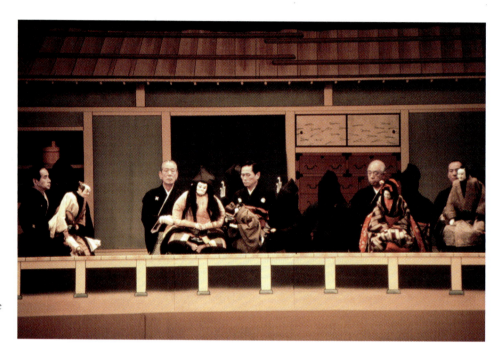

5.23 Bunraku performance on stage. Japan, c. twentieth century. © Michael S. Yamashita / Corbis. See also the text accompanying Figure 16.11.

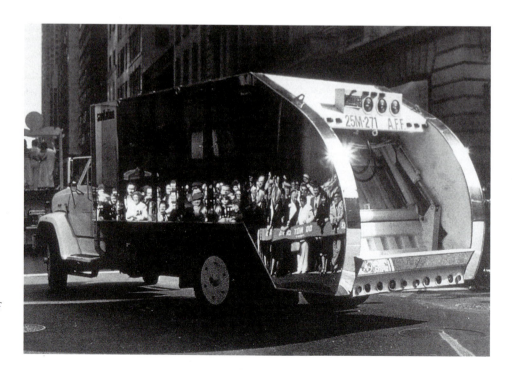

5.24 MIERLE LADERMAN UKELES. *The Social Mirror.* 20-cubic-yard New York City garbage collection truck fitted with hand-tempered glass mirror with additional strips of mirrored acrylic. USA, 1983. Photograph: The New York City Department of Sanitation. Photo: Michael James O'Brien; Courtesy of Barbara Gladstone Gallery. See also the text accompanying Figures 2.37 and 15.23.

and Pericles took those funds to build the new Acropolis shrines. The other city-states protested and accused Pericles of abusing his power. In part, this caused a protracted and disastrous civil war between Athens and its rival city-state, Sparta, a war that Athens lost.

In Japan, taxes support traditional Japanese art forms. Traditional artists are designated as Living National Treasures (*Ningen Kokuho*) because they are Bearers of Important Intangible Cultural Assets. Ningen Kokuho include musicians, dramatists, and visual artists, such as masters of Bunraku puppetry (Figure 5.23). Outstanding fine artists, such as painters and printmakers, may be honored by being appointed to the two-hundred-member Japan Art Academy.

European countries, such as the United Kingdom, France, and Austria, set aside tax monies to support artists and art making. The Austrian government actively supports artists in part because the fine art market is not very large in Austria. Also, Austrian citizens pay higher taxes (as much as 60 percent of their income) to support government programs, including those for all kinds of cultural purposes. Art galleries, too, can receive government support when they participate in international art fairs, in which galleries from many industrial countries come together to display the artists they represent.

Tax support for art in the United States consists of Percent for the Arts Program funding, in which 0.5 percent or sometimes 1 percent of the cost of any public building goes to purchase art for that building. In many states, the Percent for the Arts Program covers any federal, state, county, or city building as well as private ventures that receive tax abatements in redevelopment zones. Percent for the Arts Program funding represents considerable income for some artists. These programs have also enriched the urban environment with murals, installations, or sculptures. Sometimes government agencies support artists who make work related to those agencies' functions. Mierle Laderman Ukeles has been an unsalaried Artist in Residence for the New York City Department of Sanitation. Her work, *The Social Mirror* (Figure 5.24), was intended to raise the stature of sanitation workers as well as make people aware that they themselves are the source of trash.

The process of making public art—getting approval for work and completing the project—is hemmed in with committee review. In some cases, a competition is held, with artists invited to submit written proposals for a work that is site-specific, addressing the history of that location or the needs and values of the people who use that site. Committees of artists, members of the public, and government representatives choose a winning proposal and/or oversee the completion of the work. A few commissions go awry. For example, a public arts commission invited artist Robert Arneson to do a work on George Moscone, the assassinated mayor of San Francisco, for the new Moscone Center. Arneson made the *Portrait of George* (Figure 5.25), an informal, colorful bust mounted on a

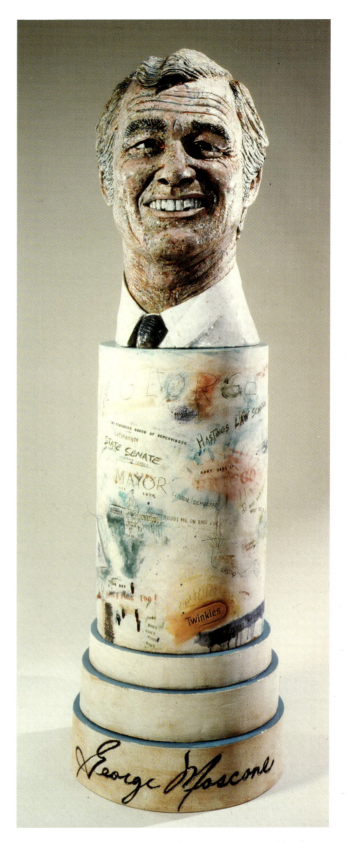

5.25 ROBERT ARNESON. *Portrait of George, USA, 1981.* Glazed ceramic, 94" × 29" × 29". Private Collection. Art © Estate of Robert Arneson/Licensed by VAGA, New York, NY. See Figure 12.30 for more on this piece and the circumstances surrounding Moscone's assassination.

column pedestal that contained references to Moscone's killer. An arts committee rejected the work, Arneson was not paid, and the bust was returned to him one week after it had been installed in the Moscone Center. Arneson's gallery later sold the work to a private collector.

SYNOPSIS

The question "Who makes art?" is answered by researching a number of issues: Who conceives the idea? Who actually makes the object? Who supplies materials and training? Who provides support?

Artists themselves fill many different roles within their cultures. Art making may reflect broader gender roles within a culture. Artists may be considered skilled workers. Science, geometry, and mathematics have overlapped in the role of artist. Artists can be priests, shamans, or ritualists in cultures in which art making is connected with religion or rituals. The notion of the artist as creative genius arose in ancient Egypt, but surfaced again in Renaissance Europe and in modern times.

The people who support art making enable artists to do their work, and sometimes greatly influence how that art looks. Other forms of support for artists include the fine art market, the tourist market, and art collectors. Taxes can be used to support art making in a number of ways. Finally, artists' livelihoods can be supported by families, by stipends and grants, and by universities.

FOOD FOR THOUGHT

Let us conclude this chapter with a few controversial ideas related to the concepts we have just covered. What do you think of the following?

- Creativity can be seen as the "job" of the artist in societies in which most other kinds of work are no longer seen as being creative. Creativity can then seem to be cut off from "real" life and become superfluous, self-indulgent, or unnecessary. How do you perceive creativity in our society? In business? In the arts? In different kinds of jobs?
- A popular Western myth portrays artists as completely asocial, isolated geniuses whose work is not recognized as important during their lifetimes. Do you think that the nonconformist (or even tragic) artist might fulfill an important role in a particular society?
- When people from first-world nations buy the art of third-world countries, they often want something "authentic," meaning that the artwork conforms to traditional styles. Museum collections also favor traditional styles. But artists alive today are subject to influences from all over the world, through media, travel, and trade. Worldwide, con-

temporary art is often a mixture of foreign and indigenous influences. What is authentic art?

- If a traditional, indigenous art object is made for the tourist market, is there any reason why it should be inherently more or less valuable than a work made for local cult use?
- Artists have tailored their work to suit the market or the tastes of a particular patron. Leonardo da Vinci was willing to devote his time to whatever activity the Duke of Mantua dictated, including either weapons building or painting. Artists making public art projects work with committees, politicians, and architects. How does this dovetail with the idea of art as personal creative expression?
- The public art process is reviewed by committees composed of politicians, the public, and artists. Can public art (or any art by committee) ever be controversial? Should it be? If taxes are used to support art making, should that art reflect the ideas of the population? If so, what percentage of the population?
- Michelangelo's *Creation of Adam* and Leonardo da Vinci's *Mona Lisa* have been (mis)used for commercial reasons, appearing on beach towels, in food commercials, in advertisements, and so on. Figure 5.26 is a souvenir pen from a

traveling Vatican exhibition with a detail of Michelangelo's *Creation of Adam.* When you move the pen, Adam's hand floats toward God's through the liquid contained in the barrel. The message on the other side is "Keep in Touch." The sale of such souvenirs to tourists supports museums and traveling exhibitions. How does this relate to the tourist trade that we discussed earlier in relation to indigenous art? How do commercial art and fine art support each other? Do they invigorate each other?

YOUR CD-ROM RESOURCES

■ Exploring Art Timeline
■ Flashcards
■ Food for Thought
■ Companion Site
    Chapter 5 Quiz
    InfoTrac® College Edition Readings
    Artists Flashcards
    Online Study Guide

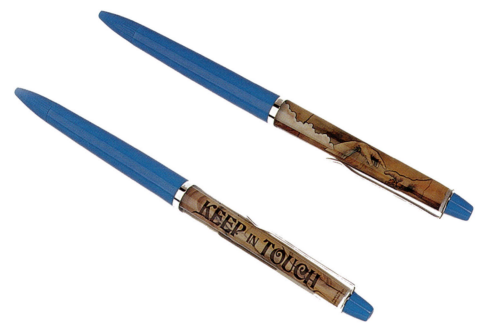

5.26 Souvenir pen from a traveling exhibition of angels from the Vatican. The right end of the barrel contains a detail of Michelangelo's *Creation of Adam,* suspended in liquid. On the reverse appear the words "Keep in Touch."

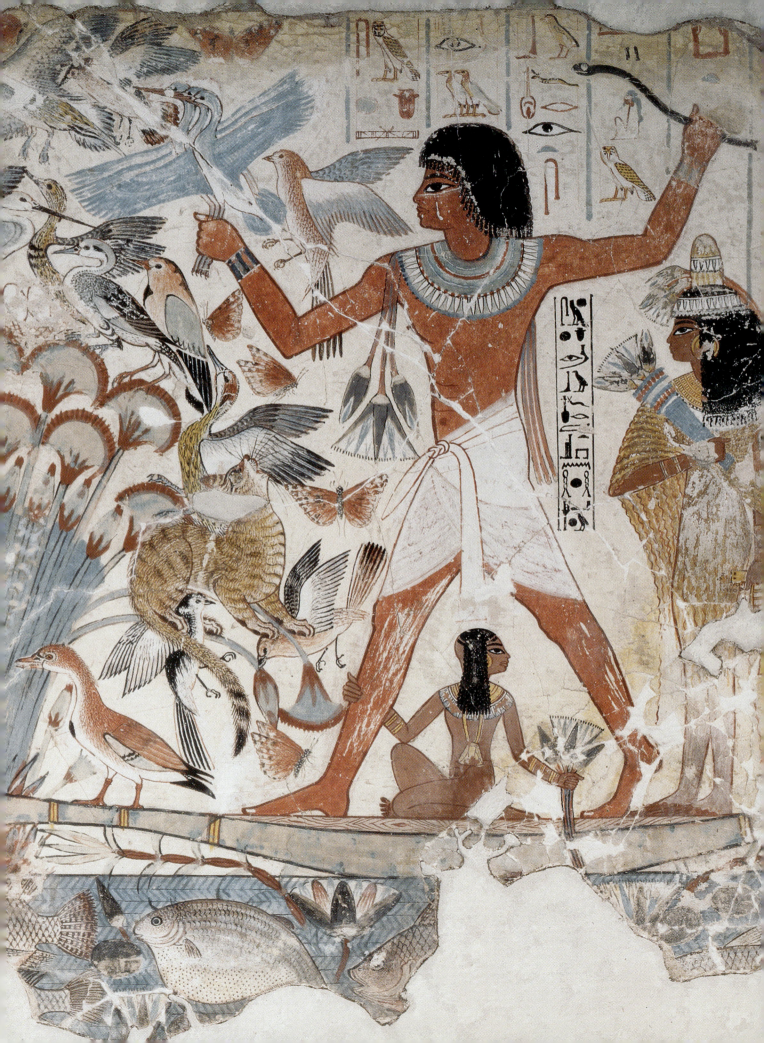

CHAPTER 6

WHAT DO WE DO WITH ART?

INTRODUCTION

A vast quantity of art treasures, from both the recent and distant past, is with us today. What do communities, nations, institutions, religious groups, armies, scholars, and others do with it?

Of course, the answer varies for different circumstances and different cultures. Consider the following questions in this chapter:

How is art displayed or performed?

How does the display of an art object change its use?

Why do nations and cultural groups keep art?

Who assembles art collections and why?

What kinds of museums keep art, and how do they operate?

For what reasons does art deteriorate?

How can art be preserved or restored?

How much effort, time, and money should be devoted to maintaining artworks?

Why do people purposefully destroy art?

What academic disciplines study art?

Fowling Scene. Detail of Figure 6.10. The British Museum, London.

USING ART

Once an art object is made, people use it, through either performance or display. The *Colosseum* (Figure 6.1), built between CE 70 and 82 in Rome, was used for centuries, from 83 until 532, to entertain the citizens of Rome. It was intended both for performance and for display. Its massive size and lavish decoration constitute the elements of display, while the extravagant spectacles that took place within were the performance elements. The Roman emperors funded the events (with tax money) to increase people's support for them.

Much Yoruba art is made for religious festivals, so it is used for performance. Masks, music, song, and dance combine in masquerades that entertain, reinforce leaders' roles, reaffirm social order, and bring cohesion to the group. When festivals are held, the masks (worn by dancers) emerge from the houses of elders (Figure 6.2). These masks celebrate the bush spirits who gave agriculture to the people. Following them are masks honoring warrior chiefs who founded new, prosperous communities, like the *Epa Headdress called "Orangun,"* from 1974 (Figure 6.3) by Bamboye of Odo-Owa. Next come masks representing herbalist priests, who possess spiritual knowledge. The final mask of the festival represents female power and the future of the community.

Art was an integral part of the ceremonies of the Kwakiutl people of the Northwest Coast, as we see in the 1914

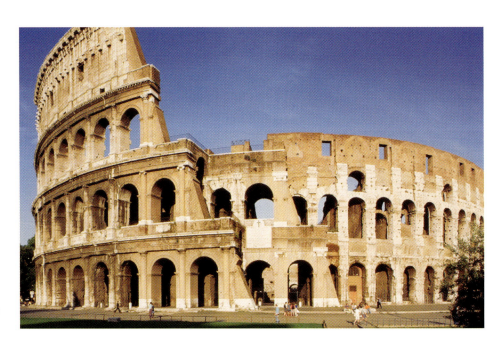

6.1 *Colosseum.* Rome, Italy, CE 70–82. © Richard Glover / Corbis. See also the text accompanying Figure 16.28.

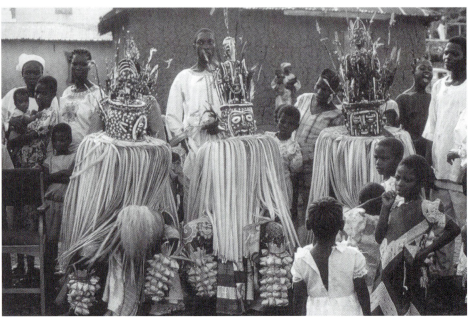

6.2 *Epa Festival at Otun.* Yoruba culture. Ekiti, Nigeria, 20th century. Photo William Rea.

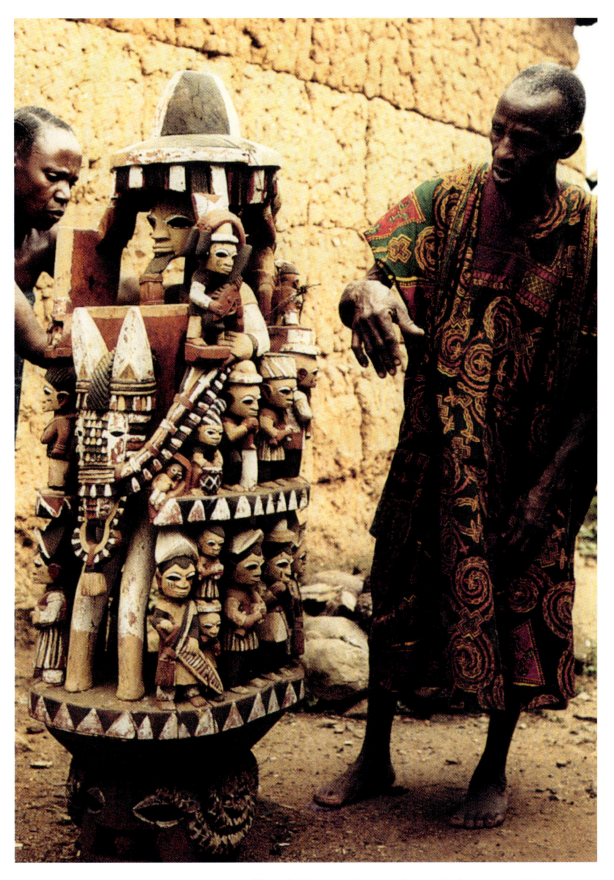

6.3   BAMGBOYE OF ODO-OWA. *Epa Headdress called "Orangun."* Wood and paint. Yoruba. Erinmope, Nigeria, 1974. Photograph by John Pemberton III. See also the text accompanying Figure 14.18 for more information on this piece.

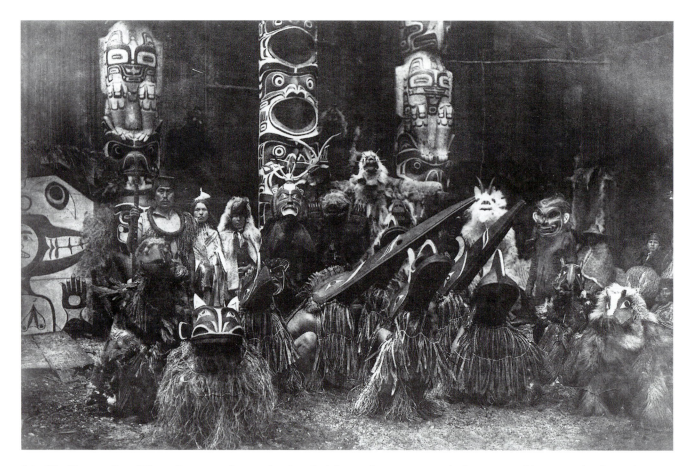

6.4 The Hamatsa Great Winter Ceremony. Costumed and masked dancers, house posts, inside the ceremonial house. Kwakiutl. Northwest Coast, British Columbia, Canada, 1914. American Museum of Natural History, New York.

photograph of the Hamatsa Great Winter Ceremony (Figure 6.4), in which participants gave thanks and praise for the riches of the land and the sea. The ceremonies also reconnected the Kwakiutl with the powerful forces of nature.

CONNECTION
In other chapters, we see Kwakiutl masks (Figure 9.13, page 235) and a house post (Figure 14.15, page 412) like those seen in this photograph.

In Western cultures since the Middle Ages, much art has been made for display, but even displayed art is used. Through Judy Chicago's *The Dinner Party* (Figure 6.5), visitors are able to piece together the lost history of many famous women. Contemporary women often feel empowered by what they see in this artwork.

An artwork's uses change when it is removed from its originally intended environment and placed in a museum. For example, small, religious devotional images, such as the *Retablo of Maria de la Luz Casillas and Children,* from 1960 (Figure 6.6), are placed as prayer offerings in front of statues of saints

in Mexican pilgrimage churches. Answered prayers increase the cult of the saint. On the other hand, retablos can be found hanging in museums and commercial galleries in the United States, no longer as prayer offerings, but as works of art. The clean, white, bare spaces of museums and galleries isolate art objects and emphasize their formal qualities. People still use the art in museums, but for aesthetic experiences.

KEEPING ART

Why do groups of people hold on to art, often beyond its original use? We will discuss art collections, both public and private, and the purposes and functions of museums, as well as art preservation and restoration.

WHY CULTURES KEEP ART

Cultures and groups keep art for the following reasons: (1) for aesthetic, civilizing, or educational purposes; (2) for religious reasons; (3) for political purposes; and (4) for commerce. People seek out art because it is pleasurable, aesthetic, and stimulating. Some even find that art gives them a transcendent or spiritual experience.

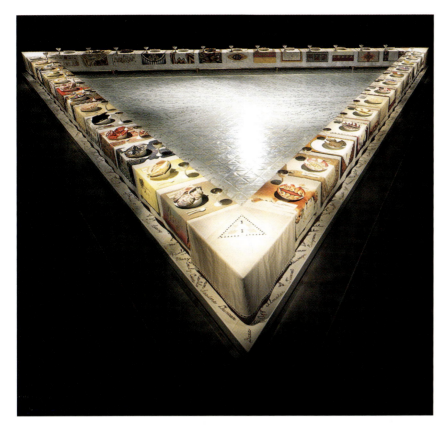

6.5 JUDY CHICAGO. *The Dinner Party.* Painted porcelain and needlework, 48' × 42' × 36'. USA, 1974–1979. Collection, "The Dinner Party" Trust. Photo © Donald Woodman © 2004 Judy Chicago / Artists Rights Society (ARS), New York. See also the text accompanying Figure 7.22.

The aesthetic, and formal qualities of the *Orangun* mask include scale changes, geometric and figurative elements, contrasting lights and darks, and strong visual rhythms. Height is important, but the bands of horizontal patterns balance it. Study of the *Orangun* mask is also demanding intellectually.

The mask has a civilizing, educational dimension, because it expands and enriches our definition of art and exemplifies Yoruba culture. By extension, we think of family structures in our own cultures and of the rituals and social structures that reinforce family functioning.

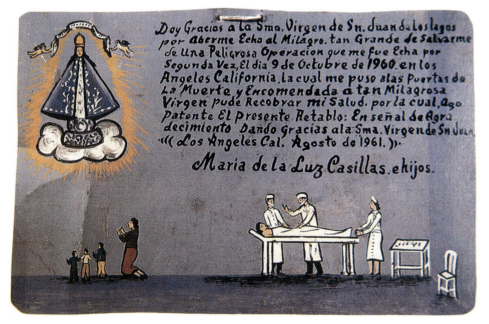

6.6 *Retablo of Maria de la Luz Casillas and Children.* Oil on metal, 7" × 10½". Mexico, 1960. Durand-Arias Collection. Photo Jorge Durand. The painting style and religious use of this retablo are also discussed in the text accompanying Figure 9.15.

Many works of art have sacred qualities. On an individual level, people keep them as aids in personal devotion. On an institutional level, many major religions have priests or officials who preserve sacred art, such as places of worship and the artwork housed in them. Collections have been made around religious shrines in Africa, in Japan, and in Islamic countries. Major Christian churches often have museums attached to them. In Mesoamerica, fabulous temples housed statues, manuscripts, and smaller art objects made of precious metals. Ancient Greek temples housed cult statues. Many mosques are lavishly covered in mosaic or decorative carving and are furnished with woven rugs and beautiful lamps.

CONNECTION
Review the many examples of religious articles and structures in Chapter 9.

Politically, art can promote the power of an ethnic group or of a nation. The Yoruba are a large ethnic group of approximately twenty million people in western Africa. They share a common language source and ethnic heritage as well as some social customs and political structures. Yet they speak different dialects and live in three separate but neighboring countries—Nigeria, Benin, and Togo. These countries are further divided into fifty separate city-states, which have waged fierce wars against each other. The Yoruba people follow various religions. The slave trade and British colonial rule disrupted the Yoruba politically and culturally.

Despite disruptions, the identity of the Yoruba is intact, in part due to their artistic heritage, which dates back nine centuries. Much of their art reinforces group cohesion, either religiously or politically. This was certainly the case with the *Orangun* mask, used in rituals that reinforce Yoruba social structure and the Yoruba identity as a whole. Another example is the *Great Beaded Crown of the Orangun-Ila* from the twentieth century (Figure 6.7), an ornate and symbol-filled work that dramatically represents and consolidates the power of Yoruba leaders. The tall cone shape is called *ibori,* and it is an ancient, persistent symbol that represents a related cluster of concepts, including power, links to the spirit world, and links to nature. This cone shape also appears in palace rooflines and can mark an important meeting place or ceremony.

CONNECTION
Two other works that deal with Yoruba rulers and sources of power are the Crowned Head of an Oni *(Figure 11.3, page 303) and the* Palace Sculpture at Ikere *by Olowe of Ise (Figure 11.12, page 311).*

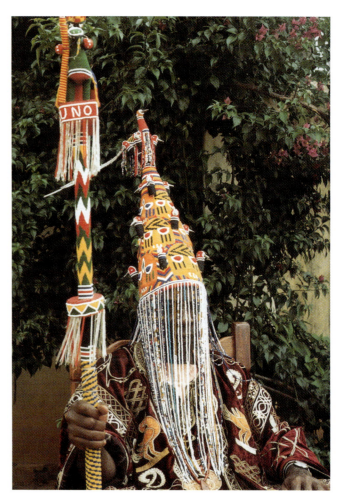

 6.7 BEADWORKERS OF THE ADESINA FAMILY OF EFON-ALAYE. *Great Beaded Crown of the Orangun-Ila.* Yoruba. Ila Orangun, Nigeria, twentieth century. Photograph by John Pemberton III, 1971. Review information about this crown accompanying Figure 14.26.

Another political reason for keeping art is national glory. Art is part of a nation's pride. It is a visual symbol that represents the nation, or it is part of the nation's aesthetic achievements. Almost every nation has distinctive artwork that it has claimed as particularly representative of itself. The Statue of Liberty, Mount Rushmore, and the Capitol Building are all works of art associated with the United States. Modern art and architecture from the 1950s onward are often related to the United States. In another example, Greece is perhaps best known for its ancient art, like the *Horsemen* (Figure 6.8) from the famous Parthenon temple, even though Greece has had an extensive history since then and is a modern nation. Many countries have established bureaucracies that manage national landmarks, monuments, museums, and preservation sites.

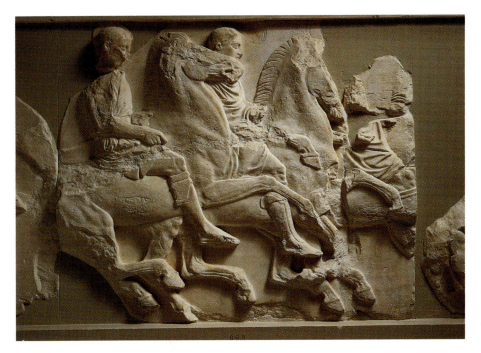

6.8 *Horsemen.* Detail of the north frieze of the Parthenon. Marble, approximately 3'6" high. Athens, Greece, c. 447–432 BCE. The British Museum, London. © Nimatallah / Art Resource, NY. See also the text accompanying Figure 9.33.

CONNECTION
See the section "Tax-Supported Art" in Chapter 5, pages 120–121, for information about Japan's Living National Treasures.

Another part of a nation's treasure is the art it seizes as booty. The last Aztec ruler, Moctezuma, gave his magnificent

Headdress (Figure 6.9) to the invading Spanish as a desperate measure to avoid his own demise. The Spanish conqueror Hernando Cortés accepted as tribute or took as plunder hundreds of Aztec works of art and sent them to the Spanish king, Charles V. The German artist Albrecht Dürer saw these objects in Brussels:

Also I saw the things which were brought to the King from the New Golden Land: a sun entirely of gold, a whole fathom

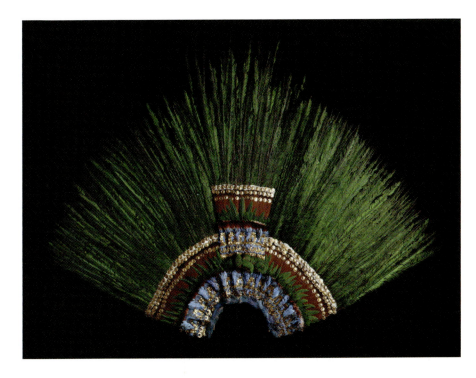

6.9 *Feathered Headdress of Moctezuma.* Quetzal and cotinga feathers, gold plaques. Aztec, c. 1519. Kunsthistorisches Museum. See also the text accompanying Figure 11.36.

broad; likewise, a moon, entirely of silver, just as big; likewise sundry curiosities from their weapons, armor, and missiles; very odd clothing, bedding, and all sorts of strange articles for human use, all of which is fairer to see than marvels. These things were all so precious that they were valued at a hundred thousand guilders. But I have never seen in all my days that which so rejoiced my heart, as these things. For I saw among them amazing artistic objects, and I marveled over the subtle ingenuity of the men in these distant lands. (Miller 1986: 202)

However, unlike Dürer, most Spaniards valued the gold used in Aztec art more than they valued the artworks themselves. Among the objects Dürer saw, every one made of gold or silver was melted down for its precious metal.

Egypt in particular has suffered from having its art treasures hauled off by foreign invaders, much to the detriment of Egypt itself. The ancient Romans took a large number of Egyptian artifacts to Rome. Some of those objects were still around centuries later, to reawaken interest in Egypt among Europeans of the fifteenth through the nineteenth centuries. In 1798, French troops under Napoleon invaded and occupied Egypt for a short time. Napoleon was motivated in part by the desire to regenerate ancient Egypt under French rule and to disrupt Britain's colonial empire. With his invading army, Napoleon sent a team of scholars to form an Egyptian Institute and seized a number of treasures that ended up in the Louvre Museum. The British later defeated the French and removed more artworks, including paintings done directly

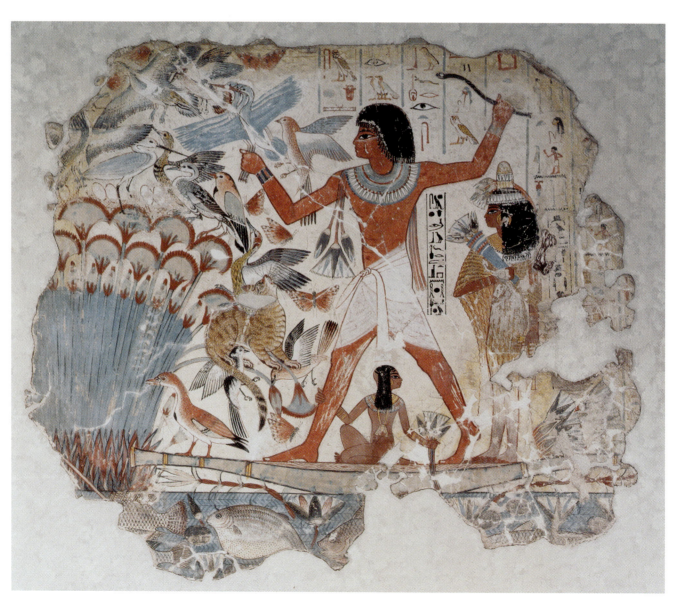

6.10 *Fowling Scene.* Wall painting from the tomb of Nebamun. Paint on dry plaster, approximately 32" high. Thebes, Egypt, c. 1400–1350 BCE. The British Museum, London. See also the text accompanying Figure 10.5.

on the walls of tombs. The *Fowling Scene* (Figure 6.10) is in the collection of the British Museum. Despite their plundering ways, Europeans increased interest in ancient Egyptian sites and began the first intensive, comprehensive study of the Egypt of the pharaohs.

The British also removed considerable amounts of art from Greece in the early nineteenth century. The *Horsemen* as well as many other sculptures from the Parthenon are currently housed in the British Museum.

Plundered art from World War II continues to be an issue. The Nazis stole thousands of works of art, and many are still missing or are in dispute. Some have turned up at art auctions, in private collections, or in public museums. The heirs of the original owners have sued for their return. In addition, Russia still holds many artworks that its armies seized after World War II from 325 German museums. Many of these artworks had been taken by the Nazis from Jewish collectors in the 1930s. Attempts to have the stolen art returned have caused international uproars. An online registry of missing or stolen art has recently been posted on the Internet, listing 3.6 million looted art objects from World War II, with detailed descriptions of 35,000.

Even more recently, U.S. and British troops invaded Iraq in 2003, causing the downfall of Saddam Hussein. Before security was established, some Iraqi museums were ransacked, and many treasures were stolen.

We have seen that victorious armies have seized small art objects. What about large monuments and buildings? The Greeks built the *Parthenon* (Figure 9.32) as a temple to Athena. But a succession of conquerors modified it for their own uses. The Romans used it as a brothel, but left the structure and sculptures essentially in their original form. In the fifth century CE, when the building was used as a Christian church, the interior was remodeled, and the large cult statue of Athena was removed and subsequently destroyed. In the fifteenth century, the Turks of the Ottoman Empire seized control of Greece and transformed the Parthenon into a mosque, adding a minaret to its southwest corner. Later, the Turks used the Parthenon to store munitions, and the structure was severely damaged in 1687 when an artillery shell exploded the gunpowder inside it. After 1,800 years of existence, the Parthenon was a ruin, but it still functions well in its most recent incarnation: the Parthenon is now a major tourist attraction.

Finally, nations keep art because art helps the economy and is good for business. Art is an economic asset that attracts tourists. The presence of a major archeological, religious, or architectural site stimulates the entire economy, and thousands of local jobs are created as a result. This is true of the Parthenon, as we just discussed, or of the *Great Pyramids* (Figure 10.2), ancient ruins in Mexico (Figure 9.36), *Versailles* (Figure 11.10), or the *Forbidden City* (Figure 11.9) in Beijing. Every day, cities are deciding which of their historic structures should be saved and which should be cleared for new development. Recently, the *Watts Towers* (Figure 14.34) in Los Angeles were saved from demolition, but only after enough people decided the sculptures were a distinctive addition to the city fabric and not merely a hazard during a big earthquake.

Popular traveling art exhibitions are also great for the economy. The Egyptian treasures from Tutankhamen's tomb and the paintings of Vincent van Gogh toured the United States, and both drew record crowds. In 1999, a traveling exhibit of van Gogh paintings from Amsterdam was reported to have been the most economically beneficial single event in the history of Los Angeles.

Art is used in advertising to sell products, promote causes, and encourage spending, travel, and donations to certain institutions. The *Creation of Adam* (Figure 6.21) has been used recently in ads for computer technology and telecommunications systems. Some statue fragments from the Parthenon appeared on billboard ads in 2000 promoting Caesar's Palace, a gambling casino in Las Vegas, Nevada. The headless statues are shown next to the words "Losing Your Mind?"

ART COLLECTIONS

Much of the art in this book is part of art collections. An art collection is an accumulation of art objects that are publicly held or are owned by private individuals. Collections can be centered on a particular (1) medium, such as ink painting on paper; (2) theme, such as portraiture; or (3) time period and source, such as early-twentieth-century sculpture from western Africa.

MUSEUMS AND PRIVATE COLLECTIONS

Since ancient times, rulers, nobles, priests, and the upper classes have collected art and kept it in palaces or temples for aesthetic pleasure, for personal or ritual use, or for the display of power. Today, many art collections are housed in museums, which is a relatively recent phenomenon. The Greeks were the first to use the term *mouseion,* which is the ancient source for our word "museum." But *mouseion* refers to an institution of philosophy, learning, debate, and contemplation, more like the modern university than a twenty-first-century museum. An example of a Greek *mouseion* is the Museum of Alexandria in Egypt, founded by the Greeks as a center for learning, with gardens, libraries, lecture halls, and banquet halls. In ancient Rome, art was displayed in baths, such as the *Baths of Caracalla* (see Figure 16.7).

The term *museum* was resurrected in fifteenth-century Europe to refer not to buildings, but to collections consisting of paintings, sculptures, coins, curios, and natural objects like ostrich eggs. These collections were often associated with libraries. Closely related to those eclectic collections are the many artworks, crafts, or exotic items that ordinary people today display in their homes. The sculptures, paintings, and personal treasures are part of the great reward of living with art, such as Kimberly Dawn Schlesier's *A Farm Is a Place to Grow,* 1970 (Figure 6.11). Full of early childhood expression, detail, and vivid colors, this painting is part of her parents' extensive, global collection of contemporary and historical art. The collection includes pieces by living professional artists, student artists, and unknown artists from early cultures. The works are diverse and affordable, acquired at home and abroad.

In the eighteenth century, *museum* came to mean a building housing a particular collection. At the same time, many industrialists, adventurers, and entrepreneurs joined the ranks of the nobility as art collectors, accumulating works in vast numbers. Many of these large personal collections remained private, but some were donated or sold to public museums for one of four reasons: (1) for personal gain, to make a profit on an investment; (2) for personal glory, to be remembered, or for social prestige; (3) to advance knowledge and culture by making a collection available to the public; and (4) to ensure the continued life of a collection, so it would not be dispersed, broken up, lost, or stolen. The wealthy private collector remains an important and influential person, often sitting on museum boards of directors that determine the mission, the budget, staffing, and exhibition calendars.

Museums became common in Europe, especially in the nineteenth century. The intellectual climate behind collecting art was shaped both by the Enlightenment of the eighteenth century, which emphasized knowledge, reason, and cultural achievement, and by the Romantic movement of the early nineteenth century, with its fascination for the unknown, the sensual, and the exotic. Museums were seen as having uplifting and civilizing influences on the general population. Capitalism, with its emphasis on ownership, control, and possession, encouraged museum growth. Colonialism was another factor supporting the establishment of museums. It provided great wealth to Europeans, which made art collections possible, and the art of colonized countries filled European museums. Colonialism also spread the European-model museum to the rest of the world.

The next segments discuss four different kinds of museums that deal with art. Each type is unique in what it shows, how it functions, and how it is funded.

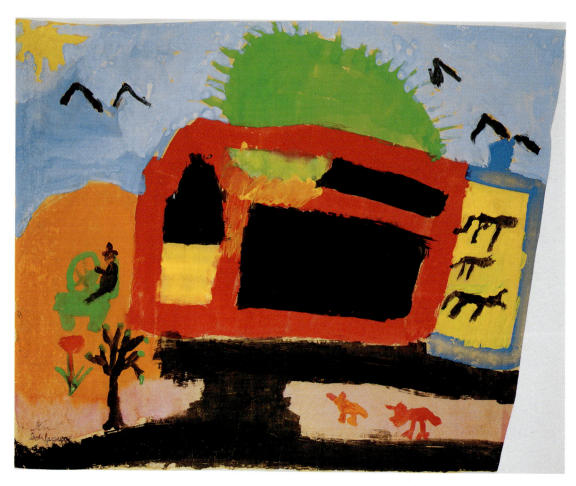

6.11   KIMBERLY DAWN SCHLESIER. *A Farm Is a Place to Grow.* Tempera paint on paper. USA, 1970. Collection of Dona and Douglas Schlesier.

NATIONAL MUSEUMS

The national museum is a large institution with collections in several areas. Many were founded in the eighteenth and nineteenth centuries, in the same general atmosphere that led to the development of the encyclopedia. Because of their size, almost all museums are funded by national governments. Their holdings consist largely of donated or purchased private collections. Our discussion will focus on the British Museum in London, but much also applies to museums like the Louvre in Paris, the Smithsonian Institution in Washington, D.C., or the Vatican Museum and Galleries. *The British Museum* (Figure 6.12) was founded in 1753 for the "inspection and entertainment of the learned and the curious, [as well as] for the general use and benefit of the public." It combined the collections of three private collectors, who became its first trustees. These first collections focused on ancient Greece and Rome and Renaissance Italy, believed to have produced the highest achievements in art. Other private collections were added, such as the Elgin Marbles, which are original sculptures from the Parthenon, including the *Horsemen* (Figure 6.8).

After an internal power struggle and a protracted debate about what constitutes art, the British Museum began accepting private collections of art from other cultures of the world. These included archaeological objects (art and artifacts excavated from ancient civilizations) and ethnographic art (artwork of nonliterate peoples). There are also major non-Western collections, notably Chinese porcelain and sculptures from India. The holdings of some large museums are truly vast and often have never been cataloged. Many items have been "rediscovered" in museum storage, after being lost for centuries.

Large museums in general benefited from conquest and colonization. Some countries have demanded the return of their lost art heritage. Greece, for example, wants the Parthenon sculptures returned. The British Museum has refused, claiming that it legally owns the works and that it saved them from damage and destruction.

CONNECTION

During the colonial era, the fascination of Europeans with "the exotic" was reflected not only in their art collections, but also in the way they conceived gender relations. See the discussion of the painting by Ingres, Grande Odalisque *(Figure 8.20, page 209).*

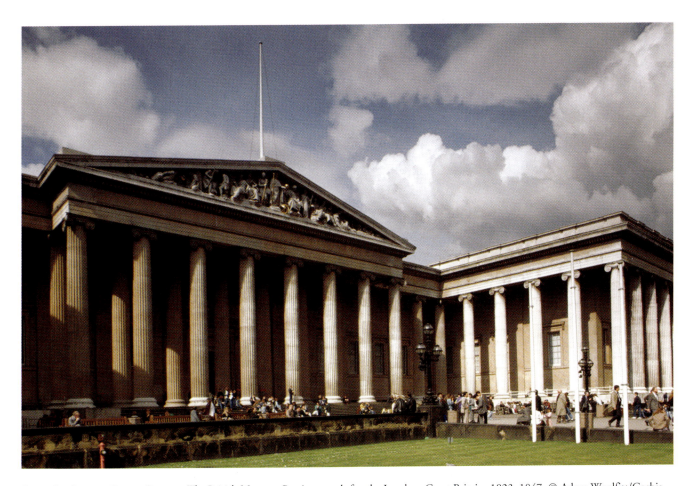

6.12   SIR ROBERT SIDNEY SMIRKE. *The British Museum.* Portico, south facade. London, Great Britain, 1823–1847. © Adam Woolfitt/Corbis.

ART MUSEUMS

The art museum displays art objects and provides aesthetic experiences. Traditionally these include painting, sculpture, printmaking, and decorative arts, but they may also include functional arts, such as furniture, and, more recently, photography, technology-based arts, and installations. Art objects are displayed in art museums to maximize their formal visual qualities: their design, texture, composition, color palette, scale, and so on. Historical, social, or political information is often omitted. Like national museums, art museums are intended to be civilizing and uplifting as well as educational. Art museums may be private institutions, public museums supported by tax money, or university-run museums.

Art museums are recent inventions. The first U.S. art museums, from the 1800s, featured plaster copies of famous classical sculptures in European collections. However, by the beginning of the twentieth century, that practice changed for several reasons: (1) painting became more important than sculpture, and the artists' unique marks made copies unacceptable; (2) abstract art challenged the central status of representational art; (3) wealthy industrialists collected original contemporary art to donate to museums; and (4) art history developed as a discipline.

Museums of modern art are a subset of art museums. They are dedicated to the most current art, which is often unusual or challenging to the public. One example is the *Solomon R. Guggenheim Museum* in New York City (Figure 6.13), a private museum housed in a famous 1950s structure designed by Frank Lloyd Wright, containing Guggenheim's collection of modern art. All modern art museums are faced with an intrinsic problem: as time passes, their collection grows old. As more works are acquired, gradually more of the museum's space,

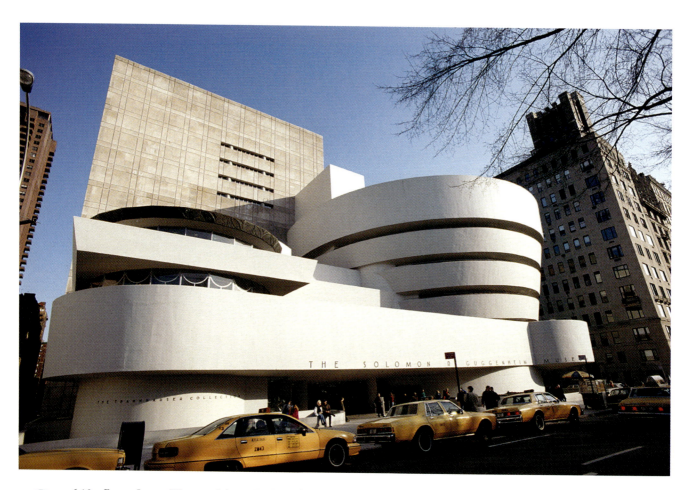

 6.13   FRANK LLOYD WRIGHT. *Solomon R. Guggenheim Museum.* New York City, USA; design begun in 1943, structure completed in 1959. © Alan Schein / Corbis. See Figure 16.5 for more information on the design and uses of this building.

budget, time, and resources go to maintaining the collection, which severely curtails the museum's ability to acquire new works. In time, the "modern art" museum ceases to be so. Recently, a number of contemporary art centers have sprung up. They generally mount exhibits of current art, but maintain no permanent collections.

REGIONAL MUSEUMS

Regional museums serve the interests of a specific locality and reflect that area's cultural history. For example, in China, the Museum of Qin Terra-cotta Soldier and Horse Figures was established to house and preserve the clay figures (Figure 6.14) and other grave goods from the tomb compound of the emperor Shi Huangdi.

A great variety exists in regional museums' missions, their collections, and the programs they sponsor. Regional museums also tend to be the most experimental type of museum, much more so than either the national museum or the art museum, because they serve local needs. For example, the Anthropological Museum at the University of Ibadan, in the Yoruba area of Nigeria, was founded in 1963 by British scholars (Nigeria was a British colony) and emphasized European-style research in archeology and museum curatorship. But this model had little appeal for African students. After independence, the museum evolved into a "vigorous meeting place. . .where new breakthroughs in political crafting as well as domestic and industrial crafts were invented." This model works better with "African peoples' traditions of visioning and thinking, and ways of praying, designing, planning, speaking and doing things; of organizing socio-politically and of exploiting the natural resources of their environmental setting" (Andah 1997: 15–16).

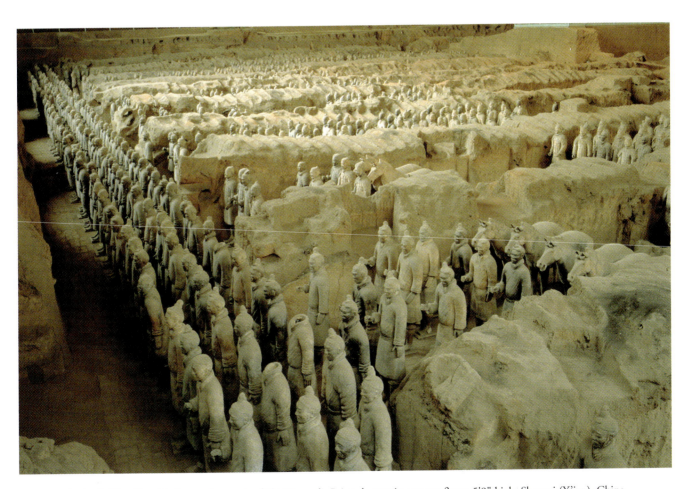

 6.14 *Soldiers from Pit 1,* near the tomb of Shi Huangdi. Painted ceramic, average figure 5'9" high. Shaanxi (X'ian), China, 221–206 BCE. Photo by O. Louis Mazzatenta/National Geographic Image Collection. See the text accompanying Figure 10.9 for more information on this terra-cotta army.

MUSEUMS AND NEW TECHNOLOGY

Recent technology has had a great influence on art, resulting in such new categories as computer-based art, interactive art, video, and, to some extent, film. These new technologies have produced two innovations in the concept of the museum: (1) the media museum, and (2) the virtual museum.

No existing media museum is older than twenty years, but their number is likely to increase. Like the art museum, the media museum exists primarily to display works of art. However, the design and function of media museums are influenced by a wide range of modern phenomena. For example, one media museum in Karlsruhe, Germany, the *Center for Art and Media,* 1997 (Figure 6.15), sees itself as resembling not only art museums, but also radio and television archives, film museums, and science centers, such as the Exploratorium in San Francisco. In addition, amusement parks such as Disney World are influential because they have raised the public's exposure to and expectations of the potential of computer-based art (Schwarz 1997: 26–33).

One special problem faced by media museums is that in addition to collecting art, they must store obsolete hardware and software to view older artworks. Because of the difficulty and cost of maintaining old computer and video equipment, one trend in media museums is to not show older works in their entirety, but to simply present stills or excerpts, with commentary. Even mounting an exhibit of current media-based artworks presents huge technological problems.

> But who is really prepared for the maintenance requirements of a Reality-Engine 2 or for correctly putting on head mounted displays or whole body suits? Who knows what strength a glass fibre cable must have, in order to transport an appropriate amount of image information to the work of art, or which LCD projector is powerful enough to provide the necessary image brightness for a work of art while maintaining a humane room brightness? Not to mention the almost insoluble problems caused by painfully competing soundtracks. There is still no model, no useful solution for how media art can be displayed appropriately and presented in a technically flawless way. A huge amount of pioneering work has to be carried out in this respect. (Schwarz 1997: 13)

Because high-end computer and video equipment is so expensive, some media museums award grants to artists to use museum equipment to produce new artworks. Thus, the Center for Art and Media in Karlsruhe functions both as display gallery (the Media Museum) and as artist workspace (the Institute for Visual Media). And the museum is better able to archive older media works if many artists use the same equipment to produce works of art.

Virtual museums and galleries are available on the Internet. The virtual museum allows all kinds of work to be dis-

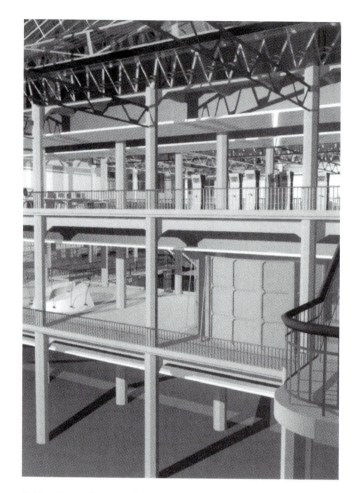

6.15 *Center for Art and Media.* View into the Media Museum. Computer simulation. Karlsruhe, Germany, 1997. Complete simulation of the Media Museum by Armen Oulikhanian © ZKM.

played to the public, without curators and collectors determining what is seen. In some cases, these virtual museums contain media art pieces made specifically for the Web, so what you are seeing is the original work itself. In other cases, the images shown are digital pictures of artwork, in which case the virtual museum really cannot replace the traditional museum nor the experience of looking at actual art objects.

MUSEUM DESIGNS

The architectural design of museums is significant, and it influences or "mediates" the viewers' expectations and experiences. Museum architecture also reflects the cultural and social circumstances prevalent at the time of construction.

The former director of the British Museum, Sir David M. Wilson, has described the outside of the British Museum as a monumental artwork in itself that influences museum visitors in the following way:

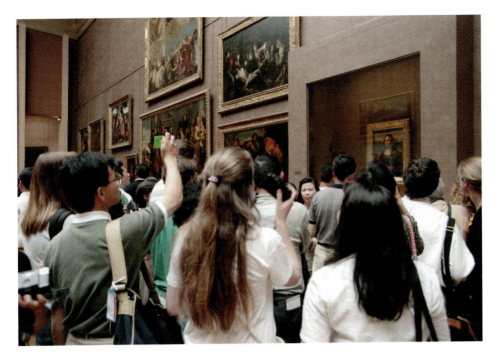

6.16 LEONARDO DA VINCI. *Mona Lisa*, as it is currently displayed behind bulletproof glass. Oil on wood, 30¼" × 21". Italy, c. 1503–1506. Louvre Museum, Paris. © Robert Holmes / Corbis.

Its great Greek Revival facade is almost the symbol of a museum. . . . Its entrance instills a sense of awe and security which enables the visitor to appreciate the treasures and the curiosities it houses not only as something it is a privilege to see, but also as something that is cared for on behalf of the whole world. (Wilson 1989: 7)

The British Museum's Greek Revival architecture (Figure 6.12), designed by Sir Robert Sidney Smirke in the early 1800s, was modeled after ancient Greek temples such as the Parthenon, appropriate for an institution originally dedicated to displaying classical art. The Greek and Roman Revival styles communicate institutional solidity and were used for many U.S. and European government buildings (for example, the Capitol Building and the White House).

The design of the *Solomon R. Guggenheim Museum* (Figure 6.13) also reflects the art it houses and many broadly held ideas of its day. Like the art inside, this museum building emphasizes abstract geometric form and monumental scale. Decoration is eliminated. The building material, reinforced cast white concrete, is treated plastically. It twists upward in a large spiral, balanced by squares and circles, like a piece of modern sculpture. The Guggenheim represents a radical innovation in museum design, a great break from previous art museums and museums in general. In this, it reflects one of the major tenets of modern art in the United States, which holds that modern art should be innovative, not imitative. The modern era was seen as new, heroic, and progressive, and not dependent upon the past.

The interior of the *Center for Art and Media* in Karlsruhe (Figure 6.15), shown here in computer simulation, resembles a number of functional, non-art structures of the late twenti-

eth century, including industrial spaces and shopping malls. The architecture is open, with no fixed walls, allowing for flexible configuration of smaller, dark projection rooms or soundproof spaces. Visually, it resembles diagrams of computer architecture and flowcharts used in software programming. The physical structure is apparent, including the columns rising from foundation to roof, the floor supports, and the prefabricated ceiling grids. The museum design affirms that the art forms contained inside have ties with industry and entertainment.

PRESERVATION AND RESTORATION

As we have seen, artworks are very valuable economically, culturally, or historically. Therefore, enormous human effort and financial resources are devoted to preserving art from the ravages of time, the environment, industrial by-products, and even other human beings. Restoring works that are already damaged presents an entirely different set of problems, and we will look at them.

Small art objects are the easiest to preserve, because they can be kept in museums and art-storage warehouses where humidity, temperature, and light are controlled and where no one can touch them. Then, art objects become enshrined or removed from everyday life. It becomes hard to remember that most works of art were made to be handled or used, and that few were ever designed specifically to be displayed in a museum.

For very famous works of art, the protective measures may become obstacles to seeing the work at all. For example, the curators of the Louvre Museum have surrounded Leonardo da Vinci's *Mona Lisa* (c. 1503–1506) with walls and bulletproof glass (Figure 6.16). The lighting on the painting itself is very subdued to better preserve it. Large crowds congregate before it, even though it is now very difficult to see. The protective measures were considered necessary to deter vandals who might attack such famous works with knives, hammers, and so on.

If art does not fit into a climate-controlled building, preservation is much more difficult. For architectural sites, preservation must counter: (1) normal weather (wind, rain, sun, temperature variations), which rusts metal, fades paint, and erodes and cracks wood, stone, plaster, or clay; (2) environmental pollution, such as smog, which deteriorates materials at an accelerated rate, and noise and vibrations, which shake structures; (3) wear and tear from tourists, including their feet, their fingers, and their breath; (4) damage by souvenir hunters, plunderers, adventurers, and vandals; and (5) damage from war.

When first discovered in 1940, the cave paintings at Lascaux, France, dated c. 15,000–10,000 BCE (Figure 6.17) were in splendid condition, having been sealed underground for thousands of years. The paintings caused an immediate sensation, as visitors flocked to see them. However, increased humidity caused by tourists' breath and sweat caused mold to grow on the walls and ceilings. With the paintings quickly disintegrating, the caves were closed to visitors in 1963. A replica was built nearby and opened in 1983, but it also was so overwhelmed with visitors that access had to be limited.

Tourists wear away ancient monuments. Where they go in great numbers, ancient stone steps and walkways become rutted and worn. Ancient relief carvings, decorations, and inscriptions on stone walls are disappearing because of tourists' touch. Yet tourists are also a financial asset to an area and are encouraged to come.

The modern world threatens the survival of artworks as never before. Vibration from traffic is causing certain ancient Roman ruins to crumble. The *Colosseum* (Figure 6.1) was for years in the middle of a traffic circle in Rome, and the constant rumble of cars, trucks, and buses was shaking apart the structure. Emissions pose a problem, too. Airplane traffic has been restricted over the Acropolis in Athens to preserve the ancient temples, including the Parthenon.

Air pollution presents an even greater threat to works of art. The modern world burns vast quantities of fossil fuels, such as gas in cars and oil in heaters. The by-products of the burnt fuel combine with humidity in the air to form a weak sulfuric acid, which we experience as acid rain or acid fog. That acidity eats away stone. The threat is worldwide. Ancient Egyptian monuments are crumbling, their wall paintings fading, and their sculptures washing away, thin layer by thin layer. In Mexico, air pollution has been particularly bad for a long time, but it has recently been aggravated by the burning of emissions from new oil wells. That pollution is eating away at ancient Mayan temples in the Yucatán peninsula. In Athens, a thin layer of marble from the Parthenon and other monuments is washed away with every downpour of acid rain.

The nation of Greece, recognizing the aesthetic, cultural, and economic value of the Parthenon and other ancient Greek monuments, has considered many possible solutions to the problem of air pollution. At one time, there was a proposal to cover the entire Acropolis with a geodesic dome. Now the government has initiated a long-term plan to replace all diesel public vehicles with electric ones. Meanwhile, all sculptures from the Acropolis have been removed to a climate-controlled building and have been replaced on-site with cast concrete copies.

Preserving film, video, and computer art presents a new set of problems. Old nitrate-based film stock gets gummy and brown and can spontaneously combust. Of all the U.S. films made before 1951, only half survive in any form. Old films on nitrate stock can be copied onto newer, acetate safety film stock, which is more durable. But even the basic copying process takes an enormous amount of time and money. To complicate matters

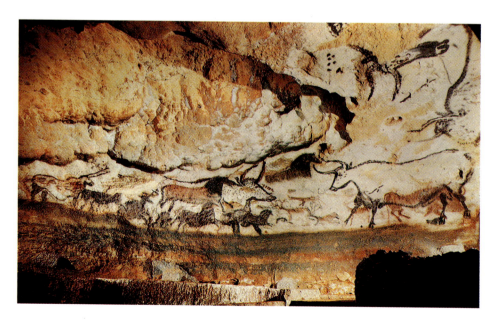

6.17 *Hall of Bulls.* Cave painting, left wall. Natural pigments. Lascaux, Dordogne, France, c. 15,000–10,000 BCE. Photo Hans Hinz. See Figure 7.1 for more on the content, style, and use of this work.

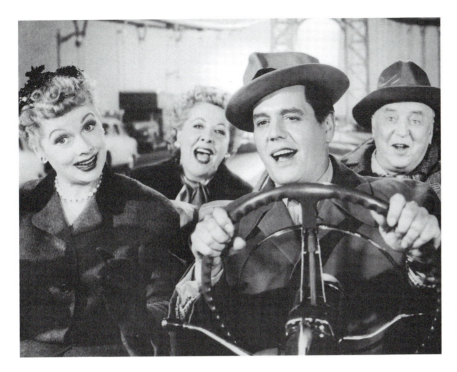

6.18 *I Love Lucy.* Television video, situation comedy (sitcom). USA, 1950–1960s. CBS Entertainment, A Division of CBS, Inc. Images of Lucille & Desi Arnaz are licensed by Desilu, Too, LLC. See also the text accompanying Figure 16.25.

further, in most cases, older films also have to be restored, as discussed in the following section. Three-strip Technicolor film stock is relatively durable. But today that has been replaced by single-strip emulsion color film, with colors that can shift and fade in as few as five years. Single-strip film is being specially stored in below-freezing, low-humidity vaults. This special storage will slow down, but not stop, the decaying process in current film stock.

A lot of old television and video has been lost. Many live television programs were never recorded. Others have been lost because the tape was improperly stored and was damaged or destroyed. Rebroadcasts of videos from the 1950s and 1960s,

such as *I Love Lucy* (Figure 6.18), tend to be low quality, especially when they are copies of copies. No one knows how long videotape lasts. Estimates vary widely, ranging from between five and twenty years to a more optimistic one hundred years. Another complication for video archiving is that old videotapes were created on equipment that is now obsolete. Even if you have intact videotape, you may have trouble finding equipment on which to play it.

As we have already seen, computer-based art is plagued by rapid obsolescence. To preserve Bill Viola's 2000 work, *Dolorosa* (Figure 6.19), requires storing the necessary computers, software, and screens in order for future viewers to experience the

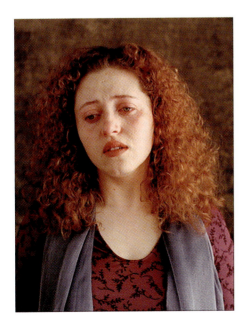
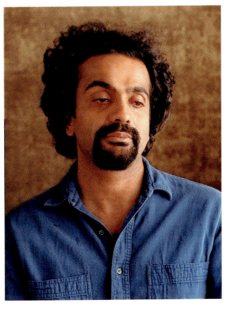

6.19 BILL VIOLA. *Dolorosa.* Production stills. USA, 2000. Photo: Kira Perov. Courtesy of the Artist. See also the text accompanying Figure 13.7.

entire work of art. Though current now, that equipment likely will be arcane in a few years, and paying technicians to maintain it can become costly and difficult. Even printed-out computer art suffers archiving problems, as many of the inks, binders, and other materials used in printing are impermanent.

RESTORATION

Art restoration is the collective technologies and efforts designed to "fix" art that has been damaged or has deteriorated and to bring it back to its original condition as much as possible.

A massive effort is under way to restore the terra-cotta army surrounding the tomb of the first emperor of China, Shi Huangdi. The army, consisting of more than six thousand clay soldiers, was broken and burned in a revolt only five years after the emperor's death. Standing in the front of the pit in Figure 6.14 are soldiers in the process of being restored, while behind them, unseen, are many that are still in pieces. The pits beyond contain still more soldiers. Each soldier was once brightly painted with mineral colors, which have almost entirely worn away. Weapons, iron farm tools, and silk, bone, linen, and jade objects were also buried with the soldiers. The clay horses of the

charioteers had bronze and leather bridles and pulled now-disintegrated wooden chariots.

The restoration of Shi Huangdi's terra-cotta army presents two major problems that frequently confront art restorers. The first is the cost. In many countries, the demands of the living compete against the relics of the past. With so many current needs, how much time, money, and energy should go to restoration efforts? According to current estimations, many generations will pass before Shi Huangdi's twenty-square-mile funeral complex has been fully excavated and restored.

The second problem confronting restorers is this: How can artworks be "restored" when we do not know what they looked like in their original condition? Even though the terra-cotta army is being painstakingly excavated to preserve all archeological evidence of its original appearance, much guesswork and dispute surround that evidence. Restored artwork shows how modern restorers think ancient artwork looked.

Even modern artworks are difficult to restore. *Gone with the Wind* (Figure 6.20), made in 1939 but recently restored, had its color and soundtrack "enhanced" during restoration. Who is to say whether the "enhancement" really represents

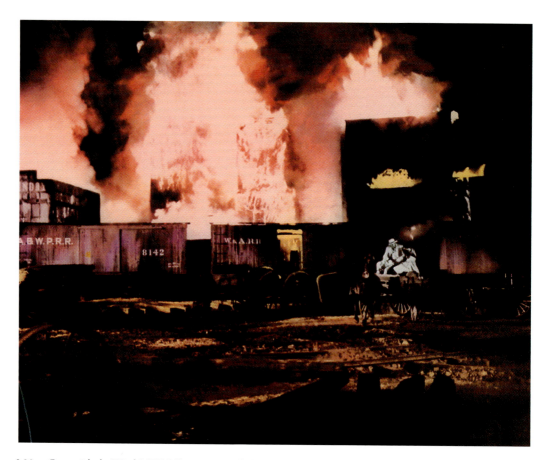

6.20 *Gone with the Wind.* MGM film starring Clark Gable as Rhett Butler and Vivian Leigh as Scarlett O'Hara. USA, 1939. Copyright Metro Goldwyn Mayer. See also the text accompanying Figure 16.24.

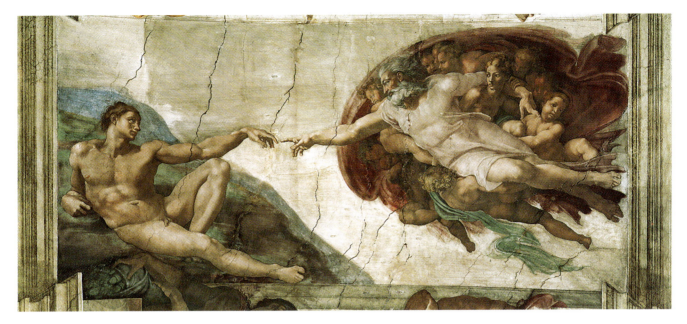

6.21   MICHELANGELO BUONARROTI. *Creation of Adam.* Detail of the Sistine Ceiling. The Vatican, Rome, Italy, 1511. View before restoration in the 1990s. © Scala / Art Resource, NY. Compare this image to the restored version, shown in Figure 9.22.

the original film version or merely reflects modern tastes for richer colors and fuller sound? In more complex film restorations, where the film stock has suffered from severe deterioration, various copies of the film have to be located and spliced together, so that damaged segments can be replaced and missing footage restored.

Sometimes the art is damaged even more while it is being "restored." In the early twentieth century, steel I-pins were embedded into the Parthenon's stones to lock adjoining blocks together. These embedded pins eventually rusted inside the stones and expanded, causing the marble to crack. Rain seeped into these cracks and froze in winter, crumbling the blocks much more than normal wear and tear might have. To undo this art "restoration," the entire Parthenon had to be x-rayed to locate each pin, and then each had to be removed.

Questionable restoration practices continue to be used. Centuries-old temples in Southeast Asia, overgrown with tropical vegetation, have been scrubbed with modern detergents and sprayed with modern herbicides in efforts to clean off mold and fungus and to retard new plant growth. Yet no one knows if the stones and carvings may have suffered long-term damage from the application of these strong chemicals.

Michelangelo's painting of the *Creation of Adam* (Figure 6.21), as well as the entire *Sistine Ceiling,* has been cleaned recently, removing layers of old varnish and candle soot that gave the painting a brown, somewhat darkened appearance. These darkened layers softened the edges of the figures, and individual muscles blended more into the overall form. Numer-

ous deep cracks snaked across the surface. For years, scholars had written that Michelangelo avoided using bright colors and favored defining forms through shading. After cleaning, vivid greens and blues emerged along with an array of pastel colors (turn to Figures 9.21 and 9.22 to see the current appearance of the artwork). Cracks were filled or minimized. Many experts argued that the restorers went too far and removed Michelangelo's final layer of paint in addition to previous restorers' layers, revealing the underpainting. To these experts, all the edges in the cleaned version have become too hard and the colors overly harsh. Other scholars respond that the cleaning was well executed and requires a rethinking of Michelangelo's use of color.

CONNECTION
Leonardo da Vinci's Last Supper (Figure 7.19, page 170) has deteriorated badly and been restored many times in the past. Of what is left, very little is actually Leonardo's painting.

Sometimes restoration may present an artificially complete view of a work. Restorers of da Vinci's *Last Supper* added watercolor painting between the old paint chips to fill in blank areas and to make the painting "look better." Several parts of the Parthenon have been replaced with concrete replicas. Do we still regard these works as "original" or "authentic"? How does

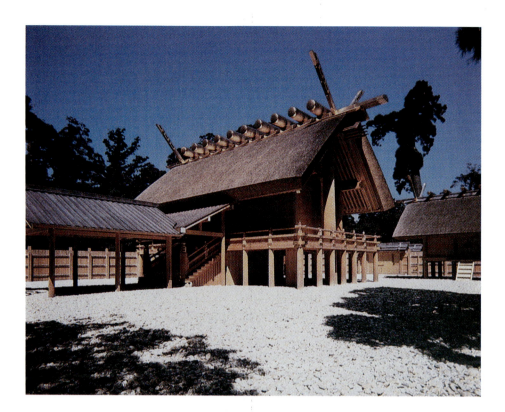

6.22 *Main Shrine at Ise.* Japan, c. 685, rebuilt every twenty years. Kyodo News International. See the text accompanying Figure 9.25 for more on this shrine.

such restoration compare to that of the Shinto *Main Shrine at Ise* (Figure 6.22) from Japan? This work is dated c. 685, but the total structure has been ritually rebuilt every twenty years, following the original plan. Everything you see is less than two decades old.

WHEN ART IS NOT SAVED

If art is so powerful and influential that great efforts go into owning, displaying, and preserving it, then the destruction of art becomes an equally powerful act, but for different reasons. Sometimes art is purposefully destroyed when one culture seeks to obliterate another. In other instances, art is created, dynamically used, and destroyed as it serves its purpose in rituals. And some artists simply choose not to make enduring art objects.

ART DESTROYED IN CONFLICTS

In national, religious, or ethnic conflicts, art is often destroyed. Such destruction may be one more insult the victors inflict upon the conquered. Or the victors may be merely negligent. At times, artwork is destroyed for religious reasons or as part of the horrible phenomenon of ethnic cleansing. We will look at several examples of art destroyed in the past, but the destruction continues today.

During the seventh and eighth centuries, early Christian icons became a source of conflict, which resulted in the destruc-tion of many. Some Christian factions of the time considered devotion to these portable religious images, usually of the Holy Family and saints, equivalent to committing the sin of pagan idolatry. Known as "iconoclasts" (the breakers of images), they sought to ban and destroy these images. At that same time, the Arabs invaded Persia, Byzantium, and Constantinople, bringing the religion of Islam. The Christian emperors of the eighth century thought God was punishing them for their idolatry by permitting the Arab invasion, and they prohibited the use of religious images. Iconoclasm reigned for a century and resulted in the ruthless destruction of thousands of these precious religious icons. Many monuments from ancient Rome were damaged or destroyed because medieval Europeans were indifferent to their artistic merit. Sculpture from the *Arch of Titus* (Figure 6.23) was damaged during the medieval era, when the arch was used as a doorway of a home. Medieval peoples stripped the *Colosseum* (Figure 6.1) of its marble facing and dug metal pins out of its stones. We have seen that the Parthenon was greatly damaged while the Ottoman Turks dominated Greece.

After the conquest of Mesoamerica, Spanish missionaries arrived to convert the native peoples to Christianity. Diego de Landa was a Spanish Franciscan priest and the first Christian bishop of the Yucatán. He was sympathetic to the native peoples and tried to help them as they suffered from European diseases, especially smallpox, and to protect them from the terrible treatment they received from Spanish authorities. He wrote the most important early book that recorded much

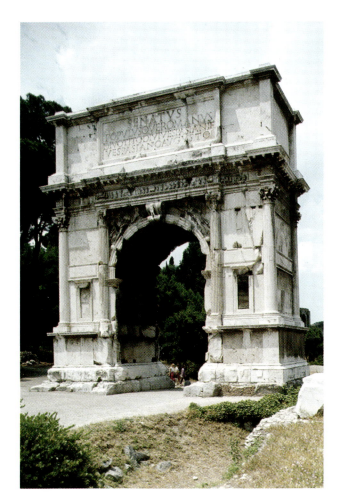

6.23 *Arch of Titus*. Marble on concrete, 50' high, 40' wide. Rome, Italy, CE 81. Saskia Ltd., Cultural Documentation. See also the text accompanying Figure 11.16.

now in the British Museum, missionaries preserved the art object and sent it back to Europe, but we have no information on the meanings or the indigenous uses of this piece. In other instances, a change in religion has meant the wholesale obliteration of the previous religion. Hindu temples in northern India are totally gone, because the conquering people, who were followers of Islam, destroyed all traces of Hinduism in areas under their control.

During World War II, in an effort to wipe out Slavic cultures, German Nazis purposefully destroyed ancient Byzantine religious icons and many monuments during their occupation of western Russia. Art continues to be lost in conflicts in Afghanistan and Iraq.

ART USED DYNAMICALLY IN RITUALS

Art can be lost or destroyed as part of rituals or dramatic performances. The Asmat men of New Guinea made *Bisj Poles,*

information about Mayan civilization, called *Relacion de las Cosas de Yucatán,* and made the first European drawings of Mayan buildings. Landa, however, was horrified by the native religions of Mesoamerica, especially the practice of human sacrifice. In his religious fervor, Landa ordered the destruction of all idols and books. He wrote, "We found a great number of these books in Indian characters and because they contained nothing but superstition and the Devil's falsehoods we burned them all; and this [the Indians] felt most bitterly and it caused them great grief"(Sharer 1994: 513). Landa's book burning has subsequently caused great grief to modern historians, archeologists, art historians, and anthropologists. The great libraries of books that he burned contained not only religious practices, but also splendid artwork and the histories of many Mesoamerican civilizations. Without a doubt, missionary efforts resulted simultaneously in the greatest destruction and the greatest preservation of Mesoamerican culture.

Missionaries to other areas of the world have contributed to the destruction of native cultures. In the case of the *Figure of a Deity: A'a Rurutu* (Figure 6.24), collected in 1820 and

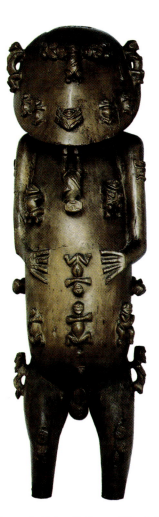

6.24 *Figure of a Deity: A'a Rurutu*. Wood, 44" high. Austral Islands, Polynesia, collected in 1820. The British Museum, London. See Figure 8.4 to review ways that this sculpture and other artworks are intended to ensure human fertility.

dated c. nineteenth to twentieth centuries (Figure 6.25), as part of rituals to promote male power, pass the spirits of the dead on to the living, and avenge the deaths of deceased clan members. Afterward, the poles were left to rot away among the sago palms, the Asmat's primary food source, to promote their fecundity. Thus, the deterioration of the art was an important part of rituals that redirected the human spirit after death.

Navajo sand paintings are also destroyed to complete the ritual for which they are made. In Figure 6.26, a mother, sitting in the middle of the sand painting, holds her sick baby to receive the medicine of the ritual. Navajo attitudes about beauty, art, and permanence are expressed in the following:

A Navajo experiences beauty most poignantly in creating it and in expressing it, not in observing it or preserving it. The experience of beauty is dynamic; it flows to one and from one; it is not

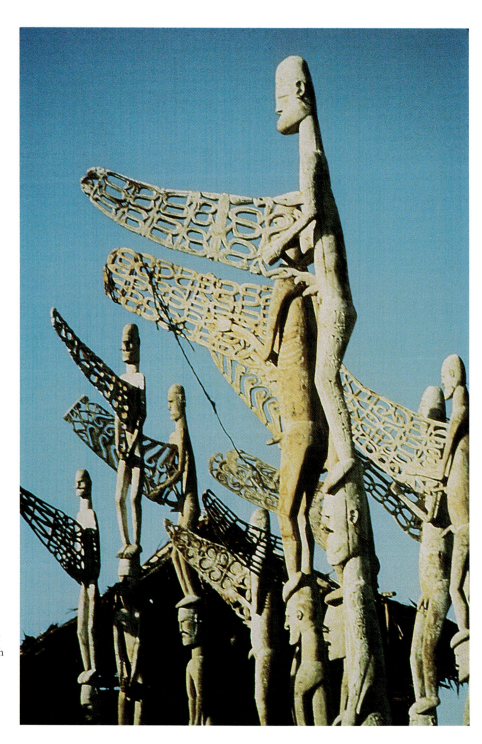

6.25 *Bisj Poles.* Wood and paint, approximately 16' high. Asmat. Buepis Village, Fajit River, southwest New Guinea, c. nineteenth–twentieth centuries. Photograph by Tobias Schneebaum. See Figure 14.17 to review the discussion of the rituals and meaning attached to the Bisj Poles by the Asmat people.

in things, but in relationships among things. Beauty is not to be preserved but to be continually renewed in oneself and expressed in one's daily life and activities. (Witherspoon 1977: 178)

Interestingly, some museum curators, scholars, and tourists make efforts to preserve the art that the Navajos themselves do not keep. Sand paintings on glue-covered boards are now sometimes made for the tourist trade. And some museums have commissioned the making of "permanent" sand paintings within the museum.

CONNECTION
To see the kinds of pigments used in Navajo sand painting, turn to Figure 5.15, page 112.

NON-OBJECT ART

Some artists choose not to make art objects. In some cases, they wish to make art an experience for people, rather than a collectible or a luxury item. Performance art is a good example of this kind of work. Yoko Ono's *Cut Piece* (Figure 6.27) from 1964 no longer exists in any material form, except for photographs that document the event. Other artists give their

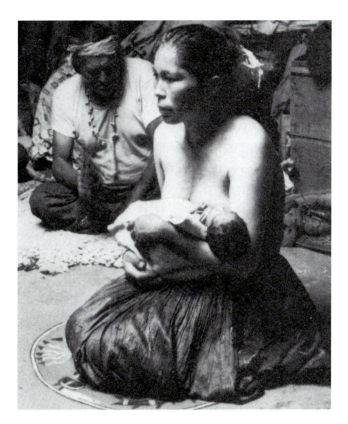

6.26 *Sand Painting.* Ritual for a sick child. Navajo. Arizona, USA, 1954. Photograph by Lee Boltin. See the text accompanying Figure 9.26.

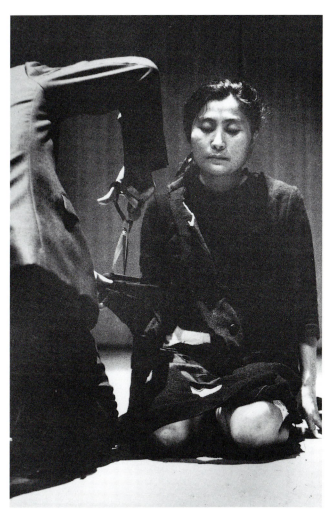

 6.27 YOKO ONO. *Cut Piece.* Japan/USA, 1964. Photo documentation of performance at Yamaichi Concert Hall, Kyoto, Japan. Collection of the artist, courtesy Studio One. See the text accompanying Figure 13.32 for more about this performance piece.

art away or sell it at minimal cost. This is especially true for artwork that can be easily copied or broadcast. The work of many Web artists is free to those who can log on.

STUDYING ART

The study of art is part of many academic disciplines, including art history, archeology, cultural anthropology, and some areas of psychology. Interestingly, all these disciplines appeared fairly recently in the nineteenth and early twentieth centuries. Each discipline is also actively evolving, with changes in scope of study or methodology.

Art history is the historical study of the visual arts. Art historians study artworks as their primary material, much as historians may study archives. Art historians develop a kind of connoisseurship; that is, they are able to study an unfamiliar art object and attribute it to a period, a style, and an artist (even specifying early or late production), and determine whether a work is authentic or a copy.

Early art historical writings were limited to artists' biographies and the formal analysis of Western painting, sculpture, architecture, and prints. Today, art historians study art within broad cultural, political, social, religious, and economic contexts, from a global perspective. In addition to painting, sculpture, architecture, and prints, art historians study photography, film, and other media. Compared to the past, more art historians now are specializing in art of Africa, the Americas, Oceania, and Asia. Art historians also study the structure of the art world: the workings of museums, the management of the art academy and the education of artists, the functioning of the gallery, the role of the collector and critic, and so on, and how each of these contributes to the "making" of art.

Aesthetics is a branch of philosophy, primarily Western, that focuses on the beautiful—its understanding and appreciation—both "universally" and within specific cultural contexts. Questions of what is beautiful are of constant debate, especially when applied to art objects. Aesthetics is a challenging and provocative vehicle for deriving meaning in art.

Art criticism consists of judgments about the value of art exhibits and events. The writings of art critics are circulated in newspapers and magazines and on radio, television, and video. Art criticism is also educational, as Robert Hughes writes: "Criticism isn't about saying 'I think this, therefore you should think this.' It's about getting people to look and to think and to do it on their own" (Preble, Preble, and Frank 1999: 113).

CONNECTION
See the section "Writings about Art" in Chapter 4, page 88, for more on the kinds of literature that art historians and critics produce.

Archeology is the scientific study of the physical remains of past human life and activity. It includes all things that are buried or thrown away, such as bones, stone tools, art objects,

weapons, utensils, and other functional objects. It also includes monuments and buildings. Archeologists conduct fieldwork in which they carefully excavate, classify, record, and date the artifacts they find. Their findings complement what is known about a civilization from written records.

In the early 1800s, archeology was in the formative state and was not entirely scholarly. Ancient sites in Egypt, as we have seen, were visited (and plundered) by European armies, adventurers, scholars, and government agents. Objects were carelessly removed, often causing damage to what was left. By the end of the 1800s, archeology had matured into a scientific, academic discipline, with controlled excavations conducted in cooperation with the host government.

Cultural anthropology is the study of humanity within cultures, including human behavior, social organization, and the creation and use of objects. Cultural anthropology uses the methods, concepts, and data of archeology, ethnology, ethnography, folklore, and linguistics, and sometimes draws on sociology and psychology. For living cultures, the cultural anthropologist does fieldwork (that is, lives with the people) and collects data on human behavior and social organization. The visual arts are important because they reflect social structure, religious beliefs, domestic practices, and aspirations of a people.

We have already discussed the Anthropological Museum at Ibadan. There, the study of archeology and art objects is contextualized into a wide range of topics, including "past climates and environments of Nigerian habitats," "early crop agriculture," "the development of towns and complex societies in African settings," and "the development of metal technology in parts of Nigeria" (Andah 1997: 21).

Art has also been used to study **human development.** Various theories of human growth and acquisition of cognitive and conceptual skills have been based on the study of drawings and diagrams made by children, adolescents, and adults. The Swiss psychologist Jean Piaget developed theories on the formative stages of childhood, based in part on the study of children's drawings. Art therapy is an area of medical treatment that uses the artwork of mental health patients to help diagnose and treat their illnesses. Because art is another language, patients can provide information visually, when perhaps words cannot be uttered.

SYNOPSIS

Art is experienced through performance or display. When people keep art, their reasons are likely among the following:

- Art provides aesthetic, civilizing, or educational experiences.
- Individuals keep sacred art for their own spiritual observances, and religious institutions maintain sacred sites.
- Political uses for art include strengthening ethnic identity, promoting national glory, and signaling the domination of one country over another.
- Art is part of commerce, tourism, and advertising.

Art is kept in private and public art collections. Museums vary in kind and in purpose and include large national museums, art museums, regional museums, and museums devoted to new technologies.

Art preservation and restoration face a variety of knotty economic, aesthetic, and technological challenges. Ancient buildings as well as yesterday's computer art are threatened by political events, environmental destruction, and technological changes.

Not all people are interested in preserving works of art. Invading armies often destroy the art of those they vanquish. Other people dynamically create, use, and then destroy their art as part of rituals or performances.

Various academic disciplines study art, including art history, art criticism, archeology, philosophy, cultural anthropology, and psychology.

FOOD FOR THOUGHT

In addition to everything else that happens to art, sometimes it is censored. Censorship is the prohibition of certain art for moral, political, or religious reasons. The German Nazis in the 1930s and 1940s practiced an extreme form of censorship. They seized or destroyed art from public and private collections that varied from the official art style, which was idealized and naturalistic and promoted Nazi policies. Artists could be banned or imprisoned if they produced abstract or surreal art or if they were non-Germanic by birth.

In the United States today, questions of censorship come up in association with art making and art exhibitions. Sometimes actual criminal charges are filed. In 1990, the director of a Cincinnati museum was placed on trial for obscenity. His institution had hosted a large photographic exhibition that included seven images that many people thought were sexually offensive. The jury acquitted him. More often, censorship means lack of funding or other support for artists and museums if politicians find their art to be offensive. In 1999, the Brooklyn Museum drew the fire of Mayor Rudolph Giuliani for an exhibit called "Sensation," which included the work of Chris Ofili (see Figure 15.5).

- What is obscene? Who defines it? What is acceptable material for an adult versus an adolescent?
- Some people claim that their tax dollars should not support art that they find offensive. Is that position different from objecting to tax dollars being spent to support a military project that some people find wasteful or medical research that some find unethical?
- Should all individuals decide for themselves what they can read, look at, or listen to? What happens if their choices conflict with community standards?
- Should art be uplifting? Should it be moral?
- Does location make a difference? Is it different if a questionable image appears in a museum, in a private gallery, on the Internet, or in an individual's home?

This subject will continue to be controversial in the United States during your lifetime, and your vote and opinion on such issues will count.

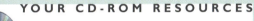

YOUR CD-ROM RESOURCES

- Exploring Art Timeline
- Flashcards
- Food for Thought
- Companion Site
    Chapter 6 Quiz
    InfoTrac® College Edition Readings
    Artist Flashcards
    Online Study Guide

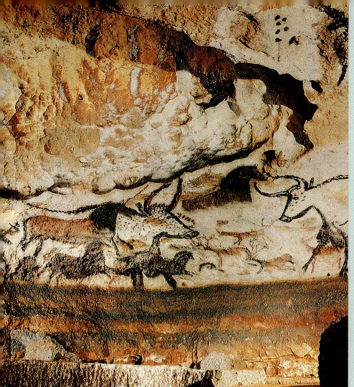

Hall of Bulls. detail of Figure 7.1. Photo Hans Hinz.

WHY DO WE MAKE ART?

Art fulfills basic human pleasures and needs. It is functional and aesthetic. In the next ten chapters, we group the discussion of why humans make art into four sections:

Survival and Beyond:

- Perceiving food as glorious, sacred, or problematic
- Looking at domestic and commercial architecture as a series of choices based on climate, available materials, and social preferences
- Constructing sexuality and the need for offspring

Religion:

- Bringing the supernatural to the human level
- Commemorating the dead and preparing for the afterlife

The State:

- Making the power of the state visible and concrete through portraiture, palaces, and fortifications
- Glorifying war, documenting war, and memorializing peace
- Protesting injustice or supporting or criticizing existing power structures

Self and Society:

- Understanding our bodies and the role of culture in shaping our perceptions of them
- Reflecting social categories of race, gender, class, and clan
- Using art as a model by which we understand the natural world
- Using art to entertain

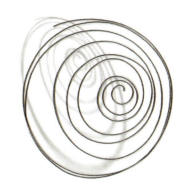

Survival and Beyond

What is basic to human survival? Food, shelter, and reproduction are ongoing concerns of humans, regardless of how civilized, socially structured, or distracted we might be in our everyday lives. What role does art play in these? Some cultures used art to actually assist in survival, usually through ritual. For other cultures, art is an aesthetic expression of social views about food, reproduction, and shelter.

The major topics in the next two chapters are:

Securing or glorifying food, and food's relationship to art, ritual, and sympathetic magic

Examining the social constructs around eating

Representing fertility, primordial couples, lovemaking, and children

Exploring gender and sexuality as seen through art

Investigating shelter for individual, group, and commercial use

CHAPTER 7 | FOOD AND SHELTER

CHAPTER 8 | REPRODUCTION AND SEXUALITY

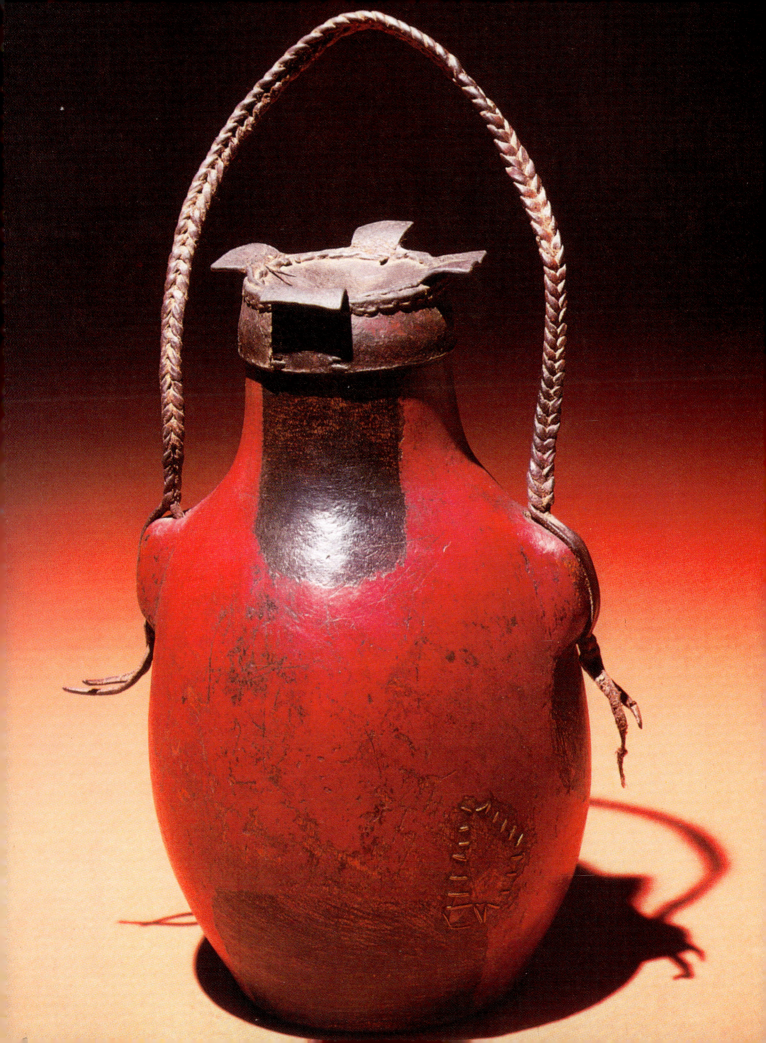

FOOD AND SHELTER

INTRODUCTION

Food is an essential element of life itself, and people need protection from extreme weather as well as from human and animal foes.

Yet our relationship to food and shelter goes beyond simple survival. People choose to live and work in settings that go far beyond functionality to aesthetically enhance and enrich their lives. And many cultures use art to help secure food, to serve it, and to store it. Artworks reflect how different peoples enjoy food. Frequently, a strong association exists among food, art, and ritual or religion.

Keep in mind the following questions regarding art in relation to food and shelter:

In what ways are food and ritual linked?

How have artists glorified food in their artworks or enhanced our experience of it?

How have artists depicted the act of eating? What significance can that act have?

What kinds of shelter have been designed for group living and for individual homes?

What architecture has been developed for the commercial world?

In this chapter, we limit our discussion to domestic and commercial architecture. For other coverage, see:

Chapter 9, Deities and Places of Worship: architecture used in religious rituals

Chapter 11, Power, Politics, and Glory: palaces and government buildings

Chapter 16, Entertainment: theater and museum design.

Milk Storage Jar. Detail of Figure 7.8. Ernie Wolff III Collection, Los Angeles. Photo by Frank J. Thomas, Los Angeles.

SECURING THE FOOD SUPPLY

Among hunters, gatherers, and farmers, food is strongly linked to art and ritual, because they can be used to invoke spiritual or magical forces to help accomplish a task, such as bringing rain for the crops. This is "sympathetic magic," in which art and ritual function together and are meaningless without each other. Ritual-based art often was destroyed if the magic ceased, or to prevent or stop the power of the magic. The artist/shaman could attain great status in society, and in some cultures still does.

Food, art, and ritual are probably linked in prehistoric cave drawings, like those at *Lascaux* in southern France, dated c. 15,000–10,000 BCE (Figure 7.1). They depict huge woolly mammoths, horses, rhinos, aurochs (wild cattle), and reindeer. Their exact purpose is unknown, but some anthropologists propose that the cave was safe and secure from animals, so rituals could be performed to ensure a successful hunt of those very same animals. By capturing the likeness of the creature, the artists may have felt they also captured its spirit. With this control, spears and arrows were painted in or actually thrown at the image of the prey, ritualistically killing it, which would ensure a successful hunt.

Other scholars argue that the painted "arrows" are few, and could be plant forms. They propose that these drawings were homage given to earth and animal spirits. Either way, the current consensus is that these images had a ritual purpose linked to bounty in nature and are thus tied to the human food supply. See also the African Rock Painting on page 191.

The ancient artists painted images deep inside the caves, through narrow and difficult passages, obviously from memory. Yet they rendered quite naturalistically the magnificent animals of their day, without showing landscape or deep space. They focused more on the energy and movement of their subjects, outlining the side view to make it most recognizable. Naturally occurring materials, such as tar and charcoal for black, colored earth for yellow and brown, and rust for red, were used for color. Dry pigment could be applied as powder or mixed with animal fat and applied with a primitive brush. Given the crude materials and the rough stone walls, the drawings are especially amazing.

Across the world in Australia, we see the same phenomenon of linked food, art, and ritual. The "Ancestor Dreaming" of the Aboriginal people of Australia is a system of beliefs and knowledge that accounted for the cosmos, from creation to death, which included food gathering. It was passed on through songs, chants, dance, and painting. As part of food-gathering rituals in the past, Aboriginal artists painted patterns and ancient secret symbols on the ground with colored dirt and natural materials. It was a kind of contour map indicating the location of precious food and water in an arid envi-

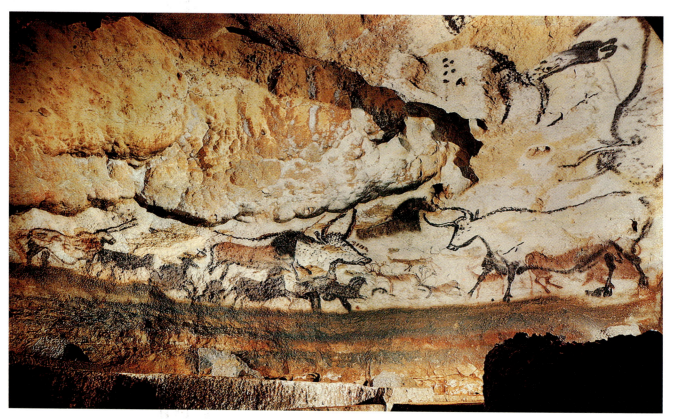

 7.1 *Hall of Bulls.* Cave painting, left wall, c. 15,000–10,000 BCE. Lascaux, Dordogne, France. French Government Tourist Office. Photo Hans Hinz. See also Figure 6.17.

ronment. The paintings were destroyed after the ritual was performed.

Since the 1970s, Aboriginal artists have been making their paintings with more permanent materials. *Witchetty Grub Dreaming*, dated 1980, is by Paddy Carroll Tjungurrayi (Figure 7.2). Taken just formally, the painting is an array of patterned dots, lines, concentric circles, and semicircles. The work is strongly patterned, with alternating lights and darks, and alternating curving and straight lines, all radiating from a center point. The painting shows the source of the ancestor grub, an important food, by the circles located in the center. The small squiggled lines represent other grubs beneath the ground waiting to be dug up for a succulent meal. The symmetrical arrangement of the painting in warm earth tones suggests the balance of the cosmos and the ancestors, which provide sustenance for human beings.

The Bamana people of Mali use masks, dance, and ritual to help ensure successful crops. Headdresses of abstracted antelopes represent the spirit of Tyi Wara or Chi Wara, who gave them the knowledge of agriculture. Our example of the *Tyi Wara (or Chi Wara) Dance Headdress* dates from the late nineteenth or early twentieth century (Figure 7.3). There are male and female antelope masks, with the female mask bearing a baby antelope on her back. Young male dancers, with

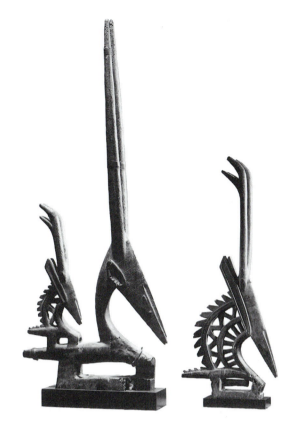

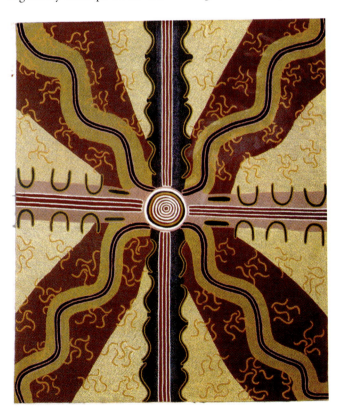

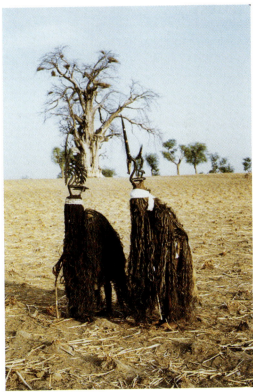

 7.2 PADDY CARROLL TJUNGURRAYI. *Witchetty Grub Dreaming*. Paint on canvas. Australia, Aboriginal, from Papunya, 1980. Photo by Jennifer Steele. © Jennifer Steele / Art Resource, NY. See Figure 2.1 for more on the formal qualities of this painting.

7.3 *Tyi Wara (or Chi Wara) Dance Headdresses*. Wood, brass tacks, string, cowrie shells, iron, quills. Female: 38.5" high; male: 31.5" high. Bamana people, Mali, Africa, late nineteenth or early twentieth century. The lower image shows Tyi Wara dancers on a field. Photo by Pascal James Imperato.

an interesting interpretation of the Passover Meal, which, in the Jewish tradition, cannot be held unless a woman is present.

In *The Dinner Party,* a large, triangular table is set with thirty-nine painted porcelain plates and stitched runners, each of which contains symbols and text that honor a woman in Western history. Each side of the triangle is composed of thirteen settings, the number of men painted in renditions of the Last Supper. The number 13 is also the number in a witches' coven. The "Heritage Floor," beneath the table, is covered with triangular tiles that are inscribed with the names of 999 other women whose accomplishments were important. The triangle is a female symbol and the symbol of the ancient Goddess thought to have brought forth all of life unaided. The china painting and needlework in this piece are usually considered "women's work."

The Dinner Party also contains historical research telling the stories of these women whose names and accomplishments may have been forgotten. An example is Theodora, an actress in the sixth-century Byzantine Empire, who married and eventually became empress despite her lowly and despised profession. As empress, Theodora worked to better the lot of actresses and prostitutes, and changed marriage laws to ensure women's property rights and to protect women from mistreatment. Her place setting at *The Dinner Party* recalls vaginal

shapes, the folds of royal robes, and the deep colors and golds of Byzantine mosaics.

CONNECTION
A portrait of Theodora's husband, the Emperor Justinian, can be seen in the mosaic Emperor Justinian and His Attendants *in Figure 11.2, page 303.*

Most meals are informal, everyday events, and are not like the ritual meals we have just described. However, even the most casual reveal how people live and their social habits.

U.S. artist Duane Hanson's *Self-Portrait with Model,* dated 1979 (Figure 7.23), presents the meal as a site for companionship. Yet there is more here. His sculptures seem real at first, and they are life-size. Hanson glorifies his subjects, but without idealizing them. The model looks down at her magazine, while the artist studies her. But here, the artist is not an exalted genius, apart from everyday society and commenting on it. He is part of the sculpture and "breaks bread" with the model, indicating that the artist and the woman are companions and are made of the same stuff. Hanson has incorporated a few details, such as the furniture, napkin holder, and salt

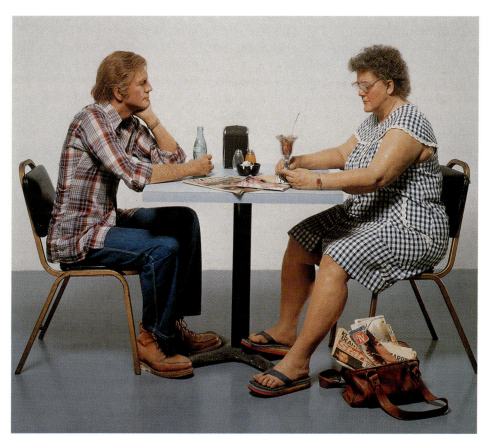

7.23 DUANE HANSON. *Self-Portrait with Model.* Painted polyester and mixed media, life-size. USA, 1979. Art © Estate of Duane Hanson/ Licensed by VAGA, New York, NY.

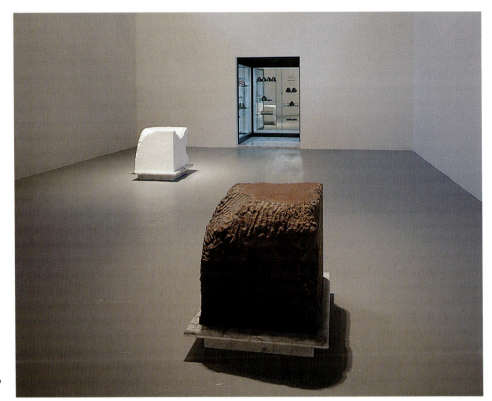

7.24   JANINE ANTONI. *Gnaw.* Three-part installation. Chocolate: 600 lbs. of chocolate gnawed by the artist; lard: 600 lbs. of lard gnawed by the artist; display: 130 lipsticks made with pigment, beeswax, and chewed lard removed from the lard cube; 27 heart-shaped packaging trays made from the chewed chocolate removed from the chocolate cube, dimensions variable. USA, 1992. Courtesy of the artist and Luhring Augustine. See also the text accompanying Figure 1.6.

and pepper shakers, to suggest the entire ambiance of a greasy-spoon diner.

The last piece on the topic of eating is *Gnaw* (Figure 7.24), dated 1992, by New York-based artist Janine Antoni. Antoni began this complex installation by fabricating a six-hundred-pound cube of chocolate and an equally sized cube of lard. She then sculpted each block by biting and gnawing the edges. The chocolate was spat out and cast into the heart-shaped trays found inside candy boxes, turning the repulsive into objects of sentimental prettiness. The lard she spat out was mixed with pigment and beeswax and cast into 130 lipsticks. The trays and lipsticks were then shown in display cabinets. Replacing the traditional hammer and chisel with her mouth, Antoni transforms the act of eating into an artistic process. The artist's sculptural methods also become a way of intimately relating to her creations—as babies put things into their mouths in order to know them, so, too, the artist consciously engages in this experience. The clean, cubic shapes of the chocolate and lard have become lumpy, gnawed masses—while in another part of the exhibition, twenty-seven pristine chocolate-cast trays are displayed with 130 lipsticks. Using materials and objects that are socially defined as female fetishes, Antoni recasts them in an art historical frame to raise questions about the position of women in art.

DOMESTIC ARCHITECTURE

Over the centuries, people have developed a wide range of houses, all serving the broad function of shelter, but done in amazingly different styles. In each case, a different house design is the result of one or more of the following factors:

- the need for protection from human foes, weather, animal predators, or insects

- historical necessity, as some event required people to change their housing styles

- the availability of materials

- aesthetic choice, as a group of people may believe that certain designs are inherently superior to or more pleasing than others

- the desire to follow precedent, or to imitate a foreign style or a palace design

- symbolic importance; the structure or decoration of houses may reflect important social values or religious beliefs

- self-identity, as the house can be a reflection of its owner's beliefs or aspirations

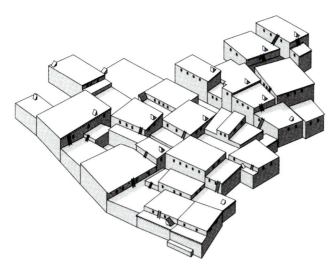

7.25   Restored drawing of Çatal Hüyük (after J. Mellaart), level VI, 6000–5000 BCE.

GROUP LIVING

Human beings tended to cluster together in communities for fortification against danger and to increase their chances of survival. The earliest examples of domestic architecture feature group living, which was popular as long ago as 25,000 BCE, with large circular or oval huts of animal hides covering a framework of light branches and accommodating several families. These huts centered around the hearth (Stokstad 1995: 38). In treeless areas of Russia and the Ukraine, where the winter is harsh, early humans used the bones of the woolly mammoth for frameworks. The long tusks spanned the doorways and reached from wall to wall to create the roof. Other bones

were placed and interlocked in a way that was both functional and aesthetic and then covered with animal hides and turf. These were much more ambitious structures than what is dictated by sheer necessity.

The Neolithic town of Çatal Hüyük in present-day Turkey was an early example of urban life. It dates from the era when agriculture was beginning, animals were being domesticated, domestic crafts such as weaving were flourishing, and copper and lead were being smelted and worked. The architectural design of Çatal Hüyük is clever (Figure 7.25). The one-story, mud-brick and timber houses were all connected and clustered around a few open courtyards placed near the center of the compound. There were no streets and no ground-level doors. Entrances were holes in the roofs, which also served as chimney vents. The Çatal Hüyük houses were sturdier and more stable than individual freestanding houses, and the solid wall without openings was an effective defense against human or natural foes. Should invaders enter, they would find themselves in a maze of spaces, none of which gave easy access to another. Yet Çatal Hüyük was a peaceful town, as there is no evidence of weapons or fortification.

Inside, Çatal Hüyük houses had plastered and richly painted walls and floors. Intermingled among the houses were many shrines, roughly one for every three houses. The shrines were richly decorated with animal and human forms representing female sexuality, male potency, and symbols to ward off evil.

Our next example of architecture for group living is *Pueblo Bonito* at Chaco Canyon (Figure 7.26), constructed by the Anasazi peoples in New Mexico, North America, around the eleventh century. The Anasazi were the northernmost extension

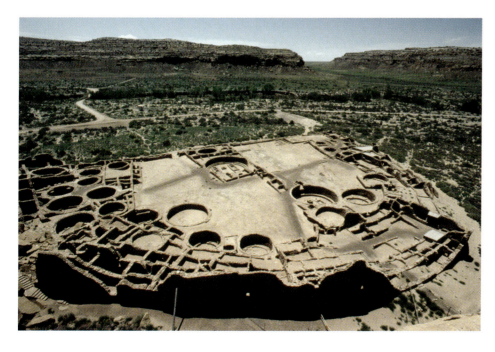

7.26   *Pueblo Bonito.* Anasazi. New Mexico, USA, eleventh century. Photo by Paul Logsdon. © Dewitt Johnes / Corbis.

of the great cultures of Mesoamerica and are believed to be the ancestors of the Hopi, Zuni, Acoma, and the peoples of the Rio Grande. They were skilled farmers in a dry climate. That they flourished is evident from the enormous piles of refuse in their trash pits.

The site of *Pueblo Bonito* had been inhabited for many centuries, and older structures were filled with earth and rubble to form a foundation for the new. *Pueblo Bonito* was a ceremonial fortress that may have been built as a center for the Anasazi elite. It was built all in one piece, in large wings, as can be seen by the precise alignment of cross-walls and the exact placement of doors. The structure itself has dramatic smooth, sweeping lines, set against and contrasting with the rough vertical cliffs behind it. The walls cover four acres, with five-story structures and approximately 660 rooms surrounding dual plazas to accommodate perhaps one thousand residents. Various clans occupied certain sections of the pueblo. The round structures in the middle of the pueblo are kivas, large rooms, totally or partly underground, which were centers for ceremony and contemplation. The masonry work at *Pueblo Bonito* is exceedingly refined and was covered with a coat of smooth plaster. Some 200,000 wood beams were hauled in from sixty miles away.

The villages of the Dogon people in Mali, Africa, date from 1200 and are currently in active use. Clinging to steep cliffs that extend for 125 miles, Dogon villages (Figure 7.27) are dense collections of adobe houses, shrines, and granaries.

Individual rooms within a single house may be irregular in shape and on different levels to make best use of available space. Land conservation is important, as almost all Dogon exist by farming, but arable land is in short supply. Houses are connected with stone and mud walls to make clusters that become joint family households or compounds. The design of houses reflects social values, as the leader's house is often larger and distinguished by checkerboard decorations, a symbol that reflects ideal human order. The houses and granaries form an aesthetically pleasing pattern of vertical geometric shapes against the cliffs. Horizontal wooden beams project from the outer walls, serving both as footholds for maintenance work and as an additional aesthetic pattern. Either flat mud roofs or conical thatched roofs cover the buildings. Unused buildings deteriorate quickly and return to the earth.

In the late twentieth century, group living again became an attractive or even a necessary idea, because of population growth, land shortage, energy costs, traffic gridlock, and the lack of a sense of community within large cities. In creating *Habitat* (Figure 7.28), Israeli/Canadian architect Moshe Safdie was influenced by several features of pueblo architecture: (1) it was energy efficient, due to its stacked design and shared walls; (2) it was climate oriented and sited to take advantage of the available natural resources; and (3) it was designed for comfortable living for many people in a relatively small space. Safdie wanted an alternative to the single-family house that created a vast, unwieldy urban sprawl, as well as the impersonal high-rise

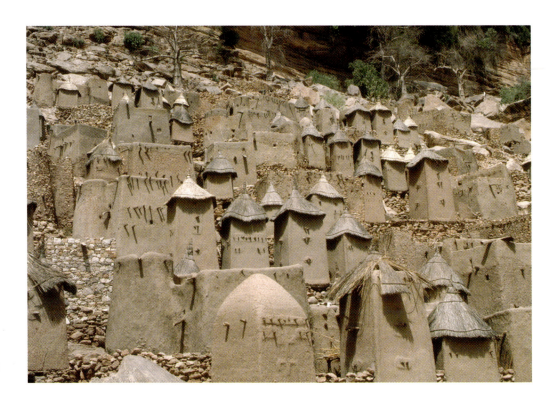

7.27 *Dogon Cliff Dwellings with Granaries,* Mali, Africa. © Wolfgang Kaehler / Corbis.

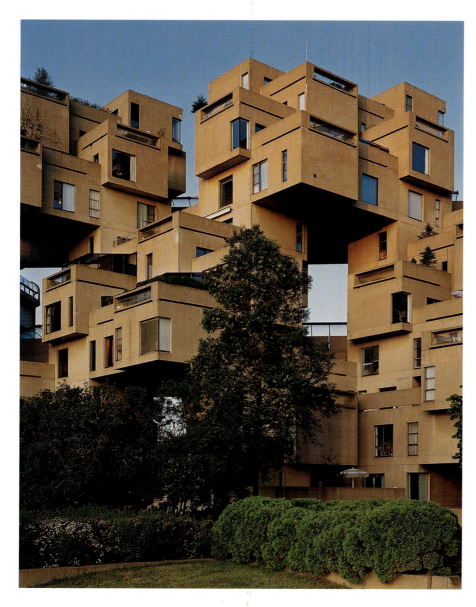

7.28 Moshe Safdie. *Habitat.* Designed for Expo '67 in Montreal, Canada. Photo Russell Thompson. The Arkansas Office, Inc. See also the text accompanying Figure 3.24.

apartment that cut its occupants off from the land. In *Habitat*, he created low-cost housing that minimized land use and that provided privacy and individualized living within a group setting. The mass-produced, prefabricated units are building blocks that can be stacked and arranged in many unique configurations. One person's roof is another's garden or walkway. Safdie himself said, "For everyone a garden." Covered parking was incorporated into the total design of the building.

Aspects of *Habitat*'s rectangular module, window design, and stacked look are taken from pueblo design, but the structure is also the product of twentieth-century modernism with the emphasis on simple geometric shapes, the lack of ornamentation, and the resemblance to abstract sculpture. *Habitat* was built for Expo '67, the World Exposition held in Montreal in 1967.

CONNECTION
See David Smith's Cubi XXVI *(Figure 15.34, page 460) for an example of modern abstract sculpture.*

INDIVIDUAL HOMES

Now let us look at the development and design of individual homes, and the ways they embody climate concerns, aesthetic preferences, and cultural choices.

In the first century CE, average Romans lived in multistory apartment buildings, called "insulae." Externally, these buildings appeared bare, with little or no ornamentation, while the insides were hot (or freezing cold!) and cramped and had no sanitary facilities. In contrast, housing for the wealthy was spacious and beautiful, like the *House of the Vettii* (Figure 7.29) from the city of Pompeii. The eruption of Mount Vesuvius in CE 79 buried the structure in ash and, therefore, preserved it. What we see now is a restoration. The exteriors of wealthy Roman houses were rather plain, but inside, the visual delights of the *House of the Vettii* are many. Open spaces brought fresh air and light into the center of the house. Figure 7.29 shows the front atrium with a pool for collecting rainwater called the "impluvium," and behind it a Greek-style garden, surrounded by a peristyle. Paintings and mosaics covered most walls and floors, and the garden was furnished with marble tables and fountains. Occupants entered individual rooms through the airy courtyards. The Roman house was organized symmetrically around an axis that ran from the entrance to the back of the house, aligning a succession of lovely views and providing illumination throughout the house.

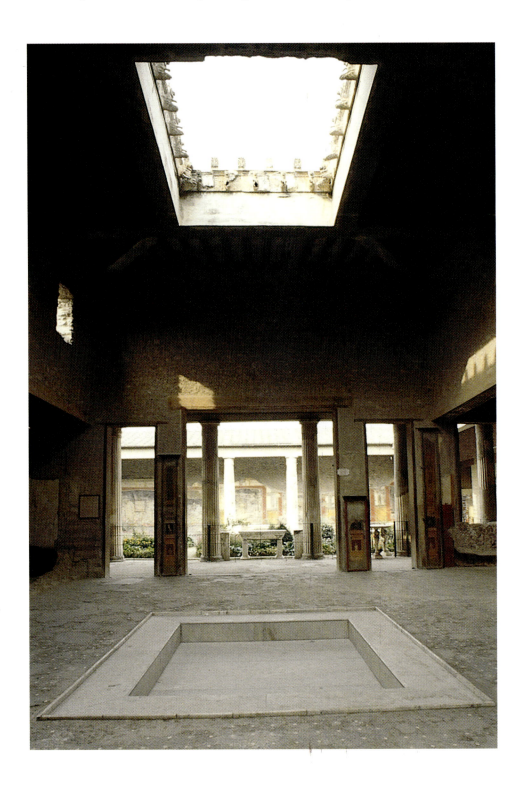

7.29 *House of the Vettii.* Atrium, reconstructed. Pompeii, Italy, CE 62–79. Naples Archaeological Museum. Henri Stierlin.

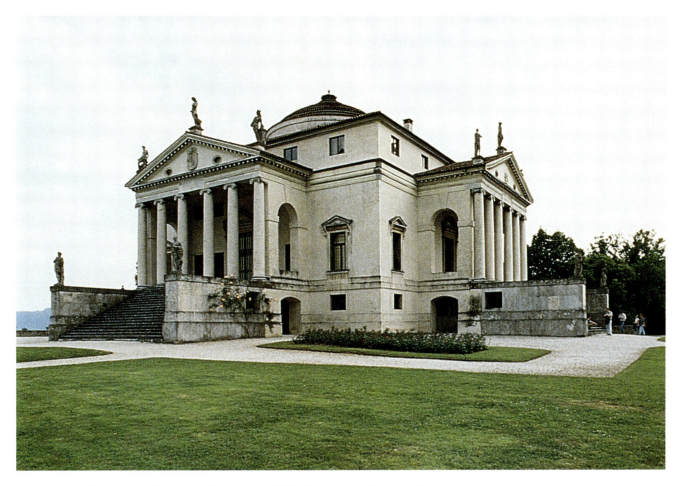

7.30 ANDREA PALLADIO. *Villa Rotonda.* Vicenza, Italy, 1552. © Scala / Art Resource, NY.

CONNECTION

An example of wall painting for a wealthy Roman residence is Gardenscape *from the Villa of Livia, Primaporta, Figure 15.14, page 446.*

The *Villa Rotonda* (Figure 7.30) is a sixteenth-century Italian house influenced by Greek and Roman designs. The designer, Andrea Palladio, was a stonemason and decorative sculptor who eventually became the chief architect of the Venetian Republic. He studied ancient Roman building and wrote books promoting symmetry and stability as controlling elements of architectural design. Centuries later, his writings influenced eighteenth-century Neo-Classical architecture in Europe and the United States, such as Thomas Jefferson's design of his home, Monticello.

All parts of the *Villa Rotonda* are worked out in mathematical relationships to the whole. The villa has a centralized plan, with thirty-two rooms and four porches, all perfectly symmetrical, with a central, dome-covered rotunda. The harmonious geometric shapes represent Renaissance philosophical principles of orderliness, hierarchy, and clarity applied to domestic architecture for the wealthy. All four facades are exactly alike, with Ionic porticos above steep flights of steps, very much like a Roman temple or the facade of the *Parthenon* (Figure 9.32). They provide different landscape views and cool breezes for personal comfort in the summertime. Built up on a platform, the villa dominates the surrounding countryside.

Traditional Chinese house design reflects different cultural values and a different response to environment than the houses we have just seen. The first emperor of China, Shi Huangdi (ruled 221–206 BCE) developed the first unified Chinese architectural style. His palaces were amalgams of the various older feudal styles, and, afterwards, wealthy Chinese built homes that were more modest versions of his palace designs. Han Dynasty houses were all wood frame, and none survived. However, we know a great deal about them from ceramic models that were buried in tombs, along with ceramic models of granaries, wellheads, and other rural structures.

The typical Han house for the wealthy consisted of large, multistoried halls, each story slightly smaller than the one below. Large roofs with wide eaves capped each level, adding a horizontal emphasis to what was basically a vertical structure. Balconies encircled the house. Ornate house decoration was important and used precious materials, such as gold and jade. Lower wood posts were finished in red lacquer, offset by white walls, with gilded doors. Roof tiles and finials featured bronze accents. The upper wooden surfaces had variegated patterns. Inside, wall paintings would have illustrated Daoist fables and Confucian aphorisms. All this was done with floral designs in brilliant colors. These features are evident in the *Tomb Model of a House,* which dates to the third century. (Figure 7.31), even though

this was not the most lavish of homes. It may have served as a watchtower and probably had one or more courtyards, where household and farming chores could be carried out. The structure itself was a timber frame house, with non-load-bearing walls of compressed earth or mud that were vulnerable to rainfall. The wide, projecting roof eaves that became so distinctive of Chinese architecture are thus both aesthetic and functional, as they protected the earthen walls from the elements. The wide eaves were supported by an elaborate wooden bracketing system that could be very ornate.

Distinctive wooden houses also were built in Indonesia, with an equatorial climate bringing year-round heavy rainfall, thick vegetation, heat, humidity, mosquitoes, and other

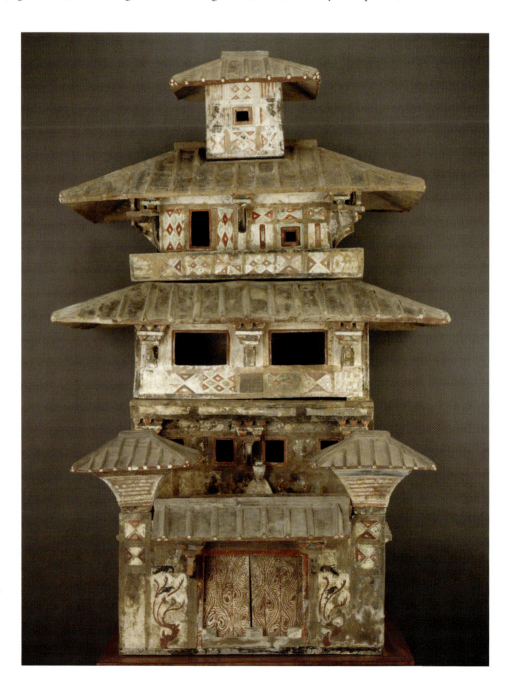

7.31 *Tomb Model of a House.* Ceramic, 52" × 33" × 27". Eastern Han Dynasty. China, first century. The Nelson–Atkins Museum of Art, Kansas City, Missouri (Purchase: Nelson Trust) 33-521. Photo by Robert Newcombe.

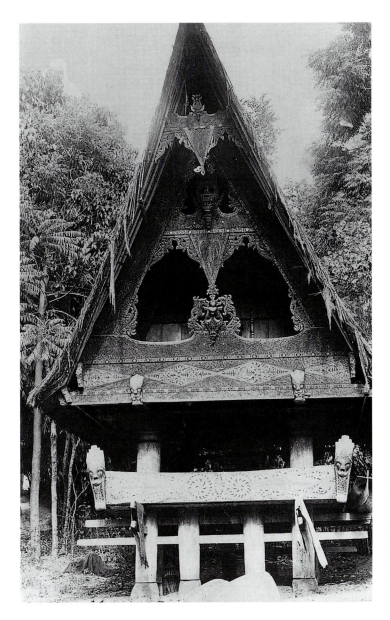

7.32 Decorated facade of *Toba Batak House*. Sumatra, Indonesia, c. nineteenth–twentieth centuries. Royal Tropical Institute, Amsterdam. See also the text accompanying Figure 3.25.

insects. Traditional houses in Indonesia, like the *Toba Batak House* (Figure 7.32), have very steep roofs that quickly shed the heavy rainfall to keep it from soaking into the thatched roof. Overhanging eaves keep the rain away from the house and shield the generous windows. When seen from the side, the roofline is highest at each end and swoops downward at the center in a gentle curve.

On the second and third levels, sleeping and storage areas were not large, so most people spent the day outdoors. The bottom level consists of stilts that raise the house above ground level, to increase breezes through the windows, keep the floor cooler, and raise sleeping people above mosquito activity. In times of conflict, the stilts make the house more secure. Sometimes animals were kept there. Huge, thick, hardwood tree trunks form the stilts and upright supports for the *Toba Batak House*. The thatched roof was heavy while the non-load-bearing walls were made of soft wood. The entire house flexes during

earthquakes, as beams are pegged instead of nailed together and the stilts sit on rocks.

In addition to the practical features of the *Toba Batak House*, the structure has symbolic meaning, as do traditional houses throughout Indonesia. The internal spaces are seen as being maternal, like a womb. The house is seen as a "transformer [that] tames the terrifying vastness of the universe and at the same time inflates human concerns with cosmic grandeur" (Richter 1994: 57). The house is likened to a human body, with stilts as legs, the roof as head, and the trapdoor entrance as the navel. On a cosmic level, the three levels are like the upper, lower, and middle worlds of the Indonesian universe; on a social level, the three levels of the house are likened to the social hierarchy separating slaves, commoners, and nobility (Dawson and Gillow 1994: 14). This house, and others by this clan, are carved and painted with black, white (lime), and red ochre pigments. Many designs are interlocking

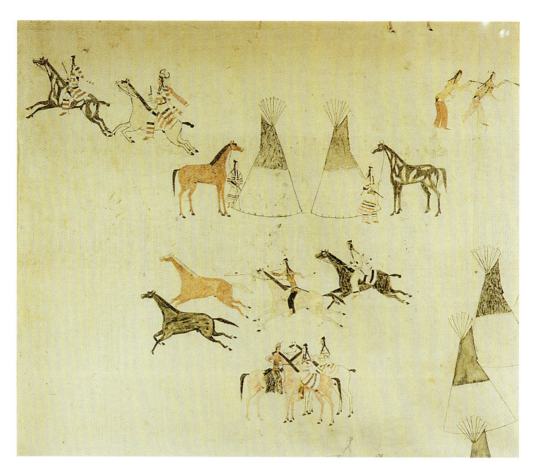

7.33 North American Sioux *Tipi* cover, decorated with images of tipis and equestrian warrior figures, c. 1880. © Werner Forman / Art Resource, NY.

curlicues, but others are figurative, such as rounded breasts or lizard earth spirits for fertility and protection.

Traditional houses are still being built in rural Indonesia, but modern homes are constructed in the growing cities, where the population has developed a taste for modern conveniences and televised entertainment. Even in traditional villages, tin roofs have replaced the thatch.

Housing can also be shaped by historical necessity. For thousands of years, the Native Americans of the Eastern Woodlands, Great Lakes, and Mississippi areas were stable populations who hunted and gathered food for their livelihood. With the coming of the Europeans, these peoples were displaced from their homelands and, for a short time, lived like nomads on the Great Plains in movable houses, like *Tipi* (c. 1880), Figure 7.33. The tipi was originally a small tent used during hunting season. When later used as year-round housing, tipis were built as large as twenty-five feet high and were moved by horses. The Crow built the tallest tipis, while those of the Cheyenne were low. Animal skins, buffalo hide, or canvas covered the framework of slender poles. Flaps that could be adjusted to keep out wind or rain formed the smoke vent at the top. Tipi covers and liners were often painted. Before the

1830s, the imagery consisted of stiff figures. Eventually the Great Plains artists adapted European styles of painting and showed scenes of nature or war. The artists likely depicted the tipi owner's personal adventures in war.

Fallingwater (1936–1938), Figure 7.34, is arguably the most famous modern house in the United States. Frank Lloyd Wright designed it for the wealthy Kaufmann family from Pittsburgh as a weekend home in the woods to balance their urban lives. Wright believed that houses should be unified wholes that merge into their natural settings. Materials should appear natural and come from the immediate surroundings. A large boulder is the base of the house's central fireplace, while the stones in the walls were taken from nearby quarries. The house is a series of geometric blocks, some vertical but most horizontal, that sit low to the ground. Decoration was eliminated from the exterior of the building, although there are contrasting textures of stone and concrete. The house is arranged to allow maximum sunlight inside, with long bands of rectilinear windows that frame the views of the surrounding trees.

Fallingwater shows much influence from Japanese and Chinese architecture, especially in its cantilevered porches, which overhang the waterfall. Interestingly, neither Kaufmann nor the

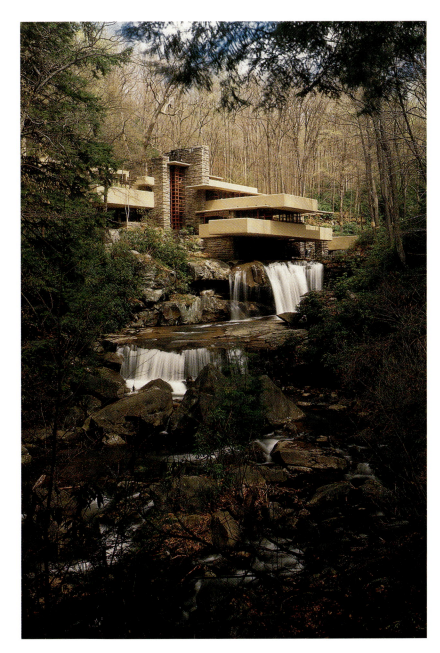

7.34　FRANK LLOYD WRIGHT. *Fallingwater*.
Kaufmann House, Connellsville vicinity,
Pennsylvania, USA, 1936–1938. ESTO
© Scott Frances. For more information, see
the text accompanying Figure 3.15.

engineers responsible for building *Fallingwater* trusted Wright's cantilever design. They had extra reinforcing steel added during construction, and one porch drooped due to the heavier weight. The cantilever was widely used in Chinese and Japanese architecture, where wide roofs and balconies projected over their vertical supports. Also, like much of the traditional domestic architecture of Asia, the walls in *Fallingwater* are not load bearing, but act as privacy screens. A timber framework hidden by the walls holds the weight of *Fallingwater*'s roof. Also from Japan was the idea of a flowing interior space, with few walls and large windows.

CONNECTION

For more on Chinese brackets and cantilevers, turn to Chapter 3, The Language of Architecture, pages 60–61.

CONNECTION

Another Wright building is the Solomon R. Guggenheim Museum, Figure 16.5, page 474.

COMMERCIAL ARCHITECTURE

Commercial architecture provides shelter for the needs of business and trade. Here are a few examples considered to be important milestones in art.

Markets of Trajan (110–112), Figure 7.35, is a large, enclosed, multistoried complex of administrative offices and more than 150 permanent shops. Its design was likely influenced by the enclosed markets of the Middle East called "souks" or "bazars." Each shop or "taberna" consisted of a single, wide doorway with a large window on top that gave access to a wooden storage attic above each shop. The markets' long "great halls" with two levels of "tabernas" on each side make it look like a modern shopping mall. Skylights and large windows illuminated the great halls. The vaulted ceiling met the new fire code that had been put in place after a terrible fire destroyed large sections of Rome in 64. Concrete was increasingly used for large projects because: (1) it was cheap; (2) it was flexible and could be poured into various forms, shaped in any way, and was not limited to straight lines and rectilinear forms as was most wood construction; (3) it was fireproof; and (4) its gray surface could be finished with a thin veneer of brick, marble, stucco, gilding, or mural paintings. Although drab today, the interior was once faced with brick veneer, with wares of all kinds on display, and vendors and shoppers filled the space.

Markets of Trajan was built on a very steep slope. The natural terrain is so steep, in fact, that a paved street winds its way through the market at about mid-level. Yet Roman innovations with concrete construction made the large, multistoried project feasible. Walls are load bearing, yet the Romans used the arch to channel the tremendous weight of the roof to massive piers, allowing large windows to pierce the walls. This was a tremendous accomplishment architecturally. The massive, muscular Roman style of architecture would have been impossible with only wood construction.

CONNECTION

For more on vaulting in general, see the section on "Arches, Vaulting, and Domes" in Chapter 3, page 62.

CONNECTION

Romans were known for their ambitious public buildings, such as the Baths of Caracalla, Figure 16.7, page 475, the Colosseum, Figure 16.28, page 491, and the Pantheon, Figure 9.28, page 246.

In industrialized nations, most people are very familiar with the downtown high-rise office building. The *Carson Pirie Scott* Building, dated 1904 (Figure 7.36), was designed by Louis Sullivan, one of the first truly modern architects who designed

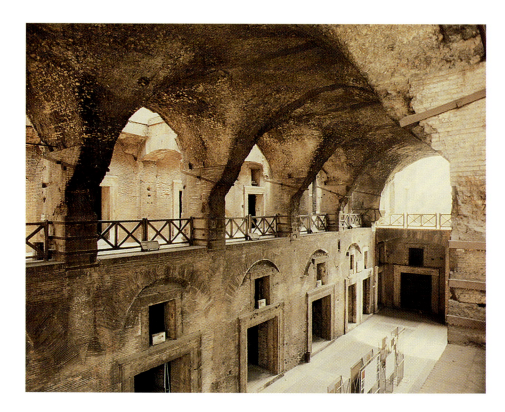

7.35 Interior of *Markets of Trajan*. Rome, CE 100–112. © Scala / Art Resource, NY. See also the text accompanying Figure 3.10.

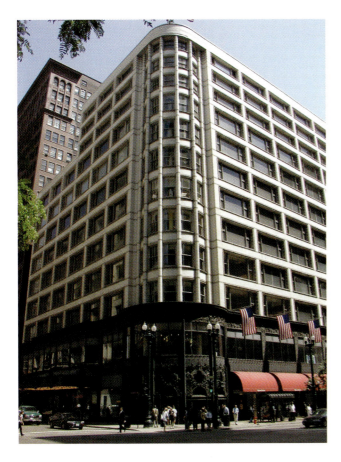

7.36 LOUIS H. SULLIVAN. *Carson Pirie Scott and Company.* Chicago, Illinois, USA, 1904. Photo courtesy of Stephen A. Edwards. See also the text accompanying Figure 3.14.

tall buildings for twentieth-century cities. (Significantly, Frank Lloyd Wright received some of his early training in Sullivan's architectural firm.) Sullivan exploited the new design possibilities of steel frame construction, coupled with the invention of the elevator. Iron and steel had been used to reinforce buildings in the past, especially in the nineteenth century, but those buildings had been sheathed in stone or brick to make them look traditional and solid and heavy. The few open steel constructions of the nineteenth century were novelty structures like the Eiffel Tower. Sullivan believed that "form follows function," meaning that buildings should not be shaped according to preconceived ideas, but, rather, that their shape be an innovative outgrowth of their function and of the materials used.

Sullivan thought of buildings as analogous to the human body, which had a rigid armature (the skeleton) with muscles and skin stretched over it. In architecture, the steel framework supported the building, with non-load-bearing walls like a skin stretched over it. Height became more important than horizontal space. The builders were constrained only by the limits of steel construction and the difficulty of providing services to the top floors.

On the ground floor, Sullivan introduced the large display windows that have become familiar fixtures in almost every retail store in the United States today. Sullivan saw these display windows as "pictures," so he framed them with cast ironwork on the first and second floors like elaborate, ornate, nineteenth-century picture frames, visible at the bottom center in Figure 7.36. Sullivan used motifs based on organic ideas of birth, flowering, decay, and rebirth of life to give expression to the structure of the building. The ornamental designs were cast in parts and installed by unskilled workers (see Figure 3.22).

In contrast, the exterior of the upper floors is relatively plain and simple, with each side of the building a regular grid of horizontal windows. The curved corner of the building provides vertical emphasis, with narrower, taller windows. Vertical space is important, and the roof is deemphasized. There are no overhanging eaves or cornices. Rather, the building has the appearance that several more floors, similar in design, could be added right on top of the existing structure. The large windows made visually evident the steel structure underneath by conforming to its grid. Thus, Sullivan achieved a greater visual unity between the exterior of the building and its internal structure.

CONNECTION
Review the section on "Steel Frame Construction" in Chapter 3, The Language of Architecture, page 67.

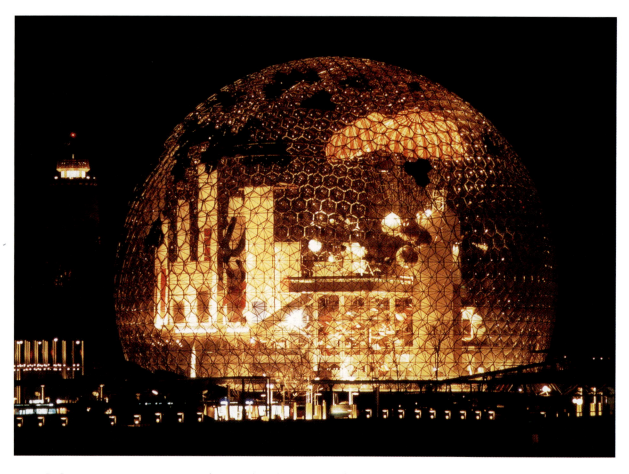

7.37   R. Buckminster Fuller. *U.S. Pavilion.* Geodesic dome, diameter 250'. Expo '67, Montreal, Canada. Comstock. See also the text accompanying Figure 3.19.

LATE-TWENTIETH-CENTURY PUBLIC STRUCTURES

Louis Sullivan had begun to exploit the new design possibilities in steel frame construction, and later-twentieth-century architects pushed the possibilities even farther. R. Buckminster Fuller was an architectural engineer, inventor, designer, and mathematician. He was interested in utopian aspects of design. He believed that by getting the maximum gain for the minimum expenditure of energy, well-guided technology could give everyone more affordable shelter with more conveniences. Fuller is probably best known for his geodesic domes, which were steel frame structures in which a grid of tetrahedrons holds up the entire building. A tetrahedron is a three-sided pyramid sitting on a triangular base. Depending upon the number of modules used, the domes could be relatively low and flat, or tall and nearly spherical, and could be made to any size. (Fuller even proposed a three-mile-wide dome to enclose midtown Manhattan in a climate-controlled environment.) The domes were efficient in a number of ways: (1) the rounded surface enclosed the largest internal volume within the least amount of "wall" surface, thus saving on materials;

(2) the framework was composed of modular, linear elements that were inexpensive and could be erected in a short time; (3) the multiplication of triangular units created a structure that was very strong against both internal and external pressures; and (4) the framework could be covered with a variety of materials, such as glass, plastic, cloth, wood, or paper.

Fuller's design for the *U.S. Pavilion* at Montreal's Expo '67 (Figure 7.37) was built along with Safdie's *Habitat*. The pavilion was a very tall, nearly spherical dome 250 feet in diameter, which created a dramatic silhouette. Lit from the inside at night, it glowed like an otherworldly orb. Because the dome is self-supporting, the space can be configured in any way desired, without supports. The geodesic dome came to be a symbol for twentieth-century innovation and progress, while its emphasis on geometry and its use of the flexible metal framework made it continuous with the innovations of Sullivan's *Carson Pirie Scott* Building. Although geodesic domes have been used in a variety of ways, as factory buildings, greenhouses, mobile living units for the U.S. Army, experimental "biospheres," and research stations, they have yet to become popular for businesses or homes.

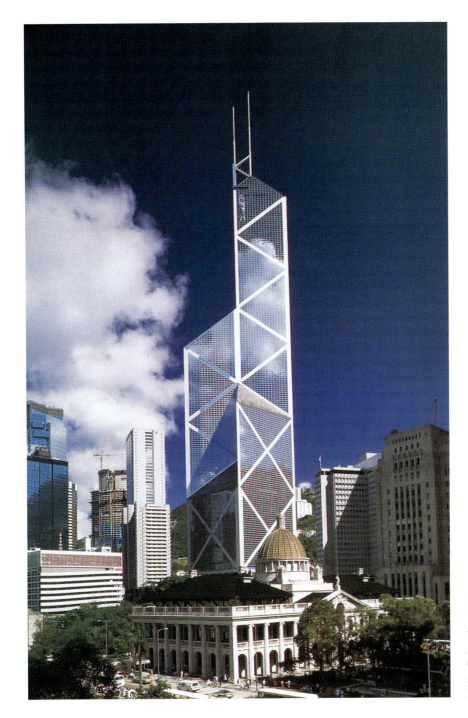

7.38 I. M. PEI AND PARTNERS. *Bank of China.* Hong Kong, 1989. Courtesy, Pei Cobb Freed & Partners. See also the text accompanying Figure 3.18.

The rectangle continued to dominate architectural design for modern office buildings, which were often spare, rectangular shafts of steel and glass that rose from street-level plazas. Ornamentation of any kind was avoided in these late-twentieth-century structures, so large buildings were often a monolithic, geometric shape. This was called the International Style because of its prevalence throughout large cities all over the world. One of the most influential architects of this twentieth-century style, Ludwig Mies van der Rohe, summarized this

aesthetic with the phrase "less is more." The unadorned, simple, geometric style was seen as new, modern, heroic, and even utopian, as architects sought to transform urban centers with functional forms.

However, within a few decades, there arose a resistance to the International Style, which some saw as sterile and oppressive. A variation on the rectangle is evident in the *Bank of China,* dated 1989 (Figure 7.38), by the architectural firm of I. M. Pei and Partners. Many shapes of the *Bank of China*

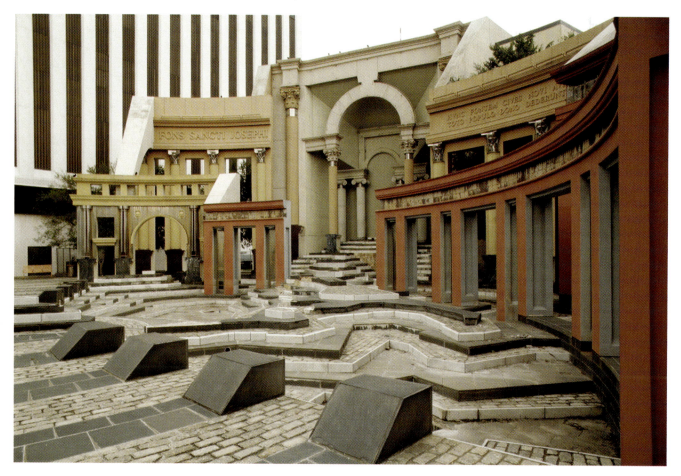

7.39 CHARLES MOORE WITH U.I.G. AND PEREZ ASSOCIATES. *Piazza d'Italia.* New Orleans, USA, 1975–1980. © Robert Holmes / Corbis. See also the text accompanying Figure 3.20.

were based on triangular shafts. In Pei's design, the square base of the building was divided into four equal triangular sections. The skeletal support for the building is innovative, composed of four massive columns at the corners of the square and a fifth, central column that begins on the twenty-fifth floor. The load from the upper floors is transmitted diagonally to the corner supports at the twenty-fifth floor. In Hong Kong, high winds and severe earthquakes are common. To make a more stable building, diagonal braces were added to the skeletal frame. Rather than hide the braces, Pei makes them an important part of the overall triangular and diagonal basis of his design.

The exterior of the *Bank of China* is gray anodized aluminum with reflective glass windows. It has an arched north entrance with a wide plaza, while the other sides feature landscaping. The interior features a vaulted lobby of white and gray granite and marble. The lower floors surround a twelve-story-high central atrium. On the top floors, dining and entertainment establishments boast spectacular views.

Other reactions against the International Style were more radical. The *Piazza d'Italia* (Figure 7.39) in New Orleans was designed by Charles Moore with U.I.G. and Perez Associates.

Moore was distressed by the sameness of modern commercial architecture and believed that cities had lost much of their unique character. He favored maintaining distinctness and the "presence of the past" in any location. The architectural style of *Piazza d'Italia* has come to be called **Postmodern,** emphasizing visual complexity, individuality, and even fun. It is symbolically complicated as well, with references and borrowed elements from a number of sources to enrich the structure. To Postmodern architects, "less is a bore." Postmodern architecture is colorful, engaging, witty, and sometimes playful. Moore looked to Disneyland as a model for modern public spaces. He was also a student of the architect Louis Kahn, who had long been an admirer of Roman architecture, and who had also departed from strict modernism in his buildings.

To design the *Piazza d'Italia*, Moore collaborated with local architects who knew the history of New Orleans and the mixed downtown setting. Because it commemorates the Italian-American community in New Orleans, the Piazza contains borrowed elements from a number of Italian sources, including the color scheme of Pompeii, the arches and columns of

Rome, and the designs of Palladio. Other influences include theaters, fountains, and villas from all over Europe. A map of Sicily sits at the center of the plaza, connected to the larger map of Italy that joins the curved architectural fragments behind it. The curving architecture recalls the apses of the *Markets of Trajan*. Water spurts up and cascades down in many places. The columns copy those of ancient Greece and the Roman Empire, and Latin inscriptions top the architecture. Modern references include the multicolored neon outlining the arches and the stainless-steel capitals on the columns. The many references make the *Piazza d'Italia* like an archeological site, where layer after layer of the past's ruins build up, one atop the other.

CONNECTION

The Classical orders are described in Chapter 3 and illustrated in Figure 3.5, page 59.

More recent still is **Deconstructivist** architecture, which rejects established professional conventions and seeks to shake viewers' expectations. Form no longer needs to follow function, as has been espoused in modern architecture since Sullivan. Rather, buildings can be disorienting and irregular, with disguised spatial relationships. The idea that a building should have a clear, conceptual design, with a front, center, and back, is no longer a given. Classical prototypes have no special merit. Deconstructivist architects derive models and drawings much as a sculptor would—for example, in Iraqi-born, London-based Zaha Hadid's *Concept Design of a Biennale Tower* (2003), Figure 7.40. In this case, gone are the expected vertical walls of structures, replaced with sensuous curves. Many designs for Hadid's buildings have a feeling of anti-gravitational space. She bases her work on the paths made by people and vehicles, and she seeks an architecture of fluidity and movement.

CONNECTION

Another example of Deconstructivist architecture is Frank Gehry's Walt Disney Concert Hall, Figure 16.6, page 475.

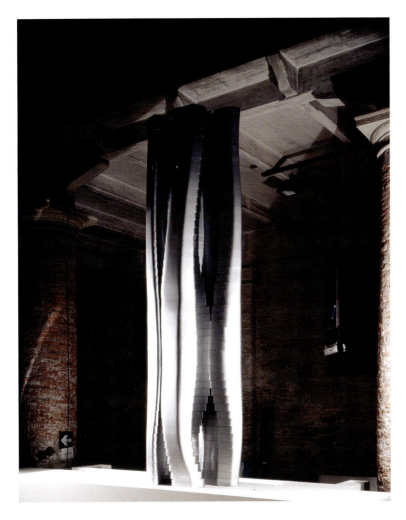

7.40 ZAHA HADID. *Concept Design of a Biennale Tower.* 2003. 200" high. Image source: Architects/Alessi. Courtesy of Zaha Hadid Architects.

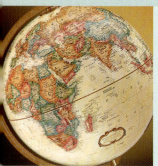

Courtesy of Replogle Globes, Inc., Broadview, IL.

Human life began in Africa, and then spread northward to Europe and Asia. Humans reached the Americas last, by crossing over the land bridge that likely existed long ago between Alaska and northeast Russia.

Our study begins in the Paleolithic era, or Old Stone Age, which began roughly 25,000 BCE. Early people hunted wild animals and gathered berries, seeds, fruits, and plants for food. They lived in small, nomadic bands, moving on to find new food sources as needed. Three major accomplishments distinguished them. First, around 500,000 BCE, people began the controlled, regular use of fire for light, warmth, and cooking. Second, they began making stone tools at least 50,000 years ago, simple at first and then more advanced, and finally made tools from bone. They cleverly crafted axes, spearheads, fishing sinkers, beads, harpoons, and even needles for sewing. This was the beginning of technology. And finally, art making began in the Old Stone Age and became an integral part of human existence.

Ancient paintings in caves and rock shelters exist in southern France, Spain, and Africa, and small sculptures in bone or stone are found much more broadly throughout Europe, Asia, and Africa. These small sculptures were made with primitive tools, but with remarkably lifelike results, whether they represented animals or were fertility figures like the *Venus of Willendorf* in

Below:
Map 1   The Spread of Homo Sapiens Sapiens (or "wise, wise humans").

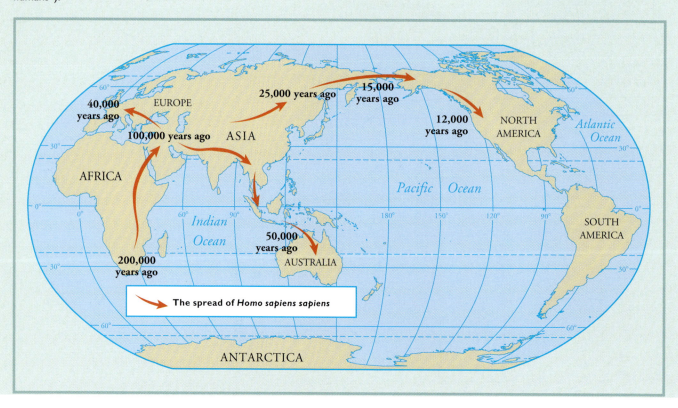

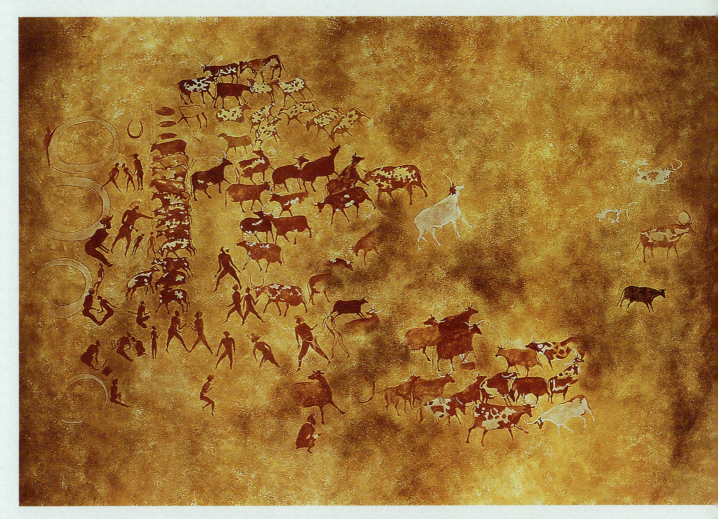

Figure 8.1. Early people found protection in caves and rock shelters, where we find amazing paintings of animals. Later on, people produced the first architecture when they built housing of mammoth bones covered with turf and skins.

Above:
African Rock Painting. Illustrates herding activities in Neolithic Africa. Fresco from Tassili N'Aijer. Henri Lhote Collection, Musee de l'Homme, Paris, France. © Erich Lessing / Art Resource, NY.

Although the Paleolithic Era was long ago, some Stone Age cultures survived into the twentieth century. An example is the Aboriginal people of Australia, hunters and gatherers whose mythology and paintings were intertwined, as in *Witchetty Grub Dreaming* (Figure 7.2).

The Mesolithic Era, or Middle Stone Age, 10,000–7,000 BCE, saw the first experiments in raising crops and animals. Humans continued to live by hunting and gathering, but older practices were intermingled with new. The African Rock Painting on this page shows people in hunting and herding scenes.

There is no clear demarcation to conclude the Old and Middle Stone Ages. The beginning of the Neolithic Period, or New Stone Age, is dated around 8,000 BCE with expanded agricultural production and the beginnings of cities, such as Çatal Hüyük (Figure 7.25).

Event	Date	Artwork
Paleolithic Era	25,000 BCE	*Hall of Bulls, Lascaux*
Mesolithic Era	10,000	
Domestication of Sheep		
Settlements in China and Chile	8,000	
Birth of Agriculture in Mesopotamia and Mexico		
Neolithic Era	7,000	
Settlements in India		
Domestication of Cattle	6,000	*Çatal Hüyük*
Mesopotamia Civilizations		
Unification of Egypt		
Irrigated Farming in Andes	2,000	
Shang Dynasty—China	1,600	
Bronze Vessel Casting, China		
	1,000	*Three-Legged Ting*
Greek Pottery	500	*Women at the Fountain House*
	200	
		House of the Vettii
Arch and Concrete in Roman Architecture	CE 1	*Markets of Trajan*
Moche, Peru	200	*Peanut Necklace* / *Tomb Model of a House*
Middle Ages, Europe	500	
Use of Cantilever in Chinese Architecture	800	
	1000	
Anasazi Culture		*Pueblo Bonito*

Event	Date	Artwork
Spread of Chinese Culture to Japan	1200	Mu-Qi: *Six Persimmons*
	1300	
Aztec Empire		
Renaissance		
Incan Empire	1400	
Ming Dynasty—China		da Vinci: *Last Supper*
Mughal Dynasty—India		*Eating Outdoors, Ramayana* / *Saltcellar* / de Heem: *A Table of Desserts* / *Tea Bowl*, Japan
Colonial Era	1700	
Industrial Revolution	1800	
Rise in Urban Population		
		Pomo: *Basket*
Steel Frame		*Tyi Wara (or Chi Wara) Dance Headdresses*
Architecture	1900	*Toba Batak House* / Sullivan: *Carson, Pirie, Scott Building*
World War II	1939	Wright: *Fallingwater*
	1960	Warhol: *Heinz 57 Tomato Ketchup* / Safdie: *Habitat* / Fuller: *Geodesic Dome, American Pavilion*
Food in Outer Space		Chicago: *The Dinner Party* / Moore: *Piazza d'Italia* / Tjungurrayi: *Witchetty Grub Dreaming* / Coe: *There Is No Escape* / Pei: *Bank of China*
	1990	Antoni: *Gnaw*
World Population 6 Billion	2000	

Many cultures have called upon art and ritual to guarantee the food supply. Some contemporary artists have used art to look critically at procedures in modern food production.

Artists have designed a wide variety of vessels to store and serve food. Often these vessels have decorative surfaces that are very meaningful to the people who use them.

Food has been a source of great pleasure to humans. Artists have made paintings, sculptures, and photographs that glorify food; that celebrate its shape, color, and texture; and that revel in the abundant bounty of the earth. These food-based works also reveal broad social values and religious beliefs.

The way food is eaten is significant. Ritual meals can be religious ceremonies or major social events. Feasts feature elaborate art objects. Paintings show us the manner in which ritual meals may be eaten. Images of informal meals reveal how and when people socialize within a particular culture.

Shelter is essential for human life, but the design of shelter is not always limited to function, as artists and architects often design it to serve a host of religious, social, and aesthetic concerns. Ancient group housing usually joins the internal need for close community with the external need for greater protection in hostile environments. Contemporary structures for group living are built for ecological reasons.

Individual houses come in a wide range of styles, which reflect broad social values, climate constraints, and historical necessity. We took a quick look at commercial architecture and studied briefly the evolution of steel frame construction and the postmodern reaction to modernism.

FOOD FOR THOUGHT

No pun intended!

An extreme attitude toward food was expressed by the Italian **Futurists** of the twentieth century, who believed that humans were machines, and that in a machinelike way, people based their actions on what they ate. Futurists wrote cookbooks designed to shock and excite the senses, but not to fill the stomach, for they believed a full stomach was dulling. In one recipe, "Raw Meat Torn by Trumpet Blasts," the diner is to take mouthfuls of raw electrified beef, and to blow loud blasts on a trumpet in between those mouthfuls of beef.

- What are your experiences of eating?
- What besides hunger is being satisfied?
- What food images have you seen today?

In the United States, housing construction makes heavy use of wood in almost all regions, for framing and for finishing. Yet hardwood forests are seriously depleted, and wood produced by tree farms is spongy and prone to warping. Some ecologists are raising alarms about deforestation. A few architects are considering building houses of rammed earth, pumice, or straw bales. Recycled steel studs, made from steel beams of demolished buildings, have been used in commercial buildings and are beginning to be used in residences. Such steel is stronger than wood and is resistant to earthquakes and termites.

What are your ideas about the following questions?

- Should architects emphasize creativity as much as artists in considering alternative building designs and materials?
- Should urban planners and architects have utopian concerns as the basis of their work?
- Should ecological concerns be on the mind of the artist/architect? Any other issues?
- What kinds of grassroots support are needed for new ideas in architecture and urban planning to be successful?

YOUR CD-ROM RESOURCES

- World History in Context
- Exploring Art Timeline
- Flashcards
- Food for Thought
- Companion Site
    Chapter 7 Quiz
    InfoTrac® College Edition Readings
    Artist Flashcards
    Online Study Guide

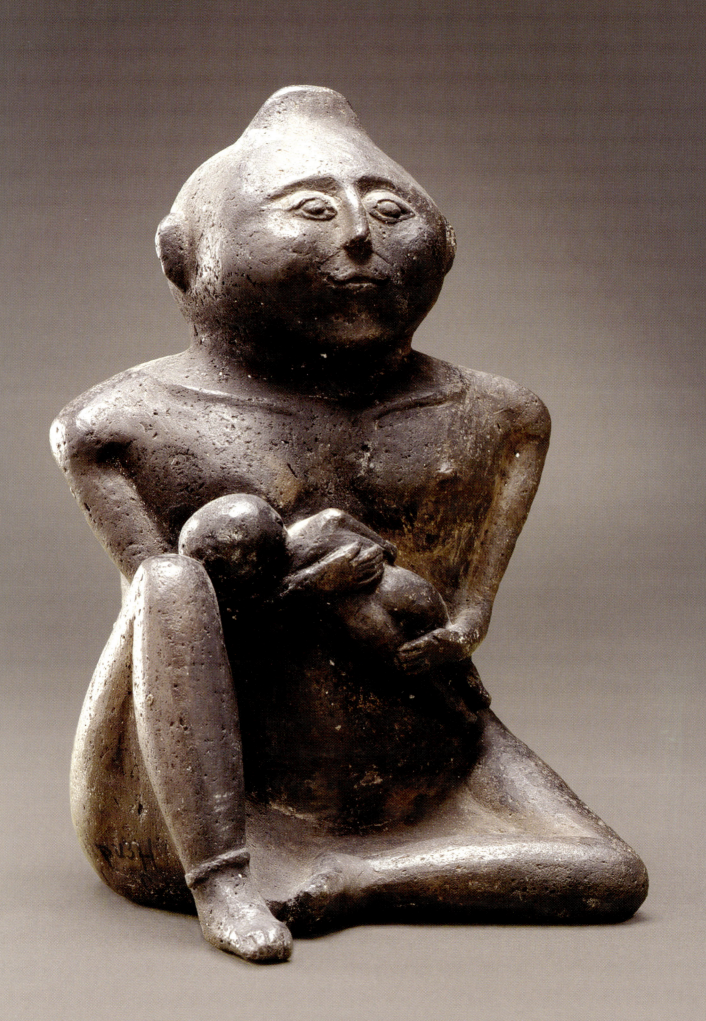

REPRODUCTION AND SEXUALITY

INTRODUCTION

Through the ages, artists have created artworks that have aided, symbolized, and depicted human fertility. The art includes small, charmlike figurines, sexually explicit sculptures, phallic symbols, fetishes, erotic prints, and photographs. Other artworks deal with pregnancy, birth, and the newborn. In this chapter, we also will look at sexuality and gender-related issues. Personal attributes of sexuality not only are private issues, but also are matters of intense social concern. Although sexuality may be genetically coded, our *attitudes* about sexuality are not; rather, they are constructed within a society and change at different times. For example, in ancient Greece, it was considered normal for men to have both male and female sexual partners, but homosexuality and bisexuality are taboo to many people in the world today.

Some art works in this chapter reinforce existing attitudes and ideas, while others use images to subvert them. In any case, the works are highly charged, powerful images that create or perpetuate ideas about reproduction, fertility, beauty, personal worth, and sexual desirability. Major topics are outlined in the following questions:

How are art, magic, and ritual intertwined to promote human fertility?

What art was made to ensure human fertility?

What primordial couples exist in various cultures?

How do primordial couples relate to images of human couples in marriage?

Why has art documented lovemaking for the sake of procreation?

How has art depicted pregnancy and offspring?

How does art show sexuality as a libidinal drive? How does it show it as social choreography with predetermined roles?

Mother and Nursing Child. Detail of Figure 8.32 St. Louis Science Center. Photo © 1985 Dirk Bakker, Detroit Institute of Arts.

THE PROMISE OF FERTILITY

As we have seen in the previous chapter, some art images and objects were created and used for the purpose of securing food. Cave paintings, elaborate masks, wood carvings, and ceramic sculptures helped the hunter-gatherer and farmer to ensure an abundant food supply. Likewise, art and art objects have functioned similarly to ensure human reproduction, again with "sympathetic magic" invoked through art objects.

FERTILITY GODDESSES AND GODS

Some of the earliest artifacts thought to relate to human fertility come from the Paleolithic and Neolithic periods of history. Some were small sculptures of female figures, depicted as abundantly fleshy and swollen, with their bellies, breasts, and thighs accentuated. They are called Fertility or Mother Goddesses, suggesting that they were part of a fertility ritual and cult.

The *Venus of Willendorf* (Figure 8.1) is a well-rounded, abstracted female figure, only four inches high, carved from a found, egg-shaped piece of limestone. The ancient artist-carver may have believed that the power of fertility was already contained in the natural egg-shape of the stone even before it was carved. Its shape, along with the natural indentation that became the navel, may have been the reason the artist chose it. The figure was discovered near a hearth at an excavation site near the town of Willendorf, Austria, in 1908. The small, Paleolithic sculpture was considered part of the Gravettian culture dating approximately between 30,000 and 18,000 BCE. The name "Venus" was given arbitrarily to the female figurines by the archaeologists who found them.

Although sometimes labeled as a "fertility goddess," the figurine was likely more a charm or a fetish, used to invoke the magic of the art object and the stone itself. The bulbous forms were carved and painted, giving repetition and pattern to the piece, emphasizing femininity in the swelling forms. Even the head, perhaps covered with curls of hair or a headpiece of some sort, repeats the bulging, round bumps. Could this featureless head symbolize a budding bloom about to burst into flower? Clearly, the figure does not realistically represent someone, but rather represents the physical essence of fertility. She is small enough to hold in the palm of your hand, yet appears to be large, strong, and robust. With her hands resting on her breasts, she suggests stability in addition to the power of fertility. People may have held the figurine for her power during childbirth or to ward off death or wish for good health. Whatever her function, she was likely a talisman for good fortune.

Thousands of years later, we see in the Cycladic Islands off mainland Greece a probable descendant of the mother goddesses. Figure 8.2 is called the *Idol from Amorgos,* from 2500–2300 BCE, and is thirty inches high. Other figures like this range from a few inches to life-size and were found buried

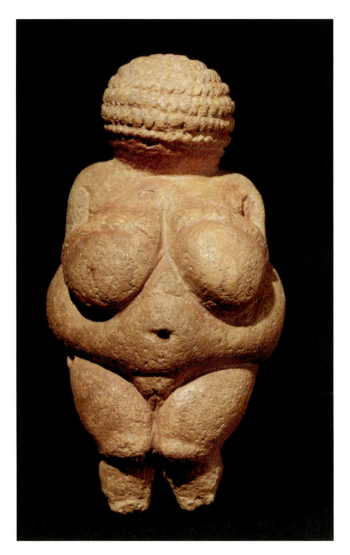

 8.1 *Venus of Willendorf.* Stone, 4³/₈" high. Austria, c. 25,000–20,000 BCE. © Ali Meyer/Corbis. See also the text accompanying Figure 2.33 for a discussion of the formal qualities of this work.

with the dead. The marble was carved with obsidian blades and polished with emery. Traces of paint were found on some figures, indicating that the eyes and jewelry (necklaces and bracelets) were accentuated in color. With her oval or egg-shaped head tilted back and her toes pointed, the *Idol of Amorgos* is thought to be a reclining figure. Slender and delicate, this abstract nude seems to emphasize feminine youth, in contrast to *Venus* and the *Female Fertility Figure* on page 219. Because these figures were found in burials, their purpose may have been to give new life to the dead, just as the young woman has the potential to give life. Sculpted very economically, the overall shapes are angular and wedge-shaped. However, the breasts, belly, and navel are subtly swelling on an otherwise stiff, plank-like body (these figures are sometimes called "plank idols"). Incised lines indicate the neck fold, arms, pubic area, legs, and toes, and connect the geometric and organic forms.

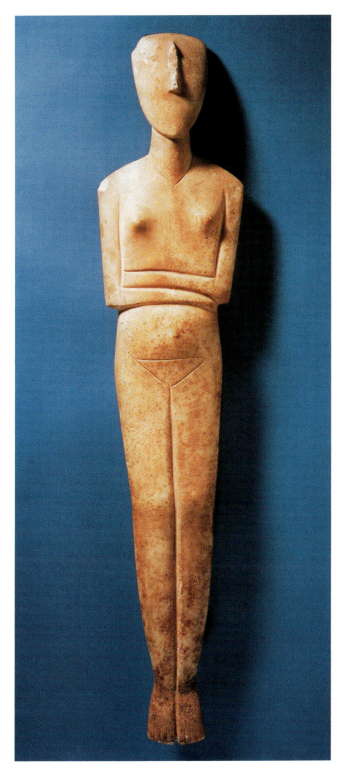

8.2   *Idol from Amorgos.* Marble, 30" high. Cycladic Islands off mainland Greece, 2500–2300 BCE. The Ashmolean Museum, Oxford.

Much later, in the nineteenth century, male fertility pieces were produced by Oceanic cultures. Figure 8.3 shows the *God Te Rongo and His Three Sons* from Rarotonga, part of the Cook Islands in Polynesia. Carved of wood and standing over

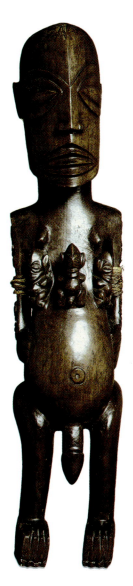

8.3   *God Te Rongo and His Three Sons.* Wood, 27³/₈" high. Cook Islands, Polynesia, c. 1800–1900s. The British Museum, London. See also the text accompanying Figure 5.19 for more on this art and on the role of the artist as priest.

twenty-seven inches high, he is balancing three small, human figures on his belly. Four more figures, in the same style but in low relief, are carved on the arm and forearm. The figure is endowed with a large penis in comparison to the rest of the figure, visually giving emphasis to the virility of *Te Rongo.* The exact character of this god is not known, as the European missionaries who collected such artworks were not interested in preserving the indigenous religion.

As we take a closer look at *Te Rongo,* we can see the precise, contained style of sculpture that is typical of works carved from a single block of wood. Careful planning was required to keep the proportion of the head equal to one-fourth of the body height. In addition, incorporating the small figures must have been challenging to the artist. The chest, a bit sunken in order to make room for the smaller figures, exaggerates the belly and penis, again suggesting reproduction. The oval shape of the head and the delineation of the facial features are repeated in the smaller figures, which clearly seem like infant images of the large figure. The surface of the wood is smooth and polished, keeping focus on the subject of the piece and less on its texture.

Male sculptures and art pieces such as *Te Rongo* were carved for religious rituals by specialists called *Ta'unga,* which is also the word for "priest." The specialist was trained through a long apprenticeship during which he acquired the skill to control and attain the *mana* (power) in the materials and tools he used. In some cultures, the art object was created for one ceremony and then discarded, whereas in others, the object was meant to endure and be passed down from one generation to the next. The more the object was used in religious ceremony, the more mana it gained. With this power, these art objects became symbols of prestige and rank, and with them, their owners displayed their place in the hierarchical order of the gods, priests, monarchs, chiefs, and people. Taboos were connected with these pieces in order to protect their status, restricting their use to those of power and rank. When passed down through many generations, the artifacts became more imbued with mana, due to their age and historical significance. They also became objects of sacred information, such as the family lineage.

Some sculptures were figures representing an ancestor. Eventually, through generations of veneration, the ancestor, who was first of a lineage, would become deified or elevated to the realm of the gods. This may have happened with *Figure of a Deity: A'a Rurutu* (Figure 8.4) from the Austral Islands in central Polynesia. These specific ancestor deities were known as *Tangaroa* figures and represented a creator in the act of creating human beings. Family lineage was critically important in Oceanic cultures, and thus this godlike creator may well have been connected to a family ancestor. The figure is forty-four

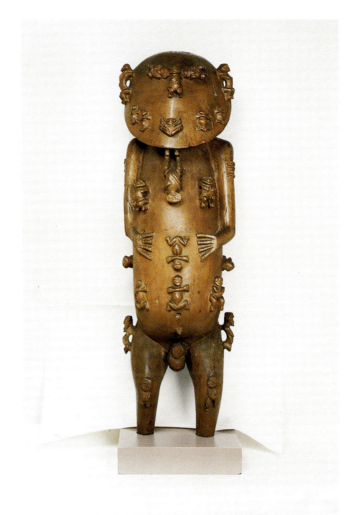

 8.4 *Figure of a Deity: A'a Rurutu.* Wood, 44" high. Austral Islands, collected in 1820. The British Museum, London. This work is also discussed in the context of art collecting in times of national or religious conflict in Chapter 6, Figure 6.24.

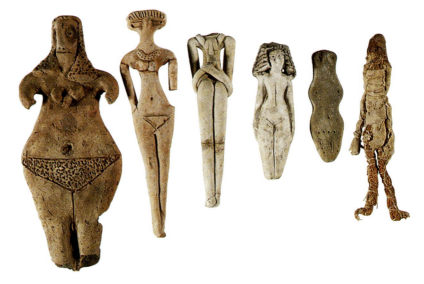

8.5 *Fertility Statuettes.* Clay, faience (earthenware covered with opaque colored glazes), linen, and reed, 6–8" high. Egypt, Middle Kingdom, 2000–1500 BCE. Photo Petri Collection, University College, London.

inches high and is carved from one block of wood. Like *Te Rongo,* this deity sculpture is rendered in a contained style, compact and stiff. However, his body is covered with crawling, infantlike figures. Even the facial features seem to be made up of the clinging little bodies. The back of the figure is hollowed out and contains additional small figures. We might be looking at the mythical creation of humankind in this figure, or the creation of a specific ancestral line.

CONNECTION
Goddesses dominated ancient rituals for thousands of years before gods came to prominence. For more on deities, read Chapter 9.

CONNECTION
The Harp Player is a male version of the early Cycladic figures. Turn to page 485 and Figure 16.21 to read more about it.

CONNECTION
Ancestry is also important among the Maori of New Zealand, another Oceanic people. Read the discussion of the Maori meeting house associated with Figure 11.14, page 313.

FERTILITY FIGURES

The next few examples are considered to be "fertility figures," probably created to aid human reproduction through the magic and power they contained. Figure 8.5 shows *Fertility Statuettes* from the Middle to New Kingdoms in Egypt, dated about 2000–1500 BCE and ranging from six to eight inches tall. The materials vary from clay and "faience" (earthenware covered with opaque colored glazes) to linen and reed, as seen in the doll-like figure on the right. These figures were found in shrines of Hathor, the Goddess of Fertility. Some of the figures have their genitals emphasized with simple incising in the clay. One is wearing the "Isis Knot" on her back and is holding a baby. The Isis Knot was an amulet worn to ensure fertility and long life. As with all cultures, the need for successful human reproduction was important to the Egyptians in order to carry on the family line and to contribute to the labor force. As is common today, it was traditional to give a son his grandfather's name. With the prayer of these fertility statuettes placed before Hathor, women hoped for many sons.

The next small sculpture is a Native American *Potawatomi Male Figure* (love doll) from Wisconsin, dated 1800–1860, and is nine inches in height (Figure 8.6). It is carved in wood and partly adorned in wool fabric. These figure-like carvings (note

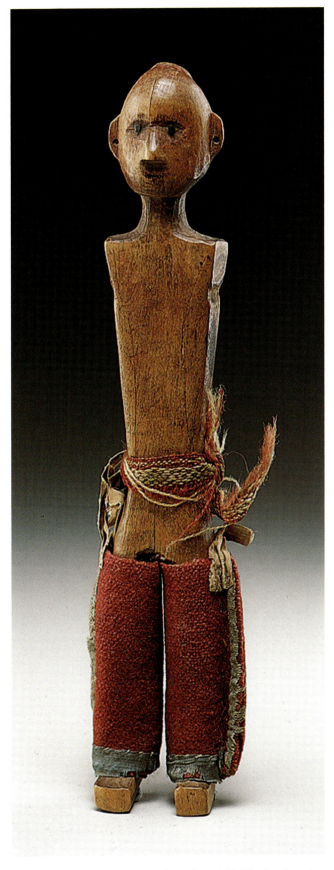

 8.6 *Potawatomi Male Figure* (love doll). Wood and wool fabric, 9" high. Crandon, Wisconsin, 1800–1860. Photo © The Detroit Institute of Arts. Cranbrook Institute of Science.

the lack of arms) were used as "medicine" to control human behaviors and health. This type of figure could be used as a love charm to cast a spell on someone whose attentions were desired. The spell could be dangerous, as those under the magic of this charm found themselves powerless and would be helpless against its strength. Ethnologist Alanson Skinner stated: "It is often that the captor tires of his or her conquest, and leaves the victim, who is still under the spell of such a charm. Such a person will become frantic, and even go crazy, following the user of the charm everywhere" (Skinner 1923: 207). To have successful "medicine," the owners of the love dolls would have to be spiritually prepared and, through dreams or visions, be given special powers by the spirits.

From the Bamana culture of Mali, Africa, the *Female Figure,* Figure 8.7, is made of wood and brass and stands twenty-one inches high. Such figures were associated with a female fertility cult and were stored in special houses created for them. On occasion, such figures were brought out for public display or for elaborate rituals to aid women having difficulties in conceiving and childbearing. This figure has sharp, angular planes and geometric forms. The head is also defined in angles, with the nose dominating the front of the face. The hair is arranged in an elegant, abstract coiffure. The shoulders and chest are fairly squared until the protrusion of the conical breasts. The elongated, erect torso has a slight swell at the navel down to where the abdomen connects to the short, bent legs. The entire figure is incised with geometric lines, some perhaps indicating body scarification. Interesting buttonlike forms vertically line her chest, ending below her breasts, again suggesting body ornamentation. Attention has been paid to the rich, shiny patina that causes finer details to show up well on the surface. The geometric forms are connected by lines, resulting in an aesthetically rich blend of the two- and three-dimensional elements in the piece.

RITUALS

Most of the fertility figures we have seen were likely used in connection with now-lost rituals. One ancient ritual has been preserved in a group of wall paintings found in the *Villa of Mysteries* (Figures 8.8 and 8.9), in Pompeii, Italy, from the middle of the first century. Pompeii was buried in volcanic ash when Mt. Vesuvius violently erupted in CE 79, which preserved the city and these mystical images for modern inquiry and appreciation. This cycle of paintings, which wrap around the four walls of a room, depict a solemn ritual of the mystery cult of Dionysos that may have been associated with sexual intercourse and fertility. The exact meaning of these paintings is not known and is disputed among scholars. However, in the pictorial succession of events, we see a young female novice being prepared to join with Dionysos, the god of wine and fertility. The novice apparently is taking the role of Ariadne, his mythological mate, who is shown along with Dionysos and

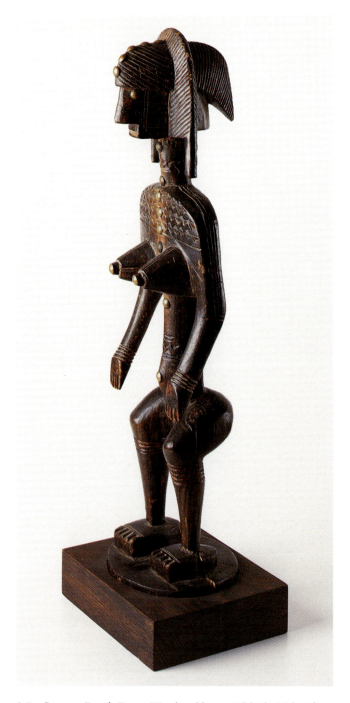

8.7 *Bamana Female Figure.* Wood and brass, 21" high. Mali, Africa, 1947. Photo courtesy Galerie Carrefore, Paris. See also the text accompanying Figure 5.2.

their accompanying entourage of mythological beings. Dionysos and the others appear to be witnessing the initiation. There is also an older woman who offers comfort to the frightened initiate, while nudes are dancing to the music played on a lute-like instrument. A priestess is ready to uncover and reveal the cult's draped sacred objects, which likely held the secrets of the mysteries of Dionysos and perhaps a concealed phallus. The event also includes a winged figure who is whipping the young initiate.

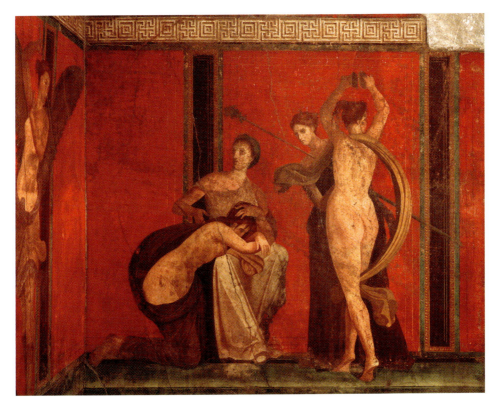

8.8 *Initiation Rites of Dionysos.* Fresco. Villa of Mysteries, Pompeii, Italy, c. CE 50. © Scala / Art Resource, NY.

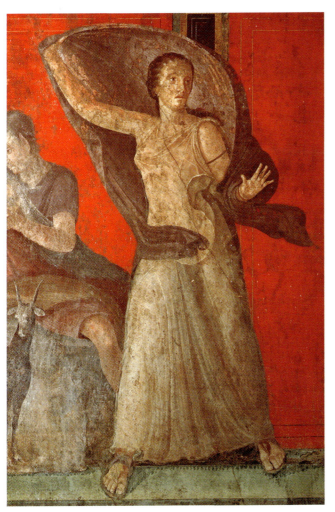

The rite takes place in an illusionist frieze, with the figures striking classic Greek poses against deep, rich, "Pompeian Red" panels. The paintings depict a shallow space, with evenly spaced columns that subdivide the running narrative into scenes. The nearly life-size figures, with convincing volume and anatomy, move and turn in that shallow space, which is a trompe l'oeil ledge. The frescoes in the Villa of Mysteries are excellent examples of Roman painting at that time. The artist paid special attention to the preparation of the walls. In many houses in Pompeii, the plaster used to cover the walls was mixed with marble dust. This was applied in several layers and then beaten with a smooth trowel, followed by polishing to a marble-like finish. The process contributed to the rich colors of the frescoes.

It is significant that this series of paintings was located in a villa, or private home, in the country. The rituals reference sex and fertility, which are often home-based. In addition, the cult of Dionysos was one of various cult religions that were practiced in Rome and were generally tolerated and even welcomed as long as they were confined to the home and did not upset the social and political order. In the case of the cult of Dionysos, the adherents were all women, who were housebound.

8.9 Detail of a figure in the fresco of the Villa of Mysteries. She is likely an initiate or a priestess taking part in the ritual. Pompeii, Italy, c. CE 50. © Scala / Art Resource, NY.

In contemporary Africa, there are sets of rituals and art dealing with fertility. The twentieth-century *Akua'mma* (Figure 8.10) from the Ashanti (Asante) culture in Ghana are fertility sculptures created solely for a ritual for women who are having difficulty in conceiving, and also to ensure a healthy and beautiful baby. *Akua* is the name of the first woman who used this ritual doll successfully and was able to conceive a baby. Consequently, *ba* (child) was added to the name *Akua;* hence, the dolls were called "Akua's child." *Akua'mma* is the plural form of the term. *Akua'mma* average about twelve to thirteen inches in height and are carved in wood.

To begin this ritual, a woman would consult a priest, who would advise her to have a doll carved. She would then adorn the doll in beads and care for it as an actual baby, carrying it wrapped on her back as mothers traditionally carry their babies. She would take care not to gaze upon any deformity in a human or *Akua'ba* doll, so her baby would not be born with these traits. Instead, she was to gaze upon the well-carved *Akua'ba* that expressed the Ashanti ideal of beauty. If the ritual was successful, the woman might place the doll in a shrine in order to recognize the power of the priest she confided in, or she might give it to her child for a toy.

In these figures, we see the interpretation of beauty reduced to uncomplicated forms. The *Akua'mma* head, neck, arms, and

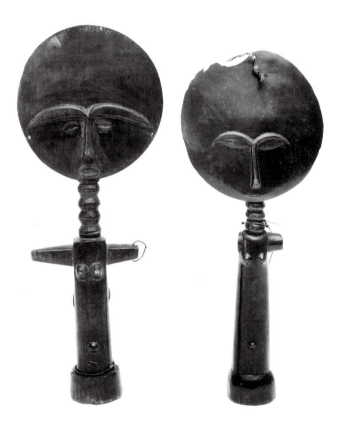

8.10 *Ashanti Akua'mma Dolls.* Wood, 13" high. Ghana, Africa, c. twentieth century. The British Museum, London. For more on the many uses of this sculpture, see the text accompanying Figure 1.1.

torso are rendered in a circular disk and a series of cylinders. The figures are always female. The canon of beauty is suggested as a round face with a small mouth, a high forehead, and a long neck and torso. The linear facial features are cleanly carved in the lower half of the smooth facial disk, which is supported by a stack of disklike forms that suggest necklaces. The breasts and navel are minimal forms, but clearly express the female gender.

ART DEPICTING PRIMORDIAL AND HUMAN COUPLES

Human couples have been depicted throughout the ages, some as primordial or first couple, the mother and father of humankind, and others as human couples representing the marriage ritual and its implications within cultural contexts. These depictions were rooted in creation myths of many religions. They also come from marriage rituals that frame procreation in many cultures.

Figure 8.11, from the Dogon culture of Africa, represents the *Primordial Couple* seated on an *imago mundi* (image of the world) stool supported by four figures. It is carved in wood and stands twenty-nine inches high. Art historians categorize its style as being part of the Sudanese Group, characterized by the use of simple tools and the lack of nonferrous metals. Like the Oceanic figures, the sculptures are usually carved from one block of wood using the subtractive method. Sometimes, naturally occurring features in the wood block, such as a bend or a knot in the wood, are incorporated into the finished sculpture.

Seated in a frontal position, the *Primordial Couple* is stately and formal. They relate the harmony of the union of the first male and female, both of whom are equally exalted in the sculpture. The union also appears to represent their fertility as well as their roles in life. The male unites the figures with his arm embracing the female at her neck and his hand resting on the upper part of her breast. His other hand is resting on his penis, symbolizing their sexual union. They wear jewelry that symbolizes their sexual power. On their backs are carved representations of the roles they have in life. As hunter, warrior, and protector, he wears a quiver, while she has a child clinging to her.

Other details in the sculpture suggest their high position and perhaps their origin. She wears a mouth ornament called a "labret," and he wears a chin beard trimmed very much like the beards worn by Egyptian pharaohs. Their headgear is similar to that worn by the people of the Peul culture, who were enemies of the Dogon. The fact that the couple is displaying this headgear could mean their domination over the Peul or their occupation by them. It could also suggest their union with the Peul, accounting for part of their heritage. The stool on which the couple is seated is supported by four figures.

The piece is vertically emphasized by the two elongated figures and their proportions and by the negative space we see

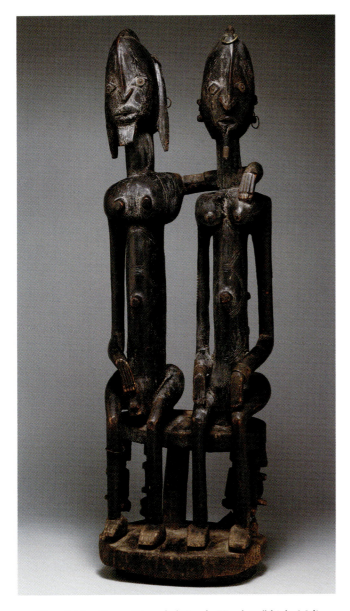

 8.11   *Dogon Primordial Couple.* Wood, 29" high. Mali, Africa, c. nineteenth–twentieth century. Metropolitan Museum of Art, New York, Gift of Lester Wunderman, 1977. (1977.394.15) Photograph © 1993 The Metropolitan Museum of Art. See also the text accompanying Figure 2.30 for more on the formal qualities of this piece.

throughout the figures. Visually there is a balance between the positive mass and the negative space in the sculpture. For the Dogon, a balanced design is a symbol for an ordered human culture (Roy 1985: 31).

Another primordial couple is Adam and Eve, found in the Jewish, Christian, and Muslim religions and depicted widely in European art. In the Bible, Genesis 1:28, their creator commanded them to "be fruitful and multiply, fill the earth and conquer it." Later in Genesis, the Fall is described, and Adam and Eve are exiled from the Garden of Eden. It is this point in the story that a young Italian Early Renaissance

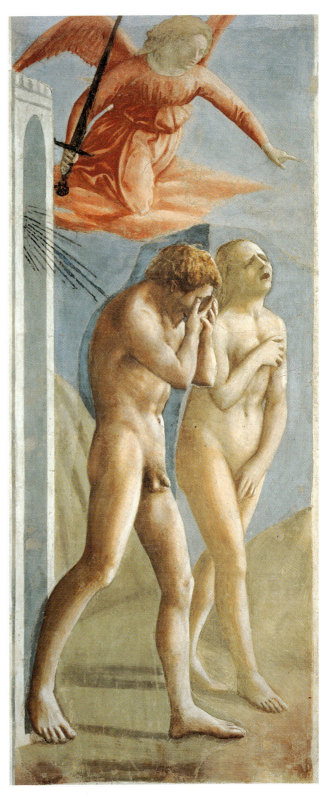

8.12   MASACCIO. *The Expulsion from Paradise.* Fresco. Brancacci Chapel, Santa Maria del Carmine, Florence, Italy, 1427. Canali Photobank.

artist named Masaccio painted in *The Expulsion from Paradise* (Figure 8.12) on the wall of the Brancacci Chapel in the Church of Santa Maria del Carmine, in Florence, Italy, in 1427.

Masaccio has captured Adam and Eve's anguish in *The Expulsion.* One can almost hear Eve's cry and feel Adam's pain as they shamefully walk from the gate. Their movement is slow, every step more agonizing than the one before. Now God's commandment to "fill the earth" has become a painful burden. The artist paid particular attention to modeling the figures, using soft contrasts of values and color. Only essential details are included with Adam and Eve, specifically the gate to the Garden of Paradise and the angel with a sword barring their return.

In a Mesoamerican chronicle, the *Codex Mendoza,* we see a pictorial documentation of a wedding of a human couple. Figure 8.13, *Aztec Marriage Couple,* depicts a man and woman seated on a mat, literally tying the knot. Aztec marriage ceremonies took place in the groom's home in front of the hearth. The codex tells us that this man is about twenty years of age, while the woman is fourteen or fifteen. The groom's parents selected a bride, aided by a matchmaker and a soothsayer who studied the couple's birth signs in order to ensure their compatibility. The bride's family also investigated the groom to be assured of his good manners. The bride's parents gave the wedding banquet, which began at noon. The bride was powdered with yellow earth and adorned in red feathers. When darkness arrived, the bride was carried on the matchmaker's back to the groom's home, where the formal vows were performed by tying together their wedding garments, as seen in the illustration. Afterward, the bride and groom prayed for four days, then were blessed by a priest and permitted to con-

summate their marriage. The man could marry additional wives (Townsend 1992: 188).

The *Aztec Marriage Couple* has outlined flat shapes, with color used decoratively. Clothing is depicted with simple flowing lines, which contrast with the angular pattern of the woven mat that surrounds the couple. The drawing of their hair provides more pattern in the image. The Aztec religion acknowledged a primordial couple, and this human couple in our image is depicted in a similar way.

The *Wedding Portrait,* or *Giovanni Arnolfini and His Bride,* from 1431 (Figure 8.14), by Flemish artist Jan van Eyck, shows Giovanni Arnolfini, an Italian businessman living in the Flemish city of Bruges, and his betrothed. More than just a double portrait, this is a wedding certificate, with both obvious and hidden symbolism. The couple is shown in their bedroom chamber rather than in church. They are joining in marriage in the place where it will be consummated, suggesting the hope for many children. Indeed, the woman holds her clothing in a way that indicates she is already very pregnant. Less obvious symbols also fill the bedroom. In the chandelier, there is one candle burning although it is daytime, representing divine presence. The couple has removed their shoes, showing they are on holy ground. In the frame of the mirror appear medallions that depict the passion of Christ. On the chest and windowsill are oranges, the golden apples of the Hesperides, representing the conquest of death. There is a dog at the feet of the couple, symbolizing fidelity. Arnolfini himself raises his hand in a gesture of blessing. The prayer for fer-

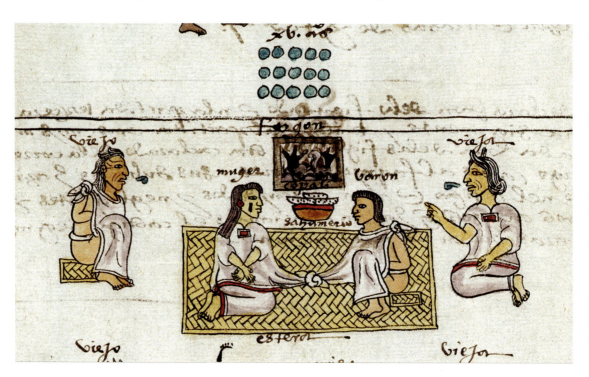

 8.13 *Aztec Marriage Couple.* From the *Codex Mendoza.* Mexico, 1434. Bodleian Library, University of Oxford, photo Peter Furst.

tility is also seen as the bed drapes are opened, and on the bedpost finial is a statuette of St. Margaret, the patron saint of childbirth. A whisk broom is also hanging on the post, suggesting setting up a household. To complete this document, van Eyck includes official witnesses, including himself. In this one-point perspective rendering, the vanishing point is located above the mirror where we see written in script, "Johannes de eyck fuit hic," which translates to "Jan van Eyck was here." And in the mirror, two figures appear, most likely the artist with a companion. Van Eyck was a pioneer in oil painting, and this work is approximately contemporaneous with Masaccio's *Expulsion.*

CONNECTION

Menkaure and His Wife, Queen Khamerernebty, *Figure 11.1, page 302, are a couple from the Egyptian culture.*

CONNECTION

Birth and death are frequently linked in art, as we will see in other examples in this chapter. Turn to Chapter 10 to see examples of funerary art that deals with the idea of rebirth, or life after death.

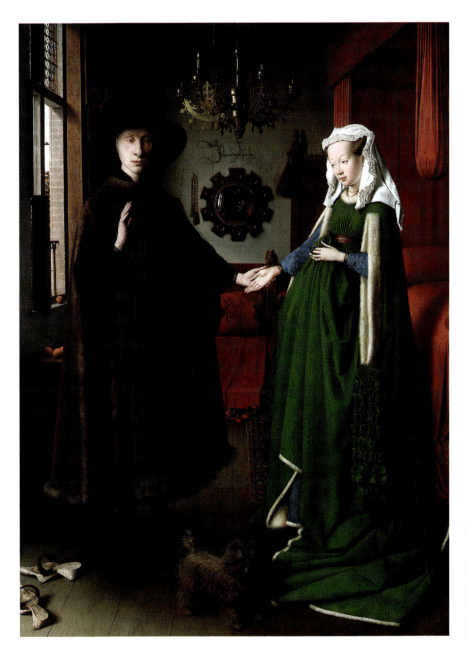

8.14   JAN VAN EYCK. *Wedding Portrait.* Oil on wood panel, 32" × 25". Flanders, Northern Europe, 1434. © National Gallery Collection; By kind permission of the Trustees of the National Gallery, London / Corbis.

(Figure 8.32) from the Mississippian Period (1200–1400), in an agricultural civilization located near the confluence of the Mississippi and Illinois rivers around Cahokia, Illinois. The Mississippians built large, truncated pyramid mounds topped with temples. Their religion strove to predict and control nature, with much attention paid to death. The *Mother and Nursing Child* was buried in a tomb that likely belonged to a high-ranking person. Tombs contained a quantity of elaborate naturalistic and fanciful funeral pottery, mostly effigies, that captured the spirit of the dead it honored. The *Mother and Nursing Child* expresses a graceful and serene image of a woman and her baby. A simple rendering, there is emphasis in the detail of the mother's face and in the nursing babe. Triangular shapes appear in the rest of the pose, as the mother's broad shoulders suggest an inverted triangle, and her folded legs suggest two other triangles. The simple, geometric form adds to the stability and calm of the figure. Representing a mother and her progeny in life, the effigy vessel may have insured her potential to bear children in the afterlife.

The mother and child is a familiar Christian icon, personified as Mary and Jesus. We will look at an example by the northern Renaissance Flemish painter Rogier van der Weyden. A student of Jan van Eyck (see Figure 8.14), Rogier became the influential master painter of Brussels in 1436, and his work was often copied in the fifteenth century. Although he

signed none of his work, his style is distinctive, with linear forms and brilliant color. *Virgin and Child in a Niche* was painted in 1432–1433 and is only 7¼ inches by 4¾ inches (Figure 8.33). Despite her size, Mary is enthroned in a delicately carved architectural space, crowned as the Queen of Heaven. Yet she nurses the newborn redeemer, holding him tenderly. Rogier's subject matter was Christian, with many paintings of the Virgin Mary. The Christian primordial couple, Adam and Eve (see Figure 8.12), appear here as carvings on the niche. Adam, who has covered himself in shame, is about to be pushed off his pedestal by a hovering angel, expelling him from paradise. Eve holds the apple under the Tree of Knowledge, while the serpent looks down from the branches. In the center above, God the Father and a dove observe the scene, completing the Trinity. The gentle and loving gaze of Mary upon her baby is calm, yet ominous in its understanding of the fulfillment of Old Testament prophecies.

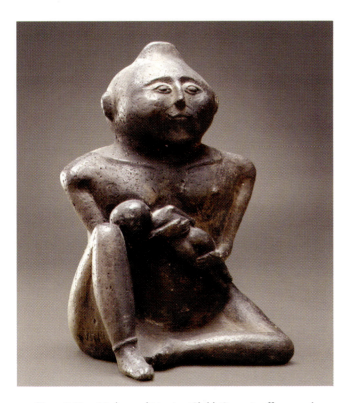

 8.32 *Mother and Nursing Child.* Ceramic effigy vessel, Mississippian Period. Cahokia, Illinois, USA, 1200–1400. St. Louis Science Center. / Photo © 1985 Dirk Bakker, Detroit Institute of Arts.

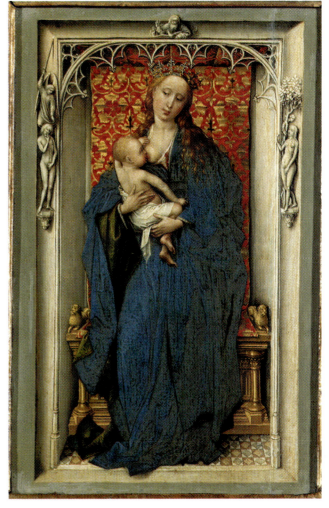

 8.33 ROGIER VAN DER WEYDEN. *Virgin and Child in a Niche.* Oil on panel, 7¼" × 4¾". Flanders, Northern Europe, c. 1432–1433. Kunsthistorisches Museum, Vienna. © Erich Lessing / Art Resource, NY.

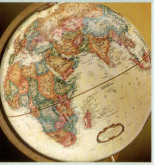

Courtesy of Replogle Globes, Inc., Broadview, IL.

During the New Stone Age, which ended around 4000 BCE, groups of people around the world began to depend increasingly on agriculture for their food in addition to hunting. They began making stone tools and continued domesticating animals. The city of Çatal Hüyük (8000–4000 BCE), located in present-day Turkey, was an early farming and trading settlement with several thousand people. They were among the first to produce pottery and make metal and obsidian objects. They connected their houses for greater protection and built many shrines (see Figure 7.25). Fertility was an important concern, and the *Female Fertility Figure* (see History Box illustration), found in a Çatal Hüyük grain bin, shows a large, powerful, enthroned woman with attending lions.

Throughout this period through about 2000 BCE, we see the emergence of civilizations around the world. The following factors influenced the growth of civilizations:

- Major rivers or bodies of water were necessary for the emergence of civilizations.

- Farming produced surplus food, which allowed for the development of cities and the division of labor within urban areas.

- Cities became political, economic, social, cultural, and religious centers.

- Trade became important among groups of people and between urban centers.

- Formal religions developed, often with many gods and with rulers as stewards of those gods.

Below:
Map 1.2   The Development of Agriculture.

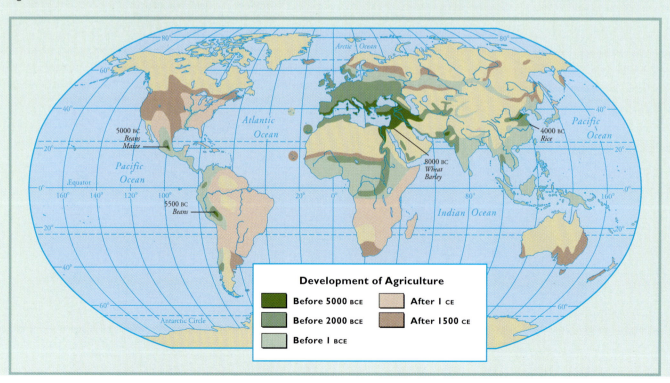

Development of Agriculture

- Before 5000 BCE
- Before 2000 BCE
- Before 1 BCE
- After 1 CE
- After 1500 CE

5000 BC Beans Maize

5500 BC Beans

8000 BC Wheat Barley

4000 BC Rice

- Political and social structures emerged, with hierarchical governments and sometimes bureaucracies. Society was organized around class systems, with priests, warriors, and the wealthy at the top.

- Writing developed in some areas.

- The military or warrior class emerged.

- Independent city-states were gradually merged into larger empires.

- Women were generally made subordinate to men.

In Mesopotamia, around 3000 BCE, a number of city-states arose along the Tigris and Euphrates rivers. They included Eridu, Ur, Uruk, Umma, and Lagash, and were located in an area called Sumer. Surrounded by walls, these cities had political and economic control over the surrounding states. Here, people first scratched cuneiform symbols and other forms of writing into wet clay tablets. Here also is the first evidence of use of the wheel. Around 2300 BCE, the ruler Sargon united several of these city-states into the Akkadian Empire.

Many agricultural communities developed along the Nile River in Egypt. Travel along the Nile was swift and relatively easy, and the upper and lower areas of Egypt were united around 3100 BCE. A series of Egyptian dynasties ruled the area for hundreds of years, and the surrounding desert kept the land relatively free from foreign invasion. The Egyptians developed hieroglyphic writing. The Old Kingdom lasted from 2686 BCE to 2125 BCE, while the Middle Kingdom (2100–1700 BCE) saw increased contact with the outside world, especially in Africa and the Middle East.

South of Egypt, around 3500 BCE, the Nubian civilization emerged. At first, Nubia was a trading partner with Egypt, but later came under Egyptian control.

Small centers of civilization emerged throughout the Americas. In 3000 BCE, skilled artisans around Lake Superior worked copper into jewelry and tools. Along the Supe River in Peru, the city of Caral flourished around 2600 BCE.

Around 6000 BCE, in the Indus River Valley (in present-day Pakistan), people began growing rice, bananas, sesame, wheat, barley, black pepper, and cotton. In 2500 BCE, the great city of Mohenjo-Daro was established, with a population of 40,000. Many craftworkers, sculptors, and potters lived in the city, which maintained a thriving trade in handcrafted and agricultural products.

In China along the Huang He (Yellow River) Valley, farmers used levees to control floods as early as 3000 BCE. Some researchers believe that as early as 2100 BCE, the Xia Dynasty brought centralized rule to a large region of China. Other researchers, however, dispute the existence of this dynasty.

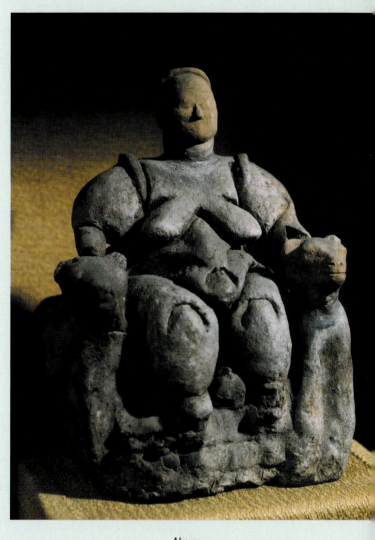

Above:
Female Fertility Figure, found at Çatal Hüyük. Terra-cotta, 7.9" high. Anatolia (modern Turkey), c. 6000 BCE.

	25,000 BCE	*Venus of Willendorf*
Paleolithic Era		
Mesolithic Era	**10,000**	
Settlements in China and Chile	**8000**	
Çatal Hüyük		
Neolithic Era	**7000**	
Settlements in India	**6000**	*Female Fertility Figure at Çatal Hüyük*
Birth of Mesopotamia	**4000**	
Unification of Egypt	**3100**	
Old Kingdom	**2500**	*Idol from Amorgos*
Civilizations in Crete		
Irrigated farming in Andes	**2000**	*Fertility Statuettes in Egypt*
Shang Dynasty—China	**1600**	
Moche and Chavin cultures	**1000**	*Moche Pottery Depicting Sexual Intercourse*
	200	*Kidder Figure*
	100	
Roman Empire		
	CE 50	*Initiation Rites of Dionysos, Villa of Mysteries*
Romanesque Era	**1000**	*Mother and Nursing Child*
Cahokia Civilization		*Relief Carving from the Kandarya Mahadeva Temple*
		Moche Pottery Depicting a Woman Giving Birth Assisted by Midwives
Gothic Era, Europe		
Aztec Empire	**1400**	van der Weyden: *Virgin and Child in a Niche*
Ming Dynasty—China		Jan van Eyck: *Wedding Portrait*
Mughal Dynasty—India		Masaccio: *Expulsion from Paradise*

		Aztec Marriage Couple
Benin Kingdom—Africa	**1700**	Utamaro: *A Pair of Lovers*
Captain Cook's voyages in Oceania		*Krishna and Radha in a Pavilion*
U.S. Revolutionary War		
French Revolution		
	1800	*God Te Rongo and His Three Sons*
		Figure of a Deity: A'a Rurutu
		Potawatomi Male Figure (Love Doll)
		Ingres: *Grande Odalisque*
		Manet: *Olympia*
Russian Revolution	**1900**	
World War I	**1915**	*Dogon Primordial Couple*
		Ashanti Akua'mma dolls
		O'Keeffe: *Grey Line with Lavender and Yellow*
		Brancusi: *Torso of a Young Man*
	1925	
World War II	**1939**	
		Bamana Female Figure, Mali
	1970	Neel: *Pregnant Woman*
Desert Storm	**1990**	Bourgeois: *Blind Man's Bluff*
		Kruger: *Untitled (Your body is a battleground)*
		Hershman: *Deep Contact*
		Aguilar: *In Sandy's Room*
		Opie: *Justin Bond*
	1995	Koons: *Made in Heaven*
	2000	

Art has been used to ensure, teach, record, and document human fertility, reproduction, sexuality, and sexual issues.

Early, small, figurative sculptures of fertility "gods" and "goddesses" from the Stone Age and early Greek cultures were likely used to aid human fertility. Similar figures were found more recently in the Americas, Africa, and Oceania. Murals from Pompeii depicted possible fertility rituals.

Sculptures and paintings have witnessed, documented, and commemorated the coupling and marrying of human beings. Images depicting lovemaking and sexuality are numerous. Some are straightforward, while others push the limits of cultural taboos. Hinduism teaches that sexuality and sexual acts reflect the relationship between humans and the divine. Gender relationships within cultures can be seen in artworks depicting the female body. We discussed the issue of the "gaze" to show the importance of the audience for whom such images are made. Other artworks complicate the usual formula of the male gaze upon the female body. High-technology, mass media, and personal choices are often presented in sexual wrappings. Sexual imagery can be realistic or abstracted.

Examples of pregnancy, childbirth, and offspring images from different cultures were examined.

FOOD FOR THOUGHT

Much of the art in this chapter comes from cultures in which human reproduction was actively promoted or even ritually aided. Having children was seen as an absolute good. Early pregnancy was common, and large families were a blessing. However, in the last several decades, that attitude has changed. Teenage pregnancy or marriage is not viewed positively in the United States today. Abortion and birth control put more choices along the way to becoming parents. Sexuality has been emphasized more for personal pleasure rather than procreation; however, the threat of sexually transmitted diseases complicates this new attitude. As the human population tops six billion, many believe that there are too many people for the planet to sustain. Indeed, the world's most populous country, China, has already legislated population control measures.

- How do you see these various attitudes reflected around you in the art made today?
- What attitudes do you see in images from popular culture—in movies, comics, fashions, dolls, advertisements, magazines, calendar art, billboards, and so on?

We saw the odalisque appear in several guises in this chapter, as harem girl, as Paris prostitute, and as a lesbian. Thus, an image like the odalisque carries with it all its past meanings as well as new meanings given to it by each successive artist.

- How do we determine when an image is being used for oppressive ends?

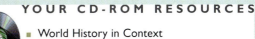

YOUR CD-ROM RESOURCES

- World History in Context
- Exploring Art Timeline
- Flashcards
- Food for Thought
- Companion Site
  Chapter 8 Quiz
  InfoTrac® College Edition Readings
  Artist Flashcards
  Online Study Guide

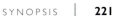

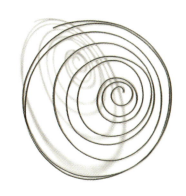

Religion

The supernatural realm lies beyond our senses, yet in almost every age and culture, people have attempted to create diagrams, symbols, and pictures that express to some extent their understanding of divinity.

How can humans make pictures of God? How can we account for the earth, ourselves, the stars, the entire cosmos? What kinds of places of worship have humans built, where they can feel a divine presence? What kinds of art have been made in reaction to—or in preparation for—death?

In the next two chapters, we will look at art from world cultures for perspectives on the following topics:

- Understanding the supernatural and communicating with divinity through art
- Using architecture and art to structure spaces that seem divine
- Building large-scale sacred architecture, and its relationship to secular power
- Employing art in creating houses and memorials for the dead
- Incorporating nature into religious and mortuary shrines, through art

CHAPTER 9 | DEITIES AND PLACES OF WORSHIP

CHAPTER 10 | MORTALITY AND IMMORTALITY

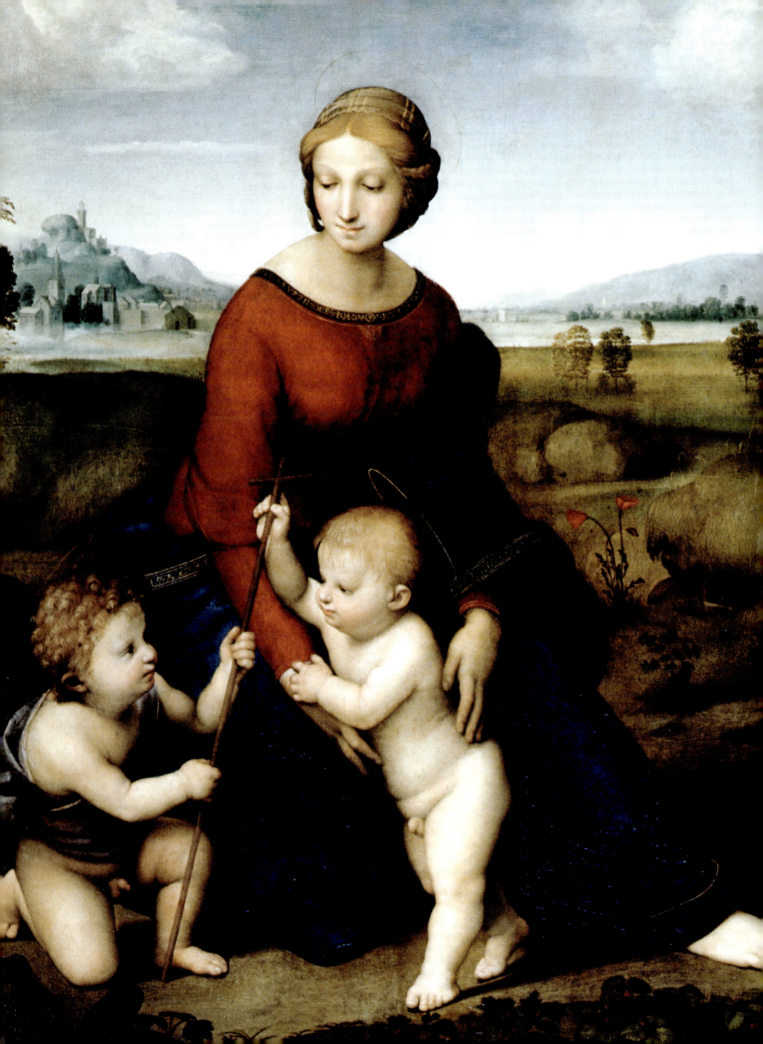

DEITIES AND PLACES OF WORSHIP

INTRODUCTION

By definition, the divine realm is beyond human ability to understand, but humans strive constantly to grasp this other world, to communicate with it or to be joined with it. Rituals, oral tradition, sacred writings, meditation, prayer, and music are but a few paths used by humans to connect to the Transcendent. Art is another.

Some basic inquiries in this chapter are the following:

What can art tell us about deities of very ancient religions?

How can a spiritual being be shown or symbolized in an artwork?

How can art become a form of prayer, or how can it be used to express it?

How do artists depict the cosmos?

What are some general characteristics of places of worship and sacred structures?

How does the use and design of a sacred space reflect the religious experience there?

How do people use art forms other than architecture in sacred spaces?

How can large-scale sacred architecture also be an expression of political power?

IMAGES OF SPIRITUAL BEINGS

Artists make images or sculptures of gods and goddesses and other holy beings to aid people in some religions' rituals. The faithful may believe that the deity is actually present in the artwork, or just represented by it.

Simple geometric shapes often symbolize God. The sphere and dome are significant in Islamic architecture, as they stand for the heavens and the oneness of God. In the Hindu religion, the circle can symbolize the unknowable Supreme Being. The triangle stands for the Christian Trinity. Words can also be symbols of God, such as in Islamic calligraphy. In many religions, light is a symbol for God.

Animal features or natural phenomena can represent, act as metaphors for, or symbolize deities. For example, the sun can be a symbol for God and, at other times, can actually be worshiped as a deity itself. In Christian art, Jesus is symbolized by a sacrificial lamb, and the Holy Spirit by a dove or by fire. Other religions are animistic, with natural elements or animals as deities or inhabited by spirits. The earth is often understood to be a female force because of its ability to generate life. Other religions depict God anthropomorphically—that is, with human attributes. Gods may be gendered and have humanlike personality traits.

In many religions, God is not pictured. Most African religions and the Hindu religion recognize a completely unknowable Supreme Being. In the Islamic religion, Allah is never depicted.

Let us now look at a few ways that deities are depicted in artwork.

EARLY DEITIES

The Earth Mother is the original deity in almost all areas of the globe—the giver of life and fertility and the carrier of death. In ancient myths of nomadic cultures—hunters and gatherers—the Goddess existed first. Later, she created her male counterpart, with whom she mated to produce the rest of Creation. As agriculture increasingly replaced hunting and gathering as the primary source of food, the importance of paternity increased, along with land ownership, animal breeding, cities, and hierarchical classes. Powerful goddesses continued to be worshiped in many religions, but alongside important male gods.

The *Snake Goddess,* 1600 BCE (Figure 9.1), probably evolved from the Earth Mother in the Minoan civilization on Crete from 2000 to 1200 BCE. The open bodice and prominent breasts tie this figure to early fertility goddesses. Her intense expression and upraised arms energize this piece. She holds snakes, which may have represented male sexuality because of their shapes. Female fertility and regenerative powers may also

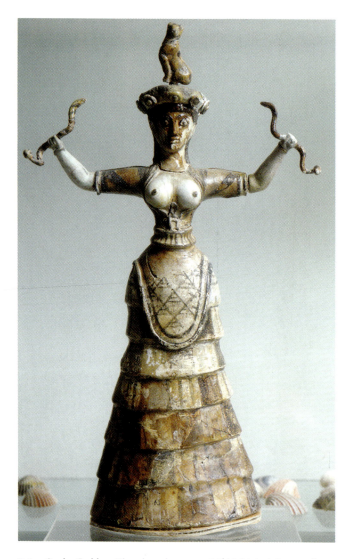

9.1 *Snake Goddess.* Glazed earthenware, 13¹/₂" high. Minoan, from the palace at Knossos, c. 1600 BCE. Archeological Museum, Heraklion. © Nimatallah / Art Resource, NY.

have been connected to the snake's periodic shedding of its skin. The leopardlike animal on her head may have symbolized royalty. Her tiered dress and hairstyle likely represent the garb of Minoan women at that time.

CONNECTION
For more on early goddesses, see the sections "Fertility Goddesses and Gods" and "Fertility Figures" in Chapter 8.

The deities of ancient Egyptian religion were mostly personifications of natural forces, such as the daily rising of the sun, the ripening of crops, and the annual flooding of the Nile River. These divine beings required worship and sacrifice from humans, who appealed to them for special needs. Most were represented as animals or as animal-human combinations.

The goddess Hathor, associated with the sky, stars, love, mirth, and joy, was depicted as a cow or as a combination of a woman and a cow. In *The Goddess Hathor and the Overseer of Sealers, Psamtik,* sixth century BCE (Figure 9.2), she encompasses and hovers protectively over Psamtik, an Egyptian official. Her horns surround the head of a cobra, a sign of royalty, and the sun disk with a crown of feathers. Even in images of Hathor as a woman, her head is usually topped by the same combination of horns and sun disk, which symbolize royalty and divinity. The side view of this piece shows the entire length of the cow striding forward, with bone and muscle beautifully sculpted. In our front view of her calm, majestic face, we see more stylized features, such as the repeated ridges above the eyes and the radiating pattern in the ears. Psamtik keeps pace with Hathor. His standardized face and body show conventional divisions of breast, rib, and belly, while the arms and hands are presented frontally and symmetrically. His official duties are inscribed on his skirt. The work was likely commissioned by Psamtik as an offering that would have been placed in a temple to Hathor.

CONNECTION

In Chapter 10, a hawk representing Horus, the Sky God, is on the coffin case of the Pharaoh Tutankhamen (Figure 10.4, page 270).

CONNECTION

In Chapter 8, you can see the Fertility Statuettes (Figure 8.5, page 198) that were placed in Hathor's temple.

THE GREEK GODS

The ancient Greeks believed that the beginning of all life on earth was Gaia, the Earth Goddess. Her descendants, the Greek gods on Mount Olympus, had distinct personalities, and formed alliances and enmities among themselves and with humans. They were responsible for many aspects of the natural world and human life, such as love, warfare, and the seasons. The Greek gods were always in human form, as the Greeks considered themselves superior to other religions that worshiped animals or mountains. The earliest images were stiff and frontal, without fluid movement, similar to Egyptian sculpture. Later Classic depictions had convincing anatomy and movement, but were entirely idealized and flawless, conforming

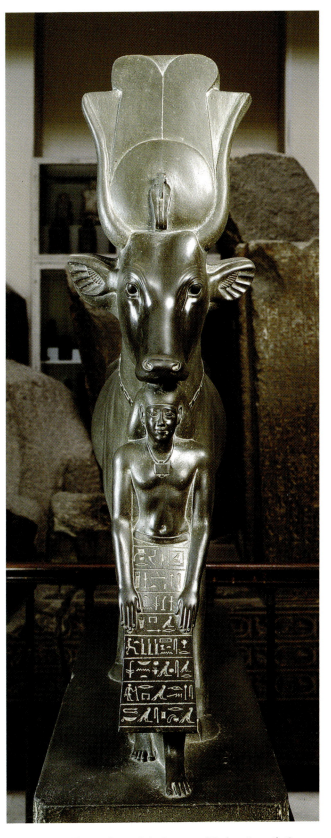

9.2   *The Goddess Hathor and the Overseer of Sealers, Psamtik.* Gray stone; base: 11¹/₂" × 43¹/₄"; height of cow to horns, 33". Saqqara, Egypt, Late 26th Dynasty, 6th century BCE. Cairo Museum, Egypt. © Sandro Vannini.

to Greek standards of beauty. Our example, *Zeus,* or possibly *Poseidon,* 460–450 BCE (Figure 9.3), is from the Classic period. Zeus, chief among the Greek gods, is usually shown as a mature bearded male with an ideal, godlike physique. His right hand probably once held a thunderbolt, an attribute of Zeus, who is associated with the sky and storms (if the figure once held a trident, then he likely is Poseidon, God of the Sea). The over-life-size figure appears monumental, muscular, and ideally proportioned. It conveys a sense of action and energy and, at the same time, poise and dignity. Fully extended, Zeus's mighty body is balanced between the backward movement of his arm and its anticipated forward movement as he hurls a thunderbolt.

HINDUISM

In the Hindu religion, there are apparently numerous gods, but this is not polytheism because they are all manifestations, or "avatars," of the Unbounded, or Brahman, who is one, pure being, pure intelligence, and pure delight, and is therefore unknowable. Although never pictured, Brahman can be partially known through the human senses because all natural things, humans, and spiritual beings reflect Brahman.

The God Shiva, one of the primary avatars, is the source of good and evil, male and female. He is the unity in which all opposites meet. He is the destroyer of life, who also recreates it—terrible and, at the same time, mild. Since the tenth century, *Shiva* has been often depicted in Hindu art as *Nataraja, or the Lord of the Dance,* seen here in a sculpture from c. 1000 (Figure 9.4). Shiva's body is shown as supple, sleek, and graceful. Cobra heads form the ends of his hair, and he stands in perfect balance. As the Lord of the unending dance, he is the embodiment of cosmic energy, yet the balanced pose also contains the concept of eternal stillness. The multiple arms tell of his power, and his divine wisdom is shown by the third eye in the middle of his forehead. His far right hand holds a small, hourglass-shaped drum, the beating of which stands for creation and the passing of time. The second right arm is coiled by a snake that symbolizes regeneration, while the hand itself forms a *mudra,* a symbolic gesture that is a sign

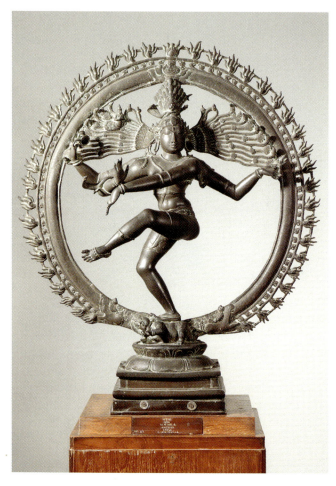

9.3 *Zeus* or *Poseidon.* Greece, 460–450 BCE. Bronze, 6'10" high. National Archeological Museum, Athens. © Nimatallah / Art Resource, NY.

9.4 *Shiva as Nataraja, or Lord of the Dance.* Bronze. Naltunai Isvaram Temple, Punjai, India, c. 1000. © Angelo Hornak / Corbis.

of protection. The far left hand balances a flame that symbolizes destruction, while the other left hand points to his feet. The left foot is elevated in the dance, indicating release from this earth, and the right foot crushes the personification of ignorance. The circle of fire that radiates around *Shiva* shows the unfolding and transformation of the universe, and its destruction.

BUDDHISM

The Buddhist religion follows the teachings of Siddhartha Gautama, a prince born in India near Nepal around 563 BCE. He fled from court life to become a homeless holy man and later achieved enlightenment, or Buddhahood. The Buddha, also known as Sakyamuni (meaning "the sage of the Sakya clan"), continued to teach for the next forty-five years until his death. Buddhists, like Hindus, hold that humans are perpetually reincarnated, most often into lives of suffering, based on the deeds of their past lives. By following the teachings of Sakyamuni, humans can overcome desires and the cycle of rebirth. Then they can attain nirvana, a transformation of their consciousness from the material world to the eternal realm.

For several hundred years after his death, Sakyamuni was represented by a set of symbols, but never as a human because he had achieved enlightenment. One symbol for Sakyamuni was the *stupa,* a sign of his death and attainment of nirvana.

Originally, a stupa was a mound tomb. It eventually was transformed into a monument that contained the ashes or relics of a Buddha. An example of an early Buddhist stupa is the *Great Stupa* at Sanchi, third century BCE to CE first century (Figure 9.5), a solid, dome-shaped mound of earth enclosed in brick or stone. The form of the mound represented the cosmos as the world mountain, the dwelling place of the ancient gods and a sacred womb of the universe. The structure is encircled with a low balustrade wall containing four heraldic gates, all highly adorned with rich carvings. The gates, called *toranas,* are located at the four cardinal points in the circular wall. The balustrades are also densely carved. Pilgrims would come from all over the world to walk around the stupa clockwise and chant, meditate, and pray as they observed the special meanings of the carvings. The square enclosure on top of the dome symbolized the heavens, surmounted by the mast with umbrellas, called *chatras,* that united the world with the paradises above. The chatres signified the levels of human consciousness through which the human soul ascends to enlightenment.

The eastern torana in front of the *Great Stupa* rises thirty-four feet. The gate contains many scenes showing episodes

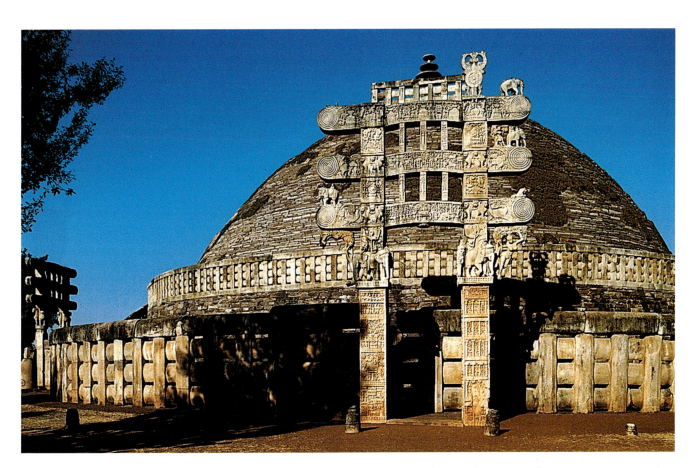

9.5   *Great Stupa.* Dome 50′ high. Sanchi, India, third century BCE–first century CE. Robert Harding Picture Library.

from the life of Sakyamuni, with Sakyamuni presented only by symbols, such as the empty throne, which represents Buddha's separation from his princely life; footprints, which represent the Buddha's spiritual journey; and the elephant, a bodily form assumed by the Buddha. Additionally, there are sensuous images of the nature deities retained from the early Vedic sculptural tradition. Small stupas carved on the gateway reliefs symbolize Sakyamuni in his attainment of Buddhahood; they look very much like the *Great Stupa* behind. The stupa as a symbol of Buddhahood spread throughout Asia, although there were local variations in its design.

CONNECTION

One of the carvings from the Great Stupa at Sanchi is the Yakshi (Figure 13.13, page 377).

As later sects emphasized a more personal Buddha, images of him in human form were produced, along with the traditional symbols. At first, these figurative sculptures were variations of older Hindu spirits, with certain Buddha-identifying attributes, such as the topknot of hair (a cranial bump indicating wisdom) and a circle between the eyebrows. Earlobes were long, since Sakyamuni was once a bejeweled prince.

In still later images, the emphasis was on the general serenity of Buddhahood. The red sandstone of the *Seated Buddha,* late fifth to early sixth centuries (Figure 9.6), has been carved and polished to a smooth, flawless finish. The statue seems to represent a generalized rather than a specific person. The body seems almost weightless. The face is rendered as a perfect oval, and the torso and limbs are simplified into graceful lines and elegant shapes. Clothing is sheer and clinging, unworldly in its draping and its perfection. The tall

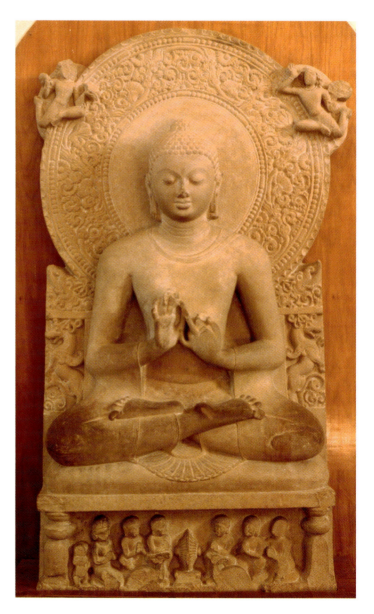

9.6 *Seated Buddha.* Sandstone, 63" high. From Sarnath, Uttar Pradesh, India, late fifth–early sixth centuries. Sarnath Museum. © Borromea / Art Resource, NY.

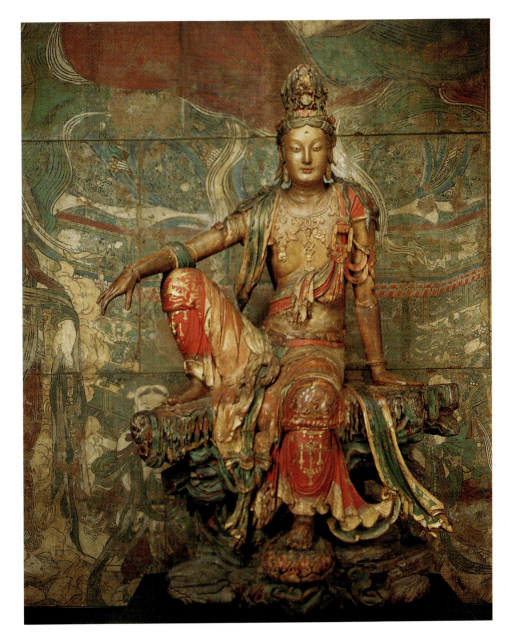

9.7   *The Water and Moon Guanyin Bodhisattva.* Painted wood, 7'11" high. China, Song Dynasty, c. 1100. The Nelson-Atkins Museum of Art, Kansas City. Purchase: Nelson Trust.

arches of the brow, downcast eyes, and quiet but sensual mouth all speak of a transcendent serenity. The Buddha is seated in lotus position on a throne, under which are carved worshippers around the Wheel of the Law. Abstracted foliage above and around Sakyamuni represents the Tree of Enlightenment. His hands are posed in a preaching gesture.

Over the centuries, Buddhist beliefs became more complex. Bodhisattvas are living beings who have attained Buddhahood, but have chosen to remain on earth to help others. While Buddhas in their serenity in nirvana may seem remote to struggling humans, the Bodhisattvas are immediate personal intercessors who give aid. *The Water and Moon Guanyin Bodhisattva,* c. 1100 (Figure 9.7), is the most powerful Bodhisattva, with a great capacity for salvation. Depictions of

Guanyin vary radically, with two to twelve arms, often crowned, sometimes with a muscular male body and sometimes with an effeminate body. In our example, the body is graceful and the face beautiful and serene. The elegance of the body and right hand, along with the lavish carving and rich colors, make this sculpture sensually appealing. The diagonals of the figure's right leg and arm balance the verticals of the torso and the left limbs, while the flowing curves of the drapery unite all.

JUDAISM

Judaism is one of the oldest religions of the Western world and also the foundation of Christianity and Islam. The Jews consider themselves the Chosen People and have a special covenant with their God and Creator, Yahweh, who alone is to be worshiped and none other. It was thought by scholars that the making of art images in the Jewish faith was forbidden because of the Second Commandment. However, images have been found in scripture illumination and on the walls of ancient synagogues. In Figure 9.8, we see the interior of the *Synagogue at Dura-Europos* dated CE 245–256, which is covered with paintings depicting Old Testament themes. Dura-Europos was an outpost in Syria and was probably founded around 323 BCE.

The *Synagogue at Dura-Europos,* originally a private home with a courtyard, was transformed into a place of worship in the second century CE. The paintings on the walls were didactic, illustrating stories found in the Hebrew Bible. The figures have stylized gestures, lack expression, mass, and depth, and, for the most part, stand in frontal rows, as a means to explain a concept or illustrate a story. Action was not depicted. Yahweh was shown as a hand emerging from the top of the panels. Evidently, this kind of image making was not forbidden for the Jews, but the worship of images was.

CHRISTIANITY

Unlike Judaism, the Christian tradition has many kinds of images of God. Some Christians understand God as a single being, while others conceive of God as a Trinity, with three persons in one, the Father, Son, and Holy Spirit. The Father is usually depicted as an aged patriarch, wise, powerful, and judging. The Son was incarnated as Jesus and founded the Christian religion. He is believed by Christians to be the Savior of souls. Images of Jesus range from a babe in arms to a young man in life, death, and resurrection. The Holy Spirit is represented as a symbol, either a dove or a flame of fire.

As an actual historical figure, Jesus is the most commonly depicted of the Trinity. In early images, he was a youthful, protecting shepherd, a comforting figure to early Christians, who were often persecuted by Romans. Once Christianity became the official state religion of the Roman Empire in the fourth century, Jesus was depicted as a royal ruler. Images of Jesus as miracle worker, judge, and teacher usually combine a narration of historical events with layers of symbolism.

In the *Madonna of the Meadow* (Figure 9.9) by Raphael Sanzio, c. 1505, Jesus is the robust, beautiful child in the center, with his cousin, St. John the Baptist, at the left, and Mary, his mother, who towers over both children. Although the children look youthful and sweet, their solemn composure and the cross they hold portends their roles of savior and prophet. All figures are totally human, but their dignity and serenity seem divine. The blues, reds, and greens add to the sense of harmony. Mary and the two children fit into an implied triangle, a stable, symmetrical, sacred shape recalling the Trinity. Mary's silhouette completely contains the form of Jesus, attesting that she is Jesus' mother and establishing her as a symbol for the Christian church, through which Jesus remains present

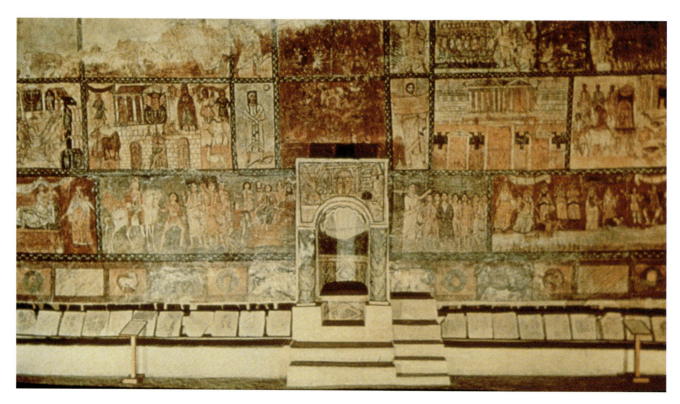

9.8 *Synagogue at Dura-Europos.* Interior, with wall paintings of biblical themes. Syria, CE 245–256. National Museum, Damascus. © Jewish Museum, NY / Art Resource, NY.

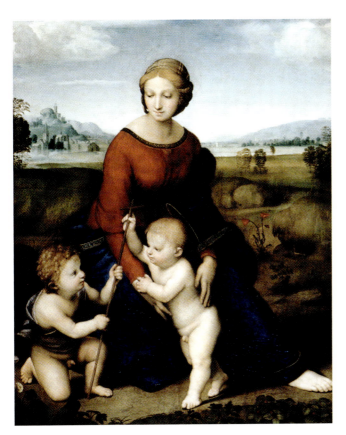

on earth. The large, sheltered body of water in the background implies a harbor, and Mary was known as the Port of Salvation.

In contrast, the *Crucifixion* from *The Isenheim Altarpiece*, c. 1510–1515 (Figure 9.10) by Matthias Grünewald, shows Jesus at death, which for Christians is a moment both of annihilation and of redemption from sin. The dark, gloomy background obliterates all landscape detail. The grisly details of Jesus' sore-ridden and scraped skin, convulsed body, and drooping head are meant to be a realistic picture of a terrible death. At the same time, the *Isenheim Altarpiece* is a conceptual rather than a realistic representation. The bottom panel, which shows Jesus' body being placed in the tomb, would sit directly above the altar, where the body of Jesus is offered at Christian Eucharistic rituals in the form of bread and wine. The lamb in the *Crucifixion* panel, holding a cross and bleeding into a chalice, symbolizes animal sacrifices conducted by Jews in the past and the current offering of bread and wine. People who were present at the Crucifixion, such as Roman

9.9   RAPHAEL. *Madonna of the Meadow.* Panel painting, 44$\frac{1}{2}$" × 34$\frac{1}{4}$". Italy, c. 1505. Kunsthistorisches Museum, Vienna. © Francis G. Mayer / Corbis. See also the text accompanying Figure 2.5 for more on this artwork.

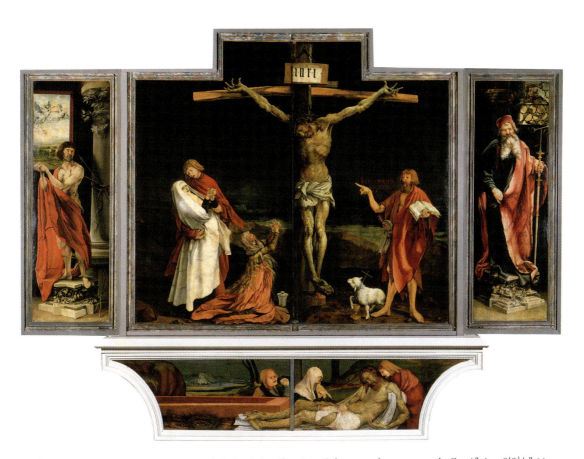

9.10   MATTHIAS GRÜNEWALD. *The Isenheim Altarpiece.* Oil on wood; center panel: *Crucifixion,* 9'9$\frac{1}{2}$" × 10'9". Germany, c. 1510–1515. Musée d'Unterlinden, Colmar, France.

soldiers, are omitted from this painting, while St. John the Baptist is shown, although he had already died. Saints on side panels were associated with cures for the sick.

The painting was a form of consolation for patients in a hospital, for they could see the horrendous suffering of Christ and relate it to their own suffering. Also, the dark, suffering-filled *Crucifixion* panel opens in the center, and behind it are three joyful scenes from the life of Jesus—his conception, birth, and resurrection from the dead, all in brilliant colors.

CONNECTION
For an example of a very early image of Jesus, see the Catacomb of Sts. Peter and Marcellinus (Figure 10.18. page 282). Turn to The Last Judgment (Figure 13.17, page 381), to see an image of Jesus as judge.

GODS FOR SPECIAL PURPOSES

Many religions are polytheistic; that is, they recognize and worship a number of gods, who are responsible for various aspects of earthly life. Mesoamerican cultures often linked the gods associated with corn and water, because water was so essential and corn symbolically stood for all food.

Having a special role as the protector of young corn plants, the maize goddess was called *Xilonen* (Figure 9.11). In our image of her, dating from 1000–1200, the head is rounded, very humanlike, and grandly adorned. She wears a headdress with ornamental bands and ears of corn, a collar with sun rays, heavy ear pendants, and a jade necklace that symbolizes crop fertility.

Tlaloc was the rain deity who made crops flourish. The most worthy of the human dead were received into Tlaloc's heaven. Images of Tlaloc were common, as were temples dedicated to him. Temple attendants would put water into urns like the ceremonial ceramic *Tlaloc Vessel*, c. 1470 (Figure 9.12) and, during rituals, break them so that the life-giving water would be symbolically poured out over the earth. Tlaloc was traditionally shown with distinctive features: circular eyes, twisted serpent nose, fanged mouth, headdress, and large ear ornaments with pendants. Tlaloc's face is flattened, with features rendered as geometric shapes.

How did the Mesoamerican artists show the divine status of Tlaloc and Xilonen? Both are represented as human, but Xilonen is shown naturalistically, yet grandly adorned to establish her divinity. Her staring eyes and down-turning mouth make her a remote, almost unapproachable goddess. The sculpture also has a monumental feel, which adds to the sense of distance. Tlaloc's face is abstractly human, making the deity seem more terrible, powerful, and removed from the experiences of every-

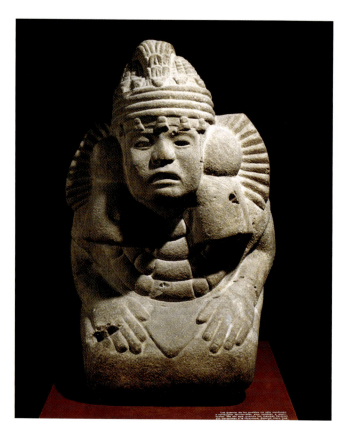

9.11 *Xilonen, Goddess of Young Corn.* Limestone, 33" high. Huastec. Tuxpan (Veracruz), Mexico, 1000–1200. © Gianni Dagli Orti / Corbis.

day life. His serpentlike features associate him with water. Divine status can be conveyed with features of powerful animals. Like Xilonen, he wears distinguishing ear pendants and a headdress.

HUMANS RESPOND TO GOD

Humans use religious ceremonies, prayers, and rituals to acknowledge God and to request what they need for earthly or spiritual existence. Many religions require humans to make offerings to the gods, as outward signs of their devotion. Art frequently is part of this process.

CEREMONIES

The Kwakiutl of the Pacific Northwest dwelled in two sites corresponding with summer food gathering and elaborate winter rituals, such as marriages, initiations, feasts, potlatches, and dramatic performances. Special houses were built for the Winter Ceremonies. Performers in full masquerade told their stories and became the supernatural beings of their masks.

Our example is the twentieth-century *Transformation Mask* (Figure 9.13)—during performance, its character changed from that of an earthly being to that of a supernatural being. At the critical moment in the story-drama, the dancer would turn and manipulate the mask with hidden strings and devices, and then turn back in a completely different mask. This surprising transformation might be the changing of a bear or a sea creature into one of the horrendous cannibal spirits. The intent of this magical event was to make humans fear the supernatural. Besides being superbly carved, the mask is exquisitely painted. Bright, bold colors in undulating shapes create overall harmonious compositions that complement the facial contours. This distinct aesthetic with its flowing curvilinear style is visible throughout Kwakiutl art forms, both past and present.

CONNECTION
Figure 7.20, page 171, shows a large Feast Dish used in a potlatch.

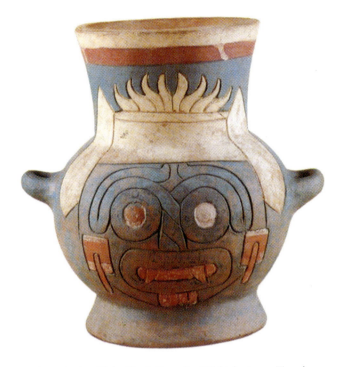

9.12   *Tlaloc Vessel.* Ceramic, 12" high. Aztec. Templo Mayor, Mexico, c. 1470. Photo © 2004, Metopolitan Museum of Art, New York. See also the text accompanying Figure 1.10.

OFFERINGS

The Balinese have many days of religious observance, which they commemorate by giving handmade offerings. They regard these offerings as artworks and consider many of their

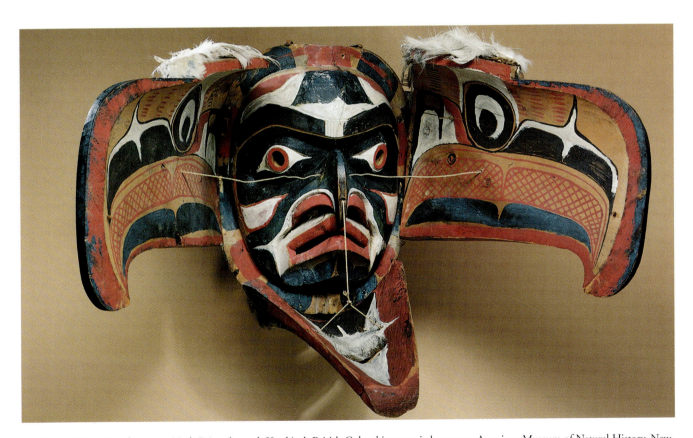

9.13   *Transformation Mask.* Painted wood. Kwakiutl. British Columbia, twentieth century. American Museum of Natural History, New York. See also the text accompanying Figures 1.17 and 2.13.

people to be artists. Religion and art are integrated components of everyday life. Often, handmade offerings are modest, but on festival days, women make and carry to temples more elaborate offerings, such as the *Offering with Cili-Shaped Crown*, from the mid-1980s (Figure 9.14), an intricate sculpture of fruit, flowers, and cut and woven palm leaves. An ancient symbol of wealth, fertility, and luck, the cili is a simplified woman's head with a large, fanlike headdress radiating from it. In temple rituals, the gods accept the essence of the offering; afterward, any foodstuff that has not touched the ground is eaten in the temple or by the family making the offering. Offerings in the Balinese sense mean to give back in thanks, and do not have the connotation of sacrificing something.

In central Mexico, hundreds of believers leave small votive paintings called *retablos* at certain important religious shrines, as a form of prayer and thanks for a divine favor. Pictures, bright colors, and text dramatically record emotional, miraculous events. These artworks also may contain holy cards, pictures of loved ones, diplomas, or legal papers.

The translated text from the *Retablo of Maria de la Luz Casillas and Children* (Figure 9.15) reads, "I give thanks to the Holiest Virgin of San Juan de los Lagos for having made me so great a miracle of saving me in a dangerous operation that was performed on me for the second time on the 9th day of October 1960, in Los Angeles, California. Which put me at the doors of death but entrusted to so miraculous a Virgin I could recover my health, which I make apparent the present retablo: in sign of thanksgiving . . ." (Durand and Massey 1995: 164). The Virgin of San Juan de los Lagos is a small statue of Mary, the Mother of Jesus, in a shrine in the central Mexican state of Jalisco. Multiple scenes are common on retablos, and, in this example, we see Maria twice, both as a

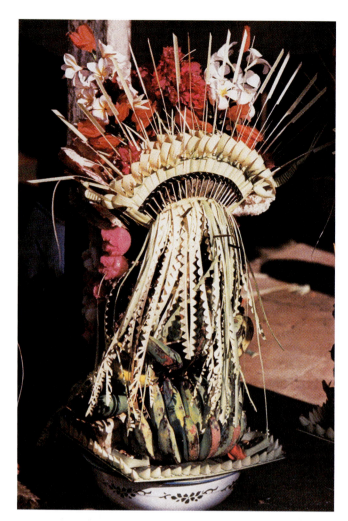

 9.14 *Offering with Cili-Shaped Crown.* Flowers, fruit, and palm leaves, approximately 24" tall. Bali, c. 1985. Photo Hans Hinz. See also the text accompanying Figure 5.8 for more on art making in Bali.

9.15 *Retablo of Maria de la Luz Casillas and Children.* Oil on metal, 7" × 10". Central Mexico, 1961. Durand-Arias Collection. Photo Jorge Durand. For more on this artwork, read the text accompanying Figure 6.6.

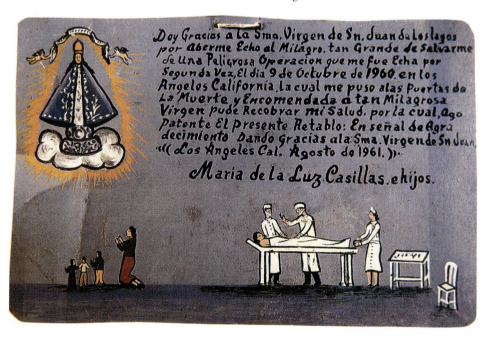

helpless and vulnerable patient on the operating table in a foreign land, and as the supplicant with her children imploring the help of the Virgin. In the retablo, the Virgin looms large in the bleak, gray room, with golden rays, miraculously intervening in a fearful episode. Extraneous details are omitted to better emphasize the victim's helplessness and the Virgin's power.

SACRIFICES

In other cultures, human offerings to God did entail sacrifice, sometimes involving the spilling of human blood. In the various Mesoamerican cultures—Maya, Toltec, Aztec, and others in Central America—the sun was believed to be ever thirsty for blood to stave off the power of the moon and was symbolized by a fiery tongue. In *Shield Jaguar and Lady Xoc,* dated c. 750 (Figure 9.16), we see an example of a bloodletting ceremony, in which the Mayan ruler holds a torch over his principal wife as she pulls a thorny rope through a hole in her

tongue. Those participating in blood sacrifices had to be high ranking, shown by their wrist bracelets, necklaces, crowns, and garb. Their flattened foreheads were signs of beauty, an unnatural effect created by binding boards on the soft skulls of very young children of the nobility. More extreme forms of blood sacrifice were practiced, such as cutting out the hearts of captured warriors or the captains of ball teams. Ballplayers were important members of society, and ball games were important religious rituals in which the ball itself and the opposing teams symbolized the terrible balance between the sun and the moon.

CONNECTION
For more on the Mesoamerican ball games and their meaning, see the Mayan ball court in Figure 16.30, page 492.

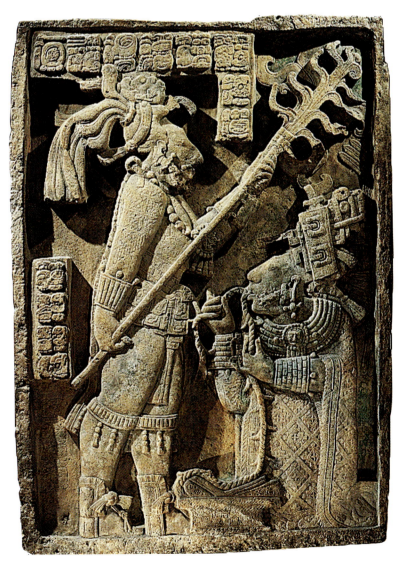

9.16   *Shield Jaguar and Lady Xoc.* Relief. Classic Maya. From a palace at Yaxchilan, Chiapas, Mexico, c. 750. © Justin Kerr.

Judeo-Christian religions recognize the offering of food-stuffs and have a history of blood sacrifice. Cain offered farm produce to God; Abel offered an animal and animal fat; the priest Melchizedek prepared a ritual meal for an offering for Abraham. One famous story of sacrifice concerns Abraham, who prepared to kill his son Isaac at the command of God, but at the last minute he was allowed to substitute the slaughter of a ram. The gilded bronze relief panel, *Sacrifice of Isaac* (Figure 9.17), sculpted by Lorenzo Ghiberti in 1401–1402, shows the emotionally intense moment when the youthful Isaac is bound on an altar of sacrifice, as his fierce-faced father Abraham holds the knife to his son's throat. The curves of their bodies echo each other, with Isaac pulling away as Abraham is poised to lunge forward. The nude body of Isaac is idealized and perfect, increasing the merit of the sacrifice. The intervention of an angel halted the sacrifice, and food, in the form of a ram (not visible in our detail), became an acceptable alternative offering. Although blood sacrifices are no longer offered in mainstream Christian religions, the Eucharistic offering of bread and wine may be celebrated, using many skillfully crafted art items.

PRAYERS

Prayer is a vehicle of communication between human beings and the gods, and it may take many forms. An example of an art object used as a form of prayer is the *Power Figure,* such as the sculpture in Figure 9.18, which would be used to counter the evil influence of enemies, whether human, animal, or spiritual. This example is dated c. 1875–1900. Sculptors carve the power figure with an open mouth, indicating that the sculpture will "speak out" on behalf of anyone beset by evil. Shamans activate them, first by ritually placing medicines in cavities in the figure's abdomen or in the back or head. Then they release the figure's power by driving in one metal nail or blade for each request for help. Once effective, the exact nail representing a particular request must be removed. This *Power Figure* is visually dramatic, with its compact form, expressive face, and bristling nails. Power figures are rarely used now, as African religious practices are evolving and rituals may be abandoned or amalgamated into other beliefs.

The Hopis of North America make small sculptures that act as a form of prayer. The Hopi believe that kachinas, or spir-

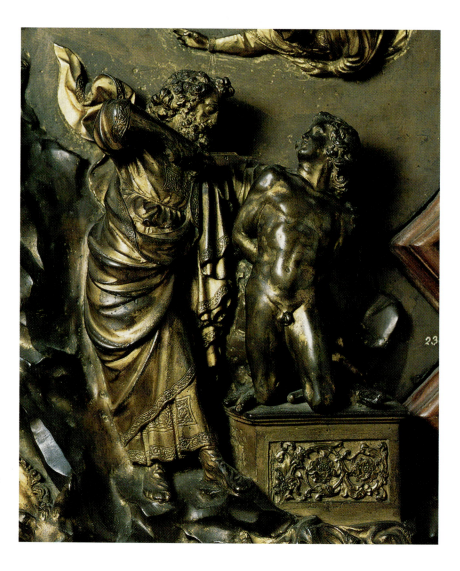

9.17   Lorenzo Ghiberti. *Sacrifice of Isaac* (detail). Gilded bronze, 21" × 17¹⁄₂". Florence, Italy, 1401–1402. Museo Nazionale del Bargello. © Scala / Art Resource, NY.

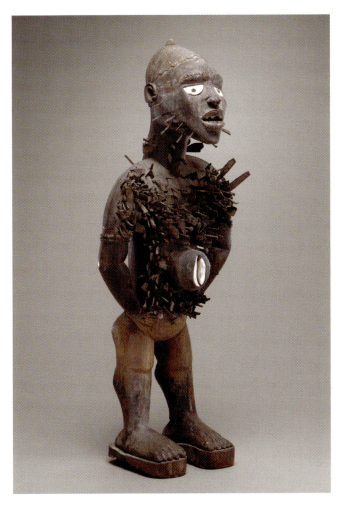

9.18 *Power Figure (Nkisi n'kondi).* Wood, nails, blades, medicinal material with cowrie shell, 46³/₄" high. Kongo, Zaire, c. 1875–1900. Detroit Museum of Art. Eleanor Clay Ford Fund for African Art. © 1998 The Detroit Institute of Arts.

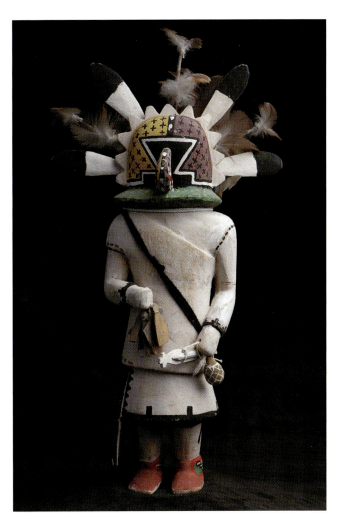

9.19 JIMMIE KEWANWYTEWA. *Ahola Kachina.* Cottonwood, paint, feathers, wool, 13" high. Hopi, Third Mesa, Oraibi, 1942. Museum of Northern Arizona. See also the text accompanying Figure 5.21.

its of dead ancestors, dwell in their community for six months in winter and spring. Kachinas ensure the welfare of the community and sufficient moisture for crops. Male members of the Hopi community perform as kachinas during religious festivals.

Kachina performers also carve dolls that reproduce the costume of specific spirits. Our example, the *Ahola Kachina,* dated 1942, by Jimmie Kewanwytewa (Figure 9.19), is the primary spirit at an important celebration. It is identifiable by the dome-shaped mask, yellow on one side and gray on the other, covered with small crosses. Other identifying attributes of the costume include the large, inverted black triangle on the face and the feathers from an eagle's tail that project from the head. The colors on the dolls, which reproduce the costumes, represent sacred directions: north is symbolized by blue or green; west by yellow; south by red; east by white; the heavens by multicolors; and the nadir by black. During ceremonies, children receive the dolls to educate them about the individual kachinas and the elaborate costumes and rituals. Women receive them as symbols of fertility. The dolls are

hung from rafters in houses as blessings and as prayers for rain and good crops. Older dolls are stiffly posed, but newer ones are more naturally proportioned and often appear in active poses. Bright acrylic colors are now used, and feathers are often carved, as certain birds become endangered.

THE COSMOS

Artists in various religious traditions have created artworks that map the cosmos, showing the origin of the world, the structure of the universe, spiritual beings, the place of humans in relation to the gods, or a diagram of time. Our first example, a mandala, is a radially balanced, geometric diagram augmented by images of deities, humans, and symbols of the universe. Together, they form a map of the structure and relationships among all entities of the cosmos, in accordance with Hindu or Buddhist beliefs. By meditating on the mandala, people can begin to grasp these cosmic relations and understand their place within them.

The mandala begins with a circle, which symbolizes the void before all creation. Into this emptiness the image of the God will appear. In our example, the *Mandala of Samvara*, dated c. sixteenth century from Tibet (Figure 9.20), the deity Samvara (also referred to in this work as Cakrasamvara, who rules and sets into motion the universe) erotically embraces his female Buddha consort, Vajravarahi. Samvara, an angry emanation of the Absolute Being, is shown with blue skin and multiple arms, symbols of his power and divinity. He is pictured here with a donkey face, because those meditating on this image learn the illusory nature of the physical body. Radiating from this center are eight paths, which terminate at the sides or corners of a square. These paths refer to rays of light, the cardinal directions, and elements, such as fire, water, wind, and earth. Other fierce deities, combinations of animal and human forms, occupy these paths.

While the inner circles contain deities, the large outer circle encloses charnel fields, where vultures, wild dogs, or cremation fires consume the bodies of the dead (there are generally no graveyards in Southeast Asia). The details are both gruesome and gleeful, vividly depicting harmful forces. Immediately outside the ring of the charnel fields are eight auspicious signs, such as a lotus blossom and a white conch shell, that represent divine gifts offered to Buddhas. The outermost areas of the mandala are populated with images of monks, mystics, and more deities.

The underlying geometry makes the mandala both simple and complex. During meditation, it can be followed from the outside inward to the center circle, indicating stages of increasing enlightenment. In reverse, the mandala represents the emanation of the creative force responsible for all life, which originates from Samvara. The mandala reinforces the belief that the cosmos, including the physical and spiritual worlds, is an uninterrupted whole of continually fluctuating energy states. Red is a common color of Tibetan mandalas and predominates here. The brilliant blue comes from lapis lazuli, an expensive pigment derived from grinding semiprecious stones. Thus, the work was probably commissioned by a wealthy patron.

The images on the *Ceiling of the Sistine Chapel*, painted by Michelangelo (Figure 9.21) from 1508 to 1512, present the origin of the universe, of human beings, and of sin. Pope Julius II commissioned the work; more accurately, the pontiff's strong

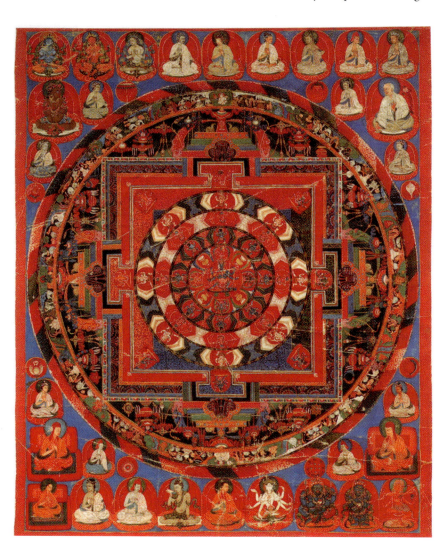

9.20 MANDALA OF SAMVARA (*Kharamukha Cakrasamvara Mandala*). Water-based pigments on cotton cloth. 23" high, 18" wide. Tibet, c. sixteenth century. The Zimmerman Family Collection. Photo Otto Nelson. See also Figure 4.5 and the accompanying text for more on this artwork.

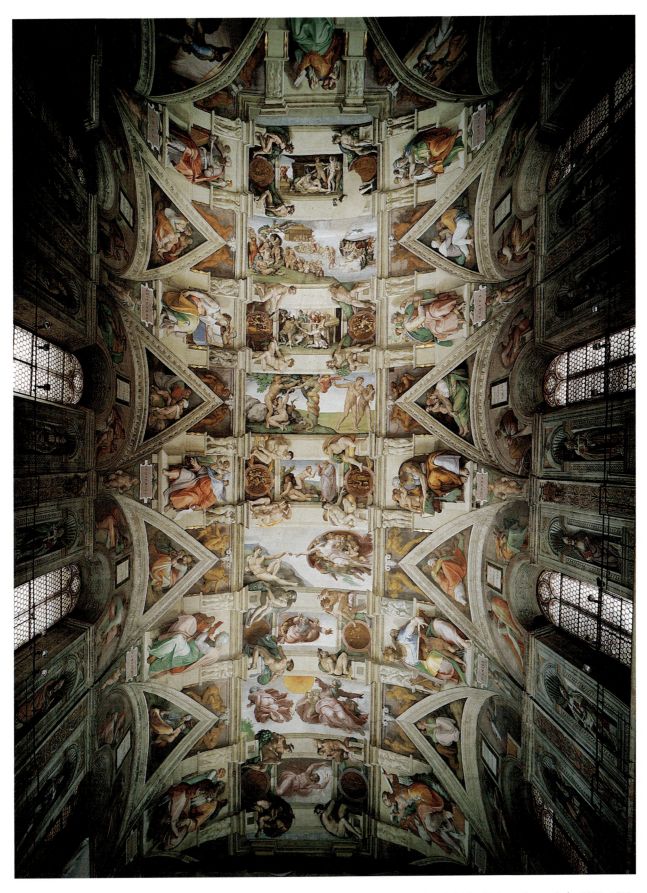

9.21 MICHELANGELO. *Ceiling of the Sistine Chapel.* Fresco, approximately 128' × 45'. The Vatican, Rome, Italy, 1508–1512. Photo Vatican Museums. See also the text accompanying Figure 6.21.

will triumphed and Michelangelo reluctantly acquiesced. The artist felt that he was a sculptor and that painting was a less noble art form. Originally, the work was to consist only of the twelve apostles with some other ornamentation. But as Michelangelo proceeded, he changed the imagery from the apostles to nine scenes from Genesis, along with seven prophets and five sibyls. Illusionistic marble frames subdivide the broad expanse of the ceiling.

At the center bottom of Figure 9.21 is a panel showing God as a powerful-bodied, older man in pink robes, separating the light in the lower right from the darkness in the upper left. Next, God creates the sun and the moon and then separates the water from land. Following are the creation of Adam, then Eve, and original sin, in which Adam and Eve break God's commandment and are expelled from Paradise. The three center panels at the top are concerned with stories of Noah, the patriarch of the human race after a devastating flood destroyed most life on earth. These cosmic moments are depicted in bright, clear colors against plain backgrounds, emphasizing the bodies' dramatic shapes.

The *Creation of Adam* (Figure 9.22) shows the moment when God transmits the spark of life into the body of Adam, thus creating the human race. The cosmic relation between the human and the divine realms is depicted here. God's bursting energy contrasts starkly with the languor of Adam, clearly distinguishing the creator from the created. Yet, human and divine bodies are similarly powerful and similarly posed, indicating the Christian beliefs that humans are created in the likeness of God and that, with God's help, humans can attain

heaven. Under God's arm is a woman identified either as Eve or as Mary with the child Jesus at her knee. Since neither Eve nor Mary existed at the moment of Adam's creation, their inclusion indicates the belief that God always contains all potentiality and the means of salvation. In other spaces are prophets and learned teachers who pointed to the coming of Jesus. The nudes may symbolize ideal humans perfected through Jesus. The Mass celebrated in the Sistine Chapel commemorates these events, linking the past to current ritual.

PLACES OF WORSHIP AND THEIR GENERAL CHARACTERISTICS

Since prehistory, people have set aside special places for religious worship. All of them, from simple to grand, are designed to reveal something of the spiritual realm and to provide an experience beyond the normal and mundane. Across cultures and religions, places of worship may

- shelter a congregation
- house sacred objects
- incorporate elements of nature
- are sites for repeated religious celebrations
- incorporate symbolic geometry in their dimensions or the determination of their location
- incorporate the concept of journey or are a destination for pilgrims

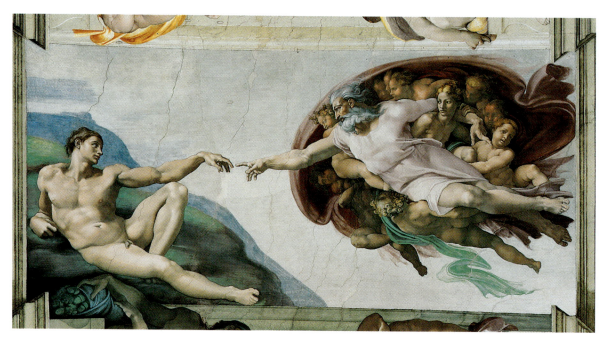

 9.22 MICHELANGELO. *Creation of Adam,* from the ceiling of the Sistine Chapel. Fresco, 18'8" × 9'2". The Vatican, Rome, Italy, 1508–1512. Photo Vatican Museums. See also Figure 6.21.

Regarding the first point, it is sufficient to say that places of worship were often designed to house a large group of people, all of whom are participating at the same time in ritual observances.

The other five characteristics are explained more fully here.

HOUSING SACRED OBJECTS

Many places of worship were built specifically to house a sacred image, text, or artifact of a religion. In the Jewish religion, the Temple of Solomon contained the sacred scriptures called the Torah and other sacred objects. The most holy structure, called the *Ark of the Covenant,* was a special tabernacle that held these sacred objects and is depicted in Figure 9.23. Moses constructed the *Ark* according to instructions from Yahweh, so that the prophet could communicate with and receive revelations from him during the exodus from Egypt. Our image is a mosaic from the fourth century CE, which depicts the *Ark* in the center of the composition. Sanctuary implements, including elaborate seven-branched candelabra, flank the tabernacle.

Because the Jewish peoples seldom had a permanent homeland in the early years of their history, a tent was likely their early place of worship as well as a temporary temple. Later, King Solomon built the Temple in Jerusalem, which was destroyed in 586 BCE. Part of the wall remains, and Jews from all over the world still go there to pray. In more recent centuries, the synagogue has evolved as a community house of worship, assembly, and study. Even modern synagogues, however, still house sacred objects: each contains an Ark, scrolls of the Law, an eternal flame, and candelabra.

CONNECTION

The Roman Emperor Titus led troops into Jerusalem and destroyed the Second Temple in CE 70. Relief carvings on the Arch of Titus commemorate the emperor's victory in Jerusalem and depict his soldiers carrying the booty from the Temple in a victory parade. See Figure 11.16, page 315.

Other religions also house sacred objects in their places of worship, as we shall see later in this chapter. Often, these are specially constructed buildings, such as temples or churches. In many cases, however, formal structures are not necessary. For example, among many African religions, shrines that hold sacred objects are part of ordinary houses. This is an important aspect of many African religions, as they weave spiritual forces with everyday life.

INCORPORATING ELEMENTS OF NATURE

Places of worship can be natural sites: mountains, springs, and sacred trees or groves. Mountains have been meeting places between heaven and earth or dwelling places of divine beings. Rocks can be seen as containers or symbols for spirits and deities. The earth and water are the sources or sustainers of life. Trees may be seen as sources of truth and symbols of the cosmos, existing simultaneously in the underworld, the earth, and the heavens. Fire, light, and the sun are divine symbols or sometimes spirits themselves.

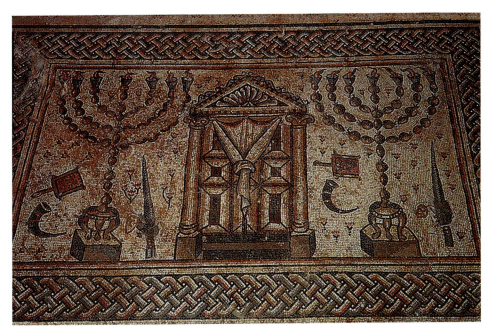

9.23 The *Ark of the Covenant* and sanctuary implements. Mosaic. Hammath, near Tiberias, fourth century. Israel Antiquities Authority, Jerusalem. Photo: Zev Rodovan, Jerusalem.

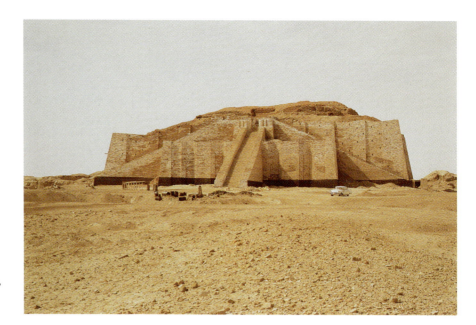

9.24 *Ziggurat at Ur* (partially reconstructed). Third Dynasty of Ur, Iraq, c. 2150–2050 BCE. Hirmer Fotoarchiv. Photo Erwin Bohm.

The *Ziggurat at Ur* (Figure 9.24), dated c. 2150–2050 BCE, is a sacred artificial mountain erected by the Sumerians of the city of Ur to honor their special deity from among the Sumerian pantheon of gods. Its corners point toward the four points of the compass, reflecting the movement of the sun. The word *ziggurat* itself means "mountain" or "pinnacle." Surrounded by flat land, this terraced tower of rubble and brick seemed to reach into the heavens. The *Ziggurat at Ur* has three broad staircases, each with one hundred steps, leading to a temple-shrine forty feet above the ground, dedicated to protective gods and goddesses and attended to by special orders of priests and priestesses.

The Shinto religion in Japan teaches that forests and enormous stones are sacred dwellings of the gods of nature, who are called the *Kami*, all connected to growth and renewal. Our example, the *Main Shrine at Ise* (Figure 9.25), is located in a forest, on a holy site. Through ritual, the Kami are prevailed upon to enter the shrine, where their powers are worshiped and their aid solicited. A mirror placed inside facilitates their coming into the shrine.

The *Main Shrine at Ise* is made of natural materials, primarily wood and thatch. It is rebuilt every twenty years to exactly the same specifications, so what we see in Figure 9.25 is both a new building and a structure that dates from c. 685.

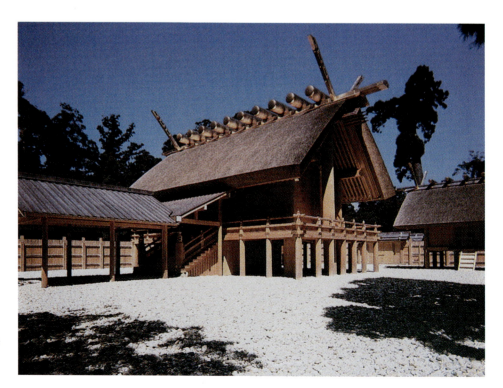

9.25 *Main Shrine at Ise* (exterior). Japan, c. 685, rebuilt every twenty years. Kyodo News International. See also the text accompanying Figure 6.22 for more on this shrine.

With each rebuilding, the builders observe careful rituals and express gratitude as they take wood from the forest. Boards taken from the same tree are placed together in the building of the shrine. The wood is left plain and unpainted to retain its natural character, and it is carefully fitted and joined with pegs. Nails are not used. The golden color of the wood and the simple but striking geometry are dramatic and impressive.

CONNECTION

Compare the basic design of the Shinto shrine to the Toba Batak House, Figure 7.32, page 181.

PROVIDING SITES FOR SACRED CEREMONIES

Places of worship are sites where sacred ceremonies are performed. Sometimes there is no special architecture, only the use of the arts—music, dance, singing, literature, or the visual arts. In the Southwest United States, the making of sand paintings has constituted an essential part of Navajo religious ceremonies for centuries. These impermanent paintings are made directly on clean-swept floors of houses and are destroyed in the course of the ceremony. Very few have ever been photographed or documented; however, the rituals are fixed and certain symbols must be repeated each time. To cure illness, ensure success in hunting, or promote fertility, the artist-priest chants and prays

while making the painting using the natural elements of colored sand, crushed stones, charcoal, and pollen. The person in need sits in the center of the painting to receive the supernatural power. Sometimes ceremonies are performed for the earth itself.

Figure 9.26 shows a Navajo mother sitting in the middle of a sand painting, holding her sick child, as a healing ritual is being performed. Color in sand paintings range from black to white, with red, blue, yellow, and brown tones. Shapes are bold and geometric. Symmetry is a frequent component. Imagery is dependent upon and determined by the painting's purpose. For example, paintings dealing with fertility may feature rivers and native plants. The Navajo restrict the photographing of their sand paintings because of their sacred nature.

CONNECTION

The cave paintings at Lascaux and Aboriginal paintings were essential parts of rituals. See Figure 7.1, page 156, and Figure 7.2, page 157.

USING GEOMETRY SYMBOLICALLY

Many cultures use geometry and symmetry to symbolize divinity, all-encompassing totality, perfection, and timelessness. Such geometry may determine the placement or orientation of religious sites, or a building's plan, layout, or elevation.

Stonehenge, dated c. 2000 BCE (Figure 9.27), in Wiltshire, England, was built at a time when religion and science were not separate, but were a single unified means of understanding natural forces. Thus, *Stonehenge* is likely an altar for religious rituals as well as an astronomical device that maps solar and planetary

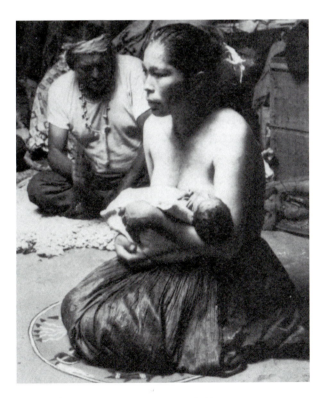

9.26   *Sand Painting.* Ritual for a sick child. Navajo. Arizona, USA, 1954. Photograph by Lee Boltin. See also Figure 6.26, as well as Figure 5.15, for examples of sand painting pigments.

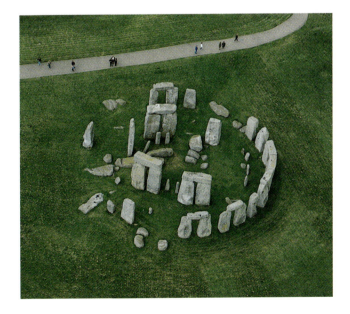

9.27   *Stonehenge.* Diameter: 97'; upright stones with lintel, approximately 24' high. Wiltshire, England, c. 2000 BCE. Pubbli Aer Foto.

movement upon the earth. The stone arrangement marks the midsummer solstice, essential to an agrarian civilization dependent on successful crop planting. Other Neolithic stone arrangements in the area align with *Stonehenge,* creating a larger network that may have mapped force fields within the earth.

The first building phase of *Stonehenge* was a gigantic circular ditch, with rubble piled to create an outer bank. The later core of *Stonehenge* consists of a ninety-seven-foot-diameter ring of colossal sarsen stones, twenty-four feet high with their capping lintel. An inner ring of bluestones in turn surrounds a horseshoe-shaped stone arrangement and, finally, an altar stone in the center. A heel stone, separate from the circle, marks the solstice. Builders dragged the stones twenty-four miles, pounded and rubbed them to shape, and likely set them in place using ropes and earthen ramps. *Stonehenge* includes several large rings of holes dug into the ground that conceptually connect the center stones to the surrounding earth.

Centuries later, simple geometric shapes formed the basis of a Roman building that alluded to divine qualities of perfection and completion. The *Pantheon,* 118–125 (Figure 9.28), is a shrine to the chief deities of the Roman Empire. A 142-foot-diameter sphere fits into the interior space, making the width of the building equal to its height. The dome, a perfect hemisphere, is the top half of that sphere. A thirty-foot circular opening at top (the *oculus,* or eye) creates a shaft of sunlight that dramatically illuminates the interior. Squares are inscribed in the dome and wall surfaces and are the basis of the pattern on the marble inlay floor. The entire structure is symmetrical, both inside and out, and creates the impression of loftiness, simplicity, and balance.

In fact, throughout this chapter, we will see the circle and square and verticality in many religious structures, and geometry was important for their placement and orientation.

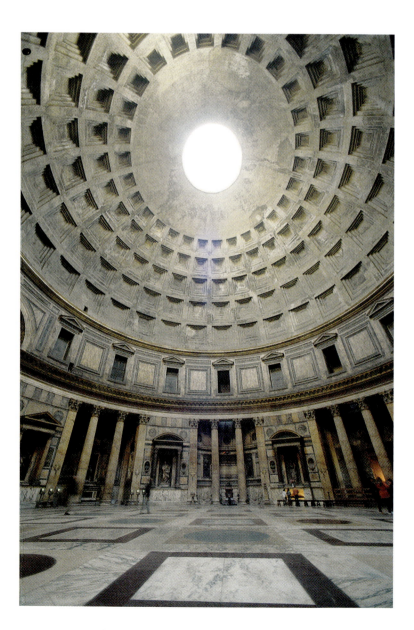

9.28 *Pantheon.* Concrete and marble; 142' from floor to opening in dome. Rome, Italy, 118–125. Henri Stierlin. See also the text accompanying Figure 3.12.

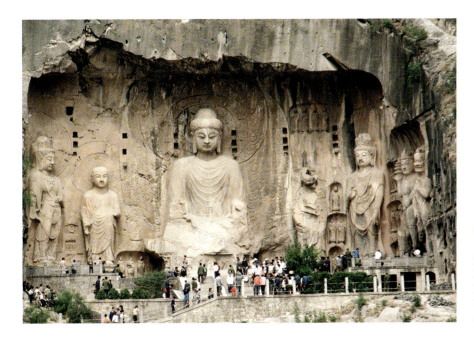

9.29   *Shrine to Vairocana Buddha.*
Natural rock carving, 50' high.
Longmen, Luoyang, Valley of the
Yellow River, China, c. 600–650.
© Lowell Georgia / Corbis.

PROVIDING DESTINATIONS FOR PILGRIMAGES

A pilgrimage is a journey to a shrine or sacred place for believers hoping to receive special blessings or deepening of faith. The concept of journey is both metaphoric and actual, as the soul's spiritual search for understanding has been likened to a physical journey. Almost all major religions incorporate the concept of pilgrimages into their belief systems, and so Muslims journey to Mecca, Jews to Jerusalem, Catholics to various sites such as Lourdes, Hindus to shrines dedicated to various deities, and so on.

Our first example is from the Longmen Caves in China, a huge complex of cave-shrines housing thousands of sacred statues, which is a Buddhist pilgrimage destination. At Long-

men, 1,352 caves have been carved into the limestone mountains, with over 97,000 statues and 3,600 inscriptions dedicated to Buddha. The largest of these is the monumental *Shrine to Vairocana Buddha,* dated c. 600–650 (Figure 9.29), who is the universal principle dominating all life and all phenomena. He is attended by demons and lesser buddhas who govern their own worlds, a model used by tyrant emperors in China to justify their rule. In fact, the carvings at the Longmen caves were supported by imperial patronage. The Buddha at the center is serene, massive, and volumetric, with drapery defined with a few simple curves, to enhance the colossal scale of the carving.

Notre Dame du Haut (Figure 9.30), a Catholic chapel in the Vosges Mountains of France, built between 1950 and 1955,

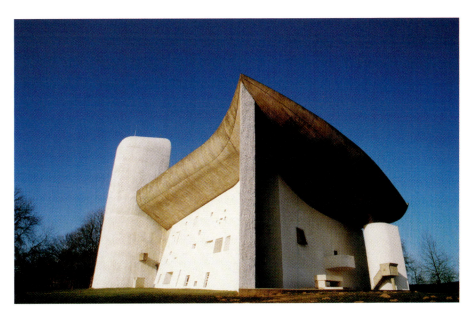

9.30   Le Corbusier. *Notre Dame du Haut.* Ronchamps, France, 1950–1955. © Archivo Iconografico, S.A. / Corbis. © 2004 Artists Rights Society (ARS), New York / ADAGP, Paris / FLC.

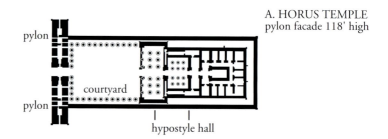

A. HORUS TEMPLE
pylon facade 118' high

pylon

pylon

courtyard

hypostyle hall

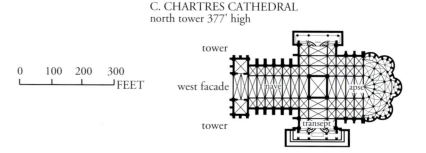

B. ACROPOLIS
Parthenon approximately 60' high

to marketplace

Parthenon

slopes of the plateau

9.31 Comparison of the plans of various places of worship. Notice that all plans are drawn to the same scale and vary tremendously in size. Heights vary tremendously also; they are indicated next to each plan. A. *Horus Temple* (top left), B. *Acropolis* (middle left), C. *Chartres Cathedral* (lower left), D. *Pyramid of the Sun* (top center), E. *Kandarya Mahadeva Temple* (right), F. *Masjid-i-Shah* (lower center). See Figure 9.42 for the plan of the Buddhist temple compound, the *Altar of Heaven,* which is too large to be shown at scale here.

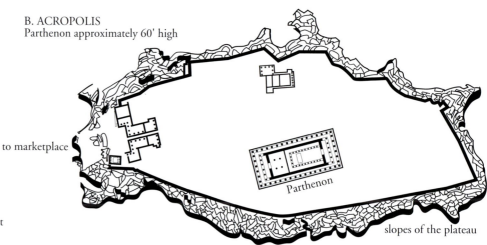

C. CHARTRES CATHEDRAL
north tower 377' high

tower

west facade   nave   apse

tower   transept

| 0 | 100 | 200 | 300 |
FEET

is a pilgrimage destination. The design recalls praying hands, the wings of a dove, and the shape of a boat, all Christian symbols of divine generosity to humans. The shape of the structure resembles sculpture. To accommodate very large crowds on holy days, the church was fitted with an outdoor altar and pulpit (visible toward the right in this photograph), so that services could be conducted for twelve thousand pilgrims on the lawn. Then, the building's exterior becomes a monumental sculptural backdrop for the religious event. The interior of *Notre Dame du Haut* is a relatively small space with limited seating, almost mystically dark and cavelike, with deep-set, square, colored-glass windows piercing the walls.

TEMPLE COMPLEXES AND LARGE-SCALE SACRED ARCHITECTURE

Some religious sites are more grand, extensive, and complex than what we have already seen. They are some of the most famous works of art in the world. They all incorporate the general characteristics of sacred sites that we saw at the beginning of this chapter. But we will see that they do infinitely more than that. When a religion has become firmly established and tied to political power, these expensive, labor-intensive, long-term projects are possible. Thus, grand

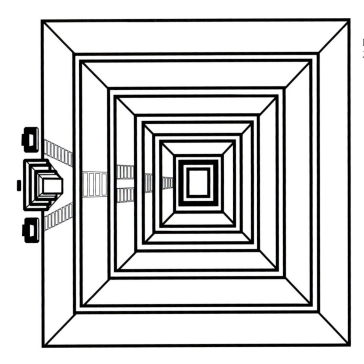

D. PYRAMID OF THE SUN
215' high

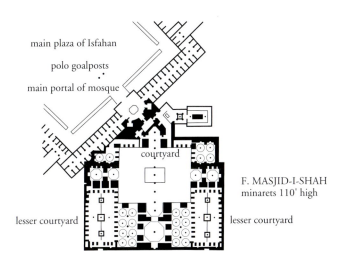

main plaza of Isfahan

polo goalposts

main portal of mosque

courtyard

lesser courtyard

lesser courtyard

F. MASJID-I-SHAH
minarets 110' high

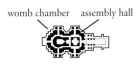

womb chamber   assembly hall

E. KANDARYA MAHADEVA TEMPLE
130' high

```
0    100   200   300
|_____|_____|_____|FEET
```

places of worship are expressions of temporal power, religious power, and broad cultural values. With imposing size and lavish detail, these structures are spectacles, amazing to see. In ceremonies, the individual is reduced to spectator, part of the throng that adds to the religious importance of the site.

First, compare the plans of six of the seven major sites we will study (Figure 9.31). All are drawn to the same scale. Even the smallest, the *Kandarya Mahadeva Temple,* is imposing with its 130-foot height. The largest, the *Pyramid of the Sun* in Central Mexico, is truly enormous. The plans also reveal how important geometry is in these designs to suggest perfection,

completion, balance, and formality. Symmetry is an excellent visual metaphor for political power and divinity.

The plan of the seventh major site, the Buddhist *Altar of Heaven,* is shown in Figure 9.42. The temple compound is integrated into the design of a quarter-mile-wide park and will be discussed in that context.

Let us begin our study of religious compounds and large-scale sacred architecture with the Greeks.

THE GREEK TEMPLE

In studying Greek temple design, we will use the Parthenon in Athens as our example.

Athens is situated on a plain surrounded by mountains, with a high plateau in the center dedicated to the city's patroness, Athena. This plateau, the Acropolis, forms a dramatic setting for temples and is a mountain to climb in the pilgrimage journey. Smaller buildings, clustered along the steep approach, contrast dramatically with the large temples and open space at the top (see plan). It is visually impressive from many surrounding viewpoints.

TEMPLE DESIGN

The *Parthenon* (Figure 9.32) is a good example of a standard Classical Greek temple. Following a three-hundred-year precedent, it is a two-room structure with pediments above the short sides and a colonnaded porch all around. It is more graceful and refined than older temples, but, like them, was covered using the post-and-lintel system. This particular style (or "order") of temple was called Doric and could be easily identified by its column. The Doric column had no base, a simple cushion capital, and a shaft that was fluted, or carved from top to bottom with thin, vertical channels. High-quality marble blocks were carefully stacked and finished so that the columns originally appeared seamless.

In designing the *Parthenon,* the architects Iktinos and Kallikrates often treated it more like a piece of sculpture than architecture. Like a pedestal, the steps form the base for the structure. They are higher at the middle of each side and lower at the corners, to counteract the illusion of sagging in the middle. Thus, the *Parthenon* contains optical illusions. The corner columns are thicker and placed closer to neighboring columns to compensate for the glaring bright sky behind them that would make them seem thinner. Outer columns lean slightly toward the middle of the building to make the *Parthenon* more visually cohesive. The shaft of the Doric column swells slightly at the middle, called *entasis,* to give the column a feeling of organic flexing.

CONNECTION

Greek columns appear on the Roman Colosseum in Figure 16.28, page 491. See also Figure 3.5, page 59, for diagrams of the Doric, Ionic, and Corinthian orders.

SCULPTURE AND RELIEF CARVING

The *Parthenon* had two interior rooms for housing sacred objects, rooms that only a few priests entered. Religious ceremonies took place outside, so originally the exterior was richly adorned with sculpture and brightly painted. Large sculptures

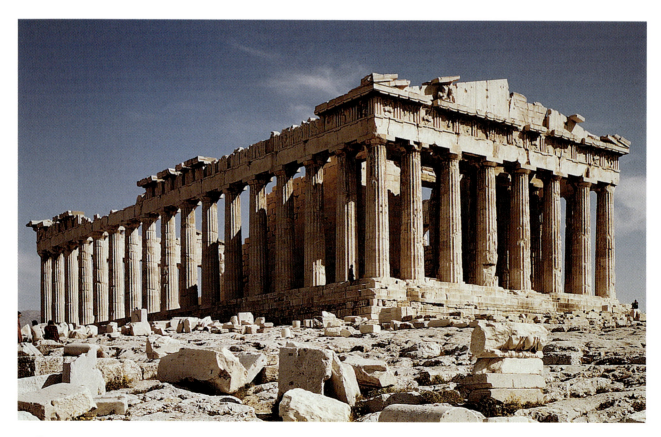

 9.32   Iktinos and Kallikrates. *Parthenon.* Pentelic marble; columns 34' high, dimensions of structure 228' × 104'. Athens, Greece, 447–432 BCE. © Photodisc Green / Getty Images. See also the text accompanying Figure 3.4.

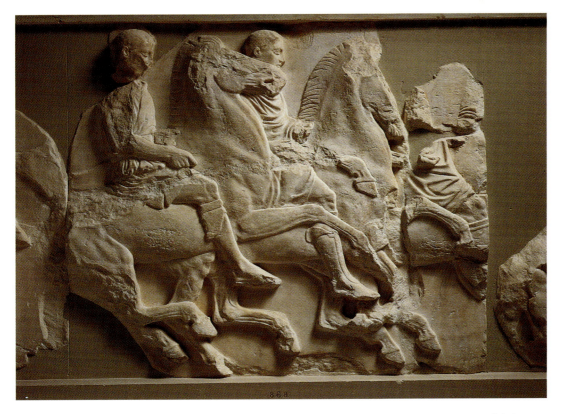

9.33 *Horsemen* (from the Parthenon frieze). Marble, 37" high. Athens, Greece, c. 440 BCE. © Nimatallah / Art Resource, NY. See also text accompanying Figure 6.8.

of the gods stood in the pediment and near the roof, and a long band of sculpture (three feet six inches high, 524 feet long), called a *frieze,* girded the top outside walls of the *Parthenon*'s two inner chambers. Carved c. 440 BCE, the frieze shows a long procession of Greek worshipers climbing up to the *Parthenon,* with marshals, youths, maidens, musicians, jar carriers, horsemen, and charioteers, some bringing animals for sacrifice. At the beginning of the procession, the worshipers are raucous and unorganized, like our *Horsemen* (Figure 9.33). Gradually, the worshipers become solemn and orderly as they approach the gods. This is probably a depiction of the special Panathenaic Festival procession, which occurred only once every four years to bring a new ceremonial tunic to robe an ancient wooden statue of Athena.

The carving on the sculptural frieze is very high quality, an especially amazing feat given that the sculpture is almost twice the length of a football field and was completed in less than a decade. Overlapping, crisscrossing diagonals—horses legs, waving hands, drapery—communicate the bustle early on. Gods and humans are similarly rendered as rounded and lifelike, with carefully carved muscles. They are dignified, composed, well-proportioned, and idealized. The frieze is carved more deeply at the top and more shallowly at the bottom to make it clearer to viewers below.

MATHEMATICAL PROPORTIONS AND GREEK PHILOSOPHY

In their science, geometry, art, religion, and philosophy, the Greeks were engaged in a search for perfection. For example, they believed that certain geometric ratios and certain musical intervals resonated with the cosmic order and were in tune with the heavens. Thus, builders used a consistent set of proportions to determine the length and width of parts within the *Parthenon,* and they balanced horizontal and vertical elements to give the structure a quality of self-containment. By not being overwhelming in size, the *Parthenon* also reflects the Greek idea of the value of the individual.

THE EGYPTIAN TEMPLE

Egyptian temple design remained relatively constant for three thousand years, and so the study of one will illustrate the qualities of many.

SETTING AND HISTORY

Protected by the desert, life in ancient Egypt was unusually stable. Natural cycles, such as night and day and the annual flooding of the Nile River, provided powerful symbols for the Egyptian religion. The Egyptians used symbolic geometry to demarcate sacred alignments in the landscape. East-west marked the path of the sun god, Re, symbolizing life, death, and resurrection. The north-south axis paralleled the Nile River. Generally, cult temples, which were used to worship gods, were located on the east bank of the Nile, like the rising sun, while funerary temples were on the west. Cult temples were often parts of large sacred cities. Successive pharaohs would add new temples to the complex or expand existing ones.

CONNECTION

Other than cult temples, much Egyptian architecture, such as the Mortuary Temple of Hatshepsut *(Figure 10.6, page 272), consists of tombs and funerary temples.*

TEMPLE DESIGN

The *Horus Temple at Edfu* housed the sacred cult image of the sun falcon, Horus. Because cult temples were believed to be the actual dwellings of the gods, they were modeled after the residences of nobles and pharaohs (see plan, Figure 9.31). Courtyards and halls were like reception rooms, leading to the sanctuary that corresponds to the private family bedrooms. For purity, amulets protected the temple's foundations, and its outer edges were walled.

The *Great Pylon of the Horus Temple at Edfu,* built c. 237–57 BCE Figure 9.34), is a temple front entrance, with two large, symmetrical, geometric "mountains" flanking the large doorway. The image may have been derived from the Nile River flowing between cliffs. Visually, the pylons both define the entrance and act as barriers; indeed, the lower classes of the Egyptian population were forbidden to enter. Statues and carvings animated the great surfaces, and they were painted to make the temple facade very colorful. The four vertical niches once held tall poles with flying banners.

All doorways and open areas were aligned to create a straight-line path that continues throughout the temple, suggesting the flow of the Nile River and echoing the Egyptians' sanctified experience of nature. The temple floor was painted

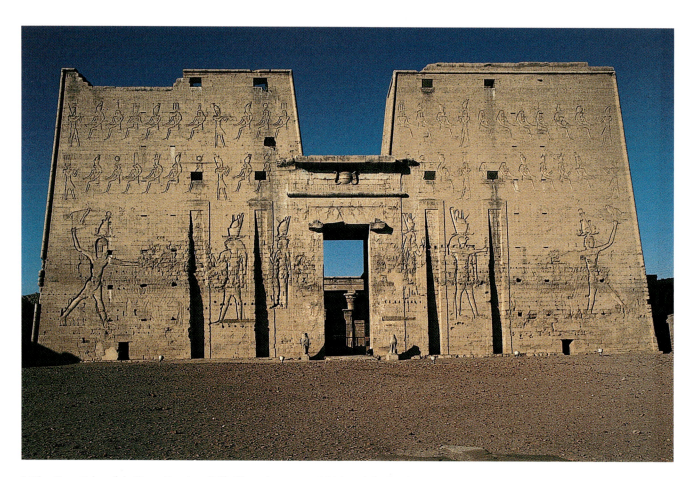

9.34   *Great Pylon of the Horus Temple at Edfu.* The pylons are 118' high and the façade is 230' wide. Unlike most Egyptian cult temples, this one is located on the west side of the Nile River. Egypt, c. 237–57 BCE. Ronald Sheridan Ancient Art & Architecture.

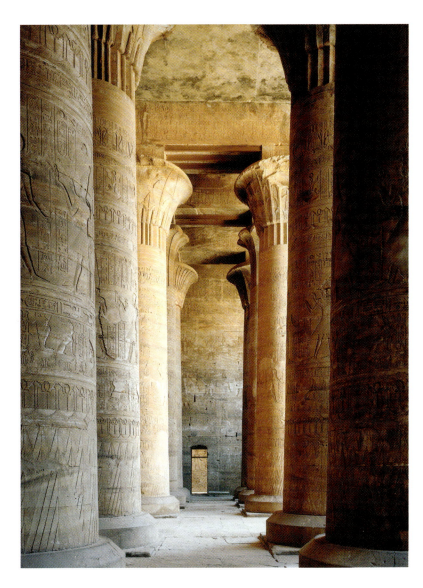

9.35 *First Hypostyle Hall, Horus Temple at Edfu.* The roof slabs are 50' from the floor. Egypt, c. 237–57 BCE. © Scala / Art Resource, NY. See also the text accompanying Figure 3.3.

to depict a river, and the ceiling was decorated with sun rays and the stars of the night sky. Two covered rooms are located beyond the entrance courtyard at Edfu (see plan). They were hypostyle halls, with parallel rows of columns that supported the ceiling. In the *First Hypostyle Hall* at Edfu (Figure 9.35), the columns are huge and closely spaced, clogging the interior space. The stone roof necessitated closely spaced supports. The concept of the passageway is again emphasized, as the space is not really usable as a room. The shapes of the columns and capitals were probably derived from the bundles of reeds used to build the very early Egyptian buildings. To express divine permanence and power, Egyptians translated that original organic material into massive and monumental granite and limestone. The stone capitals often resemble lotus buds, blossoms, or palm fronds. The shafts of the columns swell like the flexing of organic materials. At Edfu, the columns of the hypostyle hall are fifty feet tall; at another temple site, Karnak, the central columns in the hypostyle hall are sixty-six feet

high, and the capitals at the top are twenty-two feet in diameter, large enough to hold one hundred people. The massive stones are held in place solely by their tremendous weight.

The temple became darker with each succeeding room, and rooms became smaller, with lower ceilings. To help protect its purity, the sacred image of Horus was kept in the sanctuary at the very back, sealed by heavy doors covered with bronze or silver and decorated with precious stones. The holiest areas were opened only on special occasions and could be approached only by a very few. The sacred image of Horus did not always reside in darkness, however. On certain special feast days, such statues were taken out and rejoined with the sun to recover their vigor.

THE MESOAMERICAN TEMPLE

Mesoamerican temples often took the form of a pyramid with a small structure on top. Indeed, the pyramid or the mound was a frequent holy site throughout the Americas, from Illinois to Peru.

HISTORY AND SETTING

Thirty miles north of today's Mexico City, the Teotihuacános, a pre-Aztec people, built a vast religious center in a large city high on a plateau surrounded by mountains, a center that reached its peak from 100 to 400. Teotihuacán, or "Place of the Gods," had 200,000 residents, enormous temples, and numerous and lavish palaces, and governed a wide area. Unlike in previous rambling Mesoamerican cities, the streets of Teotihuacán were rigidly laid out on a grid oriented to north, south, east, and west, and even a river through the town was channeled to conform to that grid. The main north-south corridor, the *Avenue of the Dead,* formed the religious center of the city, with more than one hundred temples in two miles. The incredible scale of the Avenue of the Dead dwarfs any of the places of worship we have seen so far. Still, the style of architecture is remarkably consistent throughout, and the overall design emphasizes both space and mass: the pyramids as solid mass, with plazas as voids that were often the same size as the bases of the pyramids. Ball courts were also included.

The very building and growth of Teotihuacán directly led to its decline, as forests were leveled to fire plaster kilns, resulting in soil erosion, failure of rains, and the decline of the city.

TEMPLE DESIGNS

In the middle of the Avenue of the Dead was the *Pyramid of the Sun,* begun before 150 (Figure 9.36), and probably dedicated to sun worship. It was aligned east-west and along the rising of the star cluster Pleiades on the days of the equinox, and once had a temple atop it. The pyramid is quite simply staggering in size, covering 7.5 acres and rising 215 feet. The Teotihuacános did not use the wheel and had no beasts of burden, so people carried the 2.5 million tons of earth, stone, and rubble to the site. Probably three thousand laborers worked thirty years to complete the pyramid. The ledges, tiers, vertical insets, and square corners visually separate the pyramid from the rounded mountains that surround it. To prevent erosion, it was built with a relatively low profile, with embedded stone walls set perpendicular to the outer face.

The entire earthen mound was once covered with huge clay bricks faced with stone, and finished with a coat of smooth, white, polished lime plaster. It must have looked like a gleaming white mountain, with certain parts painted in

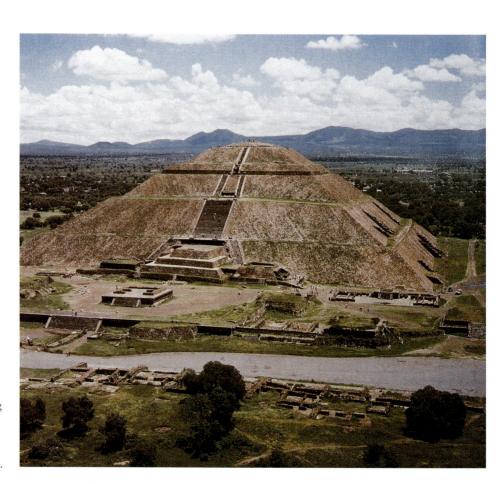

9.36   *Pyramid of the Sun,* with the *Avenue of the Dead* in the foreground. Pyramid is 768' along one side of the base. Teotihuacán, Mexico, begun before 150. Photo courtesy Ester Pasztory. See also the text accompanying Figure 1.15.

color. Ceremonies with splendid pageantry were likely held on the steps and ledges.

CONNECTION
There are many similarities between the Pyramid of the Sun and the Ziggurat at Ur (Figure 9.24, page 244), seen earlier in this chapter.

TEMPLE PAINTING

Early temples had sculptural ornamentation, but after the third century, paintings were used, like the restored copy of the *Tlalocan Painting* (Figure 9.37), from a palace in Teotihuacán. A large frontal figure at the center is a water god with green water droplets springing from her hands. Plants populated with butterflies and spiders grow from her head, while two priests, shown symmetrically and smaller in scale, attend and make offerings. The colors in this restored version are bright, with an especially intense red background. The deity is distinguished by her larger size, frontality, and the profusion of symmetrical patterns that ornament her. In fact, the entire piece shows the Teotihuacános' fondness for elaborate symmetrical patterns, both in framing and in depicting characters.

THE HINDU TEMPLE
THEOLOGY AND TEMPLE DESIGN

Hinduism is based on two belief systems. The first is nature-based and venerates the various spirits responsible for the incredible abundance of plant and animal life in India. From this came the concept of reincarnation, an infinitely repeating cycle of death and life. Around 1500 BCE, invaders brought the second belief system—an understanding of the cosmos in symbolic, geometric terms. The circle stood for the totality of the universe; the square was that divine force made physical in life on earth; a vertical pole was the pillar between heaven and earth, a link that also ensured their separation. A good person would eventually break the cycle of rebirth and death and move into a changeless, timeless union with the Supreme Consciousness, Brahman.

Temple architecture gives form to these spiritual beliefs. The earliest temples were cave temples carved into mountains, like opening the earth's womb to find the divinity enshrined inside. Other temples were freestanding, thick-walled cubes, containing a womb-chamber that housed the cult image or symbol of the deity. A heavy tower, like an abstract mountain, covered it, and a few relief sculptures adorned the exterior. Worshipers brought offerings, meditated, and made sacrifices individually, but remained outside. Priests tended to the deities housed inside and acted as intermediaries for the worshipers. Thus, the Hindu temple was more like sculpture with a small interior. There is no collective service in the Hindu religion, and the temple is the dwelling of the deity.

Later Hindu temples and precincts became much more elaborate, but the same basic formula of womb-chamber and mountain remains. In now-deserted Khajuraho, an important political capital in the tenth and eleventh centuries, was a grouping of thirty temples, symbolizing abundance and proliferation.

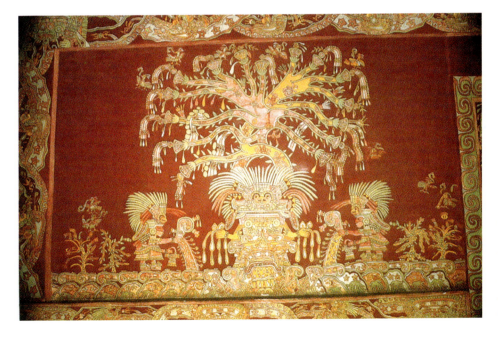

9.37 *Tlalocan Painting.* From Tepantitla compound, Teotihuacán, Mexico. Copy by Agustin Villagra. Original: pigment on stucco. Photo by Mary Ellen Miller.

One was the *Kandarya Mahadeva Temple* (Figure 9.38), dedicated to Shiva in his manifestation as Mahadeva who maintains all living things. The *Kandarya Mahadeva Temple* is still an artificial mountain that surmounts the small, dark womb-chamber. The basic shapes are symbols of male and female sexuality, representing sexual energy and the procreative urge. Then, almost lifelike, they break down into multiplying, cascading forms that are fantastic in their variety and number. Several attached porches and a front assembly hall add to the proliferating forms.

Despite the multiplicity of forms, visual unity is maintained because of the basic mountainlike form and because of the simple umbrella shape (which represents the Unbounded) that surmounts the tallest tower, above the womb-chamber. Thus, the temple exterior was an instrument of meditation on reincarnation. Up close, the relief carvings become more readable, with images of deities and of smaller shrines. Many are openly erotic, because the Hindu religion believes that carnal bliss reflects divine union with the Unbounded.

CONNECTION
Figure 8.19, page 209, shows an erotic scene from the Kandarya Mahadeva Temple.

GEOMETRY AND ITS SIGNIFICANCE

The plan of the temple (Figure 9.31) is a mandala, a geometric drawing that symbolizes the universe, which we saw in Figure 9.20. Four porches on the temple pointing in the cardinal directions mark the four sides. Then the squares and circles, which have cosmic meaning, are repeated, rotated, and overlaid, and then expanded into space, to create the fantastic compilation of shapes proliferating to become the outer layer of the temple, which still relates to the inner sanctum.

THE GOTHIC CATHEDRAL

The imposing, mystical **Gothic** cathedral is one of the most famous forms of a Catholic church. Christians believed that the body and earth are profane and sinful, while the soul is sacred. They saw the church building as the heavenly Jerusalem on earth. Abbot Suger, a leading cleric during this era, remarked upon entering a Gothic church, "I see myself existing on some level . . . beyond our earthly one, neither completely in the slime of earth nor completely in the purity of Heaven."

Gothic cathedrals were all funded by and built in cities, indicating the rise of cities and monarchies and a decline in feudalism. The modern humanist view that values the individual was beginning to develop at this time. Gothic churches are remarkable human achievements. While they evoke the spiritual realm, they do so by giving pleasure to the senses.

CONNECTION
The early Christians worshiped in homes or catacombs. An example of a catacomb, the Catacomb of Sts. Peter and Marcellinus, can be seen in Figure 10.18, page 282.

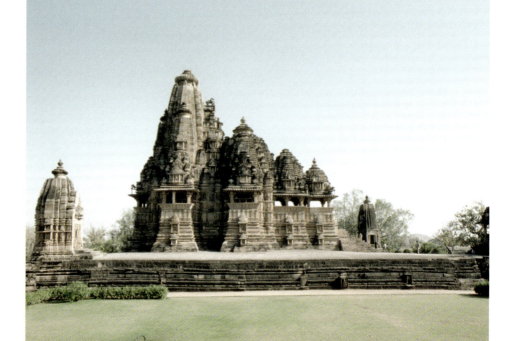

9.38 *Kandarya Mahadeva Temple.* Khajuraho, India, tenth–eleventh centuries. This is one of thirty temples at this site, dedicated to Shiva, Vishnu, or Mahavira. Main tower is 130' high. © Brian A. Vikander / Corbis.

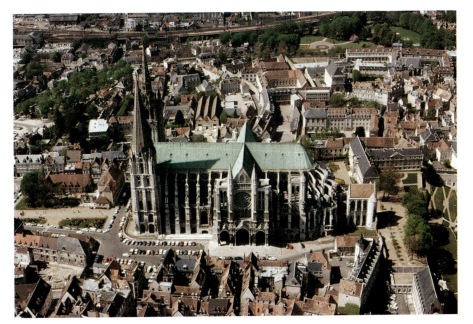

9.39   *Chartres Cathedral.* Chartres, France. South tower 344' high, north tower 377' high); the cathedral itself is 427' long. A rose window is visible at the middle of the church. Although parts of the west front date from 1145–1170, most of the exterior of this structure was built between 1194 and 1220. © Marc Garanger / Corbis. See also the text accompanying Figures 3.11 and 5.3.

PLAN AND DESIGN

Gothic cathedrals towered over the towns around them, which is evident in *Chartres Cathedral* (Figure 9.39), built between 1194 and 1220. The spires symbolized the church's role linking heaven and earth. Flat, blank walls are almost nonexistent. Large windows are filled with tracery, a lacy stone framework that holds sections of glass in place. Blank spaces are covered with figurative sculptures or decorative carvings, showing Jesus, saints, rulers, and sometimes demons. Flying buttresses create a visual pattern of forms that jog in and out, as can be seen in Figure 9.39. Towers, arches, buttresses, and arcades create vertical lines that continue from ground to roof. The plan of *Chartres* is symmetrical, while its shape (Figure 9.31) is a cross, symbolizing Jesus' crucifixion as the act of salvation that redeemed sinful humanity.

The emphasis on verticality continues inside (Figure 9.40). Long lines rise from the floor, up the piers, and between the windows, and flow gracefully up the pointed groin vaults. The vaults seem to billow overhead rather than being stone structures that weigh tons. There is also a strong horizontal pull toward the altar, with the large windows at the apse end that are like bright beacons.

WINDOW DESIGN

The large stained-glass windows were not only incredible technical achievements, but also powerful symbols of heavenly radiance. Previously, churches tended to be very dark, but these windows fill the Gothic church with muted light. The flying buttresses on the outside make the enormous windows possible, because the buttresses and not the walls are holding up the vaults above.

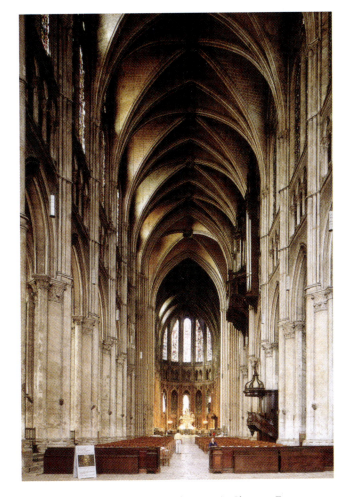

 9.40   *Chartres Cathedral* (interior). Chartres, France, completed 1194–1260. The center space, called the nave, is 130' long, 53' wide, and 122' high. Clerestory windows can be seen below the vaults on the sidewalls and around the altar, at the center. Photo Francois Lauginie. See also the text accompanying Figures 3.11 and 5.3.

The *Rose Window,* from 1233, on the north transept of Chartres (Figure 9.41), shows rings of Old Testament prophets and kings surrounding Mary with her child Jesus. This illustrates the Christian concept that the Old Testament culminated in the birth of Christ. Mary's central location indicates the raised status of women. (In fact, the church is dedicated to Mary.) The female model was now Mary, mother of the savior Jesus, rather than sinful Eve. Geometry was used to locate the various small scenes in this window by inscribing and rotating squares within a circle. The window is shaped like a blooming rose, a symbol of Mary.

CONNECTION
For an example of the English style of Gothic architecture, see the Chapel of Henry VII, *Figure 10.20, page 284.*

THE BUDDHIST TEMPLE

Distinct versions of Buddhist temples sprang up in India, Southeast Asia, Indonesia, China, Japan, and Korea. For now, we will confine our discussion to just one Buddhist temple compound from China, the *Altar of Heaven,* and to one temple within it, the *Temple of Heaven.*

The *Altar of Heaven* (Figure 9.42), constructed over the fifteenth and sixteenth centuries, is a large, tree-filled temple compound located in Beijing, south of the palace core. Surrounded by a four-mile wall, the compound is square at its southern end and semicircular at its northern end. To the Chinese, the round shape symbolized the heavens, while the square represented the earth.

The major structures and roadways of the complex are laid out on a north-south axis. Altars and temples face south, the source of temperate weather and abundance, while the north was the source of evil influences. Temple complexes were also carefully sited relative to the forces of wind and water (*fengshui* means "wind and water"), because wind disperses the breath of life and must be stopped by water. All structures are symmetrical and enclosed by walls, railings, terraces, or gates, expressing the Chinese values of seclusion and order.

DESIGN OF A PAGODA TEMPLE

Three or four times a year, the emperor used the *Temple of Heaven* (Figure 9.43), built in 1420 and restored in 1754, to officiate at religious-political ceremonies, mostly dedicated to the earth and crops. The temple is a lofty, three-tiered pagoda, a cone-shaped structure distinguished by its layers of eaves and gilded orb on top. Its shape is a geometrically simplified mountain form, like the Hindu temple. The entire structure is 125 feet high, and nearly 100 feet across. The wide eaves pro-

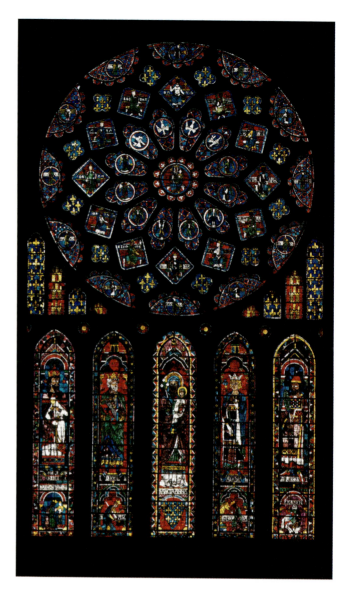

9.41   *Rose Window.* From the north transept of *Chartres Cathedral.* Chartres, France, 1233. © Angelo Hornak/Corbis.

vide shelter from bright sun and rain. The colors and patterns in this wooden building are brilliant. It has a gently curving, violet-blue tile roof, similar to the color of a dark blue sky. The outside walls are deep red, offset with bands of gleaming gold. The interior is red lacquer with foliage patterns in gold and blue and contains green and white beams. Twenty-eight tall posts on the interior entirely support the roof. There are no walls, only doorlike partitions pierced with latticework. The four central posts represent the four seasons, while other columns represent months of the year and the division of day and night. In the center of the stone floor is a marble slab with a design incorporating the dragon and phoenix, symbols of the emperor and empress.

The *Temple of Heaven* sits atop three terraces surrounded by richly carved, lacelike, white marble balustrades. Worshipers

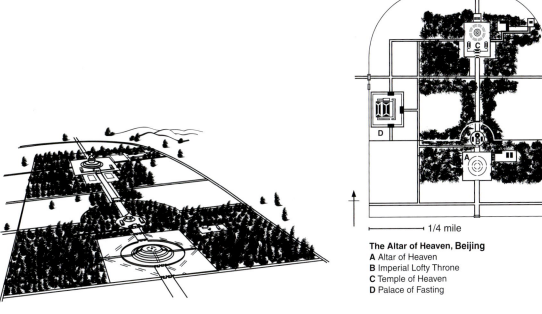

9.42 *Altar of Heaven.* Beijing, China, fifteenth–sixteenth centuries. Plan and artist rendering.

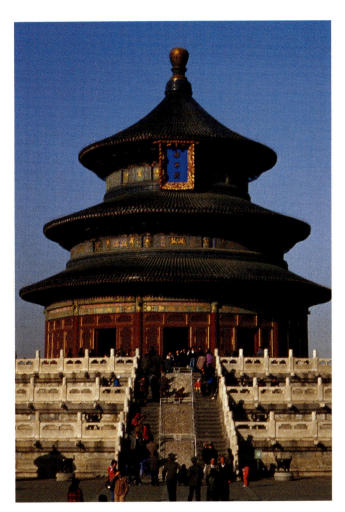

circumnavigate the round structure at different levels to symbolize the achievement of wisdom. The temple's symmetry and order contrast strikingly with expanses of wooded areas.

THE ISLAMIC MOSQUE

The religion of Islam requires that its adherents pray five times a day while bowing toward Mecca, the birthplace of the prophet Mohammed. On Friday, men are required to attend collective prayer services in mosques, a word derived from the Arabic *masjid,* which means "prostration." The faithful ritually cleanse themselves and then assemble on beautifully patterned rugs facing Mecca for prayer, sermons, and readings from the Quran, or Koran, the Islamic book of sacred texts.

It is thought that the plan of Mohammed's house in Medina influenced the design of early mosques, which were simple courtyards with shaded areas. On the wall facing Mecca was the *mihrab,* a special marker niche. A stepped pulpit called the *minbar* was usually located next to the *mihrab.* The tall minarets could be seen from afar, giving hope to weary travelers. There are no icons, statues, or images in Islamic worship or in mosques.

9.43 Round hall from the *Temple of Heaven.* Wood with tile roof. Beijing, China, begun 1420, restored 1754. © Liu Liqun/Corbis.

LATER DEVELOPMENTS IN MOSQUE DESIGN

One of the most beautiful mosques ever constructed is located in ancient Persia, or present-day Iran. Shah Abbas I (the Great) sought to make Persia an important center and undertook an ambitious urban renewal program in the capital city, Isfahan. With the *Masjid-i-Shah,* or *Royal Mosque* (Figure 9.44), dated 1612–1637, the individual parts of the mosque became elaborate and were given separate identity. The portals, for example, became separate, large structures distinguished by elaborate decoration and pattern to awe and draw in the viewer. The once-simple courtyard evolved into a two-story arcade covered with blue-patterned tiles, with four huge, porchlike portals, where schools of Islamic theology could be assembled. The covered prayer hall is physically and conceptually separate from the open courtyard. Worshipers move through a series of interlocking areas to leave the profane world and enter the sacred realm. The single minaret has multiplied to four.

The *Masjid-i-Shah* has a very rough exterior finish, contrasting with the lavishly decorated interior. The spaciousness and symmetry of the mosque represent the infinity and completeness of Allah.

PATTERN

Ornamentation is profuse and serves several purposes: (1) it symbolizes Allah in its suggestion of infinity and creation; (2) it enhances the sacred character of the mosque; (3) it identifies and makes visually distinct the various parts of the mosque, so that portals, porches, windows, domes, and the mihrab are easily recognizable; and (4) the ornamentation disguises the mosque's mass, although not the form. The mosque walls seem to be merely thin screens of incredible color and delicate pattern, rather than thick, heavy, massive brick walls.

Other elements add more pattern. Windows are covered with decorative screens that break up the light into patterns as it reflects off the patterned tiles. Reflecting pools are common, and this mosque has one in the courtyard. Seen reflected in pools, the buildings seem smaller but more beautiful. Disturb the water, and the image vanishes. Text passages on mosque walls are a favored form of decoration. Calligraphic lettering was stylized to become very elegant and, in some instances, almost indistinguishable from geometric or foliage patterns. The panels on either side of the doorway in Figure 9.45 resemble Persian weavings and tapestries. In the Islamic world,

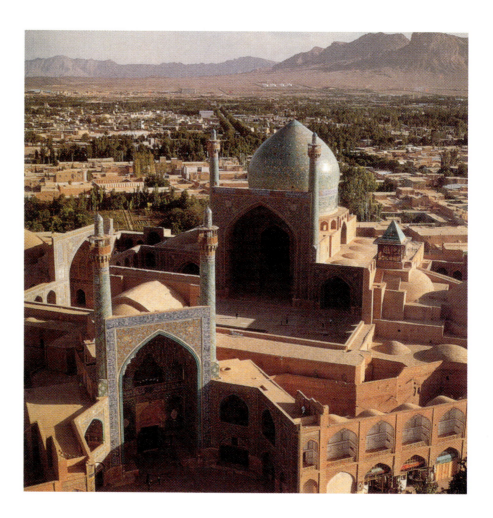

9.44 *Masjid-i-Shah,* or *Royal Mosque.* Isfahan, Iran, 1612–1637. The arch of the main portal, to the left in this picture, is 90' high; the minarets are 110' high. © Roger Wood/Corbis. See also Figure 5.18 and accompanying text for more on the dome design.

weavings serve utilitarian functions in the home, palace, and mosque, but they are also high aesthetic achievements and signs of favor. As treasured portable objects, they recall the early nomadic Arabs and the founding of Islam. The *mukarnas (muqarnas),* or vaults, in the upper left in Figure 9.45, are also pattern elements. The hanging quarter-domes break up the structure and disguise the mass of the building.

The entire complex is unified by the enormous, patterned turquoise dome that dominates the Isfahan skyline. The circular dome stands for the heavens and symbolizes the oneness of Allah.

CONNECTION

The Taj Mahal, Figure 10.21. page 285, and Figure 10.22, page 286, is an Islamic structure decorated with carved and inlaid stones.

CONNECTION

Figure 5.18, page 114, is a diagram of the dome of the Masjid-i-Shah that shows its patterned mosaic decoration.

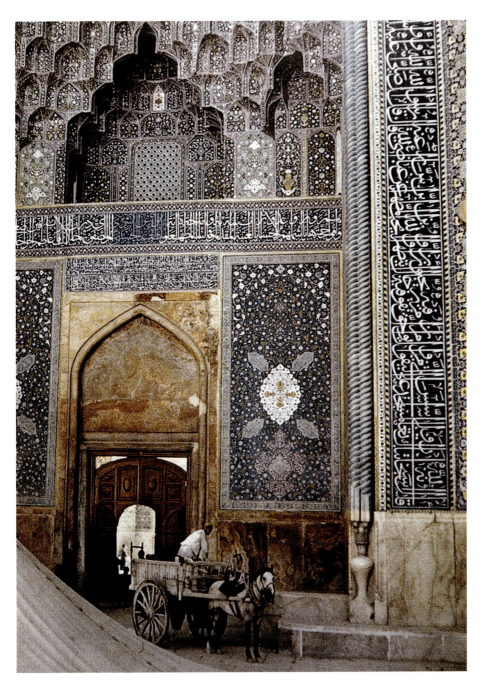

9.45   *Masjid-i-Shah,* or *Royal Mosque* (detail of the main portal). Isfahan, Iran, 1612–1637. Photo: Wim Swaan, Getty Research Library. See also the text accompanying Figures 2.12 and 5.18.

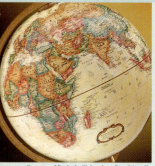

Courtesy of Replogle Globes, Inc., Broadview, IL.

The civilizations of the Middle East continued to grow and flourish and to create more amazing works of art. Babylon was a center of religious worship, with tall ziggurats topped by temples, not unlike the earlier *Ziggurat at Ur* (Figure 9.24). Between 1792 and 1750 BCE, Hammurabi recorded his Code of Law, covering the tax system, fair wages and prices, property rights for women, and criminal punishment. In 1350 BCE, the Assyrians conquered the Fertile Crescent, including Babylonia and, later, Egypt. They built extensive roads, developed a political system of provinces and governors, and established libraries of cuneiform tablets.

The Hebrew people went to Egypt in 1800 BCE because of drought in Canaan and were put in bondage. In 1250 BCE, Moses led the Exodus, and by 1000 BCE, they conquered the people of Canaan and established Jerusalem. Their religion was monotheistic and became the roots of Judaism, Christianity, and Islam.

On the island of Crete, the Minoan civilization flourished through seafaring and trade. The Minoans produced a number of fertility figures and goddesses, like the *Snake Goddess* (Figure 9.1). Around 1200 to 800 BCE, another maritime culture, the Phoenicians, prospered in small city-states in present-day Lebanon, with colonies in Carthage and North Africa and an active trade economy. They are also known for their alphabet, based on sounds of the human voice.

The Persians lived east of the Crescent Valley from 550–330 BCE, with their capital at Persepolis. Their religion included the teachings of Zoroaster, which were written down in the book *Avesta*.

Below

Map 3 The Assyrian and Persian Empires.

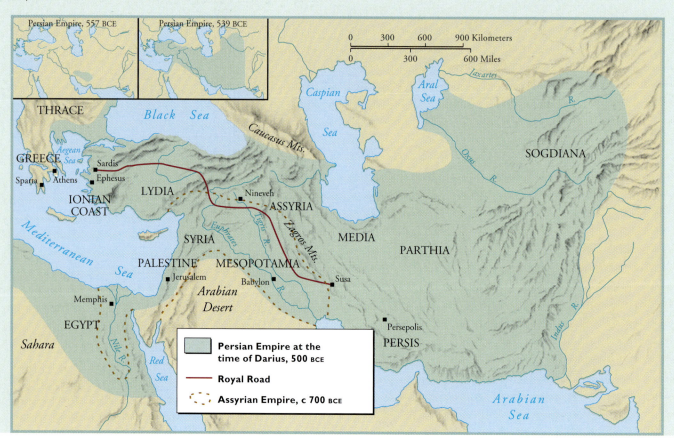

Persian Empire, 557 BCE

Persian Empire, 539 BCE

THRACE
Black Sea
Caspian Sea
Aral Sea
Jaxartes R.
GREECE
Aegean Sea
Sardis
SOGDIANA
Sparta Athens Ephesus
LYDIA
Nineveh
Oxus R.
Caucasus Mts.
IONIAN COAST
ASSYRIA
Zagros Mts.
MEDIA
PARTHIA
Mediterranean Sea
Euphrates R.
Tigris R.
SYRIA
PALESTINE MESOPOTAMIA
Jerusalem Babylon Susa
Arabian Desert
Memphis
EGYPT
PERSIS
Sahara
Persepolis
Nile R.
Indus R.
Red Sea
Arabian Sea

0   300   600   900 Kilometers
0   300   600 Miles

Legend:
- Persian Empire at the time of Darius, 500 BCE
- Royal Road
- Assyrian Empire, c 700 BCE

The long-lived Egyptians had three kingdoms. During the Old Kingdom, 2700–2200 BCE, the Great Pyramids and Sphinx were built. From 2100 to 1800 BCE, Egypt was ruled by invaders, but later recovered. In the New Kingdom, 1600–1100 BCE, remarkable temples were built that were similar in style to the later *Horus Temple at Edfu* (Figures 9.34 and 9.35).

The Greek civilizations established city-states, the strongest being Athens and Sparta. The ancient Greeks are credited with developing the early forms of democracy. Around 500 BCE, the Golden Age of Greece began, producing great advances in philosophy, the arts *(Parthenon,* Figure 9.32), architecture, writing, crafts, medicine, mathematics, and Olympic sports. Between 750 and 500 BCE, the Etruscan people ruled Central Italy. In 500 BCE, the Romans overthrew them, drove them out, and established the Roman Republic.

In India around 1500 BCE, nomadic peoples formed a new culture that incorporated Hinduism and the Sanskrit language. Later, the sacred text of the *Rig-Veda* was written. In 563 BCE, Siddhartha Gautama was born. He would later become the Buddha, the Enlightened One, founding the religion of Buddhism (see *Seated Buddha,* Figure 9.6).

From 2000 to 1500 BCE, China was cultivating millet and wheat, using the potter's wheel (producing black pottery), and domesticating animals. Later, the Shang Dynasty (1500–1122 BCE) was known for developing writing, cultivating silkworms, and producing white pottery, bronze works, and marble, jade, and ivory artworks. They practiced ancestor worship. Between 1123 and 256 BCE, the Chinese invented the crossbow and perfected lacquer.

In Africa, the Kush people lived in the Sudan between 2000 and 350 BCE. In 732 BCE, they conquered Egypt and ruled for one hundred years. In 600 BCE, they were conquered by the Assyrians.

On the American continent, the Olmec civilization existed on the coast of the Gulf of Mexico between 1200 and 400 BCE. They built great temples, pyramids, colossal heads, and monuments. They also invented an accurate calendar and a counting system. In northern Peru, the Chavin culture existed from 1000 to 200 BCE. They built temples with stone carvings and produced fine pottery and gold work. Mound builders, farmers, and potters lived in central North America.

Around 2000 BCE, Europe was still in the New Stone Age, with megalithic structures built over a widespread area. Religious rituals were mixed with astronomy and agriculture, as at *Stonehenge* (Figure 9.27).

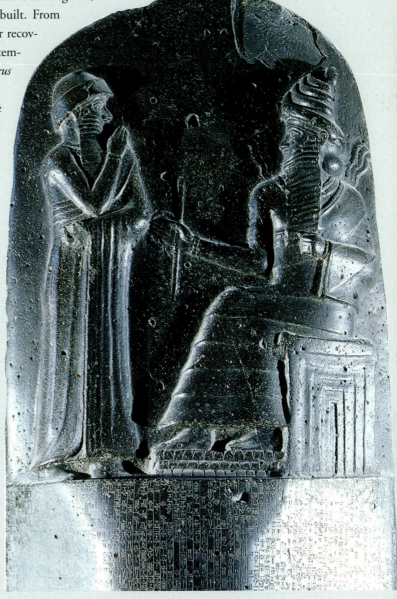

Above:
Hammurabi Stele. Relief, 28" high. Detail showing the king standing before the sun god and god of justice Shamash, who commanded Hammurabi to record the law. From Susa (modern Shush, Iran), 1792–1750 BCE. © Réunion des Musées Nationaux / Art Resource, NY.

Old Kingdom—Egypt	**2700 BCE**	
Middle Kingdom—Egypt	2100	*Ziggurat at Ur*
Babylon	2000	*Stonehenge*
Early Greek Civilizations		
Neolithic Europe		
Hebrew Culture	1800	
Hammurabi's Code		
Minoan Civilization	1700	
New Kingdom—Egypt	1600	*Snake Goddess*
Indian Civilization, Hinduism and Sanskrit		
Shang Dynasty—China		
	1400	
	1300	
Assyrians Conquer the Fertile Crescent		
Phoenician Civilization	1200	
Olmec Culture in Mexico		
Chavin Civilization—Peru	1000	
Etruscan Civilization		
	700	
	600	*The Goddess Hathor and the Overseer of Sealers, Psamtik*
Birth of Buddha		
Roman Republic	500	
Golden Age of Greece		
Persian Empire		
		Zeus (or Poseidon)
		Parthenon
		Great Stupa
	400	*Horus Temple*
Roman Empire	100	*Pantheon*
Birth of Jesus	4	
		Synagogue at Dura-Europos
	CE 200	*Pyramid of the Sun*
		Tlalocan Painting

		Ark of the Covenant mosaic
	600	*Seated Buddha*
Founding of Islam		*Main Shrine at Ise*
	700	
Crusades: Wars between Christians and Muslims for the Holy Land		*Kandarya Mahadeva Temple* *Shield Jaguar and Lady Xoc*
	1000	*Shiva as Nataraja, or Lord of the Dance*
		Xilonen, Goddess of Young Corn
	1100	*The Water and Moon Guanyin Bodhisattva*
Gothic Era—Europe		*Chartres Cathedral*
	1200	
Mali Empire—Africa	1300	
Aztecs Build Tenochtitlan		
	1400	*Ghiberti: Sacrifice of Abraham*
		Tlaloc Vessel
	1500	*Raphael: Madonna of the Meadow*
		Grünewald: Isenheim Altarpiece
		Michelangelo: Ceiling of the Sistine Chapel
		Mandala of Samvara
		Altar of Heaven
	1600	*Masjid-i-Shah, or Royal Mosque*
Height of the Ashanti Empire—Africa		
	1800	
		Power Figure
	1900	*Kewanwytewa: Ahola Kachina*
		Le Corbusier: Notre Dame du Haut
		Retablo of Maria de la Luz Casillas and Children
		Offering with Cili-Shaped Crown
		Transformation Mask
	2000	

In creating images of gods, goddesses, and other holy beings, artists use (1) geometric symbols, especially circles, squares, and triangles; (2) symbols taken from the natural world; (3) animal forms, which may be gods or symbolize gods; and (4) the human body, usually idealized. Religions that worship many gods often assign particular spheres of influence to various deities.

Art is part of the process of communication between humans and God, either as thanksgiving, an act of sacrifice, or a prayer in a ritual.

Many cultures believe that geometry can be symbolic in architecture and make a site sacred. Most sacred architecture is extraordinary in some way, in location, size, elaborate forms, decoration, or other aspects. It often incorporates elements of nature and/or the concept of a journey.

The materials used in construction and decoration are meaningful. Stone may communicate the idea of eternity or the majesty of mountains, while unadorned natural wood may echo animistic beliefs. Brilliant color or luminosity helps relate the idea of transcendence. Very large religious structures are usually expressions of both religious and secular power.

FOOD FOR THOUGHT

Try to visit an important religious site during a ceremony, when people are using it in prayer. It becomes alive, and other senses are invoked in rituals and processions: the sound of music and singing; the movement of bodies; the smell of incense, sacred oils, candles, and sacrificial fire, and so on.

Think about the many paradoxes and contradictions embedded in the human attempt to give image to the divine. For example, the visible is a vehicle to grasp the invisible. Diagrams of incredible complexity are paths for understanding Oneness. States of powerlessness can be required to come in touch with supernatural power. The material world can be both a divine manifestation and the total opposite of it.

- Can you think of art examples where contradictions are purposely used to point to the extraordinary?
- Why is it that human beings have often attempted to create images of divine or spiritual beings, only later in some cases to have them banned or destroyed?

- Do you think that the artists who created images of spiritual beings were divinely inspired?
- Could there be worship of a deity without the aid of the arts and architecture?
- How has art or architecture been a part of your own religious experience?

YOUR CD-ROM RESOURCES

- World History in Context
- Exploring Art Timeline
- Flashcards
- Food for Thought
- Companion Site
  Chapter 9 Quiz
  InfoTrac® College Edition Readings
  Artist Flashcards
  Online Study Guide

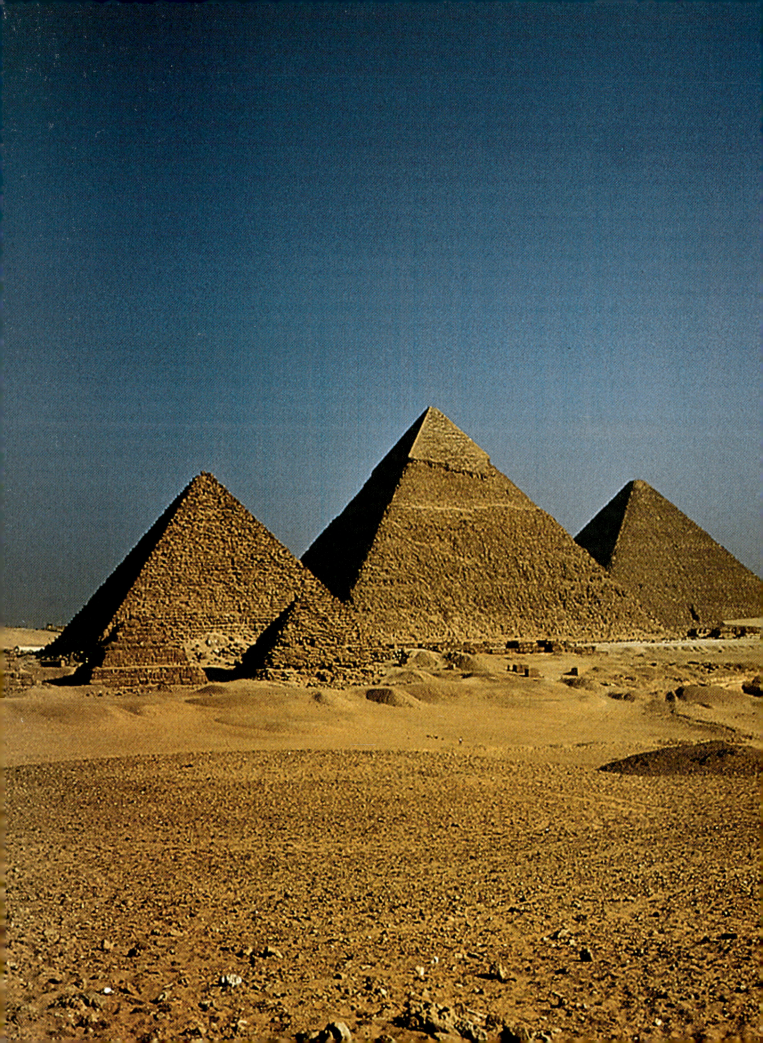

MORTALITY AND IMMORTALITY

INTRODUCTION

Tombs are among the very oldest works of art that humans have constructed. They are monuments to human mortality and to the persisting human faith in immortality in the afterlife.

Funerary art exists to honor the dead. Some wealthy and powerful individuals build ostentatious tombs for themselves, lavishly furnished to provide for their afterlife. Others build impressive tombs to preserve their fame with future generations. Friends and relatives may visit tombs for a personal connection with their departed loved ones. Governments build funerary monuments for deceased leaders and heroes for patriotic or political purposes. Elaborate rituals may accompany the burial of a person and often continue on certain feast days and anniversaries.

Think about the following questions:

How do tombs and funeral rituals reflect the cultures from which they come?

How do tombs reflect various concepts of the afterlife?

How do religions intertwine burial art and rituals?

How can tombs and commemorative art be used for political and social purposes?

How do urban development and landscape design affect burials?

MOUNDS AND MOUNTAINS

The very earliest tombs in many cultures are shaped like hills or mountains. The Egyptians built pyramids, which were geometric mountains. Others built funeral mounds that look like naturally occurring grass-covered hills, some small and others quite large. They contain hidden burial chambers, usually for elite members of a society. Some were lavishly furnished. The locations of mound graves were often tied to a natural phenomenon, such as the movement of the sun. Mound graves can be found in Europe, Asia, the Middle East, and the Americas.

ANCIENT BURIALS

The tombs we will see in this section date from periods in which funerary practices, religion, agriculture, and astronomy were often interrelated. Among the oldest tombs are the late Stone Age mounds in western Europe. They were rock and earthen hills built over large stones that were set upright to form the walls of inner burial chambers. The megalithic passage tomb at *Newgrange* (Figure 10.1) in Ireland is an early example of a mound grave, dating from 3200 BCE. It is part of a complex of tombs and monolithic rock structures. One of the largest mounds ever built, *Newgrange* is composed of 220,000 tons of loose stone with a white quartz–rock facing, ringed around the bottom with large boulders and covered on top with grass. A long, thirty-six-inch-wide passageway led to a cross-shaped interior chamber, made of forty-ton stones and sealed to prevent water seepage. Five bodies were buried there.

Many rocks along the passage were decorated with spirals, curves, or other geometric patterns, perhaps indicating celes-tial bodies. The builders of *Newgrange* had sophisticated methods of marking time. They oriented *Newgrange* so that for about two weeks around the winter solstice, a burst of brilliant morning sunlight shines through a specially constructed slit above the doorway, penetrates the entire passage, and illuminates one patterned stone at the far end of the burial chamber.

Over time, many mound graves erode and are blended into the natural landscape. After the fourth century, *Newgrange* was an abandoned and undisturbed site until 1699, when it was rediscovered by men quarrying for building stone.

Like *Newgrange*, the *Great Pyramids* of Egypt are very old, very large, very influential in style, and oriented to the sun. They are the tombs of the pharaohs, the rulers of Egypt who were believed to be the sons of the most powerful of all the gods, Re, the Sun God. The pyramids, standing dramatically on the edge of the Sahara Desert, are artificial mountains on a flat, artificial plane. They are part of a necropolis, composed of tombs and mortuary temples, that extends for fifty miles on the west bank of the Nile. The pyramids of pharaohs *Menkaure,* c. 2525–2475 BCE, *Khafre,* c. 2575–2525 BCE, and *Khufu,* c. 2600–2550 BCE (Figure 10.2) are the largest among all the pyramids. The numbers associated with the very largest, the pyramid of *Khufu,* are often recited, but still inspire awe: 775 feet along one side of the base; 450 feet high; 2.3 million stone blocks; average weight of each block, 2.5 tons.

The Egyptians used the pyramid form to create the meeting place between earthly life and eternity. It is where the *ba* and *ka* return to the mummified remains of the deceased. According to Egyptian belief, a human possessed a soul with both a ba and a ka. The ba is part of the soul whose seat was the

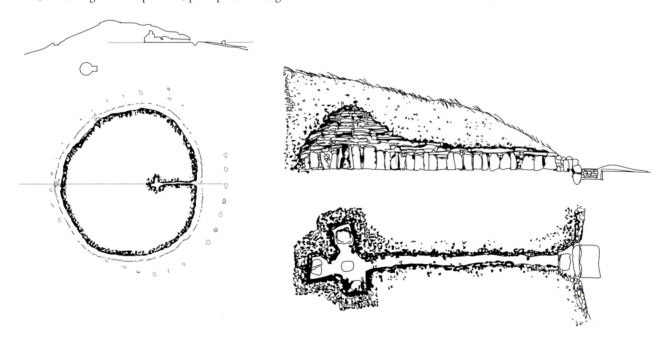

10.1   *Newgrange.* Plan and elevation. County Meath, Ireland, 3200 BCE. Adapted from A.T. Mann, Sacred Architecture 1993, p. 61. Used with permission of Element Inc. Rockport, Massachusetts.

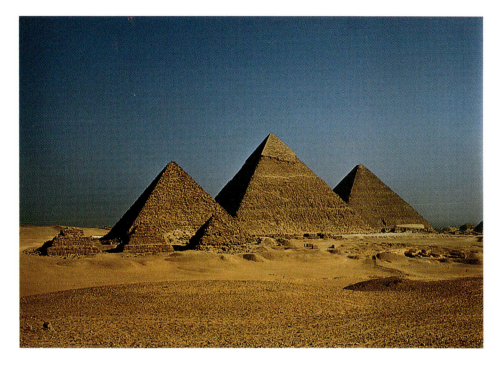

10.2 *Great Pyramids.* From left, *Menkaure,* c. 2525–2475 BCE; *Khafre,* c. 2575–2525 BCE; *Khufu,* c. 2600–2550 BCE. Gizeh, Egypt. © E. Strouhal / Werner Forman / Art Resource, NY. See also the text accompanying Figure 5.1 for more on the building of the pyramids.

heart or abdomen in the body. It is depicted as a human-headed bird. When humans take their last breath, the ba flies from the body. After the body has been mummified seventy days later, the ba returns, hungry and thirsty. A well-prepared tomb is filled with provisions to satisfy the needs of the ba in the afterlife, including water, wine, grains, dates, cakes, and even dehydrated beef and fowl. The ka is the mental aspect of the human's soul. It is symbolized by two outstretched arms or by an attendant figure that represents the double of the personality. The ka dwells in a lifelike statue of the deceased, which is placed in the tomb. It was important for both the statue and the sarcophagus to have a strong likeness of the dead person, so that both the ba and ka could easily recognize their destinations. The ba and the ka were thought to enter the tombs

through a small chimney or an air vent. Provisions for the ka would include chairs, beds, chariots, models of servants, kitchen utensils, dishes, and simulated food (unlike the real food the ba required). Combs, hairpins, and ointments were also included, along with games for entertainment. Rich treasures of gold and silver as well as carriages and boats for the ka's journey to heaven have also been found in the more elaborate tombs.

Disassembled and buried in a trench at the base of the pyramid of Khufu were two wooden boats, called barques, discovered in 1954. These boats were made from long planks of cedars, imported from Phoenicia (modern Lebanon). One reassembled *Barque,* dated 2600–2550 BCE (Figure 10.3), has a cabin to house passengers or precious freight; ten rowing oars; two rear oars for steering; and a canopy to protect the

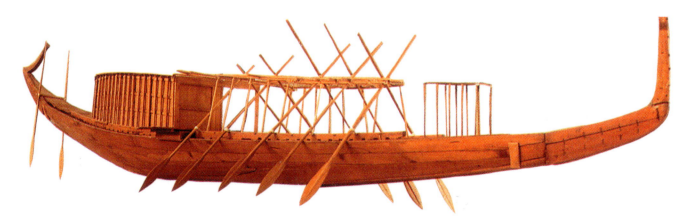

10.3 *Funerary Barque of the Pharaoh Khufu* (found at the base of his pyramid). Lebanon cedar, 143' long. Gizeh, Egypt, c. 2600–2550 BCE. Solar Barque Museum, Gizeh. Stierlin, Henri, The Pharaohs Master-Builders (Paris: Terrail. 1992).

crew from the fierce sun. It was entirely assembled with knotted cords. No nails, pegs, or rivets were used. Long and sleek, with distinctive sternposts, these boats were used to navigate the Nile during the pharaoh's lifetime; in death, they were used to bring the body and possessions of the dead pharaoh from the east to the west bank of the Nile, to the city of the dead. This last journey of the pharaoh recreated the path of his father, the Sun God, in his chariot across the sky. Thus, these boats were called "solar barques." Like the pyramids themselves that face the compass points, the Egyptian funeral ceremonies reflect the movement of the sun.

FURNISHED TOMBS

Many cultures believed that the afterlife was similar to this life, and that the dead continued to "live" in the tomb and needed furnishings like those used when they were alive, such as furniture, clothing, utensils, and precious items.

EGYPTIAN TOMBS AND MORTUARY TEMPLES

The ancient Egyptians provide the supreme examples of furnished tombs. The *Great Pyramids* we have just studied have interior chambers that are quite small, and, when opened in modern times, contained only empty stone crypts. Archeologists presume that the tombs contained scrolls, riches, and provisions, but were robbed shortly after they were sealed. In an effort to thwart grave robbing, which was rampant in ancient Egypt, the pharaohs stopped building enormous, ostentatious tombs like the pyramids. Instead, they were buried in chambers cut deep into the sides of mountains, with hidden entrances. These hidden chamber burials were also considerably less costly than erecting pyramids.

Despite the pharaohs' efforts, however, royal tombs were still robbed long ago, except that of King Tutankhamen, which was only partly plundered and then resealed. Ironically, it was saved from further theft by grave robbers who, while stealing treasures from a nearby tomb, happened to heap more debris on the entrance to Tutankhamen's tomb, which remained undisturbed until 1922. Among the amazing treasures found in Tutankhamen's tomb was his *Innermost Coffin*, dated c. 1325 BCE, in Figure 10.4. It is beaten gold, weighing nearly three-quarters of a ton, and is inlaid with semiprecious stones. Two other, larger coffin cases of gold fit over it, and together they encased the mummy. There were also inlaid chests, gilt chairs, and other wooden items covered with gold; carved watchdogs, life-size guardian statues, jewels, and so on. To provide for the comfort of those of high rank, clay statues of servants were included in the tombs.

Tutankhamen was an Eighteenth Dynasty pharaoh who ruled for about nine years and died unexpectedly before the age of twenty. There was little time to prepare his tomb, as mummification, funerary rites, and burial had to be completed

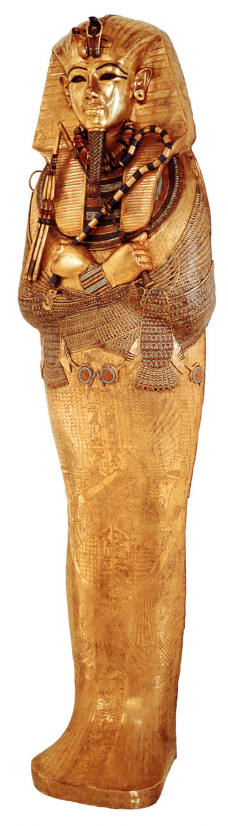

10.4   *Innermost Coffin of Tutankhamen.* Gold inlaid with enamel and semiprecious stones, 6'1" long. Thebes, Egypt, c. 1325 BCE. Egyptian Museum, Cairo. © Boltin Picture Library.

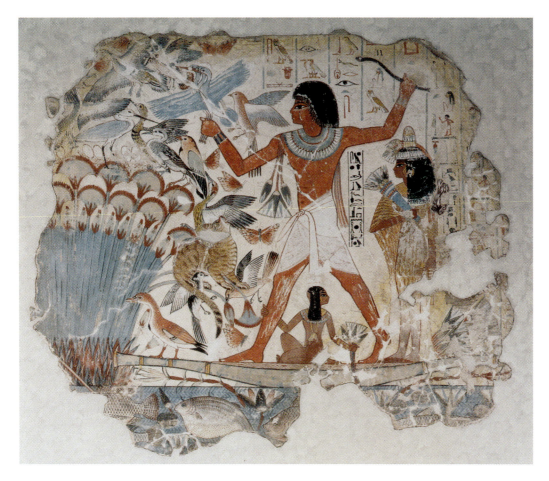

 10.5 *Fowling Scene.* Paint on dry plaster, approximately 32" high. Wall painting from the tomb of Nebamun. Thebes, Egypt, c. 1400–1350 BCE. The British Museum, London. Photo © British Museum. See also Figure 6.10.

in seventy days. Archeologists believe that his tomb was surely less lavishly furnished than those of pharaohs with long reigns. His burial chamber was small and decorated only with paintings, while other rulers buried near him were interred in large, barrel-vaulted chambers with relief carvings on the walls.

The body was mummified to preserve it as much as possible and to make it recognizable to the gods. This process involved removing internal organs, chemically treating the cadaver, and wrapping and rewrapping the body in layers of linen, while special prayers and anointments were performed. The ancient Egyptians installed likenesses of the deceased in the tomb to serve as substitute receptacles for the spirit should something happen to the mummy. For pharaohs, the portraits were stone statues or effigies in gold, like the *Innermost Coffin.* The wings of the god Horus protectively encircle the coffin, and Tutankhamen holds insignia of his rank. Certain features are standard on Tutankhamen's face: the distinctive eye makeup; the false beard, a symbol of power; the striped head-cloth; the cobra head to frighten enemies. Although the face is stylized, it is indeed a portrait of Tutankhamen. Several other sculptural likenesses were also placed in his tomb.

Many tombs were decorated with wall paintings and carvings that recreated the pleasures and labors of earthly existence. The *Fowling Scene,* a wall painting from the tomb of Nebamun, c. 1400–1350 BCE (Figure 10.5), shows an Egyptian noble hunting along the Nile River, taking pleasure in the abundance of fish, fowl, and flora in the fertile marshes. The air is filled with birds of all sorts, painted with care and distinction, and the water is thick with fish. Pattern is an important element in this image. Water ripples were rendered as linear patterns; the birds in the nobleman's hand create a repeating image; and the tops of the marsh grasses fan out in a beautiful but rigid decoration. Depth is not shown in ancient Egyptian paintings, so everything is distributed vertically or horizontally. The repetition of pattern elements is a visual metaphor for the seasonal cycles of the Nile, the rigidity of the culture, and the vast desert that surrounds the river valley.

In this wall painting, humans dominate the scene. The noble is shown in the formal manner reserved for exalted persons: head, shoulders, legs, and feet in profile; eyes and shoulders frontal. Size was an important indicator of rank, so the

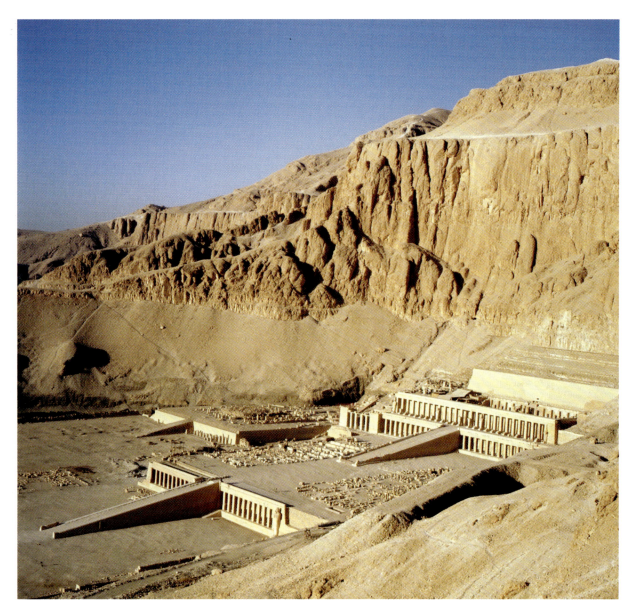

10.6 *Mortuary Temple of Hatshepsut.* Deir el-Bahri, Egypt, c. 1490–1460 BCE. © Dallas and John Heaton / Corbis. See also the text accompanying Figure 3.23 for more on the architectural features of this temple.

nobleman is larger than his wife and daughter, indicating their lower status.

When high-ranking Egyptians began to hide tombs in hillsides, the funerary temples that formerly were appendages to pyramids were enlarged and emphasized. The *Mortuary Temple of Hatshepsut,* 1490–1460 BCE (Figure 10.6), of the Eighteenth Dynasty, shows this later development in Egyptian funerary architecture. The temple was the monument to her greatness. It once housed two hundred statues of her and many brightly painted reliefs showing her divine birth, coronation, military victories, and other exploits.

The *Mortuary Temple of Hatshepsut* is impressively large, but its design is open, light, and clean, without the solid mass and ponderous weightiness of the earlier pyramids. The simple vertical columns contrast with the vertical rock formations of the bare cliffs. The terraces in front were once verdant, filled with exotic plants and aromatic trees. A quarter-mile-long forecourt contained a garden with a pool and papyrus and with rows of frankincense trees. The garden represented one of the great pleasures of Egyptian life and, thus, was prominent in their afterlife imagery. An inscription from another tomb says: "May I wander round my pool each day for evermore; may my soul sit on the branches of the grave garden I have prepared for myself; may I refresh myself each day under my sycamore."

The *Mortuary Temple of Hatshepsut* was pillaged and vandalized shortly after her death by her successor, Pharaoh

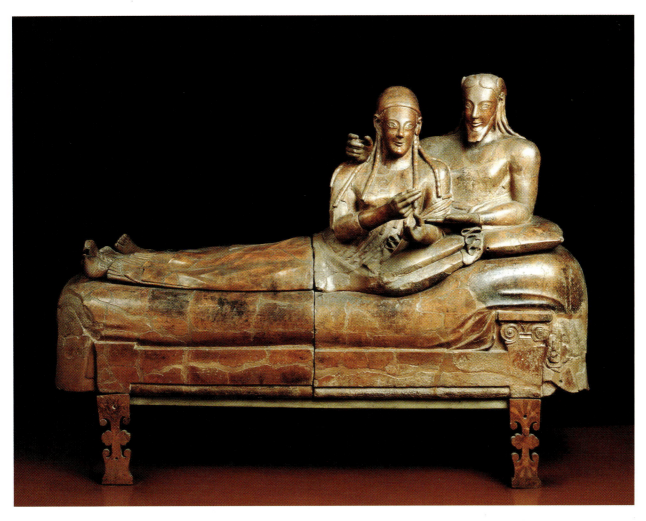

10.7   *Sarcophagus with Reclining Couple.* Painted terra-cotta, 45¹/₂" tall. From a cemetery near Cerveteri, Etruria (Italy), c. 520 BCE. Museo Nationale di Villa Giulia, Rome. © Araldo de Luca / Corbis.

Thutmose III, who was angered that her two-decade rule had delayed his accession to the throne of Egypt. Almost all her images were destroyed with the exception of her two obelisks at the Karnak temple complex.

ETRUSCAN TOMBS

The Etruscans were another ancient people who buried their dead in earthen mounds furnished for the afterlife. The Etruscan civilization was a loose band of city-states in west-central Italy. It developed in the eighth and seventh centuries BCE, flourished, and then was overtaken by the expanding Roman Empire in the fifth and fourth centuries BCE. Around the city of Cerveteri, the Etruscans buried their dead under row after row of earthen mounds arranged along "streets" in a necropolis. The Etruscan tombs often had several modest-sized rooms, laid out much like houses. These tomb chambers were carved directly out of the soft bedrock, called tufa. Furnishings, such as chairs and beds and utensils, were sometimes carved in

relief on the underground rock surfaces. They simulated a domestic interior. In contrast to those of other civilizations, the Etruscan tombs are not grand monuments to powerful rulers, but reminders of a society that emphasized sociability and the pleasures of living.

The freestanding terra-cotta sculpture *Sarcophagus with Reclining Couple,* c. 520 BCE (Figure 10.7), comes from a tomb in Cerveteri. The clay sarcophagus, with life-size figures, was molded in four pieces. The wife and husband are shown at the same scale, reclining together at a banquet, sharing the same couch. This reflects the fact that Etruscan women had more rights than women in most other cultures. The facial features are similar and standardized on both figures, and their hair is represented as a geometric pattern. Their bodies are somewhat flattened and unformed from the waist down. Despite these unnatural features, the wife and husband still give the impression of alert liveliness, health, and vigor. Their gestures are very animated.

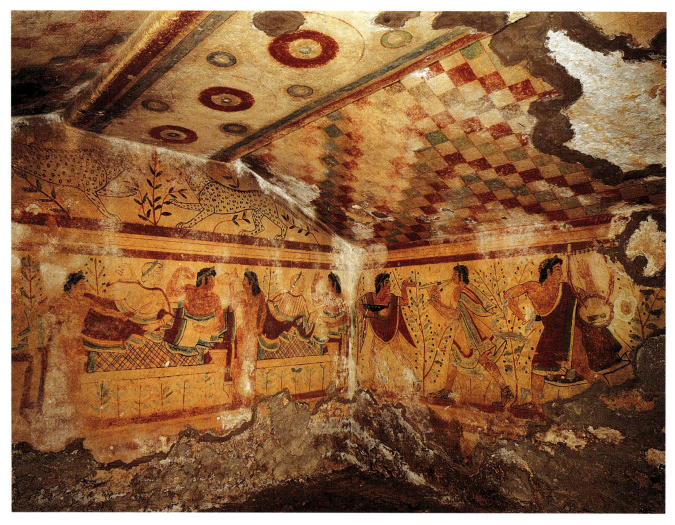

 10.8   *Banqueters and Musicians.* Mural painting from the *Tomb of the Leopards.* From a cemetery near Tarquinia, Etruria (Italy), c. 480–470 BCE. Hirmer Fotoarchiv.

Etruscan tomb art emphasizes pleasure. In tombs carved into cliffs near the Etruscan city of Tarquinia, the walls were often covered with paintings. One example is *Banqueters and Musicians,* from the Tomb of the Leopards, c. 480–470 BCE (Figure 10.8), so named for the leopards painted on the wall near the ceiling. To the left, banqueters recline on couches while servants bring them food and drink. The women are shown with light skin and men with dark, according to conventions of representation at that time. One man holds an egg, a symbol of rebirth. To the right, musicians dance across the wall. Gestures are lively and animated and are made more visible by the oversized hands. Golds, reds, and greens predominate, and the circle and checkerboard patterns on the ceiling add to the general colorfulness of the scene.

FUNERAL COMPLEX OF SHI HUANGDI

One of the most extensive tombs ever constructed was that of Ying Cheng, who at age thirteen succeeded his father to become the ruler of the Qin state in 259 BCE. By 221 BCE,

he had subdued the rival neighboring states to unify China and found the Qin Dynasty. He assumed the title *Shi Huangdi,* the "First Emperor." To consolidate his power, Shi Huangdi ruthlessly homogenized Chinese culture. He decreed the burning of all historical books and had scholars burned or buried alive to eradicate old traditions and all opposition. He destroyed the arms and fortifications of individual states, and former ruling families in rival states were forcibly moved to his capital, away from their land holdings and centers of power. He then reorganized the country into provinces administered by civil servants whom he selected and controlled, laying the groundwork for an administrative bureaucracy that continued for centuries in China. He built the *Great Wall* (see Figure 11.21) for the northern defense of China, using forced labor from conquered tribes. New highways and canals facilitated travel throughout the recently unified lands. He standardized weights, measurements, axle widths, currency, and script styles.

Shi Huangdi built for himself an underground funeral palace that was large and lavish. Very little of it has been

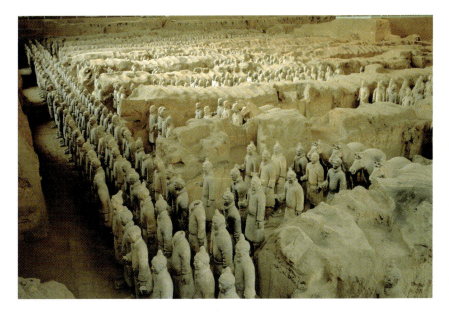

10.9   *Soldiers from Pit 1.* Painted ceramic; average figure height, 5'9". Near the tomb of Shi Huangdi, Shaanxi, China, 221–206 BCE. The soldiers visible in this picture represent only one-eighth of the length of each column, and there are eleven columns in all. Photo by O. Louis Mazzatenta / National Georgraphic Image Collection. See also the text accompanying Figure 6.14.

excavated. In 1974, peasants digging for a well uncovered pieces of a huge, buried terra-cotta army composed of more than six thousand life-size figures, the eternal guards for the afterlife palace complex. Since then, archeologists have concentrated on excavating and restoring the terra-cotta army.

The *Soldiers from Pit 1* (Figure 10.9), from 221–206 BCE, are arranged in eleven columns, with four soldiers abreast in nine of the columns. This image shows only one-eighth of one column of soldiers. Just imagine the total length of this column, eight times longer than what you see. Then multiply that by eleven columns wide, and then add at least two other pits also filled with life-size clay soldiers! Each soldier is made of low-fire ceramic clay mined from the area. The torsos are hollow, while the solid legs provide a weighty bottom for support and balance. The modeling on the bodies is standardized and formulaic: frontal, stiff, and anatomically simplified. Certain features, such as hands, were mass-produced in molds. Each of the thousands of faces is individualized, as we can see with the *Infantry General* (Figure 10.10), and sculpted with great skill and sensitivity. No two are alike. Their carefully detailed hair shows individualized knotting and braiding, typical of the coiffures worn by the Chinese infantry of the time. The clay soldiers were outfitted with bronze spears, swords, and/or crossbows. The person in Figure 10.10 is presumed to be the commander of all the troops. He wears a helmet and more armor than any other soldier, and he is five inches taller than the rest.

The soldiers were originally painted in vivid colors, adding to their grand appearance. Each column of this buried army stood on a brick "street" that was fifteen to twenty feet below ground level. Separating the columns were rows of compressed, pounded earth that supported wood beams that once covered the entire pit. Fiber mats and plaster were placed over the beams to seal the pits and prevent water seepage. Finally, the entire roof of the pit was hidden under a low, flat mound of dirt.

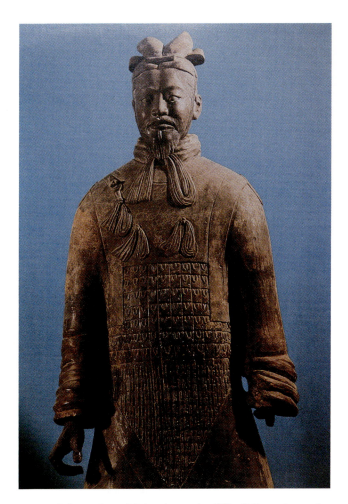

10.10   *Infantry General.* Painted ceramic, 6'4" tall. From the tomb of Shi Huangdi, Shaanxi, China, 221–206 BCE. Cultural Relics Publishing House, Beijing. See also the text accompanying Figure 6.14.

ROYAL TOMBS OF THE MOCHE CIVILIZATION

In the late 1980s and 1990s, more than 350 Moche tombs in Peru were carefully excavated and their contents examined. The burials range from simple, cloth-wrapped bodies in shallow pits to elaborate burial chambers that held not only the dead, but also a large number of lavish ceremonial items. This difference in burials indicates that the Moche society was highly stratified, with a continuum ranging from rich to poor. Without a doubt, furnished tombs were the privilege of rank within a prosperous society. Gold and silver metalwork was reserved for the elite, while pottery was available to all classes of people and was not used as a mark of class distinction. A class of full-time artisans, who were extremely skilled and technically very inventive, created these ceremonial and funerary objects.

Warrior priests apparently ruled the Moche civilization, because their grave sites were the most richly furnished. The primary reason for warfare in Moche society was to capture prisoners for sacrificial ceremonies.

The excavation of a Moche *Royal Tomb* (Figure 10.11) shows its treasures were dated c. 300. It was the tomb of a warrior priest. Flat mats made from thousands of tiny shell beads decorated his shoulders and chest. Large, shiny gold and corroded silver peanut beads were also found; when assembled, they made a peanut necklace that can be seen in the reconstruction of the warrior priest's attire in Figure 10.12.

All the objects and bodies from this tomb had to be painstakingly cleaned, sorted, identified, and reassembled. There emerged several sets of ceremonial gear for the warrior priest, including several layers of jewelry, breastplates, weapons, and ornamental feathers. The mannequin in Figure 10.12 is dressed in a small portion of the objects found in the tomb. He is wearing a cloth covered with gilded platelets, shell beads cover his wrists and shoulders, and a truly striking helmet crowns his head. Other face apparel includes a nose plate, suspended from a hole in the nasal septum, and large ear ornaments. This nose plate is plain gold; others have elaborate

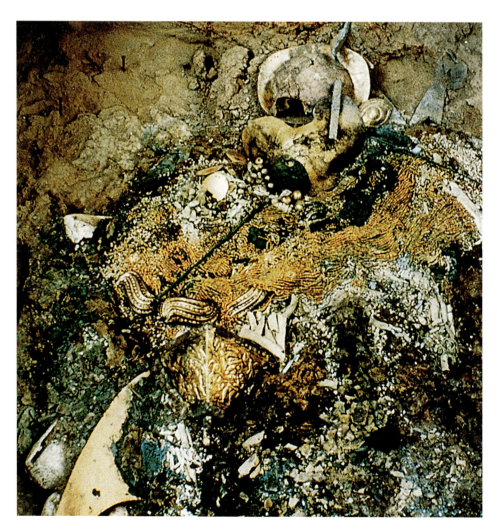

10.11   *Royal Tomb of Sipán.*
Excavation of tomb 1. Moche. Gold, silver, copper, and shell ornamentation overlaying a human skeleton (cranium visible at top). Peru, c. 300. The Fowler Museum of Cultural Heritage, University of California, Los Angeles.

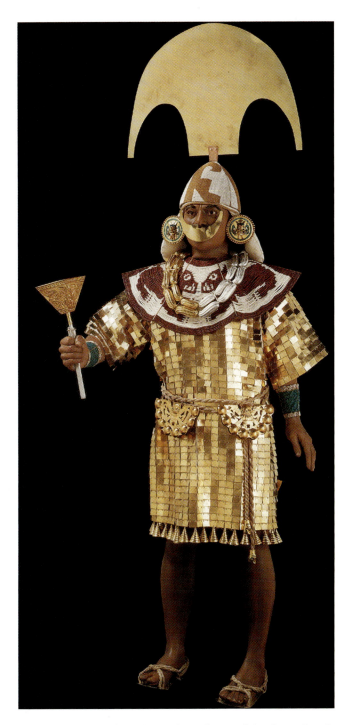

small scale. Two symmetrical figures in profile on either side are lesser priests, indicated by their smaller size.

In the Moche civilization, gold and silver were used in symmetrical and matching arrangements. The *Peanut Necklace* (Figure 7.17), for example, contained ten gold peanut beads that were worn over the warrior priest's right shoulder, and ten silver ones worn over the left. An identical pair of weapons was found in one tomb, one in gold and one in silver. In another tomb, a gold ingot was found in the deceased's right hand, and a silver one in the left. Some examples of nose plates are fabricated in symmetrical halves, one gold and one silver.

VIKING SHIP BURIAL

The Vikings were maritime raiders from Scandinavia with settlements in areas as far-flung as Iceland, England, northern France, and Russia in the ninth and tenth centuries. Their tombs, therefore, reflect how important sea travel was to their civilization. The objects found in the Oseberg ship burial, excavated in 1904 near Oslo, Norway, are the richest source of information on Viking art and funerary practices.

10.12   Mannequin dressed in replicas of some of the objects found in tomb 1, *Royal Tomb of Sipán.* Moche. Peru, c. 300. The Fowler Museum of Cultural Heritage, University of California, Los Angeles. For more on the Peanut Necklace, see Figure 7.17.

decoration and inlay on them. From his waist hang crescent-shaped bells that would have jangled with every step.

Figure 10.13 shows one of a pair of *Warrior Ear Ornaments.* The central frontal figure is shown in an outfit very similar to the one worn by the mannequin, reproduced in

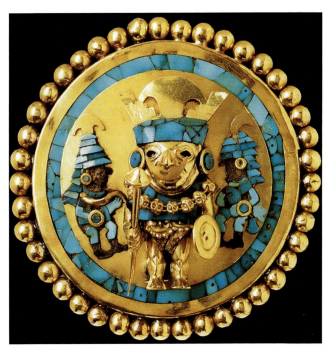

 10.13   *Warrior Ear Ornament* (restored). Gold with inlay of turquoise, 4" diameter. From tomb 1, *Royal Tomb of Sipán.* Moche. Peru, c. 300. The Fowler Museum of Cultural Heritage, University of California, Los Angeles.

The tomb of a high-ranking Viking woman from the ninth century was located under a mound approximately 20 feet high and 130 feet long. The tomb had been robbed centuries ago, but large items were left behind. The *Viking Ship* (Figure 10.14) was probably the private vessel of a wealthy family, intended for use near the coast and on inland waterways. It was outfitted with a mast and sail and had rowlocks for thirty oarsmen. The graceful curves of the low, wide ship culminate with high, spiral posts at stem and stern; the one at the front is carved like a coiled snake. Rising up each post are relief carvings of animal forms that have been elongated and interlocked into a complex, twisting pattern. The animals' bodies form the main curves of the carving, while their long, attenuated limbs interlock in thin lacy lines around them.

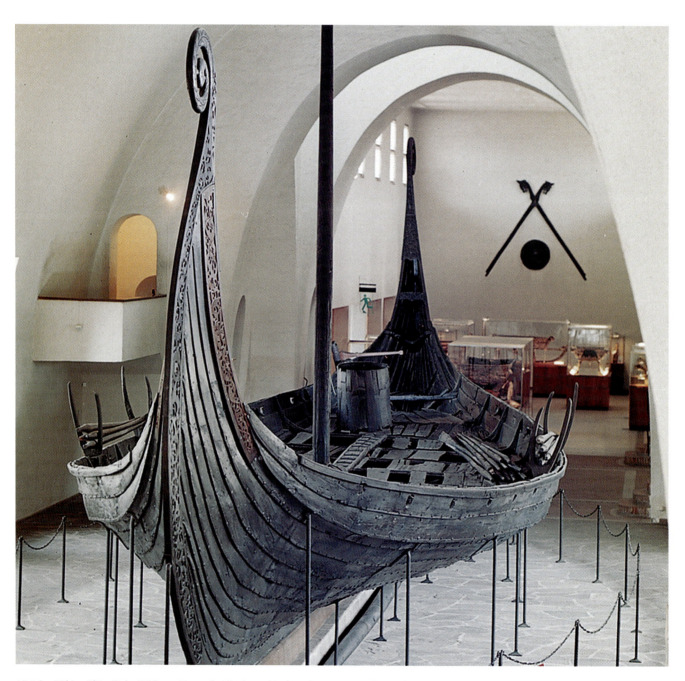

10.14 *Viking Ship*. Oak, 65' long. From the Oseberg ship burial, Norway, early ninth century. Viking Ship Museum, Oslo, ninth century. Photo University Museum of National Antiquities, Oslo, Norway.

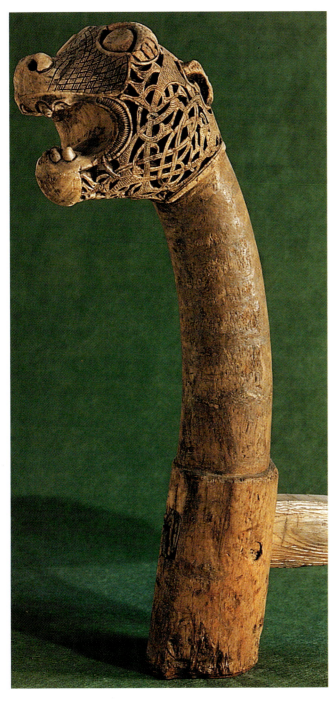

 10.15 *Animal-Head Post.* Wood, 5" tall. From the Oseberg ship burial, Norway, early ninth century. Viking Ship Museum, Oslo. Photo University Museum of National Antiquities, Oslo, Norway.

Each animal's body is further adorned with crisscross or zigzag lines carved into its surface. Although all the animals seem similar, each differs in its intricate detail work.

In addition to the stem and stern of the ship, other wooden objects in the burial (for example, beds, carts, and sledges) are covered with complex carvings, mostly animal forms, such as imaginary birds or totally unidentifiable beasts. In some, the individual animal forms are clear and large, while others are confused, entangled, and ambiguous. Yet all the animal carvings convey a feeling of wild agitation, firmly contained within the margins of the carving. They grip, bite, interpenetrate, and twist around each other. The background wood has been carved away, so that the animal forms stand out in relief. Traces of paint in some sledges' carvings suggest that they were once painted with a black background and outlines of vivid color on the animals, enhancing and emphasizing the interlaced design.

The *Animal-Head Post* (Figure 10.15) from Oseberg conveys that same sense of ferociousness, agitation, and energy. Its mouth is drawn back in a snarl, baring its large teeth. Its wide, short snout is covered with a pattern of squares, and its eyes bulge from striped sockets. Drastically elongated interlaced birds form a complex, curved pattern on the sides. This carving was executed with such a level of precision, intricacy, and control that it may have been made by a jeweler. Similar animal interlaced designs are found on Viking jewelry.

DEVELOPMENT OF CEMETERIES AND GRAVE MONUMENTS

During the first millennium BCE, a long transition took place from mound tombs to other forms of funerary art and architecture. A fundamental conceptual shift accompanied this change: tombs no longer served as permanent homes for the dead and repositories of the items they needed. Rather, tombs commemorated the departed individuals.

The ancient Greeks developed the earliest commemorative funerary architecture in Europe and the Middle East. Among the wealthy and powerful, the tradition arose of erecting very grand monuments, like temples, that housed the bodies of the deceased and elevated them to a semidivine status. Like the Greeks, the rulers of ancient Rome built large commemorative mausoleums.

While large mausoleums were the privilege of the wealthy, cemeteries near Greek and Roman cities were laid out for the burial of the merchant and working classes. Among nomadic or farming communities, the disposal of the dead presents no problem. But as cities developed and populations became denser in and around them, cemeteries with small plots marked by upright monuments became practical.

In ancient Greece, the most common monuments were (1) small columns that supported vases, urns, or small statues; (2) life-size freestanding figures of young men or women; or (3) relief carvings on stone slabs. The *Grave Stele of Hegeso,*

c. 410–400 BCE (Figure 10.16), is an example of the third type. Hegeso is represented as a seated woman, whose servant has brought her a piece of jewelry to examine. Quiet, everyday moments were often depicted on Greek grave markers. A simple, architectural frame encloses the scene. The geometric curves of the chair make a pleasing transition from the straight edges of the frame to the complex folds of the drapery and the organic curves of the women's bodies. The bodies are rounded and naturalistic, but they also are idealized in their propor-

tions and in their overall serenity and composure. Grave markers such as this were once colorfully painted, brightening up a gloomy graveyard.

In ancient Rome, the dead were buried outside the city walls, along roadways entering the city, because Romans wanted their funerary monuments to be highly visible. The funerary monument was one important means of ensuring an individual's fame, and it served as an enduring testament to the entire family's honor and standing in society. The tomb

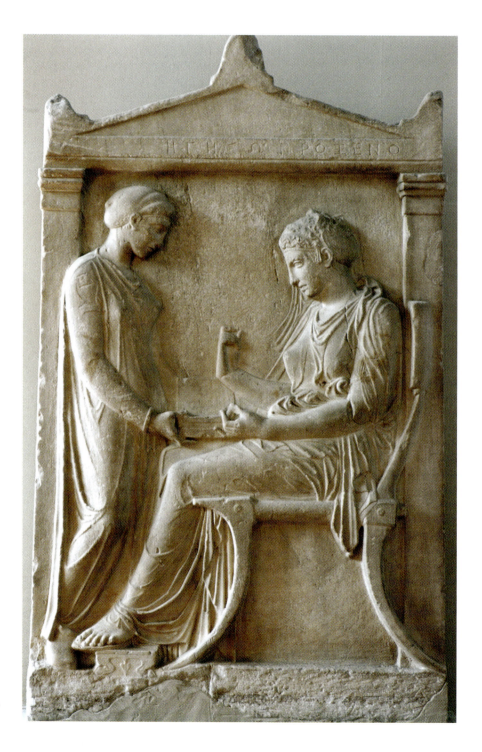

10.16 *Grave Stele of Hegeso.* Marble relief, 5'2" high. From the Dipylon cemetery, Athens, Greece, c. 410–400 BCE. National Archeological Museum, Athens. © Saskia.

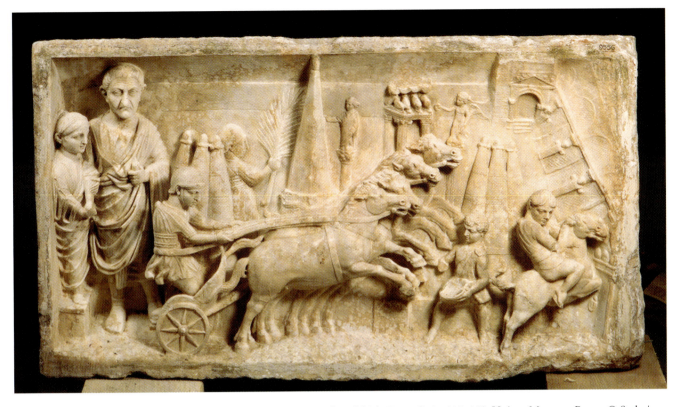

10.17 *Funerary Relief of a Circus Official.* Marble relief, approximately 20" high. From Ostia, 110–130. Vatican Museum, Rome. © Scala / Art Resource, NY.

was the meeting place of the living and the departed, and feasts would be held regularly at the family tomb in which all would partake; food and drink were poured out for the dead to enjoy.

Roman family tombs and mausoleums were built in several styles. They could be altar-tombs. Others were towers, modified Greek temples, diminutive Egyptian pyramids, or combinations of these. Almost all afforded ample space for inscriptions and relief carvings, with narratives and details that announced the fame of the individual or family interred there. The sculpture on the tombs of the wealthy was lavish and tended to imitate Greek styles, with dignified, idealized figures filling an uncrowded space. The *Funerary Relief of a Circus Official,* dated CE 110–130 (Figure 10.17), was produced for a working-class person's tomb and is very different in style. The space on the Roman relief is cramped. However, its purpose was to tell complex ideas and narratives, so it features numerous characters, varying scale, and symbolic details.

The largest figure is that of the official himself, holding hands with his wife at the far left. In Roman art, the handshake symbolized marriage. The wife is smaller, as she is of lesser status, and stands on a pedestal as a sign that she died before him. The faces of the official and his wife are frank, unflattering portraits. The Romans had a long tradition of realistic portraiture, in which the nonidealized likenesses of

older people were recorded in stone—in this case, with forehead wrinkles, protruding ears, and a drooping nose and mouth. The official and his wife are crowded to the side to give space for the Circus Maximus. Only one team of horses is shown, but they leap forward to communicate the speed and competitiveness of all the chariot teams that raced there. The space of the racecourse is tilted up and shrunken down behind the chariot, while the charioteer is shown twice, once driving the team and again holding a palm branch of victory. The deceased may be officiating the race, or he may be the charioteer himself, shown in his younger days.

CONNECTION
For an example of Roman portraiture, see Head of a Roman Patrician *(Figure 14.13, page 410).*

BURIAL IN PLACES OF WORSHIP

In some cultures, a preference arose for being buried in holy sites. In this way, the deceased was seen as closer to God. This practice can also be a sign of prestige. The most sanctified

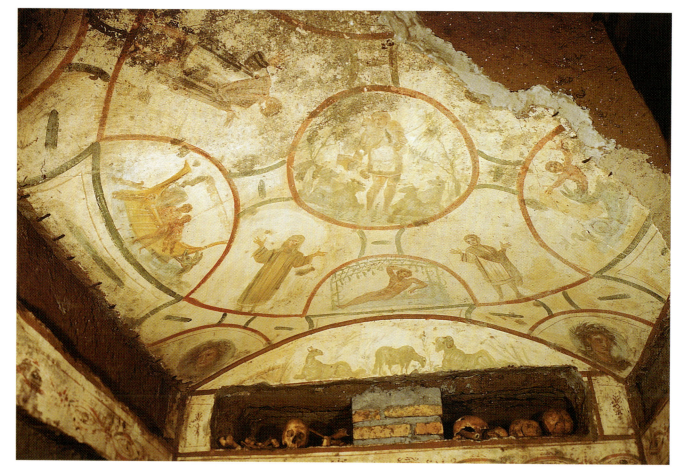

10.18 *Catacomb of Sts. Peter and Marcellinus.* Ceiling painting from a cubiculum. Fresco. The center circle shows Jesus as the Good Shepherd; surrounding half-circles show scenes from the biblical story of Jonah and the Whale. Rome, early fourth century. © Madeline Grimoldi.

places for burial were reserved for those with the greatest wealth, power, or religious standing.

CHRISTIAN BURIALS

Early Christians buried their dead rather than cremating them, as was the common practice in the Roman Empire, because they believed the body would be resurrected and would rejoin the soul at the end of time. Outside Rome and other nearby cities, the dead were buried in vast underground networks of tunnels and chambers called *catacombs,* dug out of the same soft bedrock, or tufa, as the Etruscan burial chambers. Catacombs were used from the second through the fourth centuries, and some were dug as many as five levels deep. Passageways were lined with openings the size of a body, one above the other, stack after stack. At death, a Christian's body would be placed into an opening, which was then sealed and decorated with painted plaster or carvings (such openings, now unsealed, are visible in Figure 10.18).

The catacombs became sanctified places for a variety of reasons. The Roman imperial government periodically tried to suppress Christianity because its followers refused to recognize

the divinity of the emperor or pay token tribute to Roman gods; therefore, the religion was considered destabilizing to civil order. During two great periods of persecution, in 249–251 and again in 303–306, Romans killed, imprisoned, or harassed Christians for their beliefs. During times of persecution, the catacombs were used to bury martyrs, to hide fugitives from the Romans, and, occasionally, as places of worship.

At various intervals in the catacomb passageways, small rooms were carved out to be used as mortuary chapels. These chapels were often plastered and painted. An example of a painted ceiling in a mortuary chapel from the fourth century is shown in Figure 10.18, from the *Catacomb of Sts. Peter and Marcellinus,* in Rome. The style of the catacomb painting and much of its imagery are very similar to Roman secular painting. The feeding and resting lambs are taken from Roman landscape painting, for the Romans were very fond of pastoral scenes, often having them painted on the walls of their homes. But here the lambs are transformed into the Christian "flock" of followers who were protected by Jesus, the Good Shepherd, who is shown in the central circle of the ceiling painting. Decorative motifs of birds, foliage, and little angels as well as images of the seasons were also taken from Roman secular painting. The background of catacomb paintings was usually white, for better visibility in the dark tunnels, and wall surfaces were often subdivided by red and green lines. Figures were usually lively and energetic, rendered in quick, sketchy brushstrokes. There was no attempt to show deep space in perspective.

The status of Christianity changed radically under Constantine, the emperor of Rome from 306 to 337, who legalized Christianity in 313. During his lifetime, Constantine funded the construction of lavish churches over the tombs of some of the most famous martyrs. One of these was Old St. Peter's in Rome, a church built over the tomb of St. Peter, the first head of Jesus' church. His tomb lay in the ground, but was marked by six twisting marble columns and a crown-shaped candelabrum.

By the sixteenth century, Old St. Peter's, a timber church, had deteriorated and its size no longer befitted the grandeur of the expanded Catholic Church, and so a newer, grander St. Peter's was constructed in stone. The tomb of St. Peter continued to be the focal point of the new church, and a new canopy in bronze, called a *Baldacchino* (Figure 10.19), was erected to

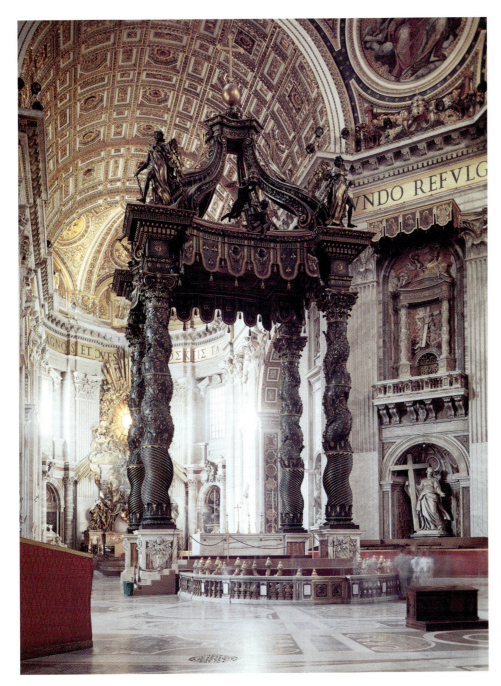

10.19 GIANLORENZO BERNINI. *Baldacchino.* Gilded bronze, 100' high. St. Peter's, Rome, Italy, 1624–1633. © Scala/Art Resource, New York.

mark the site. The canopy, designed by Gianlorenzo Bernini between 1624 and 1633, is a grand, lavish, richly decorated structure, taller than an eight-story building. Its design recalls the cloth canopies that originally covered the tombs of early martyrs, and its curving columns recall those placed by Constantine in Old St. Peter's. The vine-covered, twisting columns seem to leap up and support the grand canopy as if it were weightless, instead of tons of bronze (which was stripped from the nearby Pantheon [see Figure 9.28] and melted to make the *Baldacchino*).

Although the tradition of burying the dead in church developed very early in Christianity, it was discouraged repeatedly, as the interior of churches rapidly became completely overtaken by tombs. The poor and working classes were eventually buried outside in cemeteries and in rural parish churchyards. Despite periodic bans, the rich and powerful could continue to be buried in churches, in part because many churches were built and operated with donations from the wealthy, who wanted the prestige and protection of a church burial.

An example of church burial is the *Chapel of Henry VII,* dated 1503–1519 (Figure 10.20), attached to Westminster Abbey in London, England. This large chapel, almost a separate church on the back of the older abbey, was built to house the tomb of Henry VII and his wife, Elizabeth of York, and to promote the growing cult of veneration around his already-deceased uncle, Henry VI, who was expected to be canonized a saint. After years of engaging in warfare and royal intrigue, Henry VII felt the need to include numerous provisions for the welfare of his soul in his will. He donated major funds to Westminster Abbey for the construction of his chapel. He also donated money to many charitable institutions. The monks at Westminster Abbey had lobbied heavily for the chapel, as the royal burial represented such generous endowments and established the fame of the abbey, making it a destination for pilgrims.

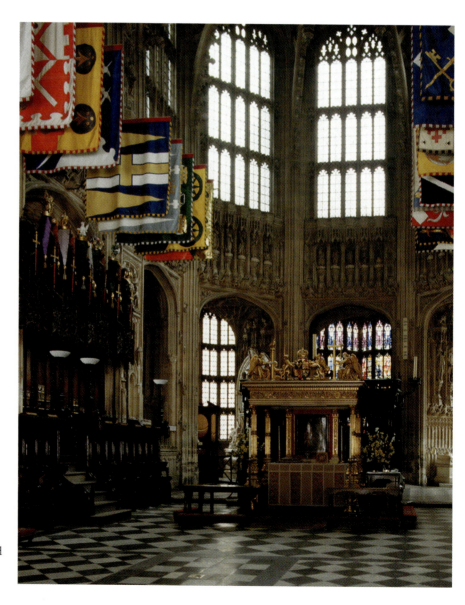

10.20 *Chapel of Henry VII.* Interior, toward east. Westminster Abbey, London, England, 1503–1519. © Corbis.

The chapel is built in the **English Perpendicular** style, a variation of the **Gothic** style. Here, the vaults are intricate, lacy, and elaborate. The ceiling seems to rise up on slender piers between the windows, and then fan out gracefully and drape downward. Window tracery and carvings add to the overall effect. Sculptures of saints fill the remaining wall space. The great height of the interior and its delicate patterning make a fitting symbol of royal power at the end of the age of chivalry. A carved wooden screen encloses the tombs of Henry VII and Elizabeth, which have bronze effigies atop them. The tombs are located directly behind the altar, at the most venerable location in the chapel.

Westminster Abbey, with the *Chapel of Henry VII,* continued to be used for royal burials until the eighteenth century. Its fame has also been enhanced by the numerous tombs and memorials it houses for illustrious people, such as statesmen, military leaders, and poets.

CONNECTION

Compare the French Gothic cathedral emphasis on verticality with the elaborate Perpendicular style of the Chapel of Henry VII. *See Chartres Cathedral, Figures 9.39 and 9.40 (page 257).*

ISLAMIC MAUSOLEUMS

The wealthy and powerful among Islamic societies were sometimes buried in mausoleums adjoining mosques. For example, Shah Abbas the Great, ruler of a seventeenth-century Persian empire, was buried in a mausoleum attached to the *Masjid-i-Shah* (see Figure 9.44).

Possibly the most famous Islamic mausoleum is the *Taj Mahal,* the final resting place of Mumtaz Mahal, wife of Shah Jahan, ruler of the Mughal Empire in India. Both Shah Jahan and Mumtaz Mahal were of Persian ancestry, descendants of invaders who established an Islamic state in northern India. She died in 1630 while giving birth to their fourteenth child. Mumtaz Mahal was apparently very beloved by the emperor; she may have been his trusted adviser. The *Taj Mahal* shows the influences of a number of cultures, including Afghanistan, Turkey, Iran, and indigenous India.

The *Taj Mahal,* built between 1632 and 1654 (Figure 10.21), sits at the north end of an expansive walled and gated garden, like some in Turkey and Iran. Such gardens symbolized Paradise and were also earthly recreations of it. The *Taj Mahal's* thirty-five-acre garden is subdivided into four equal squares by cypress-lined canals that meet in the center at a large reflecting pool. Each of the four squares is further subdivided into four garden plots. The four canals symbolize the

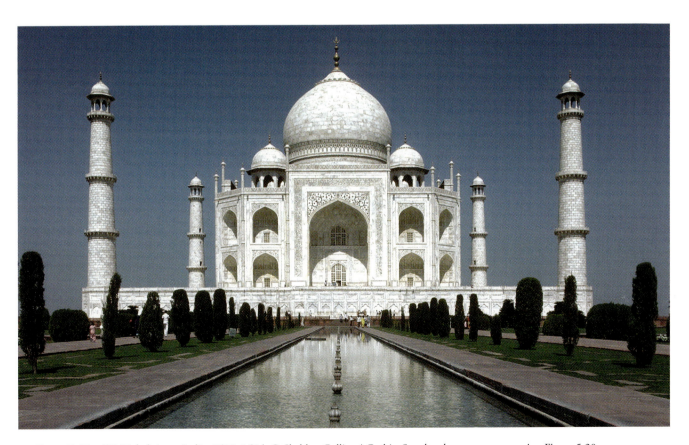

 10.21 *Taj Mahal.* Agra, India, 1632–1654. © Sheldan Collins / Corbis. See also the text accompanying Figure 5.20.

four rivers of Paradise in the Quran. An inscription on the main gate of the garden reinforces the association between the garden and Paradise:

> But O thou soul at peace,
> Return thou to the Lord, well-pleased, and
> well-pleasing unto Him.
> Enter thou among my servants,
> And enter thou My Paradise.

(THE QURAN SURA 89)

The mausoleum sits at the far end of the garden, not central in it, so that the garden retains its autonomy and symbolic significance. The *Taj Mahal* itself symbolizes the throne of God, a celestial flowering that rises above Paradise, the garden. This divine vision is well buffered from the outside world, with a river to the north and a forecourt in front of the garden's main gate. In addition to symbolizing Paradise and serving as a mausoleum, the entire complex may have been intended as a monument to Shah Jahan's own greatness.

CONNECTION
In the manuscript painting Babur Supervising the Layout of the Garden of Fidelity *(Figure 15.17, page 448), we see an example of a walled garden from Persia.*

Although the *Taj Mahal* is located at the end of the garden, it is undoubtedly the focus for the entire compound. It is flanked by a mosque and by a guesthouse, both in red sandstone that contrasts with the white marble of the mausoleum. In this respect, the *Taj Mahal* differs from some examples in which tombs are attached to larger places of worship. The *Taj Mahal* is a compact, symmetrical, centrally planned structure, on a raised platform and surrounded by four minarets. The huge dome dominates and unites the entire building, but the various parts, from arched portals to windows to porches, main-

tain their own identity while being integrated into the overall design. From a distance, its billowing dome and apparent whiteness make the *Taj Mahal* seem to rise up rather than hunker down; the sheerness and airiness of the structure, combined with its reflection in the pool, give an impression of floating.

The *Taj Mahal* has a primarily brick core, with some rubble. The building is sheathed in white marble and, in less-noticed areas of the interior, in white plaster. Up close, however, neither the floating whiteness nor the integration of architectural elements is its most striking feature. Inside and out, the *Taj Mahal* is covered with an abundance of delicate floral decoration and elegant calligraphy, all set in stone (Figure 10.22). The center area of the interior, under the dome, is enclosed by a screen of carved and pierced marble. It surrounds the cenotaphs, the false tombs that act as commemorative monuments to Shah Jahan and Mumtaz Mahal, whose bodies are actually buried in a crypt below. The cenotaphs themselves show a richness of decorative work. They are made of white marble into which have been laid strips and pieces of onyx, red sandstone, agate, jasper, cornelian, lapis, coral, jade, amethyst, green beryl, and other semiprecious stones. The walls throughout the *Taj Mahal* are decorated with inlaid or carved floral designs, while the floor is white with black geometric patterns inlaid.

RELIQUARIES

In some religions, bones, tissues, and possessions of deceased holy persons are kept and venerated. Since the first centuries after Jesus' death, the faithful sought out the relics of Christian saints and martyrs for special intercession with God. The practice continued in medieval Europe, where pieces of clothing or body parts were separated from the buried remains of saints, moved to major churches throughout Europe, and housed in small, precious shrines, called *reliquaries*. Almost all prominent medieval churches were pilgrimage sites, as the faithful would travel great distances to ask special intercession of a

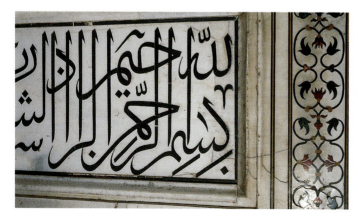
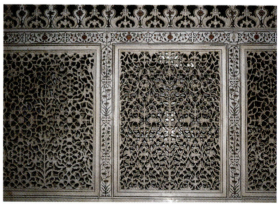

10.22   *Taj Mahal.* Two details from the interior. Inlaid and carved marble. Agra, India, 1632–1654. Black Star / Dinodia. See also the text accompanying Figure 5.20.

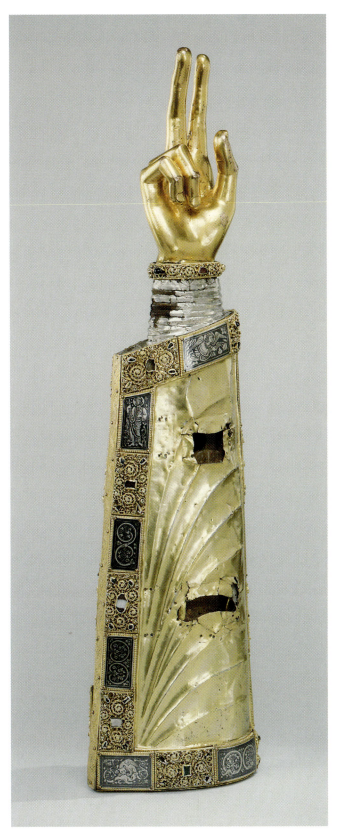

saint whose relics were located there. One example is the *Reliquary Arm*, c. 1230, (Figure 10.23). Reliquaries frequently had sculptural representations of the body part contained within. This example was built to hold pieces of arm bone from an unknown holy person. Clergy used it to bless the faithful or heal the ill. Reliquaries were very expensive to produce, as was appropriate for items used to house precious relics. In addition to the decorations of precious metals and stones, there are also scenes from the lives of Saints Peter and Paul. Reliquaries were related more to the jeweler's craft than to sculpture.

Let us look at an example of a reliquary from Africa. Rather than saints and martyrs, ancestors are venerated among most African religions. Many sculptures from Africa are part of rituals to honor ancestors. Ancestors are believed to affect the welfare of the living in many ways, and, accordingly, ancestors must be properly honored with offerings at their grave site or at shrines dedicated to them.

One example of a sculpture used in the veneration of ancestors is the *Reliquary Guardian Figure* (Figure 10.24) from

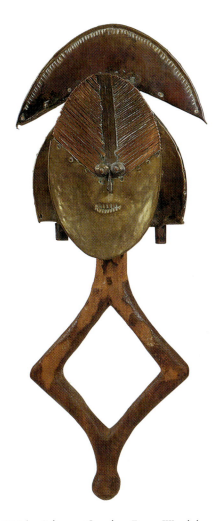

10.23 *Reliquary Arm.* Silver over oak; hand: bronze-gilt; appliqué plaques: silver-gilt, niello, and cabochon stones; $25^{1}/_{2}$" × $6^{1}/_{2}$" × 4". Mosan (Belgium), c. 1230. The Metropolitan Museum of Art, The Cloisters Collection, 1947. (47.101.33) Photograph © The Metropolitan Museum of Art.

 10.24 *Reliquary Guardian Figure.* Wood, brass, 24" high. From the Kota-Obamba regions of Gabon, Africa. Stanley Collection, University of Iowa Museum of Art.

Gabon in west-central Africa. This kind of sculpture was placed on a bag or basket that contained the skull and long bones of the ancestors who founded a clan, both to protect these relics from any kind of evil and to obtain help for food, health, or fertility from these ancestors. The sculpture, combined with the relics, was considered the image of the spirits of those dead ancestors. Offerings were made to them.

This *Reliquary Guardian Figure,* and others like it, were constructed over flat, wide, wooden armatures, and then covered with brass or copper sheets or wires. The faces were oval and usually concave, with flat shapes projecting from the sides and top like the elaborate hairstyles traditionally worn in the area. The guardian figure probably evolved from full-body anthropomorphic sculptures with hollow torsos in which bones were originally placed, which became impractical as more bones were accumulated. In their present form, these figures could also be used in dances. These sculptures, when they first became known among European modern artists, were extremely influential in the development of twentieth-century art styles.

MODERN COMMEMORATIVE ART

We will now look at some examples of commemorative art from the past two centuries. These examples are varied and include monuments that deal with personal loss, memorials for large populations, and monuments for important political leaders. These works draw from fine art, architecture, popular culture, folk art, and craft. They all represent attempts to express loss, preserve memory, and transform the experience of death.

MODERN CEMETERIES

From the middle of the eighteenth century and into the nineteenth century, cemeteries within cities in Europe reached a crisis point. Burials generally took place in churches or in the churchyard, which had become overcrowded and often neglected. As urban populations increased, cities expanded and surrounded these cemeteries, which were believed to be sources of pollution and dangerous to health. As a result, civil authorities gradually removed control of burial practices from

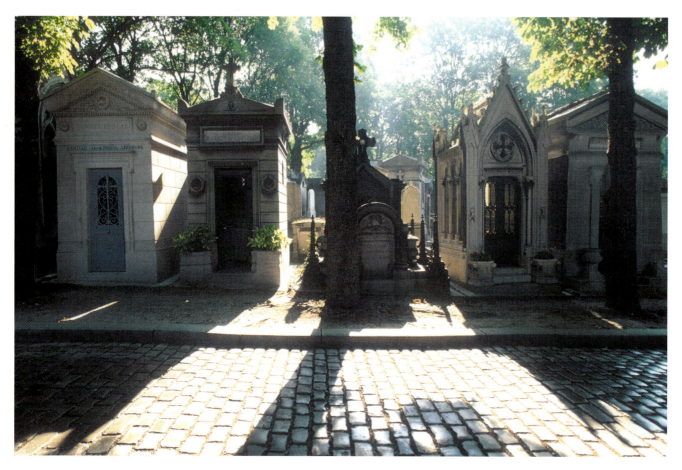

10.25 *Père Lachaise Cemetery.* Paris, France, opened 1804. © Alamy.

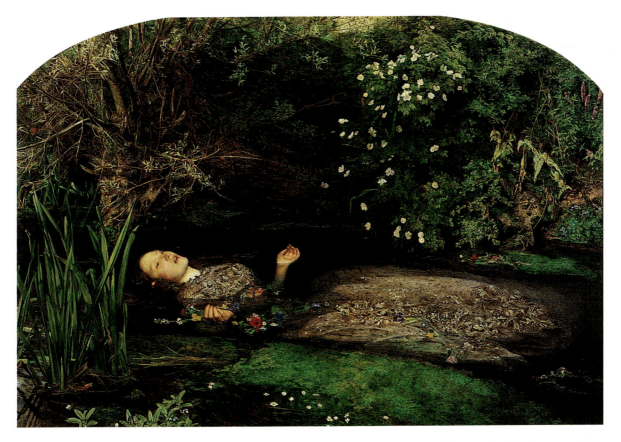

10.26   JOHN EVERETT MILLAIS. *Ophelia.* Oil on canvas, 30" × 44". England, 1852. Tate Gallery, London / Art Resource, NY.

the churches and established new, large, suburban cemeteries. The link between religion and burial ground had been broken; many new cemeteries buried the deceased who followed any (or no) religion.

In Italy, the new cemeteries were rigidly organized around tight grids. In northern Europe, people favored the picturesque cemetery, such as the *Père Lachaise Cemetery,* opened in 1804 (Figure 10.25), originally on the outskirts of Paris. The design of this cemetery was influenced by **Romanticism,** a major art and cultural movement of the nineteenth century, which emphasized a return to a simpler, rural way of life, just as the Industrial Revolution was creating ever more packed cities, greater pollution, and mechanization of life. The cemetery was laid out with meandering paths on a hilly site, with massive trees forming a canopy overhead. As families could own plots in perpetuity, they often constructed elaborate and fantastic memorials. The monuments in *Père Lachaise Cemetery* run the gamut from Egyptian, Greek, Roman, Byzantine, and Gothic to modern art nouveau styles. The small mausolea reflect a similar range of styles. Urns, columns, and obelisks abound. Their exotic qualities are further manifestations of Romanticism. The famous and the obscure are buried together here, making the cemetery a national tourist attraction, like many burial places in this chapter.

Ophelia (Figure 10.26), painted by John Everett Millais in 1852, is contemporary with some of the monuments in *Père Lachaise Cemetery.* Ophelia is a character in the Shakespearean play *Hamlet* who becomes incapacitated from grief, falls into water, floats a while unknowingly, and then drowns. This painting exhibits the same feeling toward picturesque nature that is apparent in *Père Lachaise Cemetery.* Nature is painted with deep color, lushness, accurate detail, and extraordinary delicacy. The beautiful, young Ophelia floats before us with gracefully outstretched hands, her flower-strewn dress and pose already suggesting the casket. The whole scene is lacking in the grisly details of madness and death by drowning, but rather is permeated with tragedy and poetic feeling. At *Père Lachaise Cemetery,* a planned cemetery, many monuments echo the sensibilities expressed in this painting, with sculptures of family members reaching for each other or lying together in death.

One of the most famous planned cemeteries in the United States is Forest Lawn, in Glendale, California, a city in the greater Los Angeles metropolitan area. The planner of Forest Lawn aspired to create a culturally uplifting and happy cemetery, in a benevolent, nondenominational Christian setting. Tombstones were forbidden, because they would be blots on the green rolling hills, so all grave sites are marked by inconspicuous bronze plaques set into the ground. Artwork plays a prominent part in the Forest Lawn landscape, as the theme of the park is "Great Art of Western Civilization." Although the collection contains many original works, it is better known for its copies of masterpieces of the Italian Renaissance, like *Leonardo da Vinci's Last Supper* (Figure 10.27), rendered in stained glass by Rosa Caselli Moretti between 1924 and 1930. Forest Lawn drew many visitors and was a cultural center for art in an era before many U.S. citizens traveled to Europe. It was an enormous success because of its benevolent, controlled, cultural atmosphere and its picturesque settings for remembrance of loved ones.

CONNECTION

But is it art? Forest Lawn's art collection includes not only the Last Supper in stained glass, but also copies in marble of every major Michelangelo sculpture. For more on the relationship between original work and copies, high and low art, popular culture and kitsch, see Chapter 1.

CONTEMPORARY MEMORIAL ART AND PRACTICES

The art and rituals of today that surround death serve broad social, political, and personal needs.

Among Mexican people, the Day of the Dead is a popular celebration. The feast day, a mixture of Christian and Aztec beliefs, is celebrated in Mexico and in the United States with local variations. Marketplaces become sites for parades and spirited celebrations, with vendors selling drinks, treats, and flowers. In private homes, altars are set up commemorating the family's dead, with incense burned and pictures of the departed placed next to their favorite foods to welcome their returning spirits. Families may spend the night at the graveyard with the deceased. After the grave sites are tended, hundreds of candles are lit throughout the vigil.

The Day of the Dead is so important that it is depicted among a series of murals of Mexican history and culture that were painted by Diego Rivera in the Ministry of Education building in Mexico City. The painting *Día de Los Muertos,* executed in 1923 (Figure 10.28), shows the urban observance of this feast day; two other panels depict more traditional rural observances. Great crowds fill the marketplace in a raucous celebration. In the foreground are food vendors and children in skull masks. Hanging under the awning in the background are satirical skulls and skeletons of various characters, including a priest, a general, a capitalist, and a laborer. In Mexico, the carnival atmosphere of Day of the Dead invites political satire and commentary. Rivera painted his figures in a simplified, rounded, monumental style. He insightfully recorded different individuals' personalities, and he captured the crush and excitement of the crowd and the spirit of the event.

Complex memorial festivals are held among the peoples of New Ireland and nearby islands, located in the Pacific Ocean

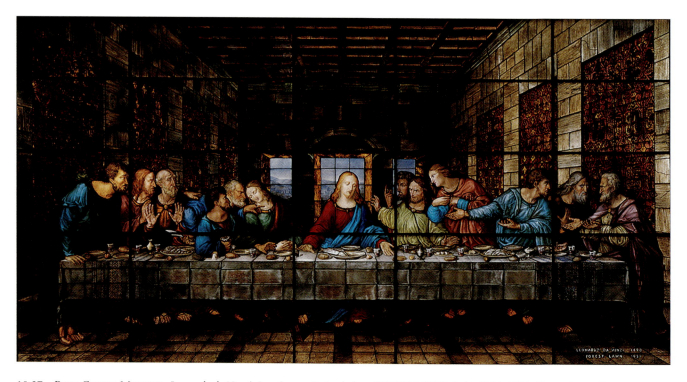

10.27   Rosa Caselli Moretti. *Leonardo da Vinci's Last Supper.* Stained glass, 29'10" × 13'9". Italy, 1924–1930. Forest Lawn Cemetery, Glendale, California, USA.

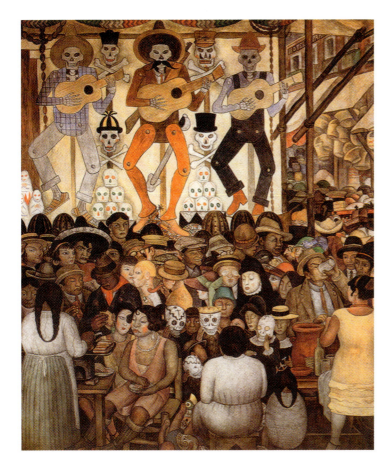

 10.28 DIEGO RIVERA. *Día de Los Muertos.* Fresco. Detail showing the city fiesta. South wall, Court of the Fiestas, Ministry of Education, Mexico City, 1923. Photo © Bob Schalkwijk.

northeast of Australia. Both the festivals and the sculptures carved for the occasions are called *malagans* (also spelled *malanggan*). The sculptures and festivals honor ancestors, but they also strengthen clan ties and stimulate the economy. When a member of a clan dies, both the first phase of mourning and the burial rituals are held immediately. But several months or even years later, a village organizes a malagan that may commemorate several deceased clan members at once. Planning takes several months, as special crops must be planted, pigs raised for the feast, and sculptures carved for the occasion. The malagan, which lasts several days, involves a great expenditure of effort and wealth to appropriately honor the dead. It requires the coordinated efforts of several surrounding villages, resulting in the exchange of money and stronger intervillage alliances. Because they fulfill many purposes, malagan rituals continue to be enacted in New Ireland, although they have evolved due to foreign religious and political interference.

Malagan carvings made for the event are intricate sculptures of humans, birds, fish, snakes, and, sometimes, boars, combined so that parts transform from one creature to another or merge ambiguously. Figures often seem to swallow or struggle with other creatures. Only certain patterns of malagans are made, and a clan must buy the rights to use a pattern. There are several different types of malagans, including masks, pole sculptures, long horizontal friezes, and dance ornaments. The exact meaning of all carved elements is not known, as clans keep many of their rituals secret and missionaries and traders acquire sculptures without knowing or caring about their ritual significance. The rich and brilliant colors are symbolic, but the context changes the exact meaning. Red is usually associated with danger. The frieze in Figure 10.29, called a *walik,* has a fish head at each end of the carving, indicating a coastal clan. Two pairs of male and female figures (the deceased) clasp stretched snakes. The snakes and four-legged animals

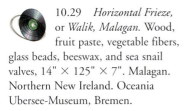 10.29 *Horizontal Frieze,* or *Walik, Malagan.* Wood, fruit paste, vegetable fibers, glass beads, beeswax, and sea snail valves, 14" × 125" × 7". Malagan. Northern New Ireland. Oceania Ubersee-Museum, Bremen.

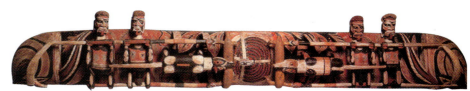

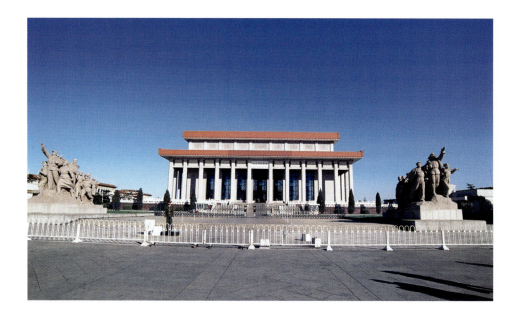

10.30 *Mausoleum of Mao Zedong.* Tiananmen Square. Beijing, China, latter half of the twentieth century. © Lee White / Corbis.

bite at the center, containing a fire eye. Visually, the malagan is complex: animal forms are detached from the background; the entire piece is intricately cut and painted; the human heads, carved and attached separately, vary the piece's silhouette. Friezes such as this are dramatically displayed in a ceremonial hut during the malagan festivities, while other malagans are used in dances. The rituals and sculptures together provide an opportunity for spirits to be present in a village. Once a ceremony is over, some malagans are never used again and may be destroyed or sold to foreign collectors.

The Day of the Dead and malagan rituals not only commemorate the dead, but also serve social needs. Our next work has both a commemorative and a political function. The *Mausoleum of Mao Zedong* (Figure 10.30) not only houses the body of the leader of the Communist revolution in China, but it also asserts the authority of the Communist government to rule China after centuries of imperial rule. Mao came to power in 1949, after years of civil war and Japanese invasion. His historical accomplishments included helping to restore Chinese independence and redistributing land to the peasants.

The layout of the Chinese capital city, Beijing, symbolizes the power of the ancient Chinese emperors. Its major axis runs north-south, and official buildings, palaces, public grounds, and city gates were placed along this axis. Also aligned on the axis is the Forbidden City, a walled complex with hundreds of buildings, including the Imperial Palace containing over nine thousand rooms. This alignment signifies the authority of the imperial dynasties. In front of the Forbidden City is Tiananmen Square, a large, important ceremonial space. Located in the square, along the major north-south axis of Beijing, is the *Mausoleum of Mao Zedong,* placed deliberately as a sign of the

legitimate authority of the Communist leaders as the rightful successors to the emperors.

CONNECTION
See the discussion of the elaborate Forbidden City *and the* Hall of Supreme Harmony *in Chapter 11 (Figure 11.9, page 309).*

CONNECTION
Like the tomb of Mao Zedong, the Vietnam Veterans Memorial *(Figure 11.33, page 328) stands on politically significant ground, the Mall in Washington, D.C.*

The *AIDS Memorial Quilt,* shown here in 1996 (Figure 10.31), is a commemorative work with a personal and political impact. The quilt is composed of thousands of individual three-by-six-foot panels, approximately the size of a twin-bed blanket, which would cover the body of one person who died from AIDS. Each panel is submitted as a remembrance by friends or family and is personalized, sometimes only with initials, but often more elaborately, with photographs, memorabilia, or details of a life story. The *AIDS Memorial Quilt* is not the product of a single artist. The work is organized by a group called the Names Project in San Francisco, and most people contributing quilt pieces have no art training. The format of a quilt is especially appropriate for this collaborative, grassroots product of loving remembrance. After only a few years, the *AIDS Memorial Quilt* has become truly vast, and its

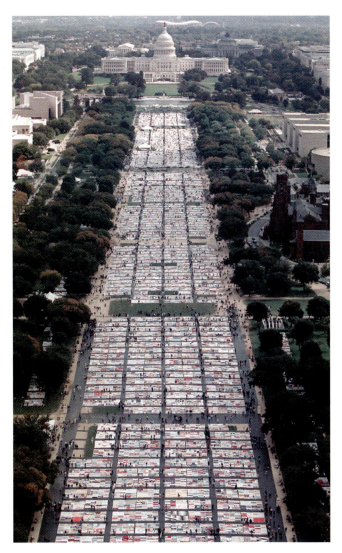

size makes it a public spectacle. It also communicates the enormity of the epidemic and its toll in the United States alone. The quilt changes every time it is displayed. The setting where it is shown contributes to the meaning. In Figure 10.31, the quilt's proximity to the White House and government buildings means that the disease was recognized publicly as a crisis and a tragedy by the U.S. government.

Our last example is the moving memorial for those who died in the tragedy of the September 11, 2001, terrorist attacks. For one month in 2002, *Tribute in Light* (Figure 10.32), designed by three architects and two artists, projected two powerful beams of light into the night sky where the twin towers of the World Trade Center once stood. A dramatic vertical juxtaposition next to the broken New York City skyline, the memorial strikingly reminded viewers of what happened that day. The "towers" of light appeared architectonic, because each was composed of 44 high-powered lamps that, combined, resembled a three-dimensional column with fluting. As light, the beams referenced hope and aspiration, but because they were immaterial, they also recalled the transitory nature and vulnerability of earthly things. The design of the permanent memorial, as well as the new structures at the World Trade Center site, are discussed in Food for Thought, page 297.

10.31 *AIDS Memorial Quilt.* Displayed on the Mall in Washington, D.C., October 11, 1996. Organized by the Names Project, San Francisco. © AP / Wide World, Ron Edmonds. See also the text accompanying Figure 5.9.

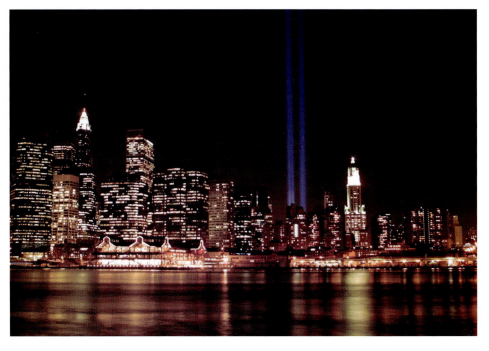

10.32 JOHN BENNETT, GUSTAVO BONEVARDI, RICHARD NASH GOULD, PAUL MYODA, JULIAN LAVERDIERE, AND PAUL MARANTZ. *Tribute in Light.* High-power lamps. World Trade Center Memorial at Ground Zero, New York City, 2002. © Rommel Pecson / Topham / ImageWorks.

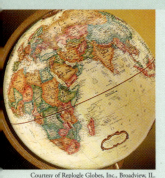

Courtesy of Replogle Globes, Inc., Broadview, IL.

Below
Map 4 Trade Routes of the Ancient World, centering around China at the time of the Han Dynasty.

The year 500 BCE brought the Golden Age of Pericles to Athens. The structures on the Acropolis were restored, including the Parthenon (see Figure 9.32). Later, in 404 BCE, at the end of the Peloponnesian War, Athens fell to Sparta. In 334 BCE, Alexander the Great from Macedonia invaded Persia and defeated King Darius. Alexander's empire stretched from Greece to India and included the Middle East.

In 500 BCE, Rome overthrew the Etruscans and established a republic in which male citizens chose their governors. This early form of democracy lasted until 27 BCE. In the second century BCE, Rome grew more powerful and conquered Europe and all the lands around the Mediterranean Sea. By 146 BCE, Rome had conquered Carthage in North Africa after the Punic Wars, which lasted one hundred years. In 46 BCE, Julius Caesar took power. He had a relationship with the famous Cleopatra, who wanted to rule the empire with him. After Caesar was mur-

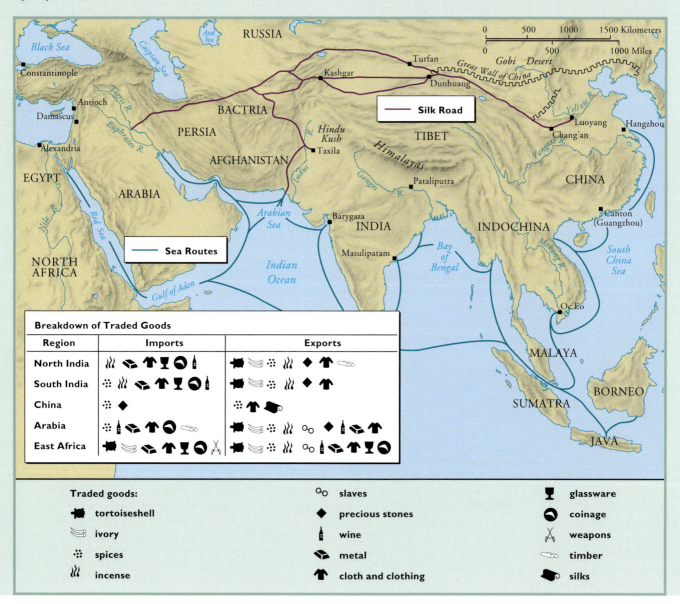

Breakdown of Traded Goods

Region	Imports	Exports
North India		
South India		
China		
Arabia		
East Africa		

Traded goods:

- tortoiseshell
- ivory
- spices
- incense
- slaves
- precious stones
- wine
- metal
- cloth and clothing
- glassware
- coinage
- weapons
- timber
- silks

dered by senators who thought he had too much power, Cleopatra aligned herself with Mark Antony, but was defeated by Caesar's son Octavius, who then took power. Octavius became known as Caesar Augustus, and his reign was the beginning of the *Pax Romana* (Roman Peace), which lasted for two hundred years. Jesus Christ was born during Augustus's reign.

In 290 CE, the Roman emperor Diocletian divided the huge empire into two sections: Rome in the west and Constantinople in the east. In 312, Constantine made Christianity legal, and eventually it became the religion of the empire. Nomadic tribes from northern Europe migrated southward and threatened Roman rule. The Huns conquered the Western Empire in 500, but the Eastern Empire survived for another thousand years.

In India, the Mauryan Empire united most of the country with a central government between 321 and 185 BCE. The major rulers were Chandragupta and Asoka. The empire included northern and central India (modern Pakistan and part of Afghanistan). The Golden Age of India occurred between 330 and 500 CE during the Gupta Empire, begun by Chandragupta I. During this time, India prospered, and the arts were highly developed.

In China, the Zhou Dynasty ended in 256 BCE. During this dynasty, Confucianism and Daoism were practiced and the art of lacquering was developed. From 221 to 206 BCE, Shi Huangdi unified China, established the Qin Dynasty, and built the Great Wall. A life-size ceramic army (see Figure 10.9) guarded his monumental tomb. Later, the prosperous Han Dynasty (202 BCE to 222 CE) developed the iron sword, made Confucianism the official policy, and grew soybeans. Arts included wall painting and sculpture. There was a major expansion of both domestic and foreign trade (see Map 4).

In Africa, the Great Empire of Ghana was established in 300. The Ghanaians set up trade routes and controlled trade in gold and salt. South of Egypt, the independent state of Kush thrived, due to vigorous trade. In 400, the Bantu people settled in South Africa.

In Mesoamerica, the Maya developed writing, a calendar, sophisticated architecture, painting, and sculpture between 250 and 900. In Peru, the Chavin culture flourished between 1000 BCE and 200 CE and developed agriculture and art. Later, the Moche, whose culture dates from 200 to 800, built pyramids, buried their dead in elaborate tombs, and made fine pottery (see Figure 8.31).

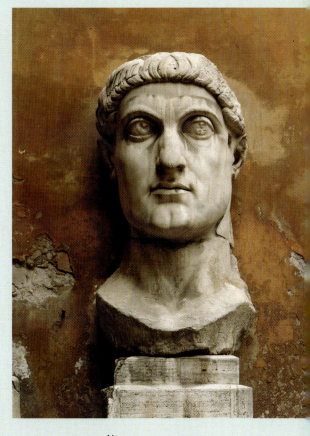

Above:
Head of Constantine the Great. Marble. Rome, fourth century CE. © Araldo de Luca / Corbis.

	BCE	
	4000	
Unification of Egypt		Newgrange burials
	3000	
		Funerary Barque
Old Kingdom—Egypt		Great Pyramids at Gizeh
Middle Kingdom—Egypt		
	2000	
New Kingdom—Egypt		
		Mortuary Temple of Hatshepsut
		Fowling Scene
		Coffin of Tutankhamen
Chavin Culture—Peru	1000	
Etruscan Civilization		
		Sarcophagus with Reclining Couple
Golden Age of Greece		
		Banqueters and Musicians
		Grave Stele of Hegeso
First Emperor—China		Soldiers from Pit 1
Qin Dynasty		Infantry General
	CE	
Roman Empire	100	Funerary Relief of a Roman Circus Official
Moche Civilization—Peru		
		Royal Tomb of Sipán
		Warrior Ear Ornament
		Catacomb of Sts. Peter and Marcellinus ceiling painting
Byzantine Empire	500	
Islam Religion founded		
		Viking Ship
		Animal-Head Post
	1000	
Gothic Era		
		Reliquary Arm
Mali Empire at height		

	1500	
Renaissance begins		Chapel of Henry VII
Baroque Era begins	1600	
		Bernini: Baldacchino
		Taj Mahal
Age of Enlightenment	1700	
Colonization of the Americas and Africa		
	1750	
Industrial Revolution		
American Revolution		
French Revolution		
South American Revolution	1800	Père Lachaise Cemetery
Mexican Independence from Spain		
	1850	Millais: Ophelia
Mexican Revolution		
Russian Revolution	1900	
World War I		
		Rivera: Dia de Los Muertos
		Moretti: Leonardo da Vinci's Last Supper
World War II		
		Malagan Frieze (Walik)
People's Republic of China		
	1950	Reliquary Guardian Figure
Vietnam War		
Death of Mao Zedong		Mausoleum of Mao Zedong
Desert Storm		AIDS Memorial Quilt
	2000	
September 11 terrorist attacks		
	2002	Tribute in Light

SYNOPSIS

The living make tombs and commemorative art that express their ideas about death and reflect the values of their cultures. Religion is closely tied to burial art and rituals. Many commemorative monuments serve political and social purposes. Tombs can help establish power or guarantee fame.

Ancient tombs were often oriented to the movements of celestial bodies, reflecting that spiritual, agricultural, and scientific concepts were intertwined. Tombs also reflect changing concepts about the afterlife. In some cultures, furnished, sealed tombs were permanent homes for the afterlife. In other cultures, tombs are meant only to contain bodies while spirits are believed to dwell elsewhere. Either kind of tomb is a commemorative monument, to preserve the memory of the deceased person.

Urban development and landscape design have influenced burials. Ancient Egypt and the Etruscan civilizations both established elaborate cities of the dead. In eighteenth- and nineteenth-century Europe, new ideas in city planning led to the development of the suburban cemetery.

FOOD FOR THOUGHT

Birth and death are often linked in art. We saw the rising sun that shone into the tomb at *Newgrange,* the egg imagery in the Etruscan Tomb of the Leopards, and the continued living of the Egyptian soul in their tombs. We also saw the birth–death link in several works in Chapter 8, Reproduction and Sexuality.

- Are life and death linked in your experiences of death?
- How is death handled in the news media, locally, nationally, and internationally? Look at both the deaths of celebrities and the deaths of relatively anonymous people.
- Do elaborate burials reflect only an underlying hope of afterlife, or do they in fact guarantee fame, which is a form of life after death?
- Are funerary art and ritual really for the living rather than the dead, since the living must contend with their own mortality?

Studio Daniel Libeskind has developed models for reconstructing the World Trade Center site, as shown in the *Computer-Generated Design to Rebuild the World Trade Center Site,* 2003 (Figure 10.33 on page 298). The proposal includes a ring of lower office buildings, and one large Freedom Tower, a tapering, twisting 70-story skyscraper, topped by an openwork cable superstructure and a spire. The Freedom Tower will be 1,776 feet tall, commemorating the year of the Declaration of Independence. The goal of the architect and design teams is to have the tower symbolize the spirit of the United States, while being extremely safe, secure, and not competing with the design of the old World Trade Center.

The area in the middle of the ring of buildings will be left open for a tree-covered plaza and permanent memorial to those who died at the site on September 11, 2001. Michael Arad and Peter Walker's design has been chosen for that permanent memorial, *Reflecting Absence* (Figure 10.33), consisting of two sunken reflecting pools. Access areas beneath the pools feature walls with the victims' names inscribed, a meditation room, and a site for leaving mementos. The sunken pools mark the footprints of the old towers.

Research the new center buildings and memorial as they are being built. What kinds of political, aesthetic, and security issues are influencing the design? What changes are being made to the original proposals, and why? Do you think this design is an appropriate memorial for the 9/11 event and for this site?

YOUR CD-ROM RESOURCES

- World History in Context
- Exploring Art Timeline
- Flashcards
- Food for Thought
- Companion Site
   - Chapter 10 Quiz
   - InfoTrac® College Edition Readings
   - Artist Flashcards
   - Online Study Guide

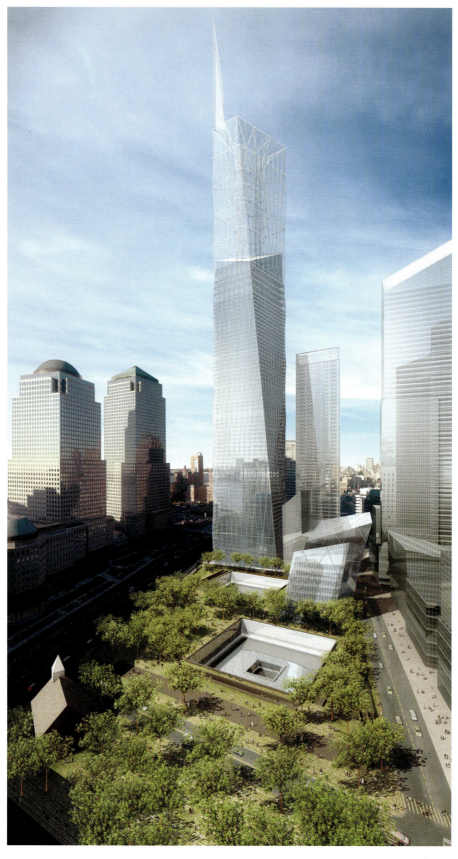

 10.33 Studio Daniel Libeskind. Selected design for World Trade Center Site Memorial—*Reflecting Absence* by Michael Arad and Peter Walker, copyright 2004 LMDC. Rendering by dbox. Courtesy of Lower Manhattan Development Corp.

The State

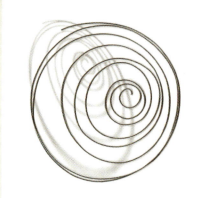

Rulers and governments understand well the power of art. They use it to celebrate and spread their earthly power. Art is also used in war, either for creating weapons and armor for it or by making images that promote it. Art also gives us images of peacemaking and monuments for peace.

If art can be a powerful tool for the state, it can be an equally strong voice of protest. People who hold values different from those of their rulers use art to affirm their ideas and to protest against warfare, social oppression, or political policy.

SECTION

3

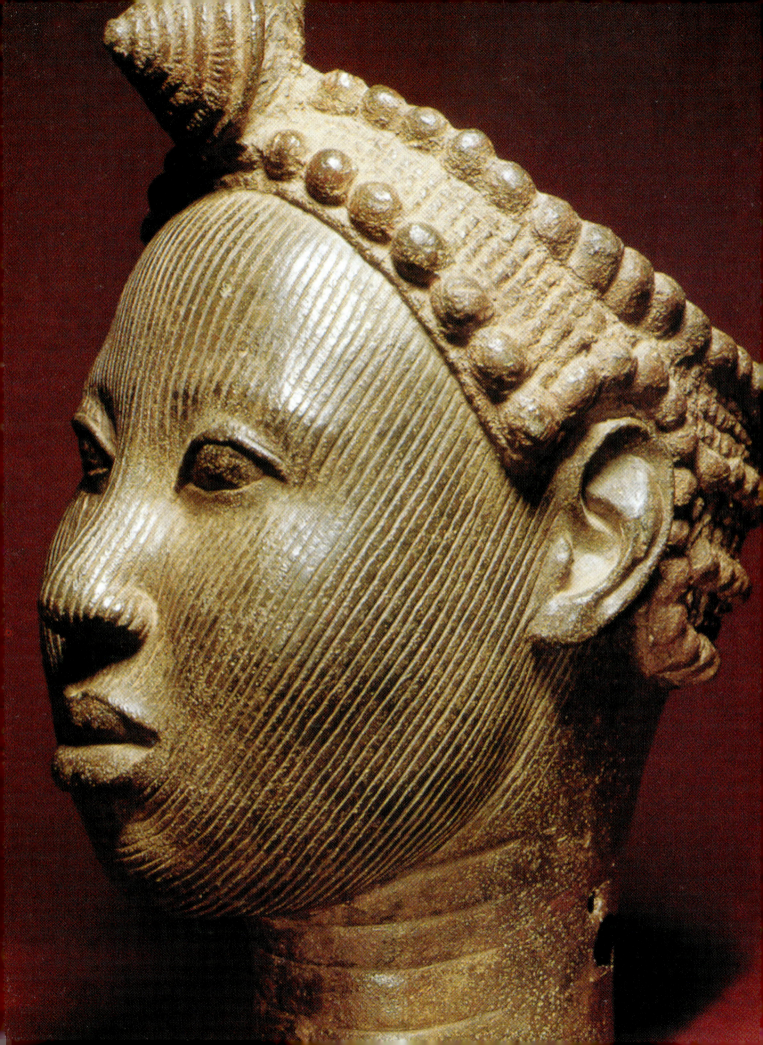

POWER, POLITICS, AND GLORY

INTRODUCTION

Throughout human history, a vast amount of artwork has empowered, popularized, and propagandized governments as well as their rulers. Art has depicted war and helped shape our reaction to it. Art has also celebrated peace. Think about the following questions while reading this chapter:

In what ways can art be used in the service of the state and rulers?

What kinds of art and architecture have been so employed?

Do politics influence the design of architecture?

Why have the designers of objects of war included aesthetic considerations in their creations?

How has war influenced the form and function of architecture?

How has art documented both war and peace?

Crowned Head of an Oni. Detail of Figure 11.3. Museum of the Ife Antiquities, Ife, Nigeria.

THE GLORY OF THE RULER

The following artistic devices are often used to glorify a ruler's image:

- *the idealized image:* the ruler's face or body or both are depicted without flaw and often with youthful vigor; the idealized image often includes a dignified demeanor

- *symbols:* details are included that indicate omnipotence, authority, or divine blessing

- *compositional devices:* the ruler often occupies the center of a picture and may be shown larger than attendants or other figures; the ruler's clothing may attract attention

DIVINE RULERS AND ROYALTY

Many heads of state through history have considered themselves to be heaven-sent or members of a divine family. Images helped them to spread and communicate that idea.

An early example of a royal portrait is the Egyptian royal couple, *Menkaure and His Wife, Queen Khamerernebty,* dated c. 2600 BCE (Figure 11.1). They stand side by side, united by the queen's embrace, placing the same foot forward. Young, strong, and confident, they display the Egyptian ideal of beauty and maturity. Note that Khamerernebty is shown as large as Menkaure, as pharaonic succession was traced through the female line. The compact pose makes the sculpture more durable and permanent, befitting the pharaohs as divine descendants of the Sun God, Re.

The sculpture was carved from a slate block, a very hard type of stone. One view was likely sketched on each side, according to the Egyptian canon of proportions, and then carved inward until all four views met. The sculpture was evidently painted, as traces of paint were found on the piece. Menkaure was the pharaoh who built the third and smallest of the *Great Pyramids* at Gizeh (see Figure 10.2). This shrine-like statue was found in his valley temple.

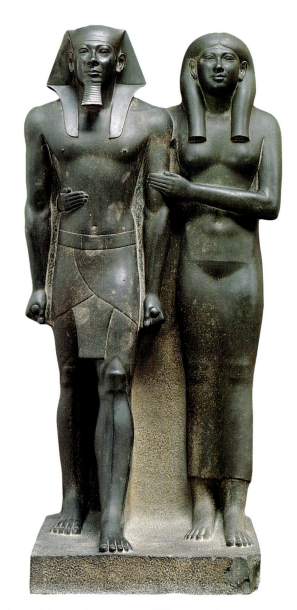

11.1 *Menkaure and His Wife, Queen Khamerernebty.* Slate, approximately 4'6¹/₂" high. Gizeh, Egypt, Fourth Dynasty, c. 2600 BCE. Museum of Fine Arts, Boston.

 CONNECTION
Look at another Egyptian portrait, the Seated Scribe (Figure 14.23, page 418), to see how portraits of lesser officials were handled compared to rulers.

Another royal portrait is *Emperor Justinian and His Attendants,* from the Church of San Vitale in Ravenna, Italy, built in the sixth century (Figure 11.2). Justinian was a famous and powerful ruler of the Byzantine Empire, which was an outgrowth of the old Roman Empire. In this image, Justinian is located in the center and dominates the focus of the viewer,

just as he dominated his empire. He was a devout Christian, so his portrait frames him firmly between figures of the church at the right and of the military and state at the left. Facing the viewers stiffly and with little expression, the figures seem to be part of a religious procession, with Justinian holding a golden bowl with bread used in Christian ritual.

As emperor-priest, Justinian wears a purple cloak and a magnificent jeweled crown and carries the golden bowl. He has a solar disk or a halo behind his head, a device used in Egyptian, Persian, and late Roman art to indicate divine status. The emperor is flanked by twelve figures, alluding to Christ and the twelve apostles. The clergy at right hold sacred objects: the crucifix, the book of Gospels, and the incense

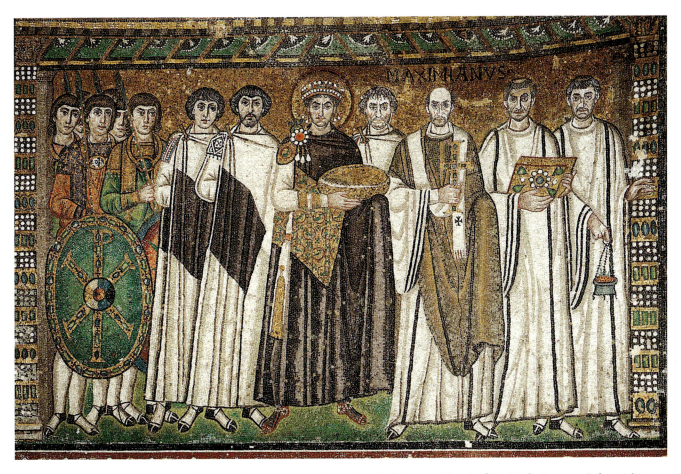

11.2 *Emperor Justinian and His Attendants.* Mosaic on the north wall of the apse. Church of San Vitale, Ravenna, Italy, c. 547. Canali Photobank. See also the text accompanying Figure 2.11.

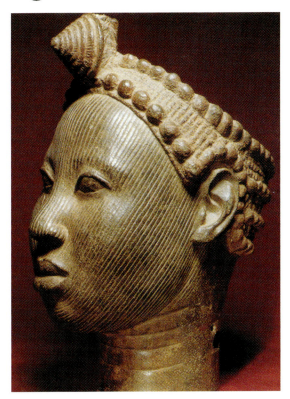

11.3 *Crowned Head of an Oni.* Zinc, brass. Yoruba. Wunmonije Compound, Ife, Nigeria, twelfth–fifteenth centuries. Museum of the Ife Antiquities, Ife, Nigeria.

burner. Even the soldiers are marked with holy symbols: the shield at left displays an ancient symbol of Christ.

A similar mosaic (not pictured here), *Empress Theodora and Her Attendants,* faces the Justinian mosaic in the sanctuary of the Church of San Vitale. Theodora, Justinian's wife, was an able and effective co-ruler, and her image indicates her equal rank and power. Both the Justinian and the Theodora mosaics have rich colors and use gold lavishly, further signs of rank. The figures seem to float in a celestial space.

In the next example, the head alone carries the exalted qualities of a ruler. In west-central Africa, several superb portrait heads were made in the twelfth to fifteenth centuries, each very much like the *Crowned Head of an Oni* (Figure 11.3). The delicately detailed portrait is in a naturalistic style that contrasts with more abstracted art from much of Africa. The face has a remarkable sense of calm and serenity, with beautiful flowing features, making it an outstanding example of an idealized royal portrait. Scholars still debate the exact identity and use of these portrait heads, but many believe each head represents a Yoruba or Benin ruler, who traced their rule back to the mythic first human ancestor. The crown was likely a royal insignia. The lines on the face may indicate scarification or perhaps strings of a beaded veil. Also visible are neck rings that are similar to those worn today among the Yoruba. The making of this portrait required considerable skill, with highly sophisticated mold making and metallurgy (see Chapter 2 for a description of the lost wax process).

CONNECTION
To see the range of styles in African art, contrast the naturalistic quality of the Crowned Head of an Oni *with the more abstracted style of the* Reliquary Guardian Figure *(Figure 10.24, page 287).*

CONNECTION
Yoruba leaders today are identified by such headgear as the Great Beaded Crown of the Orangun-Ila, in Figure 14.26 (page 421). These contemporary crowns are ancient forms that may date back to those worn by the early onis.

We could look at many other royal portraits from various cultures and see repeatedly how similar attributes convey an exalted quality: the idealized face/body, the symbolic details, or the centralized composition.

OBJECTS OF ROYALTY AND PRESTIGE

Royalty have always availed themselves of exquisite objects of power and have adorned themselves in elaborate garments and dazzling jewelry. Already in this chapter, we have discussed crowned rulers and royal robes of the richest materials. If crowns and robes are lacking, some other object usually proclaims the ruler's exalted status.

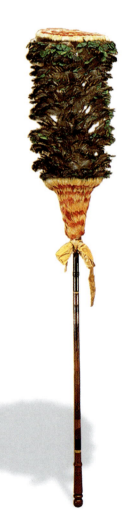
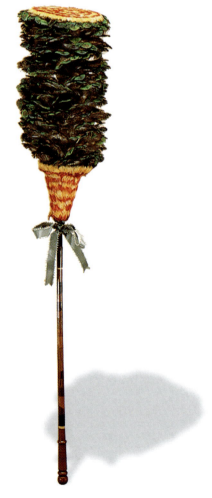

11.4 *Royal Kahili*. Feather work approximately 10' high. Hawaii, eighteenth century. Bishop Museum, Honolulu, Oahu, Hawaii.

Hawaiian royal objects were made of materials that were taboo to all others in the society, unlike the gold and gems found in a European crown, which any wealthy individual could possess. Hawaiians considered feathers sacred and connected with the gods, so only royalty could own or wear them. Some Hawaiian royal objects were common objects transformed into luxury items, sometimes losing their functional appearance completely. This can be seen in the *Royal Kahili* (Figure 11.4), from the eighteenth century, which basically were elaborate fly whisks.

The kahili signified the maternal genealogy that joined new rulers with preceding rulers and divine ancestors. Averaging ten feet tall and held only by royal males, the kahilis were displayed in splendid array, especially during funerals, processions, and state ceremonies. Our example features the large black and green feathers of the frigate bird, which symbolized fearsomeness.

CONNECTION
See Moctezuma's Headdress in Figure 11.36 (page 330) to compare Hawaiian and Aztec feather work.

The kahili may be a relatively unique royal object, but thrones and chest ornaments are used in many cultures. Among the Mesquakie people around Tama, Iowa, in the mid-1800s, grizzly bear claws were signs of high status, just as diamonds and pearls might be of value in other cultures. The prairie grizzly's nails—over three inches in length—were rare and difficult to acquire. Bear claws were considered a great trophy. The *Mesquakie Bear Claw Necklace* (Figure 11.5) represented the strength and tenacity of the bear, which added to the dignity of the owner. This necklace contains long claws alternating with colored glass beads, along with otter pelts and silk ribbon. The unassembled materials would be given to the designated people who owned the rights to create the neckpiece. The striking repetition of delicate curves suggests the lethal potential of each claw. The pelt of the otter is decorated in beads and attached to the necklace to become an elegant train.

CONTEMPORARY POLITICAL LEADERS

Images of contemporary political leaders are fundamentally different from those of the past, just as the concept of *ruler* has evolved. Today, almost no rulers openly consider themselves to be of divine descent, although some are believed to have been sent by a god. And with photography, the images of rulers come to us not as works of art, but as a flood of newspaper or television images. There is a great difference between images that are produced under the ruler's control and those over which the ruler has little or no control. In 1934, Adolf Hitler

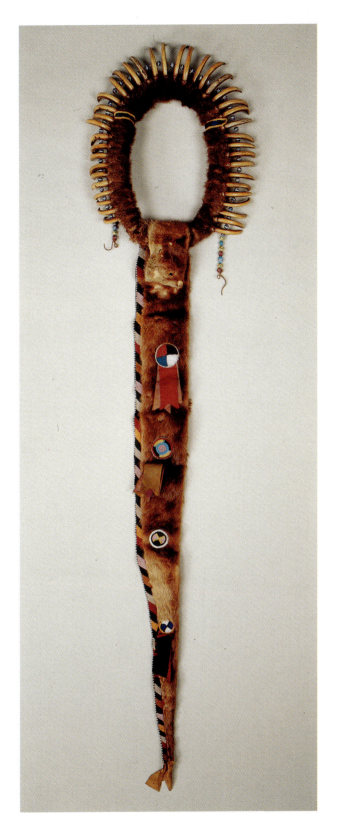

 11.5 *Mesquakie Bear Claw Necklace.* Otter pelt, grizzly claws, glass beads, silk ribbon, 16$^{1}/_{4}$" long, 14$^{1}/_{4}$" wide, 3$^{1}/_{8}$" high. Tama, Iowa, USA, c. 1860. Photo archive of the National Museum of the American Indian. Photo by Carmelo Guadagno. See also the text accompanying Figure 2.35.

commissioned the film *Triumph of the Will* (Figure 11.6), directed by Leni Riefenstahl, to glorify his rule, his military strength, and the Nazi order of Aryan supremacy. A work of brilliant propaganda, Riefenstahl's film established Hitler as the first media hero of the modern age.

Given unlimited funding by Hitler, Riefenstahl had a staff and crew of over 130 people, sixteen cameras, four sound trucks, and cranes and dollies for dramatic shots. The sound tracks, with speeches, parades, cheering crowds, and the lush music of the popular German composer Richard Wagner, were skillfully edited into the film. *Triumph of the Will* covered a six-day rally celebrating Hitler at Nuremberg. Although it was a documentary, the imagery was entirely staged. Of course, all film and photographic content is manipulated to

some extent at the time the picture is taken and can be further retouched and altered. In this case, Riefenstahl carefully set the scene so that Hitler is presented to and worshiped by the masses as Germany's savior. In close-ups of Hitler's smiling face, his charisma is evident. At the end of the film, we see an impressive aerial shot of an enormous, troop-filled field, with flags, an elevated podium, and monuments (Figure 11.6). A mass of military power in absolute formation is under Hitler's total control. This utopian image of harmony and strength would appeal to those whose lives were in disorder, and human history would experience one of its most tragic and horrendous episodes.

One can wonder about the motivation of Leni Riefenstahl. Perhaps she was a devout believer in the dogma of Hitler and his party, or perhaps she was seduced by the opportunity

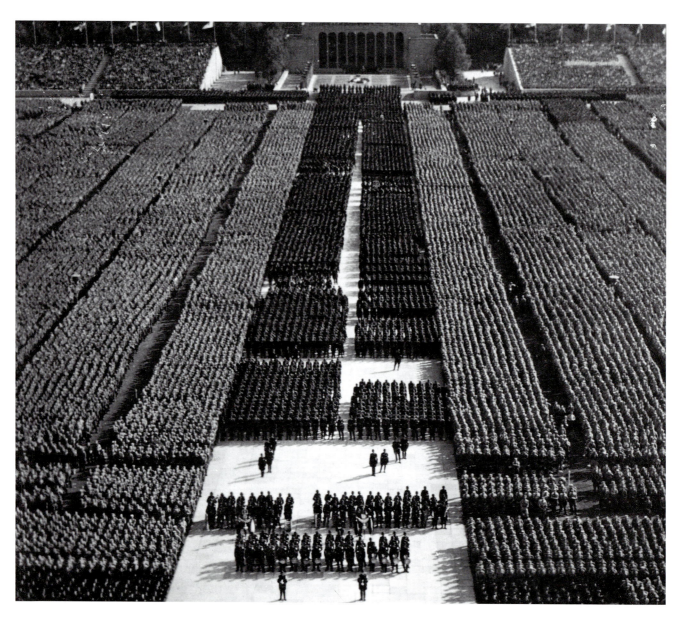

11.6 *Triumph of the Will.* Film, directed by Leni Riefenstahl. Germany, 1934. Kobal Collection.

to work in a new art medium with unlimited funds at her disposal. Whatever the case, Riefenstahl created a prototype in film that would impact future campaigns for political elections as well as lay the foundation for consumer advertising.

THE POWER OF THE STATE

Now we will look at palaces, government buildings, and monuments to see how architecture can contribute to the power and glory of the state and the ruler.

PALACES

Palaces are official residences of kings, emperors, and high-ranking religious leaders. They are visual representations of the power of the state, and often the government is administered in the palace. Palaces often have the following qualities:

- They are distinguished from ordinary residences by their grand size.

- They are usually lavishly ornamented.

- Their height is very often an important element.

- They feature art prominently, often adding symbolic content.

An outstanding early example of a palace comes from the Achaemenid civilization in ancient Persia, the largest in the Near Eastern world. The Achaemenids produced a body of monumental art whose splendor was difficult to match. The palace of Persepolis, begun by Darius I in 518 BCE and

destroyed by Alexander in 331 BCE, took fifty years to build. The heavily fortified palace citadel was located on a terraced platform measuring 1,500 feet by 900 feet, with mud walls that reached sixty feet high. The mud brick walls were sometimes ornamented with carved stone slabs and glazed brick panels and had gates with stalwart human/animal guardians (see a similar creature in the *Lamassu,* Figure 11.11). Most of the grand ceremonial rooms and apartments were hypostyle halls (interior spaces in which the roof is supported by columns). The windows were made of solid blocks of stone with cutout openings. Stairs were also chiseled from stone blocks and then fitted into place. You can see examples of the columns, windows, and staircases in Figure 11.7.

The *Royal Audience Hall* and its grand staircase (visible at the right in Figure 11.7) were two hundred feet square and sixty feet high and may have held up to ten thousand people. The walls of the grand staircase, cut directly from natural rock formations, were covered with reliefs depicting subjects presenting tribute to the king. But it is the grand use of columns that makes Achaemenid architecture so unique. The fluted drums of unequal heights were crowned with elaborate capitals with curving scrolls and foreparts of bulls or lions. Some had human heads. One hundred of these grand capitals supported the massive wood beams of the ceiling.

Like the Persians, the Mayans of Central America used high platforms, relief sculpture, and large buildings to create palace structures. The Mayan culture at Palenque is dated c. 514 to 784. Located deep in a rain forest and abandoned before the Spanish conquest, Palenque remained unscathed but was completely overgrown by tropical flora until it was

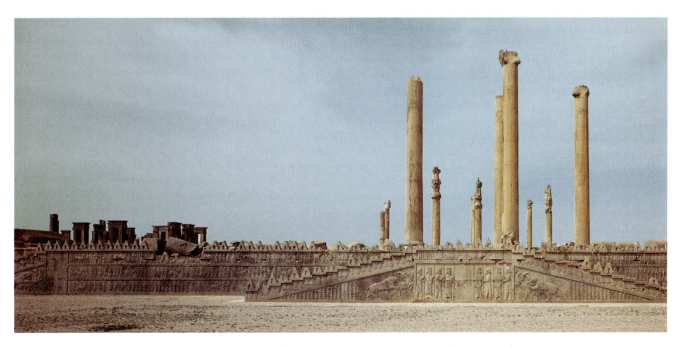

11.7 *Royal Audience Hall and Stairway.* Darius I. Persepolis, Persia (Iran), c. 500 BCE. Oriental Institute, Chicago.

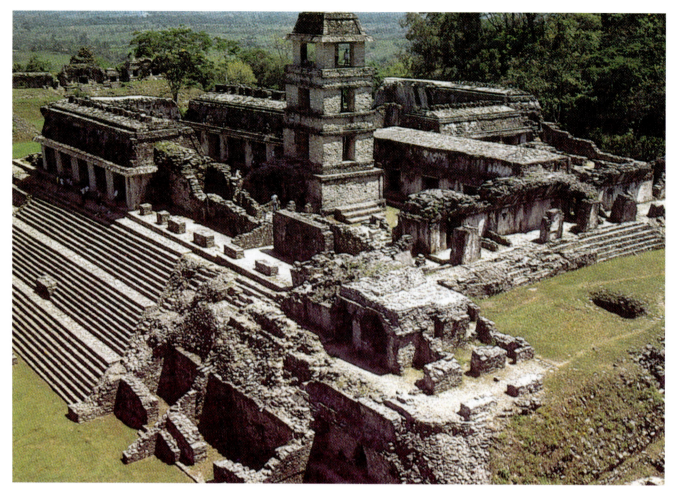

11.8 *Palace at Palenque.* Maya. Chiapas, Mexico, 514–784. Photo Mary Ellen Miller.

rediscovered in modern times. Palenque had the living quarters for the Mayan royalty, a center for religious rites, facilities for astronomical studies, and an administrative precinct.

The design of the *Palace at Palenque* (Figure 11.8) featured four courts, each surrounded with rooms and galleries, likely used for administrative purposes. A number of thrones were found within the galleries. Built on a thirty-foot-high platform, the complex measures 250 feet long by 200 feet wide. Large, painted stucco masks of human faces once adorned the ends of the terraces. A nearby vaulted underground aqueduct brought water to the *Palace.* Height was important and the seventy-two-foot-high tower on the southwestern corner adds verticality to the overall horizontal building. Large windows in the tower facing the four cardinal points suggest an astronomical as well as a defensive use. The profusely decorated interior was covered by parallel rows of corbel arches and vaults. This allowed for thin walls and large airy rooms that made life comfortable in the fierce heat and humidity of the tropics. The outer walls were pierced with T-shaped windows and doorways.

Chinese royal architecture was an important vehicle for maintaining the emperor's rule as Son of Heaven, father of the people, and the one who maintained Heaven on Earth. The Forbidden City was a palace compound so enormous (at one time, it had 9,999 rooms) that it resembles a city unto itself within Beijing. Only the elite, and no commoners, were allowed to enter. The major structures of the Forbidden City have gleaming yellow tile roofs and walls painted a rich vermilion, connected by pure white marble staircases and terraces, one courtyard after another. Along with the imperial buildings were mansions of princes and dignitaries, lush gardens, artificial lakes, theaters, and a library, laid out in a symmetrical plan. The major axis of the city is north-south, with most structures facing south, as the South is the source of fruitfulness, while the North is the source of evil influences. The *Imperial Throne Room* (Figure 11.9) is one example of the interior decoration. The majestically high ceiling is covered with elaborate patterns subdivided by grids. The focus of the room, the throne, is framed by columns and elevated on a stepped platform.

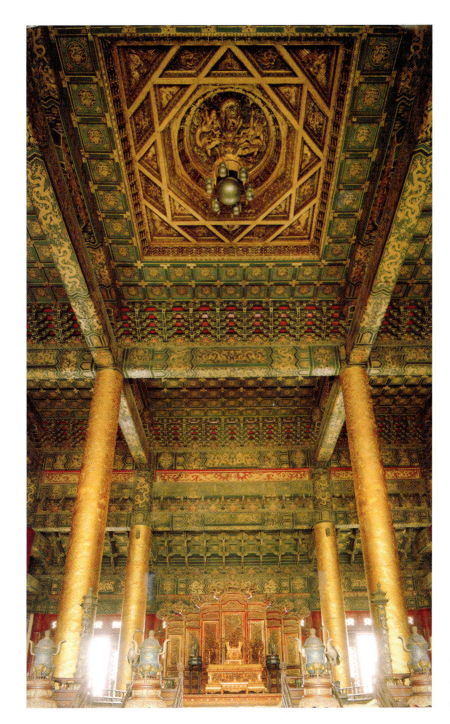

11.9 *Imperial Throne Room,* in Hall of Supreme Harmony. Forbidden City, Beijing. China Photographic Publishing House, Beijing. See also the text accompanying Figure 3.21.

CONNECTION
Other Chinese examples of ambitious royal building projects are the Soldiers from Pit 1 (Figure 10.9, page 275) from the tomb of Qin emperor Shi Huangdi, and the Great Wall of China (Figure 11.21, page 319).

Like the Forbidden City, the palace complex at Versailles was both a sign of power and an instrument for maintaining that power. It was built by King Louis XIV of France, who identified himself with Apollo and called himself the Sun King. Louis moved his entire court from Paris to the palace complex of *Versailles* in 1682 in order to better control them. Originally Louis's grandfather's hunting lodge, *Versailles* was extensively enlarged and remodeled. Approximately thirty-six thousand workers took twenty years to complete *Versailles* to Louis's liking. Grand spaces, dramatic embellishment, theatrical display, and high contrasts all contributed to the **Classical Baroque** style. The connected buildings measure two thousand feet wide and are surrounded by expansive parks covering seven square miles. Over four million tulip bulbs were planted in the parks' flower beds (see illustration on page 395).

The exterior of *Versailles* is visually overwhelming, and the interior matches it, particularly in the *Hall of Mirrors* (Figure 11.10). Measuring 240 feet in length, this dazzling grand corridor connects the royal apartments with the chapel. The ceilings were covered with marvelous frescoes, and the long, mirrored room was embellished with gilded bronze capitals, sparkling candelabra, and bejeweled trees. Just as Louis XIV dominated the French church, nobility, and peasants, he also controlled the arts, fashion, and manners. He established the French Royal Academy of Painting and Sculpture to ensure a steady supply of works that would glorify his person and reign.

CONNECTION

For more on the French Royal Academy, see Chapter 5, Who Makes Art?

CONNECTION

At Versailles, Louis XIV stripped the nobility of their power, so they occupied their time in games of romance and intrigue, as in Fragonard's The Swing (Figure 14.25, page 420).

Some palace sculptures have special symbolic value. The mighty *Lamassu* (Figure 11.11), from 720 BCE, is an enormous sculpture that stood guard at the palace gates at Khorsabad, capital of the Assyrian Empire. The Assyrians, known for their ruthlessness and brutality, dominated the Near East for over three hundred years. With enormous size and glaring stare, two large *Lamassu* guarded the palace gate, to terrify and intimidate all who entered. A form of divine genie, the winged creature is part lion or bull, with the head of a human being. The three-horned crown symbolizes the divine power given to the king. Carved from one large block of stone, the *Lamassu* has five legs, a clever device to show movement and stability at the same time. From the oblique vantage point, the *Lamassu* appears to be striding forward toward the viewer. The front view, however, shows the beast at a stalwart standstill, blocking the viewer's forward movement. A combination of stylized and natural elements aptly expresses the beast's human and fantastic character. Hair and wings are depicted with stylized linear and repetitive patterns, while the strong muscular legs are more naturally rendered, as are the facial features.

CONNECTION

We will look at other fantastic animals, and the reasons humans invented them, in Chapter 15, Nature, Knowledge, and Technology.

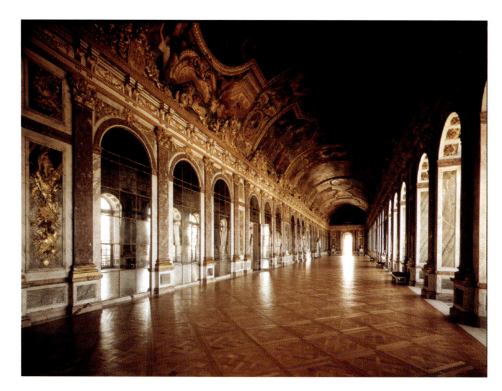

11.10 JULES HARDOUIN MANSART AND CHARLES LE BRUN. *Hall of Mirrors.* Versailles, France, c. 1680. © Scala / Art Resource, NY. See also the text accompanying Figure 3.9.

Another example of symbolic sculpture is a carved court-yard column in the Palace at Ikere, the residence of a local ruler in Nigeria. The *Palace Sculpture* (Figure 11.12) by Olowe of Ise shows the senior wife, the queen, standing behind the enthroned king. Significantly larger than the king, the royal female is revered for her procreative power, as are all women. She crowns the new king, because she is the source of his power. On top of his conical crown is a bird, a symbol for mothers and the reproductive power that female ancestors, deities, and older women possess. The interlocking forms of king and queen visually convey monumentality and elegance. Attention to detail, especially in the pattern of body scarification, adds authenticity and authority to the sculpture. Yoruba aesthetic values are evident: "clarity, straightness, balance, youthfulness, luminosity and character" (Blier 1998: 85).

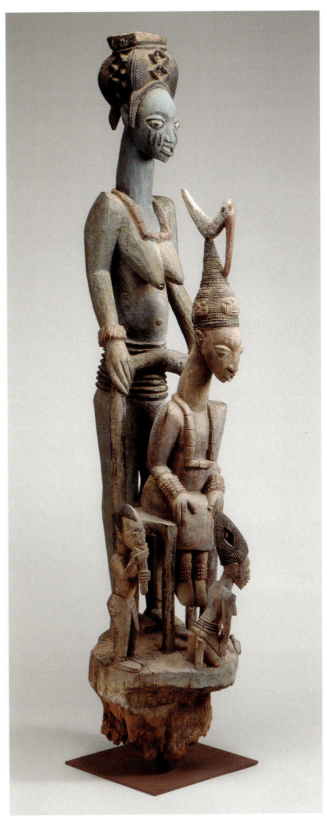

11.12 OLOWE OF ISE. *Palace Sculpture.* Wood and pigment, 60^7/$_8$" × 13^1/$_4$". Yoruba. Ikere, Nigeria, 1910–1914. Photograph by Bob Hashimoto. Reproduction: The Art Institute of Chicago. See also the text accompanying Figure 4.2.

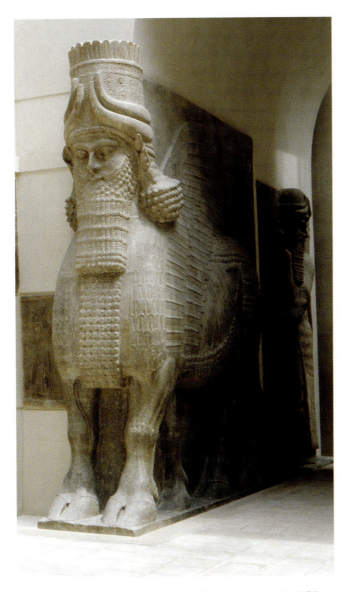

11.11 *Lamassu.* Limestone, 14' high. Khorsabad, Iraq, 720 BCE. © RMN / Art Resource, NY.

Yoruba kings would seek the best artists to make artwork for their palaces, as a way to increase their prestige. Olowe of Ise spent four years (1910–1914) at the Palace at Ikere producing around thirty pieces. So excellent was this sculptor's work considered that songs or poems of praise (*oriki*) were composed about him:

> Handsome among his friends.
> Outstanding among his peers.
> One who carves the hard wood of the iroko
> tree as though it were as soft as a calabash.
> One who achieves fame with the proceeds of his carving.
>
> (BLIER 1998: 85)

Thus, across several continents and several centuries, we have seen palaces built with certain distinguishing features: large size, height, terraces and/or platforms, decorated interiors, and symbolic sculptures.

SEATS OF GOVERNMENT

Social and political pressures help determine which styles of architecture are used in government buildings. We can see an example of such pressures in the designing of England's *Houses of Parliament* (Figure 11.13). In 1836, England's old Houses of Parliament burned. A new design was sought for rebuilding the seat of government to coincide with England's desires to create a "national identity" and express patriotic spirit. Architect Charles Barry designed the general plan, while A. W. N. Pugin was responsible for the exterior and interior ornamentation. Although most official architecture at that time was influenced by Classical Greece, Barry and Pugin were inspired by Gothic aesthetics, for they felt that this style—the style of the magnificent, soaring medieval cathedrals—would be appropriate for a Christian nation. The availability of new building materials, such as cast iron, enabled the **Gothic Revival** style to flourish on a grand scale.

Pugin and Barry were hotly criticized for breaking away from neoclassic architecture, which had been used for public and government buildings in many Western nations, including England, France, and the United States. The painter John Constable argued that the new Gothic Revival design of Parliament was a "vain endeavor to reanimate deceased art, in which the utmost that can be accomplished will be to reproduce

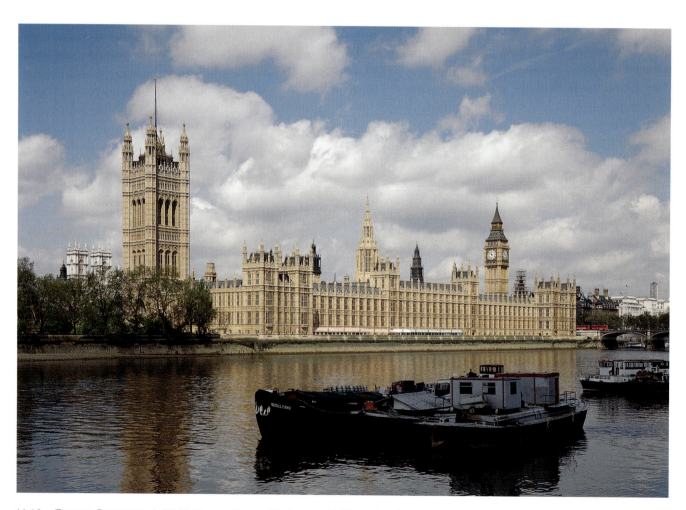

11.13   CHARLES BARRY AND A. W. N. PUGIN. *Houses of Parliament.* 940' long. London, 1840–1860. © A. F. Kersting.

a body without a soul" (Honour and Fleming 1995: 621). Pugin, however, felt that Gothic art never died and therefore did not lose its "soul." He believed that Gothic was a principal, rather than a style, "as eternally valid as the teaching of the Roman Church" (1995: 621). On the other hand, Pugin reasoned that contemporary Greek temples would be mere imitations and would have no integrity.

As we look at the impressive structures, we see a long, horizontal block of buildings topped with a series of spires and towers. Victoria Tower is on one end while the famous clock tower, with Big Ben, is on the other. Ironically, the building's plan is clearly symmetrical with repetitive ornamentation, qualities of Classical architecture. However, when one views the buildings, a medieval church or a castle-fortress comes to mind, visually housing Parliament in a metaphor of the church's strength and the government's power.

CONNECTION

Chartres Cathedral *(Figure 9.39, page 257) and the Chapel of Henry VII in Westminster Abbey (Figure 10.20, page 284) are two examples of Gothic architecture, which inspired the design of the Houses of Parliament.*

Just as a new architectural style was developed for the *Houses of Parliament,* a new form of architecture would evolve on the island of New Zealand, in response to political and social needs. In the nineteenth century, the Maori nation was undergoing tremendous change due to European colonization. The Maori Meeting House, *Te Mana O Turanga* (Figure 11.14), from 1883, was a visual representation of old tribal values that reaffirmed clan ties. The Meeting House developed from the design of the chief's home, but was much more art-filled, elaborate, and symbolic.

Metaphorically, the entire house is transformed into the body of a powerful ancestor, who is the source of clan power. Once inside, the living became one with their ancestors. In this potent environment, chiefs, priests, and houseguests would conduct tribal affairs and ceremonies. The porch is considered the brains of the ancestor, while the large boards of the overhanging roof symbolize the ancestor's arms and hands. The ridgepole of the roof represents the ancestor's backbone, and it terminates at the front with a mask of the ancestor's face. It has figures of the original ancestral parents, sometimes engaged in sexual intercourse, carved on it. The rafters and the wall slabs represent the ancestor's ribs and are covered with carved and painted vines that symbolize all the clan's generations.

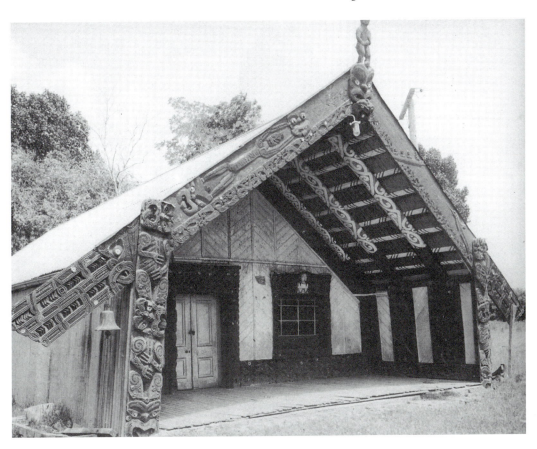

 11.14   RAHARUHI RUKUPO AND OTHERS. *Te Mana O Turanga.* Exterior of Maori meeting house. Carved and painted wood. New Zealand, opened 1883. From *Whakairo–Maori Tribal Art* by David Simmons, 1985, pp. 38–39. Reprinted by permission of Oxford University Press, New York.

The sculptures on Maori meeting houses are visually overwhelming and are meant to be. These profuse carvings, swirls, lines, and frightening imagery empower clan members, while intimidating any outsiders. The interior back wall of *Te Mana O Turanga* (Figure 11.15), from 1883, contains various carvings of ancestors and images from the history of the tribe, concentrating on battles, migrations, and land and fishing rights. These images, combined with inspirational stories about clan heroes, pass on clan history, traditions, and values. Thus, not only is the past preserved, but some part of the Maori way of life is guaranteed for the future. This house dates from a period of transition for the Maori. It has the traditional-style carving with spiral patterns and intricate detail as well as the European-style portrait of Agnew Brown and his dog, a settler who gave money to help build the meeting house.

MONUMENTS

A final category of government art is the monument, which commemorates a person, an event, an era, or a culture, either past or present. Many monuments share such features as imposing size, a mixture of architecture and sculpture, use of inscriptions, and/or figurative sculpture.

The Romans built triumphal arches to commemorate military victories or major building projects. The *Arch of Titus* (Figure 11.16) was built along the *Via Sacra* (the Holy Road) in Rome, by Titus's brother Domitian, to record Titus's apotheosis. The inscription at the top reads roughly, "[The Senate

and the People of Rome] . . . dedicate this arch to the god Titus, son of the god Vespasian."

This single-passageway arch (others have two passageways; most have three) is a mini–barrel vault. The vault's opening is framed with engaged columns that are a composite of Ionic and Corinthian elements, a Roman synthesis of Greek orders. The columns support the entablature upon which rests the attic, the uppermost section with the inscription. "Winged victories" in the spandrels symbolize Titus's military successes. In the center on the ceiling of the vault, a relief depicts Titus being carried up to heaven on the back of an eagle, giving a visual image of his deification. On the inside walls of the arch are relief carvings of his military victories.

The *Monumental Heads,* or *moai* statues (Figure 11.17), have always been a bit of a mystery. Believed to date from the fifteenth century, they are located on Easter Island, which is part of Polynesia. As in other Polynesian cultures, such as the Maori, genealogy was the source of the Easter Islanders' existence and importance in the community. It is likely that the carvers of these gigantic figures linked them to their ancestors. Over six hundred heads averaging twelve to twenty-five feet in height have been found in pieces on the island. The statues were carved in pits, out of volcanic rock called tufa, a fairly soft material that hardens with age. After completion, each piece was raised and fitted onto a basalt platform without the use of mortar. The largest one found in a pit is forty feet high, and one started in a quarry is sixty-nine feet high. The largest topknot is estimated to weigh thirty tons. Carved with primitive

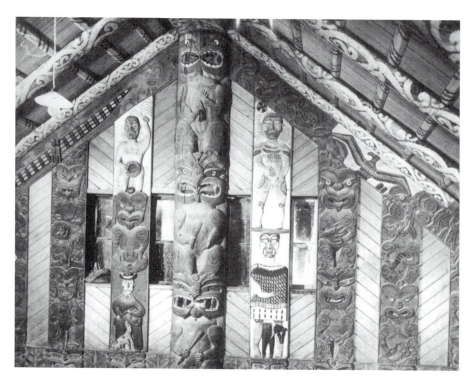

11.15 RAHARUHI RUKUPO AND OTHERS. *Te Mana O Turanga.* Interior back wall of Maori meeting house. Carved and painted wood. Whakato marae, Manutuke, New Zealand, opened 1883. From *Whakairo–Maori Tribal Art* by David Simmons, 1985, pp. 38–39. Reprinted by permission of Oxford University Press, New York. See also the text accompanying Figures 4.6, 5.22, and 11.14.

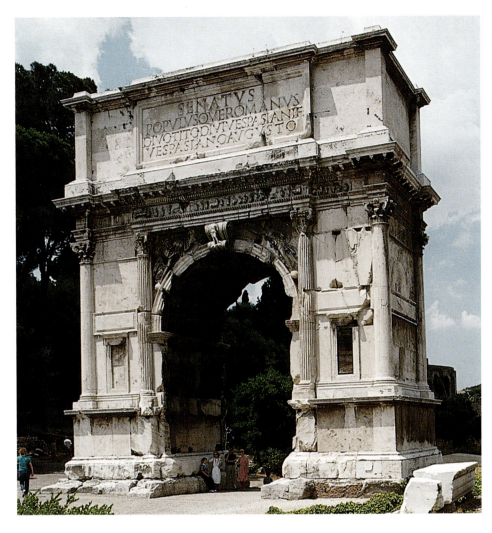

11.16 *Arch of Titus.* Marble on concrete, 50' high, 40' wide. Rome, Italy, CE 81. Saskia Ltd., Cultural Documentation. See also the text accompanying Figure 6.23.

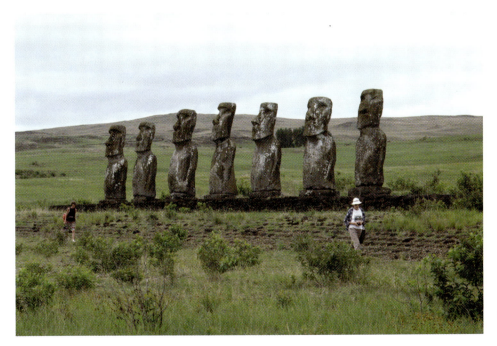

11.17 *Monumental Heads.* Volcanic tufa. Easter Island (Rapa Nui), Polynesia, c. fifteenth century. © Wolfgang Kaehler / Corbis.

basalt picks, the figures were rendered in large minimal forms. When fully exposed, the statues have full-length torsos with long slender arms. Most are male figures, although a few females have been found.

We have studied only two monuments here. Undoubtedly, in your city, you can find many monuments to past events, civic leaders, and military victories.

CONNECTION
The monuments in this section specifically relate to the power of the state. Later in this chapter are monuments relating to war and peace. The Portrait of George (Figure 12.30, page 360) is a monument to slain San Francisco mayor George Moscone.

WAR

War is part of the history of most civilizations and cultures, and it is part of the story of power, politics, and glory.

ART DEPICTING WARRIORS

Warriors have been depicted in art since the earliest times, as far back as 8000 BCE on rock walls. Warrior images can be found in almost every culture since then. How is a menacing attitude conveyed in these works? Frequently, such art contains the following qualities:

- Warriors are often depicted as very large.
- Armor, weapons, or regalia of power are emphasized.
- Facial expressions are usually aloof or fierce.

We will begin our brief survey in Mesoamerica, in the Toltec city of Tula in central Mexico. Impressive, colossal *Tula Warrior Columns* were erected upon a pyramid between 900 and 1000 (Figure 11.18). These tall, blocky figures loomed above a temple platform and reached sixteen to twenty feet high, three times life size. Stiff and frontal, these formidable warriors were carved in basalt and painted in bright colors. The columns were made of four drums and held together by dowels. They were supporting structures, functionally and figuratively holding up a temple roof. Carved in low relief, the warriors were adorned in Toltec garb with elaborate headdresses, and each held *atlatls*—spear-throwers—at their side. They were uniformly carved as well, giving one an impression of an army of robots that would crush anything in their path. Stylized butterflies, carved on their chests, were the souls of past warriors.

Before the modern era, the warrior on horseback was one of the most feared. In equestrian monuments, the strength

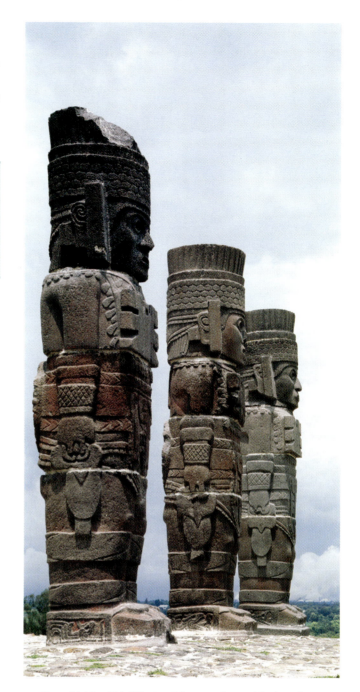

 11.18   *Tula Warrior Columns.* 16' to 20' high. Toltec. Mexico, 900–1000. © Superstock.

and speed of the steed becomes joined with the determination of the rider. A fine example of this art form is Andrea del Verrocchio's colossal bronze *Equestrian Monument of Bartolomeo Colleoni* (Figure 11.19). Colleoni was a *condottiere,* or mercenary soldier, who fought many campaigns for the city-state of Venice during the fifteenth century. The statue is fifteen feet in height and is raised on a high pedestal. Looking up at this monument from under the horse's raised hoof, the viewer

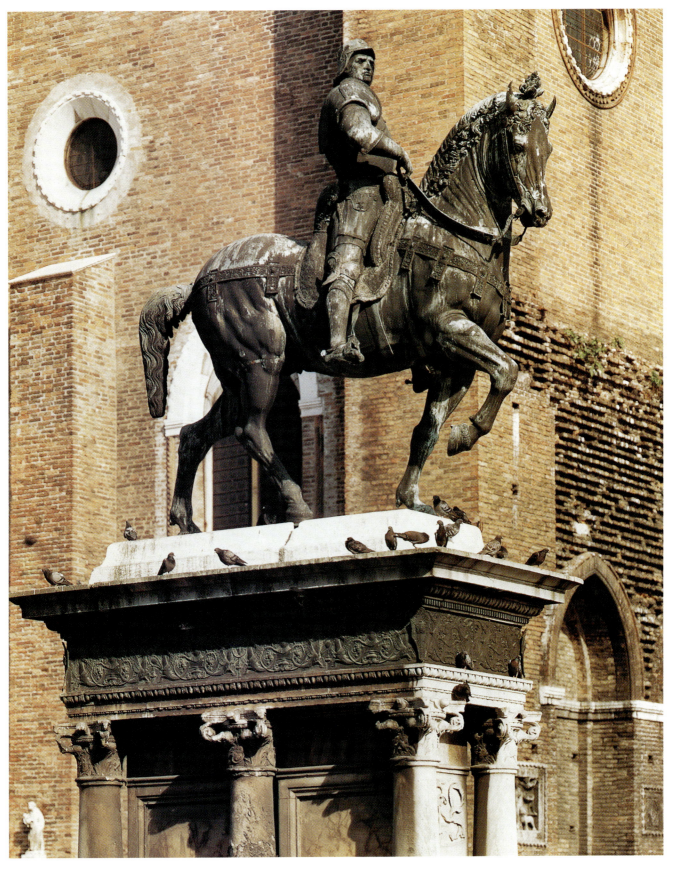

11.19 ANDREA DEL VERROCCHIO. *Equestrian Monument of Bartolomeo Colleoni.* Bronze, 15' high. Campo Ss. Giovanni e Paolo, Venice, Italy, c. 1483–1488. © Scala / Art Resource, NY.

feels the strength, determination, and aggressive spirit of the Renaissance. The horse's tense bulging muscles, the twisted attitude of the figure, the scowling face, and the determination in the eyes of the rider convey the feeling that this soldier might charge at any moment.

The brass *Plaque with Warrior and Attendants* (Figure 11.20) depicts an impassive Nigerian warrior king from the seventeenth or early eighteenth century. The central king figure is larger in scale than his two attendants and is in classic African figurative proportion, approximately three heads high. His apron and shield have leopard imagery, which was the regal symbol. Dominating the composition are the warrior's spear, helmet, and shield. The warrior is depicted as powerful royalty, with his strength being his absolute authority, while at the same time appearing aloof. Benin bronze plaques documented kings, warriors, and famous events, and they were placed prominently in the halls of Benin palaces. The plaques represented the king's power and literally were his image among his people, since he rarely appeared in public except to wage war and to officiate at religious ceremonies.

CONNECTION

Because Benin artworks were sculptural reliefs in a rectangular format, rather than the more-common freestanding sculpture, some scholars suggest that these plaques were influenced by the Portuguese, who had been trading in that area since the sixteenth century, as we saw with the Afro-Portuguese Saltcellar (Figure 7.11, page 163).

FORTIFICATIONS, ARMOR, AND WEAPONS

Architecture and paraphernalia for war need to function offensively and defensively. Battle effectiveness, however, can have aesthetic and religious dimensions as well, as we shall see. Beautiful objects function better.

One of the most ambitious and amazing accomplishments in the architecture of war is the *Great Wall* of China (Figure 11.21). Begun in 206 BCE during the Qin Dynasty, with major additions during the Ming Dynasty (CE 1368–1644),

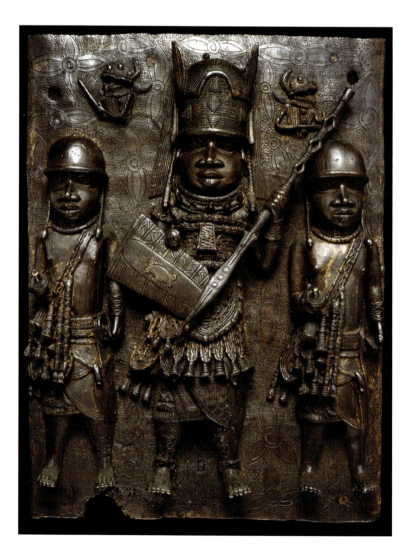

11.20 *Plaque with Warrior and Attendants.* Brass, 19¼" high. Benin. Nigeria, seventeenth or early eighteenth centuries. Peabody Museum of Architecture and Ethnology.

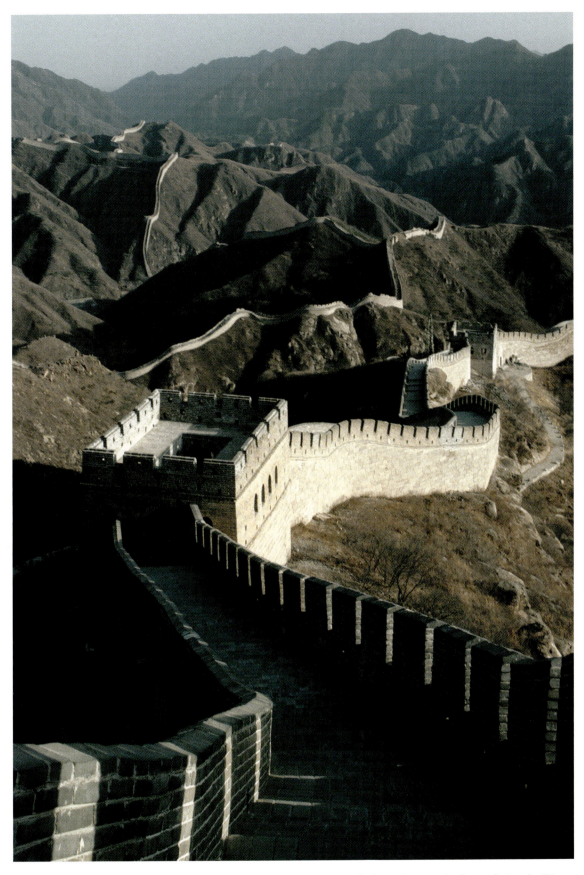

 11.21 *The Great Wall.* Brick faced, average height 25', 1,500 miles long. Construction began during the Qin Dynasty in 206 BCE with major work occurring during the Ming Dynasty, CE 1368–1644. China. © Michael Howell/Index Stock Imagery/Picturequest.

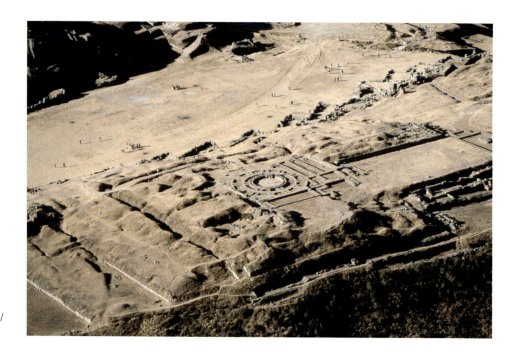

11.22 *Sacsahuaman.* Inca. Peru, c. 1480. © Yann Artuhus-Bertrand / Corbis.

this 1,500-mile-long wall is a "wonder of the world" and is visible from the moon. New pieces of it are still being discovered, and the section near Beijing has been restored. The wall averages twenty-five feet in height and width and is faced in brick. It creates a beautifully flowing line that defines and accents the curves of the hills. Its light colors contrast strikingly with the surrounding vegetation. Strategically placed watchtowers punctuate its undulating length and provide points of visual emphasis. The towers contained embrasures for cannons and were used as signal stations, with smoke by day and fires by night.

Another example of architecture motivated by war is the Incan fortress of *Sacsahuaman,* located high in the Andes Mountains on the west side of the sacred city of Cuzco, Peru (Figure 11.22). It contained within its walls several important Incan structures, among them the holiest, the Temple of the Sun. The aerial view of *Sacsahuaman* shows its layout and its many walls that still exist. Some of the hard limestone blocks in the lower walls reach over fourteen feet in height. Many were irregular blocks that, amazingly, were shaped to fit precisely against the adjacent stones without using mortar. Some walls were plastered and painted, while others were decorated with beaten gold. The walls were usually thicker at the base and tapered above in a gradual slope, and they were pierced with gold-trimmed, trapezoidal doors, windows, and niches. The roofs were covered in a lightweight patterned thatch. This style of construction is very sturdy, and many Incan walls still stand, even though earthquake tremors have crumbled the later Spanish colonial structures built on top of them.

Dressing for war means being protected in both body and spirit. Figure 11.23 shows a life-size ceramic sculpture of an Aztec *Eagle Knight* (c. fifteenth century). Like their later North American neighbors, the Aztecs considered the eagle to

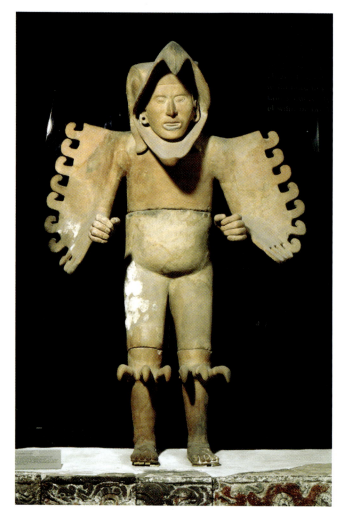

11.23 *Eagle Knight.* Earthenware and plaster, 66⁷/₈" × 46¹/₂" × 21⁵/₈". Aztec. Museo Templo Mayor, Mexico, c. fifteenth century. © John Bigelow Taylor / Art Resource, NY.

be fearless, brave, and daring. It could also gaze at the sun (which, for the Aztecs, was looking directly at their God, a feat that humans dare not attempt). The highest earthly reward for a successful Aztec warrior was induction into the Order of the Eagle or Jaguar Knights. The Eagle Knights wore an open-beaked eagle on their heads, while their arms were sleeved in full plumage. This ceramic representation of the knight is made of five pieces precisely fitted together and was at one time covered with painted stucco feathers. According to the Aztec religion, warfare and daily human sacrifice were necessary to preserve the Sun God, who otherwise would succumb completely to the Moon Goddess and night. Therefore, warriors enjoyed special privileges.

CONNECTION
Mesoamerican ball games recreated the rivalry between the Sun and the Moon and ended with human sacrifices. For more, see the Great Ball Court (Figure 16.30, page 492).

Ironically, the Aztecs, who made war to achieve heaven, were conquered by the Spanish, who made war to save "heathens" for the Christian heaven. Both, of course, were motivated by material as well as spiritual gain. Our next example, *Boy's Dress Armor of Archduke Charles* (Figure 11.24), was

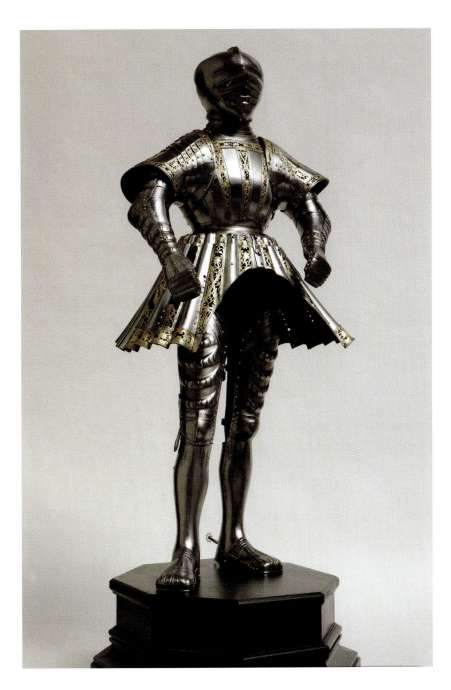

11.24   *Boy's Dress Armor of Archduke Charles* (later King Charles V). Steel, silver gilt, velvet, leather, 59" high, 27¹/₂" wide. Spain, 1512–1514. © Kunsthistorisches Museum, Vienna.

never used in battle, but may have resembled what some of the conquistadors wore as they entered the Aztecs' pristine city of Tenochtitlán. Impressive dress armor was designed not only to protect the warrior but also to arouse fear in the foe. Imagine the Aztecs' terror as they saw a steel-covered man mounted on a steel-covered horse, an animal they had never seen before, with deadly thunder sticks that blew humans apart.

The *Boy's Dress Armor of Archduke Charles* was commissioned by Maximilian I in 1512 for his twelve-year-old grandson, who later became Charles V of Spain. The designer, Konrad Seusenhofer, was Maximilian's court armorer. A gifted craftsman, Seusenhofer was also a fashion designer and patterned Charles's armor after the "long coat," a pleated skirt worn as part of Dutch men's clothing. The armor's gilded, interlaced, recessed bands of metal have black velvet inserts to enhance the detailing of the metal "lace." Symbols of the Cross of St. Andrew, the Order of the Golden Fleece, and the flint and sparks of Burgundy are interwoven throughout the bands. The front of the skirt is opened to a half circle to facilitate horseback riding. The etching and decoration in silver were executed by the best artists in Augsburg.

Our next example is approximately contemporary with the armor we have just studied. The highly ornamented Islamic *Battle Axe* (Figure 11.25) was probably used for ceremonial purposes. The axe is inscribed with the name and titles of a Mamluk sultan, along with prayers for his victory and praise to Allah. In many cultures, prayers and weapons are combined through art, as warriors all over the world seek the protection of their religion. The aesthetics of a weapon can enhance its spirit and function or elevate the status and power of its owner.

The axe has two styles of calligraphy: an older, square style on the socket for the handle, and a newer, curving style on the circle in the blade. Each style of calligraphy fits beautifully within the shape allotted for it. In addition, the differing styles contrast strongly with each other, adding to the decorative richness of the axe's design. Calligraphy is an important Islamic art form, and many variations have been developed. The iron blade is damascened in gold with rich arabesques.

WAR SCENES

Artists throughout time have documented the events of war. In our examples, we will see three different approaches. The first approach presents war as a memorable, even glorious, action-filled event. The second, using examples from the nineteenth century, shows how art can document battles from various points of view. The third approach, with examples from the twentieth century, emphasizes the horrors of war.

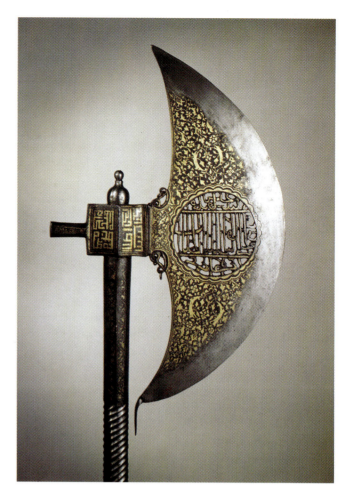

11.25   *Battle Axe*. Iron damascened with gold, 38⁷/₈" long. Mamluk, Egypt, late fifteenth century. Kunsthistorisches Museum, Vienna.

GLORIFYING WAR

Our first example of art that glorifies war is the *Palette of King Narmer* (Figure 11.26), a relief carving from ancient Egypt, dating from 3000 BCE. This object would have been used to mix the black eye makeup both men and women wore. The carving records the forceful unification of Egypt five thousand years ago, when Narmer (also called Menes), king of Upper Egypt, was victorious in a war over Lower Egypt. On the back in the center of the top band is the pictograph of King Narmer's name: a horizontal fish, which corresponds to *nar*, and below it a vertical chisel for *mer*. Flanking Narmer's name are two images of Hathor, the cow goddess of beauty, love, and fertility, who was the king's protector. In the next large register below, in hierarchical order, is the biggest figure on the palette, King Narmer, wearing the tall white crown of Upper Egypt. He is about to administer a deadly blow to the enemy he grasps by the hair. Behind him is a servant who is carrying his sandals, his bare feet suggesting that this is holy ground and that this

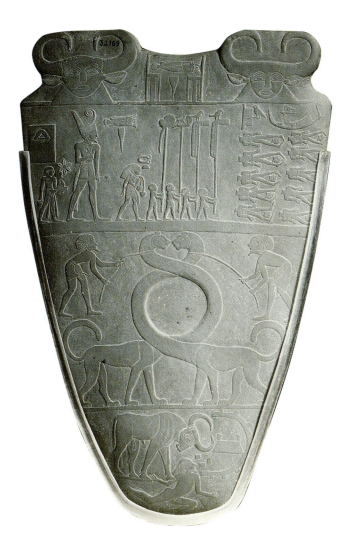
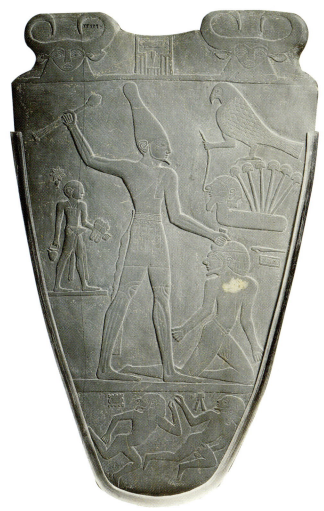

 11.26 *Palette of King Narmer.* Slate, 25" high. Egypt, c. 3000 BCE. © Jurgen Liepe, Berlin. See also the text accompanying Figure 2.34.

event was divinely predisposed. The falcon represents Horus, the god of Upper Egypt, standing triumphantly on a head and papyrus, both representing Lower Egypt. In the bottom register are dead prisoners.

On the other side of the palette, we again see the triumphal Narmer uniting Egypt by war, now wearing the cobra crown of Lower Egypt. Preceded by standard-bearers, he inspects the beheaded prisoners lined up in rows with their heads tucked between their feet. The intertwined necks of beasts may represent unification of Egypt.

Looking at the figure of Narmer, we see the standardized pose of the human body that became so typical of the Egyptian style. Size indicated figures of greater or lesser status, while horizontal divisions enabled the information to be understood easily.

 CONNECTION
You can see another example of the Egyptian style of figure representation in the Temple of Ramses II, *Figure 14.22 (page 417).*

Next is a battle scene from medieval Japan, during the Kamakura era, when civil war and two invasions by the Mongol emperor Kublai Khan convulsed Japan. Warfare and artistry were particularly interwoven at this time. The martial arts were elevated to a precise art form, and literature featured long tales of war and battle, in contrast to the period immediately preceding, which featured tales of courtly love. One tale of war was the *Heiji Monogatari,* the story of a power feud

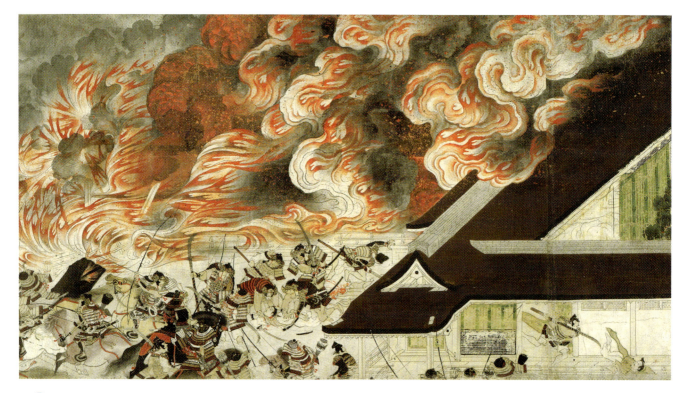

11.27 *Burning of the Sanjo Palace.* From the *Heiji Monogatari*. Hand scroll (detail), ink and color on paper; 16¹/₄" high, 22'9" long. Japan, Kamakura period, late thirteenth century. Museum of Fine Arts, Boston.

between two clans that lasted approximately four years in the twelfth century. A scroll illustrating the story, nearly twenty-three feet long, was unrolled one scene at a time, to be viewed privately by two or three people. Our scene shows the *Burning of the Sanjo Palace* (Figure 11.27) and effectively illustrates the tumult and disorder of warfare. As flames and smoke erupt, the raiders dash away to the left, trampling their victims or leaving them trapped in the burning rubble. To make the raid seem even more disorderly, the artist used strong visual contrasts. Jumbled shapes contrast with the clean lines of the palace roof. Groups are juxtaposed with single figures to build and then diffuse dramatic moments.

NINETEENTH-CENTURY BATTLE SCENES

In the preceding examples, the artists had license to exaggerate or even fantasize about the battles and their heroes. The nineteenth- century invention of the camera changed that. Although photographers could still make romanticized portraits of the War Hero, they also began to make gritty, horrific representations of the battlefield. *Dead Confederate Soldier with Gun* (Figure 11.28), a U.S. Civil War photograph by Mathew B. Brady (or staff) from 1865, is but one of the 3,500 photographs he took covering both sides of the conflict. Brady was the first to photographically document war.

Brady took care to frame and compose his shots, and he often advantageously arranged "props," such as the rifles, to enhance the visual beauty of the picture and emphasize the sense of tragedy. The rough texture of the ground fills the entire image, except for the dramatically lit planes of the soldier's face. The fallen tree trunk forms a horizontal barrier that forever separates the dead soldier from the living. The guns and rubble in the background line up in parallel diagonals, setting up a visual cadence that echoes the line of the soldier's body. He is visually trapped and squeezed by the tree trunk and the rifle.

In some cases, art can provide us with an alternative record of events, one that differs from the official record. The *Battle of Little Big Horn* (Figure 11.29), painted in 1880 by the Sioux artist Red Horse, presents the Native American point of view, which was conspicuously absent in Western art and history. The painting is a colorful depiction of the defeat of Lieutenant Colonel George Custer and his troops. The Sioux had been given land in a treaty with the U.S. government, but the government then tried to revoke the treaty under pressure from gold prospectors, settlers, and the railroads. The flamboyant Custer tracked Sitting Bull, the Sioux leader, to Little Big Horn, thinking that his capture of this renowned chief would help him to be elected U.S. president. As the painting illustrates, Custer fell, and the Sioux won their final victory as a nation. In this image, Sioux warriors

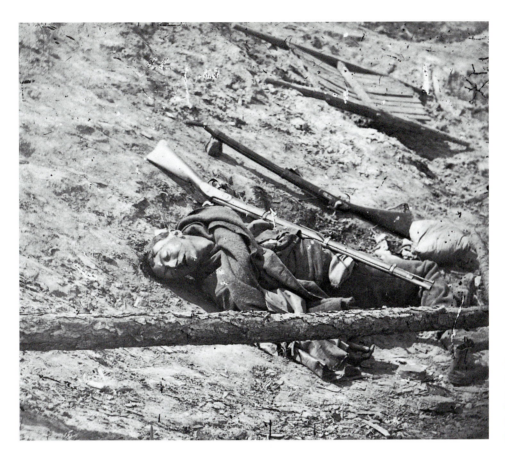

11.28 MATHEW B. BRADY (OR STAFF). *Dead Confederate Soldier with Gun.* Civil War photograph. USA, 1865. Reproduced from the Collections of the Library of Congress.

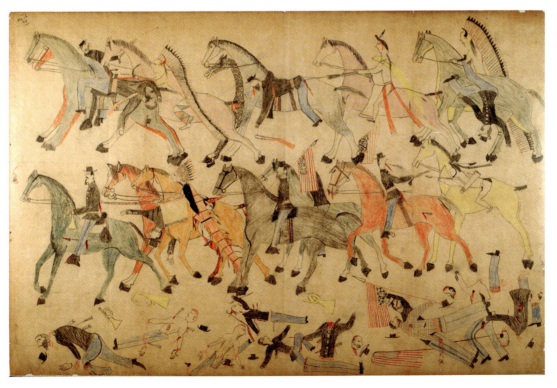

11.29 RED HORSE. *Battle of Little Big Horn.* Sioux. USA, 1880. National Anthropological Archives, Smithsonian Institution, Washington D.C.

advance from the right, killing U.S. soldiers, who fall from their horses. The dead and wounded from both sides occupy the bottom of the image. Red Horse visually organizes the overlapping and nonoverlapping figures, both to convey the crowdedness of the battle scene and to record detail clearly.

TWENTIETH-CENTURY IMAGES OF WAR

Although war is still glorified in twentieth-century art, as we saw in Riefenstahl's *Triumph of the Will* (Figure 11.6), more and more images present the horrific side of war.

After the revolution of 1917 in Russia, Communist leader Vladimir Lenin saw the advantages of film as a new medium and supported the development of filmmaking. Sergei M. Eisenstein was commissioned to glorify the collective heroism and martyrdom of the Soviet people in his masterpiece film, *The Battleship Potemkin,* made in 1925 (Figure 11.30). A great admirer of U.S. filmmaker D. W. Griffith, Eisenstein expanded the expressive vocabulary of film. His camera shots varied from full to medium to close up to extreme close up, and included pan, iris (blurred edges), and traveling (moving from front to back or back to front). Flashbacks and crosscutting (two events edited together for dramatic effect) were also part of his compositions. But Eisenstein's genius was his editing. He used a rapid form of "montage," a kind of cinematic collage of images that allowed the viewers to conclude the action of the multiple scenes.

In the Odessa Steps Massacre sequence in *Battleship Potemkin,* Eisenstein bombards the audience with a climactic montage showing the horrendous results of a failed historic uprising against Czarist Russia in 1905. In four minutes and twenty seconds of film, 155 separate shots, all from different camera angles, show Czarist soldiers opening fire on unarmed people crowded into the port of Odessa. Fleeting images include the soldiers firing, a mother holding a dead child, a soldier swinging a club, the bloodied face of a beaten woman, a baby in a carriage that careens down the steps, a horrified student, and the dreadful aftermath of the dead lying on the stairs of the port. Viewers finds themselves caught in the action of the scene, feeling the terror and panic.

CONNECTION
In Chapter 12, we will see several artworks effectively used in protest against war, including Francisco Goya's Executions of May 3, 1808 *(Figure 12.1, page 338).*

One of the greatest twentieth-century paintings is *Guernica* (Figure 11.31) by Pablo Picasso, dramatizing the 1937 destruction of the Basque capital during the Spanish Civil War. Three forces of thirty-three Nazi German planes, each

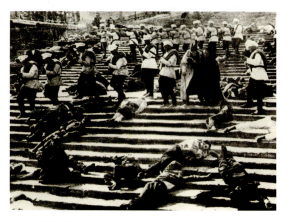
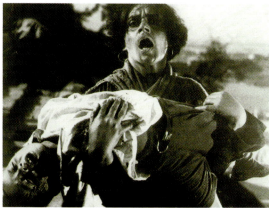
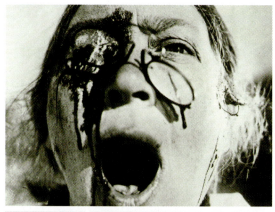
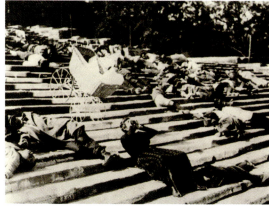

11.30 SERGEI M. EISENSTEIN. *The Battleship Potemkin.* Film stills. Russia, 1925. © Kobal Collection.

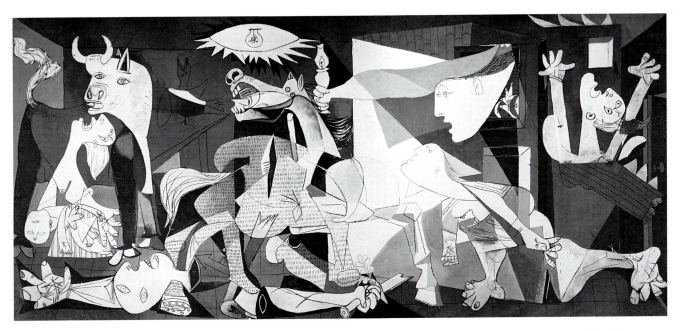

11.31   PABLO PICASSO. *Guernica.* Oil on canvas, 11' × 28'8". Spain, 1937. Prado Museum, Madrid. Institut Amatller D'art Hispanic © Museo del Prado. © 2004 Estate of Pablo Picasso / Artists Rights Society (ARS), New York. See also the text accompanying Figure 1.18.

armed with three thousand pounds of bombs and hundreds of incendiary cylinders, bombarded Guernica for several hours. Three days later when the fires died down, over one thousand people were dead.

In Paris, Picasso received the news of the Guernica massacre. Shocked and outraged, he immediately set down sketches for the painting. Using imagery that had been part of his visual vocabulary in previous works, Picasso blended the nightmarish aspects of Surrealism with his own style of Cubism to create a powerfully expressive work. The bull represents Fascist Spain, doomed to be tortured and suffer a slow, inevitable death. The gored, dying horse rearing in agony is the Spanish Republic, while the fallen soldier holding the broken sword represents the spirit of resistance against tyranny. In the dimmed light of an oil lamp, the looming, profiled head expresses shock while witnessing this suffering and carnage. The electric light bulb in the eye-shape at the top of the painting suggests that the world is being shown its inhumanity. All the figures, abstracted, contorted, and distorted, profoundly allude to unbearable pain.

Picasso experienced a conversion after the holocaust of Guernica. In earlier work, he was more concerned with the formalistic elements in art. Subsequently, his role as an artist and his political commitment changed. He said, "Painting is not done to decorate apartments. It is an instrument of war for attack and defense against the enemy."

WAR MEMORIALS

An entire book could be devoted to monumental art dedicated to the glory of victories, battles, and the dying of the brave.

In this chapter, we have already seen the *Arch of Titus* (Figure 11.16), which served the dual purposes of enhancing the fame of the emperor and memorializing his battle victories. War memorials can vary dramatically, as in the following examples.

The *USA Marine Corps War Memorial* (Figure 11.32) sculpted by Felix W. Weldon and dedicated in 1956,

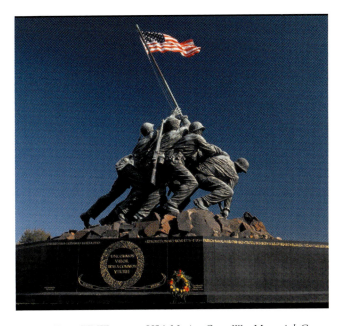
11.32   FELIX W. WELDON. *USA Marine Corps War Memorial.* Cast bronze, over life-size. Arlington, Virginia, 1954. © Andre Jerry / Picturequest #527094.

commemorates the 6,800 U.S. soldiers who died in the victorious battle for Iwo Jima Island in World War II. The war memorial recreates an actual event, in which Marines charged up Iwo Jima's Mt. Suribachi and planted the U.S. flag there. The pose and figures in the sculpture were copied from an Associated Press news photograph taken by Joe Rosenthal, which was staged after the event. Weldon's bronze sculpture is over life-size, grand and dramatic at the same time. The triangular shape formed by the figures suggests strength and solidity, while the numerous diagonals within give a sense of tumbling, hurrying forms. The sculpture blends the commemoration of the past event with present-day reality: every day, a real flag is raised and lowered on the flag pole in the memorial.

Built in 1982, the *Vietnam Veterans Memorial* by Maya Lin (Figure 11.33) is located on the Mall in Washington, D.C., a long, grassy park with several historical and patriotic monuments, surrounded by numerous government structures. It commemorates almost 58,000 Americans who died in the Vietnam War, from 1959 until 1975, with each name chronologically listed and carved on its black granite face, like a gravestone. The memorial is low, long, and V-shaped, set into the ground with one end pointing to the Washington Monument,

a symbol of national unity, and the other end pointing to the Lincoln Memorial, a monument to a nation grievously divided by civil war. This reflects the national anguish over the soldiers who served and died in a war about which the general population was ambivalent. Magazine and newspaper coverage had brought the blunt realities of the war into U.S. homes, as evident in *Brigadier General Nguyen Ngoc Loan summarily executing the suspected leader of a Vietcong commando unit* (Figure 11.34), a war photograph from 1968 by Eddie Adams. This imagery informed people's concept of the Vietnam War. Its harshness contrasts severely with romanticized images of war.

When first proposed, the *Vietnam Veterans Memorial* was very controversial, and, later, figurative sculptures of soldiers and of nurses were added near the site to glorify the troops. The *Vietnam Veterans Memorial* moves observers to private meditation or mourning, rather than celebration. Its polished surface reflects the faces of the living and superimposes them on the names of the dead, which forces a personal connection between the two. Relatives linger over the memorial to their loved ones, take rubbings of the names, and leave all kinds of remembrances, such as poems, childhood mementos, or personal items.

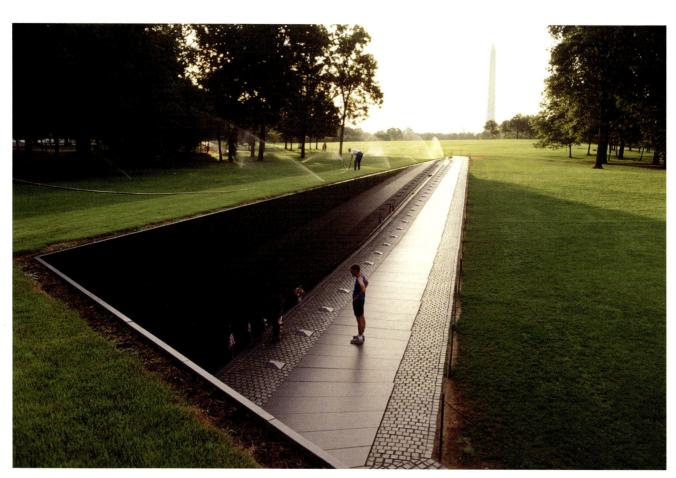

 11.33 MAYA YING LIN. *Vietnam Veterans Memorial.* Black granite, 492' long; height of wall at center, 10'1". Washington, D.C., USA, 1982. © Frank Fournier / Contact Press Images.

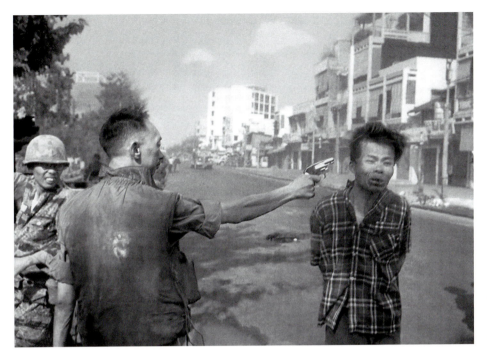

11.34 EDDIE ADAMS. *Brigadier General Nguyen Ngoc Loan summarily executing the suspected leader of a Vietcong commando unit.* Saigon, South Vietnam, February 1, 1968. © A/P / Wide World Photos.

PEACE

Although many works of art relate to war, relatively few deal with peace.

ART ABOUT PEACE

One image that expresses the concept of peace is Edward Hicks's *The Peaceable Kingdom* (Figure 11.35), painted between 1830 and 1840. Hicks, a Quaker convert, based his image on the following biblical passage:

> The wolf also shall dwell with the lamb, and the leopard shall lie down with the kid; and the calf and the young lion and the fatling together; and a little child shall lead them. (Isaiah 11)

Hicks was motivated in part by his own struggles with "drink and riotous living," but he was also inspired by the Quaker

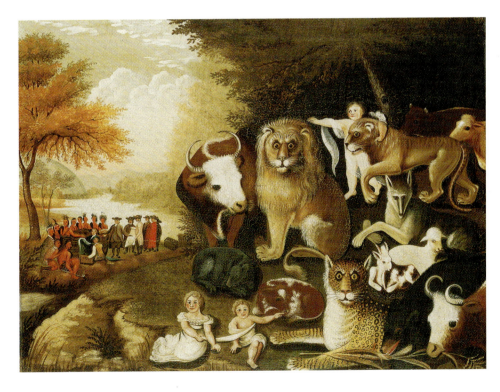

11.35 EDWARD HICKS. *The Peaceable Kingdom.* Oil on canvas. USA, 1830–1840. Brooklyn Museum of Art. See also the text accompanying Figure 1.4.

William Penn and his treaty with the Indians. Hicks copied this detail, visible in the background, from a famous painting by U.S. artist Benjamin West. In the scene, Penn brokers peace between warring factions of settlers and Native Americans, who meet in a circle with Penn in the center. The image came to signify a utopian new world.

The metaphors Hicks used throughout his painting have become standard language for expressing the concept of peace. A luminous sky glows in the background, while lush vegetation frames the foreground figures. The animals are rendered in a flat, decorative, imaginative style. Their wide, staring eyes and the patterns of their fur are emphasized. There is a feeling of innocence and peace, without strife and turmoil. Hicks was not inhibited by academic rules of proportion and style. Along with his natural talent, his only art training occurred on the job as a sign maker and carriage decorator.

PEACE OFFERINGS AND PEACE MONUMENTS

Art is used both as an exchange offering for peace and a memorial to peace. When agreements are made and peace treaties are signed, gifts are often exchanged to seal the arrangement. Precious objects might also be offered to show submission or to avoid further confrontation.

Our first example is the splendid *Moctezuma's Headdress* (Figure 11.36), believed to have belonged to the last Aztec ruler. Moctezuma may have given it to the Spanish leader Cortés as a peace offering or as a desperate last measure to avoid his own demise. Objects made of feathers are frail, and feather working is a rare skill. Not many examples of feather

work survive. This one is exceptional. Moctezuma's four-foot-high headdress is constructed of brilliant, iridescent green feathers from the tail plumage of the quetzal. It is trimmed in blue feathers from the cotinga interwoven with small gold disks. The feathers came from royal aviaries that were attended by three hundred workers. The feather work of our example is believed to have been done by Moctezuma's wives and concubines.

A few centuries later, Native Americans created objects designed exclusively for peaceful exchange. Around 1820, the Ottawa tribe of the Great Lakes received the *Presentation Pipe Tomahawk* (Figure 11.37). Its function as a weapon has been superseded by its aesthetics and the ritual giving as a peace offering. Crafted only for presentation purposes, this fine example is made of hickory wood, silver, iron, and lead. On the handle top in a silver inlay is engraved the name "Ottokee," the recipient of the gift. Inlaid also in silver in the handle are a naturalistic fish and an abstract curvilinear pattern. On the head and blade of the tomahawk are engraved an acorn, a heart, and a half moon. The style of the engravings is reminiscent of the *Boy's Dress Armor of Archduke Charles* (Figure 11.24), suggesting European influences. The pipe tomahawk may have been crafted by European, American, or Ottowan metalsmiths.

An example of a peace monument is the *Ara Pacis Augustae* (Figure 11.38), from 13–9 BCE. The monument was built upon Emperor Augustus's return to Rome after quelling the civil wars between Spain and France. This altar of peace sits on a podium that is enclosed by a rectangular wall, with twelve steps to the entrance. The walls are covered with reliefs inside and out.

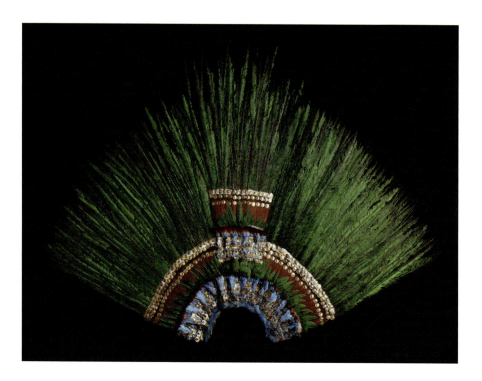

11.36 *Moctezuma's Headdress.* Quetzal and cotinga feathers, gold plaques. Aztec. Mexico, c. 1319. Kunsthistorisches Museum. See also the text accompanying Figure 6.9.

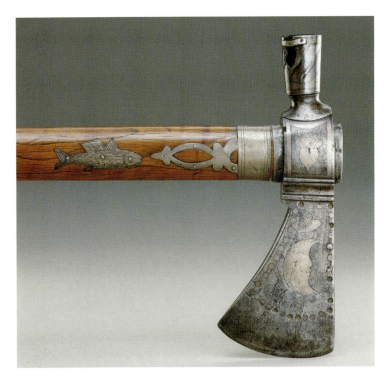

11.37 *Presentation Pipe Tomahawk.*
Wood, inlaid metal. Ottawa. USA,
c. 1820. The Detroit Institute of Arts.

The lower section of the outer walls is decorated with a wide band of foliage ornamentation, while above, wrapping around three sides of the monument, are figurative reliefs depicting the Earth Mother, Tellus; Aeneas, the legendary founder of Rome; and two long processions led by Augustus. Carved foliage and fruit garlands symbolize the golden age of plenty as well as fecundity, ripeness, and peace, all under the rule of Augustus. Sacrificial offerings of animals and humans are indicated. The whole piece was probably brightly painted. Although the *Ara Pacis* promoted peace as a value held dear by the Roman Empire and, more specifically, by Emperor Augustus himself, it can also be seen as a victory monument and a vehicle of propaganda or personal aggrandizement.

Not long ago, in the twentieth century, memorials to peace were constructed in Hiroshima, Japan, and in Los Angeles, California. These "peace parks," not shown here, were built to heal wounds of war. Hopefully, more monuments and memorials to peace will be created and become part of human history.

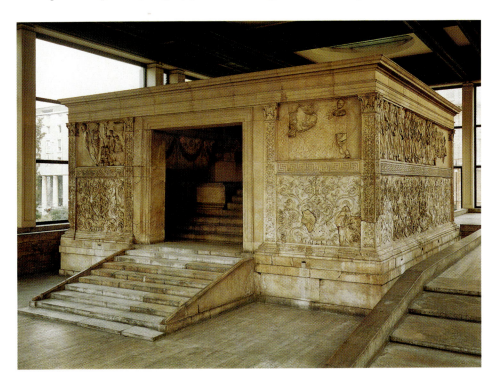

11.38 *Ara Pacis Augustae.* Marble; outer wall 34'5" × 38' × 23'. Rome, 13–9 BCE. © Scala / Art Resource, NY.

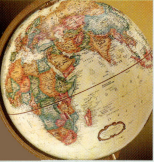

Courtesy of Replogle Globes, Inc., Broadview, IL.

Below:

Map 5 The Expansion of Islam, the Byzantine Empire, and the Migration of Germanic People into Southern Europe

Art on a grand scale, lavish and made with the best materials by the best artists, is imposing and overwhelming. All the art in Chapter 11 was made for the state's political or military reasons. World history from 500–1300 witnessed the rise and fall of many kingdoms, with rulers using art to increase their prestige.

Civilization centers flourished throughout the Americas. The Moche civilization (200–800) of coastal Peru produced great temples of sun brick and had elaborate burials filled with metal, jewels and ceramic treasures. The Incan civilization in the Andes Mountains was shortly to emerge (see the Fortress at *Sacsahuaman,* Figure 11.22). North American centers included the Mississippian culture (c. 800), and the Anasazi (1000–1300), who built the famous cliff dwellings in the southwest United States.

Central America saw the succession of many great empires with ambitious architecture and advances in learning, especially in mathematics and astronomy. All were hierarchical societies, governed by a supreme ruler with warrior and priest classes. Teotihuacán reached its height around 600. The old Maya Empire in the Yucatan Peninsula thrived until around 900, with grand temples and palaces, like the *Palace at Palenque* (Figure 11.8). From the Toltec culture (900–1200) around Veracruz came the *Tula Warrior Columns* (Figure 11.18). Beginning in the thirteenth century, the Aztec built a powerful empire in central Mexico, with engineering feats that included irrigation and drainage systems and road building.

During this period, the Byzantine Empire and the expansion of Islam dominated Eastern Europe, the Middle East, central Asia and northern Africa. One of the great rulers of the Chris-

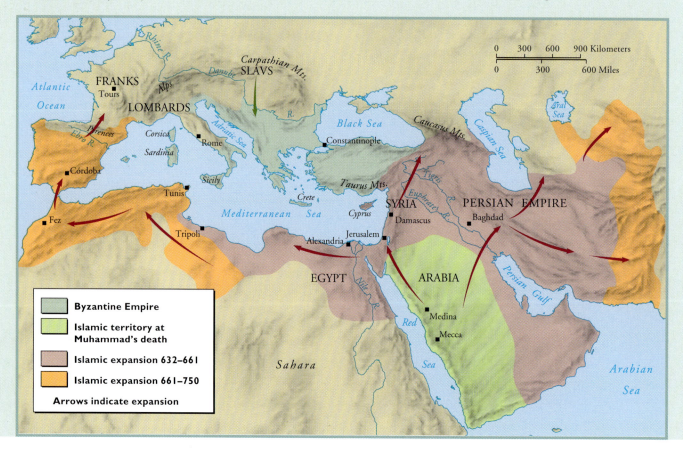

Legend:
- Byzantine Empire
- Islamic territory at Muhammad's death
- Islamic expansion 632–661
- Islamic expansion 661–750
- Arrows indicate expansion

tian Byzantine Empire (476–1453) was Justinian (Figure 11.2), whose churches had notable mosaics and design. Wealthy Byzantium had many centers for learning and for preservation of ancient knowledge. It began to decline around 1100, due to warfare with Muslims.

The prophet Muhammed founded the Islamic religion in the early seventh century. Islam spread quickly through warfare, with Muslim armies conquering northern Africa, Spain, and the Middle East within one hundred years and advancing on India beginning in 1000. Important Muslim kingdoms include the Umayyad Caliphate in Spain (c. 750–1050), the Abbasid Caliphate in Baghdad (c. 750–1250) and the Ottoman Empire in Turkey (fourteenth–twentieth centuries). The Muslims were known for their accomplishments in algebra, geometry, astronomy, optics, and literature, as well as for the creation of great universities and libraries.

This was the Middle Ages in Europe, beginning with the dissolution of the Western Roman Empire, and concluding with the early forms of the modern European nation-states. Large monasteries and the Catholic Church in Rome were more powerful than any other European government. Almost all art was religious. Until 600, Europe experienced upheaval as Germanic peoples migrated south and east. They also created small, precious art objects. Once they settled, they founded Christian kingdoms with architecture and art influenced by Rome and Byzantium. The Crusades (1095–1291), a series of wars for control of the Holy Land, brought the Germanic Europeans in further contact with Byzantium and the Muslim Empire. Feudalism was the main form of social and economic organization. The Black Death (1347–1351) ravaged Europe, killing one-third of the population. By 1200, a distinctive art form, Gothic, developed in Northern Europe.

Africa also saw the emergence of several early empires. Northern empires were Islamic, while southern empires followed native African religions. Powerful and wealthy Ghana (c. 700–1200) controlled the area's trade in salt and gold. Its ironworks produced powerful weapons. Later in the same area, Mali became a large Islamic empire. Farther south, in Ife, the twelfth century saw the founding of the Yoruba civilization, with its famous *Crowned Head of an Oni* (Figure 11.3). Also in the south, the Zanj people thrived on trade with China, Arabia and India from 1200 to 1500, and the kingdom of Zimbabwe flourished, with its great stone buildings.

India experienced a resurgence of Hinduism beginning in the sixth century, and many huge temple complexes were constructed. After 1000, Muslims invaded and established the Mughal Empire in northern India. In the south, strong Hindu dynasties continued, with ambitious building programs. Indian art and architecture spread to Southeast Asia and Indonesia throughout this period.

The Tang Dynasty (618–906) was a golden age in China for poetry, literature, art and music. Contact with central Asia brought wealth and an exchange of ideas. The Song Dynasty (960–1279) saw the inventions of the magnetic compass, paper money, and book printing. In the arts, the Imperial Court promoted painting and ceramics. Next, conquering Mongols led by Kublai Khan established the Yuan Dynasty (1279–1368). Gunpowder was invented. Trade abroad increased. The Ming Dynasty replaced the Yuan, and began an ambitious building program,

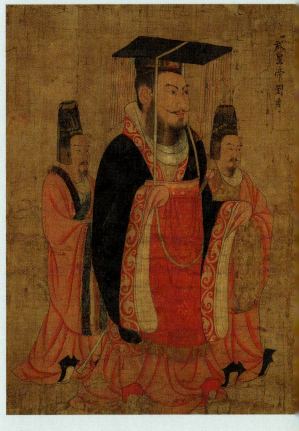

Above:
Chinese emperors were believed to be Sons of Heaven. Their lavish attire, serene expression, and relatively large size all attested to their brilliance. Yan Liben: *Portraits of the Emperors* (detail). Ink and colors on silk, 17.5" high. China, seventh century. Museum of Fine Arts, Boston.

including the Forbidden City (Figure 11.9). China was an international naval power. Ceramics, painting and literature were promoted.

Japanese recorded history begins around the year 600. The Japanese imported the Buddhist religion, mathematics, architecture, the arts, and agricultural methods from the Chinese, but eventually modified them. Shinto is the native Japanese religion. Japan produced the world's first novel, *The Tale of the Genji*, by Lady Murasaki Shikibu, illustrated in the handscroll, *Heiji Monogatari* (Figure 11.27). From the eighth century through the nineteenth, Japan was essentially a feudal state, with a hierarchy of military leaders under the shogun.

Event	Date	Artwork
Unification of Egypt	3200 BCE	Palette of King Narmer
		Menkaure & Khamerernebty
	1500 BCE	
	1000 BCE	
Achaemenid Persia	500 BCE	Persepolis
Roman Republic		Royal Audience Hall and Stairway
		The Great Wall
	100 BCE	
Roman Empire		Ara Pacis Augustae
		Arch of Titus
Teotihuacán	200 CE	
German migration Europe	400	
Byzantine Empire begun	500	
		Emperor Justinian & Attendants
		Palace at Palenque
Tang Dynasty—China	600	
Islam founded		
Japan historic era		
	700	
		Lamassu
	800	
Yoruba Culture founded	900	
Maya-Toltec Culture		
Song Dynasty—China		
Romanesque Era	1000	Tula Warrior Columns
Anasazi Culture		Crowned Head of an Oni
	1100	
	1200	
Gothic Era		
Yuan Dynasty—China	1300	Burning of the Sanjo Palace
		Moctezuma's Headdress

Event	Date	Artwork
Aztec Empire		Eagle Knight
Black Death		
Incan Empire	1400	Fortress at Sacsahuaman
Ming Dynasty—China		Verrocchio: Colleoni
Mughal Dynasty—India		
		Monumental Heads: Easter Is.
Forbidden City begun	1500	Imperial Throne Room
		Boy's Dress Armor
		Battle Axe
	1600	
		Hall of Mirrors
Benin Kingdom—Africa	1700	Royal Kahili
		Plaque with Warrior & Attendants
U.S. Revolutionary War		
French Revolution	1800	Mesquakie Bear Claw Necklace
		Maori Meeting House
		Presentation Pipe Tomahawk
		Hicks: The Peaceable Kingdom
		Houses of Parliament
		Dead Confederate Soldier with Gun
		Red Horse: Battle of Little Big Horn
Russian Revolution	1900	Olowe: Palace Sculpture
World War I		Eisenstein: Battleship Potemkin
World War II		Triumph of the Will
	1950	Picasso: Guernica
		Weldon: USA Marine Corps War Memorial
		Adams: Brigadier General ... executing ...
Vietnam War		
	2000	Lin: Vietnam Veterans Memorial

Art has played a tremendous role in promoting the power of an individual ruler. Portraits and royal paraphernalia denote power, as do the materials used to make them. Prestige comes from the ownership of special objects. Political leaders also have relied on art to proclaim their political achievements. In part, the rulers' greatness comes from the awesome works of art they create for their own names and states.

The state also benefits from the contributions of art, especially architecture and monuments. The design and embellishment of palaces and seats of government must meet political and societal needs.

A warrior's paraphernalia is made with aesthetic considerations, whether to enhance the spirit and function of the weapon or to elevate the status and power of its owner. War scenes can exalt the drama of war, give nonidealized or alternate views of battle, or emphasize its horror. War memorials may evoke deep patriotism or private mourning and contemplation.

Peace itself is given an image in painting, and beautifully crafted art objects may become peace offerings. Peace memorials may glorify the abundance possible when there is no war.

FOOD FOR THOUGHT

As we have seen, leaders and states depend upon art and media to communicate their power to the broad population and to other states.

- Can the high cost, in money and lives, be justified in the grand works of art and architecture that were commissioned by "divinely empowered" individuals or totalitarian states?
- Would works of art and architecture as ambitious and grand as some we have seen in this chapter ever have been created without such commissions?

We have analyzed war objects and imagery from many different cultures. You can use the same tools to analyze imagery in popular culture.

- How are war and peace presented now in contemporary mass media—in comic books, television shows, movies, or computer games?
- Does one group or the other seem to have justice on its side?
- How are warriors and battles framed and depicted?
- How are winners and losers presented?
- Are there instances in which peace or peaceful situations are fully imagined, visualized, or explored?

Finally, photography is often associated with factual reporting. But "factual" reportage, by necessity, is edited or limited. With video, viewers may watch events as they happen, as in the World Trade Center and Pentagon disasters. But the video camera records only one point of view, and that can be edited. Photographers choose which pictures to take and which to ignore. Editors select only a few images to print. Governments can control the press's access to events and thus influence coverage, as happened in the early 1990s during Operation Desert Storm.

- Is the news factual?
- Is art factual?

YOUR CD-ROM RESOURCES

- Your CD-ROM Resources
- World History in Context
- Exploring Art Timeline
- Flashcards
- Food for Thought
- Companion Site
    Chapter 11 Quiz
    InfoTrac® College Edition Readings
    Artist Flashcards
    Online Study Guide

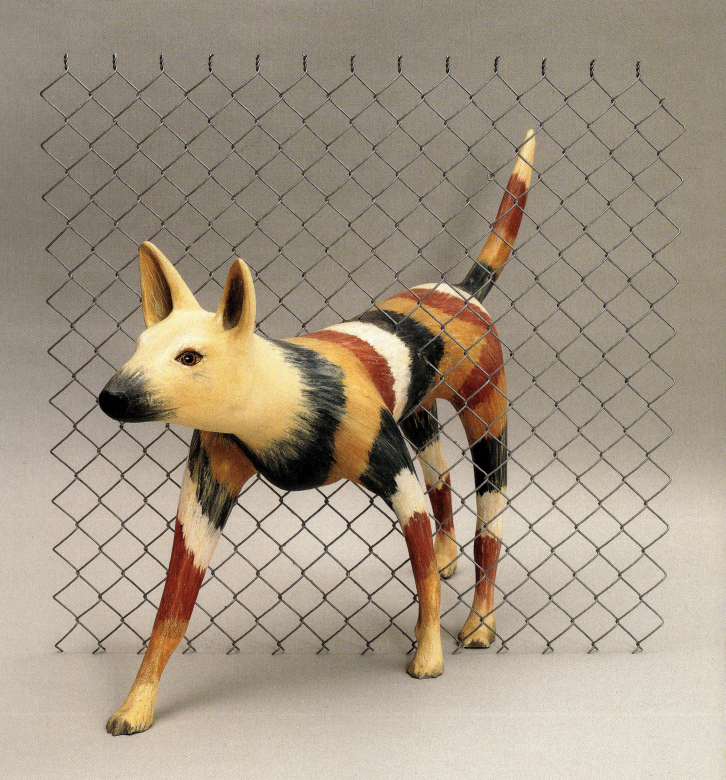

CHAPTER 12

SOCIAL PROTEST/AFFIRMATION

INTRODUCTION

Humans have done terrible things to other humans, and specific instances of injustice have spurred many artists to protest through their artwork. Art is a useful and effective tool here: villains can be identified, heroes honored, and causes promoted with emotional and visual impact unequaled by the written word.

We will focus our discussion on these questions:

Protests against Military Action:

- When have most antiwar artworks been made?

- What kinds of events have they decried?

Fighting for the Oppressed:

- Whose causes have artists championed?

- What kinds of strategies have artists used to make their work more effective for political and social change?

- How have artists affirmed the values of minority groups?

Questioning the Status Quo:

- What is "normal" in society?

- What do artists have to say about all-pervasive normalcy?

- What types of social power are used to control or oppress people?

Dingoes; Dingo Proof Fence. Detail of Figure 12.22. National Gallery of Australia, Canberra.

Artists use humor, shock tactics, beauty, drama, or understatement to convey their protest messages. Yet protest art is a form of affirmation, because behind it are the fundamental beliefs that human dignity must be respected and that change is possible. Implicit also is the belief that artwork should play a challenging role in society and politics.

Two other chapters contain images related to this topic. Chapter 11, *Power, Politics, and Glory,* has artworks that show war as horrible. In Chapter 14, *Race, Gender, Class, and Clan,* are artworks that protest unfair racial or gender practices.

PROTESTS AGAINST MILITARY ACTION

For thousands of years, artists have made paintings and sculptures about war. Some glorify victors, while others portray (sometimes with sympathy) the defeated and those killed or wounded.

Not until two hundred years ago, however, did artists begin to make art that protests a particular war or the idea of warfare altogether. One likely reason is that a sizable percentage of past art was made for political or religious leaders, usually victorious and powerful ones. Warfare was one means to gain power, and art was a way to display that power. The nineteenth century saw the first antiwar images in the West, while in the twentieth century, and especially in the years since World War II, artworks that protest military action have grown in number. The protested military action includes full-blown war, police actions, covert operations, and guerrilla activity.

A pivotal piece in the history of protest art is *The Executions of May 3, 1808* (Figure 12.1), from 1814. The artist, Francisco Goya, based his painting on sketches he had made of the actual event as it happened six years earlier. This work represents the Spanish point of view in the conflict, but Goya's interpretation goes beyond partisanship and could stand for any mass execution. The citizens of Madrid rose up against Napoleon Bonaparte's occupational army in 1808. In suppressing the uprising, the French soldiers captured many of the rioters and executed them a short distance outside the city. In Goya's painting, our sympathy lies with the Spaniards about

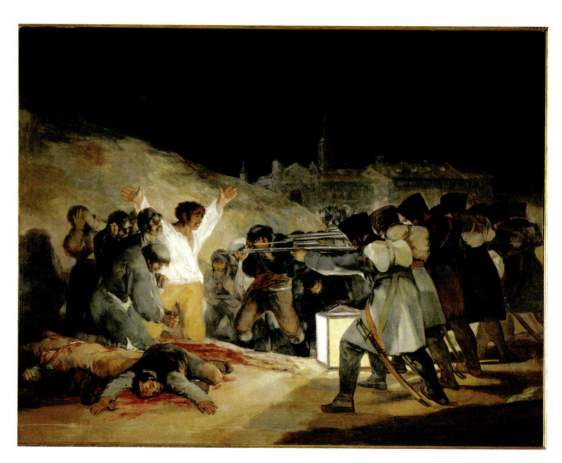

 12.1   FRANCISCO GOYA. *The Executions of May 3, 1808.* Oil on canvas, 104³/4" × 135³/4". Spain, 1814. Prado, Madrid. © Erich Lessing / Art Resource, NY.

to die, as they tremble, pray, or protest as they face the firing line. They all share a common fate, yet Goya individualized them, so that we identify with their horror. We particularly focus on the man in white with outstretched arms who cries out against the executions. Goya posed him like the crucified Jesus, and surrounded him with light colors, against the pervasive gloom. In contrast, Goya has dehumanized the French soldiers, with repeated poses and hidden faces. The barrels of their pointing rifles are rigidly organized, like a war machine.

Käthe Kollwitz dedicated her art to ending war and poverty, and she always showed the faces of anger, betrayal, loss, and death. Kollwitz lived in Germany through the two world wars, losing a son and a grandson in the fighting. In her artwork, however, she frequently turned to past conflicts to show the destructive energy of war. *The Outbreak ("Losbruch")*, dated 1903 (Figure 12.2), is the fifth in a series of seven prints that tell of the Peasant War in Germany in the early sixteenth century. The peasants were miserably poor, worked the land under extremely difficult conditions, and were subject to all kinds of exploitation and abuse by the ruling class. In the first four prints in the series, we see the causes for the uprising: poverty, crushingly hard work, rape of the women. In the fifth image, *The Outbreak ("Losbruch")*, the peasants revolt, charg-

ing forward, their wretched living conditions propelling them to rebel at any cost.

The composition of the work is remarkable. The fury of the peasants' charge is expressed in their postures. They gather steam at the right, grouping and lurching forward, their bodies leaning, while already at the left side of the image they are propelled at deadly speed, nearly horizontal, attacking their oppressors with crude weapons and farm tools. The dark woman at the front becomes the leader and the conscience for the group. Her upraised arms incite them to action, while her bony, twisted hands and arms are documents to the incredible harshness of the peasants' life. Lights and darks alternate and flash across the image, visually conveying the emotions of the moment. The leaden quality of the bent backs, dull faces, and twisted bodies is transformed; they release their energy in a flash, catapulted forward with anger and speed. The colors are stark black and white.

Kollwitz shows a woman leading the revolt, breaking old stereotypes about women's passivity. This also attests to the misery of the peasants' lives—in the end, the women rose up. The uprising was unsuccessful, as the forces of the ruling class suppressed the peasants with brutality. The last two prints of the Peasant War series show a mother who searches for her dead son among piles of bodies, and peasant prisoners bound together awaiting execution.

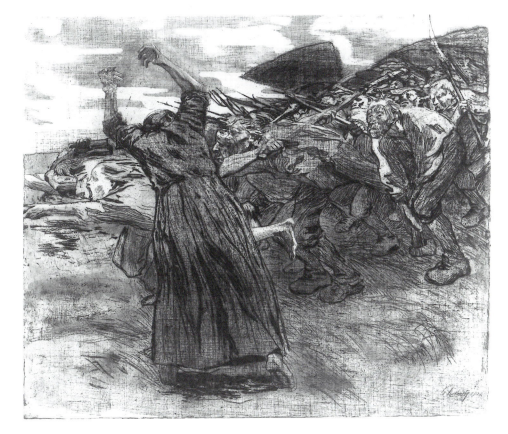

12.2   KÄTHE KOLLWITZ. *The Outbreak ("Losbruch")*. Etching, 20" × 23$^{1}/_{4}$". Germany, 1903. Reproduced from the collections of the Library of Congress, Washington, D.C. © 2004 Artists Rights Society (ARS), New York / VG Bild-Kunst, Bonn. See also the text accompanying Figure 2.2.

Other artists who lived through the world wars dealt with their experience. *Fit for Active Service* (Figure 12.3), a 1918 pen-and-ink drawing by George Grosz, exposed the behind-the-scenes workings of the German army in World War I. All armies are composed of the soldiers who fight on the front line and, in the background, the military machine that commands them. Grosz's image protests the bloated doctors and self-absorbed officers, secure in their bureaucratic assignments, who sent elderly, sick, or very young men to the front lines to fight for Germany near the end of World War I. (All able-bodied men had been sent out much earlier.) With grim wit, the artist's pen outlines the smug, laughing faces of the officers in the foreground, who cynically continue the fighting although their soldiers are in pathetic condition. Farther back, two toadying soldiers stand at attention. Their conformity is made evident by the way the seams in their uniforms line up with the floor and the window frames. They are subsumed into the structure, and an independent conscience does not exist in them. The doctor at the center seems almost happy as his arm reaches around the skeleton, and his examination has found another body for the front lines. Outside, factories contentedly belch out the machinery of war. In contrast to the spare and flattened manner in which the other figures are portrayed, the skeleton is rounded, detailed, and visceral, adorned with rotting organs and tufts of hair.

John Heartfield dedicated much of his art to exposing and condemning the horrors of Nazi Germany. Heartfield was born in Germany as Helmut Herzfelde, but later chose to anglicize his name. *Goering the Executioner,* dated 1933 (Figure 12.4), is a photomontage, in which news photographs are combined and manipulated with drawing to express Heartfield's outrage. The subject is Field Marshal Hermann Goering, one of the major leaders of the Nazi party. Heartfield pulled Goering's head forward, increasing the thickness of the neck and emphasizing the aggressiveness of his bullying face. Behind him burns the Reichstag, the German parliament building, which was destroyed in 1933 by an act of terrorism that was likely perpetrated by the Nazis, but "officially" blamed on Communists. The burning of the Reichstag ended any vestige of a democratic government in Germany, and gave the Nazis the excuse to seize absolute power. This photomontage was the front-page illustration for the September 14, 1933, edition of the newspaper AIZ (Arbeiter-Illustrierte-Zeitung), published in Prague.

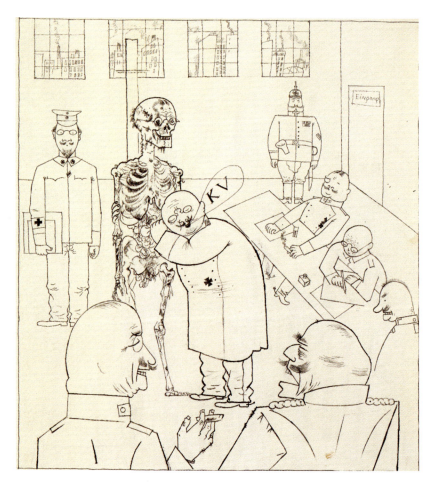

12.3 GEORGE GROSZ. *Fit for Active Service.* Pen and ink, 14¹/₂" × 13¹/₂". Germany, 1918. The Museum of Modern Art, New York. © Digital Image © The Museum of Modern Art / Licensed by Scala / Art Resource, NY. © Estate of George Grosz/ Licensed by VAGA, New York, NY.

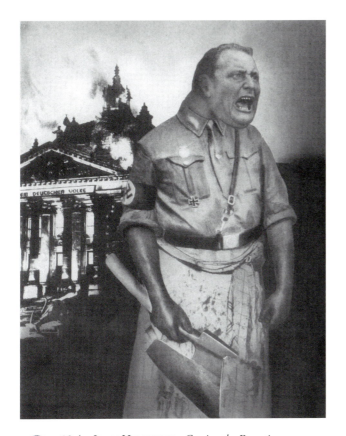

 12.4 JOHN HEARTFIELD. *Goering the Executioner.* Photomontage cover for *AIZ.* Germany, 1933. Reproduced from *John Heartfield,* by Wieland Herzfelde Dresden: VEB Verlag der Kunst, 1964. © 2004 Artists Rights Society (ARS), New York / VG Bild-Kunst, Bonn.

The use of black-and-white elements gives the image an unvarnished, blunt quality. Goering's meat cleaver and stained apron have the quality of factual truth, even though the artist added those props. Heartfield's warnings of Nazi bloodshed in this work proved to be prophetically true. Heartfield was forced to leave Germany and spent much of the 1930s and 1940s in England.

In the mid-1930s, Spain was engulfed in a civil war that in many ways was a prelude to World War II. In 1937, David Alfaro Siqueiros painted *Echo of a Scream* (Figure 12.5) in response to the horror of the Spanish Civil War. There were many innocent victims of that war, including children, and Siqueiros uses the incessant scream of a pained child to express horror at the gross destruction of modern warfare. All of humanity, symbolized by the child, sits amid piles of debris. The child is alone and helpless, and knows only physical and emotional pain. The sky is filled by the large, detached head—the child's head repeated—a massive cry that symbolizes the combined pain of all the victims we do not see. The dark tones and blue-gray colors of the painting add a somber note to the ugliness of the surroundings. The painting also alludes to the

urbanization and industrialization that blot out nature, and to the endless piles of waste that are the result of "progress" and "innovation."

Siqueiros knew his subject matter firsthand. He was a Mexican citizen who fought in Spain as a volunteer in the International Brigade, along with volunteers from fifty other countries who were fighting for the Spanish Republic against the Fascists, who were backed by Nazi Germany. He was also a political activist and social reformer, in addition to using his paintings as vehicles to call for change.

CONNECTION

See Pablo Picasso's Guernica *(Figure 11.31, page 327) for another artwork that deals with the Spanish Civil War.*

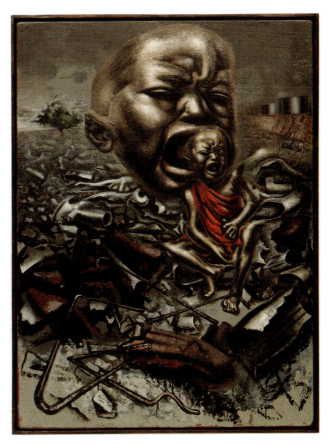

 12.5 DAVID ALFARO SIQUEIROS. *Echo of a Scream.* Enamel on wood, 48" × 36". Mexico, 1937. Gift of Edward M. M. Warburg. (633.1939) The Museum of Modern Art, New York, NY. © Estate of David Alfaro Siqueiros/SOMAAP, Mexico City/VAGA New York. See also the text accompanying Figures 1.5 and 2.21.

Robert Motherwell painted the *Elegy to the Spanish Republic XXXIV* from 1953 to 1954 (Figure 12.6), several years after the Spanish Civil War. It was part of a series of over 150 paintings dedicated to mourning the loss of liberty in Spain after the Fascist forces were victorious. The paintings do not tell a story. However, Motherwell believed that abstraction communicated, in universal terms, the struggle between life and death and between freedom and oppression. The large size of the painting makes these struggles seem monumental. The use of black and white also suggests death and life. Motherwell was influenced by the **Surrealist** process of expression called "automatism," which incorporates intuition, spontaneity, and the accidental when creating artworks, similar to the **Abstract Expressionist** style. His black-and-white forms suggest several Spanish motifs, according to Robert Hughes (1997: 496). They are bull's testicles, the patent leather berets of the Guardia Civil, and living forms (represented by the large, ovoid shapes) that are being crushed by the black bands.

On the other side of the world, atrocities of war have also occurred. Tomatsu Shomei's *Woman with Keloidal Scars* (Figure 12.7) is one of a series of photographs of victims of the atomic bombing of Nagasaki, Japan, at the end of World War II. The blast was so powerful that it vaporized the victims who were nearest the center of impact. The bodies of many were never found. Those farther away suffered terrible burns and injuries, with children stunted and deformed, and adults severely

scarred. Tomatsu's photograph is technically beautiful, with a full range of deep blacks and silvery grays. But the lacy texture is excessive fibrous tissue stretched over the woman's skull. Her pained, fearful expression seems withdrawn and reserved. Her psychological and physical injuries, although inflicted a long time ago, seem still fresh. Yet there is a strange sense of normalcy, as if she were out sightseeing. Tomatsu made this series to document past horrors and to protest against U.S. troops who were stationed in Japan. These troops participated in the Korean War and in cold war standoffs. Since World War II, there has been a strong movement in Japan for complete, permanent demilitarization of the country.

Leon Golub's painting, *Mercenaries I* (Figure 12.8), shows the violence and terrorism that occur whenever authority is imposed on unwilling people. In this painting from 1976, two "guns for hire" dangle a bound victim between them, using brute power in the service of a repressive government. These professional fighters are devoid of any ideological stance; they are simply paid thugs. The mercenaries are flattened figures against the flat background. The victim has no identifying traits and is totally dehumanized; it could be anyone; it could be us. Their larger-than-life size makes the mercenaries seem imposing and their brutality uncontrollable. They are pushed aggressively to the foreground, and we, the viewers, are dwarfed by the nearly eleven-foot height of the painting. We have approximately the same view as the victim, looking up at the merce-

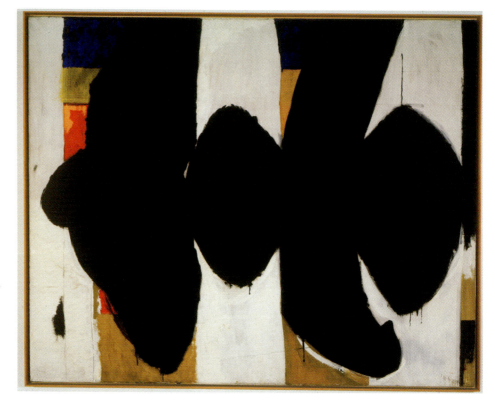

12.6 ROBERT MOTHERWELL. *Elegy to the Spanish Republic XXXIV.* Oil on canvas, 80" × 100". USA, 1953–1954. Albright-Knox Art Gallery, Buffalo, N.Y. © Dedalus Foundation/Licensed by VAGA, New York, NY. See also the text accompanying Figure 1.14.

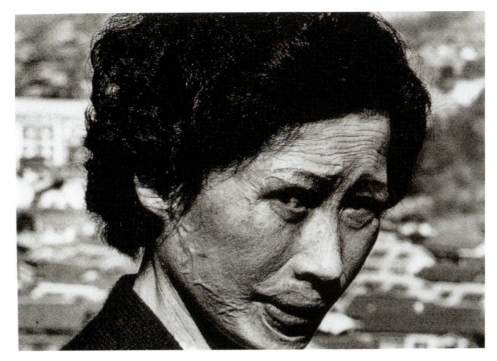

12.7 TOMATSU SHOMEI. *Woman with Keloidal Scars* (from the series *11:02 – Nagasaki*). Gelatin Silver Print, 11.5" × 16". Japan, 1966. Courtesy of the artist.

naries. The paint, applied thickly at first, has been scraped repeatedly so that the surface seems raw and nasty. When rendered this way, flesh looks particularly repulsive, whether it covers the cruel face of the mercenary or the tortured skin of the victim. The colors are jarring and acid.

Golub insists that his images realistically report everyday events in the world. Many of the conflicts of the late twenti-

eth century were guerrilla wars or ongoing civil wars, and the media broadcast many videos and still photographs of atrocities. Golub works from news photographs to create his paintings. Although Golub's images may refer to actions far from home—"out there"—there is an immediacy to them for two reasons. First, the ugliness of the pieces is overwhelming. Second, because the world's politics and economies are entangled,

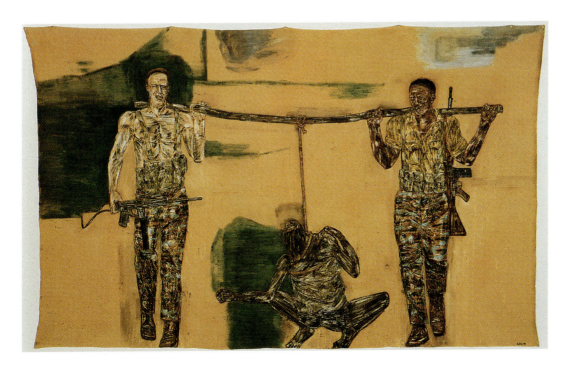

12.8 LEON GOLUB. *Mercenaries I.* Acrylic on canvas, 116" × 186¹/₂". USA, 1976. The Broad Art Foundation © Leon Golub/Licensed by VAGA, New York, NY. Courtesy Ronald Feldman Fine Arts.

democratic governments often assist (directly or indirectly) regimes as repressive as those Golub shows.

FIGHTING FOR THE OPPRESSED

Artists who are fighting for the rights of economically or politically repressed peoples use several strategies to make their points most forcefully. These include beauty, illustration, narrative, humor, and shock. Art also affirms the values of those who have been held down or marginalized. Most social protest works are designed to affect public consciousness in general ways, rather than to prescribe specific changes.

STRATEGIES FOR PROTESTING OPPRESSION

Interestingly, beauty and excitement can be very effective elements in protest art. In Eugène Delacroix's *Liberty Leading the People,* painted in 1830 (Figure 12.9), Liberty has been per-

sonified as a partially nude woman—apparently flesh and blood—but reminiscent of a Greek goddess in her profile and in her idealized body. Energized and oblivious to danger, she carries a rifle and the flag of the French Revolution. She forms the peak of a triangle that is made up of merchants, students, laborers, soldiers, and even young boys rising to follow her call. Excitement grows as they emerge from the smoke, debris, and dead bodies to move toward the light that surrounds Liberty. The lower and middle classes throughout Europe revolted many times against the ruling classes in their countries in the late eighteenth and early nineteenth centuries. Specifically, this work is an homage to the Paris revolt in 1830 to overthrow and replace a repressive monarch.

Delacroix's painting is a rather jarring mixture of realism, idealism, and romantic views about revolution. Realistic are the faces of the men, who look like Parisians of the day, and the details of the clothing, weapons, and the Paris skyline in the background. Elements of idealism include the goddesslike figure of Liberty, and the belief that revolution will lead to a bet-

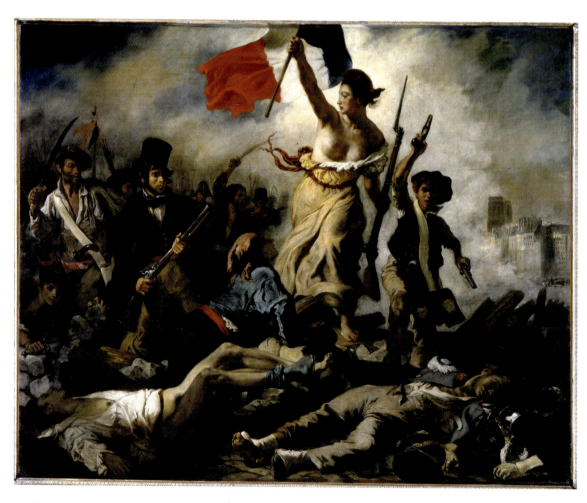

 12.9   Eugène Delacroix. *Liberty Leading the People.* Oil on canvas, approximately 8'6" × 10'8". France, 1830. Louvre, Paris. © Réunion des Musées Nationaux / Art Resource, NY.

ter way of life. The work is romantic in its portrayal of fighting as thrilling, dangerous, and liberating; added touches of romantic drama come from flashes of red in the painting and the brilliance around Liberty in contrast to the overall gloom. Compare this work to Siqueiros's *Echo of a Scream* (Figure 12.5), to see a work in which warfare is not romanticized.

One of the most direct ways to make social protest art is to illustrate the oppressive situation. At the beginning of the twentieth century, sociologist and artist Lewis Hine used photographs to show the miserable labor conditions and slum housing of the poor in the United States. He was particularly known for his photographs of children working in mines and textile mills, as child labor was common and children were used for the lowest-paying, most tedious jobs. Because of their small size and agile fingers, children often worked close to moving machinery where adults could not fit. Injuries and deaths were not uncommon. *Leo, 48 Inches High, 8 Years Old, Picks Up Bobbins at 15¢ a Day*, from 1910 (Figure 12.10), shows a young boy who dodges under textile looms to pick up loose thread spools. Children typically worked ten- to twelve-hour shifts, six days a week, in the mills. With schooling thus impossible, child laborers were destined to remain illiterate, poor, and overworked. Hine wrote detailed titles for his photographs to fully document the youthfulness of the child laborers. Yet in some ways, the long titles were unnecessary. Hine carefully framed his image so that we can see the large scale of the weaving machines—their great length and height—that dwarf the child. We can clearly see Leo's young face, his tentative posture, his bare feet. Also apparent are the gloomy darkness, poor lighting, and littered floor of the mill, and the other workers, who are women, another underpaid group. Hine's photographs are particularly effective because his subjects become real as individuals, and thus the pictures are harder to forget than are ideological arguments, pro or con, on labor conditions.

Hine was part of the loosely organized Progressive Movement of the early twentieth century, which sought reform for a number of problems resulting from urbanization and industrialization. Hine made photos for the National Child Labor Committee, a private group dedicated to protecting children in the work environment. He lectured widely, and his images were published in progressive magazines. With this backing, Hine's images were unusually successful in changing both public opinion and public policy. Child labor was eventually outlawed in the 1930s.

Ben Shahn used narrative as a means of social protest against injustice. He compressed space and time in *The Passion*

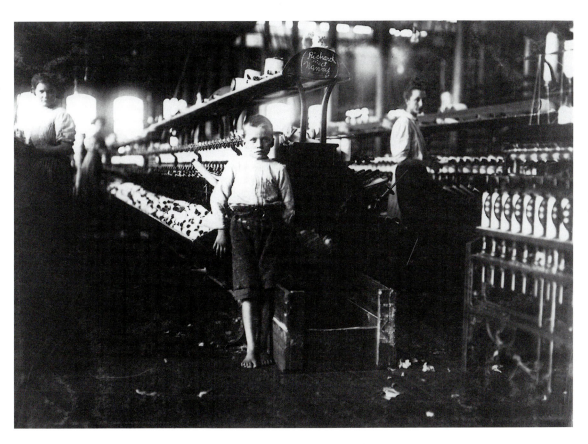

12.10   Lewis Hine. *Leo, 48 Inches High, 8 Years Old, Picks Up Bobbins at 15¢ a Day*. Photograph, 8¹/₂" × 11". USA, 1910. University of Maryland Library, College Park, Maryland. Reproduced from the collections of the Library of Congress.

of Sacco and Vanzetti, dated 1931–1932 (Figure 12.11), to tell the story of the conviction and execution of Nicola Sacco and Bartolomeo Vanzetti in the United States in the 1920s. The political climate then was tense, as conservative elements felt threatened by extremist political groups and the large influx of immigrants. Sacco and Vanzetti were Italian immigrants who were active in labor organizations, avoided the draft in World War I, and were political anarchists. They were arrested and convicted for robbery and murder, despite several witnesses who testified that they were elsewhere at the time of the crime. Many people believe that Sacco and Vanzetti were convicted because

of their politics, as the judge allowed the prosecution to make many inflammatory statements about their political beliefs during the trial. In his painting, Shahn collapses time, as we see simultaneously the courthouse steps, the framed portrait of the judge who presided over the original trial, and the ashen faces of Sacco and Vanzetti as they lie in their coffins. Prominent in the middle are the portraits of three commissioners who reviewed the trial and declared it to have been legal, thus allowing the execution to take place. The expressions of the three commissioners are dour and righteous; they seem unmovable; they are bolstered by institutional rigidity. The harsh colors of the painting, with the preponderance of blacks, the sickly blue tones in faces, the acid green grass, all express Shahn's distress at the death of the two men, whom Shahn and many others felt were heroes.

Jacob Lawrence also used narrative to tell stories, in this case in a series of paintings that recount the history, accomplishments, challenges, burdens, and oppressions of the African community uprooted to the Western Hemisphere by slavery. He made a series of thirty-one paintings on the life of Harriet Tubman and twenty-two on John Brown. The paintings often have lengthy, narrative titles to make the story even clearer. These works are meant to be reconstructions of the past, like history lessons. Our example is *No. 36: During the Truce Toussaint Is Deceived and Arrested by LeClerc. LeClerc Led Toussaint to Believe That He Was Sincere, Believing That When Toussaint Was Out of the Way, the Blacks Would Surrender* (Figure 12.12). It is one of forty-one paintings Lawrence made from 1937 to 1941 on the life of François-Dominique Toussaint-L'Ouverture (Jacob Lawrence used the spelling "L'Ouverture" in naming this series, although the name at time also appears as "Louverture"), a slave who led a revolt in Haiti that resulted in the abolition of slavery there in 1794. After the revolt, Toussaint was able to establish a semiautonomous black government and resist French, English, and Spanish attempts to control Haiti. Napoleon Bonaparte's brother-in-law, Charles LeClerc, led an army to Haiti. He deceived and captured Toussaint, who died a year later in a French prison. The French forces were eventually overcome, resulting in Haiti's achieving complete independence from France in 1804 and becoming the first black-governed country in the Western Hemisphere.

Lawrence completed the forty-one preliminary drawings and then worked on all the paintings simultaneously, so that the series has a remarkable formal cohesion, especially in color use and drawing style. Colors are limited, with black and white punctuating the images, giving them strength and starkness. *No. 36* shows Toussaint's betrayal and capture by Napoleon's troops. The crossed swords in the center pin Toussaint; the four white faces that surround him symbolize his struggle against the better-supplied and better-trained forces of the French army. The floor tilts up, and the walls of the room trap him at the

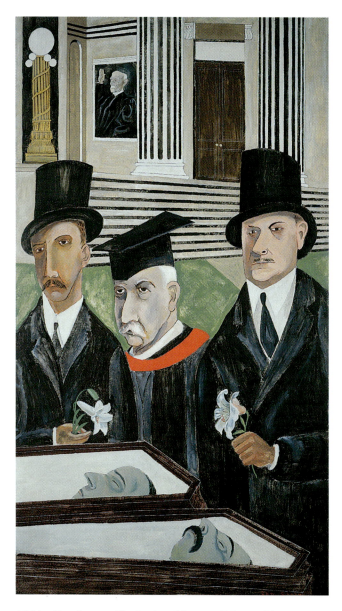

12.11   BEN SHAHN. *The Passion of Sacco and Vanzetti.* Tempera on canvas, 84 1/2" × 48". USA (Lithuanian born), 1931–1932. The Whitney Museum of American Art, New York.

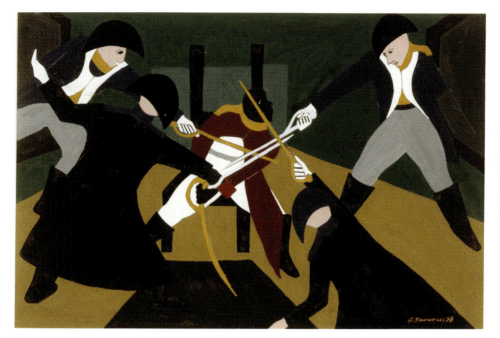

12.12 JACOB LAWRENCE. *No. 36: During the Truce Toussaint Is Deceived and Arrested by LeClerc. LeClerc Led Toussaint to Believe That He Was Sincere, Believing That When Toussaint Was Out of the Way, the Blacks Would Surrender.* Tempera on paper, 11" × 19". USA, 1937–1938. Photograph courtesy of Gwendolyn Knight Lawrence / Art Resource, NY © 2004 Gwendolyn Knight Lawrence / Artists Rights Society (ARS), New York. See also the text accompanying Figure 2.15.

intersection of colors. The black chair he sits on reads like bars of a prison. Lawrence's style is bold, flat, and simplified. Broad sections of yellow and green in the background unify the image, while the center, with its greatest density of detail, provides a forceful focal point. By eliminating many details, Lawrence simplifies his scenes so that they read more universally. His images were not just of the past, but were meant to inspire African Americans of today.

CONNECTION
Lawrence trained in Harlem during the Harlem Renaissance, supported by such people as those in James VanDerZee's Society Ladies, Figure 14.2 (page 401).

The Rent Collection Courtyard, sculpted in 1965 (Figure 12.13), narrates instances of injustice from Chinese history in

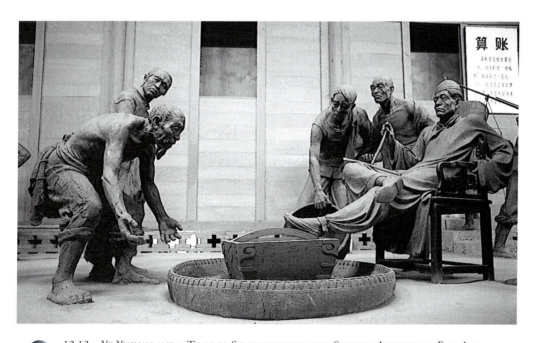

 12.13 YE YUSHAN AND A TEAM OF SCULPTORS FROM THE SICHUAN ACADEMY OF FINE ARTS, CHONGQING. *The Rent Collection Courtyard* (detail). Clay, life-size figures. China (Dayi, Sichuan), 1965. See also the text accompanying Figure 5.7.

several tableaus. Although the work is officially credited to an anonymous team of sculptors, Ye Yushan and others at the Sichuan Academy of Fine Arts made it. With more than one hundred life-size figures, the *Courtyard* comprises several scenes. Here, a bent, aged peasant farmer is bringing his harvest to the landlord to make his tax payments. Because of the landlord's excessive taxes, peasants remained in poverty and were often forced to mortgage their future crops. Many sold their children into servitude. In another vignette from the work, not shown here, the landlord's thugs seize a peasant, tie him, and take him to prison, while his family pleads for him. One thug turns to kick the peasant's wife, groveling on the ground with an infant in her arms. In the final scenes in the original version of this work, the peasants are rising in revolt.

Realistic details and life-size figures make viewers feel as if they are witnessing the actual event. The poses make clear where our sympathies should lie. The peasant is bowed in awkward submission. The bones of his hands and feet are thick and twisted from hard labor; his clothing is ragged. In contrast, the relaxed, haughty, well-dressed landlord shows no sign of having ever worked. The *Courtyard* was meant to validate the existing Chinese Communist government, which instituted land reforms in the 1950s that eliminated the powerful land-

lords. *The Rent Collection Courtyard* was first displayed in the courtyard of the mansion of one of these landlords (Liu Wencai in Dayi) where the events depicted actually took place.

CONNECTION

Contrast the idea of the anonymous artist working at the service of others with the notion of art stars and the artist as genius in Chapter 5, Who Makes Art?

CONNECTION

The Rent Collection Courtyard is similar to the USA Marine Corps War Memorial in Figure 11.32 (page 327), in that both are highly realistic, both memorialize past events, and both essentially affirm the existing government of each nation. They do, however, commemorate different kinds of events.

Shocking ugliness can be used in the service of protest art. In *The State Hospital*, from 1966 (Figure 12.14), artist Edward Kienholz criticizes the way society deals with people it

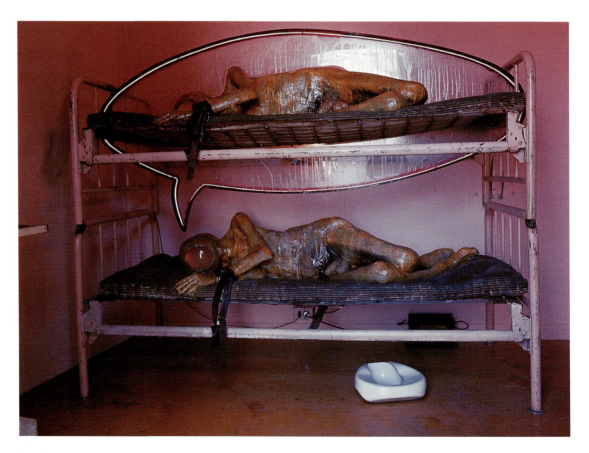

 12.14   EDWARD KIENHOLZ. *The State Hospital* (detail). Mixed media, 8' × 12' × 10'. USA, 1966. Moderna Museet, Stockholm. © Edward Kienholz.

deems incompetent. The outside of this work, not shown here, is a grim, boxlike cell with bare, reinforced walls and one barred, locked, grimy door. To look inside, one has to peer between the bars of a small window to see the naked mental patient strapped to his bed. His mattress is thin and filthy; the bed-pan below is streaked with excrement. His head is replaced by a fish bowl with two black fish swimming aimlessly inside. Encircled in neon is the cartoon balloon above his head that shows another image of himself. The patient has no world outside himself and his wretched cell. He is completely isolated and does not leave this room. *The State Hospital* is so effective and gruesome in part because Kienholz used actual objects from such an institution: the bed frame, the urinal, the rolling table (barely visible at left). The strongest impact, however, comes from the pathetic body of the patient—his bony knees; his sagging, exposed genitals; his leathery skin. As in *The Rent Collection Courtyard*, the realism makes the sculpture seem more immediate to the viewer.

Kienholz based his work on his experiences as an employee in a mental hospital. He saw, for example, a staff member repeatedly hit a patient in the stomach with a soap bar wrapped in a towel, so there would be no surface bruises. But the artist's criticism does not stop with the institution. When viewers look through the barred windows, they take on the role of guards or surveillance cameras. Thus, Kienholz implicates everyone on the outside, the "normal" ones who set up such institutions in which the aged, the infirm, the poor, and the powerless are mistreated.

Cildo Meireles made *Insertions into Ideological Circuits: Coca-Cola Project* (Figure 12.15) in the 1970s in response to Brazil's military government, which was "selling" the country to foreign investors, mostly from the United States, and supporting its regime with outside money. Much of the natural environment as well as the cultures of indigenous peoples in Brazil were destroyed, and continue to be destroyed, because of such policies. Meireles and others wanted to affirm and bolster Brazil's autonomy and resist becoming a market for foreign goods, but art that was openly critical of the government was repressed. So Meireles took empty Coca-Cola bottles, screen printed subversive messages on them, and then returned them for refilling. The added writing on the bottles is almost invisible when they are empty. Only the person holding the bottle close while drinking the soda can easily read the message. Using Coca-Cola bottles as vehicles for political messages was clever in many ways: first, because Coca-Cola is everywhere; second, because Meireles took advantage of the already-existing system of

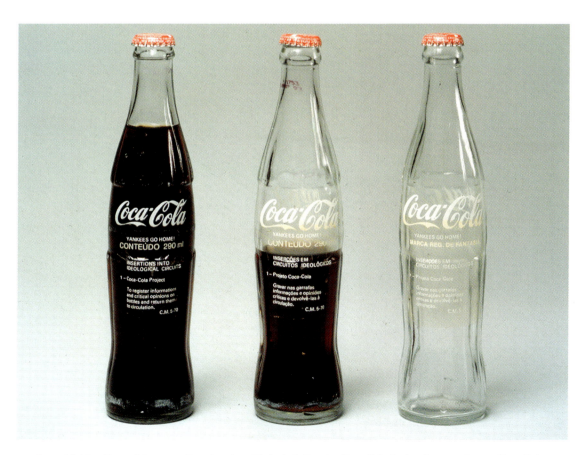

 12.15 CILDO MEIRELES. *Insertions into Ideological Circuits: Coca-Cola Project.* Screen print on Coca-Cola bottles. Brazil, 1970. Courtesy of the artist and Galerie Lelong, New York. See also the text accompanying Figure 4.13.

reusing bottles; and third, because Coca-Cola is a popular symbol for U.S. culture.

CONNECTION

Some would say that writing "Yankees go home!" on Coca-Cola bottles is not art. Others would argue that an artist's job is to increase the viewer's awareness. For more, see Chapter 4, Deriving Meaning.

Humor is another strategy for effective protest. In *Sun Mad,* dated 1981 (Figure 12.16), Ester Hernandez takes familiar imagery from popular, commercial culture and subverts it. For decades, the raisin growers around Hernandez's hometown heavily used insecticides that contaminated the groundwater the local population used for drinking and bathing. Hernandez took the packaging of the best-known raisin producer, Sun Maid, and changed the usual image of healthy eating into a message of death. Her work is effective precisely because it uses grim humor to turn around something familiar to us; it is memorable because the raisin industry advertising is so successful and we

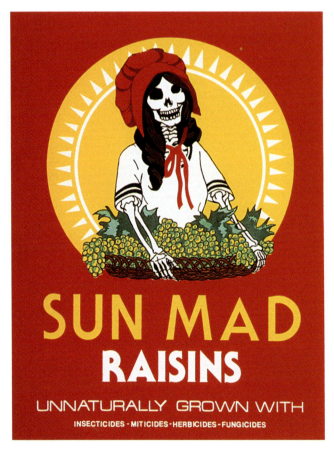

12.16 ESTER HERNANDEZ. *Sun Mad.* Color serigraph, 22" × 17". USA, 1981. © 1981 Ester Hernandez.

know the original image. Hernandez has chosen an art form that allows her to reach many people, just as advertising does. Rather than create a single painting to hang in a gallery, she designed a color screen print that has been reproduced and widely disseminated on T-shirts and postcards. Even though Hernandez was reacting to a specific instance of contamination, her work reaches out to everyone who may unknowingly ingest pesticide residue. In addition, the work echoes the struggle of farmworkers who protest the practice of spraying pesticides on fields as they are working, exposing them to unacceptable levels of poisons.

Yinka Shonibare uses historical quotes, clothing, and humor to protest the colonial past and to show the complexity of world trade and culture in his *Mr. and Mrs. Andrews Without Their Heads,* 1998 (Figure 12.17). A contemporary artist of Nigerian origin (Nigeria was a British colony), Shonibare has created a three-dimensional parody of a famous eighteenth-century painting by British artist Thomas Gainsborough, called *Mr. and Mrs. Andrews.* In Gainsborough's painting, Mr. Andrews shows off his possessions, including his estate, his wife, his dog, and his gun. In his version, Shonibare has beheaded the aristocrats, recalling the treatment given to the ruling class during the French Revolution. The most complex aspect of the piece, however, is the printed cotton cloth, the kind associated with idealized African culture, which Mr. and Mrs. Andrews are wearing. The cloth is not African at all, but is made in the batik method that the Dutch and English manufacturers learned in Indonesia, and then sold in West Africa. Shonibare shows that all cultures are intertwined and hybridized, and although many people may like the idea of cultural purity, it does not exist.

Some art dealing with past injustices and oppressions is met with mixed responses, even from people who are descendants of the oppressed. Kara Walker is an African American artist who creates life-size, cutout silhouette figures based on racist imagery of the slave era in the United States. Petticoated plantation mistresses, slaves with their masters' heads under their skirts, bastard children, black women squeezing out multiple babies between their legs, slaves being tortured or murdered—all are depicted as elegant flat shapes, both humorous and shocking. The imagery is based on fact and fantasy, primarily from pulp fiction sources dealing with subjugation and titillation. In works like *"They Waz Nice White Folks While They Lasted" (Says One Gal to Another),* from 2001 (Figure 12.18), Walker's cutouts are enhanced with projections in darkened galleries, so that viewers participate in the action by casting their own shadows on the wall, joining the animated and raucous silhouettes hung there. Walker has received many letters of protest from black people who believe that she should refrain from presenting negative images of African Americans. Walker responds that she makes these images because they are controversial and should be discussed.

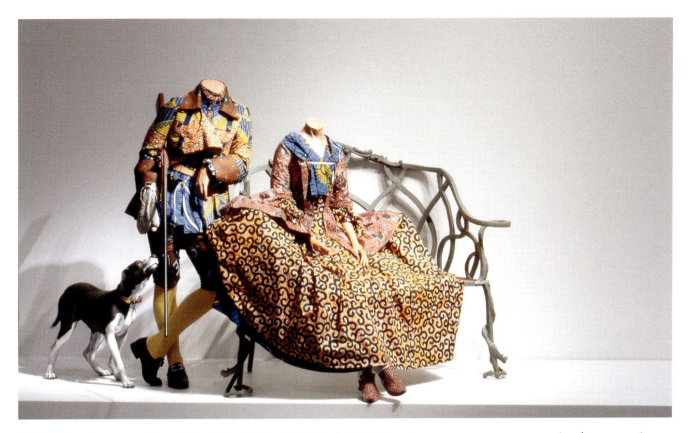

12.17   Yinka Shonibare. *Mr. and Mrs. Andrews Without Their Heads,* 1998. Wax-print cotton costumes on mannequins, dog mannequin, painted metal bench and rifles, 65" × 224" × 100". Courtesy Stephen Friedman Gallery, London. Collection of the National Gallery of Canada, Ottawa, Canada.

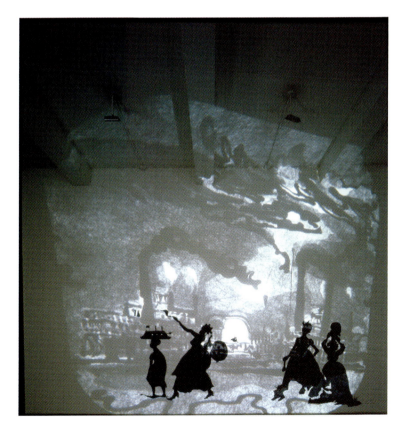

12.18   Kara Walker. *"They Waz Nice White Folks While They Lasted" (Says One Gal to Another).* Cut paper and projections on wall, 14' × 20'. USA, 2001. Courtesy Brent Sikkema, New York City.

AFFIRMING THE VALUES OF THE OPPRESSED

When a group of people is oppressed, their way of life and their values tend to be discounted or ridiculed. To be completely effective, protest movements must not only fight against unjust oppression, but also affirm the lifestyles of the downtrodden group to increase cohesiveness and bolster a sense of identity. Art is an especially effective tool for doing this.

When Ambrogio Lorenzetti painted the fresco *Allegory of Good Government: The Effects of Good Government in the City and in the Country* in 1338–1339 (Figure 12.19), Italy was a patchwork of city-states regularly thrown into turmoil by competing political factions, overthrown governments, and petty tyrants. In contrast, Lorenzetti showed how common citizens prosper when Justice, Prudence, Temperance, and Fortitude reign. In a climate of security, businesses flourish, culture thrives, and the fields are fruitful. Virtues are represented as allegorical figures hovering above. This late-**Gothic** painting is full of delightful details of everyday life in fourteenth-century Italy. The sweeping panorama was a remarkable achievement in Italian painting of the era. It is still a testimony to the rights of people to live free of tyrannical or unjust rulers.

Mario Cravo Neto made a series of photographic portraits of people from Bahia, Brazil, a culturally diverse area with a mulatto majority and a mix of Portuguese, African, and indigenous populations. Many practice syncretic religions that combine the beliefs of traditional African and European reli-gions. *Voodoo Figure,* dated 1988 (Figure 12.20), is a photo-graph of a hunched, brooding man, a follower of Candomblé, an African religion with elements of Roman Catholicism. Can-domblé emphasizes the community as a sacred sphere of mutual well-being. To worship spirits, the Candomblé follower under-goes trances and performs ritual tasks and animal sacrifices.

Voodoo Figure was the result of an actual ritual performed in Cravo Neto's studio. Rather than planning a shot, posing his subject, and "taking" a photograph, Cravo Neto collabo-rated with his sitter and did not know what would happen before the photo session began. The *Voodoo Figure* loses his individual identity and becomes an image of a spiritual state, a portrait of mystical energy. The body position is from the Candomblé rituals. The muscles of the shoulders and arms are sculptural, while the hair, the woven fingers, and the paint splatters add textural variety. The lighting ranges from the darkness of the abdomen to the well-lit shoulders. The pose is symmetrical overall. The paint splatters connote two things: (1) the working class, with the splattered body of the laborer or housepainter; and (2) the ritual experience, as the body is changed by the transformative power of religion. Cravo Neto's work shows the divisions between the upper and lower classes in Brazil, where Christian and capitalist, Western-influenced groups marginalize those most involved in mystic religions.

Aboriginal artists have used art to affirm their cultural val-ues, which have been suppressed by Australians of European

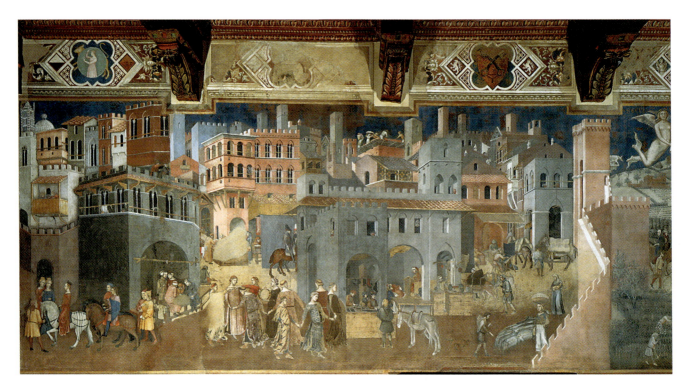

12.19 AMBROGIO LORENZETTI. *Allegory of Good Government: The Effects of Good Government in the City and in the Country* (detail). Fresco. Italy, 1338–1339. Sala della Pace, Palazzo Publico, Siena, Italy. © Scala / Art Resource, NY.

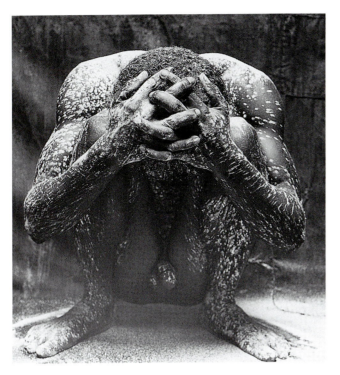

descent. Colonization has left a tragic legacy of land theft, displacement, and genocide, and the Aboriginal people are examining past injustices and reclaiming lost history. While the rest of Australia was celebrating the two hundredth anniversary of Captain Cook's "discovery" of Australia, the Aboriginal population commemorated "Invasion Day." Many artists collaborated to make *The Aboriginal Memorial,* installed in 1988 (Figure 12.21). The work is composed of two hundred logs, one for each year of settlement, hollowed out as traditional Aboriginal coffins. They are memorials to all the native peoples who died as a result of European settlement and were never given proper Aboriginal mortuary rites. Forty-three participating artists painted the logs with their important clan Dreamtime symbols, continuing the vitality of traditional Aboriginal culture, which was undermined and, at times, outlawed. Many of the poles are imposing, reaching ten feet high, and seem like living growths springing up with vibrating patterns and vigorous animals as one walks through the installation (Caruana 1993: 206).

12.20   Mario Cravo Neto. *Voodoo Figure.* Photograph. Brazil, 1988. Courtesy Sicardi Gallery, Houston, TX.

CONNECTION

For more on Aboriginal culture and Dreamtime imagery, see Witchetty Grub Dreaming *in Figure 7.2 (page 157).*

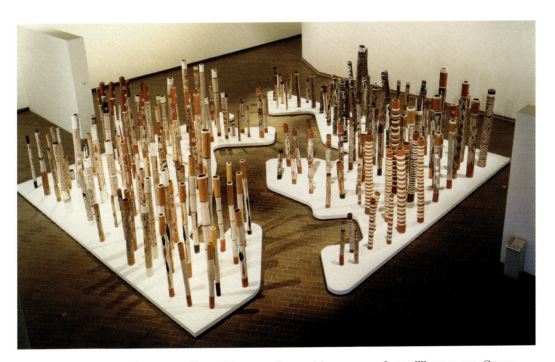

 12.21   Paddy Dhatangu, David Malangi, George Milpurrurru, Jimmy Wululu, and Other Artists from Ramingining. *The Aboriginal Memorial.* Natural pigments on 200 logs; heights: 16" to 128". Australia, 1988. National Gallery of Art, Canberra. © 2004 Artists Rights Society (ARS), New York / VI$COPY, Australia. See also the text accompanying Figure 2.3.

Lin Onus's *Dingoes; Dingo Proof Fence,* dated 1989 (Figure 12.22), alludes to the difference between Aboriginal and European land use. The Aborigines hunted for and gathered what they needed, leaving the natural environment relatively untouched. Europeans aggressively changed the natural environment for pastoral use; they cleared, fenced, farmed, or grazed it, and subdivided it for individual ownership. Twenty thousand Aborigines and two thousand settlers died in land wars. In this piece, the dingo, a wild dog, alert and energetic, effortlessly passes through a fence. Onus's work upholds the animals' rights to the land, in the face of the thousands of miles of dingo fence erected by settlers to protect the imported cattle and sheep. In a twist of humor, the "dingo-proof fence" turns out to be considerably less than so. In non-Aboriginal slang, *dingo* has come to mean a coward or contemptible person, but Onus reinvents the dingo as the first native of the land, and its right to the land has become a metaphor for Aboriginal rights (Caruana 1993: 194). The dingo sculpture is painted red, yellow, black, and white, the four basic Aboriginal colors, to further identify the wild dingo with the Aborigines and affirm their views of land use.

Puerto Rican–born Pepón Osorio's mixed media installation, *The Scene of the Crime (Whose Crime?),* 1993–1999 (Figure 12.23), affirms the worth of Puerto Rican culture in New York, while protesting how the people are depicted in mass media. He has recreated a "typical" Puerto Rican house, cluttered with kitsch statuettes, inexpensive religious objects, plastic

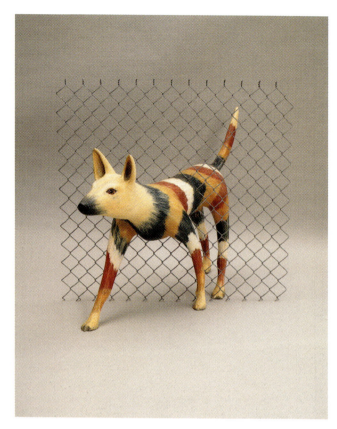

12.22   LIN ONUS. *Dingoes; Dingo Proof Fence* (detail from the series *Dingoes*). Synthetic polymer on fiberglass, wire, metal, 37^1/$_2$" high. Aboriginal. Australia, 1989. National Gallery of Australia, Canberra. © 2004 Artists Rights Society (ARS), New York / VI$COPY, Australia.

12.23   PEPÓN OSORIO. *The Scene of the Crime (Whose Crime?).* Mixed media installation, dimensions variable. Puerto Rico/ USA, 1993–1999. Bronx Museum of the Arts. Purchased through funds from the H. W. Wilson Foundation and the National Endowment for the Arts, 1999.1.4. Courtesy Ronald Feldman Fine Arts, New York.

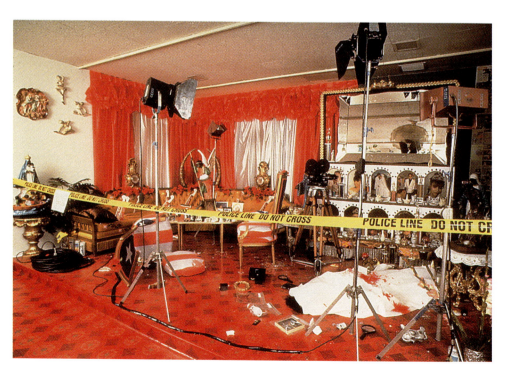

plants, sentimental family photos, trophies, covers of *TV Guide,* and so on. Police tape and bright lights indicate a crime has happened, and a mannequin corpse lies face down at the back of the installation, but everything is remote and no details are given. A welcome mat in front reads: "Only if you can understand that it has taken years of pain to gather into our homes our most valuable possessions; but the greater pain is to see how in the movies others make fun of the way we live." Osorio's installation is like a historical tableau with much of it just out of the viewer's line of sight or obscured, so viewers' reactions are based on stereotypes or narratives from mass media. Stereotypical reactions include assumptions of drugs and crime in the culture, or class-based condemnations of the décor. Like Kara Walker (see Figure 12.18), Osorio at times has received negative responses, some from Latino viewers who want to distance themselves from these cultural stereotypes.

Mona Hatoum is an artist of Palestinian descent who has lived in London since 1975, when she was forced to flee fighting in Beirut. Her work deals poetically with personal identity, the body, surveillance, and control. *Light Sentence,* 1992 (Figure 12.24), is an installation of wire mesh lockers in a dark room, stacked to human height. In the middle, a bare light-bulb swings around, casting wildly rocking shadows so that the cell-like room seems to sway. The swinging bulb is like a sometimes-blinding prison searchlight, implying surveillance. Lockers should hold private possessions safely, but here everything is exposed. The piece suggests animal cages in an experimental laboratory, and also connotes the architecture of deadeningly uniform high-rise housing for low-income residents. *Light Sentence* reveals the instability that those without power endure.

QUESTIONING THE STATUS QUO

The status quo is the existing state of affairs, which appears natural or inevitable, instead of constructed and evolving. In this section, artists take a critical look at the "normal," at all those underlying systems, beliefs, and ways of operating within a culture that have become so accepted that they are almost invisible.

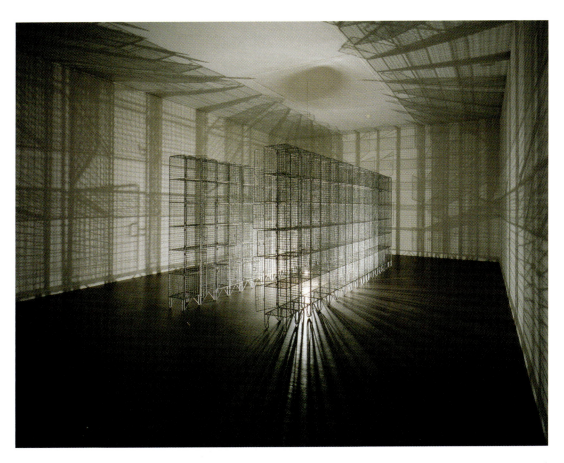

12.24 MONA HATOUM. *Light Sentence.* Mixed media, dimensions variable. Palestine/England, 1992. Musée National d'Art Moderne, Centre Georges Pompidou. © Courtesy the artist and Jay Jopling / White Cube (London). © CNAC/MNAM/Dist. Réunion des Musées Nationaux / Art Resource, NY.

THE SOCIAL ENVIRONMENT

William Hogarth satirized the English upper classes in a series of six paintings called *Marriage à la Mode,* dated c. 1745, a comedy mixed with criticism and condemnation. In the second of the six images, *Breakfast Scene* (Figure 12.25), the wall clock indicates past noon, but the couple is just meeting over the breakfast table. Hogarth does a great job of storytelling through body language and details. The large rooms are filled with the columns, rugs, and other finery that are signs of class. The disheveled, bored, sulky husband has been out all night. The puppy sniffs at his pocket where another woman's lingerie hangs. The young wife stretches after a night of cards and music. The overturned chairs indicate that the evening became a bit raucous. She casts a flirting glance at her husband, but he is completely unresponsive. A vacuum of unconcern separates them, and their marriage is a legal agreement only. The paintings on the walls indicate a taste for sexual intrigues, despite the presence of classical busts and religious images for propriety. At left, a servant rolls his eyes, clutching unpaid bills.

The earlier scene from this series shows the young, penniless nobleman whose father arranges for him to marry the daughter of a wealthy merchant. The arranged marriage brings status, and the girl has become Lady Squanderfield. The series,

however, ends miserably with infidelity, scandal, and death by duel. Hogarth's paintings were turned into inexpensive prints that were enormously popular and received widespread distribution among the English middle class.

While Hogarth satirized the upper classes in eighteenth-century England, George Tooker looked critically at the systems and structures of the modern world, showing them to be oppressive and inhuman. His paintings of places like subways and cafeterias show people pushed together in tight, artificial environments, yet isolated from or fearful of each other. In *Government Bureau,* painted in 1956 (Figure 12.26), Tooker attacks excessive bureaucracy with long lines, spawned by large, unresponsive governments. The office is deadeningly uniform. A maze of cubicles holds an endless numbers of clerks, who peer or listen through holes, surveying the people outside. Tooker's scene is a distillation of every person's experience with modern bureaucracies, like the motor vehicles department or a university's registrar. The faces of the clerks are mostly hidden, and no one has either power or responsibility.

Yayoi Kusama looks at the commercial and gender underpinnings of society. *Accumulation No. 1,* dated 1962 (Figure 12.27), is a fringed armchair covered obsessively with sewn, stuffed protrusions. Kusama appropriated the male phallus

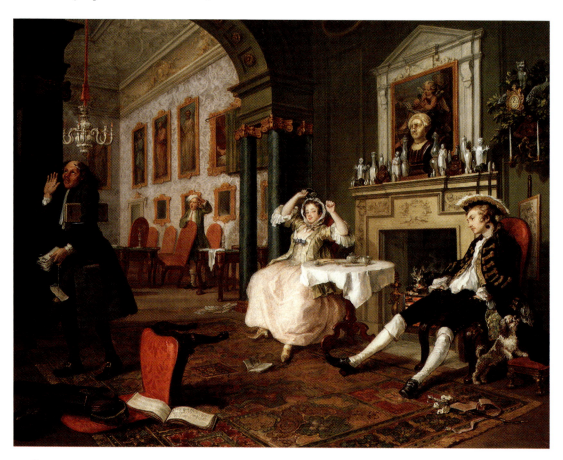

 12.25   WILLIAM HOGARTH. *Breakfast Scene* (from the series *Marriage à la Mode*). Oil on canvas, 28" × 36". England, c. 1745. National Gallery, London. © National Gallery Collection; By kind permission of the Trustees of the National Gallery, London/Corbis.

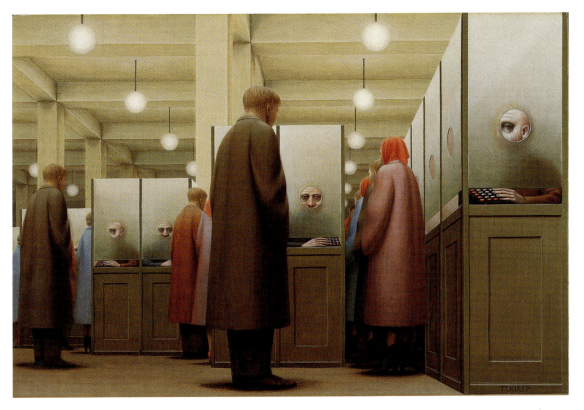

12.26   GEORGE TOOKER. *Government Bureau.* Tempera on gesso panel, 19⁵/₈" × 29⁵/₈". USA, 1956. The Metropolitan Museum of Art, New York, George A. Hearn Fund.

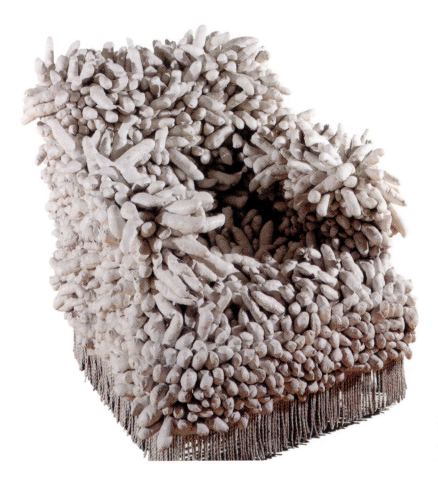

12.27   YAYOI KUSAMA. *Accumulation No. 1.* Sewn stuffed fabric, paint, fringe on chair frame, 37" × 39" × 43". Japan/USA, 1962. Beatrice Perry Family Collection. The Los Angeles County Museum of Art. See also the text accompanying Figure 5.12.

and proliferated it outrageously. She has done similar work on a sofa, a vanity, an ironing board, a stepladder, and a rowboat. Some pieces also have spike-heel shoes among the phalluses. Although many are all white, some are made of polka-dot or striped fabric. Taken together, they make a frightening, crude, and humorous ensemble of familiar domestic items engulfed by the groping, organic growths.

Kusama's work refers to many underlying presumptions and power relations that, almost unseen, make up the modern world. The profusion of phalluses that take over everything stems from her experience of Japan's traditional, authoritarian, patriarchal society. In contrast, Kusama herself sewed and stuffed all the phallic forms, thus mimicking traditional feminine work that tends to be undervalued, anonymous, and monotonous. The phalluses and high-heel shoes refer to the sex industry and sexual appetites that, in many cultures, coexist with religions that teach very different morals. In addition, Kusama's work points out social conformity through the uniformity of the soft forms covering this armchair and other pieces. It also refers to the consumer society, because the phallic forms are like the vast quantities of standardized objects that surround us. Imagine the sameness and sheer numbers if, lined up before you right now, were every bar of soap you will have used in your life, every candy bar eaten, every tube of toothpaste, every box of breakfast cereal, every can of beer.

Kusama called her work Obsessional Art, because of the almost compulsive drive and amount of time required to make her repetitive forms. A kind of self-obliteration comes from constant, compulsive repetition, a tendency seen in the work of several Japanese visual artists and dancers at this time. It may have stemmed from the post–world war sense of void. As a teenager, Kusama experienced the annihilation of World War II and the postwar Americanization of Japan.

Magdalena Abakanowicz's *Backs,* dated 1976 to 1982 (Figure 12.28), consists of eighty slumping, hollow backs that are more than life-size, but without legs, heads, and hands. They hunch forward, immobile, in lines all facing the same direction. *Backs* alludes to the human condition in times of great distress. Abakanowicz lived in Poland during World War II, saw her mother's arm shot off at the shoulder, and wit-

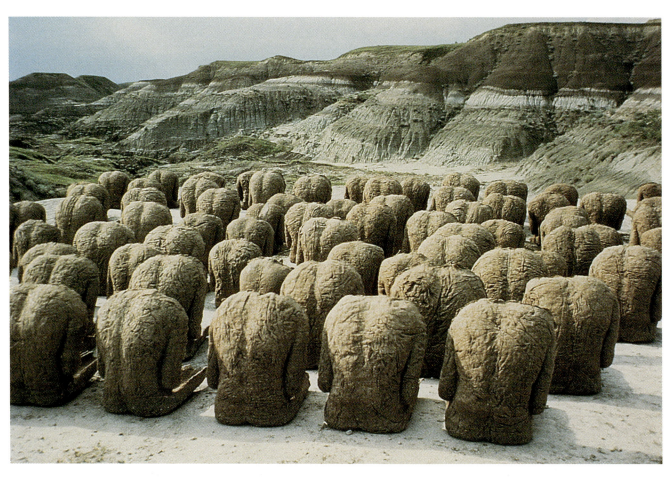

12.28   Magdalena Abakanowicz. *Backs*. 80 pieces, burlap and glue, each over life-size. Poland, 1976–1982. © Magdalena Abakanowicz. Courtesy of Marlborough Gallery, New York. See also the text accompanying Figure 2.31.

nessed death, pain, and destruction. In postwar Soviet-dominated Poland, she encountered many hardships in her struggle to make artwork. *Backs* certainly recalls some aspects of World War II, but it also suggests the modern malaise of uniformity, of loss of self and of individuality.

Organic fibers were pressed into the same plaster mold to make all eighty backs, so that each is very similar to the others. However, small degrees of individuality emerge. The fibers are not alike, and each back has a unique posture caused by distortion after being removed from the mold. The thick, twisted fibers suggest wrinkled skin, knotted muscles, and visceral tissue. The fibers are very organic, emphasizing our physicality and our ties to the natural world. The backs seem weary but, at the same time, suggest endurance, strength, and survival. The work also changes depending upon where it is displayed. Outdoors, the figures seem rooted to the very earth, but that association is lost in the white gallery interior.

Jenny Holzer focused on the mass of implicit beliefs that are widely held and accepted in the United States today, in *Untitled (Selected Writings)* dated 1989 (Figure 12.29). Holzer wrapped electronic signs around the spiral interior of the Solomon R. Guggenheim Museum in New York City and placed a circle of red granite benches below. The stream of words jumps out from the darkened interior of the museum. They start at the bottom, and then whirl around and up until they disappear far above at the top of the spiral. The phrases seem familiar, but as a whole, they sound contradictory or even a little idiotic. As Holzer herself says, "They're about how we

drive ourselves crazy with a million possibilities that are half correct" (Auping 1992: 55). "A sincere effort is all you can ask" is countered with "Enjoy yourself because you can't change anything anyway." The partial truths, taken together, are boggling. Another example is, "Protect me from what I want," written in a culture where money can buy almost anything. The phrase points out the negative aspects of consumer culture and the high level of personal danger we accept in our surroundings.

The electronic signs flash words, like an attack, and then they quickly slip away almost before we can grasp them, like the barrage of messages in a media culture. In contrast, the words carved in the stone benches below are permanent, but just as conflicting and contradictory. The sheer number of phrases, the speed at which we see them, and their contradictory messages destroy thought, although we normally think of words as the carriers of meaning.

CONNECTION *For more on the design of the* Solomon R. Guggenheim Museum, *see* Figure 16.5 (page 474).

ART VERSUS POLITICS

In Chapter 11, Power, Politics, and Glory, we saw art that promoted the personal glory of a ruler or the power of a state. In this section, we will see art as the opposite, and look at art that does not dovetail with the political status quo.

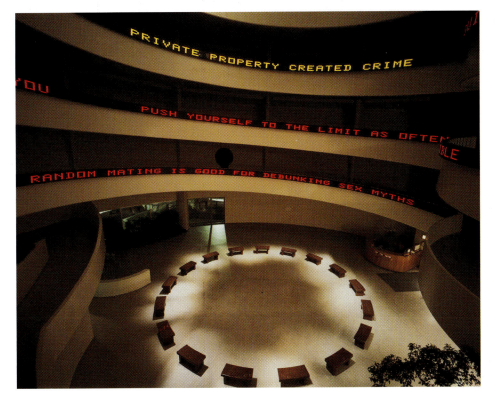

12.29 JENNY HOLZER. *Untitled (Selected Writings).* Extended helical LED electronic signboard, with selected writings; 17 Indian Red granite benches. Installation view at Solomon R. Guggenheim Museum. USA, 1989. Photo: David Heald, courtesy Solomon R. Guggenheim Museum. © 2004 Jenny Holzer / Artists Rights Society (ARS), New York. See also the text accompanying Figure 2.22.

Portrait of George, dated 1981 (Figure 12.30), by Robert Arneson, is a bust portrait of George Moscone, a popular mayor of San Francisco in the late 1970s. Moscone's big smile, with crooked teeth and squinting eyes, is distinct and alive, and the surface of splattered colors animates the face. The bust sits on a column casually covered, graffiti-like, with phrases recalling Moscone's background, some of his more memorable sayings, and events from his life and death. Arneson's piece was to have been placed in the Moscone Center, a new civic center in San Francisco named after the deceased mayor. Moscone and another politician had been assassinated three years earlier by a disgruntled San Francisco city supervisor named Dan White, who had disagreed with Moscone on most political points, including issues concerning homosexuals.

Arneson's *Portrait of George* departs from the status quo of bland, bronze portrait heads of political leaders that are common in parks and in lobbies of many public buildings. This sculpture is irreverent, colorful, and very large, and the viewer cannot pass by without noticing it. It was the pedestal below the head, however, that caused the greatest controversy. Among the words, bullet holes apparently pierce the column, making a comment on the ubiquity of guns in the United States today. A yellow, phallic Twinkie is prominent. Dan White received a light sentence of voluntary manslaughter for his crimes. His lawyers claimed that he had been unbalanced at the time of the shootings because he had eaten too many Twinkie snack cakes. Many San Franciscans protested the lighter sentence, and there was a night of rioting. Arneson's *Portrait of George* was a vivid, permanent reminder of the circumstances that surrounded his death, the recent riot, and the tensions in the city. One week after the unveiling at the Moscone Center, politics intervened. *Portrait of George* was officially removed because the pedestal was deemed crude and inappropriate. The work was later sold to a private collector.

Art has been used for political lobbying or public relations in the United States recently. In the past few decades, many museums have found themselves in financial difficulties, as operating budgets increased, tax support decreased during recessions, and the cost of artwork skyrocketed in the 1980s. Increasingly, museums rely on corporate support for funding, but corporate motives for giving money to museums are often less than pure. Hans Haacke's *MetroMobiltan,* dated 1985 (Figure 12.31), deals with an art exhibition that was sponsored by a large corporation for political purposes. In the mid-1980s, protest groups criticized Mobil Corporation for selling supplies to the South African police and military. Mobil profited from the violent enforcement of apartheid, the white South Africans' political and economic repression of the native African population. At the same time, Mobil gave considerable funding to sponsor the New York Metropolitan Museum of Art's blockbuster exhibition, "Treasures of Ancient Nigeria." Although the corporation's sponsorship undoubtedly promoted the arts,

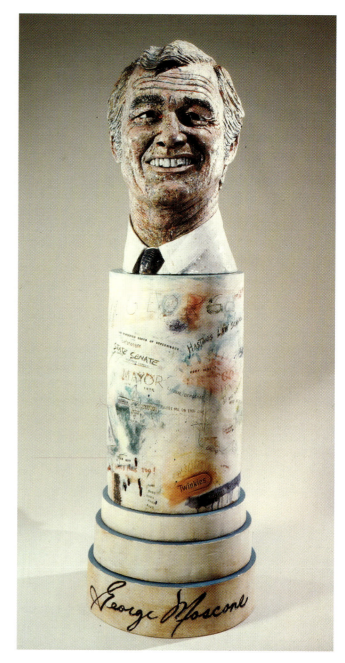

12.30   ROBERT ARNESON. *Portrait of George.* Glazed ceramic, 94" × 29" × 29". USA, 1981. Private Collection. Art © Estate of Robert Arneson / VAGA, New York, NY. Courtesy of George Adams Gallery, New York. See also the text accompanying Figure 5.25.

many saw it as simultaneously a public relations move to counter Mobil's negative image in connection with apartheid.

Formally, *MetroMobiltan* is like a stately altar, raised on a platform, frontal and symmetrical, adorned with silk banners, and topped by a large, classical entablature like a roof. The grand decor obscures a stark, black-and-white photomural, showing a funeral procession for black South Africans shot by police. The phrases on the end banners are excerpts from Mobil's board of trustees' refusal to church groups that had

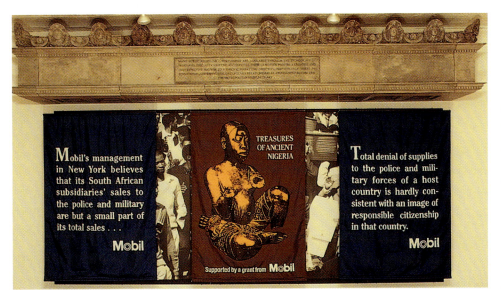

asked the company to stop supporting apartheid. *MetroMobiltan* also points out the complicated ties between museum and corporation. The carved inscription on the entablature was taken from a Metropolitan Museum pamphlet encouraging corporate donations. It says, in part, that sponsoring museum programs offers "creative and cost effective answers" if a corporation is experiencing difficulties in "international, governmental or consumer relations." Thus, the donation helps both the money-starved museum and the corporation with image problems. The entablature recalls the majestic façade of a grand museum, a site for many conflicting political, economic, and cultural forces.

For our last example of protest art, we turn to contemporary El Salvador, with Miguel Antonio Bonilla's *The Knot*

(Figure 12.32), from 1994. The two ominous figures represent the country's police and politicians, who conspired in the 1980s to create an oppressive regime in El Salvador. The knot that connects them seems to be made of two extended, elongated phalluses. In this way, Bonilla referred to the chauvinism in his culture that allows factions to dominate and damage others. On a domestic level, these same social forces result in violence and abuse in the home, which Bonilla addresses in other paintings.

Bonilla took a political risk in this painting because of its criticism of the political status quo. He also took artistic risks, because he chose to make the painting purposefully ugly, to shock. The style of this work was contrary to prevailing Salvadoran aesthetics for painting at that time.

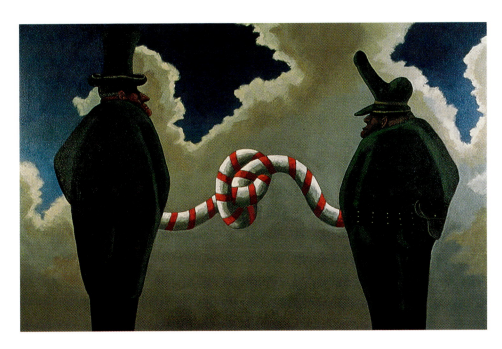

12.32 MIGUEL ANTONIO BONILLA. *The Knot.* Acrylic on canvas, 51" × 78". El Salvador, 1994. Museum of Latin American Art.

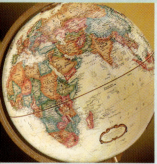

Courtesy of Replogle Globes, Inc., Broadview, IL.

The world in 1300 was still a patchwork of relatively autonomous, relatively isolated regions. Two hundred fifty years later, much of that had changed.

China during this period was ruled by two dynasties: the Yuan dynasty of the Mongolian invaders, which ended around 1400, and the native Ming dynasty, known for its territorial expansion as well as its amazing building program, which included rebuilding the Great Wall and constructing the Forbidden City. Wealth was distributed to lower classes through the Civil Service and land ownership. This was a period of stability, prosperity, religious tolerance, and a high standard of living. Chinese ships traveled to India and Africa, and the Portuguese landed at China's ports in 1514.

Islam continued to expand in Asia, Africa, and southeastern Europe. Around 1280, the mighty Ottoman Empire was established with Turkey as its center, and it expanded its territories in North Africa and the Middle East. Many Ottoman rulers were art patrons, great builders, and conquerors. They generally tolerated other religions. Likewise, the Mughal Empire in India was known for its ambitious building program, its humane rulers, and its illuminated manuscripts. The Safavids ruled Persia after 1500.

At this time, Europe saw the end of the Middle Ages and the beginning of the Renaissance. The rise of Christian humanism in the fourteenth and fifteenth centuries brought an emphasis

Below:
Map 6 The Slave Trade.

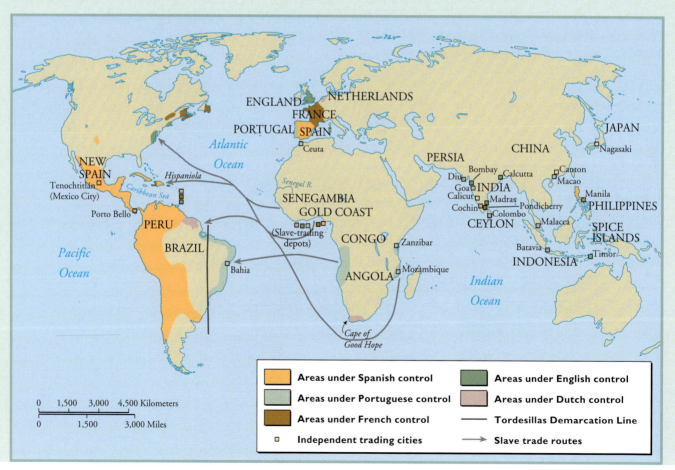

on reason, human abilities, and intellectual achievement. This humanistic tradition has continued to grow, and, because it promotes the inherent worth and dignity of all human beings, it is the basis for much social protest art. Small areas of Italy had republican governments, notably Florence and Siena (see Figure 12.19). In Italy, the era brought increased prosperity and the rediscovery of Greco-Roman culture. Beginning in 1300, the secular power of the Catholic Church slowly declined. The Church's religious authority was challenged in the 1500s when the Protestant Reformation divided European Christians between the Protestants and Catholics.

This was the beginning of the age of exploration and expansion. European sailors undertook amazing voyages of discovery, most notably in the Americas in 1492. Advanced civilizations had flourished earlier in Central America, especially the Maya/Toltec culture, with hieroglyphics, ball courts, and palaces. In 1500, the Aztecs dominated central Mexico and had a complex society with accomplishments in painting, architecture, astronomy, and cosmology. The Aztec *Calendar Stone* (see history box illustration) is a large sun disk and calendar that demarcates the creation/destruction cycle of past and future worlds. In 1519, the Spaniards conquered the Aztecs; later, they also conquered the Incas of Peru and established a large colonial empire in America.

Other adventurers circled the globe, visiting ports in Asia and India. Trade expanded greatly in the 1500s and reached many parts of the world. For Europe, the spice trade with Southeast Asia and the slave trade with Africa were important. Other traded commodities included fur, fish, timber, tobacco, rice, silver, gold, sugar, cacao, coffee, diamonds, tea, silk, cotton, and ivory.

The Kingdom of Zimbabwe flourished from 1300–1450 in Africa. Other central areas of Africa remained free of Europeans, but African slaves from coastal areas were brought to Europe and the Americas beginning in the 1500s. England, Portugal, and France as well as Spain established American colonies. In still-isolated Australia, the Aboriginal peoples were growing in population and developing long-distance trading among themselves.

Above:
Calendar Stone. Relief carving; diameter: Approximately 11'6". Aztec. Tenochtitlán, Mexico, c. 1502–1520. Museo Nacional de Antropología, Mexico City.

Year	Event		Art
1000	Chola Kingdom—India		
	Yuan Dynasty—China		
	Maya/Toltec Culture in Mesoamerica		
1300			Lorenzetti: *Allegory of Good Government*
	Black Death in Europe		
	Ming Dynasty—China		
	Great Wall of China rebuilt		
1400	Renaissance in Europe		
	Ottoman Empire in Turkey, North Africa, and Middle East		
	Christopher Columbus		
1500	Portuguese arrive in China		
	Spanish conquest of the Aztecs and Incas		
	Martin Luther and the Reformation		
	European colonies in the Americas		
	Slave trade begins: Africa, Europe, and the Americas		
	Spice trade—Dutch East Indies and Southeast Asia		
	Mughal Empire in India		
1600	Japan closed to Westerners		
1700	Rise of merchant class in Japan		Hogarth: *Breakfast Scene*
1800			Goya: *The Executions of May 3, 1808*
	Displacement of Native Americans from Western U.S.		Delacroix: *Liberty Leading the People*
	Aboriginal decline in Australia		
1850	Colonial rule established in Africa		
	Civil War, U.S.		
	End of Slavery in U.S.		

Year	Event		Art
1900			Kollwitz: *The Outbreak ("Losbruch")*
			Hine: *Leo, 48 Inches High . . .*
			Grosz: *Fit for Active Service*
1920	Harlem Renaissance		
1930	Great Depression		Shahn: *The Passion of Sacco and Vanzetti*
	Stalin and the U.S.S.R.		Heartfield: *Goering the Executioner*
			Lawrence: *No. 36: During the Truce Toussaint Is Deceived . . .*
	Spanish Civil War		Siqueiros: *Echo of a Scream*
1940	World War II		
1948	U.N. Universal Declaration of Human Rights		
	People's Republic of China		
	Cold War, 1950–1990		Motherwell: *Elegy to the Spanish Republic XXXIV*
			Tooker: *Government Bureau*
1960	Civil Rights Movement, U.S.		Kusama: *Accumulation No. 1* Shomei: *Woman with Keloidal Scars*
	Cesar Chavez and the United Farm Workers		
			The Rent Collection Courtyard
			Kienholz: *The State Hospital*
1970			Golub: *Mercenaries I*
	Six-Day War—Israel		Meireles: *Insertions into Ideological Circuits*
	Islamic Revolution in Iran		Abakanowicz: *Backs*
1980			Hernandez: *Sun Mad*
	Nicaraguan Civil War		Arneson: *Portrait of George*
			Cravo Neto: *Voodoo Figure*
			Haacke: *MetroMobiltan*
			The Aboriginal Memorial
			Onus: *Dingoes; Dingo Proof Fence*
			Holzer: *Untitled (Selected Writings)*
1990	Iraqi Invasion of Kuwait		
			Shonibare: *Mr. and Mrs. Andrews Without Their Heads*
	Apartheid ends—South Africa		Hatoum: *Light Sentence* Bonilla: *The Knot*
	World Conference on Global Warming		Osorio: *The Scene of the Crime (Whose Crime?)*
2000			Walker: *"They Waz Nice White Folks . . ."*

Art can depict the cruelty and destruction of war as a means of protesting it. Art can expose cynical or vicious military leaders who cause people to die. Even abstract art can express the human struggle for liberty against totalitarian forces.

Artists have protested many forms of oppression, such as the exploitation of laborers, repressive governments, and acts of betrayal. Art has been used to protest colonization and pollution as well as to affirm indigenous values.

The conditions under which we all live and that we accept as normal are reexamined by artists and, in many cases, found wanting. Half-truths, stultifying bureaucracies, police states, and upper-class greed and mindlessness are all targets for artistic critique. Other artists look at consumerism, oppressive patriarchy, the status of women, and corporate funding for museums.

FOOD FOR THOUGHT

Here are a few questions to think about in relation to protest art.

- If protest art is shown only in galleries or museums, is it reaching a wide enough audience to be effective?
- With protest art, the artist often has a clear political message to deliver, presents it in a persuasive way, and hopes to cause change. Is that different from propaganda?
- Can propaganda be art?
- Finally, some recent artists and art writers have been critical of social protest work like Hine's *Leo, 48 Inches High* . . . . Hine's photograph did not really change the existing power structures, even if it did help to alter people's opinions about child labor abuses. The wealthy and privileged remained insulated. The photographs enabled them to gaze upon people like the mill workers (who cannot see them in return), but did not change the distance between them. The status quo was maintained, although the privi-

leged might have been moved to "reform" the situation out of their own benevolence. Or they might not. What do you think of criticisms such as this?

YOUR CD-ROM RESOURCES

- World History in Context
- Exploring Art Timeline
- Flashcards
- Food for Thought
- Companion Site
  Chapter 12 Quiz
  InfoTrac® College Edition Readings
  Artist Flashcards
  Online Study Guide

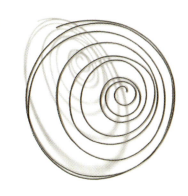

Self and Society

In this section, the artworks deal with the human body, social structures, and the world around us. The next four chapters explore the following major topics:

Idealizing body types through art and mass media in different cultures.

Revealing the nature of humans in general and individual personalities in particular through figurative art.

Examining race and gender as biological categories that are surrounded by culturally determined attitudes, which are made evident through art.

Reinforcing and distinguishing social and economic classes through art.

Defining changing concepts of "family," from large clan to extended family to nuclear family to contemporary realignments, by portraying them in art.

Revealing through artwork the shifting relationship of humans to animals and humans to the land.

Expanding knowledge about ourselves and the world around us through art.

Making art that entertains us, pleases us, diverts us, and educates us.

SECTION

4

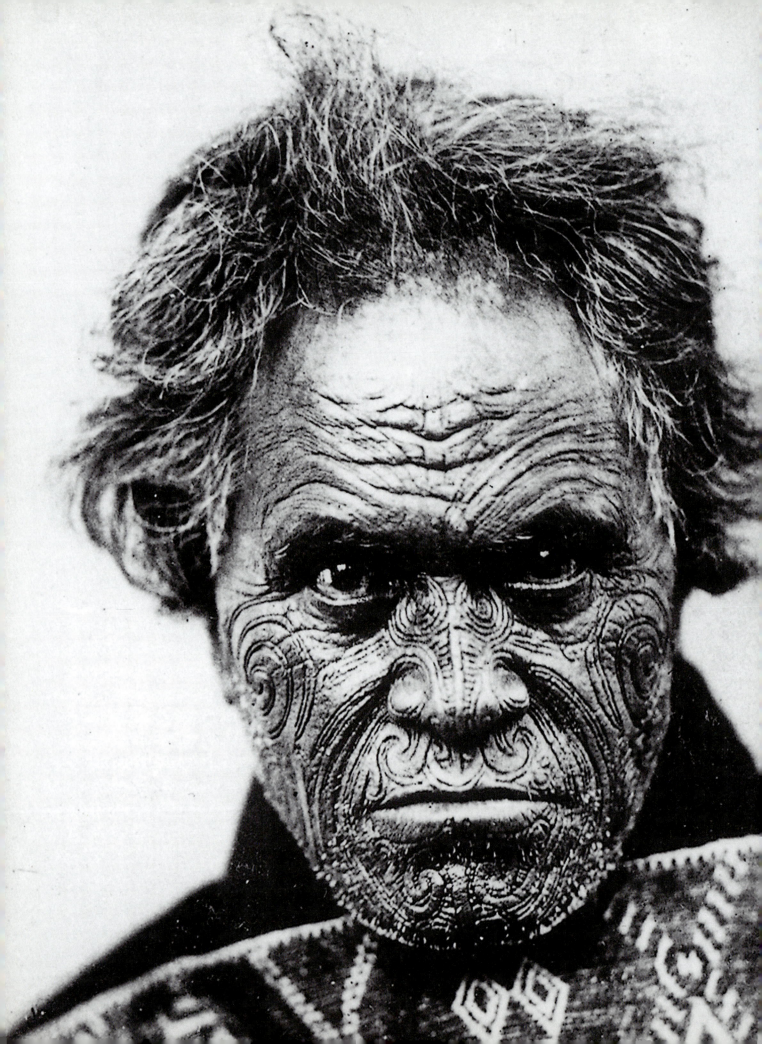

CHAPTER 13

THE BODY

INTRODUCTION

The body is very personal: this is my body, this is me.

The body is very social: we study each other intensely; we use our bodies to communicate attitudes; the ways we dress and walk are meaningful to the group.

The body reflects the personal experience of an individual as well as larger social trends and ideas. Through art, different cultures show their concept of human nature and what they consider to be ideal, powerful, or beautiful.

Most images in this chapter are of human beings, although deities and mythic heroes are included when they illustrate important concepts of human nature. The following questions are important:

How does portraiture reveal the individual?

What do depictions of the body indicate more broadly about human nature?

What are the boundaries between the self and the world, both physical and spiritual?

What is the experience of sickness and death?

How is the human body used in art, both as material and as tool?

The body in art also appears in these chapters:

Chapter 8, Reproduction and Sexuality: female and male bodies as powerful forces in the creation of offspring

Chapter 9, Deities and Places of Worship: images of deities and how they compare to humans

Chapter 11, Power, Politics, and Glory: the imposing images of rulers

Chapter 14, Race, Gender, Clan, and Class: images of family and of different classes; social dictates regarding men's and women's roles and appearances; race in society

Tomika Te Mutu of Coromandel. Detail of Figure 13.20. Photo: John Hillelson.

DEPICTING THE BODY

The following sections, "Portraits" and "Self-Portraits," reveal personal aspects of an individual. Later, in "The Physical Body," artworks reflect ideas about human nature in general.

PORTRAITS

In Oscar Wilde's nineteenth-century novel *The Picture of Dorian Gray*, Gray remained handsome and youthful in appearance throughout his life. However, hidden in a closet, Gray's portrait aged, becoming ugly and blemished as he lived a reckless and dissolute life.

Like this example from literature, a successful portrait in art is usually considered to be someone's likeness, both in face and in character. Faces are important to humans and, in fact, are the very first things to which newborn children respond. Humans are extremely perceptive in determining—or imagining—another person's state of mind by nuances in facial expressions. As adults, we continue to study our own faces and the faces of others for hints of character and experiences.

CONNECTION
Chapter 14 includes portraits used to strengthen clan ties, like the Head of a Roman Patrician (Figure 14.13, page 410).

The first attribute of a portrait is usually individualized features, as in the *Olmec Head* (Figure 13.1) from the Olmec culture that first thrived along the Gulf coast of Mexico near modern Veracruz around 1500 BCE. This ceramic head may have been made originally as part of some kind of offering. Others like it were carved from jade. The individualized face is strikingly modeled, with subtle curves in the cheeks and brows, and a sensitive rendering of the mouth. Although a portrait, it also points to Olmec social customs. The head was probably purposely deformed after birth, to conform to Olmec ideals of beauty. There are five locks of long hair that fall down the back of the neck, indicating that this is a woman.

CONNECTION
Another ancient head modeled with refined, portrait-like sensitivity is the Crowned Head of an Oni (Figure 11.3, page 303).

The *Study for the Portrait of Okakura Tenshin,* painted in 1922 (Figure 13.2), records the face of a shrewd, intelligent individual who was at the center of social, political, and aesthetic controversies in Japan during his time. Okakura was a

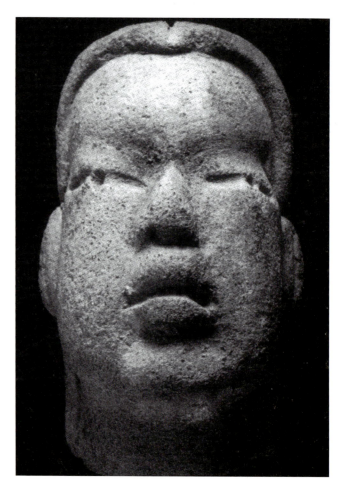

 13.1 *Olmec Head.* Ceramic, 2" high. Olmec. Mexico, 900 BCE. Museo Nacional de Arqueologia y Etnologia, Guatemala City.

writer, aesthete, educator, and art curator who lived from 1862 until 1913, a time when rulers of Japan were ending three hundred years of isolation and embarking on a period of rapid Westernization. Eastern-influenced music, literature, religion, and medicine were suppressed and replaced with Western modes. The one exception was the visual arts, in which traditional and Western styles—and mixtures of the two—flourished. Traditional Japanese paintings and prints were popular and sold well not only in Japan but also in the West. They influenced a number of Western artists, such as Vincent van Gogh (see Figure 13.3).

Okakura and a U.S. scholar, Ernest Fenollosa, wrote the first Western-style history of Japanese art and established a Japanese museum, an academy of art, and art appreciation societies, which were essentially Western cultural institutions. Before this, traditional Japanese paintings and prints had not been considered fine art in the Western sense of the term. Later, Okakura wrote *The Ideals of the East,* in which he created the concept of Asia as the East in contrast to the West. Eventually, he moved to the United States and became an assistant cura-

believed that only the combination of modernism and tradition meant progress in art. His face is the focal point of the composition, sitting atop the triangular shape of his body, and his features make a great study of shrewdness, toughness, and perception.

CONNECTION

For an example of a face rendered in traditional Japanese style, with outlines only, see Komurasaki of the Tamaya Teahouse (Figure 14.33, page 428).

Often artists reveal as much about themselves as they do about their subjects. In the *Portrait of Dr. Gachet*, dated 1890 (Figure 13.3), Vincent van Gogh painted a free-thinking, eccentric, homeopathic doctor with the foxglove flower to symbolize his profession. Gachet's portrait is also a vehicle for van Gogh to make observations about modern urban life in general, which van Gogh found to be full of suffering. With a melancholy face and pose, Gachet leans on two nineteenth-century novels about tragic and degenerate life in Paris. Van Gogh himself found life in Paris to be unhealthy and miserable,

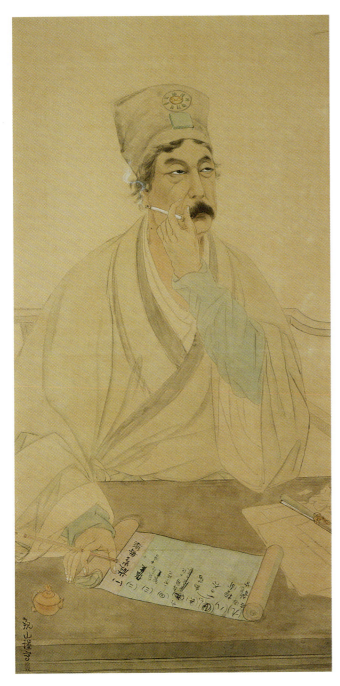

13.2　SHIMOMURA KANZAN. *Study for the Portrait of Okakura Tenshin.* Pigment on paper, 53$^{1}/_{2}$" × 26". Japan, 1922. Art Museum, Tokyo National University of Fine Arts and Music.

tor in the Japanese and Chinese Department of the Boston Museum of Fine Arts.

The very style of *Study for the Portrait of Okakura Tenshin* reflects much of the controversy that raged around Japanese art during his time. Japanese-style contour lines and flat shapes are apparent here, especially in Okakura's left hand and sleeve. But the face and hat are rendered with Western chiaroscuro—that is, by dark and light shading. Okakura smokes a Western cigarette while wearing traditional Japanese garb. Okakura

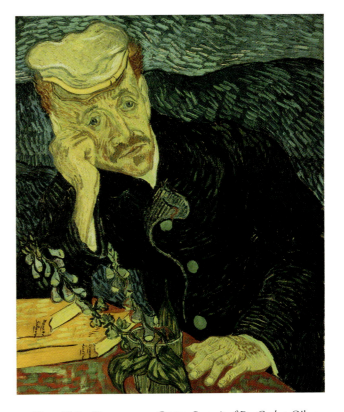

13.3　VINCENT VAN GOGH. *Portrait of Dr. Gachet.* Oil on canvas. 26$^{1}/_{4}$" × 22". Netherlands, 1890. Photo courtesy Christie's. Copyright © Christie's Images, Inc. / Christies Images—All rights reserved. See also the text accompanying Figure 1.20.

and he took refuge in his art, in the countryside, and in medical help. At this time, van Gogh was painting at a feverish pace, but was less than two months away from his own suicide. Thick paint animates the entire surface, with emphatic dashes and tight swirls that model form, increase color saturation, and indicate van Gogh's own agitation and intensity. Thus, Gachet's likeness was both an image of Gachet and a reflection of van Gogh's own inner state.

In *Fanny (Fingerpainting),* dated 1985 (Figure 13.4), artist Chuck Close has painted an elderly woman's head in great detail, at an enormous scale (more than nine feet high). Her face fills the foreground space of the painting, pushing toward us her lizardlike eyelids, her watery eyes and cracked lips, and the sagging skin of her neck. With this painting, we can stare

curiously at a person's face, an action considered impolite in U.S. culture. Also, we could not focus on a real face for long periods at very close quarters, but this very large, detailed portrait allows us to do so.

The pose is ordinary, like that on a driver's license. Her nonidealized features are lit unflatteringly from both sides, leaving dark shadows at the center of her face. But the scale and amazing surface make her face forceful and imposing. The artist works from photographs. Like his photographic sources, this painting is in sharp focus in certain areas, with soft focus in others. The center of the face is clear, but all points closer (the tip of the nose) and more distant (the hair, base of the neck, and shoulders) fall out of the depth of field of the camera and are blurred. The expression on the woman's face also

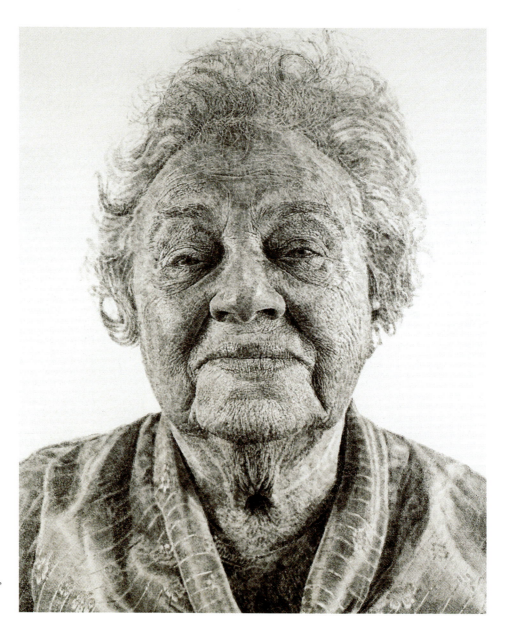

13.4 CHUCK CLOSE. *Fanny (Fingerpainting).* Oil on canvas, 120" × 84". USA, 1985. Washington, National Gallery of Art, donation of Lila Acheson Wallace.

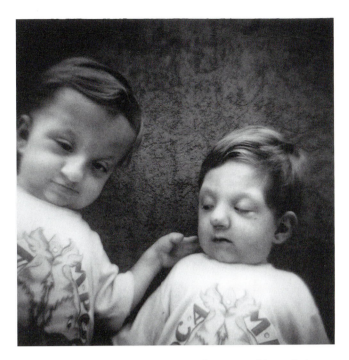

13.5 NANCY BURSON. Untitled image from *Faces.* Silver gelatin print, 15" × 15". USA, 1992. Twin Palms Publishers, Santa Fe, New Mexico. Courtesy of the Artist.

makes evident the photographic source: her eyes are focused on the camera that is close to her nose, and she seems both tolerant of and slightly affronted by the camera.

In the 1992 series called *Faces,* Nancy Burson also gave us the opportunity to indulge our curiosity about other people's faces. She used a cheap plastic camera to make grainy, fuzzy photographs of children with unusual faces due to genetic conditions, accident, or disease. The low-quality lens produced surprisingly beautiful images, with blurred edges, softened highlights, and grainy but luminous shadows. Burson's photographs reveal some aspects of the children's personalities, such as friendliness, dreaminess, caution, concern, curiosity, and boldness. Our untitled example (Figure 13.5) shows the boy at left obligingly posing and encouraging the other to do so also, while the other boy remains reluctant and suspicious of manipulation. Framing makes the child at left seem to be moving, while the other appears more pinned at the center.

Burson's photographs act as a mirror to the viewers, who reveal themselves in their reactions to the images. Burson noted that people who dwell on disaster see these children as disasters, whereas others react to them as they would to other children. Thus, degrees of "normal" and "abnormal" are more the viewers' judgments than objective standards.

Full-body portraits include posture and body type, which may reveal more about the sitter's personality. *Leigh under the Skylight,* painted in 1994 (Figure 13.6), is one of Lucian Freud's many full-body portraits. During the long process of sitting for a painting in Freud's studio, the sitters unintentionally

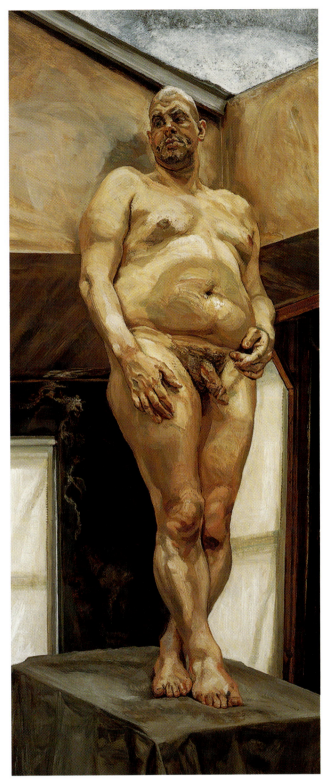

 13.6 LUCIAN FREUD. *Leigh under the Skylight.* Oil on canvas, 90" × 48". Britain, 1994. New York, Acquavella Contemporary Art. By permission of the Artist.

reveal clues about their most intimate selves, primarily through their poses and facial expressions. The figure of Leigh is massive, and from the low point of view assumed by the artist, he

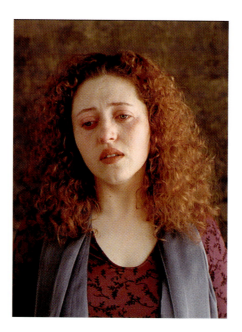 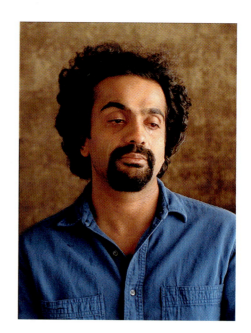

13.7 BILL VIOLA. *Dolorosa* (production stills from the video installation). 2000. Photo by Kira Perov. Courtesy of the Artist. See also text accompanying Figure 6.19.

appears to be almost gigantic. Yet the flesh is soft. The crossed legs, deeply lined face, and furrowed brow communicate a sense of tightness. The figure appears almost stuffed up against the space of the skylight, wary and exposed. The paint is thick and buttery in the lower legs and the top of the belly, but congealed and clotted in the lower face, nipples, navel, and genitals. The excess of texture is both fascinating and repulsive. This full-size nude is definitely a portrait of an individual man, in contrast to the full-size nude *Doryphoros* (see Figure 13.14), which is a depiction of "Man."

Video allows artists to make moving portraits. Bill Viola's *Dolorosa* (Figure 13.7) consists of two flat-panel monitors arranged like a diptych or a double-frame portrait showing a weeping man and woman. At first glance, the videos look like paintings, because the color is so saturated, the picture so sharp, and the movement so excruciatingly slow. Only after a few minutes of study do we see the subtle changes in their faces, expressing a deep, almost unbearable sorrow. Viola made this work and more than twenty others in a series titled *The Passions,* based on Renaissance and Baroque paintings of figures in sorrow, ecstasy, or astonishment. Rather than restage the old paintings, Viola sought to expand their emotional and spiritual dimensions. Viewers can study faces as never before.

SELF-PORTRAITS

We will look at four artists who have made many pictures of themselves. Rembrandt van Rijn made at least sixty-two self-portraits. Frida Kahlo painted herself fifty-five times, which represents almost one-third of the artwork she did in her entire lifetime. Cindy Sherman has photographed herself hundreds of times in various guises and settings. Likewise, Mariko Mori

has made multiple images of herself that cross the boundaries between fine art, consumer culture, and kitsch.

Rembrandt's records of his face can be strong, vulnerable, cloddish, or sophisticated, and range from youth through old age. The paintings are emotional barometers as well, showing happiness, worry, sorrow, humor, or resignation. In *Self-Portrait,* painted in 1669 (Figure 13.8), Rembrandt records both a human face and a human soul. His lit face emerges from the void of the background. Light seems both to reflect off the surface of his face and to emanate from inside his head. His eyes express gentleness, pain, and knowledge. The left side of his face is in soft shadow, a fitting visual metaphor for a man of wisdom facing his own death. In fact, Rembrandt died later that year. Earth tones, blacks, dull reds, and luminous yellows predominate in this painting. The paint surface is rich and thick.

Rembrandt studied himself in a country where both religion and the state promoted individualism. The Netherlands were Calvinist Protestant, a religion that believed industriousness and spirituality were the measure of an individual. Humanist philosophy flourished in leading Dutch universities, and learning was valued in upper and middle classes. Power in the country was distributed among wealthy bourgeois families, rather than concentrated in a monarchy.

In her fifty-five self-portraits, Frida Kahlo conducted a long inquiry into her inner and her outer being. Her face stays almost the same in all her paintings: distinctive, unemotional, and with an unblinking gaze that looks back. She surrounds herself with signs and images of the different factors that shaped her life, such as her ancestry, her physical body, her nearly fatal accident and chronic pain, the indigenous Mexican culture, the landscape, the Christian religion, and her relationship

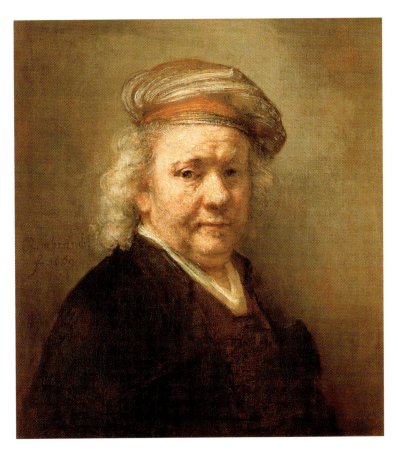

13.8 REMBRANDT VAN RIJN. *Self-Portrait.* Oil on canvas, 23¼" × 20". Netherlands, 1669. The Hague, Mauritshuis. © Scala / Art Resource, NY.

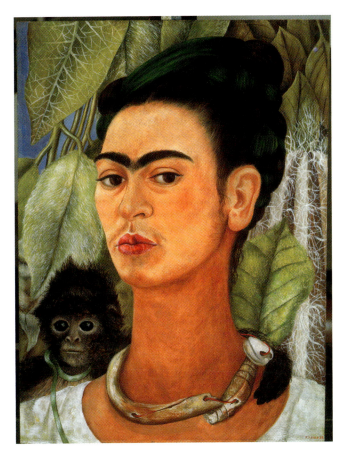

with Diego Rivera, a prominent Mexican artist. In *Self-Portrait with Monkey,* painted in 1938 (Figure 13.9), Kahlo's face is central, studying us as we study her. Her long hair is braided and pulled on top of her head in traditional Mexican style, to show her identification with the peasant culture. Lush foliage from the Mexican landscape surrounds her head. For Kahlo, the monkey was her animal alter ego. In other self-portraits, Kahlo uses such symbols as hummingbirds, which stood for the souls of dead Mayan warriors, and blood, which alludes to the crippling injuries she suffered in a bus accident, to Mayan bloodletting ceremonies, and to the Christian crown of thorns.

CONNECTION
For an example of Diego Rivera's work, see Dia de Los Muertos (Figure 10.28, page 291).

13.9 FRIDA KAHLO. *Self-Portrait with Monkey.* Oil on masonite, 16" × 12". Mexico, 1938. Albright-Knox Art Gallery, Buffalo, N.Y. Bequest of A. Conger Goodyear, 1966. See also text accompanying Figure 2.16.

CONNECTION
A Mayan relief depicting a bloodletting ritual, Shield Jaguar and Lady Xoc, *appears in Figure 9.16, page 237.*

Kahlo's and Rembrandt's self-portraits show the inner self of a unique, deeply feeling person. Cindy Sherman photographed herself hundreds of times, but the cumulative effect is one of fragmentation, not of piecing together a unique individual. Each image of Sherman reflects a socially prescribed or media-disseminated role. Our example, *Untitled Film Still #35* (Figure 13.10), is one of a series of sixty-nine fake film stills she made between 1977 and 1980. They were all black and white, eight by ten inches, the exact format of B-film stills. She wears a wide range of costumes and poses in all kinds of settings, with

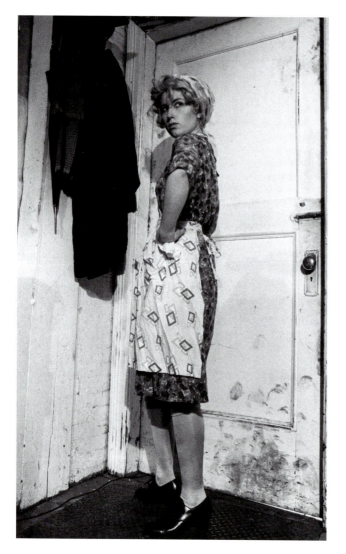

13.10   CINDY SHERMAN. *Untitled Film Still #35.* Gelatin Silver Print, 8" × 10". USA, 1979. Collection of Eli and Edythe Broad, Los Angeles. Courtesy of the artist and Metro Pictures. See also the text accompanying Figure 4.10.

a vast array of props, as if unaware of the camera. Yet Sherman often reveals the mechanics of her self-portraiture; in this picture, the shutter release cable that Sherman operates is visible on the floor at left.

In the photos, Sherman is sometimes almost unrecognizable as she reenacts roles for women that are given to us by the media, such as the sweetheart next door, the housewife, the girl left behind, or the vulnerable hitchhiker from a slasher film. In *Untitled Film Still #35,* Sherman appears as a poor woman who is hardened, trapped, sullen, and sexy. The grimy setting and costumes seem to be taken from the 1930s. The kick marks on the door allude to an atmosphere of violence. This image is the reversal of the independent, single, working girl who becomes the happy homemaker. Sherman suggests that we have no built-in sense of identity, but rather compose ourselves from pieces of popular culture. The *Film Still* self-portraits are collectively a portrait of familiar female types, as represented through the media.

Japanese-born Mariko Mori is an artist and a former fashion model and fashion designer living in both New York and Tokyo. She creates photographs and performances "starring" herself in various roles, such as geisha or cyberchick, which she sees as total fabrications. Embracing the commercial world that uses models to sell messages, she sees her artwork as part of pop culture and wants to connect art with movies and fashions. In *Birth of a Star,* she photographed herself as a teen rock star in a shiny, plastic, plaid skirt and spiked purple hair, surrounded by computer-manipulated floating bubbles. Afterward, she translated that same image into *Star Doll,* 1998 (Figure 13.11), an edition of ninety-nine dolls. Because her identity is a totally fabricated hybrid, her work raises the question, What is "self"? Mori's work collapses distinctions among the categories of art, toy, fashion, kitsch, frivolity, and serious inquiry.

THE PHYSICAL BODY

Artists use the body to address ideas about the essence of humanity.

THE IDEALIZED BODY

Our first four examples present the human body in ideal terms, although that varies from culture to culture. *Torso,* dated c. 3000 BCE (Figure 13.12), is a carving from the ancient Harappan civilization that was centered on the Indus River in what is now Pakistan. The sculpture is an idealized version of the human body, with a supple, rounded form. The arm sockets suggest that the figure originally included several arms, possibly representing a youthful deity. The somewhat distended stomach suggests a yogic breathing posture. The stone has been so sensitively shaped that it gives the impression of living flesh, smooth muscle, and a little pad of fat. The outlines and forms are smooth and curving, suggesting grace, flexibility, sensuality, and even vulnerability.

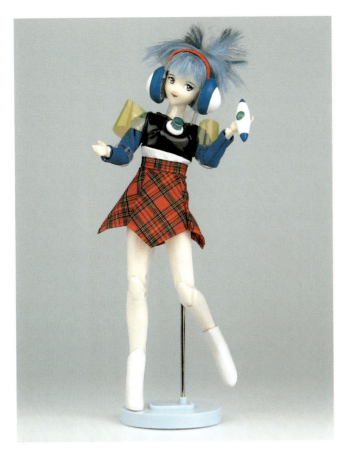

13.11   MARIKO MORI. *Star Doll,* 1998 (edition for Parkett 54, 1998–1999). Multiple of doll, 10¹/₄" × 3¹/₈" × 1⁹/₁₆" (irreg). Publisher: Parkett, Zurich and New York. Manufacturer: Marmit, Tokyo. Edition: 99. © 1998 Mariko Mori and Parkett.

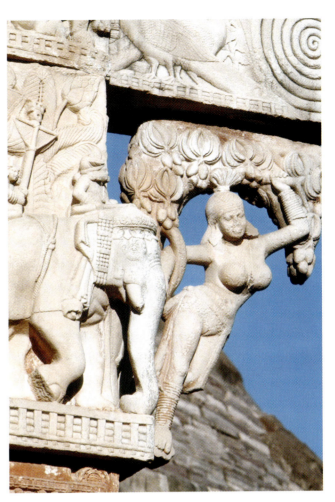

13.13   *Yakshi* (detail of East Gate, Great Stupa). Sandstone, approximately 5' high. Sanchi, India, early Andhra period, first century BCE. Robert Harding.

Yakshi, dating from the first century BCE in India (Figure 13.13), continued the rounded form and sensuality of the *Torso.* "Yakshi" is a nature spirit who represents fertility; her breasts are exaggerated to emphasize her powers—her touch caused trees to flower. Her nearly nude body is curving and rounded and can be seen through her transparent skirt with the hemline draping across her shin. *Yakshi* twists with incredible flexibility, looking natural in a pose that would leave a human totally off balance. Jewelry adorns her lower arms and legs, giving interest to the less-curving features of her body. Her belt visually emphasizes her broad hips in contrast to her small waist. For the next several centuries, India produced an enormous amount of splendid figurative sculpture, and the twisting pose and voluptuous form appear often. Thus, in

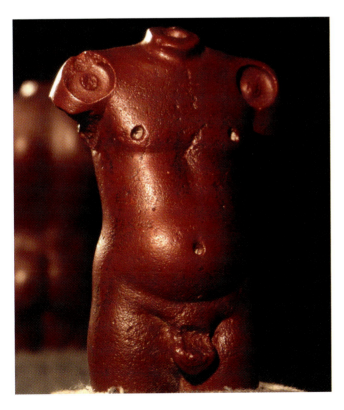

13.12   *Torso.* Red sandstone, 3¹/₂" high. India (Harappa, Pakistan), c. 3000 BCE. National Museum, New Delhi. © Borromeo / Art Resource, NY.

India, sensuality seems to be an important and central characteristic of human nature.

Protagoras said, "Of all things, the measure is man," and the ancient Greeks had a great respect for the human mind and human body, esteeming the arts, sciences, philosophy, and athletics. The democratic government, although limited, meant that individuals were self-governing. Athlete, philosopher, scientist, statesman, playwright, and warrior were all ideal occupations for men. The Greeks believed that humans were capable of near perfection, defined as a fit body guided by a keen mind. Emotions were generally considered less important than the intellect and should be properly contained. Nudity was common in art and in athletic events, both of which glorified the unclothed, idealized human form. *Doryphoros,* which means "Spear-bearer," is dated 450–440 BCE (Figure 13.14). This sculpture by Polykleitos is a slightly larger-than-life-size nude male that reflects the Greeks' deep appreciation of the human body. The figure is idealized in a number of ways: (1) in the balanced pose; (2) in the internal proportions; (3) in the restrained emotions; and (4) in the roles depicted—youth, athlete, and warrior.

The pose is simple, balanced, and understated. The statue's straight leg and arm create a vertical line on the left, balanced by the bent leg and arm on the right. Balance is also expressed across the body. The straight leg and bent arm are tensed, versus the hanging arm and flexed leg, which are relaxed. The action is minimal and at the same time complex in its subtleties, with small twists, stretches, and compressions. This *contrapposto* (counterbalanced) stance is the way many people stand, and so the sculpture recreates an image of a living, flexing body.

Polykleitos invented and applied a now-lost system of mathematical and geometric proportions, called the Canon, which harmonized one body part with another in his sculptures. *Doryphoros* was originally conceived as a sculpture that would illustrate and demonstrate the Canon. A few of the simpler proportions of the Canon are still known; for example, the length of the longest finger equaled the length of the palm of the hand, and together they were used as a measure for the length of the arm. The breast nipples are one head-length below the chin, and the navel is another head-length below the nipples. This system also determined the placement of all the muscles. Polykleitos and the Greeks of his era believed that mathematical proportions resulted in a harmonious figure that was morally and aesthetically good. (In fact, the body is blocky, the result of the application of the Canon.)

Emotionally, *Doryphoros* is reserved and self-contained. The statue does not imply the presence of another figure or even the presence of the audience. This restraint complements its minimal but complex body movement. Polykleitos chose to represent a young, physically fit athlete and warrior, versus some-

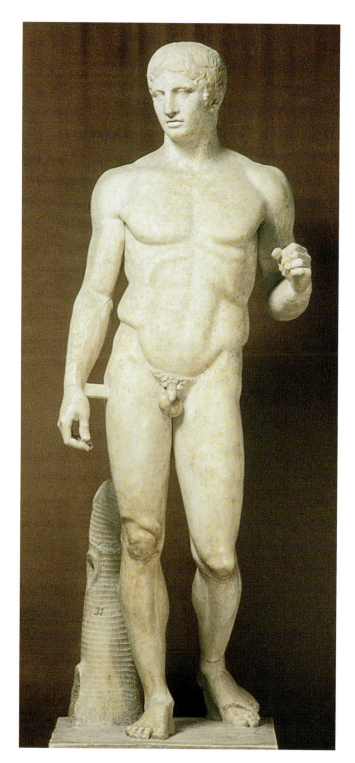

 13.14 POLYKLEITOS. *Doryphoros (Spear-bearer).* Marble after a bronze original, 6'11" high. Rome, c. 450–440 BCE. Museo Nazionale, Naples. See also the text accompanying Figure 1.13. Saskia Ltd.

one aged or ill or engaged in a tedious occupation. The total combination of balance, proportion, restraint, and youthful heroism made *Doryphoros* one of the most famous nudes of its time as well as the Roman era and the Italian Renaissance.

CONNECTION

See Zeus/Poseidon (Figure 9.3, page 228) to compare the similarity between images of gods and humans in Greek Classical art.

CONNECTION

The original Doryphoros was executed in bronze, which would have had a very refined surface and brought more vigor to the pose. Our example is a marble copy, which required greater support around the legs. For more, see the "Art Materials and Media" section of Chapter 2, The Language of Art.

It is interesting to compare *Doryphoros* with the *Male Torso* (Ancestor figure) in Figure 13.15, which was likely carved in the twentieth century in the Baule area of Africa. Internal proportions, idealized character, harmony of parts, and restraint are important elements here as in *Doryphoros,* but the visual result is very different. In most traditional African sculpture, the front view of the human figure was sculpted symmetrically; arms are in parallel positions, legs both on the ground, head facing forward. This formal, frontal pose contributes to the dignified, almost solemn aspect of the sculpture. In contrast, the side view features counterbalanced curves: the abdomen and knees project forward, balanced by the buttocks to the back. The straight neck and back interrupt the curves. The distinctive silhouette of the head is the focus for the entire work. This sculpture is likely the depiction of an ancestor.

In some African traditions, the head and neck were considered the most important parts of the body, and thus were apportioned one-third the height of the entire figure. The torso occupied another third, and the legs the last third. The sculptor's first cuts set these proportions. The major forms were sculpted next, and, finally, decorative patterns enlivened the surface. The patterns represent scarification and carefully combed, braided, twisted, or beaded hair. The pattern elements are all confidently carved without mistakes or reworking, because African sculptors generally were well trained as apprentices. The *Male Torso* combines naturalistic and abstracted features; for example, the mouth, nose, and eyes are relatively naturalistic compared to the stylized hands. This echoes tendencies in African sculpture as a whole, which runs the gamut from realistic to very abstracted.

LESS-THAN-PERFECT HUMANITY

Having looked at idealized human forms, we turn now to some works that present a less-idealized image of humanity.

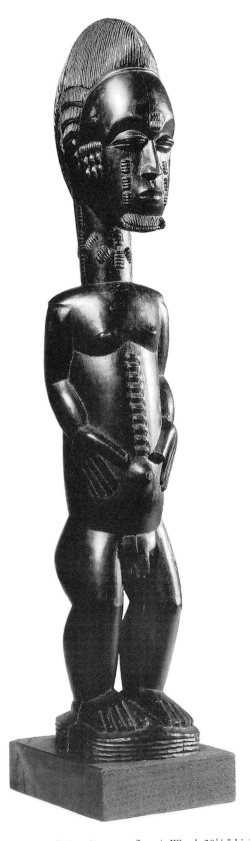

13.15 *Male Torso* (Ancestor figure). Wood, 20½" high. Baule. Africa, c. nineteenth–twentieth century. The British Museum, London. See also the text accompanying Figures 1.12 and 5.17.

The first is *Laocoön and His Sons,* dated 300 to 100 BCE (Figure 13.16). In the two or three centuries that followed the making of the "perfect" image of *Doryphoros,* the Greeks turned to depicting humans engaged in violent action, vulnerable to age, injured, diseased, and subject to feelings of pain, terror, or despair. Two cults were particularly influential in Hellenistic Greece: Stoicism, in which individuals were urged to endure nobly their fate and state in life; and Epicureanism, which advocated intelligent pleasure seeking in life because death was the end to existence. Both philosophies imply a kind of resigned acceptance of fate and a withdrawal from the Classic Greek ideal of the active, heroic, involved person.

Laocoön and His Sons shows these changing concepts of the human body and human nature. In *Laocoön,* the human bodies are impressively muscular, an inheritance of the Classical Greeks. But the balance of mind and body, and the contained emotion, has here burst apart in a scene of high drama and sensationalism. Laocoön was a Trojan priest who tried to warn his fellow citizens against accepting the Trojan Horse as an apparent token of surrender from the Greeks who had been warring against them. Greek warriors hid in the horse, and they overcame the Trojan forces once the horse was inside the fortifications. The gods, who sided with the Greeks against the Trojans, sent sea serpents to strangle and kill Laocoön and his sons, even as they were making offerings at an altar! The story seems to be one of great injustice, as a virtuous man helping his fellow citizens is cruelly crushed by the gods. Human vulnerability and lack of control of one's fate are well demonstrated.

The figures are like a group of actors on a stage, all facing forward as if performing for an unseen audience. Their struggles are theatrical. Their bodies are idealized, but the father's is overdeveloped and muscle-bound, more spectacular than heroic.

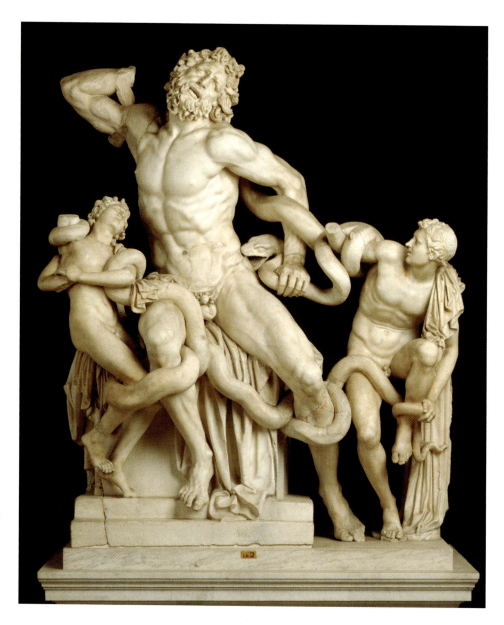

13.16 AGESANDER, ATHENODORUS, AND POLYDORUS OF RHODES. *Laocoön and His Sons.* Marble, 7'10" high. Greek, Hellenistic (Roman patronage), late second–early first century BCE. Vatican Museums, Rome. © Araldo de Luca/Corbis.

Emotionality is increased with the high contrast between the lights and the darks; the great space the sculpture occupies; the numerous negative spaces that add to the complexity of the piece; and the various textures and surfaces, from skin, to hair, to cloth, to serpent.

In medieval Europe, human nature was held in very low esteem. Medieval Christians saw a great split between the purity of God's divine realm and the natural world, a transitory place of sin and corruption. The mortal body was given over to appetites and lusts that led humans into sin and endangered their immortal souls. Salvation with God was possible only through the Church. In *The Last Judgment,* dated c. 1130 (Figure 13.17), from the main entrance of the Church of St.-Lazare, human bodies are depicted as miserable, frail, and pitifully unattractive. The scene illustrates the end of time, when every person rises from the ground to be judged forever as worthy of heaven or condemned to hell. In the lower section of this carving, the cowering humans rise from their boxlike graves and huddle in line until a pair of large hands, like oversized pliers, clamps around their head. All are then plucked up and deposited on the scales of Judgment, where they risk being snatched by demons and stuffed in hell for eternity. The saved clutch fearfully at the robes of the angels.

Because human nature was considered so base, the Greek nude was inconceivable, and the concept of a naturalistic body as beautiful and good had long since disappeared. The body in medieval art was distorted to communicate moral status. Thus, naked humans are puny. Good angels are elongated and serene, their anatomical distortions emphasizing their distance from earthly beings. The demons, however, seem to have been modeled on a flayed human corpse, with the exposed ribs and muscles of a tortured body, while their faces grimace horribly. Their claw feet are beastlike, and indeed the human body was associated with animals, which were seen as even more distant from God. Jesus is depicted in a grand manner reigning over heaven and earth, frontal and symmetrical, and much larger than all others.

Attitudes about human nature shifted again in Europe as the Renaissance flourished in Italy. Humanistic philosophy of this time celebrated the glory of humanity: Italian philosopher Giovanni Pico della Mirandola declared in the fifteenth century, "There is nothing to be seen more wonderful than man,"

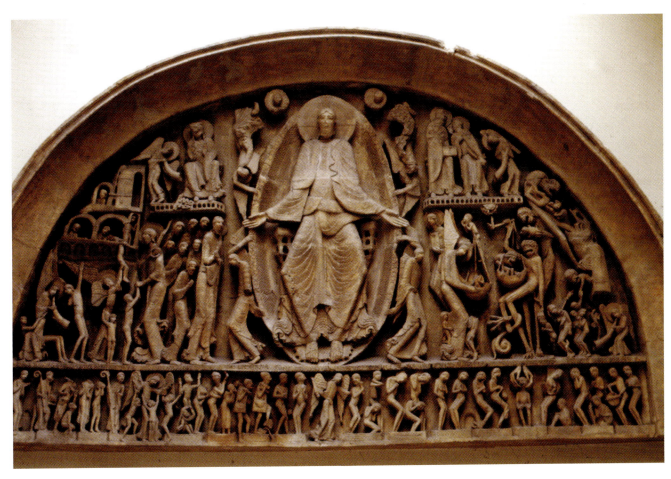

13.17   GISLEBERTUS. *The Last Judgment.* Stone carving, 21' wide, 12' high. West tympanum of the Church of St.-Lazare, Autun, Burgundy. France, c. 1130. The bottom band shows humans raised from the dead on the last day, while Heaven is shown on the upper left, and the scales of Judgment and Hell are on the upper right. Ronald Sheridan / Ancient Art & Architecture.

reflecting an attitude very similar to the Greeks'. Michelangelo Buonarroti, the famous painter, sculptor, and architect of the Italian Renaissance, believed that the human form was the most perfect and important subject to depict. He believed that his work was an echo of God's divine creation of humanity. Like most other Italian artists of that time, he was strongly influenced by Hellenistic and Roman sculptures that were being excavated in central Italy. The nude as an ideal form became popular again.

But Renaissance nudes were different from the Classical nudes. On the one hand, the body was seen now as a work of God and deserving of respect and honor. Yet the medieval beliefs persisted regarding the enduring soul versus the aging, rotting body that often leads to sin and damnation. *David*, dated 1501 to 1504 (Figure 13.18), represents the Israelite youth who fought the giant warrior, Goliath, saved his people, and later became the greatest king of the Old Testament. Michelangelo chose the moment that the young David first faces Goliath. Tension is apparent in his frown, tensed muscles, and protruding veins. The sculpture is not self-contained, in contrast to *Doryphoros* (see Figure 13.14); the turning figure of David is "completed" by the unseen Goliath. The head and hands are oversized, indicating youthful potential still maturing and a greater potential violence, all attributes that differ from the restrained, relaxed *Doryphoros*. David's inner tension speaks of the core of being, the soul, that is separate from the body. The body is ennobled and emphasized, but only as a vehicle for expressing the soul.

David reflects some broad trends. During the Renaissance, there was also a growing interest in scientific inquiry and the study of human anatomy. Michelangelo, Leonardo da Vinci, and other Italian artists performed dissections to assist them in rendering muscles. Also, David versus Goliath was a popular story in the republic of Florence, the city-state in central Italy for which this sculpture was made. Florence was ruled by a group of wealthy families rather than by a single leader, and Florentines saw themselves as much more self-determining than citizens of other areas ruled by tyrants.

CONNECTION

See Andreas Vesalius's Fourth Plate of Muscles *(Figure 15.24, page 454) for more on Renaissance scientific studies of anatomy.*

CONNECTION

Ambrogio Lorenzetti's Allegory of Good Government *(Figure 12.19, page 352) was a tribute to republican governments in central Italy.*

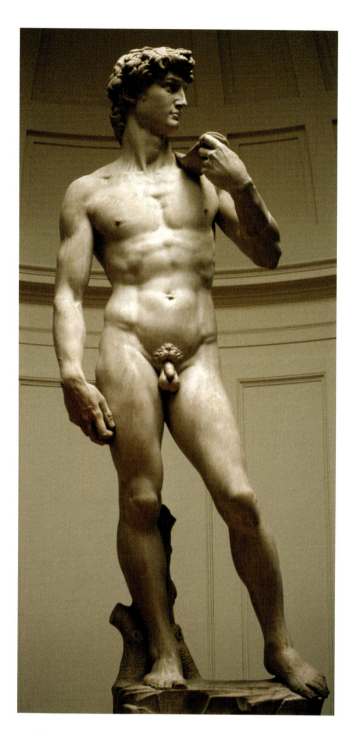

 13.18 MICHELANGELO BUONARROTI. *David*. Marble, 14'3" high. Italy, 1501–1504. Galleria dell'Accademia, Florence, Italy. © Michael S. Yamashita/Corbis. See also text accompanying Figure 2.32

By the nineteenth and twentieth centuries, religious models for human nature held less sway in Europe and were increasingly challenged and displaced by concepts of human nature based on scientific inquiry. This shift was apparent in artwork, also. One indicator was the training of young artists, who now studied in academies, where art training was standardized and systematized. New technologies, such as photography, changed

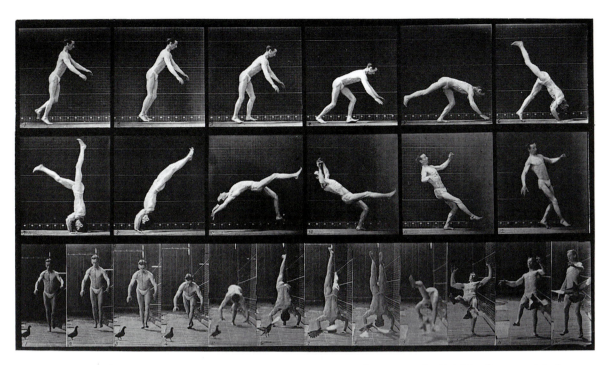

 13.19 EADWEARD MUYBRIDGE. *Handspring, a flying pigeon interfering, June 26, 1885.* Print from an original master negative, Plate 365 of *Animal Locomotion.* England/Scotland/USA,1887. International Museum of Photography at George Eastman House, Rochester, New York. See also the text accompanying Figure 2.25.

the understanding of the human body and the way art was made. With photography, human movement could be stopped and observed as never before. *Handspring, a flying pigeon interfering, June 26, 1885* (Figure 13.19) is a study of the human body in action made by Eadweard Muybridge and subsequently published with other such studies in the book *Animal Locomotion.* Muybridge invented a special camera shutter and then placed twelve cameras so outfitted in a row. When the athlete performed the handstand, his movements broke the series of strings stretched across his path, thus progressively triggering each of the twelve cameras.

For Muybridge, the human body was an object of detached, scientific study and not a powerful presence like *David* or the *Male Torso* from Baule. With Muybridge, the concept of the human body was altered and was recognized as being modified by time and space. Muybridge made similar studies for all kinds of human and animal movement. He also developed a cylindrical device that allowed his images to be mounted, rotated, and viewed to give the illusion of motion. In this respect, his work was a precursor of cinema.

 CONNECTION
Turn to Chapter 16 for a discussion of film and television in art.

THE LIMITS OF THE SELF

Is the individual person a discrete entity? What are the boundaries between the self and the environment, between the self and the spiritual realm, or between the self and technology?

Many Oceanic cultures of the South Pacific conceive of the person as an amalgam of life forces, physical substances, and ritual knowledge that come from many sources. That amalgam of external forces, which is at this moment a particular person, is in fact constantly changing and transforming and also in danger of coming apart. All of existence is divided into two realms: first, the earthly world of light, and second, the domain of darkness, which includes the gods, fertility, creativity, and dissipation and death. A newborn has just emerged from darkness and is considered sanctified, but also unstable and dangerous to the living. Birth was the result of powerful forces, forces that threatened the living and that had to be contained by ritual. The infant is not a complete being, but one that transforms through rituals at important stages of development: these include birth, initiation, circumcision, and marriage.

Ritual tattooing was one way of strengthening the individual and was used throughout the more eastern islands of the South Pacific. On the Marquesas Islands, the entire body was tattooed, while tattooing was confined to the buttocks and thighs of the women of Fiji and of the men of Samoa, Tahiti, and Tonga. Extensive tattooing subjects a person to severe pain for a long time, but the result was generally seen as a kind of ritual empowerment. Extra eyes, for example, gave the tattooed person more power and decreased vulnerability. Tattooing is often part of initiation rites that gradually harden the human body for adulthood.

The tattoos of *Tomika Te Mutu of Coromandel* (Figure 13.20), a nineteenth-century Maori tribal chief, were seen as an extra protective shell and a new ritual skin. Tattooing was effective in war, as it distracted and confused opponents. The tattoos also identified the individual. Among the Maori, facial tattoos were often considered more memorable than the person's natural features, which is true of Tomika Te Mutu. The chiseled whorls emphasize his scowl, piercing vision, hot breath, and fierce mouth. Traditional Maori tattooing is done with chisels, which gouge deep grooves in the skin. Curves and spirals are like the patterns in Maori woodcarving. Tattoos are treated in various ways once a tattooed person dies. The tattooed heads of deceased Maori chiefs were preserved by steaming, smoking, and oiling them. In contrast, the people of the Marquesas rubbed the skin off a deceased relative to remove

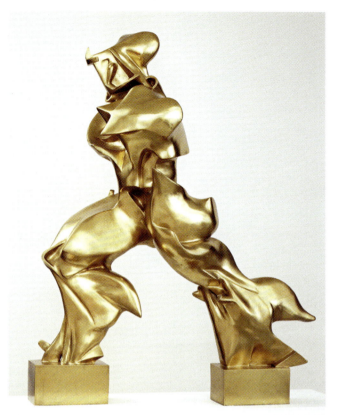

13.21 UMBERTO BOCCIONI. *Unique Forms of Continuity in Space.* Bronze (cast 1931), approximately 43" high. Italy, 1913. The Museum of Modern Art, New York; acquired through the Lillie P. Bliss Bequest. © Digital Image © The Museum of Modern Art / Licensed by SCALA / Art Resource, NY. See also the text accompanying Figure 2.24.

the tattoos, because they were barriers to the person's reentering the realm of darkness.

CONNECTION
Turn to Figure 11.14, page 313, to see Maori wood-carving on a traditional meeting house.

If ritual beliefs can shape the concept of the human being, scientific discoveries and technological advances can do so, also. A vast range of environmental factors influence the living body. The human being is seen now as permeable and as an integrated part of the total world.

In *Unique Forms of Continuity in Space* (Figure 13.21), from 1931, artist Umberto Boccioni dissolves the conventional belief that the skin layer defines the body's outer edge. To him, the body is a mass of wave energy defined by its movement through a fluid atmospheric medium. Significantly, the body is considered less as a human and more as a form that is continuous with others in space. Muscle and bulk are implied, but the sculpture resembles a map of aerodynamic turbulence and the dis-

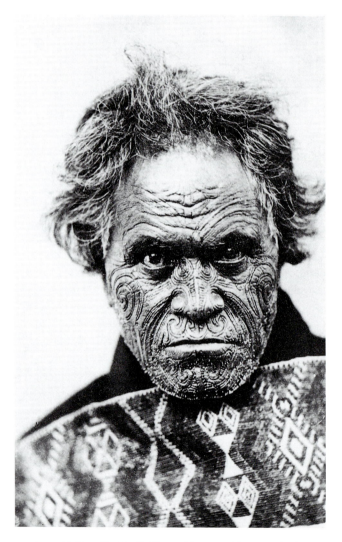

13.20 *Tomika Te Mutu of Coromandel.* Maori chief. New Zealand, nineteenth century. Photo: John Hillelson.

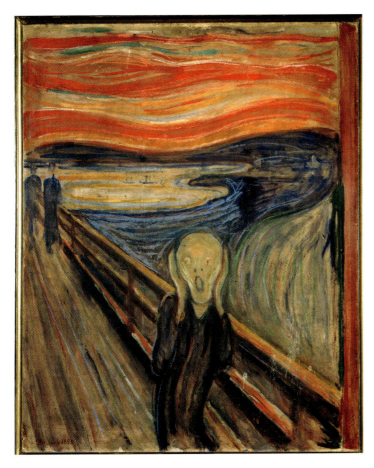

13.22　EDVARD MUNCH. *The Scream.* Oil painting, 35³/₄" × 29". Norway, 1893. National Gallery, Oslo, Norway. © Erich Lessing / Art Resource, NY. © 2004 The Munch Museum / The Munch-Ellingsen Group / Artists Rights Society (ARS), New York.

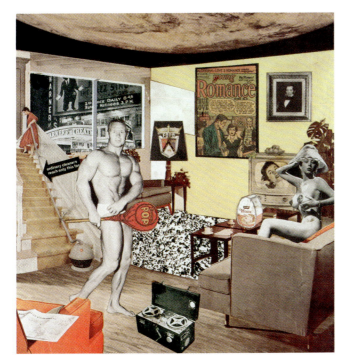

13.23　RICHARD HAMILTON. *Just What Is It That Makes Today's Homes So Different, So Appealing?* Collage, 10¹/₄" × 9³/₄". England, 1956. Kunsthalle Tubingen, Germany. Bridgeman Art Library © 2004 Artists Rights Society (ARS), New York / DACS, London #NUL 108077.

torting effects of air currents on forms. Boccioni was part of an art movement called **Futurism,** which celebrated violence, speed, energy, motion, force, and change.

The body can also be affected by a host of internal forces. In *The Scream* (Figure 13.22), painted by Edvard Munch in 1893, the distorted body is the vehicle for expressing inner terror, anxieties, and pressures. Realism has been abandoned to give form to these internal emotions. At this time, Sigmund Freud had propagated his theories of repression and neurosis as both social and personal ills, which influenced Munch and other artists. The central character glances back at distant figures, but it is unclear whether they are part of the scene or disinterested bystanders. Whatever the situation, fear in the mind has twisted the body and reduced the face to a near skull. The figure stands in complete physical and emotional isolation, cupping its hands over its ears and screaming at a pitch that reverberates in the landscape and in the sky. The colors are emotionally distorted and heightened.

In an era of consumerism, people often gauge their worth by the purchases they can make, not by character, deeds, fate, or karma. Advertising undermines people's self-esteem and then convinces them to buy certain products to improve themselves and their lives. And in an age of consumerism, body shape becomes something that can be bought.

In the 1956 collage *Just What Is It That Makes Today's Homes So Different, So Appealing?* (Figure 13.23), by Richard

Hamilton, we see the aestheticized body ideals of the late twentieth century: the buff, muscular man of amazing sexual prowess (the Tootsie pop) and a super-thin, sexy woman with a fashion-model pouty face. The faces and bodies have been molded through implants, plastic surgery, and the latest abdominal workout machine. In addition, the couple's attractiveness is enhanced by their acquisition of trendy props, which in the 1950s included modern furniture, the latest appliances, and new media products. Hamilton took his imagery from popular magazines and billboards. The rug is a designer version of a Jackson Pollock action painting, which we will see at the end of this chapter. The cluttered composition, with all things new and chic, makes everything seem arbitrary and faddish. Hamilton's lampoon of modern consumer culture reveals the effectiveness and ridiculousness of advertising, because it projects ideal body images that are so extreme, images to which we can never (but must always try to) measure up.

CONNECTION
Hamilton's work is fine art with mass media imagery, and he is critical of both. For more, see "Art, Popular Culture, and Kitsch," in Chapter 1.

Installation artist Jin Soo Kim was born and raised in South Korea, trained as a nurse, and immigrated to the United States at age twenty-four. Much of her work has consisted of Environments, in which she transforms discarded refuse into works that allude to the human body and to self, as evident in the installation view of her 2003 exhibition at the Chicago Cultural Center (Figure 13.24). Organic and architectural forms blur, as objects covered in gauze bandages "bleed" rust, while wrapped ropes and furniture resemble skeletons and viscera. Pieces of furniture seem to become creatures. All forms together

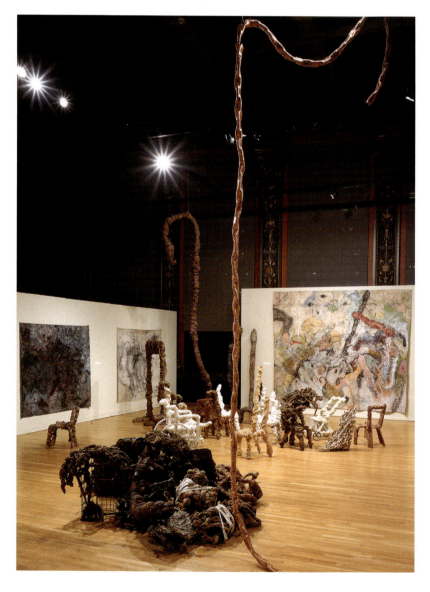

13.24 JIN SOO KIM. Installation view of various artworks at Chicago Cultural Center, 2003. Sculptural works date from 1983–2003. On walls left to right: *Winter*, 1986; *Untitled XV*, 1990; and *Untitled (from Environment D)*, 1984, all acrylic and charcoal on canvas. Photo by Tom Van Eynde, Courtesy Chicago Department of Cultural Affairs, Jin Soo Kim.

suggest a vulnerable, living, interconnected environment of bodies and the things humans build. Kim's work suggests that the human body is completely one with its surroundings. She also suggests that the human "self" is not just the body or a person's character, but also the objects that one carries through life.

Andrea Zittel believes that modern humans "are so inundated with material weight that it finally loses its ability to anchor and satisfy." Her artwork, which straddles art and design, is based solely on the real needs of the physical body and the needs of the psychological self for comfort, serenity, and security. She seeks to eliminate excess materialism, excess choice, and shoddily designed products in everyday life through her *A to Z Administrative Services.* For example, her piece *A to Z Clothing* is a total wardrobe for a woman and consists of only three items: one suit, one jumper/smock, and one jacket/utility coat. That is all. For Zittel, art collecting is a subtractive process, because when art collectors purchase her pieces, they must agree to discard other redundant items in their homes and lives.

Although Zittel does not make images of the human body, her work is totally designed around and is an extension of the body and its needs. The *A-Z Time Tunnel: Time to Read Every Book I Ever Wanted To Read,* 2000 (Figure 13.25), is a compact, beautifully designed living pod to which a person can retreat, close the lid, and escape the rest of the world. There is no timepiece in the pod, because Zittel wanted people to have new experiences, not by adding something to their lives, but by eliminating the artificial way that time is measured in modern cultures. All of Zittel's work is impeccably designed and crafted, and the *Time Tunnel* is no exception, from its flawless

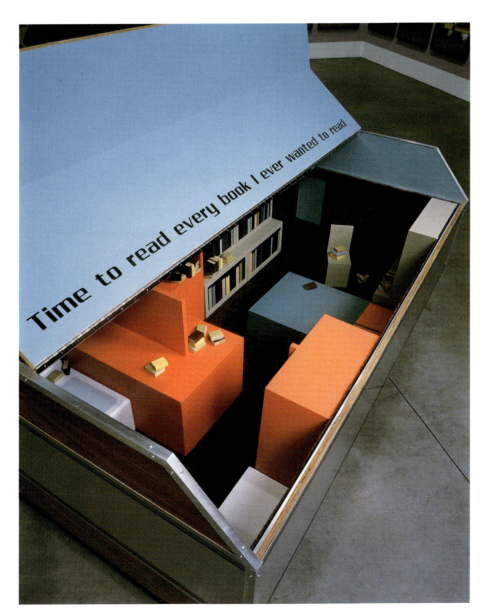

13.25 ANDREA ZITTEL. *A-Z Time Tunnel: Time to Read Every Book I Ever Wanted To Read.* Walnut, wood, steel, carpet, paint, vinyl adhesive, aluminum, MDF, electrical lighting, sound machine, 39" × 48$\frac{1}{4}$" × 80$\frac{1}{2}$" (closed without ladder), 46$\frac{3}{4}$" × 38$\frac{1}{4}$" × 94$\frac{1}{4}$" (open with ladder). USA, 2000. Courtesy Andrea Rosen Gallery, New York; © Andrea Zittel.

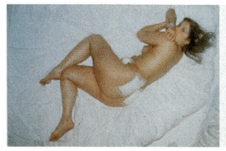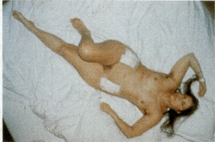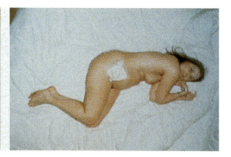

 13.26 HANNAH WILKE. *Intra-Venus*. Chromogenic supergloss photographic prints (13); each panel: 26" × 39¹/₂". USA, 1992–1993. Courtesy Ronald Feldman Fine Arts, New York.

exterior finish to its interior furnishings. Her work has an aspect of performance art (see Antin, Mendieta, and Ono later in this chapter), but in her case, it is the audience who performs within the given constraints, not the artist.

SICKNESS AND DEATH

Intra-Venus, dated from 1992 to 1993, is a series of large-scale photographs that the artist, Hannah Wilke, made with her husband, Donald Goddard, as she struggled with and eventually succumbed to cancer. In this series, both cancer and its medical cures transform and ravage Wilke's body. In many cases larger than life, the photographs present her body to us as it weakened, bloated, and bled. The size makes the physical reality of sickness apparent; it is "in your face." In one bust-

length portrait, we see her bald scalp, mottled skin, and bleeding, pus-filled tongue, all resulting from her cancer treatment. Yet many of the images show that her body possessed a kind of monumental beauty, and that Wilke was still a person of humor and strength.

In three panels from *Intra-Venus* (Figure 13.26), Wilke assumes three poses derived from images of sexually attractive nudes taken from fine art and from magazines, such as *Playboy*. Her glance implies the presence of a sexual partner, as she poses herself as the object of voyeurism. Her posture speaks of narcissistic pleasure. She is Venus, the goddess of love and beauty, even with the ravages of disease and surgery. Wilke reclaims sexuality for herself in sickness and, thus, challenges conventional ideas of attractiveness. In doing so, her last work continued her earlier art. Before the onset of cancer, her body conformed to

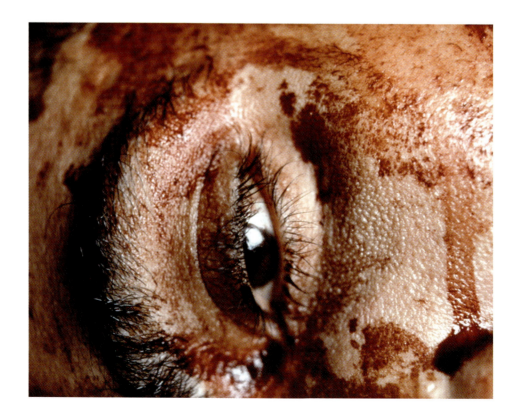

 13.27 ANDRES SERRANO. *The Morgue (Hacked to Death II).* Cibachrome, 49¹/₂" × 60". USA, 1992. Musee d'Art Contemporain, Montreal. Courtesy Paula Cooper Gallery, New York.

"fashion model" looks, and she frequently used her body in her artwork to undermine or critique how female beauty is currently defined and consumed in the United States.

CONNECTION

For more about the sexual meaning of gaze and gender roles in images, see Olympia *by Edward Manet (Figure 8.21, page 210).*

The Morgue (Hacked to Death II), dated 1992 (Figure 13.27), is one of a series of twenty large-scale photographs by Andres Serrano, showing close-up details of the bodies of people in morgues who have died as a result of accidents, violence, or disease. The location is not important, however, as Serrano's images block out the surroundings. In some images, it is not clear if the person is lying on the side of a road or asleep in bed. No body is shown in entirety, so the individuals have no identity. They are close and intimate to the viewer.

The Morgue (Hacked to Death II) is a disturbing image, not only for its content, but because it is impossible to see this death as distant, as one would see a death on the evening news. We can see each hair as it grows out of the person's pores, study the dirt ground into the skin, trace the blood where it flowed and congealed. We cannot miss the dull, unfocused eye in dead center of the image. Serrano's framing, focusing, and manipulation of tones is artful and aesthetic; the refinement and beauty of the image jar with its content.

CONNECTION

Compare this image of death with those from war, such as Mathew Brady's Dead Confederate Soldier with Gun *(Figure 11.28, page 325).*

THE BODY IN ART AND AS ART

The body is not only depicted in art. It is used in making art, or it is transformed to become artwork itself.

THE BODY AS ART MATERIAL

The human body is material for art making. It can be painted or sculpted, or it can be part of a performance or spectacle. In all these instances, the living body energizes, personalizes, or adds emotional content to the artwork. We have already seen an example of body art in the tattooed face of *Tomika Te Mutu* (see Figure 13.20), where his skin is the canvas upon which the artwork is made. The marks on the face of the *Male Torso*

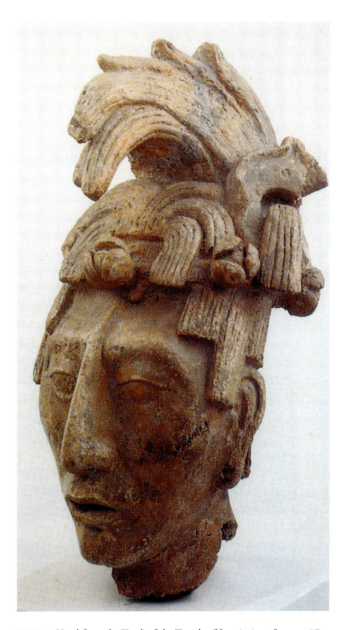

13.28 *Head from the Tomb of the Temple of Inscriptions.* Stucco, 17 inches high. Maya. Palenque, Chiapas, Mexico, mid–late seventh century. Museo Nacional de Antropología, Mexico City. Photo © 2004 Metropolitan Museum of Art, New York.

(Ancestor figure) (see Figure 13.15) from Baule may be scarification patterns. In both cases, the body art has great cultural significance.

The Mayan *Head from the Tomb of the Temple of Inscriptions* from Mexico (Figure 13.28), dated mid to late seventh century, shows how the human body is plastic and moldable, a kind of raw material from which works of art can be made. To the Mayans, a flat, sloping forehead was beautiful and aesthetically pleasing, so they bound and compressed infants' heads to deform the shape as they were growing to achieve the desired results. Hair was bluntly cut at different levels and woven with jade ornaments, cotton threads, and flowers. The stair-step cut on the sides and the top plume of hair were common designs. The resulting human head was a living artistic creation, the image of which is reproduced in this stucco sculpture in the round, which was once brightly painted. This portrait sculpture of a ruler known as Shield II (or *Pacal II* in Mayan) was found next to his tomb. Likewise, the *Olmec Head* (see Figure 13.1) represents a person whose skull had been purposely distorted according to cultural ideals.

Body ornamentation is an art form in many traditional African cultures, where rituals are the supremely important events for the community, governing all aspects of life, death, everyday survival, and interaction with the spirit world. In many of these cultures, body painting is equivalent to wearing masks or costumes. Among the Ngere people in the late twentieth century, girls after initiation paint their torsos white and their faces in brilliant colors, as in *Ngere Girl Prepared for a Festival* (Figure 13.29). The patterns of color are similar to the way the face can be abstracted and broken down into parts in sculpture, while the parallel lines in the white paint echo both chisel marks and sculptural hair patterns. Body painting, like tattooing, makes the living body into a work of art, expands its power and its protection, announcing the status of the person in the community—in this case, an initiated girl.

The sculpting of the human body was the subject matter in Eleanor Antin's *Carving: A Traditional Sculpture,* documented in 1972 (Figure 13.30). Her performance was the attempt to create a traditional Greek sculpture from her own

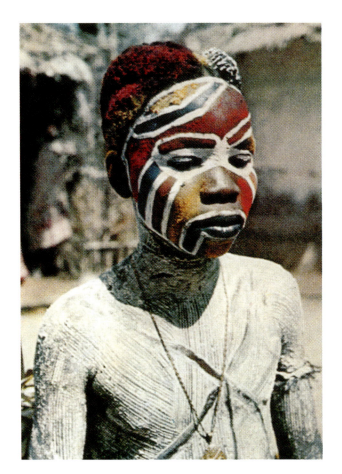

 13.29 *Ngere Girl Prepared for a Festival.* Body painting. Africa, late twentieth century. Photograph by Dominique Darbois.

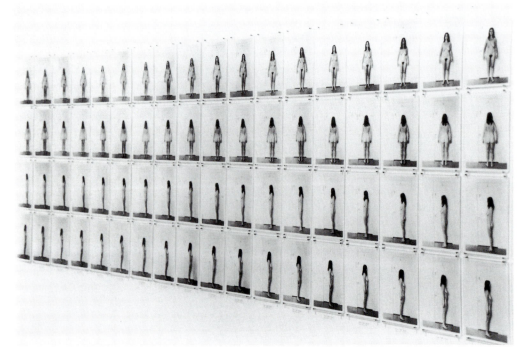

13.30 ELEANOR ANTIN. *Carving: A Traditional Sculpture* (detail). Photographic documentation. USA, 1972. Collection of the Art Institute of Chicago. Courtesy Ronald Feldman Fine Arts, New York.

body, according to the process outlined in *Greek Sculptors at Work* by Carl Bluemel (Phaidon, 1969):

> The Greek Sculptor worked at his block from all four sides and carved away one thin layer after another; and with every layer removed from the block, new forms appeared. The decisive point is, however, that the Greek sculptor always removed an entire layer right around the statue. He never worked just a leg or an arm or a head, but kept the whole in view. . . . Thus the figure which started as a block was worked over by the sculptor at least a hundred times . . . becoming increasingly richer, more rounded and lifelike until it reached completion. (quoted in Sayre 1989: 77)

Antin used her body as art material, and dieting was her method of removing layer after layer from her body until it "reached completion." She lost ten pounds over thirty-six days of dieting, and photographed herself every day from all four sides to document her body's daily changes, minimal yet perceptible. All together, *Carving: A Traditional Sculpture* covered twenty running feet of wall space with nudes. Antin's work was finished when she, as artist, reached an "ideal image." Her photo documentation of her efforts to carve the ideal body show just the opposite: she (and, in fact, all other living women) always falls short in the eyes of a faultfinding observer.

Antin's work points out that what appears to be her own concept of the ideal female form is the product of the fashion, fitness, and diet industries that glorify thinness and have created the contemporary phenomenon of eating disorders. Antin's photo documentation mimics the format of before/after makeovers that are common in fashion magazines. The format of her work also recalls Muybridge's studies of human and animal locomotion (see Figure 13.19), giving them the quality of scientific documentation and investigation. It reveals how much science is based on and believes in the idea that vision/observation leads to truth.

CONNECTION
Peter Paul Rubens's Abduction of the Daughters of Leucippus *(Figure 14.8, page 406) shows the ideal European female body in the 1600s.*

Ana Mendieta created a number of outdoor performances that dealt with her body directly or the trace of her body on the earth. Individual works in the series, called *Silueta* (Silhouette), were performed in Iowa and in Mexico from 1973 until 1980 and exist now only as documentary photographs. In *Arbol de la Vida, No. 294,* dated 1977 (Figure 13.31), Mendieta made herself into a body sculpture covered with mud and straw. She posed against a tree in a manner reminiscent of ancient fertility goddesses, leaving traces of mud on the bark. The site of

her performance was very dramatic, with a massive tree growing at the edge of a deeply cut creek bed. In other works in the *Silueta* series, Mendieta sculpted the mud or used stones or flowers to trace the outline of her body on the earth. It was important to use her living body in these performances because they became like rituals in which the energy of her living being was joined with that of the earth, which she believed was a force that was omnipresent and female. For both Antin's and Mendieta's performances, photo documentation is all that remains.

CONNECTION
Review the discussion of ancient fertility goddesses, such as Idol from Amorgos *(Figure 8.2, page 197).*

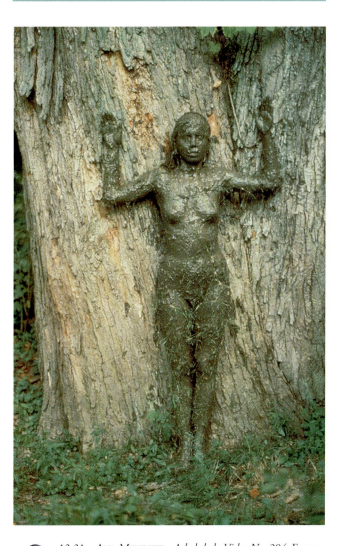

 13.31 ANA MENDIETA. *Arbol de la Vida, No. 294.* From the series *Arbol de la Vida/Silueta* (Tree of Life/Silhouette). Color photograph documenting the earth/body sculpture with artist, tree trunk, and mud, at Old Man's Creek, Iowa City, Iowa. Cuba/USA, 1977. Collection Ignacio C. Mendieta. Courtesy of Gallery Lelong, New York.

In some cases, the artist relinquished control in a performance. Yoko Ono wrote scripts that set up situations for artworks, but the exact outcome of the pieces was determined by chance or by spontaneous audience participation. In a 1964 performance of *Cut Piece* (Figure 13.32), Yoko Ono entered an empty stage clothed in a black dress, and sat/knelt in a traditional position for Japanese women. She held aloft scissors and then placed them in front of herself, as if preparing for *seppuku* (ritual suicide). She then invited and encouraged audience members to cut away her clothing. As the performance proceeded, she sat without showing emotion. Long pauses occurred during the performance. Ono was influenced by John Cage, a composer who believed that the silences between sounds were as

important as the music. More and more skin showed until she was nearly nude and bare chested, and the performance ended as she gasped and covered herself.

Cut Piece alludes to a number of ideas: the traditional male sexual prerogative over the female body; the display of the body for the consuming gaze; violation and control; and herd mentality among humans. Roles are confused in the piece: Ono, apparently the violated, also set up the situation. Yet the audience members acted freely, as it was beyond her control to dictate what they did. The artist's body and the actions of the audience are the art piece, not the photo document we see in this book. The physical presence of real bodies, the quality of spectacle, the uncertainty, and the palpable

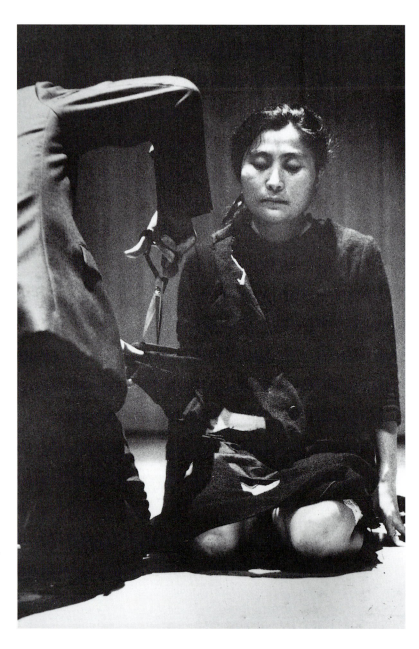

13.32   YOKO ONO. *Cut Piece.* Photo documentation of performance at Yamaichi Concert Hall, Kyoto. Japan/USA, 1964. Collection of the artist, courtesy Studio One. See also the text accompanying Figure 6.27.

experience of time passing are potent elements that a photo still cannot convey. Ono was part of the **Fluxus** movement in New York, which sought to create a kind of anti-art or non-art. In Fluxus, art was conceived as an artist-initiated experience rather than an object, like a painting or sculpture.

CONNECTION *In Chapter 16, the section titled "The Visual Arts within the Performing Arts" provides more discussion of performance art.*

THE BODY AS AN ART TOOL

The first and most important tools of artists are their bodies: their fingers, hands, and arms, guided by their minds. In making works of art, artists continually touch the entire surface of their works. This is obvious with sculptors who model clay with their hands. But even painters work the entire surface of their images with sensitive brushes and often adjust or finish their work with their fingertips. Although the touch of photographers and computer artists may leave no mark on their works, their hands are nonetheless essential and present. In *Fanny (Fingerpainting),* which we saw in Figure 13.4, artist Chuck Close created the woman's enormous head in detail, showing the texture of her hair, skin wrinkles, her watery eyes, and the cloth of her dress. The entire work was painted with the artist's hand and fingerprints. Although it looks like a photograph, the face in fact is a mass of smudges, a record of

everywhere the artist touched. The mark of the hand relates to fossils and the handprints in prehistoric cave paintings and to the first marks we made as children.

When Jackson Pollock painted *Lucifer* (Figure 13.33) in 1947, the motion of his entire body was very significant. This style of painting is called "gestural abstraction" or "action painting." The "action" came from the movement of the artist himself. The canvas was laid down on the ground, and Pollock poured, dripped, and flung paint upon it as he stood at the edges or walked across the surface. He lunged and swirled about in furious outbursts, which were followed by periods of reflection. His body movements were fixed and recorded in the paint surface, which is a rhythmic mesh of drips, congealed blobs, and looping swirls.

Pollock's act of painting and the painting itself were frequently described in quasi-combat terms. He saw the canvas on the ground as a plane of action, but when hanging on the wall in front of the viewer, it became a plane of confrontation. Pollock believed his spontaneous, energetic painting style fit the mood of the United States immediately after World War II. He also believed that the power of his unconscious mind was being released in action painting and that his painting style was a burst of primal energy and a release from civilized constraints. The action painter was seen as being an isolated genius, almost always male, whose work had no morals and no narrative, just pure paint and pure body action. Pollock as a painter of action reflected the ideas that made the cowboy or the "rebel without a cause" so appealing. His paint handling was seen as sophisticated and a mark of artistic genius.

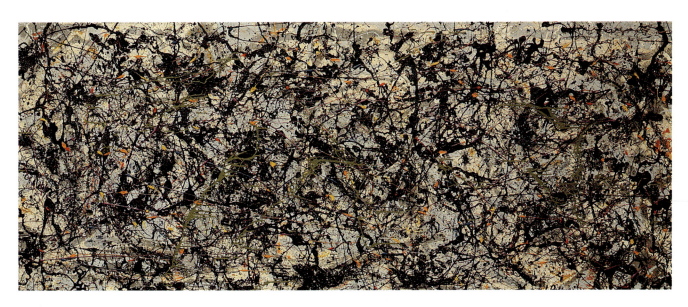

 13.33   JACKSON POLLOCK. *Lucifer.* Oil, aluminum paint, and enamel on canvas, approximately 3'5" × 8'9". USA, 1947. Collection of Harry Ward and Mary Margaret Anderson. © 2004 Pollock-Krasner Foundation / Artists Rights Society (ARS), New York. See also the text accompanying Figure 4.4.

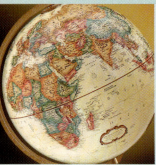

Courtesy of Replogle Globes, Inc., Broadview, IL.

This era saw the increased development of centralized states, in some cases formed around ethnic units. Also, beginning in 1700, the world population grew dramatically for four reasons: better immunity to diseases that had been spread by the first explorers; a period of climate warming, which improved agricultural conditions; new food sources through trade; and the invention of gunpowder, which allowed rulers to control larger areas with their armies and to create more stability.

The Ottoman Empire in Turkey and the Middle East continued to flourish, in spite of unsuccessful bids to conquer areas of Central Europe. Africa's heartlands continued to be self-ruling and

Below:

Map 7 Latin America in the Eighteenth Century.

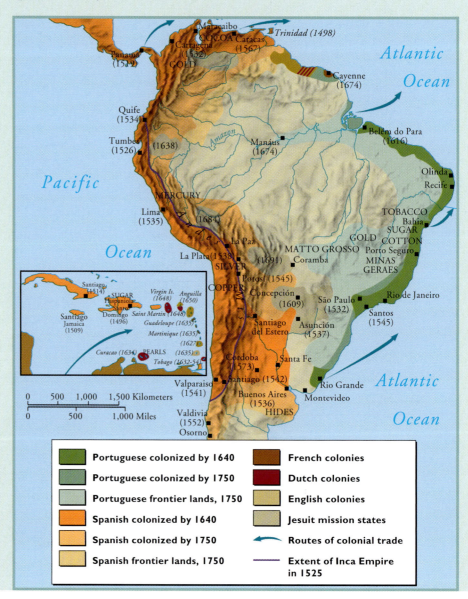

Legend	
Portuguese colonized by 1640	French colonies
Portuguese colonized by 1750	Dutch colonies
Portuguese frontier lands, 1750	English colonies
Spanish colonized by 1640	Jesuit mission states
Spanish colonized by 1750	Routes of colonial trade
Spanish frontier lands, 1750	Extent of Inca Empire in 1525

relatively isolated, although the coastal regions were engaged in the slave trade with Europe. The Ashanti Kingdom was established in West Africa in 1680. Likewise, in Southeast Asia, Dutch and English traders continued in the lucrative spice trade, but the mainland areas were generally unaffected and self-ruled.

The Mughal Empire continued in India, and Akbar (1556–1605) oversaw a period of humane rule, peace, and prosperity. The empire subsequently weakened throughout the eighteenth century. After a long peasant uprising that ended in 1644, China also saw a period of remarkable tolerance, prosperity, and unity, especially under the reign of Kangxi (1661–1722). Japan continued to be ruled by local warlords until 1603, when Tokugawa Ieyasu unified Japan under his command and closed the country to foreigners. The Japanese merchant class grew in numbers and wealth for the next few hundred years.

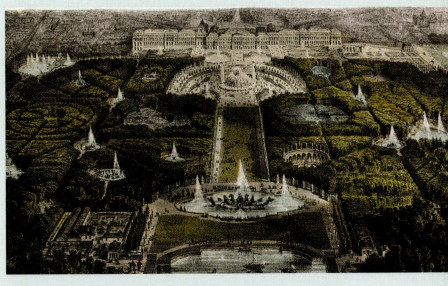

Above:
Versailles. Anonymous seventeenth-century painting. © Bettmann / Corbis.

Europe had already embarked on a period of global expansion. With the exception of limited access to a few ports, Europeans were kept out of China, Japan, and India. However, they rapidly colonized the Americas. North America was divided into English, French, and Spanish colonies. The population in the English colonies continued to be mostly European, both racially and culturally. Spanish rule was the most extensive, covering western North America, Central America, and most of South America, except for Portuguese Brazil. At this time, Latin America (see map) began to emerge as a cultural entity, although it was composed of many individual states. Latin American societies were multiracial, reflecting intermarriage among native populations, Europeans, and Africans since the 1500s. Because Latin America was more remote, European rulers exercised less direct control, and large, local landowners developed extensive power.

In Europe itself, 1560–1650 was a period of crisis, caused by religious wars between Catholics and Protestants, competition for colonial lands, and hardship caused by crop failures. In response to the unrest, new centralized powers emerged after 1650. In some cases, these were absolute rulers who governed all aspects of their country with tight control—for example, Louis XIV of France, Peter the Great of Russia, and the rulers of Prussia. Louis XIV lived in his lavish palace, *Versailles* (see image in history box), a fitting setting for his absolute rule as the Sun King, which also helped him to control the nobility. The Habsburgs ruled Austria, but the nobility maintained considerable power. England developed a constitutional monarchy.

This was also the period of the Enlightenment, which saw advances in philosophy, science, literature, and human rights. Increasingly, learned people believed that men were entitled to life, liberty, the pursuit of happiness, property ownership, and individual rights. That belief contributed to the power and prosperity of the Dutch middle class, which Rembrandt (see Figure 13.8) depicted in many paintings. The rising support for human rights eventually led to the curtailing of the power of kings and contributed to the American Revolution in 1776 and the French Revolution in 1789.

Indus River Civilizations	**3000 BCE**	*Torso* (Harappa)
Olmec Civilizations	**900**	*Olmec Head*
Classical Greece	**400**	Polykleitos: *Doryphoros*
Hellenistic Greece		
Mauryan Dynasty founded in India		
	100	*Laocoön and His Sons*
		Yakshi
Mayan Civilization	**600 CE**	*Head from the Tomb of the Temple of Inscriptions*
	1100	Gislebertus: *The Last Judgment*
Renaissance—Europe		
Reign of Akbar—India	**1500**	Michelangelo: *David*
Tokugawa Shogunate—Japan		
Thirty Years War—Europe, 1618–1648		
Louis XIV of France	**1650**	Rembrandt: *Self-Portrait*
Kangxi of China		
Enlightenment		
	1700	
Latin American Independence Movement		
Victorian Era—England	**1850**	
		Tomika Te Mutu
Freud and Psychoanalysis		Muybridge: *Handspring*
	1890	van Gogh: *Portrait of Dr. Gachet*
		Munch: *The Scream*
	1900	*Male Torso* (Ancestor), Baule
End of the Ottoman Empire		Boccioni: *Unique Forms of Continuity in Space*

World War I	**1920**	Kanzan: *Study for the Portrait of Okakura Tenshin*
	1940	Kahlo: *Self-Portrait with Monkey*
	1950	Pollock: *Lucifer*
Death of Stalin		
Khrushchev era—Soviet Union		
	1960	Hamilton: *Just What Is It . . . ?*
		Ono: *Cut Piece*
Death of Mao Zedong—China	**1970**	Antin: *Carving: A Traditional Sculpture*
		Mendieta: *Arbol de la Vida, No. 294*
	1980	Sherman: *Untitled Film Still #35*
		Close: *Fanny (Fingerpainting)*
		Ngere Girl Prepared for a Festival
Tiananmen Square Uprising—Beijing		
Reunification of Germany	**1990**	Burson: *Untitled image from Faces*
Creation of the European Union		Freud: *Leigh under the Skylight*
		Wilke: *Intra-Venus*
		Serrano: *The Morgue (Hacked to Death II)*
Digital Video, Digital Imaging		
Mandela Becomes President of South Africa		Mori: *Star Doll*
	2000	Viola: *Dolorosa*
		Kim: *Installation*
		Zittel: *A-Z Time Tunnel*

In portraiture, we might intimately encounter either a unique individual or a person who conforms to mass media types. The body has been idealized in art and alludes to a range of ideas about human nature. Other artwork emphasizes the tragic or the debased in human nature. The body can be measured and studied like a machine.

Increasingly, humans include themselves as part of the larger physical, spiritual, and technological world. This dissolving of boundaries transforms the human body, first at the skin layer and then below the skin with the very structure of the skeleton and muscles. Physical and psychological pressures can distort the body. More frequently, there is a strong tie between the human body and the things that humans build.

In artwork that deals with sickness and death, the horrible and the beautiful often are mixed.

The body can be either art material or art tool. It is malleable and can be scarred, sculpted, or painted. It is a primary element in performance art. It is the most wonderful art-making tool we have.

FOOD FOR THOUGHT

A number of the artworks we studied in this chapter seem to fall outside strict definitions of art. In the United States, we generally do not consider tattooing as art, nor body painting, weight loss, or hair styling. Yet probably we have all seen examples of piercing, tattooing, hair cutting, and styles of dressing that seem like artistic expressions. In some cases, the boundary between art and fashion is hard to determine.

■ What do you think are the most powerful ways in which individuals express themselves visually in your world today?

Science and medicine are meant to serve humans and their bodies. However, the fascination with scientific measurement and comparison can result in disaster. For example, in the late nineteenth century, criminologists believed that certain skull shapes indicated individuals capable of deviant behavior; thus, you could be condemned if you had bumps in the wrong places. Also, at times, some medical cures have caused huge amounts of suffering.

■ What social tools do we have to keep science and medicine in check?

YOUR CD-ROM RESOURCES

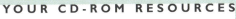

■ World History in Context
■ Exploring Art Timeline
■ Flashcards
■ Food for Thought
■ Companion Site
    Chapter 13 Quiz
    InfoTrac® College Edition Readings
    Artist Flashcards
    Online Study Guide

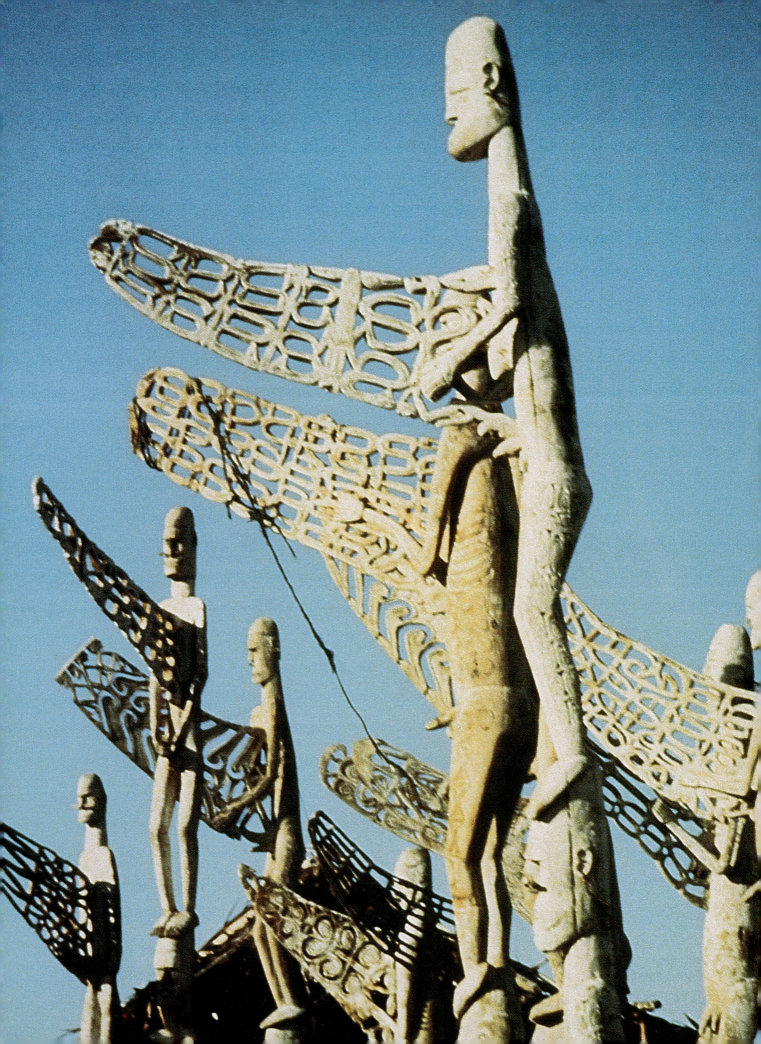

CHAPTER 14

RACE, GENDER, CLAN, AND CLASS

INTRODUCTION

All people are born with a particular combination of racial background, gender, class standing, and genealogy that will contribute to their personal status and life experience. Humans are social beings. We seek community. We develop our very selves by imitating others or reacting to them. Most people live intimately within families or clans. Most regularly socialize within their class.

On the downside, these factors may trigger prejudice and discrimination. Waves of prejudice have inundated the United States throughout its history. Moreover, although gender may be a matter of genetics, gender roles are not. How should men and women look? What roles should they have in society? How should power be distributed between them?

Because these factors are so central to our lives, it is hardly surprising that they figure prominently in many works of art. Some questions for this chapter are:

How does art help forge racial identity?

How is gender tied to ideas of what is beautiful or what is heroic?

How should men and women look? How does art make that clear?

How does art identify a clan?

When are ancestors important to a clan, and how does art help to make that relationship possible?

How do paintings and drawings give us images of the ways different classes live?

How does art reflect the tastes, ideas, and needs of different classes?

Why does possession of a certain kind of art indicate a person's class status?

Bisj Poles. Detail of Figure 14.17. Photograph by Tobias Schneebaum.

RACE AND ART

This section contains a number of artworks that deal with race. In some instances, art is used to purposefully form a cohesive identity for a racial group, by memorializing the group's history or recording its distinct ethnic culture. Other artworks challenge negative attitudes that majorities develop about minorities living among them. Still others look beyond national boundaries.

ART THAT PROMOTES ETHNIC HISTORY AND VALUES

These works of art examine or illustrate the history or values of a certain ethnic group.

In the 1800s and early 1900s in Russia, Jews were considered outsiders because of laws and traditions originated and maintained both by the Jews themselves and by the Russians. The Jews actively maintained their own identity by speaking their own language and supporting a separate educational system. But Russian law also enforced separateness—Jews were allowed to live only in certain areas and were restricted from attending universities. That separateness was often passively accepted, but at times Jews were massacred and villages burned in acts of anti-Semitic terrorism. Even so, Russian Jews were often cultural innovators and, in many cases, were known throughout Europe as artists, musicians, and writers. This occurred in part because of the rise of secular humanism, which allowed people to seek good in others, regardless of their religion.

Marc Chagall was a prominent Jewish artist who grew up in Russia but spent most of his long life in Paris, France. Many of his paintings imaginatively recreated Jewish village folklife in Russia at the turn of the twentieth century, which was in fact disintegrating due to political, religious, and economic pressures. Chagall's imagery was a personal, sometimes incoherent, reordering of bits and pieces of his experience. Nevertheless, he depicted many aspects, both negative and positive, of Jewish village life in Russia, including folktales, festivals, marriages, funeral practices, and suffering and death caused by antisemitism. In *Over Vitebsk,* dated 1915–1920 (Figure 14.1), Chagall painted a large, solitary figure floating over his own village, representing thousands of Eastern European Jewish refugees who fled to Russia, displaced by World War I. Many of these people later immigrated to the United States. In Yiddish, "passing through" is expressed as wandering "over the village," which Chagall painted literally by means of the floating figure, the refugee. A sense of rootlessness and upheaval pervades the picture. The space in the foreground of the picture appears fractured, and Chagall used the cubist device to represent instability. The picture contains Chagall's memories of

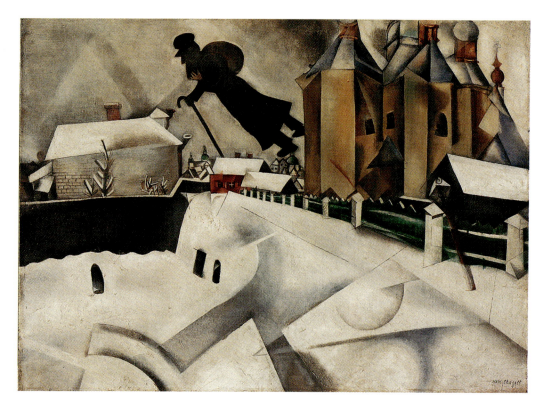

14.1   MARC CHAGALL. *Over Vitebsk* (after a painting of 1914). Oil on canvas, 26¹/₂" × 36¹/₂". Russia/France, 1915–1920. The Museum of Modern Art, New York. Acquired through the Lillian P. Bliss Bequest, 1949.
© MOMA / Art Resource, NY / © 2004 Artists Rights Society (ARS), New York / ADAGP, Paris.

Vitebsk, its architecture, its streets, its icy winter landscape. The colors are **Fauvist,** an art movement that originated in Paris in which color was exaggerated in paintings for greater power and expression.

James VanDerZee was a commercial studio photographer whose works are a record of the Black Renaissance of Harlem, generally dating from 1919–1929 (he continued to photograph the Harlem residents through the 1940s). VanDerZee's photographs contrast strongly with the two kinds of images of African Americans from that time. The most common were crude racial caricatures of African Americans from postcards, comics, magazines, picture books, and greeting cards. On the other hand, a few photographers depicted African Americans as helpless victims of racism, and their situation as a problem to be solved. VanDerZee, however, was photographing his peers, his friends, and his community. In his images, African Americans are confident, autonomous, healthy, and self-aware. VanDerZee was part of the black middle class, like the women pictured in *Society Ladies,* photographed in 1927 (Figure 14.2). They were intellectuals, merchants, and writers who demanded full participation for blacks in U.S. politics and culture. The furniture and trappings of comfort surround his well-dressed sit-

ters. Their poses convey a variety of emotions, including confidence, humor, directness, and dreamy wistfulness.

VanDerZee was influenced by films of the 1920s and 1930s, and encouraged sitters to take poses from the films. At times, VanDerZee provided costumes and props that allowed his sitters to expand their personalities. He manipulated and retouched his images. The results were confident, proud portraits that cannot be seen as racial caricatures or images of victims.

CONNECTION

Another artist of the Harlem Renaissance, Jacob Lawrence, painted the history of African Americans in the Western Hemisphere. For more, see No. 36, During the Truce Toussaint . . . (Figure 12.12, page 347).

ART THAT CRITICIZES RACISM

Unflattering images of African Americans have been common in popular culture over the past 150 years—for example, the pickaninny, Little Black Sambo, and Uncle Tom. Another is

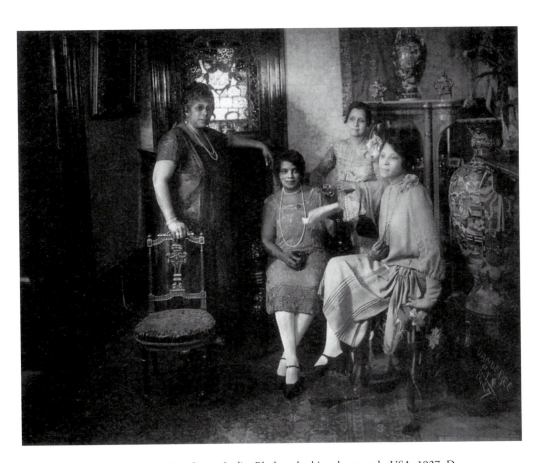

 14.2 James VanDerZee. *Society Ladies.* Black-and-white photograph. USA, 1927. Donna Mussenden VanDerZee.

Aunt Jemima, a domestic servant whose title of "aunt" was a commonly used term of subordination and familiarity for African American domestic servants, nannies, and maids. Aunt Jemima is a caricatured jolly, fat character who has been used recently to sell commercially prepared pancake mix. In the 1972 mixed-media piece *The Liberation of Aunt Jemima* (Figure 14.3), Betye Saar uses three versions of Aunt Jemima to question and turn around such images. The oldest version is the small image at the center, in which a cartooned Jemima hitches up a squalling child on her hip. In the background, the modern version shows a thinner Jemima with lighter skin, deemphasizing her Negroid features. The older one makes Jemima a caricature, while the new one implies she is more attractive if she appears less black.

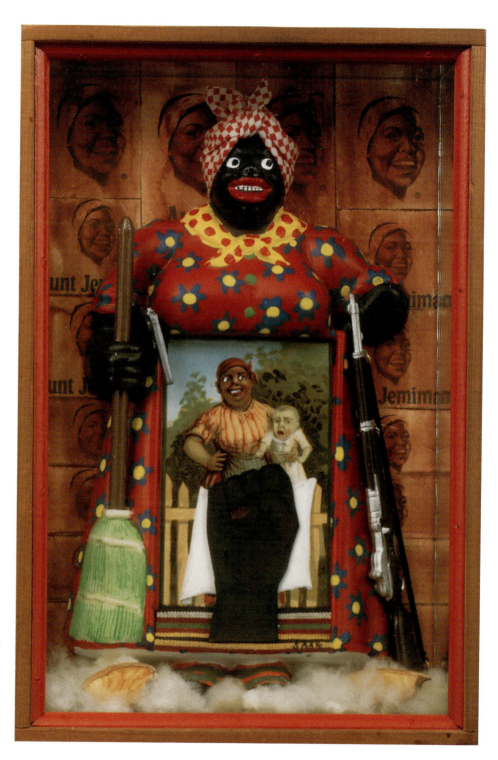

14.3   BETYE SAAR. *The Liberation of Aunt Jemima.* Mixed media, 11³/₄" × 8" × 2³/₄". USA, 1972. University Art Museum, University of California, Berkeley. Purchased with the aid of National Endowment for the Arts funds.

The middle Jemima is the largest figure and the most emphasized. Her checked and polka-dotted clothing is very bright and colorful. Her black skin makes her white eyes and teeth look like dots and checks, too. This Jemima holds a rifle and pistol as well as a broom. A black-power fist makes a strong silhouette shape in front of all the figures, introducing militant power to the image. The idea of Aunt Jemima, in any of its forms, can no longer seem innocuous. Saar enshrined these images in a shallow glass display box to make them venerable. Symmetry and pattern are strong visual elements.

In *The Artifact Piece,* performed in 1986 (Figure 14.4), Native American artist James Luna challenged the way contemporary American culture and museums have presented his race as essentially extinct and vanished. In this performance piece, Luna "installed" himself in an exhibition case in the San Diego Museum of Man in a section on the Kumeyaay Indians, who once inhabited San Diego County. All around were other exhibition areas with mannequins and props showing the long-lost Kumeyaay way of life. Among them, Luna posed himself, living and breathing, dressed only in a leather cloth, with labels around him pointing out his scars from wounds suffered when drunk and fighting. Various personal items were displayed in a glass case, including contemporary ritual objects used currently on the La Jolla reservation where Luna lives, recordings by the Rolling Stones and Jimi Hendrix, shoes, political buttons, and other cultural artifacts. The mixture of elements revealed a living, developing culture.

In this striking piece, Luna challenged the viewer to reconsider what museums teach about cultures and what constitutes a cultural artifact. Museum artifacts may be simply the things that, by chance, happened to survive. In other cases, the white culture chooses to keep and view certain objects and ignore or destroy others. Thus, we learn less about Native American culture than we learn about the white culture's ideas about Native American cultures. In addition, museums often discount or eliminate living cultures of today. Museums (and museumgoers!) are often only interested in their own preconceived idea of "cultural purity." "Authentic Indians" are those who are long dead. Native Americans who are alive today are less interesting to museums, because they are cultural mixtures who may wear Reeboks rather than moccasins. Luna sees himself in a new way. Although he still considers himself a warrior, he is a new one who uses art and the legal system to fight for Native Americans. In *Artifact Piece,* Luna also touches on the effects of alcohol on Native Americans.

WHO IS LOOKING AT WHOM?

In the United States, hundreds of images are produced every day that deal with other cultures, so we develop ideas about foreign or ethnic groups from the mass media images we consume. But who is making those images of others, and why? And what about the viewer? The position of the viewer is a privileged position, "consuming" the images of other people without directly interacting with them. Art and cultural critics

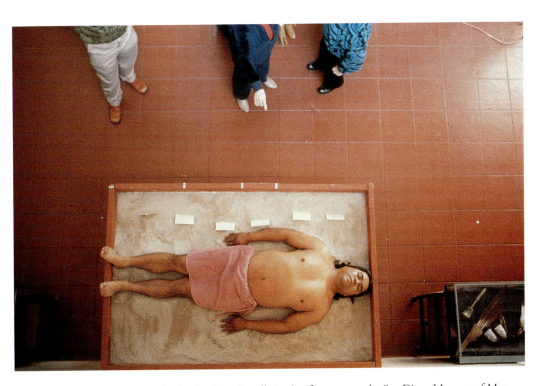

14.4   JAMES LUNA. *The Artifact Piece.* Installation/performance at the San Diego Museum of Man. USA, 1986. Museum of Man, San Diego.

have written extensively about this issue of the gaze, considering how the artwork is used, by whom, and for what purpose. How can the use of imagery reflect a power relationship in the "real world," or how might it be used to maintain such a relationship?

Tseng Kwong Chi turned around the act of looking in a series of photographic self-portraits, such as *Disneyland, California,* photographed in 1979 (Figure 14.5). While Western industrial countries have produced a wealth of images of peoples from the rest of the world, Tseng Kwong Chi produced images of Asians looking at the West and made them for a Western audience. In his many self-portraits, he posed in front of tourist sites in the United States, such as the Grand Canyon, Mount Rushmore, and the Statue of Liberty. In all his images, he wore a Mao jacket to emphatically identify himself as Chinese, rather than Japanese, Korean, or any other Asian ethnicity. He took his own picture—the shutter release cable is evident—to show that he was the author of his own image. He appears as a tourist, but with mirror glasses. We cannot see his eyes, while he critically appraises what he sees of the West from an Asian point of view. He is unyielding and severe next to the goofy, grinning Mickey Mouse. We, the viewers of this photograph, have been displaced from our positions of power, as Tseng has taken on the role of the non-interactive viewer.

Tseng also took on the issues of individuality in situations in which racial stereotypes make everyone in a group seem alike. Tseng's rigid pose is repeated in all the self-portraits in this series to emphasize his unmistakable, unique individuality from picture to picture. This was done to counter the stereotypes that Asians are all alike, that they shun any show of public individuality, or that they avoid making themselves stand out.

CONNECTION

We also encounter the issue of the gaze in Lewis Hine's Leo, 48 Inches High . . . (Figure 12.10, page 345; see especially the Food for Thought section of Chapter 12). In Chapter 8, review the section on "The Feminine Body and the Gaze," page 209.

GENDER ISSUES

Every culture sets up standards and roles to which both genders are expected to conform. Society dictates and constrains acceptable behavior for women and for men. Artwork from different eras and cultures often gives us clues about those social restrictions and, in some cases, is actually part of making them.

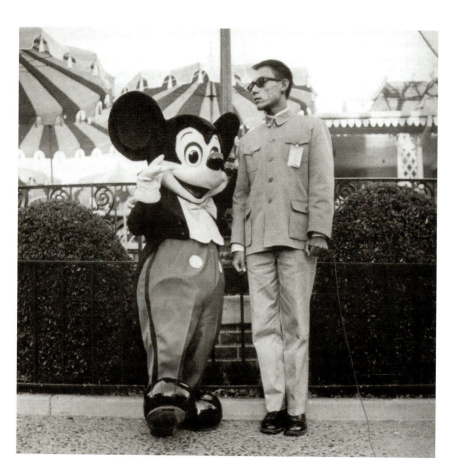

14.5 TSENG KWONG CHI. *Disneyland, California.* Gelatin Silver Print, 36" × 36". China/USA, 1979. © 2004 Estate Tseng Kwong Chi / Artists Rights Society (ARS), New York.

ART AND RITUAL PERPETUATING GENDER ROLES

We will begin by examining gender concepts, ritual, and art among the Sepik people of New Guinea in the South Pacific, focusing on the early twentieth century, before foreign influences had seriously disrupted the indigenous social order and religion. Gender differences and the power relationships between men and women were extremely important to the Sepik tribes. Men dominated women in much of Sepik life, and art and rituals reinforced and dramatized this relationship. Sepik art also made men powerful in war.

These rituals, called "Tambaran," took place in large A-frame cult houses, with carved beams and paintings on the gables and ceiling. The largest were eighty to one hundred feet high. They contained the sacred carvings, masks, and musical instruments used in initiations. When rituals were in progress, woven mats covered the entrances and preserved secrecy. The cult houses were gendered; that is, the Sepik men saw the ridgepole as phallic and the interior of the house as the belly of a woman. Men saw their rituals as creating men from infants, usurping women's procreative power. Unlike the Western notion that an individual exists from birth, many South Pacific peoples believed that a person's very being is built through a lifetime of ritual experiences.

Men invested their vigor into the paintings and carvings that hung in the cult house. They gave them away to pass their spirits on to those at lower stages of initiation. These objects do not explain the Tambaran cult or illustrate it. Rather, they become effective or invigorated when they are used in cult rituals.

Sepik men made many different styles of hooks so that spiritual items or food bags could be suspended from the roof beams of the cult houses. The *Stylized figure of a spirit, known as Yipwon* (Figure 14.6) is one kind, with aesthetic embellish-

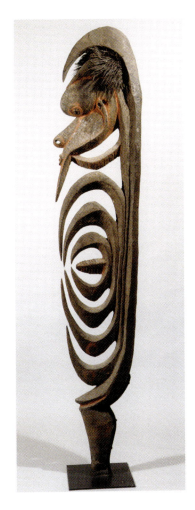

14.6 *Stylized figure of a spirit, known as Yipwon.* Yimar culture, Sepik River region, Papua New Guinea, c. twentieth century. Wood. Collection Philip Goldman, London, Great Britian. Werner Forman/Art Resource, NY.

ments that can compromise functionality. Yipwon is the spirit of hunting and warfare, and the sculpture has a series of aggressive, rhythmic C-shapes, which may be abstracted ribs or phallic shapes. It was intended to be seen in profile. Large yipwon figures were the property of the whole clan. Smaller versions were also carved. They were owned by individual men, who carried them as amulets.

Paintings could be ritually powerful, too. In the *Painting from a Cult House* at Slei (Figure 14.7), from the early twentieth century, the curves create multiple faces, with gaping, tooth-filled mouths, large noses, and numerous eyes. Faces can be read stacked or superimposed on each other. The curves and spirals fill the triangular shape of the painting—cramped and small at the edges, swelling into large, aggressive forms in the middle. The colors—black, red, and off-white—are bold, with high contrast from dark to

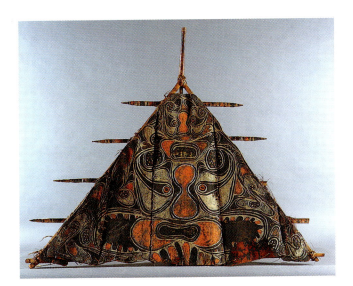

14.7 *Painting from a Cult House.* Palm leaves on a bamboo frame, painted with earth pigments, 44" × 61^1/$_2$". Slei, Middle Sepik Region, Papua New Guinea, c. twentieth century. Museum der Kulturen, Basel, Switzerland. See also the text accompanying Figure 5.16.

light. Major forms, such as mouths and eyes, are outlined repeatedly in alternating black and white lines, resulting in vibrating patterns that express the idea of fearsome vigor. The arrangement of the paintings in the cult house indicated the specific family and clan relationships among the men. The paintings were made on bark or natural fibers from trees in the area.

We have seen how gender roles are related to maintaining power and to art making. Although we focused only on the Sepik people, most cultures, past or present, incorporate these relationships.

GENDER REFLECTED IN ART AND ARCHITECTURE

Gender roles are often revealed in art and are reflected in architecture and fashion.

Our first work, *Abduction of the Daughters of Leucippus,* painted by Peter Paul Rubens in 1617 (Figure 14.8), is another example of the European fascination with sexual exotica, like the *Grande Odalisque,* which we saw in Chapter 8. The scene comes from Greek mythology. Castor and Pollux were twin sons of Zeus, and they captured a philosopher's two daughters as they were out horseback riding. Aided by Cupids who hold the horses' reins, the two immortals lower the women, who resist with dramatic but ineffective, fluttering gestures. Interestingly, this painting is also commonly referred to as *Rape of the Daughters of Leucippus,* as an old meaning of *rape* was "the carrying away of someone by force."

Blue skies, shimmering cloth, and a variety of textures add to the rich surface of the image and the sensual color harmonies. The composition places all figures in a diamond shape, which is compact and yet expressive of movement because of its instability. Darks predominate on the left, acting as a foil to the lighter areas in the center and at the right. The forms are modeled in color and lit with a marvelous glow. Various textures, such as armor, satin, flesh, and hair, are all expertly painted.

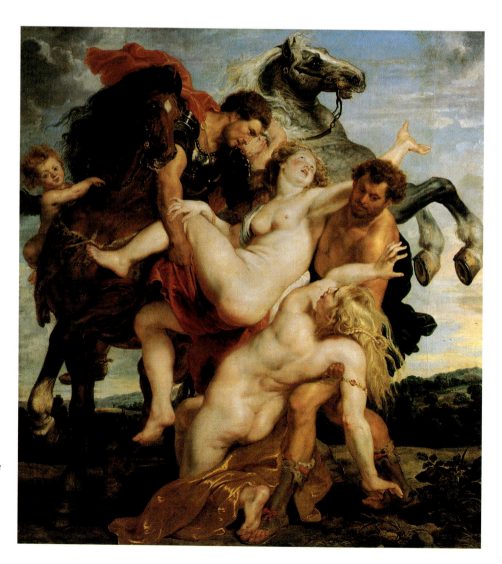

14.8   PETER PAUL RUBENS. *Abduction of the Daughters of Leucippus.* Oil on canvas, 7'3" × 6'10". Flanders, 1617. Alte Pinakothek, Munich. © Scala / Art Resource, NY. See also the text accompanying Figure 5.6.

Through poses, behavior, and clothing, the painting indicates what was considered masculine and feminine during that era. All figures represent ideal body types for their time. The women's voluptuous, soft fleshiness was considered sexually attractive and a sign of health and wealth. Outdoor activity was appropriate for the darker-skinned, muscular men versus the pale women who occupy the domestic interiors. Not only does the painting represent ideal body types, however; it also represents current ideas of gender behavior. Men had privilege over women's bodies. Women learned to be helpless, and they relied on social structures to protect their virtue. The expressions of the men are subdued and determined, while the women's bodies and faces are much more emotional. The men are at least partially clothed—one is in armor—while the women are unclothed and displayed. Throughout Western art history, we see numerous examples of the female nude providing lascivious pleasure for male viewers, legitimized because it was "art."

All kinds of trappings can serve as indicators of masculinity or femininity. In *Oath of the Horatii,* painted in 1784 (Figure 14.9), Jacques-Louis David represents a scene from the early history of ancient Rome, in which three brothers vow to represent the Roman army in a fight to the death against three representatives of an opposing army. Their father hands them their swords, reminding them of the manly virtues of courage and patriotism, while their sisters swoon at the right, in dread and sorrow at the anticipated killing (one of the sisters was to

marry a representative of the opposing army). Heroic actions are a mark of masculinity, reinforced by the women's passivity. In a moment of male bonding, forged in the face of danger, the three brothers become a single force, a part of each other, and each willing to die for the others and for an external cause.

There are other gender indicators. The male dress is rendered in angular lines that contrast with the soft curves of the female attire. The men hold weapons as their job is war, while women's jobs are concerned with children. The architecture's symmetry and the composition's overall balance suggest the orderliness of this world. In this work, images both reflect the "reality" of gender roles and create that "reality." They spring to some extent from existing social conditions, but they also entrench those conditions and make them seem "natural," not just social conventions. The more we see such works, the more we believe them.

In this painting, the classical architectural background is an indicator of masculinity, which was popular during the French Revolutionary era when this painting was executed. The use of classical elements in art and architecture at this time formed a style called **Neo-Classicism,** which was a revival of Greek and Roman aesthetics after the discovery of Pompeii and Herculaneum. Also at this time, French citizens were about to overthrow the oppressive, parasitic French monarchy and aristocracy. The nobility favored decorative architecture called **Rococo,** such as that seen in the

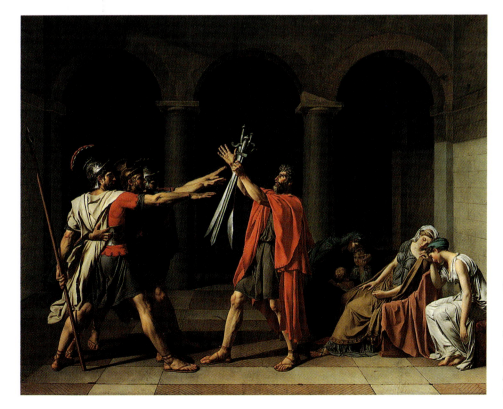

14.9　Jacques-Louis David. *Oath of the Horatii.* Oil on canvas, 10'10" × 14'. France, 1784. Louvre. © Réunion des Musées Nationaux / Art Resource, NY. See also the text accompanying Figure 4.7.

Hall of Mirrors, dated 1734–1739 (Figure 14.10), by François de Cuvilliès. Rococo architecture was seen as female, with its emphasis on the delicate, the curving, the colorful. Square walls and ceilings dissolve in curves, and these curves themselves dissolve under the abundance of nature-based decoration and the reflecting mirrors, crystal, and silver. The ceiling appears to be an open sky, with birds flying from branch to branch of gold-leafed stucco trees. All elements—the architectural shell, the precious materials, the detailed, graceful decorations—contribute to the entire exquisite effect. The French middle class, on the verge of revolt, chose the clean, simple, austere architecture that we see in the background of *Oath of the Horatii* to distinguish themselves from the aristocracy, and as an appropriate symbol for their ideas.

Indeed, in Western culture, architecture is gendered; that is, different styles come to mean or be associated with certain qualities, and those qualities in turn are associated with masculinity or femininity. This goes back at least as far as the ancient Greeks, who saw the Doric Order as masculine and the Ionic as feminine. Although the architecture behind the Horatii was considered manly while the *Hall of Mirrors* was considered feminine and elegant, there is nothing inherent in these styles that requires them to be understood in this way. In another situation, the Horatii background might be seen as bare and oppressive, and the *Hall of Mirrors* to be considered uplifting and stirring to the imagination. The gendered associ-

ations of Western architectural styles continue, as writers commonly associate the modern, bare, high-rise skyscrapers of the late 1960s and 1970s with masculinity.

CONNECTION

The Doric and Ionic Orders are illustrated in Figure 3.5. The Swing (Figure 14.25, page 420) is a Rococo painting by Jean-Honoré Fragonard and reflects the same sensibilities as the Hall of Mirrors.

CRITIQUING GENDER ROLES

In many cultures, people change their bodies to enhance their femininity or masculinity, usually by dieting, plastic surgery, implants, scarification, and various bindings that mold body parts, most often the skull, waist, neck, or feet. These practices can be widely accepted at times. But in times of cultural change, they can become very controversial.

In her work, artist Hung Liu has examined foot binding, practiced in China from the Song Dynasty (960–1279) until the beginning of the twentieth century. Many Chinese women's feet were bound from birth to artificially confine their growth, distorting them into small, twisted fists that were sexually attractive to men. With bound feet, walking was extremely difficult,

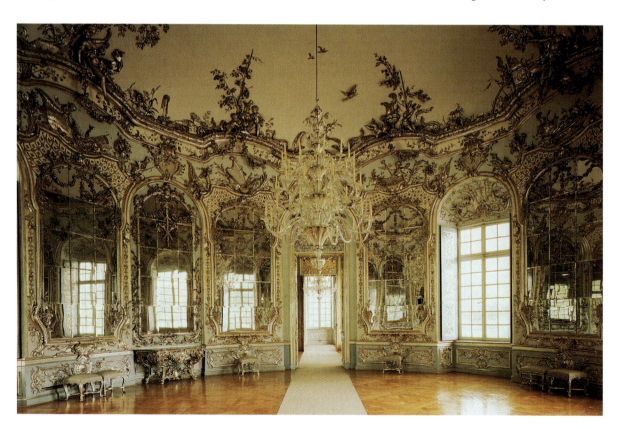

 14.10 FRANÇOIS DE CUVILLIÈS. *Hall of Mirrors.* Amalienburg, Nymphenburg Park, Munich, Germany, 1734–1739. © Scala / Art Resource, NY.

but the mincing steps were considered delicate and lovely. Bound feet left women handicapped, which also ensured that they remained subservient. Many resorted to prostitution when the Chinese Communist government came to power and mandated physical labor for all able-bodied people.

Liu ties oppressive gender practices to broader political repression. In *Trauma,* dated 1989 (Figure 14.11), the woman at the center publicly shows her bound feet. Although bound feet were considered erotic in private, public exposure was a shameful act. Below her is an image of a dead Chinese student, killed by Chinese government forces when they violently crushed the demonstrations for freedom in 1989 in Tiananmen Square. Liu sees the killings in Tiananmen Square as a shameful event for China. The outline map of China behind the woman's head is upside down, while its reflection below, cut out of red felt, becomes a bloodstain on the floor below the student. The bowl is a symbol Liu sometimes uses. It is a vessel often emptied and filled, but never in exactly the same way. Poetically, the empty bowl represents China and the artist herself, emptied and then refilled by the cycles of history. Because of their long history, the Chinese commonly make associations between contemporary events and events of the distant past, a habit of thought that is evident in Liu's work.

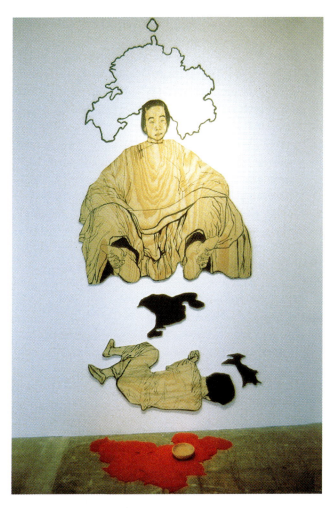

14.11 HUNG LIU. *Trauma.* Ink on plywood cutouts, acrylic on wall, felt cutout, and wooden bowl, 108" × 52" × 26". China/USA, 1989. Courtesy of the Artist.

CONNECTION
Eleanor Antin's Carving: A Traditional Sculpture *(Figure 13.30, page 390) examined the notion of dieting and body perfection for Western women.*

The Guerrilla Girls' *Do women have to be naked to get into the Met. Museum?* (Figure 14.12) seeks to correct a specific kind

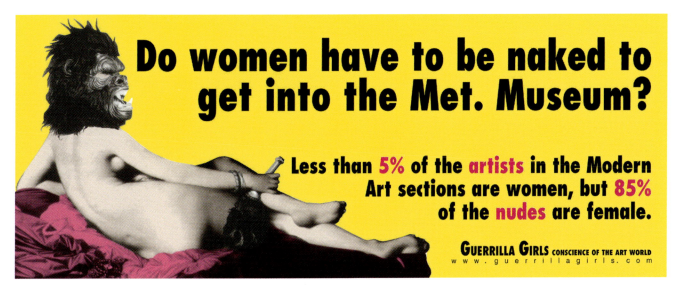

14.12 GUERRILLA GIRLS. *Do women have to be naked to get into the Met. Museum?* Street poster. USA, 1986. Courtesy www.guerrillagirls.com. See also the text accompanying Figure 4.12.

of gender discrimination. In 1986, when the poster was made, high-profile art exhibitions in prestigious museums often included very few women artists. In other words, a naked woman painted by a man might be shown in a museum, but a painting by a woman artist was not likely to be. On the poster, the woman's body is that of the *Grande Odalisque* (see Figure 8.20 in Chapter 8, Reproduction and Sexuality), whose aesthetically pleasing elongated torso reclines on cushions, on display for male viewers to enjoy and "consume." However, her head has been obscured by a gorilla mask, like those the Guerrilla Girls wore in public appearances to maintain their anonymity and to liken themselves to revolutionary guerrillas who seek to overthrow a dominant power.

The Guerrilla Girls is a collective of anonymous women artists and arts professionals protesting racial and gender discrimination in the art field. Their mass-produced, inexpensive posters feature text, image, and humor presented with a strong graphic design sensibility. The Guerrilla Girls in masks would show up at galleries and museums hosting high-profile art events where women were underrepresented. The purpose of their work was to cause exposure, embarrassment, and, eventually, change. The Guerrilla Girls also protested the fact that women artists had fewer exhibition opportunities, had fewer tenure-track teaching jobs in universities, made approximately 33 percent of the income from art that male counterparts earned, were infrequently discussed in scholarly works, and so on. Later posters were concerned with both gender and racial imbalances in museums, exhibitions, and teaching opportunities.

CLAN

A clan is a group of people joined by blood or marriage ties. It could be as small as two people. In its extended form, a clan is a group of families who share a common ancestor, bear the same name, and recognize one member as leader.

THE EXTENDED FAMILY

Art helps solidify extended families in three ways: (1) art makes major ancestors available to the living clan members; (2) art depicts important events in the clan's history; and (3) art is an important element in rituals that bring the entire clan together.

ANCESTORS

For many, the founding members of a clan have a major impact on the prestige of the living people and on their ability to function with power and authority among the living. Ancient Romans believed their ancestry was tremendously important. They preserved portraits of their ancestors and venerated their memory, as a way of establishing their own importance as they went about the business of living. At first, these ancestor por-

traits were simply death masks, made by pressing soft wax on the face of a deceased family member shortly after death. However, the wax masks deteriorated after a few years and looked like death, with sagging tissue and sunken eyes. Around the first century BCE, affluent Romans began having copies of the death masks made in marble for permanence, and so the face could be sculpted to appear energetic or even monumental. The faces were enough for the Romans, unlike the ancient Greeks, who integrated body and head into their sculpture.

The *Head of a Roman Patrician,* from Otricoli, dated c. 75–50 BCE (Figure 14.13) is an excellent example of a Roman portrait bust made to worship an ancestor and to glorify the lineage. The face is aged, but it reflects a determined, experienced, prosaic individual. Although the bust is a factual record of the ancestor's appearance, personality comes through in the wrinkles of the brow and the curling lip. Ancestor portraits were treated with respect and were frequently copied for various family members; having a unique art object was not important. They were kept in a shrine in the family home and brought out at funerals and family ceremonies. Upper-class

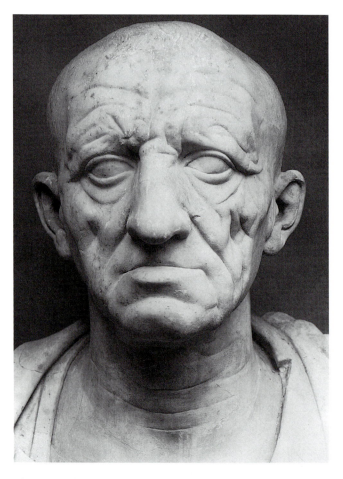

14.13 *Head of a Roman Patrician.* Marble, approximately 14" high. Otricoli (Italy), c. 75–50 BCE. Museo Torlonia, Rome. DAI, Rome.

Romans would ridicule prominent people who could not produce and display impressive busts of their own ancestors.

Among the Zapotec people of Oaxaca in southern Mexico, ancestors were so important that the living interred the dead in tomb chambers under their houses and consulted them on pressing problems. By displaying their ancestors' leg bones, the rulers ensured their right to rule.

Tombs were lavishly decorated, houselike crypts, with sculpture and painting to make ancestors available to the living. Figure 14.14 shows *Portrait Heads from Tomb 6,* from the town of Lambityeco, in Oaxaca. They are life-size heads sculpted in stucco, and date from 640–755. The heads seem very lively and create a strong presence. The male head on the left has a goatee, a beaded necklace, and earrings, and his hair is pulled up and tied in a bun above his forehead. Lines through his eyebrows and below his eyes are actually ancient symbols or glyphs that identify him. The wife's head, to the right, is lined with age. Her hair is styled with ribbons very much like that of Zapotec women today. The faces have individualized features and are definitely portraits. They likely represent the founding parents of a clan. Both were important as lineage was traced through the male and female sides. These portrait heads are located on the lintel above the entrance to the tomb and probably represent the first ones buried within.

Important ceremonies for living members of the clan took place in ancient Zapotec tombs. The tombs would be reopened every time the head of the clan died, which was a profoundly important event for the entire clan. The deceased was seen as a giver. The power, energy, and wealth of the deceased were released to the living, and the power structures within the clan shifted. In contrast, the birth of a new clan member did not cause such a profound change. The newborn was passive and powerless within the clan.

CONNECTION
Among the present-day Zapotec, this belief in the power of the dead continues. They celebrate Dia de Los Muertos, as in Diego Rivera's painting (Figure 10.28, page 291).

CLAN HISTORY

Art is also instrumental in preserving clan history, which helps ensure clan cohesion and thus increases its power.

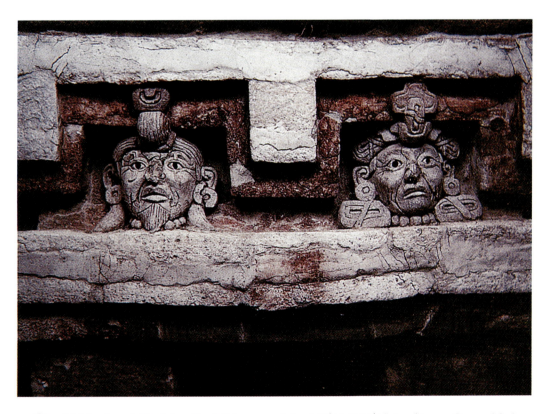

 14.14 *Portrait Heads from Tomb 6.* Stucco, each head 10¹/₂" × 11¹/₂". Lambityeco, Oaxaca, Mexico, 640–755. Photo by Arthur G. Miller.

The *Interior House Post,* dated c. 1907, in Figure 14.15, was one of four carved by Arthur Shaughnessy for the Raven House of the John Scow clan of the Northwest Coast of North America. The Raven House, completed in 1916, was a lineage house, built when a new lineage was founded because of death or marriage. When first built, these houses were used for festivities when the new leader assumed his ceremonial name. Guests would be invited to several-day celebrations called potlatches, with elaborate singing and masquerades. Later, the interior was subdivided to create living quarters for several clan families.

The carvings in lineage houses were visual aids that accompanied the telling of clan legends and history. The carvings were concentrated in significant areas, specifically around doorways, on totem poles that stood in front of the houses, and on the house posts, as we have seen. The carvings might represent specific ancestors, like animals in European family crests, or important deities, or a human in animal form. House posts both physically support the house and symbolically represent the spiritual and mythical foundation of the clan. The top of our *Interior House Post* has a mythical thunderbird with spread wings, representing a chief. Its powerful curved beak and curved ears suggest supernatural powers. Extra eyes are placed on the wings and torso, again to imply power.

The thunderbird is always shown with spread wings to create a large, imposing shape. The feathers are examples of formline design, typical of much Northwest Coast art. The intention of the Northwest Coast artist is not to invent new forms, but to invest old ones with new life and energy. The formline (Figure 14.16) divides and merges, creating a continuous flowing grid that beautifully unifies the overall decoration. The ovoid is always convex on its upper side with the lower side slightly concave; the shape possibly was inspired by

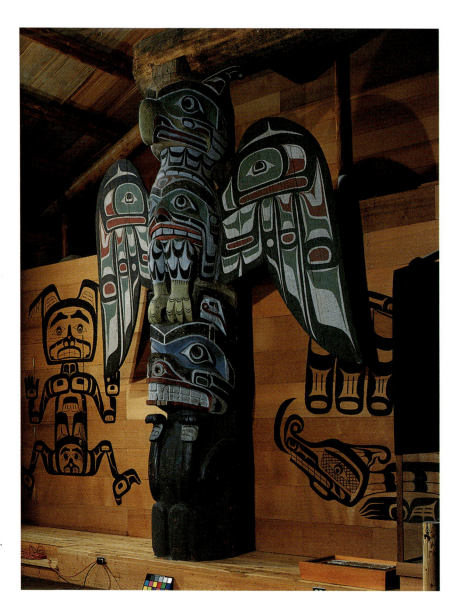

14.15 ARTHUR SHAUGHNESSY. *Interior House Post.* Carved and painted red cedar, 180" × 132" × 34". Kwakiutl. Gilford Island, British Columbia, Canada, c. 1907. Seattle Art Museum. Gift of Mr. John H. Hauberg. See also the text accompanying Figure 4.14.

the elliptical spots on a ray fish. We also see two examples of the U form (Holm 1995: 29, 37–41). Black emphasizes the major shapes, while red, white, green, and yellow are added for brightness and high contrast. For this *Interior House Post*, Shaughnessy used formline design extensively in the thunderbird's wings, painted with newly available commercial paint for brighter colors. Older works were painted with natural pigments, so their color is less saturated.

The figure below the thunderbird is a bear, a common figure on family crests, often associated with an elder or a high-ranking person. It has bared teeth and an upturned nose with circular nostrils. Its arms and legs are drawn up in a compact position that is also used in rendering figures of humans and other four-legged animals. Bodies were usually compressed, but heads were oversized, often one-third the total figure. Essential features were emphasized and shown in a highly stylized manner, while less important features were understated or even omitted. Again as symbols of power, many sets of eyes frequently would cover a figure. In this example, the bear's claws are given prominence—an extra face is painted on each paw—while the torso is generalized, without musculature or surface detail. The claws and muzzle were separate pieces added to the trunk, again increasing the dynamism of the carving.

CONNECTION
For more on the potlatch, see Charles James's Feast Dish, *Figure 7.20 (page 171).*

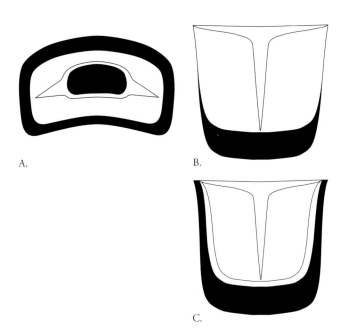

14.16   Examples of formline design in Northwest Coast art. A: ovoid form; B: typical U complex with semiangular curves; C: split U with outline (after diagrams by Bill Holm).

ART USED IN CLAN RITUALS

Clan ties are strengthened through rituals, and art is often an essential part of those rituals. Among the Asmat people of Irian Jaya, of Western New Guinea, the living engaged in elaborate rituals to pass on the life force of the deceased clansmen to the rest of the group. They carved and erected tall poles called *Bis* or *Bisj Poles* (Figure 14.17), up to sixteen feet high, which were named and represented the deceased clansmen, now called ancestors. The large openwork projections on the top figures are penises, representing power in warfare and in fertility. The height and intricate carving make the poles impressive. The negative and positive shapes and snarling faces speak of bristling warlike energy. Sometimes poles were painted in high-contrast colors. As recently as the 1950s, the Asmat were headhunters, and part of their rituals involved avenging a clansman's death, as they believed that death is not natural, but

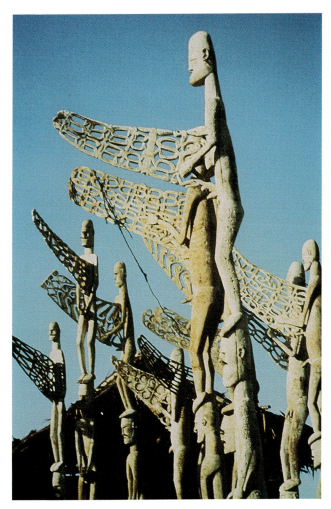

 14.17   *Bisj Poles.* Wood and paint, approximately 16' high. Asmat. Buepis Village, Fajit River, southwest New Guinea, c. nineteenth–twentieth century. Photograph by Tobias Schneebaum. See also the text accompanying Figure 6.25.

caused by enemy warfare or magic. After the men carved and painted the *Bisj* poles, the ritual feast prepared them for actual headhunting. Warriors stood before the poles and bragged about their power and received the strength of the ancestors for success in headhunting. These rituals were also tied to fertility, as successful warriors were rewarded with sexual favors.

After the rituals, the poles were traditionally left to rot in groves of sago palms, where they would pass their vitality on to the plants that provide a staple food for the Asmat. Art for the Asmat, then, was the experience of the rituals and the feasts, not the preserved art object. Headhunting has now been suppressed, but the Asmat continue to carve the poles and conduct the rituals. Recently, some *Bisj* poles have been sold after

rituals to collectors and museums rather than rotting, while others are made exclusively for the tourist trade.

Art, ritual, and clan identity are intertwined among the Yoruba people of west-central Africa. The Epa Festival is held every other year for three days in March to promote fertility and the well-being of the community. The *Epa Headdress called "Orangun"* (Figure 14.18), sculpted by Bamgboye of Odo-Owa, was used in masquerades to honor the family. The base of an Epa headdress is a helmet that fits on top of the performer's head, and it is carved with grotesque Janus-like faces, front and back. Above the helmet is a large structure with an equestrian figure, the nomad warrior chief who founded several towns. Other characters represent important members of

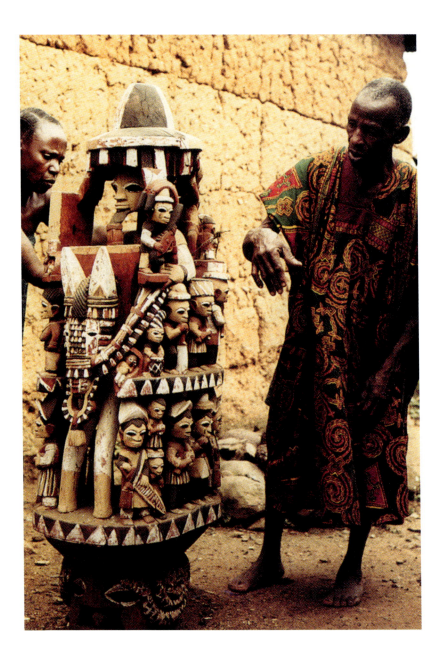

14.18 BAMGBOYE OF ODO-OWA. *Epa Headdress called "Orangun."* Wood and paint. Yoruba. Erinmope, Nigeria, 1974. Photo by John Pemberton III. See also the text accompanying Figure 6.3.

the household. Although such masks weigh more than fifty pounds, young dancers would perform athletically in them.

We have seen that clan strength and identity are often tied to art, because art gives access to ancestors, records clan history, and figures prominently in clan rituals.

THE NUCLEAR FAMILY

In highly industrialized societies, where individuals have great mobility, the extended family has lost much of its strength, and the clan has dwindled to the nuclear family. Artists have examined the nuclear family, to find its strengths, its changes, and its points of tensions.

The Family, dated 1962 (Figure 14.19), by the artist Marisol, presents us with a mother and her children arranged as if sitting for a photographer. Feelings of both mutual affec-

tion and personal awkwardness emanate from the three older children, as they present themselves to the world as family members and as individuals. The mother in the center is dignified, solid, and thoughtful, but not elegant. She links all the figures and elements. The doors and decoration behind suggest the domestic setting, but they seem generally poor. Marisol's figures are blocks of wood, drawn on and minimally carved, each maintaining its own separateness while interlocking with the group. The shoes and doors are real, found objects that Marisol incorporated into her work. *The Family* contrasts with the uniformity, happiness, and affluence of the nuclear family as it was commonly presented on U.S. television in 1962, with shows like *Leave It to Beaver* and *Father Knows Best.*

Artists sometimes allude to their subject without presenting it literally. Such is the case with *Sail Baby,* dated 1983

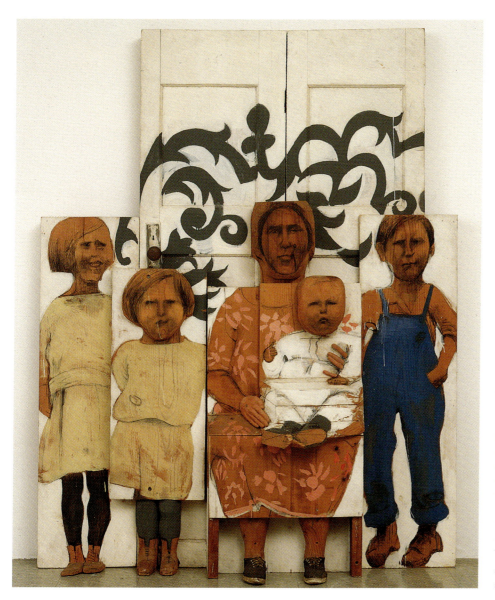

14.19   MARISOL. *The Family.* Painted wood and other materials in three sections; overall, 6'10⅝" × 65½" × 15½". USA, 1962. Advisory Committee Fund (231.1962.a-c), The Museum of Modern Art, New York. © The Museum of Modern Art, New York / Art Resource, NY. Art © Marisol Escobar / Licensed by VAGA, New York, NY. For more about the formal qualities of this artwork, see Figure 2.29.

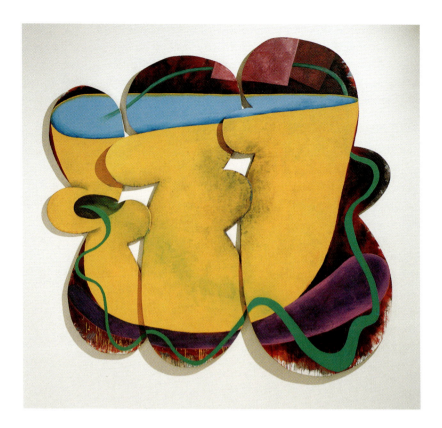

14.20 ELIZABETH MURRAY. *Sail Baby.* USA, 1983. Oil on three canvases, 126" × 135". Walker Art Center, Minneapolis, Minnesota. For more about the meaning of this artwork, see the text accompanying Figure 4.8.

(Figure 14.20), by Elizabeth Murray, which is a painting about family life. Three rounded canvases suggest the bouncy, energetic bodies of infants or children. The bright colors recall the palette of childhood. The yellow shape becomes a cup, referring to the role of parents, the domestic sphere, and feeding. The grouping of the three shapes suggests the closeness of siblings, all with similarities and, at the same time, each a unique individual. The ribbon of green reflects their relatedness and the intimacy of their lives. The artist, in fact, has said that this painting is about her own siblings and her children, while her other abstract paintings refer to different family relationships, such as mother-daughter and husband-wife.

As the twentieth century drew to a close, the definition of family had been expanded. *Baby Makes 3* (Figure 14.21), from the late 1980s, is by General Idea, the Canadian collective of three artists, A. A. Bronson, Felix Partz, and Jorge Zontal, who had been working together since 1968. General Idea presented a homosexual approach to the nuclear family, showing three men in bed in the clouds, looking tranquil and impish. The work both ridicules the idea of the happy nuclear family and shows how gays and lesbians recreate family and social structures. *Baby Makes 3* also alludes to recent discoveries in science that suggest the possibility of means other than heterosexual reproduction to generate a biological family. The image appeared on the cover of *File,* which was General Idea's parody of *Life* magazine. General Idea critiqued many aspects of popular culture that so heavily promote the heterosexual nuclear fam-

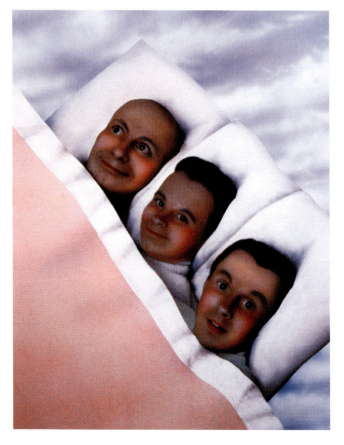

14.21 GENERAL IDEA. *Baby Makes 3.* Lacquer on vinyl, 78³/₄" × 63". Canada, 1984–1989. By permission of General Idea.

ily. They created their own versions of TV dinners, postage stamps, boutique items, videos with commercials, and so on. With their versions blending into the popular culture mainstream, General Idea hoped to alter preconceived ideas, specifically in the case of the nuclear family.

CLASS

A group of people sharing the same economic, social, or ruling status comprises a class. In some cultures, class distinctions are rigid, while in others, people can easily move up or down the "social ladder." Members of the same class tend to hold the same values.

Class becomes like a very large extended family, a group in which individuals often find their identity and their social circle. Art and class structure can be linked in several ways: (1) members of different classes may be depicted with distinctive body styles and poses; (2) artwork can show the environment, accoutrements, and activities that mark members of a

certain class; and (3) a work of art can be a status item, the possession of which indicates the class of the owner.

CLASS STATUS AND BODY STYLES

In ancient Egypt, the human body was sculpted in different ways, depending upon the class of the person. Upper classes, consisting of the pharaoh and his family, the nobility, and the priests, were depicted in formal, highly standardized ways that indicated immediately their importance in the social hierarchy. The four gigantic statues at the *Temple of Ramses II* at Abu Simbel, dated c. 1270 BCE (Figure 14.22), are examples of official images of the pharaoh. Befitting his semidivine status, he is enormous. The repetition of the image reinforces the idea of his imposing grandeur (and, as if four large, seated images were not enough, there are another eight standing statues just inside the doorway, each standardized, each thirty-two feet high!). The seated pose is frontal, composed, and symmetrical, with few breakable parts. It is absolutely standardized, the same formula being used repeatedly to depict the divine ruler of Egypt. The expressionless face and staring eyes

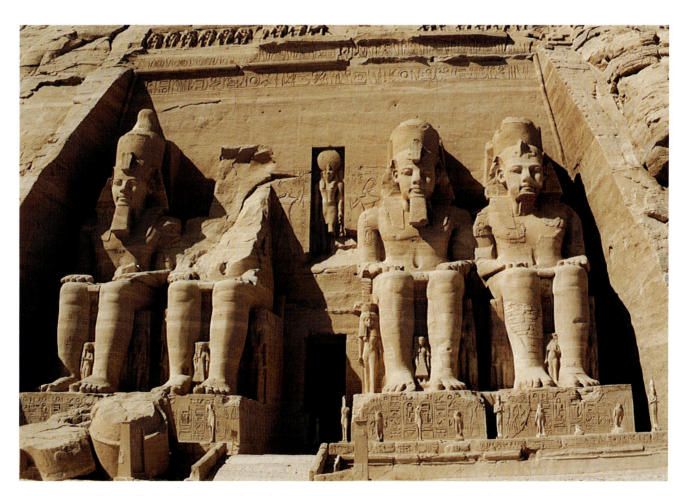

14.22   *Temple of Ramses II*. Abu Simbel (now relocated), Egypt, XIX Dynasty, c. 1275–1225 BCE. Each colossal statue is 65' high. John P. Stevens / Ronald Sheridan Ancient Art & Architecture Library.

look outward in timeless serenity. The body of Ramses II is well developed and flawless, frozen forever in idealized, youthful prime. Smaller figures at Ramses' knees and feet are members of his family, their smaller size indicative of their lesser rank. Enormous projects of this kind were very costly and demanded the skills of the best carvers, reinforcing the status of the very highest classes. The formula we see for sculptures of the pharaoh is also used for images of nobility, who are shown with large, idealized bodies, taking standardized poses.

The colossal statues of Ramses II were intended to be permanent memorials to him, as befitting his rank. In 1968, the statues were moved to higher ground and affixed to artificial cliffs to avoid their being submerged in the back pools of the new Aswan Dam. Their permanence remains.

By contrast, the *Seated Scribe,* dated 2500–2400 BCE (Figure 14.23), is a portrait of an Egyptian court official of much lesser rank than the pharaoh. The sculpture is limestone, a relatively soft, inexpensive stone considered to have an unattractive finish, so the work was painted. The result is more lifelike, and thus less eternal and permanent than the monumental stone image of Ramses II at Abu Simbel. As befitting those of lower class, there is much less formality and idealization in the portrait of the scribe. His pose is more relaxed, and the figure is

cut away from all backing stone. His face is expressive and personalized, rather than eternally calm and divine. He seems intelligent, alert, and aware. His body shows the effects of age, with sagging chest muscles and a potbelly, attributes that would be considered disrespectful in a portrait of a pharaoh.

The Egyptians depicted class by using different body styles. More often, artists depict class by people's dress, their environment, the things they hold or use, and what they are doing. Our next section looks at art showing the lifestyles and activities of various classes.

CONNECTION
The Egyptians were not the only people to create idealized images of their leaders. See images of rulers in Chapter 11, such as Emperor Justinian and His Attendants *(Figure 11.2, page 303).*

CLASS ACTIVITIES AND LIFESTYLES

Art records not only the lifestyles of the rich and famous, but also the more mundane existence of the lower classes. We will look at a cross-cultural selection of images that reflect class activities and class lifestyles. It is important to remember that the great majority of these images are made by the ruling class or middle class, often of themselves but also of classes below them.

THE RULING CLASS

Upper-class and ruling families in Europe in the last millennium have used art to define and maintain their high rank. Portraits were often records of high positions, and indeed, only the wealthy could afford to commission or own an oil painting.

The title of *Las Meninas* (Figure 14.24), painted by Diego Velazquez in 1656, means "Maids of Honor," which by itself marks the upper class. At the center of the composition is the blond Infanta Marguerita, the daughter of King Philip IV and Queen Mariana of Spain, the focus of considerable attention and energy. She is shown almost casually in the painter's studio. The informality of this painting is understandable, because it was not meant for public display, but for the king's private office. Although the Infanta is not painted in a throne room or with a crown, we can understand her exalted position through many elements in the painting. Her location at the center of the picture, the light that floods her, and her glowing white dress all mark her as the most important figure. As the presence of servants is also a sign of rank, she is attended by two young ladies in waiting, two dwarfs, and two adult chaperones, male and female, in the shadowy right background. Her parents, the king and queen, are reflected in the mirror against the back wall; presumably, they are standing where the viewer of the painting would be.

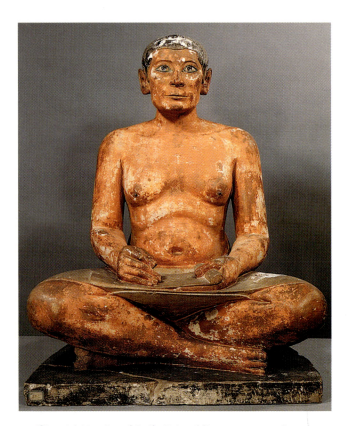

14.23 *Seated Scribe.* Painted limestone, approximately 21" high. From a mastaba tomb at Saqqara, Egypt, V Dynasty, c. 2500–2400 BCE. Louvre, Paris. © RMN / Art Resource, NY.

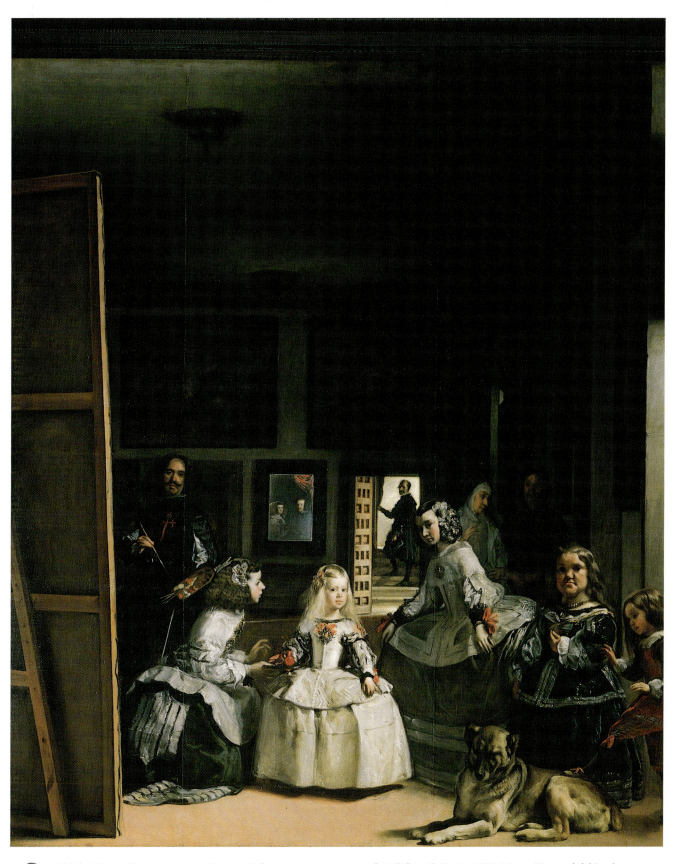

14.24   DIEGO VELAZQUEZ. *Las Meninas.* Oil on canvas, approximately 10'5" × 9'. Spain, 1656. Museo Nacional del Prado, Madrid. Institut Amatller d'Art Hispanic © Museo del Prado.

The space of the painting is majestic: light floods the foreground; the room is grand; the deep space extends back in the distance. The space is also made complex by mirrors. One we see. The other we cannot, but its presence is implied by the fact that Velazquez peers outward, presumably into a mirror, to paint himself. Velazquez is the standing figure at the left of the painting, working on a large canvas, perhaps this very picture.

Size is important. This painting is ten and one-half feet by nine feet. A physical object this large is a sign of rank and a mark of distinction, as well as is owning, possessing, or commissioning such an artwork. Diego Velazquez was a celebrated and famous artist. His prestige is an important addition to the royal commissions.

Sometimes class was indicated by its members' activities. *The Swing* (Figure 14.25), painted by Jean-Honoré Fragonard in 1766, shows the frivolous sexual escapades of the French aristocratic class in the mid-eighteenth century. During that period, they enjoyed tremendous wealth and privilege and had few responsibilities, as most of their power had been assimilated by the French king and most of their duties assumed by an ever-growing middle class. The aristocracy was effectively transformed into a leisure class, with little to do but become embroiled in their own intrigues.

In *The Swing*, a young, aristocratic woman enjoys a moment of swinging, assisted by the bishop in the shadows who pulls the ropes. Hidden among the bushes in the lower

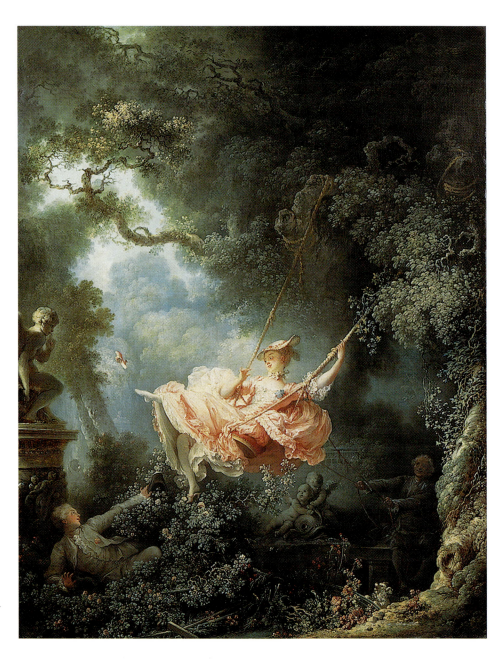

14.25 JEAN-HONORÉ FRAGONARD. *The Swing.* Oil on canvas, 35" × 32". France, 1766. Photo Wallace Collection, London.

left is a young nobleman, enjoying a peek up the woman's skirt as she playfully kicks off her pink shoe at a statue of Cupid. All details speak of the wealth and the lack of purpose of the aristocracy: the lush parks of their beautiful estates, sprinkled with statuary; their rich clothing; the complete frivolity of their days' activities; and their interest in sexual intrigues. Fragonard's rich colors, delicate details, and sensual textures lend a sweetness to the scene, and a sense of fragility. In fact, the aristocratic class was shortly to be brutally eliminated by the French Revolution, which began in 1789.

Dress and other paraphernalia are often a sign of rank. We see this often among royalty and nobility, as well as with members of the military and even the Boy or Girl Scouts. Priests of most religions dress distinctively to show their status. We could look at hundreds of examples in art where class hierarchy is made apparent by dress, but we will limit ourselves to just one example: the *Great Beaded Crown of the Orangun-Ila* (Figure 14.26), from the Yoruba people of Nigeria in Africa. The image shows not only the crown, but also the robe and staff that are signs of rank. Crowns such as this

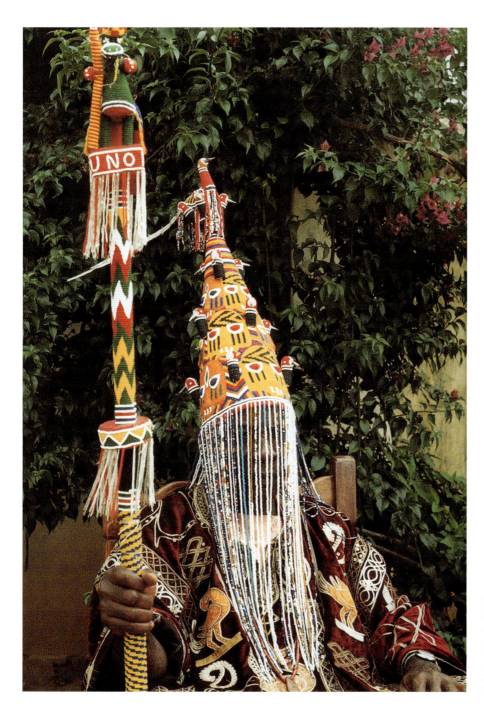

14.26   Beadworkers of the Adesina Family of Efon-Alaye. *Great Beaded Crown of the Orangun-Ila.* Yoruba. Ila Orangun, Nigeria, twentieth century. Photograph by John Pemberton III, 1971. See also the text accompanying Figure 6.7.

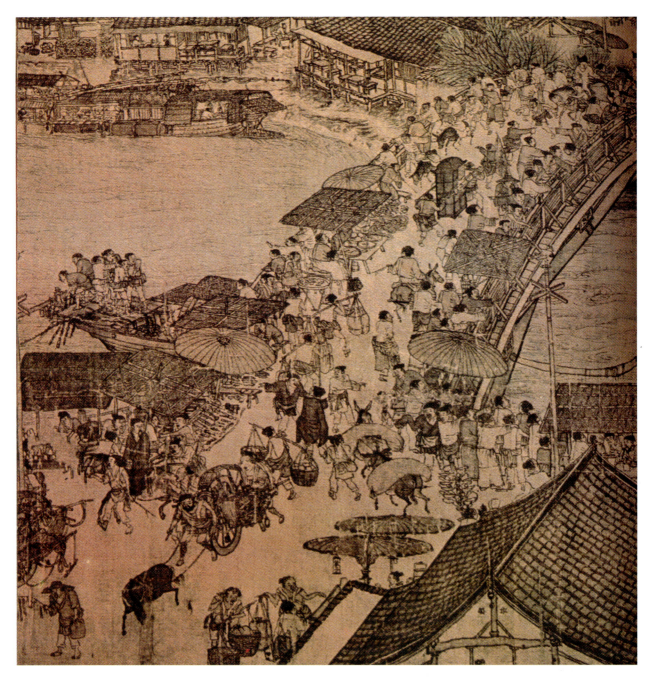

14.27 ZHANG ZEDUAN. *Spring Festival Along the River* (detail). Handscroll, ink on silk. 10" high × 207" long. China, late eleventh–early twelfth centuries. The Palace Museum, Beijing.

one are worn by high-ranking territorial chiefs and are similar to the headgear worn by priests and the supreme ruler. Rank is made apparent through dress in a number of ways: (1) the shapes of the clothing or headgear; (2) the materials used; and (3) the meaning of the decorative symbols. The conical shape of the crown is a highly significant Yoruba symbol. It represents the inner self, which, in the case of those of rank, is connected with the spirit world. The cone shape is repeated in the umbrella that protects the chief from the sun and in the peaked-roofed verandas where he sits while functioning as the ruler. The material used in crowns is also significant, as beads have been used in Yoruba crowns at least since the 1550s and in all likelihood even earlier. The birds on the chief's crown and robe represent generative power, closely associated with women's reproductive abilities and the life-giving, stabilizing structure of Yoruba society. The long, white feathers at the top of the crown are from the Okin, called the royal bird by the Yoruba people.

CONNECTION

For an example of the conical shape used in Yoruban art, see the Palace Sculpture *by Olowe of Ise (Figure 11.12, page 311).*

THE WORKING CLASS

The middle class flourishes in cities, where the dense population provides opportunities for commercialization and specialization. Merchants, skilled workers, laborers, restaurateurs, entertainers, and a whole spectrum of other workers find livelihoods in urban settings.

Kaifeng, the longtime capital of China, had 260,000 households in the year 1105. Scenes of its urban culture are recorded in the scroll painting, *Spring Festival Along the River* (Figure 14.27), by Zhang Zeduan, from the late eleventh or early twelfth century. A painting this size was undoubtedly commissioned by a member of the aristocracy, and so this image represents an upper-class concept of middle-class life. Our example here shows the ideal working class, animated with crowded, bustling activity. Details show merchants selling goods in booths, people eating in restaurants, farmers delivering produce, and so on. Urban life was marked by friendliness and sociability, as neighbors were helpful and involved with each other. For example, many onlookers shout advice and gesture from the bridge and banks as boatmen steer their vessel under the Rainbow Bridge. Each small scene is rendered with the same amount of detail and similar color, and the accumulated scenes give a picture of busy, contented, unassuming middle-class life.

The Kitchen Maid (Figure 14.28), painted by Jan Vermeer in 1660, shows a maid in a modest home in the Netherlands of the seventeenth century. In this painting, the working class

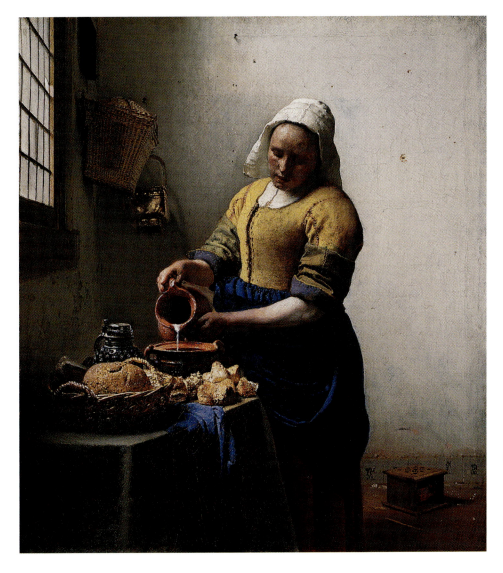

14.28 Jan Vermeer van Delft. *The Kitchen Maid.* Oil on canvas, approximately 17" × 15". Netherlands, 1660. The Rijksmuseum Amsterdam.

is elevated in dignity. The mundane tasks of pouring milk and arranging bread seem almost sacred. The gentle light bathes, outlines, and gives a strong sense of the physical presence of a humble woman, an image with such simplicity and directness that she almost personifies virtue. Her work seems healthy and life sustaining. Everything around her seems similarly transformed: the woven basket, the crust of the bread, the earthen jug, the texture of the wall are all painted so that their distinct surfaces seem familiar, burnished with age, and glowing. The color harmonies of cream, gold, and rust are earthen versions of the strong primary colors red and yellow.

Vermeer often painted unimportant, ordinary scenes from everyday life, a category of paintings called "genre paintings." This was part of an overall tendency in the Netherlands of the seventeenth century to emphasize and elevate middle-class domestic life, where music, reading, and culture flourished and

basic needs were met. The maid, from an even lower social level, is treated with the same grace and dignity. The sphere of women was the home, and *The Kitchen Maid* reflects the ideals of womanhood at that time: virtue, modesty, hard work. As a middle-class country without a king or an aristocracy, the Netherlands focused on the family and family life and the individual. Portraits were common, as were moralizing genre scenes that criticized such vices as laziness, drunkenness, and lust.

CONNECTION

The Self-Portrait (Figure 13.8, page 375) by Rembrandt van Rijn reflects the same sense of individual worth and the sacredness of a modest life as does Vermeer's Kitchen Maid.

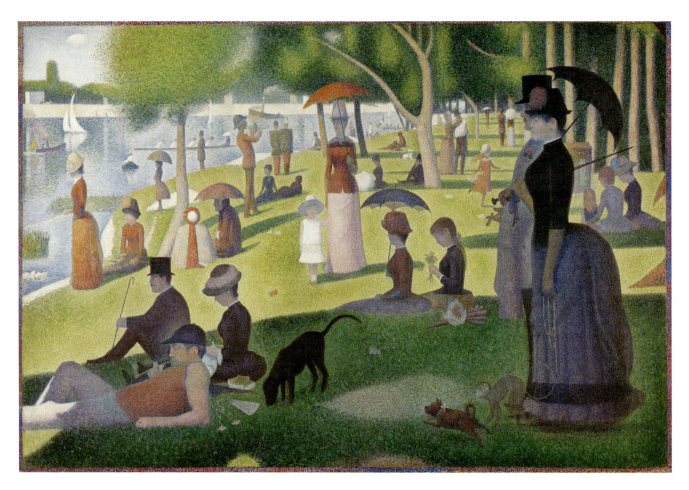

14.29   GEORGES SEURAT. *La Grande Jatte* (also called *A Sunday on La Grande Jatte—1884*). Oil on canvas, approx. 6'9" × 10'. France, 1884–1886. The Art Institute of Chicago, Helen Birch Bartlett Memorial Collection. Photo © The Art Institute of Chicago. All Righs Reserved. For more on the cultural context surrounding this painting, see Figure 1.21.

In *A Sunday on La Grande Jatte,* dated 1884–1886 (Figure 14.29), Georges Seurat painted a middle class that was enjoying the increased wealth and leisure that accompanied nineteenth-century industrialism. The very creation of parks was the result of the affluent middle class's desire to reintroduce nature into increasingly crowded cities. The painting shows a collection of strangers outdoors on a modern holiday. Unlike villagers attending a local festival, the groups do not know each other. The figures are proper, composed, and orderly. Details of middle-class dress are carefully recorded. Almost all figures are shown rigidly from the side, front, or back. Diagonals are reserved for the left side of the painting and are stopped by the orderly verticals on the right. Shadows mass in the foreground, and light in the back.

The painting reflects the growing emphasis on and awareness of science. The woman in the right foreground holds a monkey on a leash, and the similarity between the monkey's curved back and the bustle on her dress shows an awareness of Charles Darwin's theories of evolution and the resulting social Darwinism, which placed women closer on a continuum to the rest of nature than men were placed. Also, Seurat was influenced by the science of color and optics, especially the works of the scientist Eugène Chevreul, as he painted with small dots of intense colors laid side by side. He followed Chevreul's theories in the placements of contrasting colors to either intensify or nullify each other. The dots of bright colors eliminated muddy mixtures, and in fact, this painting up close is a somewhat dizzying and disorienting mass of small dots of bright colors. So labor-intensive was this process that it took Seurat more than two years to complete the work.

THE POOR

Art provides us a record of the poor, their way of life and their struggles. Art itself, however, is often an upper- or middle-class luxury, and so the following artwork represent how the more affluent classes saw the very destitute. In our second example, the image reflects a growing political pressure for change to alleviate the plight of the poor.

Roaming Beggars (Grotesque Figures) (Figure 14.30) was painted by Zhou Chen during the late fifteenth or early sixteenth century. Four portraits show homeless peasants, a relatively common sight in China in the fifteenth century, when taxes, natural disasters, and the grasping aristocracy combined to uproot many from the lands where they had long lived and worked. These ink-and-color sketches capture the precarious, desperate, and crazed existence of these people, as they resort to scavenging or looting for food. The line quality is quick, jagged, and spare. The faces are scruffy or demented and the bodies lean, some to the point of emaciation. The figure on the left scavenged for firewood, while that on the far right survived by catching snakes, which was a kind of sideshow entertainment. The snakes could also be sold to be eaten as a delicacy.

CONNECTION
For an example of how the poor might view the rich, see The Rent Collection Courtyard, *Figure 12.13 (page 347), which shows an instance of exploitation and oppression.*

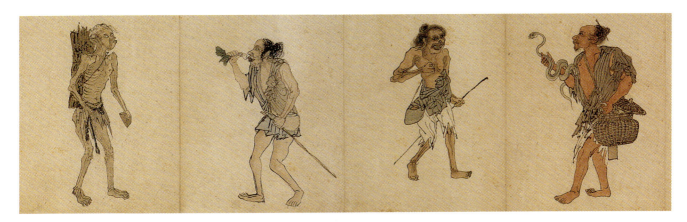

14.30   ZHOU CHEN. *Roaming Beggars (Grotesque Figures)* (details from two sections). Ink and color on paper. 27'7^{1}/$_{2}$" long, 12^{7}/$_{8}$" high (overall); 8'1^{1}/$_{2}$" long, 12^{7}/$_{8}$" high (painting only). China, late fifteenth–early sixteenth centuries. Honolulu Academy of Arts.

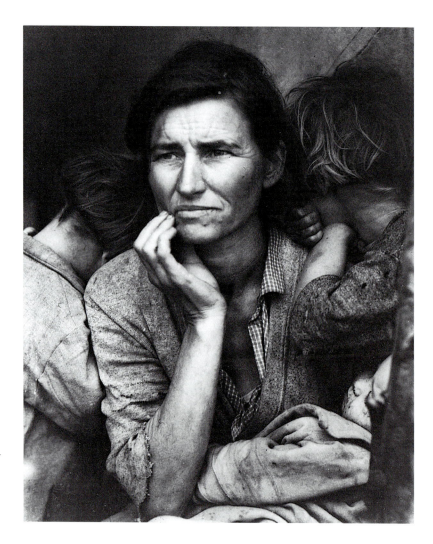

14.31 DOROTHEA LANGE. *Migrant Mother, Nipomo Valley.* Gelatin Silver Print. USA, 1936. From the Collections of the Library of Congress. See also the text accompanying Figure 4.1.

Migrant Mother, Nipomo Valley (Figure 14.31), photographed by Dorothea Lange, is one of many workers who were starving at a migrant camp Lange visited in 1936. Lange's field notes tell us about the woman: "Camped on the edge of a pea field where the crop had failed in a freeze. The tires had just been sold from under the car to buy food. She was 32 years old with seven children." The woman's face and pose express both strength and desperation. Skin, clothes, and hair show signs of poverty and hard times. Fear and uncertainty permeate the scene, made more acute because we also see the emotional ties of the family and the fear of the children. *Migrant Mother, Nipomo Valley* is an example of documentary photography, which purports to record facts objectively and in a straightforward manner. In actuality, we know that this family posed for Lange, that she made several exposures of them, and that she edited her prints for the most effective image. Nevertheless, it is important that we understand the photograph to be factual, whether or not it was staged or manipulated. We are more drawn to the image because photography here seems to record facts and does not appear as artistic invention.

Lange was a New York commercial photographer who was moved by the plight of migrant workers in the United States during the Great Depression. She was hired by California and federal agencies to document migrant farmworkers in the United States. Her depression-era photographs were especially effective because she made her subjects so human and so immediate. Her photographs were credited with improving conditions for migrant workers in California. The black-and-white photograph was an especially effective medium to use to express conditions of poverty, to concentrate on the facial expression, and to lend the aura of truth.

CONNECTION
Many other U.S. artists took up the cause of the poor or laboring classes throughout the nineteenth and twentieth centuries. Turn to Ester Hernandez's memorable print, Sun Mad (Figure 12.16, page 350).

CONNECTION

For more on the apparently objective nature of photography, see Chapter 4, Deriving Meaning.

ART OBJECTS THAT INDICATE CLASS STATUS

Finally, different kinds of art are often indicators of class. Art objects are made for and reflect the needs and tastes of specific classes. Again, we could have chosen from almost innumerable examples to illustrate this concept, but we will focus first on two from the era of the Tokugawa Shogunate (1573–1868) in Japan. Then, we will conclude with an example from the United States of the twentieth century.

Historically in Japan, classes were kept rigidly distinct. The ruling class consisted of the imperial family, and the warrior class, who divided the land and were its feudal rulers, led by the shogun. The very poorest class consisted of the peasants, who farmed the land that belonged to the warrior class. In addition, a middle class of urban dwellers began to emerge, starting in the mid-1600s and continuing into the twentieth century. This class was composed primarily of merchants, manufacturers, and laborers, and the largest concentration of them was in the city of Edo, known today as Tokyo. As each group was kept separate and distinct, they all developed their own cultural spheres. For example, the emperor and warrior class preferred a restrained, sophisticated, understated style of theater known as Noh, while the middle class favored the more expressive Kabuki theater.

Likewise, different art styles developed for each class. The warrior-rulers built for themselves splendid stone castles that were both fortresses and self-aggrandizing monuments. Because of the stone construction, rooms in these castles were large, gray, and dimly lit. The warrior-rulers commissioned large screens, sliding doors, and wall paintings to lighten and decorate the dark, drab interiors. For example, *Uji Bridge,* from the sixteenth or seventeenth century (Figure 14.32), is a large screen more than five feet tall. The bridge arcs across the top of the screen, partly obscured by mists. In the foreground, the river rolls past a water wheel. Dramatic willow branches contrast with budding leaves. The dark branches stand in stark contrast to the golds and reds of the background. The painting expresses qualities of simplicity and beauty, perishable with the passing of the moment.

The artwork of the middle class was likely the ukiyo-e print. These prints were modest in size and produced in large numbers, so that the cost of each was within the reach of the middle-class merchant. They were kept in drawers and therefore did not require a castle to house them, as did the gold screen we just saw. The ukiyo-e prints were eclectic in style, combining Japanese, Chinese, and, later, Western styles. Because they were inexpensive to produce, the artist who drew

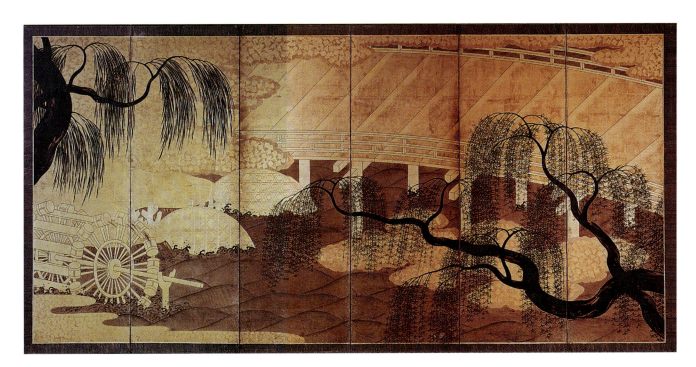

14.32   *Uji Bridge.* Six-fold screen, color on paper, 62" high. Japan, Momoyama period, sixteenth—seventeenth centuries. Tokyo National Museum.

the original design was able to be innovative. For lavish screens like the *Uji Bridge,* artists had much less latitude in the designs they produced.

Ukiyo-e prints showed generally one of three subjects: famous Kabuki actors, beautiful young women, and landscapes. *Komurasaki of the Tamaya Teahouse* (Figure 14.33), designed by Kitagawa Utamaro in 1794, is an example of the beautiful woman theme, showing the courtesan Komurasaki. The image is beautiful, but fleeting and simple. The woman is charming, but human existence is transitory; thus, the beautiful can add a melancholy note, making humans ache all the more for life's passing. This wistfulness is a quality of many Japanese images, as we saw even with the *Uji Bridge* screen. The colors are exceedingly delicate, with yellow ochres, olive tones, dull reds, grays, and blacks—not blazingly bright. The line quality of the prints was splendid—delicate and fine, curving and graceful (or, in the case of prints of the energetic Kabuki actors, vigorous and even wild). The lines in the face and hair are especially refined, while the folds of the drapery are expressed in bold marks and curves. Geishas and courtesans were depicted in ways that would make them outlets for male desires; the market for these pictures was married men who would see in these women for hire a fleeting beauty and an erotic perfection that they desired. Especially famous courtesans and geishas would be depicted in popular prints, and their images circulated and collected.

CONNECTION
You can read more about ukiyo-e prints with A Pair of Lovers (Figure 8.16, page 207). The production of ukiyo-e prints, and the printers, carvers, and artists who contributed, is discussed in Chapter 5, Who Makes Art?

Our last example, *Watts Towers* (Figure 14.34), was made by a working-class man for a working-class neighborhood in Los Angeles. Beginning in the 1920s when he was in his late forties, Simon Rodilla (also called Simon or Sam Rodia) labored for more than thirty years in his backyard to erect a nine-part sculpture, more than one hundred feet high. It was an amazing artistic and physical effort. The tower forms rise dramatically against the sky, while the openwork pattern adds an element of rhythm. The *Watts Towers* are constructed of rods and bars shaped into openwork sculptures. The concrete coating on the *Towers* was encrusted with ceramic pieces, tiles, glass, seashells, mirror pieces, and other shiny or broken castoffs, creating a glittering mosaic-like surface. An immigrant from Italy, Rodia wanted to construct a monument to pay tribute to his adopted land.

Rodia was not academically trained as an artist, and his work does not reflect the major art trends of his day. His work was not made for an upper-class audience. As a result, many critics place *Watts Towers* in categories outside of fine art. It has been variously described as folk art, outsider art, or naive art. The dense and shimmering surfaces have caused some to relate his work to crafts and decorative arts. Some have even called it "kook" art, claiming that Rodia was trying to make a transmitter to contact aliens. Some of these descriptors ("naive," "kook," "decorative," etc.) have more or less pejorative connotations, while "folk" suggests an art category of less value than fine art. But there is no denying how powerful and memorable *Watts Towers* is.

CONNECTION
Another work of "folk art" is the Retablo of Maria de la Luz Casillas and Children (Figure 9.15, page 236). Read about that work and review the discussion of "Art, Popular Culture, and Kitsch" in Chapter 1.

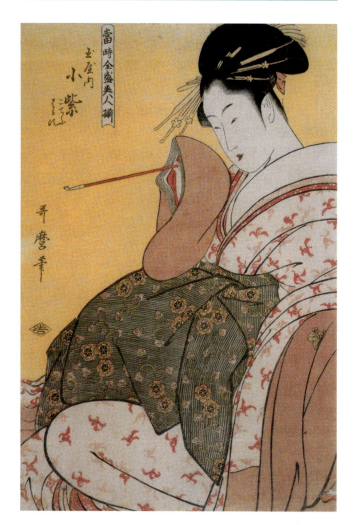

 14.33 KITAGAWA UTAMARO. *Komurasaki of the Tamaya Teahouse.* Multicolor woodblock print from the series "A Collection of Reigning Beauties," 10" × 15". Japan, 1794. Tokyo National Museum. See also the text accompanying Figure 5.13.

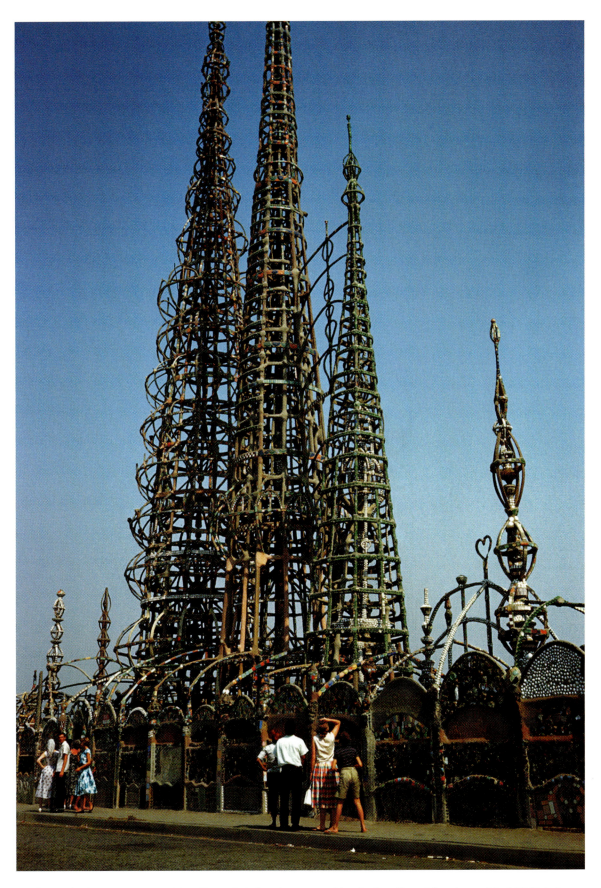

14.34 SIMON RODIA. *Watts Towers*. Reinforced concrete with mixed media and found materials; 100' high. Los Angeles, California, USA, 1921–1954. © Bettmann/Corbis. See also the text accompanying Figure 5.5.

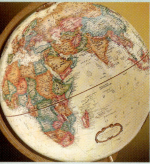

Courtesy of Replogle Globes, Inc., Broadview, IL.

The period 1750–1850 brought major changes in the history of humankind. In 1760, the Industrial Revolution was beginning in Europe—power machinery replaced hand labor and steam engines replaced water wheels and spinning mills. People moved to the cities to work in factories, and a middle class grew and gained power. This was also the Age of Enlightenment, which fostered ideas of personal liberty.

In the Americas, colonization had taken place. The French claimed land from Canada through the Great Lakes and down the Mississippi River to the Gulf of Mexico. Britain controlled the thirteen colonies, and Spain claimed Florida, Texas, New Mexico, Arizona, and California as well as vast territories in Central and South America. Britain also maintained colonies throughout Asia and Africa.

In 1775, the American Revolution against England occurred, followed by the French Revolution in 1789 in which the monarchy was overthrown. The gap in wealth and lifestyles between

Below:
Map 8 Napoleon's Grand Empire.

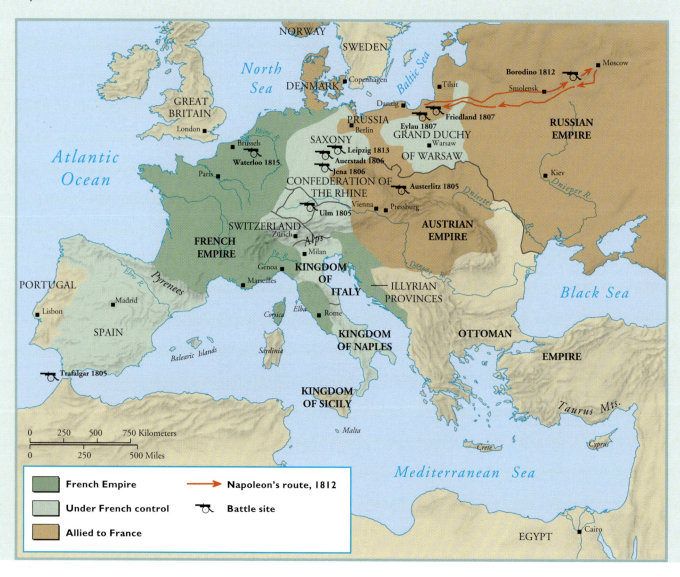

the rich and the poor in France can be seen in *Versailles* and *The Swing* (see Figures 5.4 and 14.25) and in *Third-Class Carriage* by Daumier in this box. George Washington became the first president of the United States, while Napoleon took control of France and conquered an empire (see Map 8). In 1812 in South America, Simón Bolívar and José de San Martín fought for independence from Spain. In the 1800s, Eli Whitney invented the cotton gin, workers formed the first trade unions to fight for their rights, and Karl Marx and Friedrich Engels wrote the *Communist Manifesto.*

In India, Great Britain set up colonial rule, and, later, Queen Victoria would become the Empress of India.

The Manchu Dynasty ruled in China during this period. Between 1839 and 1842, the Opium Wars broke out between China and Britain. Britain had smuggled opium from India into China causing mass addiction to the drug, which in turn greatly affected China's economy. Britain won the war and gained Hong Kong plus five ports in China for trade.

In Africa, during the 1700s and 1800s, the Dutch, Portuguese, and other Europeans colonized vast territories. Toward the latter part of this period, the empires of Zimbabwe and Ashanti came to an end.

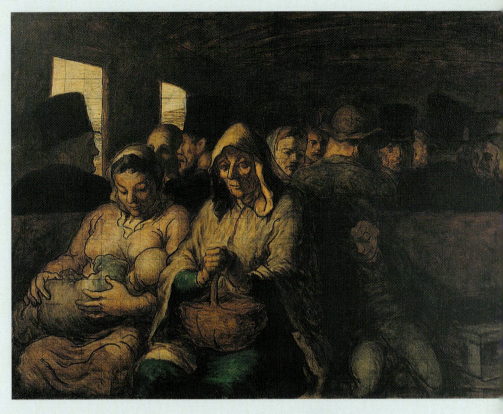

Above:
HONORÉ DAUMIER.
Third-Class Carriage.
Oil on canvas, 25¼" × 35½".
France, 1862. The Metropolitan Museum of Art, New York. Havemeyer Collection, bequest of H. O. Havemeyer, 1929.

Old Kingdom, Egypt	**2700 BCE**	
	2500	*Seated Scribe*
	2000	*Temple of Ramses II*
Roman Empire	**100**	
	75	*Head of a Roman Patrician*
Tang Dynasty—China	**600 CE**	
Historic Era—Japan		
	640	*Portrait Heads from Tomb 6*
Teotihuacán—Mexico	**700**	
	1000	Zhang Zeduan: *Spring Festival Along the River*
Renaissance Begins	**1400**	
	1500	Zhou Chen: *Roaming Beggars*
	1600	*Uji Bridge*
	1617	Rubens: *Abduction of the Daughters of Leucippus*
	1656	Velazquez: *Las Meninas*
	1660	Vermeer: *The Kitchen Maid*
Age of Enlightenment	**1700**	
England, France, Spain colonize the Americas		
Dutch and Portuguese colonize Africa		
	1734	de Cuvilliès: *Hall of Mirrors*
Industrial Revolution	**1760**	
American Revolution	**1775**	
	1776	Fragonard: *The Swing*
		David: *Oath of the Horatii*
French Revolution	**1789**	
	1794	Utamaro: *Komurasaki of the Tamaya Teahouse*
South American Revolution	**1800**	
First trade unions established		
Communist Manifesto		
Britain colonizes India		

Opium War between Britain and China	**1839**	
	1862	Daumier: *Third-Class Carriage*
	1863	
	1884	Seurat: *La Grande Jatte*
Women's suffrage begins in 1900; movement continues to present day		
	1900	Adesina Family: *Great Beaded Crown of the Orangun–Ila*
		Bisj Poles
	1907	Shaughnessy: *Interior House Post*
	1908	
World War I		*Painting from a Cult House*
	1921	Rodia: *Watts Towers*
	1927	VanDerZee: *Society Ladies*
World War II		
	1936	Lange: *Migrant Mother, Nipomo Valley*
	1949	Chagall: *Over Vitebsk*
Vietnam War		
	1962	Marisol: *The Family*
Feminist Movement	**1970**	
	1971	Bamgboye of Odo-Owa: *Orangun Epa Headdress*
	1972	Saar: *The Liberation of Aunt Jemima*
	1973	*Waupanal*
	1979	Tseng Kwong Chi: *Disneyland, California*
	1983	Murray: *Sail Baby*
	1984	General Idea: *Baby Makes 3*
	1986	Luna: *The Artifact Piece*
		Guerilla Girls: *Do women have to be naked to get into the Met. Museum?*
	1989	Hung Liu: *Trauma*

We looked at artworks that seek to preserve racial identity and the history and values of an ethnic group. Other artworks in this chapter protest racial oppression, turning negative stereotypes and racist habits into forceful criticisms of racism.

Gender roles are reinforced or challenged in the artworks we saw in this chapter, where gender identity is formed through rituals or art. Gender issues affect our interpretation of various European artworks. Gender practices can also symbolize broad political trends—for example, the oppressive practice of foot binding is linked to government suppression. Art can be a vehicle to protest unequal pay and opportunities for women in the art world.

The very identity of a clan is often supported by artwork that makes the clan's history visible or validates the power of the living rulers. Art may enhance the telling of a clan's oral history during feasts and celebrations. The nuclear family is depicted in art as a complex entity, with strong alliances, conflicting emotions, and tensions. Art can show us the closeness of siblings or the shifting definitions of family.

Upper and lower classes are depicted differently in art. In art from various cultures, class rank and distinction were made clear, through the amount of space occupied and the quality of the furnishings. Poverty, desperation, or fear mark the figures from the lowest classes.

In the last section, we saw artworks that were directly related to class because of the subject shown, the size, and the materials used.

FOOD FOR THOUGHT

We saw racism challenged in many works of art. Glorifying racial identity may have positive results. Racial glorification mixed with ideas of racial superiority leads to disaster.

- When does promoting the beautiful get confused with superiority?

The culture of the Sepik people of Papua New Guinea may seem very distant from the United States today. However, consider the following questions:

- Are you familiar with any gender-based organizations, jobs, clubs, sports, or religious practices that exist in your life now?
- Which consumer products reinforce gender roles in the United States today?

In this chapter, we did not look at art that referenced the elderly. But let us consider aging for a moment.

- What images of old people do we get from fine art and popular art forms?

Almost every art form is a reflection of the class for whom the art is made. We see repeatedly that the most lavish works are made for upper classes, while more modest works are for the lower classes. What about access to art? In many cases, the wealthy are the only ones who can afford to purchase high-profile art or develop collections around well-known artists. Most private collections are not accessible to the public. Eventually, some art collections owned by wealthy individuals end up in museums.

- Does the museum redress the class-related issues of ownership and access to art?
- Who controls what art gets into museums?
- Are there any forms of art that transcend class?
- Art is made by humans for humans, so shouldn't everyone feel comfortable with it, no matter of what clan or class?

YOUR CD-ROM RESOURCES

- World History in Context
- Exploring Art Timeline
- Flashcards
- Food for Thought
- Companion Site
    Chapter 14 Quiz
    InfoTrac® College Edition Readings
    Artist Flashcards
    Online Study Guide

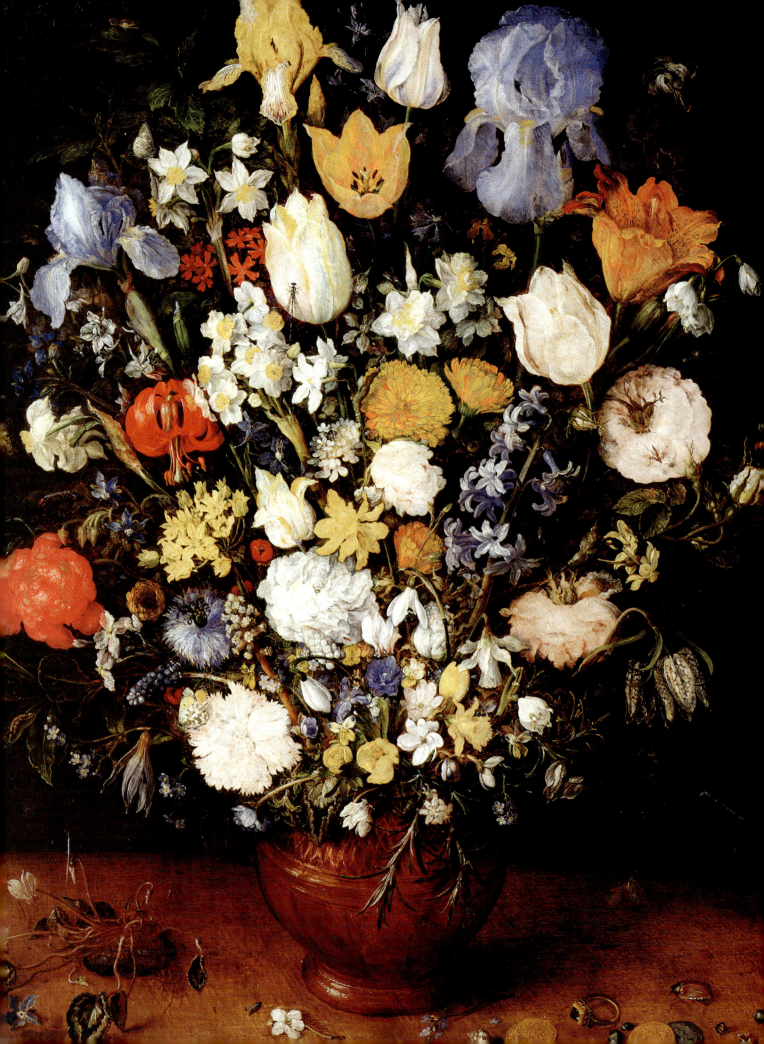

CHAPTER 15

NATURE, KNOWLEDGE, AND TECHNOLOGY

INTRODUCTION

Artists make art that imitates, admires, and judges the world around us. That world consists of animals and plants as well as human constructs: our knowledge systems, our technology, our cities. For this chapter, the basic questions are:

What do we consider ideal in nature?

How do animals in art reflect desirable or despicable qualities in humans?

What do we know about the world around us through art?

How does art advance knowledge?

When does knowledge advance the well-being of humans and the world, and when is it oppressive, manipulative, or too unwieldy to be helpful?

What are our attitudes regarding the things humans have constructed in the world?

How is technology helping us, and how is it hurting us?

The relationship of humans and animals is very complex. We hunt them, love them, and eat them. They are part of industry, as we breed some and extinguish others. We identify with animals and project our highest aspirations and deepest fears onto them. Likewise, people use landscape imagery, both the wild and the cultivated, to project their own ideals.

Human knowledge has been expanded through artwork, from educational illustrations to imagery for introspection. We will look at some examples in this wide range.

Art comments on technology, reflecting our mixed attitudes and relationships to it. We have proliferated technology wildly because of its advantages and comforts. Recently, however, we have seen its polluting side effects, the global political entanglements our dependence upon it may cause, and the ways it controls our lives.

Little Bouquet in a Clay Jar. Detail of Figure 15.16. © Archivo Iconograpfico, S.A./Corbis.

NATURE

Our natural world consists of the earth and its flora and fauna. All figure prominently in art.

ANIMALS

Animals appear in art in every culture, in forms that are both real and imagined. As far as we know, animals were the subjects of humans' first drawings. They figure in myths and religious narratives, such as "Noah and the Ark" and the *Ramayana*. Humans have observed and recorded animal likenesses and have used them as vehicles for expressing ideas about the world at large. Finally, as if animals like aardvarks, armadillos, and narwhals were not fantastic enough, humans have invented bizarre creatures pieced together with parts of other living beings.

CONNECTION
The cave drawings at Lascaux, Figure 7.1 (page 156), are among the oldest existing drawings made by humans.

FANTASTIC CREATURES

Fantastic creatures are usually an amalgam of parts from existing animals. They are the product of human imagination, fear, and desire. Because they really do not exist, their human creators can assign a meaning and purpose to them. These creatures still feed popular imagination, as mermaids, giant insects, and werewolves are alive and well in film and literature.

CONNECTION
Examples of fantastic creatures appear in previous chapters. They include serpents (Laocoön and His Sons, Figure 13.16, page 380), human-headed winged bulls (Lamassu, Figure 11.11, page 311), and totem animals (Interior House Post, Figure 14.15, page 412).

Fantastic creatures can express various forms of power. The limestone *Relief,* dated sixth century BCE (Figure 15.1), comes from the Olmec culture of ancient Mexico, which produced many instances of animal imagery that combine natural and fantastic elements. Here, a helmeted man sits in the lower center of the relief holding a bag. His accoutrements suggest that he is either a warrior or a priest. He wears an elaborate helmet formed into a mixed jaguar-serpent creature. The extended jaw of the creature forms the chinstrap, and the man's face appears in its gaping, fierce mouth. The large serpent both cradles and towers over the man. It has the realistic rattles of a

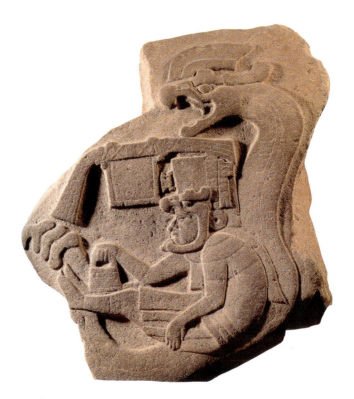

 15.1 *Relief.* Basalt, 38¹/₂" high. Olmec. La Venta (Mexico), sixth century BCE. Museo Nacional de Antropología, Mexico City. The Metropolitan Museum of Art, NY.

rattlesnake, but the heavy brows and crest suggest some sort of imaginary bird. Undoubtedly, the animal attributes are combined with human to create a being of heightened powers.

The ancient Greeks invented several fantastic creatures, but in contrast to the Olmec *Relief,* these beings generally were threats to humans or represented degraded human nature. Harpies were woman-headed birds who lured and fed on men. Centaurs were man-headed horses known for their lustfulness. Satyrs were men with goat or horse attributes and were prone to drunkenness and sexual excess. Medieval Europeans were especially interested in fantastic animals, like the satyrs and centaurs from antiquity, and made up several of their own. Medieval beasts, however, often acted like humans in narratives that had a moralizing purpose. Bestiaries were common in medieval times, filled with lions, pigs, rabbits, and dogs as well as sirens, harpies, griffins, dragons, and so on. Margins of prayer books featured small paintings of exotic animals. Church gargoyles and capitals were carved in the shapes of various tormenting creatures, a warning to humans of the danger of hell.

The unicorn is a horse with some goat features and a long, single horn projecting from its forehead. Ancient Greeks and Romans first described it, but in the late medieval era, the unicorn took on many layers of secular and religious meaning and was very popular in literature. "Unicorn" horns were expensive, prized possessions (they were actually the spiral tusk of a narwhal, an arctic whale). People believed unicorn horns could purify water and remove any poison from it. Another common belief was that the unicorn could elude all hunters. However, when it saw a virgin, it put its head on her lap and could easily be caught. The virgin was taken to represent Mary, and the unicorn became a symbol for Christ.

The Unicorn in Captivity, dated late fifteenth century (Figure 15.2), is the last image in six tapestries. Previous scenes showed the splendid animal using its horn to purify water from a fountain of life for lions, stags, and pheasants. Other scenes show the unicorn being hunted, tricked into captivity, and slaughtered. Our example shows the unicorn as a brilliant white horse captured in a paradise garden, surrounded by an abundance of decorative flowers and plants. The details are delightful, all distributed in a flat pattern that fills the space from top to bottom with carefully rendered, colorful flowers. The unicorn has a lively and soulful expression on its face. It

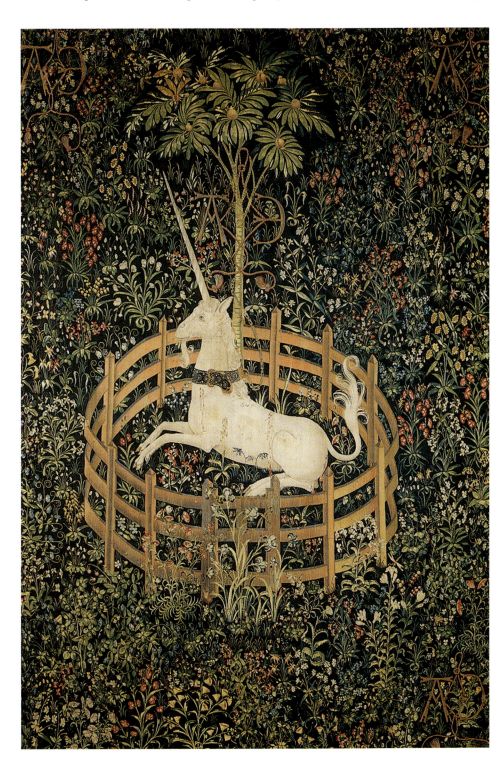

15.2　*The Unicorn in Captivity.* Wool warp, wool, silk, silver, and gilt wefts, 12'1" × 8'3". South Netherlandish, 1495–1505. Gift of John D. Rockefeller, Jr., 1937. The Metropolitan Museum of Art, New York, Cloister Collection.

is surrounded by a fence, wears a jeweled collar, and is chained to a pomegranate tree.

The unicorn represented at least two different sets of meanings in these tapestries. One is that of Jesus, believed to be the source of spiritual life, who was hunted by men and brutally killed. In the last scene, shown here, he is the indestructible, eternally Risen Christ. Or, the images may represent the course of true love, with the unicorn as the chivalrous male and the virgin the object of his desire, and the unicorn in this set of tapestries has had to endure terrible ordeals to win his beloved. The collar represents a chain of love, mentioned in medieval allegories as a sign that a gentleman submits to his lady's will. The pomegranates above the unicorn drip their red juice onto its coat; the pomegranate is a symbol both of Christ's resurrection and of human fertility. Dual meanings were common in the medieval era, as a way to acknowledge the complexity of life.

The *Shaman's Amulet,* dated c. 1820–1850 (Figure 15.3), is an example in which the combination of animal forms is a source of power and protection among the peoples of the Northwest Coast of North America. A shaman, a person having supernatural powers, was believed to be a bridge among the human, animal, and spirit worlds. The combination of animal and human forms in the amulet was both symbolic and functional; it was a visible sign of the shaman's power, and it extended that power. The most prominent animal is the sea serpent, whose head is to the right, swallowing a human. This indicated that the shaman could take on the forms of certain animals and could operate in both the animal and human

realms. Other animals include a bear, for its strength, and a bird, for its ability to fly.

The design of the amulet is engaging, as there are many details of animal forms to hold one's interest. All these details are united and contained within the smooth, arching outline of the amulet. Many internal forms, such as folded arms, lines of feathers, and the serpent's mouth, echo the outer shape. A dark patina makes the details stand out and adds to the volumetric quality of the work. The shape and size of the amulet enabled it to fit easily in the hand.

Another example of fantastic creatures comes from Thailand, a country abundant with jungles and animal life. The monsoon rains fall in deluges, and the humidity is heavy during the rainy season. Plants, birds, and beasts abound in traditional Thai art. Many powerful ones are composite beasts, but others are snakes and birds that have been associated with forces in nature. Most images have more than one meaning. Monkeys, for example, are common wild animals in Thailand, and they are metaphors for humans, who aspire to be gods. They figure in many Hindu and Buddhist tales, where they indulge in behavior and emotions unfit for humans or gods, such as lust and drunkenness. Monkeys can present the realistic side of human nature in contrast to the idealized.

Mask of Hanuman (Figure 15.4) is a headpiece representing Hanuman, the white monkey-hero and loyal follower of Rama, who is an incarnation of the Hindu God Vishnu in the Thai story *Ramakien* (called the *Ramayana* in India). Performers wear this mask when representing this fantastic creature, a divine monkey with white fur, jeweled teeth, and a

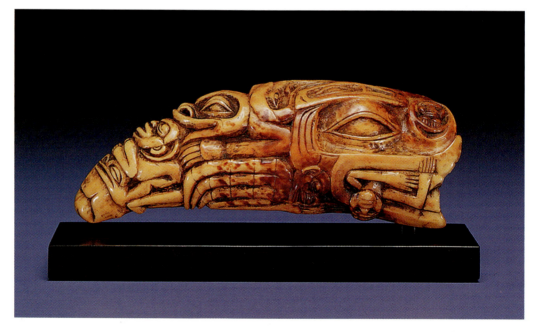

 15.3 *Shaman's Amulet.* Sperm whale tooth, 6¹/₂" long. Tlingit. Alaska/ British Columbia, c. 1820–1850. Indiana University Art Museum, Bloomington, Indiana, Raymond and Laura Wielgus Collection (RW 60–197). Photo by Michael Cavanagh / Kevin Montague.

white crest of hair atop his head that shone like diamonds. His heroic exploits were many, including helping Rama rescue his wife from a demon and bringing a mountain of medicinal plants to cure the wounded in battle. The *Mask of Hanuman* is equally fantastic, covered with gleaming, iridescent mother-of-pearl. Red, black, and green dramatically outline his facial features. His bulging eyes and snarling mouth are visually arresting, alert, and ferocious at the same time. Curves and spirals mark the contours of his cheeks and skull. Gold serpents curl at his ears. As fantastic as he is, Hanuman is modeled from an actual monkey, the leaf-eating langur from India (Taylor 1994: 35–38).

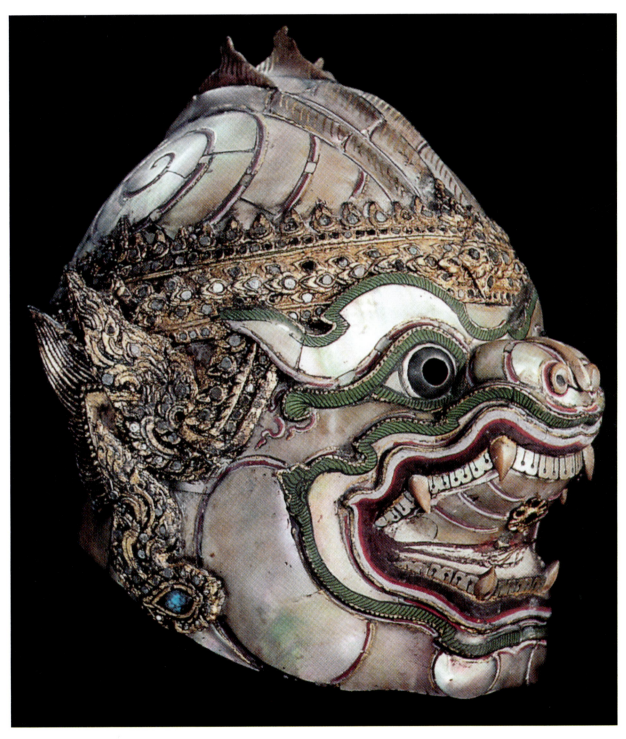

 15.4   *Mask of Hanuman.* Mother-of-pearl, gilt, gems, and other materials; fits over a human head. Thailand. National Museum of Bangkok. Photo Pam Taylor.

The monkey is again a stand-in for human behavior in Chris Ofili's 1999 painting, *Monkey Magic—Sex, Money and Drugs* (Figure 15.5). Here the monkey holds an empty turquoise vessel and tries to capture three powerful elements of life: sex, money, and drugs. Ofili has attached three clumps of dried elephant dung to the canvas, each representing one of the elements. The colored heads of straight pins inserted into the dung spell out the words. Thick beads of paint and layers of glitter make the surface colorful and shining, to emphasize the imagined rather than real quality. Ofili is a British artist of Nigerian descent, and his use of dried elephant dung references the African ritual use of the material. He often displays his paintings resting on balls of dung, because they seem then to be coming up from the earth rather than hanging on the wall.

OBSERVED ANIMALS

Animals are magnificent creatures, and, in many instances, the likenesses of animals as they actually are—without embellishment—are sufficient justification for a work of art.

An ancient set of stone reliefs shows how people admire animals and, at the same time, desire to destroy them. In *Ashurbanipal Hunting Lions*, c. 650 BCE (Figure 15.6), the lions' muscles, veins, and bones show their tremendous strength. Their faces show their fierceness, and their flexible bodies are capable of tremendous leaps. Although they greatly admired the beauty of the living lion, the Assyrian elite slaughtered them in a public spectacle, the royal lion hunt. Lions in cages were released in an enclosed arena, where the king, Ashurbanipal, accompanied by bowmen and spearmen, would kill them. The fact that the lion is a strong and admirable animal made the king's courage in facing them all the greater, as did the large number of lion carcasses piled behind him. The Assyrians believed that the longer a man or beast took to die, the higher the layer of heaven that was attained in the afterlife. This is why many lions are depicted as wounded or slowly dying.

The Assyrians made many such relief carvings to cover the mud-brick palace walls. They boasted the king's power not only in lion hunts, but also in battle campaigns and in accompanying the gods. The low relief made it possible to produce great numbers of carvings. Yet Assyrian carvers were so skilled that the bodies of the lions seem rounded and their muscles evident despite the shallowness of the carving. The curving silhouettes of the lions are particularly effective.

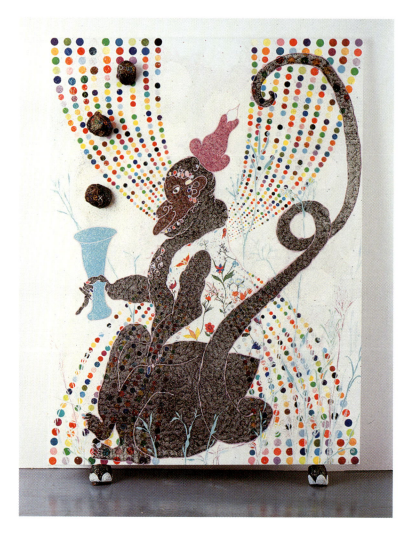

15.5 CHRIS OFILI. *Monkey Magic—Sex, Money and Drugs.* Acrylic, collage, glitter, resin, pencil, map pins, and elephant dung on canvas, 96" × 72". Great Britain, 1999. Museum of Contemporary Art, Los Angeles. Purchased with funds by the Broad Art Foundation. Courtesy Chris Ofili—Afroco and Victoria Miro Gallery.

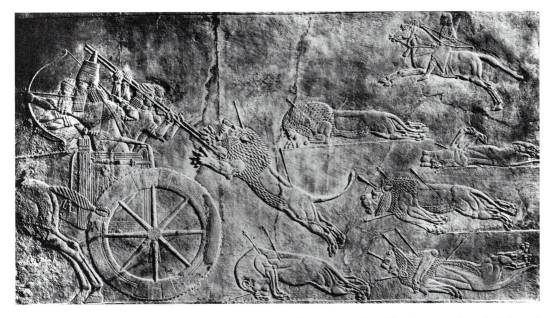

 15.6 *Ashurbanipal Hunting Lions.* Limestone relief, approximately 60" high. Assyria, from the Palace of Ashurbanipal, Nineveh (northern Iraq), c. 650 BCE. The British Museum, London. Photo: The British Museum, London.

The Nazca culture, a pre-Incan civilization in southwestern Peru, produced a group of large-scale animal drawings on a flat, rock-strewn, arid plain, devoid of vegetation. With no wind and essentially no rainfall—less than one inch over a twelve-year span—a casual footprint or scrap of litter will remain undisturbed for years. The Nazca drawings were made at least 1,400 years ago by scraping the thin, brown surface of the desert floor, revealing lighter-colored sand and stone beneath. The earliest drawings were of animals, such as birds, whales, monkeys, or dogs. Our example, *Spider* (Figure 15.7), dates from around 200–600. Later drawings consisted of large geometric shapes, spirals, and a large number of long, straight lines that extend for miles or radiate from center points. Many drawings were made right on top of previous ones.

The Nazca drawings are remarkable for their regularity. Straight lines extend for long distances, and curved lines coil perfectly back on themselves. All lines in a drawing are a single, standard width. Each outline is executed as a continuous path. The Nazca people probably used rudimentary surveying instruments and string to plot the paths. The drawings are so large and the plain so flat that most images cannot be discerned from the ground. The exact meaning or use of the lines and drawings is unknown. Some long, straight lines may have been used for astronomical sightings, while others may have been

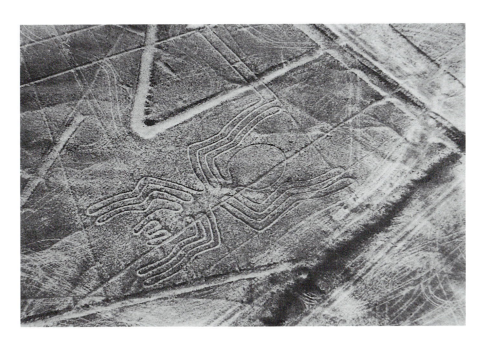

15.7 *Spider.* Large drawing created when brown surface rocks were scraped away to reveal yellowish surface below. Nazca, Peru, c. 200–600. Henri Stierlin.

paths that connected the plain's various shrines. The animal drawings may have been messages or offerings to the gods, especially water gods. In such a parched environment, underground water sources were more important than rainfall, and the later Incas believed that water gods resided in mountains, a belief perhaps shared by the earlier Nazca. The spider is still highly regarded in areas of Peru and Bolivia because it both augurs weather changes, and certain series of actions by spiders are believed to foretell rainfall.

Vessel in the Form of a Monkey, made between 800 and 900 (Figure 15.8), is from the pre-Columbian Veracruz culture in Mexico. Animal-shaped vessels were common in many Mesoamerican and South American cultures. The monkey's squatting pose, with its arms overhead grasping its own tail, and its facial structure are convincingly naturalistic to the point that its species can be identified: it is a spider monkey. The artist has captured the animated expressions and energy of the animal. In addition, small rocks sealed inside in hollow pockets rattle when the vessel is shaken, mimicking the monkey's chatter. Monkeys were kept as pets and were featured in Mesoamerican mythology. They were also linked to dancers, because of their quick, agile movements, or to uninhibited sexuality (Pelrine 1996: 75). The monkey in this example has pierced ears, like humans. On the formal side, the vessel can be enjoyed for its design: the monkey's belly in front and expanded back become the vessel. The opening is behind the monkey's head. Rounded belly shapes contrast with angular forms of the arms, as do the concentrated facial details with the smooth abdomen. Protruding forms, negative spaces, and dark hollows all add to the vessel's visual richness.

Horses have been admired in many cultures. In a detail of a small scroll entitled *Three Horses and Four Grooms,* from the late thirteenth or early fourteenth century (Figure 15.9), artist Ren Renfa portrayed the animals as very strong and, at the same time, delicately light on their feet. With subtle color and sure line, the artist captured the silken hair and details in the horses' heads and feet. They stand out against the plain back-

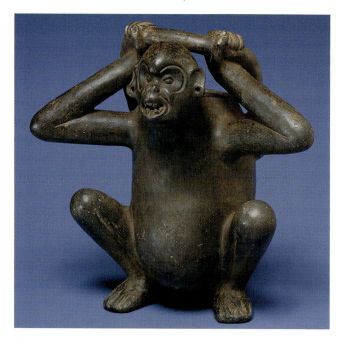

15.8   *Vessel in the Form of a Monkey.* Clay, 8$^{1}/_{2}$" high. Veracruz, Mexico, late Classic period, 800–900. Indiana University Art Museum, Bloomington, Indiana. Raymond and Laura Wielgus Collection. IUAM 100.7.4.75 (RW 62–233). Photo by Michael Cavanagh / Kevin Montague.

ground as beautiful shapes, with deep chests, long bodies, and arched necks. Horses in general were especially prized in China during the era of Mongol domination, under Genghis Khan. Khan's empire spread from Turkey to Korea, and the success of the Mongol army was due to the strong, fast horses of the cavalry. Under Mongol law, stealing a horse was a crime punishable by death. It is interesting that the grooms are depicted as Chinese, although the painting was probably commissioned by a Mongol patron.

THE LAND

This section is divided into four groups. In the first, the land is the subject of paintings and photography. The second group

15.9   REN RENFA. *Three Horses and Four Grooms* (detail). Handscroll, ink and color on silk, 11$^{1}/_{2}$" × 54". China, 1254–1327. The Cleveland Museum of Art. © Cleveland Museum of Art, Leonard C. Hanna, Jr., Fund, #1960.181.

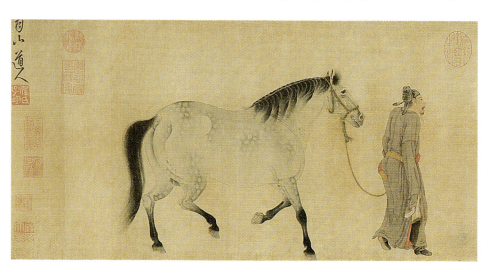

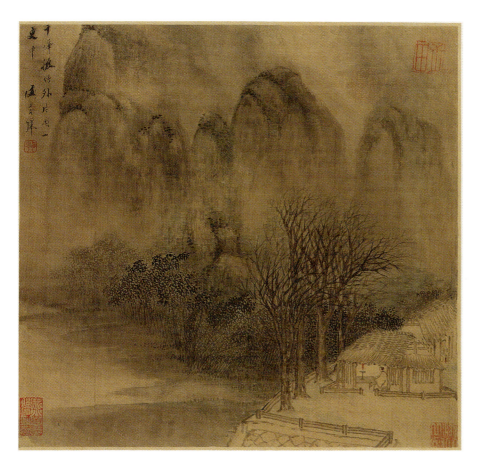

15.10 SHENG MAOYE. *Beyond the Solitary Bamboo Grove.* Ink and color on silk, 11¼" × 12". From an album of six leaves; landscapes inspired by Tang poems. China, c. 1625–1640. The Metropolitan Museum of Art, New York. Purchase, The Sackler Fund, 1969 (69.242.4).

deals with planned gardens and cultivated flowers. The third covers art in which earth is used as sculptural material. Finally, we will see art that addresses ecological concerns.

LANDSCAPE IMAGERY

Enjoying a landscape image is quite a different experience than enjoying the actual outdoors. Most landscape images are highly aestheticized, in either their compositions, their materials, or marks used to make them. In addition, they may have deeper social or religious meanings.

Landscape imagery is common in Chinese and Japanese paintings and is especially popular among upper- and middle-class urban populations in affluent times. Although they were the centers of wealth, cities were overcrowded, noisy, and polluted. The booming city of Suchou, wealthy from the European silk trade and tourists, had one park so overcrowded that a local artist called it "squalid," with "visitors flock[ing] there like flies swarming on meat" (Cahill 1966: 87). Such paintings as Sheng Maoye's *Beyond the Solitary Bamboo Grove* (Figure 15.10), from the seventeenth century, made pristine nature

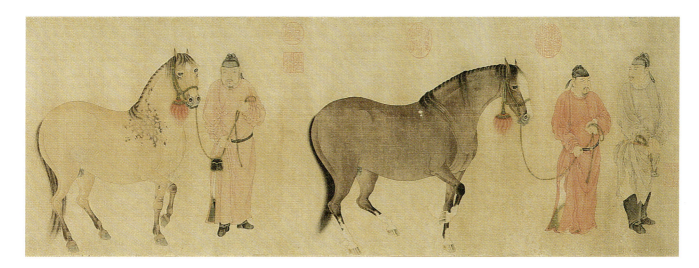

once again available. In homes, landscapes were displayed on large, hanging silk scrolls, on fans, or on smaller album leaves for private viewing. Our example shows the subtle blurring effects of mist, the isolated hut, and the distinctive silhouettes of various trees with a naturalism that seems effortless. The effects of the painting are achieved mostly through subtle washes of ink and light color, expertly painted. The soft, rounded, misty mountains in the background contrast with the crisply rendered trees and line-drawn hut in the lower right corner of the painting. Poetry was often an important inspiration for landscape painters. Many Chinese landscapes reflected religious beliefs of Daoism (or Taoism), which held that nature was a visible manifestation of the Absolute Dao, the ultimate substratum from which all things come. Nature also reflected Daoism in its rhythms, changes, and transformations. Chinese landscapes are carefully composed imaginary scenes. Artists practiced their brushwork for years to achieve a sense of effortlessness and spontaneity, qualities valued in Daoism.

Landscape paintings were particularly common in the United States and in Europe in the nineteenth century. Landscapes tended to have a nationalistic look. For example, German landscapes often were marked by melancholy or morbidity. English landscapes, however, tended to emphasize the open-air expansiveness of the countryside. John Constable's *The Haywain,* from 1821 (Figure 15.11), shows a broad meadow in the distance, while in the foreground, a farmer with his wagon fords a stream next to a white cottage framed by dark trees. The composition seems casual, direct, natural, and unstudied. Tranquility pervades all, as a warm mellow light washes over the greens, golds, and browns of the land, and brilliant clouds play against the blue sky.

Constable communicated a sense of rightness, as humans on the farm live a healthy and virtuous life, at one with nature. His work appealed especially to Europeans who had migrated in large numbers to industrial cities and felt a sense of loss of contact with nature. Constable constantly sought communion with nature. Before painting large canvases, Constable made numerous outdoor studies that he saw as being scientific (meteorology was his avocation). But his work also grows from **Romanticism,** which elevated nature and immediate experience. On his finished works, he used small dabs of bright color and white to paint the shimmering of light. His method was important later to **Impressionism.**

One impressionist, Claude Monet, is especially well known for his paintings of nature. He painted almost exclusively outdoors to capture the subtle qualities of light and reflection, and even planted his own water garden at his home in Giverny, France. In *Water Lily Pool* (Figure 15.12), from 1900, the colors are dazzling; by mixing vivid strokes of pure color, Monet achieved the effect of sunlight upon water. In Monet's later career, his paintings approached abstraction, as the emphasis on brushstrokes became more important than imagery. The Impressionists' emphasis on observation paralleled the ideas of scientists and philosophers of the day, who

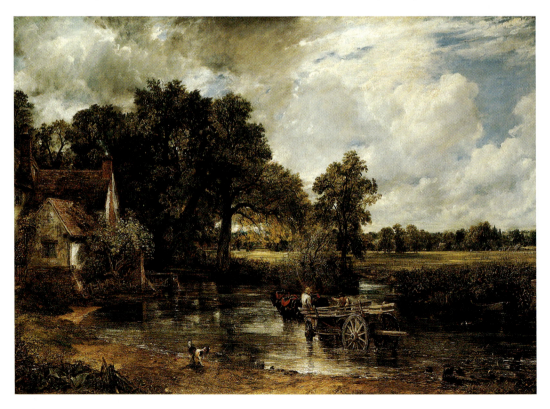

 15.11   JOHN CONSTABLE. *The Haywain.* Oil on canvas, 4'3"× 6'2". England, 1821. The National Gallery, London.

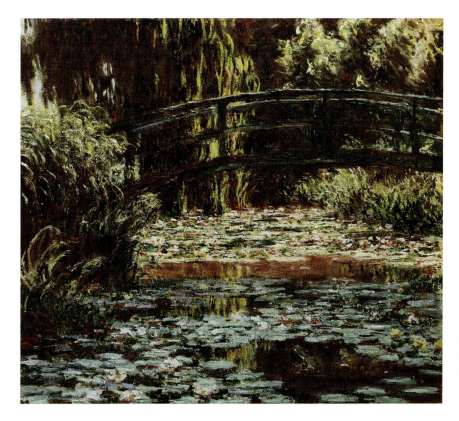

15.12 CLAUDE MONET. *Water Lily Pool*. Oil on canvas, 35³/₈" × 39³/₄". France, 1900. The Art Institute of Chicago. © 2004 Artists Rights Society (ARS), New York / ADAGP, Paris. Mr. and Mrs. Lewis Larned Coburn Memorial Collection.

posited that reality was only that which could be sensed, measured, and analyzed.

Landscape painters in the United States were influenced by European models, but they produced more images of pristine, untouched nature than the Europeans did. Even photographers in the United States were influenced by undeveloped areas of the Midwest and West. Ansel Adams was particularly well known for landscape photographs of remote areas of the West, as exemplified in *Clearing Winter Storm, Yosemite National Park, California, 1944* (Figure 15.13). His

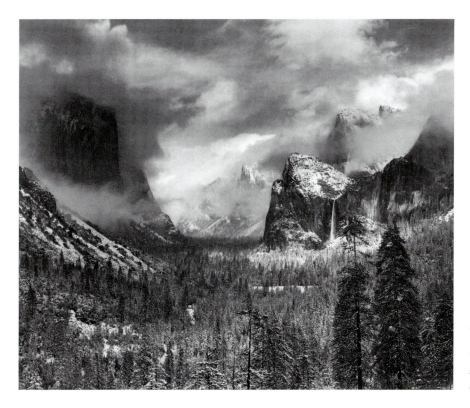

15.13 ANSEL ADAMS. *Clearing Winter Storm, Yosemite National Park, California, 1944*. Photograph. USA, 1944. Copyright © 1993 by the Trustees of the Ansel Adams Publishing Rights Trust / Corbis. All rights reserved.

photographs were particularly grand and romantic, with broad expanses of sky, dramatic peaks, and the sensual textures of flora and rock. In our example, the mist- and cloud-covered mountains are the focal point, balanced by the white-lit clouds above, whose wispy forms contrast with the textured expanse of trees below.

Adams worked very hard to get his negatives, exploring, studying, and waiting until light and form created a brilliant effect. In this case, the light had to catch the waterfall while the surrounding cliff was in dark shadow. The thin, bright, white line of water against the dark ridge becomes the focus of the work. Of course, the clouds and snowfall added further uncertainty to getting the right shot. Adams was careful to balance the squared peaks on the left with the pointed peaks on the right; the center remains clear for the seemingly infinite recession of space. Finally, Adams manipulated the photographing and printing of his images until he achieved the full range of tone available in black-and-white photography. Brilliant white contrasts with the darkest blacks.

Adams's photograph promotes the beauty of nature unaltered by the human hand, an ideal very different from that of Constable's *Haywain*. Adams's concept was similar to the Native American idea of the sacred places in nature. His landscape photographs were so brilliant and visually splendid that they helped to generate public support for national parks and for the environmental movement in general.

FLOWERS AND GARDENS

Art about flowers gives us framed, composed, distilled, and transcendent images that are based on, but different from, the real experiences of flowers. And all gardens are works of art to some degree. Earth, rock, wood, and plants are part of a living sculpture, an exotic refuge arranged for human enjoyment. Water is frequently a central motif for a garden, whether in a small backyard or next to a king's palace. Paintings of gardens attempt to capture that same sense of pleasure and release.

Two millennia ago, gardens were popular among the Romans. Like the Europeans and the Chinese discussed on previous pages, the Romans had become urban dwellers with the success of their empire, but they never lost their love of the country and their tendency to idealize life surrounded by nature. The very wealthy could afford the expense of a villa in the country. Others with means cultivated small, courtyard gardens and had distant vistas painted on walls. *Gardenscape,* dated c. 30–20 BCE (Figure 15.14), is a detail of a painting from a partly underground room of an imperial villa. From floor to ceiling and all around, the enclosing walls are dissolved by the airy depiction of flowering plants, flying birds, fruit-bearing trees, and pale blue skies. Although nearby forms are painted in detail, distant trees are pale and blurred, dissolved by atmospheric perspective. A low garden fence separates the space of the painting from the actual space of the room. The overall tones of blue and green are accented by the occasional splash of orange, white, or red fruit.

Like gardens, flowers are sources of pleasure and vehicles for greater understanding. In Japan, flower arranging is considered an important art form, on the level of painting, calligraphy, and pottery. Flower paintings were particularly popular in both China and Japan. An example from China is *Apricot Blossoms,* dated early thirteenth century (Figure 15.15), by Ma Yuan, a lyric painting with lines of poetry by Empress Yang,

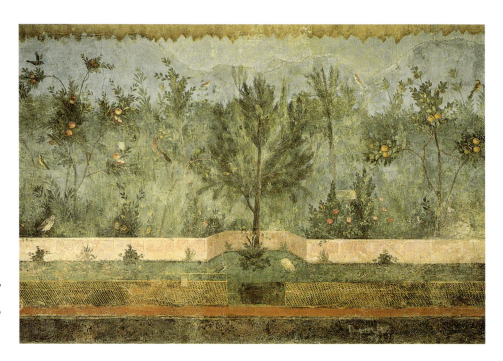

15.14   *Gardenscape.* Second style wall painting, approximately 6'7" high. Roman, from the Villa of Livia, Primaporta, c. 30–20 BCE. Il Museo Nazionale Romano–Palazzo Massimo alle Terme, Rome. Photo by Henri Stierlin.

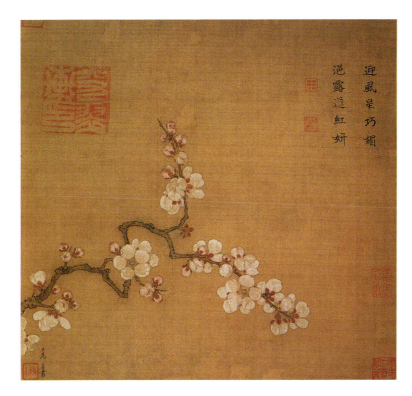

15.15 MA YUAN. *Apricot Blossoms.* Album leaf with ink and color on silk, 10' high. China, Southern Song Dynasty, early thirteenth century. National Palace Museum, Taiwan. For more about this artwork, see Figure 1.3.

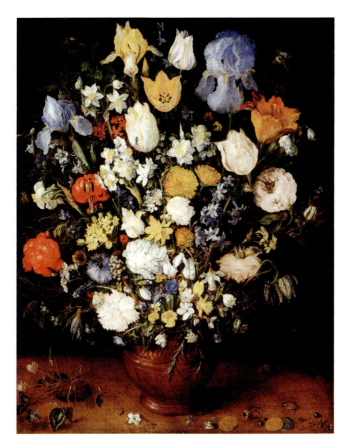

15.16 JAN BRUEGEL. *Little Bouquet in a Clay Jar.* Oil on panel, 20" × 15³/₄". Flanders, c. 1599. Kunsthistorisches Museum, Vienna. © Archivo Iconograpfico, S.A. / Corbis. For more about this artwork, see Figure 1.11.

which read: "They greet the wind with artful charm; / Boasting pink beauty moist with dew." Ma Yuan's brushwork is refined. The blossoms are outlined in elegant curves, while the ink strokes that make the branch are crisp and angular. The twisting branches bend and display themselves in an off-balance, irregular composition that captures the unexpected forms in nature. Branch and poem both seem to be suspended in the space. The rich golden color of the background and the delicate whites and pinks of the blossoms contrast with the dark branch. The beauty of the blossoms is simple and timeless, but the flowers last only a short time.

Ma Yuan was a professional court painter who collaborated with Empress Yang on other works as well. Such painters produced large quantities of small works, with poems penned by the emperor or his circle, to be given away as gifts and favors. The combination of poetry and painting was common; both poet and painter were believed to have the capacity to express ineffable beauty. Brushwork was an exacting art, requiring long practice at making subtle washes and dark strokes that captured the essence of the plant. Also, it was important that artists know how to select, combine, and distill aspects of many apricot blossoms, so that their paintings suggested the whole experience of the short-lived blooms, including their smell and their movement in the wind. Working from just one sample would likely result in detailed drawings that were painstaking but dull.

Flower paintings have also been very popular in the West. In Jan Bruegel's *Little Bouquet in a Clay Jar,* dated c. 1599 and also known as *Iris Bouquet* (Figure 15.16), the bouquet fills the frame with a joyful display of rich colors and delicate shapes. The image is teeming with vitality, not only in the fresh flowers, but also in moths, flies, beetles, slugs, and butterflies. To better capture the subtle coloration, Bruegel layered his paint so that, for example, pale blues might show through under bright yellows without turning into green. He was unsurpassed at painting the silkiness and translucency of petals. He claimed that they were lovelier than gold and gems, proving it by the rings and coins at the lower right in the painting.

Bruegel's flower paintings were a vision beyond reality. His flower arrangements never existed in actual life. He combined local meadow flowers and exotic varieties in a single vase and included specimens that bloom in different climates and in different seasons. However, Bruegel painted the individual flowers only from life, using a magnifying glass to better see each flower, studying it like a scientist. He sometimes waited months for a certain bloom; at other times, he painted in the botanical gardens of the nobility. Bruegel's flower paintings are like little pictures of paradise. He was undoubtedly

aware that flowers had been sacred symbols since medieval times. The iris was the symbol for Jesus, while the rose stood for Mary, and so on. The symbolism may have enriched the meaning of the painting for Bruegel's patrons.

We return to gardens in our next example, *Babur Supervising the Layout of the Garden of Fidelity,* c. 1590 (Figure 15.17). Gardens were very popular among the ruling classes of Persia, central Asia, and Mughal India, all areas under Islamic rulers (these areas are modern-day Iraq, Iran, Afghanistan, Pakistan, and northern India). The *Garden of Fidelity,* like many Islamic gardens, represented Paradise. Water is symbolic, functional, and central to the garden's design. Channeled in four directions through stone courses, each set ninety degrees apart, water represents the four rivers of Paradise. A large catch basin in the foreground sits on a lower level, creating attractive falling water and terraces. The basin also traps overflow and allows silt to settle. These streams subdivide the garden into squares that became the basic garden module. Squares are especially suited to the design of Islamic gardens because they can be

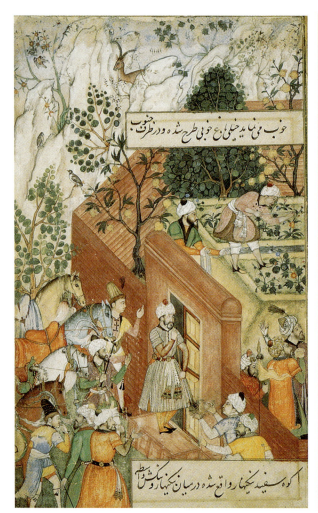
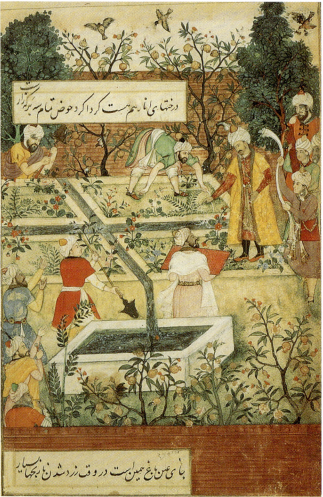

 15.17 BISHNDAS (PORTRAITS BY NANHA). *Babur Supervising the Layout of the Garden of Fidelity.* Manuscript painting, gold and gouache on paper, 8³/₄" × 5³/₄". Mughal. India, c. 1590. Victoria and Albert Museum, London, IM 276–1913. For more about this artwork, see Figure 2.20.

infinitely proliferated without destroying the integrity of the original layout. Thus, squares can be added easily around the edge of the garden, or existing blocks can be further subdivided to create more squares. The proliferation of squares represents the abundance of Allah's creation. In almost all cases, Islamic gardens are geometric in design.

The sensual appeal of Babur's garden is apparent in the lush flowering and fruit-bearing trees. Birds are nesting, and ducks and fish appear in the cool water. The outer wall provides privacy for the garden and protects it from desert wind and sand—note the bare hills outside the wall. The English word *paradise* comes originally from ancient Persian words for "walled garden," and most images of paradise from any culture are based on gardens. Many Persian gardens were originally oases in the desert.

Babur Supervising the Layout of the Garden of Fidelity is a book illumination from the memoirs of Emperor Babur, a botanist who took great interest in planning many gardens throughout the lands that he ruled, both garden oases in deserts and hanging terraces on mountainsides. In our example, he is standing near the right edge, directing an engineer who is holding plans, as a workman behind measures a section of a plot. For Babur, the garden was important in establishing his identity and securing his power. He was originally a minor prince who eventually conquered much of central Asia and northern India. To bolster his legitimacy as a ruler, Babur emphasized that he was a descendant (a very distant one to be sure) of two great conquerors, Genghis (Chingiz) Khan and Tamerlane (Timur). Establishing gardens linked him to the great rulers of the past, as horticulture was a prerogative of princes, and the garden physically separated the prince and his court from the common people. In addition, the symmetry and geometry of gardens like the Garden of Fidelity provided a visible sign of order. Babur believed his rule created order out of the chaos of the world around him.

CONNECTION
Review the discussion of the Taj Mahal (Figure 10.21, page 285) for more on Islamic gardens symbolizing Paradise.

CONNECTION
Expansive gardens were often the privilege of the ruling class and a sign of their power, as at the palace at Versailles (Figure 5.4, page 105, and the Chapter 13 World History in Context box, page 395)

In Japan, there are different traditions for gardens. One kind is planned around a pond (or lake, in larger versions). Rocks, plants, landforms, winding paths, buildings, and bridges are arranged so visitors are constantly delighted by views that are new, fresh, and changing. Everything about these gardens is deliberate, down to the way the plants are pruned. In this way, the gardens are an echo of paradise.

A different tradition in Japanese garden design is exemplified in the *Ryoanji Zen Garden of Contemplation*, c. 1488–1499 (Figure 15.18), in a courtyard of a Buddhist temple in the city of Kyoto. This kind of garden is laid out to be completely

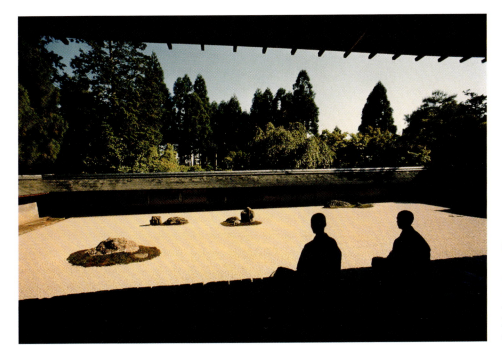

15.18 *Ryoanji Zen Garden of Contemplation.* Walled garden, 99' wide × 33' deep. Daijuin Monastery, Kyoto, Japan, c. 1488–1499. © Paul Chesley, Stone / Getty Images.

visible at once from one point of view. No one walks through this garden (except one who rakes the stones). Stillness is emphasized, as visitors sit along one edge and meditate on the minimal elements, consisting of large, dark boulders amid raked, luminous white quartz gravel. The garden elements parallel both the cosmos and Buddhist philosophy. The white quartz represents the void both of the universe and of the mind; the dark rocks represent material substances and worldly events that float through the universe and through the mind. The gravel is also likened to an ocean or a journey; it has been raked in long, parallel lines to represent waves, except for the circle patterns around each boulder, which now stand for mountains. The fifteen large rocks, each of a distinctive shape and outline, are arranged in five groups. Their shapes, sizes, and orientations contrast with each other, creating visual tension and variety. The fifteen rocks are arranged such that visitors can see only fourteen at once from any angle. Only when the viewer attains spiritual enlightenment through Zen meditation can the fifteenth stone be seen through the mind's eye.

The *Ryoanji Zen Garden of Contemplation* is very small, but it seems larger when viewed from the entrance because the largest boulder is at the front and the smaller at the back, creating the illusion of greater depth. That illusion becomes a reality as visitors meditate in the garden, filling it with their own thoughts and finding numerous ways in which the rock arrangements are like life's conditions. The rock garden is a reflection of Zen Buddhist beliefs, which hold that the world is full of change and disorder, but by silent meditation, one can reach an intuitive understanding of the oneness of the universe.

EARTHWORKS AND SITE PIECES

The earth itself is sculptural material. Hundreds of years ago, native peoples of North America used dirt to construct large ceremonial mounds. Mounds and pyramids were relatively common in the ancient world, but the North American mounds are unique in being animal-shaped, like the *Serpent* (or *Snake*) *Mound*, c. 900–1300 (Figure 15.19), in Ohio. The distended jaw of the 1,400-foot-long serpent is pointing to the upper

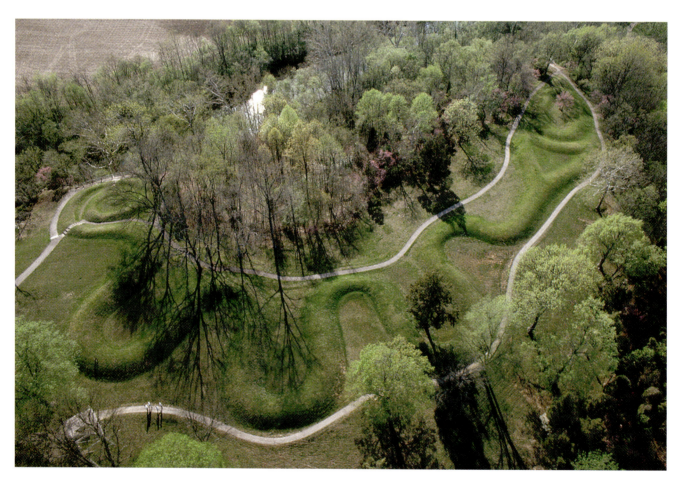

15.19 *Serpent* (or *Snake*) *Mound*. Earthen sculpture, 1,400' long. Native American. Near Locust Grove, Ohio, c. 900–1300. © Richard A. Cooke / Corbis.

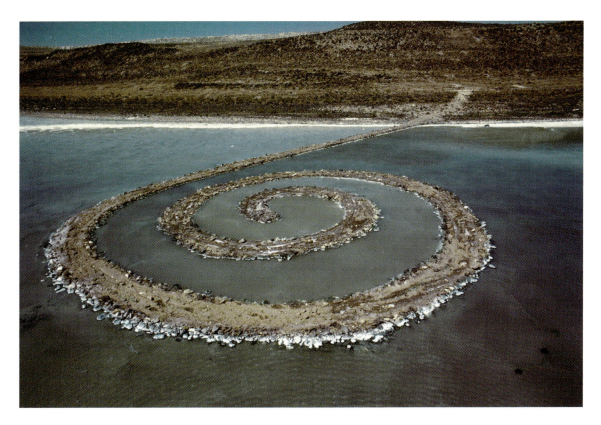

 15.20   ROBERT SMITHSON. *Spiral Jetty.* Earthwork; black rocks, salt crystals, earth, red water (algae), 1,500' long × 15' wide × 3¹/₂' high. Great Salt Lake, Utah, USA, 1970. Courtesy James Cohan Gallery, New York. Art © Estate of Robert Smithson / Licensed by VAGA, New York. See also the text accompanying Figure 5.10.

right; its body curves in rhythmic U-shapes and ends with its spiraling tail. An oval shape inside the serpent's jaw, measuring almost 79 by 158 feet, encircles a plateau with a pile of stones in the center, which may have been an altar. The exact purpose for this monumental sculpture is unknown; in fact, it could only be realized in the minds of those who built it, as they never enjoyed an aerial view of it. The builders must have had a great admiration for the snake to stamp its form so dramatically on their landscape. Much labor was required to dig and carry earth to the site. In 1846, the snake's body was five feet high and thirty feet wide, but it has since eroded to four feet by twenty feet. The serpent's body follows a natural ridge in the land near a small river, visible at the upper center. The natural formation of the landscape may have suggested the serpent shape to its ancient makers.

Contemporary earthworks are large-scale environmental pieces in which the earth itself is an important component. Earthwork artists not only use natural materials, but also are responsive to their sites. The monumental scale of their work is an attribute of both ancient and modern art. There is a minimalist emphasis on simple shapes. Robert Smithson's *Spiral Jetty,* 1970 (Figure 15.20), was made of rocks, dirt, salt, and

water, extending below the broad, bright sky and into the flat, unmoving surface of the Great Salt Lake. Smithson thought that the large spiral in the vast expanse suggested an incredible potential force, like a dormant earthquake or a raging cyclone immobilized. The work is located in a remote site. Few people saw it at the time it was made. Now, it is often inundated and invisible because of the rising lake level.

Smithson was interested in moving his art outside the gallery and away from traditional art materials. He saw his earthworks as unifying art and nature. Human design is, of course, evident in this work, as the spiral shape contrasts completely with the surrounding landscape, despite the use of earth as an art material. Less evident is what went into making the piece, which involved heavy earth-moving equipment, engineering skills, and a number of workers.

 CONNECTION
How are such artworks as Spiral Jetty *financed? For the answer, see Chapter 5, Who Makes Art?*

The Lightning Field, 1971–1977 (Figure 15.21), by Walter De Maria, consists of a large, flat plain surrounded by mountains in New Mexico, and four hundred stainless steel poles arranged in a rectangular grid measuring one kilometer by one square mile. This work of art is not fixed, but ever changing, depending upon season and weather. On clear days, the tall, bright poles with sharpened points catch the sun and glow against the distant mountains and natural vegetation. On stormy days, an occasional bolt of lightning may strike a pole, creating a fleeting, but dramatic, visual effect. The work requires some effort and endurance on the part of viewers. Like *Spiral Jetty, The Lightning Field* is remotely located. To see it, one must get permission from the Dia Foundation, which commissioned the work. Once on-site, the viewer waits for whatever happens, which may be spectacular for a split second, but most likely not, as lightning storms are few, and strikes even fewer. *The Lightning Field* is better known through photographs that document it in different conditions than it is by actual experience. In this respect, the work is also a conceptual piece, existing primarily in the mind of the viewer, who contemplates the contrast between constructed and natural elements, the passage of time as the minutes crawl by in the desolate environment, and the imagined experience of the work as known through various photographs.

ECOLOGICAL CONCERNS

We will now turn to a few works that directly address ecological issues, which are increasingly becoming of concern to artists. Neil Jenney's *Meltdown Morning,* 1975 (Figure 15.22), conveys with poetic simplicity the natural loss that would result from a nuclear accident or nuclear war. It presents a thin slice of a landscape, a view we do not normally see, with a section of a tree trunk. In the distance, in pale pinks, purples, and golds, a mushroom cloud from a nuclear explosion billows in the sky. The mushroom cloud's color is pretty, like the tints of a sunset, seemingly innocuous and comfortingly distant. The thick tree trunk with its rough bark looks substantial, but the clusters of delicate leaves, like graceful green umbrellas, make it clear how vulnerable the natural world is. The sky is luminous. There is a long history of landscape painting that aspires especially to capture the quality of light; Constable's *Haywain* (see Figure 15.11) is one. That luminosity, especially lovely at sunset and dawn, has always been one of the pleasures of human existence. Here, it is caused by a hazy nuclear glow. The thick frame, which is part of the painting, acts like the black border of an obituary notice or the thin viewing slot of a reinforced bunker.

The Social Mirror, 1983 (Figure 15.23), by Mierle Laderman Ukeles, focuses on the problem of waste made critical by growing populations and consumerism. Ukeles had a clean New York City garbage truck fitted with gleaming mirrors. The mirrors brilliantly reflect the sun, transforming and making us newly aware of the shape of the garbage truck, like a piece of sculpture. *The Social Mirror* also has a performance element. In this photograph, the truck is part of a parade, and its mirrors are reflecting the images of the parade watchers,

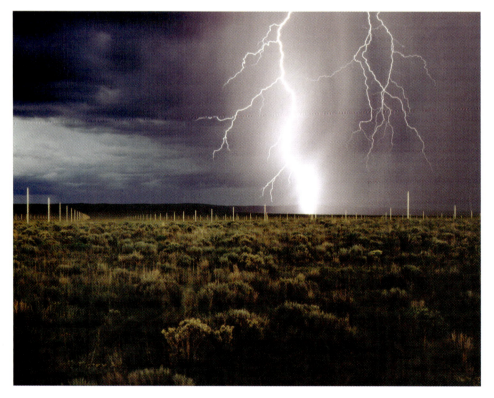

15.21 WALTER DE MARIA. *The Lightning Field.* 400 stainless steel poles, average height: 20'7"; land area: 1 mile × 1 kilometer in New Mexico. USA, 1971–1977. Photograph by John Cliett. © Dia Center for the Arts. For more about this and other earthworks, see Figure 2.36.

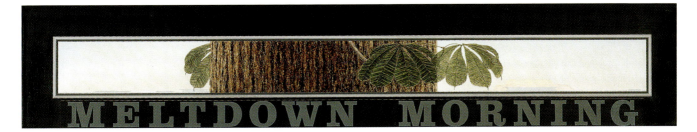

15.22   Neil Jenney. *Meltdown Morning.* Oil on panel, 25^1/$_2$" × 112^1/$_2$". USA, 1975. Philadelphia Museum of Art.

the public. It is intended to make viewers aware that they make trash and are responsible for its impact. The mirrors also glamorize the garbage truck and raise the status of sanitation workers, whose jobs are not respected, but who, according to Ukeles, keep New York City and other urban centers alive. All of Ukeles's work since the mid-1970s has focused on ecological issues of maintenance, recycling, waste management, and landfill reclamation.

KNOWLEDGE

Humans systematically study and examine the world in an attempt to understand (and often control) its course. This section focuses on art that deals directly with a body of knowledge (although all art, in some way, is reflective of a kind of knowing). The first group consists of informative images, in which art helps explain a specific body of learning. The second group provides glimpses into areas of intuited knowing. Finally, art critiques what we consider knowledge.

These same ideas—scientific knowledge, intuited knowledge, or critiqued knowledge—are found in other areas and are historically and culturally specific. German philosopher Immanuel Kant (1724–1804) challenged people to strive toward knowledge and reason, and he epitomized the era of the Enlightenment. Later, French philosopher Henri-Louis Bergson (1859–1941) promoted the value of intuition over intellect for understanding the world. Finally, the wars of the twentieth century caused many to question the use of knowledge for destructive purposes.

INFORMATIVE IMAGES

There are numerous examples of art that illustrate a specific body of knowledge. In the Low Countries in 1543, Andreas Vesalius of Brussels published *De Humani Corporis Fabrica,* a study of bones, muscles, and internal organs based on the dissection of human bodies, which is considered the beginning of modern science. Before that time, Western knowledge of the human body was based on ancient Greek, Roman, and medieval Arabic writings. These sources contained numerous

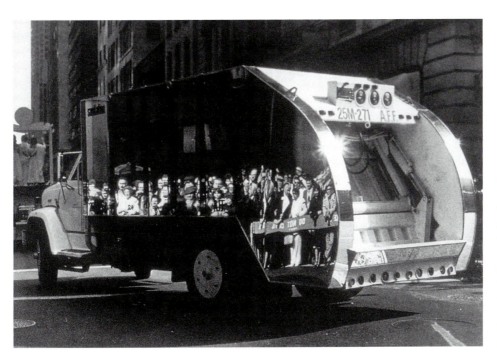

15.23   Mierle Laderman Ukeles. *The Social Mirror.* 20-cubic-yard New York City garbage collection truck fitted with hand-tempered glass mirror with additional strips of mirrored acrylic. USA, 1983. The New York City Department of Sanitation. Photo: Michael James O'Brien, courtesy of Barbara Gladstone Gallery. Courtesy Ronald Feldman Fine Arts, New York. For more about this artwork, see Figures 2.37 and 5.24.

inaccuracies, which Vesalius's studies corrected; also, Vesalius's work added a tremendous amount of new knowledge. Important here, however, is that Vesalius's book is a major work of art. Figurative artists use it to this day.

The Fourth Plate of Muscles, dated 1543 (Figure 15.24), shows the dissection process Vesalius used to understand the body. He gradually stripped the cadaver's outer muscles, but left them partly attached to make clear their relation to deeper muscles just exposed. Nonetheless, the body is standing as if alive, moving, and turning, with weight on one leg, because Vesalius wanted to emphasize the structure and workings of the living, moving body, instead of the separated parts of the dead. The engravings themselves were excellent works of Western science and art. The poses are expressive, which makes the drawings more interesting. Altogether, there are eight plates of muscles that make a lurid and fascinating narrative of dismemberment. In *The First Plate of Muscles,* the body stands like a classic statue, with an aura of grandeur mixed with a sense of pathos. Our *Fourth Plate* is both fascinating and horrible. By the time we arrive at the seventh and eighth plates, the disjointed cadaver is dangling on ropes. The works comment both on the splendidness of the human body and on its inevitable disintegration.

De Humani Corporis Fabrica is a collaborative work. Other artists produced most of the finished drawings from Vesalius's sketches and notes. Vesalius himself had become very busy and quite famous, and he was often called upon to give medical advice to the reigning kings of Europe. Another unknown artist drew the landscape backgrounds. When all the plates are placed side by side, the backgrounds make a large, continuous landscape of the Italian countryside. Another professional made the engravings.

Another famous illustrated study is John James Audubon's *Birds of America,* a very large book that contained 435 plates. Robert Havell Jr. made most of the printing plates from Audubon's original watercolor studies. *Birds of America* is an outstanding work, both artistically and scientifically. *Carolina Paroquet,* 1827–1838 (Figure 15.25), shows several birds in

15.24 ANDREAS VESALIUS OF BRUSSELS. *The Fourth Plate of Muscles.* Engraving from *De Humani Corporis Fabrica.* Flanders, published in 1543.

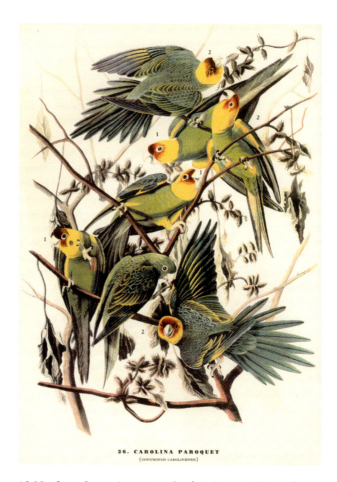

15.25 JOHN JAMES AUDUBON. *Carolina Paroquet.* Watercolor, 29¹/₂" × 21¹/₄". Original for Plate #26 of *Birds of America.* USA, 1827–1838. North Carolina Museum of Art. See also the text accompanying Figure 5.14.

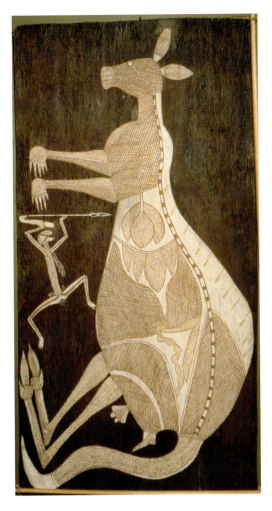

15.26 *Hunter and Kangaroo.* Paint on bark, 51" × 32". Aboriginal. Oenpelli, Arnhemland, Australia, c. twentieth century. Private collection, Prague. © Werner Forman / Art Resources, NY.

scientific detail, with all the markings and in their habitat. Audubon eliminated the background to emphasize the defining silhouettes of the parakeets and to make details clearer. The birds and branches visually counterbalance each other. The birds are arranged in two arcs, one that echoes and one that opposes the direction of the main stem. The entire work is a decorative pattern that is enhanced by the bright colors. The whole book, with its hundreds of plates, is colorful and lively, and it shows how passionately Audubon loved his subject.

Drawings in the service of science continue to be made, even though photography might seem to be an adequate substitute for them. But artist drawings can emphasize details that either do not stand out in photographs or become lost in the wealth of detail. Medical books are still enhanced with drawings, and medical illustrations are essential aids for study. Drawings also are used in studies of plants and insects and for very small items.

Our next example is an educational aid. *Hunter and Kangaroo,* c. twentieth century (Figure 15.26), is from the Aboriginal people of Australia. The painting on bark shows the instant that the hunter's spear is about to enter the animal. The animal is shown in x-ray style, meaning that both external silhouette and internal organs are evident. We can see the kangaroo's backbone, heart, and intestines. The kangaroo is larger than the hunter, because it is the subject of the painting. This work, and others like it on bark and on the walls of cave shelters, was meant to be educational and, perhaps, ritually powerful. Showing the animal's internal organs assisted the hunter in the slaughter. The hunter's body implies movement and energy. The specific form of cross-hatching associated paintings with individual clans and endowed the painted objects with spiritual force.

CONNECTION
Other Aboriginal paintings transmit knowledge from one clan member to another, as we saw in Paddy Carroll Tjungurrayi's Witchetty Grub Dreaming, *Figure 7.2 (page 157).*

Some works of art are experiential in a way that is both conceptually interesting and educational. For example, the Optical Art (or Op Art) style was popular in the United States and Europe in the 1960s. Bridget Riley's *Current,* 1964 (Figure 15.27), is a precisely painted pattern of undulating lines

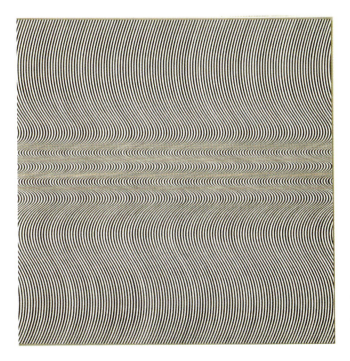

15.27 BRIDGET RILEY. *Current.* Synthetic polymer paint on composition board, approximately 58¹/₂" × 58¹/₂". Great Britain, 1964. The Museum of Modern Art, New York. © Digital Image The Museum of Modern Art / Licensed by Scala / Art Resouce, NY.

that affect our visual perception. The pattern produces visual ambiguity that makes it seem not static, but pulsating and flickering. The work is similar to experiments by visual psychologists who test the limits of visual perception to better understand how our vision works. It is also related to mathematics, as each line is a sinusoidal curve, in which the interval between each dip increases as your eyes move away from the central horizontal axis of the painting. *Current* makes evident that our vision is based on nerves, because our eyes tire and hurt if we stare at the image too long. Its large size means that, up close, the work encompasses our entire visual field, both the sharp foveal vision at the center and our peripheral vision at the edges.

CONNECTION
Georges Seurat also relied on the science of optics in his work, La Grande Jatte (Figure 14.29, page 424).

ART AND INTUITED KNOWLEDGE

For humans, the "world" consists not only of the external environment, but also of the internal realm of the mind and the metaphysical world. Art also deals with knowledge that humans can intuitively grasp without necessarily being able to articulate it. This kind of knowing is the product of dreams, visions, and speculative guessing. It is not necessarily systematic, organized, or scientific.

Surrealism was an early-twentieth-century art movement in Europe and the United States that explored the unconscious, especially through dream imagery. Surrealists posited that this unconscious or dream world is at least as real as, and probably more important than, the ordered and regimented external world in which humans function. For example, watches are devices of knowing and a means of maintaining external order. However, in his painting *The Persistence of Memory*, 1931 (Figure 15.28), Salvador Dali presents watches that are limp, flaccid, and useless. The landscape stretches out, vast and empty. The sky glows in splendid blues and golds, while the still water reflects the sun-bathed cliffs like a flawless mirror. Nothing makes "sense," but Dali has painted everything with rigorous detail and convincing realism so that book-learned knowledge fades in importance, and we enter the eerie scene with a kind of intuited knowing. Swarming ants and a fly allude to the horror dimension in dreams.

Other works of art refer to knowledge that cannot be clearly articulated in words. Mark Rothko made a series of paintings alluding to the sublime. Although he started as a figurative painter, he abandoned imagery that reflected the physical world for abstractions that hint at a transcendent state of being. This series of paintings contained large rectangles, sometimes only vaguely defined, against a field of other colors. Each color area was subtly modulated, so that the shapes, and alternately the background, seemed to emerge, float, and glow, as in *Green, Red, Blue*, 1955 (Figure 15.29). Rothko first applied thin "veils" of paint that soaked into and stained the canvas. He then applied many layers on top to create shapes that seem present and yet hard to define, hovering in a space that is real and yet not wholly knowable.

Rothko turned to abstraction as a means to address these broad and fundamental feelings/ideas, because figurative or

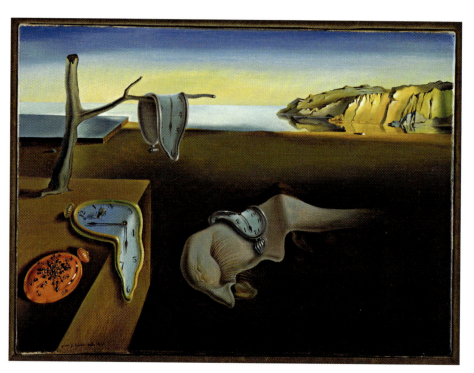

15.28 SALVADOR DALI. *The Persistence of Memory.* Oil on canvas, 9½" × 13". Spain, 1931. The Museum of Modern Art, New York. © Digital Image © The Museum of Modern Art/Licensed by SCALA / Art Resource, NY © 2004 Salvador Dali, Gala-Salvador Dali Foundation / Artists Rights Society (ARS), New York. For more on the meaning of this artwork, see Figure 4.11.

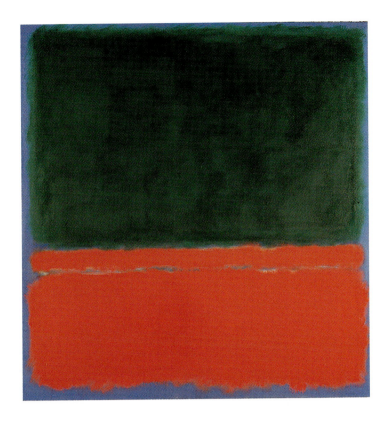

15.29 MARK ROTHKO. *Green, Red, Blue*. Oil on canvas, 81¹/₂" × 77³/₄". USA, 1955. Milwaukee Art Museum. Gift of Mrs. Harry Lynde Bradley, m1977.140. © 1998 Kate Rothko Prizel & Christopher Rothko / Artists Rights Society (ARS), New York.

narrative imagery was too specific and too limiting. In addition, Rothko's abstractions were meant to provide a kind of direct physical experience to the body. Another 1950s painter, Robert Motherwell, expressed these ideas in this way:

> [I]t is the social world that tends to appear irrational and absurd. . . . Nothing as drastic as abstract art could have come into existence save as the consequence of a most profound, relentless, unquenchable need. The need is for felt experience—

intense, immediate, direct, subtle, unified, warm, vivid, rhythmic. If a painting does not make a human contact, it is for nothing. (O'Hara 1965: 45, 50)

THE CRITIQUE OF LEARNING

Gods of the Modern World, 1932–1934 (Figure 15.30), painted by José Clemente Orozco, is a strong critique of sterile knowledge. It is a warning against the academic who is completely

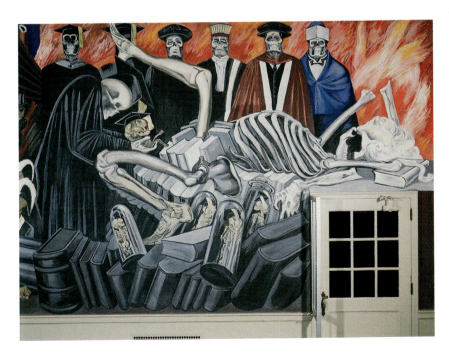

15.30 JOSÉ CLEMENTE OROZCO. *Gods of the Modern World*. Fresco, 126" × 176". Twelfth panel in a cycle of murals entitled *An Epic of American Civilization*. Mexico, 1932–1934. Baker Memorial Library, Dartmouth College, Hanover, New Hampshire. Commissioned by the Trustees of Dartmouth College, Hanover, New Hampshire.

occupied with research or learning that has no value outside academia. The black-clad university scholars line up like mid-wives to watch a skeleton give birth to miniature scholar-skeletons and stacks of obscure books. Orozco believed that sterile education passes for knowledge, but it actually keeps the young busy without giving them any real wisdom or understanding. The lurid red background suggests urgency, as if the world is on fire, but no guidance or concern can be found among the "learned." Their posture is aloof, frontal, stiff, and unresponsive. The style of the work is very striking. The rhythm of the lines is strong, from the verticals of the academic robes, to the black and white of the skeleton's ribs, to the swaying parade of book spines below. Significantly, this painting is in the library of a prestigious U.S. college, to be seen by all students and professors.

In *Breaking of the Vessels,* 1990 (Figure 15.31), artist Anselm Kiefer looks at knowledge on many different levels. The piece consists of a three-tiered bookshelf filled with massive volumes whose pages are made of sheets of lead. The books sag per-ilously, some about to fall from the shelf. Glass shards from the books have fallen, and their shattering has covered the floor all around. Above, written on a half-circle of glass, are the Hebrew words *Ain Soph,* meaning "the Infinite." Dangling copper wires connect thick stumps projecting from the sides. The piece is seventeen feet high and weighs over seven tons. The shattered glass covers several square yards of floor all around.

The piece contrasts the infinity and clarity of the spiritual realm with the thick, dull, ponderous containers of human knowledge. Human knowledge, as contained in and symbol-ized by the books, is limited and sagging under its own weight. Visually, the heavy lead pages are like the blackened pages of burned books. The knowledge contained within them seems inaccessible to most people; the book format hides knowledge rather than exposes it. The books seem as though they might even be rotting away, ready to crash to the floor. The sheer mass of the sculpture becomes a metaphor for the accumulated struggles to acquire and preserve human knowledge. But books and their contents disintegrate. The work alludes to the fact that all human endeavor is cyclical like nature; it is subject to periods of decline and entropy that eventually lead to regeneration.

The title *Breaking of the Vessels* refers to mystical Hebrew writings (the Kabbalah) that tell of the awesome, uncontain-able Divine essence whose power filled and shattered the frag-ile vessels of the universe upon Creation. The title symbolizes the introduction of evil into the world. It also refers to the atrocities of *Kristallnacht* (the Night of Crystal or the Night of Broken Glass), when the Nazis vandalized and terrorized Jew-ish neighborhoods in Germany and Austria in November 1938.

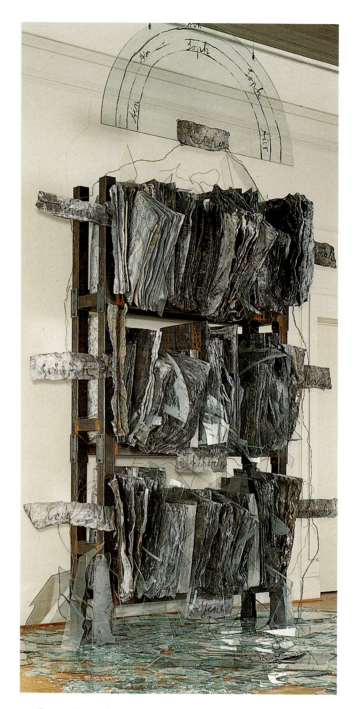

 15.31 ANSELM KIEFER. *Breaking of the Vessels.* Lead, iron, glass, copper wire, charcoal, and aquatec, 17' high. Germany, 1990. The St. Louis Art Museum. Courtesy Sperone Westwater.

TECHNOLOGY

Technology is the last component of the outside world that we will see in this chapter in relation to art. The first works regard technological advances as good, healthy, exciting, and even aesthetically pleasing. The second group evaluates our constructed world for both its positive and negative impacts.

TECHNOLOGICAL ADVANCES

In *Farm Scene,* c. 1000–1240 (Figure 15.32), we see that technology has long been part of human history and has often made life easier. A farmer and his wife operate a foot-driven pump that diverts water to flood their rice field. Beneath a shed, a water buffalo turns a larger pump for similar results. A boy fishes in the background, a boat is moored to a riverbank, and a footbridge spans the water between clumps of land. Pumps, bridges, boats, and fishing poles—all pieces of technology—fit comfortably into the overall scene. Well-placed trees shade all workers, and the generous river waters stretch out for long distances in the background. Harmony and serenity abound. Human handiwork and nature seem to belong together. The emphasis on horizontal lines, the orderly diagonals in space, the blended ochres, greens, and browns all turn what could be a scene of hard labor into an image of peaceful coexistence.

When we consider technology today, however, we most likely think of the world since the Industrial Revolution of the nineteenth century and more recent developments in transportation, manufacturing, and communication. Technology advanced rapidly in the early twentieth century, causing cities to expand and producing structures in shapes and sizes never seen before. Particularly striking were bridges, factories, skyscrapers, ocean liners, and fast trains. These forms inspired many artists, among them Fernand Léger. His painting *The City,* dated 1919 (Figure 15.33), was a tribute to geometric

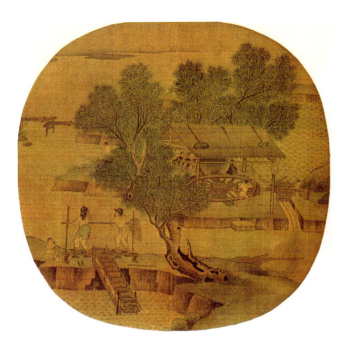

15.32   *Farm Scene.* Ink and color on silk. China, Song Dynasty, c. 1000–1240. C.C. Wang, New York.

industrial structures and the precision and efficiency of machines, all of which struck Léger as forms of beauty. The city of Léger's painting is rendered in abstract forms, but speaks of its concrete, steel, electrical power, and transportation systems. The repetition of colors and shapes suggests the

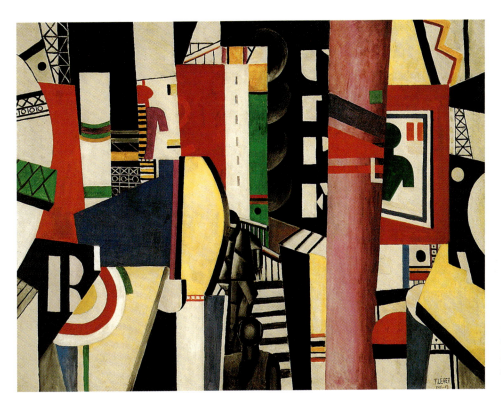

15.33   FERNAND LÉGER. *The City.* Oil on canvas, 91" × 117^1/$_2$". France, 1919. Philadelphia Museum of Art. © 2004 Artists Rights Society (ARS), New York / ADAGP, Paris.

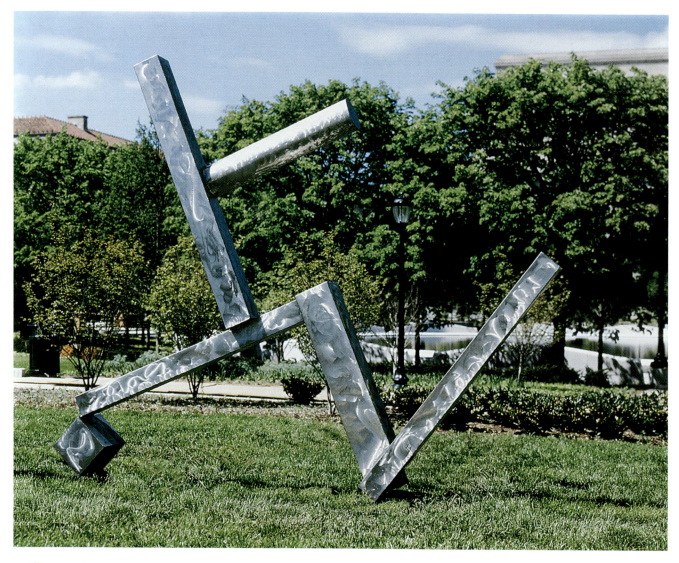

 15.34 DAVID SMITH. *Cubi XXVI*. Steel, approximately 10' × 12'6" × 2'3". USA, 1965. Alisa Mellon Bruce Fund, Image © National Gallery of Art, Washington, D.C. Art © David Smith/Licensed by VAGA, New York, NY. See also the text accompanying Figure 2.14.

staccato of city sounds. Letterforms refer to billboard advertisements. The colors are bright and artificial. Other shapes resemble a jumble of roofs and walls, bridge trestles, or factory smokestacks. Even humans are robotlike, as their bodies are composed of geometric volumes. The space seems shallow, as all forms are compressed and pushed forward, in contrast to the open horizon and distant spaces in paintings of rural scenes.

David Smith's *Cubi XXVI,* 1965 (Figure 15.34), is abstract art imitating some qualities of machines. Smith used industrial fabrication to create this stainless steel sculpture and others in this series. He learned this technology as a factory worker. His works are marked by a machine aesthetic, and thus his processes and materials are the same as those that

would be used to make a locomotive. The large, geometric shapes of stainless steel cubes, rectangles, and cylinders look machine-manufactured, with clean edges, flawless welding, and precise fits. They resemble mass-produced items. The structure, unsoftened, is bluntly emphasized. Strong, balanced forms seem to defy their weight. The metal surfaces, however, were abraded to give them a spiral pattern that seems to dissolve the solidity of the volumes. Smith emphasized gesture, so that the sculpture seems to be moving forward, like an animated stick figure of a walking person. The forms suggest vectors in space, some in opposition to each other. The work also suggests forces suspended and in movement, like components of a machine.

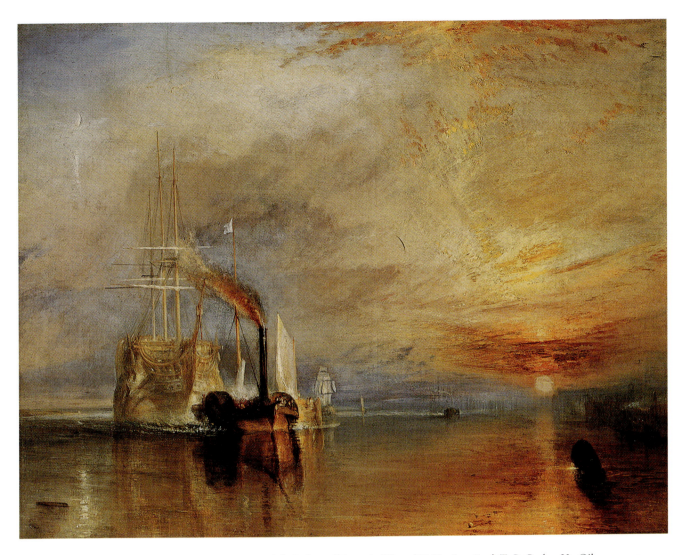

 15.35   JOSEPH MALLORD WILLIAM TURNER. *The Fighting "Temeraire" Tugged To Her Last Berth To Be Broken Up.* Oil on canvas, 35¼" × 48". England, 1838. The Tate Gallery, London. © The Tate Gallery/Art Resource, NY.

EVALUATING THE CONSTRUCTED WORLD

We have already seen Jenney's *Meltdown Morning* and Ukeles's *Social Mirror,* which were highly critical of human technology and its impact on the land. The following artists present technology to us in a way that makes clear its mixed impact.

In *The Fighting "Temeraire" Tugged To Her Last Berth To Be Broken Up,* 1838 (Figure 15.35), Joseph Mallord William Turner distinguishes between innovation and progress. He painted the tall, shimmering, white form of the elegant sailing vessel against the new powerful tugboat, which is squat, dark, and smoky. By this time, sailing vessels were obsolete for war or commerce, superseded by more modern technology. Turner marked the *Temeraire's* passing by the splendid glowing sunset

(marred by the tug's smoke!)—both ship and sunset were soon to be lost forever. Turner was famous for his facility with paint; thick blobs become an array of golden clouds, brushy strokes blend where mist meets blue sky. The scene is a conflict between light and darkness, and light is just about to be eclipsed.

Without a doubt, Turner was romanticizing archaic technology, responding to the latest innovation that seemed ugly to him. He painted this work in his old age, as a sign of his own life drawing to a close. The beautiful colors and expressive handling of the paint convey the poignant feeling of beauty and loss, transforming an otherwise nondescript harbor scene along the Thames River in London into a picture of poetic beauty.

Jean Tinguely's *Homage to New York,* 1960 (Figure 15.36), looked like a whimsical, playful, absurd machine. Tinguely constructed it with the help of an engineer, using junkyard machine parts. The work was designed so that it would destroy itself in one evening in the gardens of the Museum of Modern Art in New York City, which it did, but not according to plan. A fire in some parts necessitated the unscheduled participation of the New York City Fire Department. Tinguely was mocking the machine, and yet celebrating it for qualities very different from Léger's *The City.* To Tinguely, the machine was not magnificent because of its clean design or its efficiency, but for its unexpected results. Machines never work in exactly the way that we expect them to, nor can we anticipate all the results of using them. Tinguely's satirical work references the frenzy of the machine age and, by extension, the city of New York at that time, which in some ways could be seen as a large machine, absurd in its size, its complexity, its haphazard workings, and its entertainment value.

CONNECTION

Homage to New York *was both an environmental sculpture and a happening. For more on such works, see the sections "Engaging All the Senses" and "Chance/Improvisation/Spontaneity" in Chapter 2.*

For us now, technology includes computers and televisions. For nearly forty years, artist Nam June Paik has been exploring what that means and its impact on us as humans. *Megatron,* 1995 (Figure 15.37), is composed of over two hundred video screens divided into two groups, displaying video clips, digital distortions, and animation sequences. Paik's images are from high and popular culture, from East and West, and include scenes from the Olympic Games, experimental art events, rock concerts, and Korean rituals as well as sexual images, scenes of aggression, and, sometimes, simply a wall of white screens or a display of national flags. Visually, the piece is very dense, as images are juxtaposed or tumble one after another. Pictures are even nested inside each other, as can be seen in the upper left, in which the large shape of a flying bird is composed of smaller images. *Megatron's* visual assault is matched by the cacophonous sound track. Yet over time, the piece may have a lulling or perhaps hypnotic effect.

The viewer is restricted to the role of spectator, dwarfed and essentially silenced by the forceful presence of *Megatron.* The accumulation of screens and the large size of *Megatron* speak of the imposing presence of the mass media in everyday life, a feature in the home, in business, in sports, in entertainment, in commerce, and so on, where again the viewer is a spectator only. The making of *Megatron* was itself a technological feat, as images are fed by laser disc players and controlled by seven computers in such a way that sequences rarely repeat. In this way, the piece reflects our everyday lives, in which we

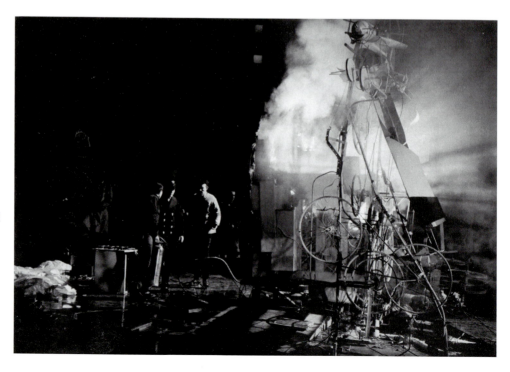

15.36 JEAN TINGUELY. *Homage to New York: A Self-Constructing, Self-Destructing Work of Art.* Mixed media sculpture. Switzerland, 1960. Photograph of the work as it self-destroyed in New York City on March 17, 1960. Photo by David Gahr. © 2004 David Gahr © 2004 Artists Rights Society (ARS), New York / ADAGP, Paris. See also the text accompanying Figure 2.27.

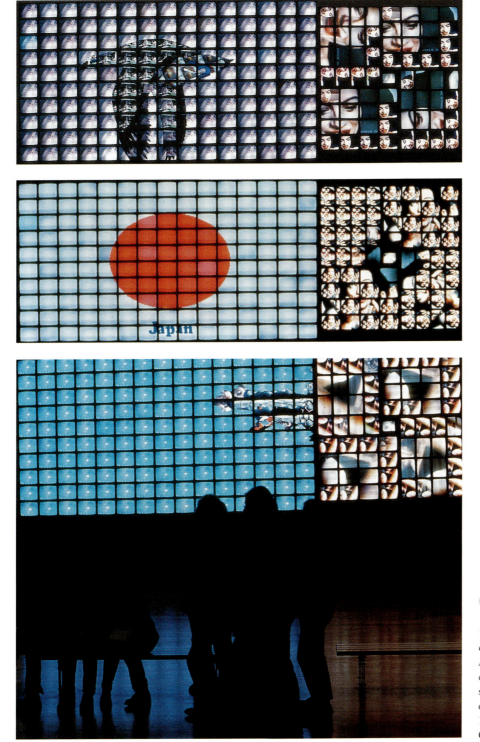

15.37 NAM JUNE PAIK, in collaboration with Shuya Abe. *Megatron* (three views). Eight-channel video and two-channel sound installation in two parts, overall size 12' × 33' × 2'. Korea, 1995. Courtesy Holly Solomon Gallery, New York.

are bombarded by disjointed but familiar images while flipping through television channels, zipping past freeway billboards at sixty-five miles per hour, or surfing the Internet.

This piece and others by Paik are about the act of perception, how reality is presented, and how we as viewers reinte-grate the random images. To Paik, the recombinations and dislocations of images are potentially playful and constructive. He sees his pieces as creative ways of thinking about the reshaping of our lives and becoming engaged in the diversity and variety in contemporary culture.

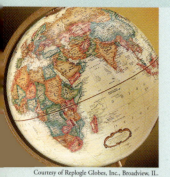

Courtesy of Replogle Globes, Inc., Broadview, IL.

Three major trends marked this period: industrialism, modernization, and nationalism. Older western European nations continued to build their colonial empires in Africa and Asia. The years from 1850 to 1914 marked the high point of colonialism, even with increased resistance and colonial independence movements. Colonies provided raw material for industrialized nations. The Industrial Revolution, which had already begun in Great Britain, spread to other areas of western Europe and the United States. The Industrial Revolution brought amazing advances in technology as well as profound social changes, including the development of a large middle class and an industrial working class, the creation of factories, great increases in population, and mass migration into urban areas.

The newly powerful middle class enjoyed greater educational opportunities and leisure time, but the working class was oppressed. Karl Marx coauthored the *Communist Manifesto* in 1848, and the labor movement was agitating for fair wages, safe working conditions, and reasonable

Below:
Map 9 World War II in Asia and the Pacific.

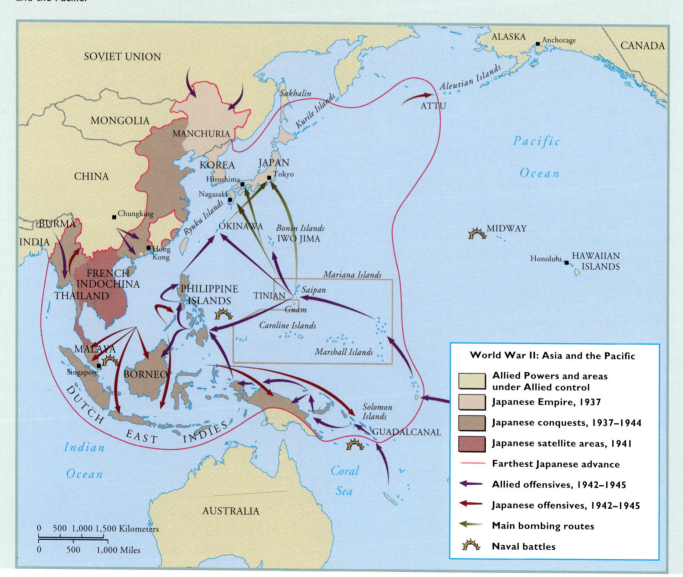

hours for workers. Civil rights movements for racial and gender equality grew in power throughout this period.

Nationalism is devotion to one's country, especially promoting that country's interests and culture above all others. Nationalistic fervor saw the formation of modern nations in South America, central Europe, and the Balkans. In the United States, the Civil War (1861–1865) reinforced the national identity.

In 1868, the old shogun rulers of Japan were overthrown. Emperor Meiji rose to power and began the rapid industrialization of Japan and modernization of its society. In 1874, Japan began a period of expansion in Asia, following the model of Western colonial empires. Japan envisioned itself as the dominant power in Asia.

The Great War (World War I) broke out in 1914 and lasted until 1918. Its causes were many, including increased friction among European nation-states, entangling alliances, internal conflicts caused by ethnic groups that had not yet achieved nationhood, and competition for colonies and trade. The war and the terms of the peace treaty embittered Germany, one of the losing nations.

Imperial rule was beginning to crumble. The 1912 revolution in China ended centuries of dynastic rule. The Russian Revolution of 1917 created a Communist state and ended the rule of the czars. The centuries-old Ottoman Empire, centered in Turkey, was broken up in 1919. Unfortunately, totalitarianism in other forms was on the rise. All people were subject to the absolute authority of the state in Stalinist Russia and Nazi Germany in the 1930s, and there was a rise of dictatorships in Latin America. Fascism dominated in Spain and Italy as well.

Another major event of the 1930s was the Great Depression, a period of severe financial hardship for industrialized nations. The Depression's unemployment and homelessness, coupled with extreme nationalism and the rise of totalitarian regimes, led to World War II. In 1931, Japan, Italy, and Germany began seizing lands around them, until war was declared in Europe in 1939 and in the Pacific in 1941. When the amazingly destructive war finally ended in 1945, at least 17 million soldiers and perhaps as many as 40 million civilians were dead, including the millions who died in German concentration camps.

The years immediately following World War II saw the founding of the United Nations, the destruction of old European colonial empires, and the establishment of Communist China (1948). Also established was the modern state of Israel, which displaced the Palestinians.

Thus, we see that today's trend toward globalization was already under way in 1850, as the foundations were laid for the global economy, global trade and resources, and global political entanglements.

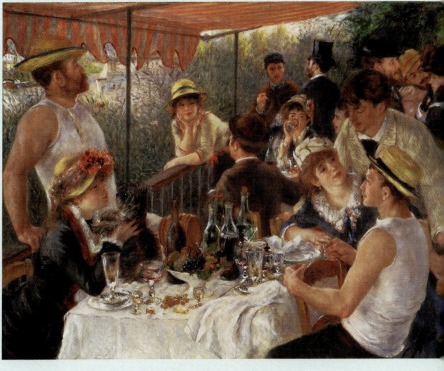

Above:
PIERRE AUGUSTE RENOIR. *The Luncheon of the Boating Party.* Oil on canvas, 51" × 68". France, 1881. The Phillips Collection, Washington, D.C. The European middle class enjoyed greater leisure time in the late nineteenth century, including pleasurable outings in nature, as we see in this painting.

Events	Date	Art
Domestication of horse and camel	**4000 BCE**	
Wheel appears—Mesopotamia Bronze casting in Sumeria	3500	
First library in Sumeria	2000	
First libraries in China	1700	
		Ashurbanipal Hunting Lions
China: The Silk Trade	600	*Relief* (Olmec)
Mouseion at Alexandria: A community of scholars	300	
	100	*Gardenscape* from the Villa of Livia
Paper first used in China	**100 CE**	
Elephants first used in warfare		
Printing invented in China	200	
Islamic Libraries established		*Spider* (Nazca)
Temple Libraries in Japan		
	800	*Vessel in the Form of a Monkey*
	1000	*Serpent (or Snake) Mound*
		Farm Scene
Moslem Paper Mills in Spain		
Medieval Universities		
	1300	Ren Renfa: *Three Horses and Four Grooms*
		Ma Yuan: *Apricot Blossoms*
Renaissance in Europe	1400	*The Unicorn in Captivity*
Gutenberg's Press		
	1500	*Ryoanji Zen Garden of Contemplation*
		Vesalius: *The Fourth Plate of Muscles*
	1600	Sheng Maoye: *Beyond the Solitary Bamboo Grove*
		Bruegel: *Little Bouquet in a Clay Jar*
		Bishndas: *Babur Supervising the Layout of the Garden of Fidelity*

Events	Date	Art
Industrial Revolution begins		
Steam Locomotive—Europe	1800	*Shaman's Amulet*
Early Experiments in Photography		Constable: *The Haywain*
Invention of Dynamite		Audubon: *Carolina Paroquet*
		Turner: *The Fighting "Temeraire"*
Edison and the Light Bulb		
Labor Movement		
Women's Rights Movement		
First Flight, Wright Brothers	1900	Monet: *Water Lily Pool*
		Hunter and Kangaroo
World War I		
	1920	
		Orozco: *Gods of the Modern World*
		Léger: *The City*
Great Depression		Dali: *The Persistence of Memory*
Early Experiments with Computers		
World War II	1940	Adams: *Clearing Winter Storm, Yosemite National Park, California, 1944*
		Rothko: *Green, Red, Blue*
		Riley: *Current*
	1960	
		Tinguely: *Homage to New York*
		Smith: *Cubi XXVI*
	1970	Smithson: *Spiral Jetty*
		De Maria: *The Lightning Field*
		Jenney: *Meltdown Morning*
Desktop Publishing	1980	Ukeles: *The Social Mirror*
Digital Imaging		
The Internet	1990	Kiefer: *Breaking of the Vessels*
		Paik: *Megatron*
	1999	Ofili: *Monkey Magic—Sex, Money and Drugs*

Artists use animals to reflect many human qualities and the human need for power. Art also shows us how much we admire animal beauty.

The land—its natural state and what we do with it—is of acute interest to artists. Landscape paintings and photographs are popular in many cultures. Humans also love to arrange plants, rocks, water, and ground into gardens that become pieces of the earthly paradise. Plant forms are also admired in art, and flowers are symbols for the beauty and fleeting nature of life. The ground itself is sculptural material in site-specific work. Other artists examine the negative impact that human technology has had on the environment.

Art is a means to deliver knowledge, either as single illustrations or in books. Some art communicates knowledge that cannot be clearly articulated; some is intended to give us the experience of the sublime. Artists also make judgments on the value of esoteric knowledge.

Finally, technology is examined in art. Artists working in many media show us the good and the bad results of our fascination with machines.

FOOD FOR THOUGHT

It is possible to think of humans as distinct and separate from nature and technology, or as part of these larger systems. For example, the computer is a tool that we have made and that therefore is at our command. But what is the nature of your presence in cyberspace? Are we disembodied, or real? If you could feel the Internet, would your e-mail course through the network like the blood pumping through your veins? Like vibrations through your skeleton?

Networks are the basis of human existence on the cellular level and in the nervous, lymphatic, and circulatory systems. However, our body's survival depends on (and is sometimes threatened by) the earth's ecosystems and by technological systems that we have constructed, such as transportation and energy grids. Databases construct our legal and financial identities. Our bodies are composed of the same materials as the animals, plants, dirt, and the stars.

- Are humans separate from animals and technology, or are we all evolving together?

- How much do we model the systems we make—whether the freeways or the Internet—upon systems within our own bodies?
- Because of ecological changes, medicines, and machines, how are we different from humans of centuries ago?
- Compare the earliest artwork produced by humankind with the most recent. What conclusions can you draw?

YOUR CD-ROM RESOURCES

- World History in Context
- Exploring Art Timeline
- Flashcards
- Food for Thought
- Companion Site
    Chapter 15 Quiz
    InfoTrac® College Edition Readings
    Artist Flashcards
    Online Study Guide

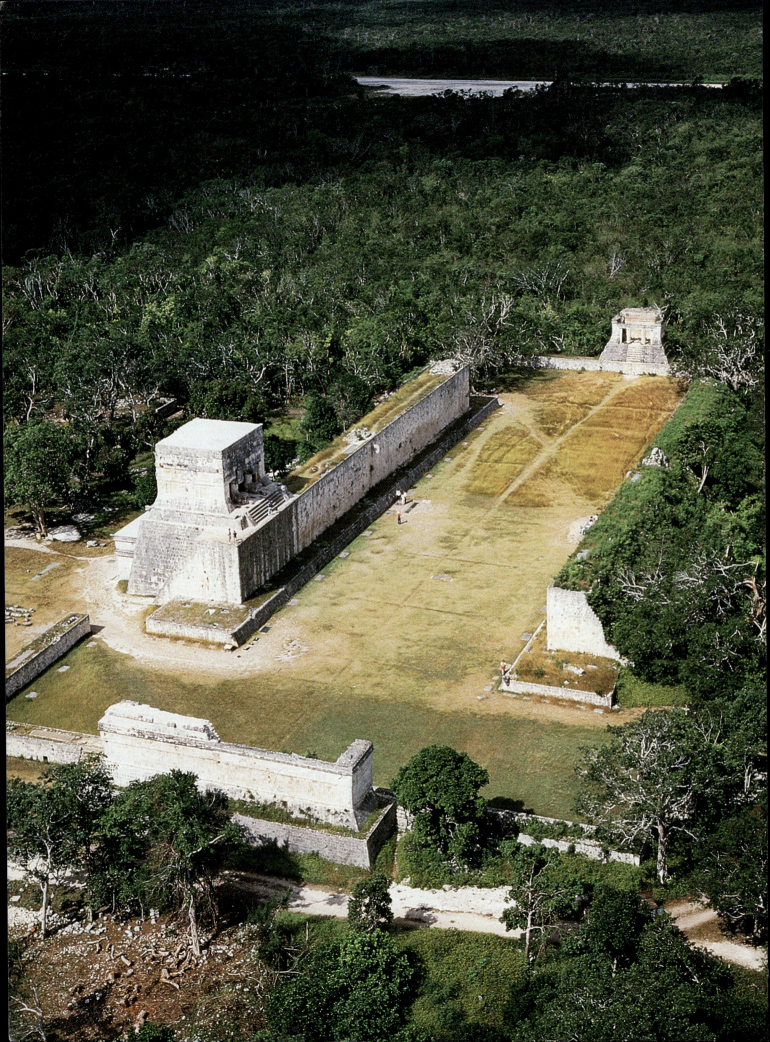

CHAPTER 16

ENTERTAINMENT

INTRODUCTION

Entertainment means "diversion or amusement." The verb *to entertain* also means "to admit into or to hold in the mind," which suggests the presence of ideas. These two definitions form the basis of this chapter. Art can certainly be entertaining while being informative and provocative.

In this chapter, we will be looking at examples that are unquestioningly accepted as art, like art museums and opera houses as well as what goes on inside them. But they also are leisure-time destinations and, thus, entertainment. Many works are combinations of art, popular culture, or tourist attraction. Is a classic film like *Gone with the Wind* a work of art or Hollywood? Is the *Open-Air Museum* in Hakone, Japan, an art museum or a park? Ritual can be added into the mix; for example, the masquerades in several African cultures incorporate visual arts, are entertaining, and may be religious ceremonies.

Keep in mind the following questions as we observe the art and architecture of entertainment:

How is art in its various forms entertaining?

How has architecture facilitated the performing arts? Arts and recreation? Arts and education?

How have visual artists contributed to theater and music?

Where are arts and crafts used in drama and performance?

In what areas do the visual and performing arts overlap?

What kinds of imagery have artists made that depict various forms of entertainment?

The Great Ball Court. Chichén Itzá, Mexico. Detail of Figure 16.30. Photograph © 1990 The Metropolitan Museum of Art, NY.

"HOUSES" FOR THE ARTS

THEATERS, MUSEUMS, AND OPERA HOUSES

Museums and performance spaces must function well and comfortably accommodate their audiences. In addition, these spaces must "look the part," by conforming to the aesthetic sensibilities and the values of the audience. Also, the exterior design must reflect the activities inside, whether the buildings are libraries, history museums, planetariums, or aquariums.

The earliest form of theater in Western cultures took place in ancient Greece, where dramatic rituals for Dionysos, god of wine and fertility, were performed in the hollows of hills. These rituals dealt with human conflict in the forms of comedy and tragedy and were performed only once during sacred festivals. The human conflict usually concerned issues between human beings and the gods, community, and fate. The plays, which included music and dance, continued for hours and involved nonstop action. The actors wore elaborate costumes with even more elaborate oversized masks. The masks both emphasized the characters' emotions and amplified the actors' voices through a megaphone-like mouth. Thousands of people attended these dramas.

CONNECTION
The cult of Dionysos is also background material for the paintings in the Villa of Mysteries at Pompeii, Italy, such as the Initiation Rites of Dionysos (Figure 8.8, page 201).

Eventually, magnificent theaters were designed to hold a multitude of people where all could see and hear the drama and have easy access to the structure. One example is the *Theater at Epidauros* (Figure 16.1), designed by Polykleitos the Younger around 350 BCE. Its plan references the Classical Greek ideal shape, the circle, although it is only a little more than a semicircle with a 387-foot diameter. The *theatron,* or seating area, has fifty-five tiers of stone and marble benches, rising at a high angle to give each spectator a clear view of the performance. Stairs connect each section. At the very center was the orchestra platform, a circle in which the chorus would dance near or around the altar of Dionysus. Behind the orchestra is a long, rectangular structure used for the stage, backed by the *skene,* a building that provided a backdrop for the plays

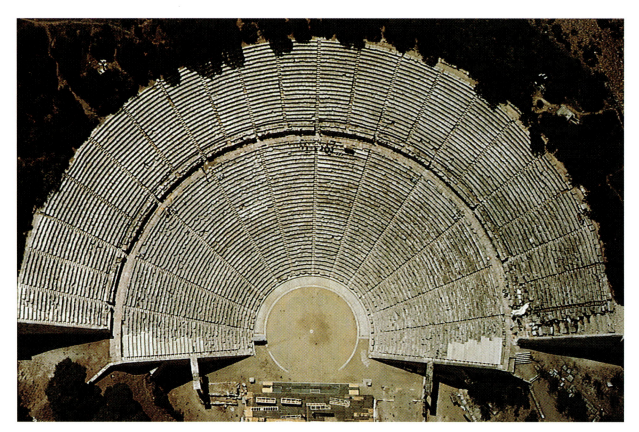

 16.1 POLYKLEITOS. *Theater at Epidauros.* Greece, c. 350 BCE. Hellenic Ministry of Culture.

and contained dressing rooms and scenery. This brilliantly designed theater could accommodate over 12,000 people and was acoustically perfect for all seats.

The *Theater at Epidauros* has had many descendants through the centuries, some that copied its design quite faithfully, and others that diverged considerably from its plan. For example, the Globe, an English Elizabethan theater in which William Shakespeare's plays were first performed, was an open courtyard encircled by three levels of galleries, holding only 2,500 spectators. The audience was often rowdy and drunk. Aristocratic men and women sat in elegant galleries, while the cheap seats were for the poor.

A very different theater was designed for the Japanese Kabuki. The word *Kabuki* literally means "song, dance, and acting," and this type of theater was intended for commoners. The subject matter for Kabuki performances came from upper-class Noh dramas, historical plays, and domestic themes that were especially enjoyed by the public. However, the literary value of Kabuki plays was less important than the actors' expressive and exaggerated body postures and vocal performances. The acting was highly stylized. The dialogue was partly sung and partly spoken, with precisely choreographed movements emphasized with percussion or wind accompaniment. Richly embroidered silks and brocades were used in Kabuki costuming, and grotesque makeup was applied to fantastic characters and villains, including painted red lines to simulate bulging veins on their faces and hands. Constant interaction took place between actors and audience during Kabuki productions. Actors interrupted the play to talk directly to the audience, and the audience would respond or call out the names of their favorite actors. (Although Kabuki was started by a woman, women soon after were forbidden to appear, so the men played female roles.) Productions lasted all day, with food served at mealtimes, although most attendees stayed only for a scene or two.

A Theatre in Edo (Figure 16.2), from 1802, shows us a packed theater with audience members dressed in their fine kimonos. The stage has a large set, which was typical in Kabuki, and a scene with several characters is taking place. The flower walk, or *hanamichi,* was a raised wooden path that allowed actors to enter and exit the main stage through the audience. With two of these paths, actors surrounded some viewers on three sides. Thus, the design of the Kabuki stage facilitated the interaction between the actors' "world" and the audience's space. This feature contrasts with Western theater design, which we saw in the *Theater at Epidauros.* It contrasts even more with seventeenth-century European theater design, in which the audience sits passively observing and facing one direction, separated from the actors by the proscenium arch.

A Theatre in Edo is rendered in a combination of contour lines and flat decorative tones. Perspective lines do not all vanish exactly to a single point, but the stage and galleries are clearly and economically depicted. Note how large the actors appear compared to the audience, perhaps to emphasize the importance of the characters or the fame of the actors.

Like the Kabuki theater, the European opera house was a space in which the middle class enjoyed entertainment that was formerly available only to the aristocracy. As the ballet in France moved from the court to the theater, the up-and-coming French middle class became an enthusiastic audience in the nineteenth century. In new, sumptuous theaters, these newly rich could socialize and show off their wealth under the guise

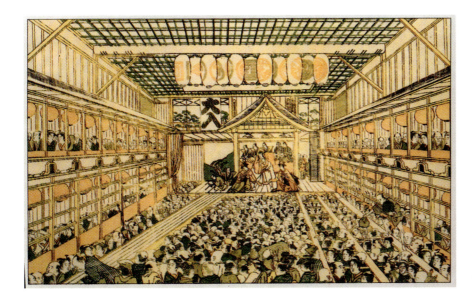

16.2 *A Theatre in Edo.* Woodcut. Japan, c. 1802. The British Museum, London.

of culture. Napoleon III responded, and his plan to modernize Paris included the grand and opulent Paris *Opera House,* designed by J. L. Charles Garnier and built from 1861 to 1874 (Figure 16.3). This piece of architecture would inspire many opera houses and, later, movie theaters that would be built all over the Western world. It remained the premier place for popular entertainment for years, until the advent of radio and television.

The ornate structure was designed not only for music and dance performances, but also for grand social encounters. Balconies, corridors, and vestibules, all laced with sparkling lamps illuminated by the latest technology, natural gas, invited the audience in and out of the building. The grand staircase, which occupies about one-third the area of the opera house, allowed for spectacular entrance fanfare. The stage was located in front of the audience and was framed by a lavishly decorated proscenium arch. Although considered **Neo Baroque** or **Flamboyant Baroque** in style, the opera house is eclectic in design, with many far-flung influences, such as the Louvre and Greco-Roman temple fronts. Large sculptures adorn the extremely dressed facade, including a fifteen-foot sculpture that celebrates the spirit of dance. Like Versailles and the Louvre,

the *Opera House* continued the tradition of extravagance and overstatement in the post-revolutionary Paris, but this time for a new breed of aristocracy.

CONNECTION
Many monuments in the Père Lachaise Cemetery (Figure 10.25, page 288) in Paris exhibit the same flamboyance and eclectic designs as the Paris Opera House.

As mentioned before, the opera house became part of the vernacular of Western architecture. One recent innovative example is in Sydney, Australia, where the graceful *Opera House* majestically stands on the edge of the harbor and greets the visitor from air, land, or sea (Figure 16.4). Designed by Danish architect Joern Utzon, the flowing forms make this structure a new type of "functional sculpture," but in architectural terms. This approach was rooted in the work of both Louis Sullivan and Frank Lloyd Wright, architects from the United States, who felt that the function of the building dic-

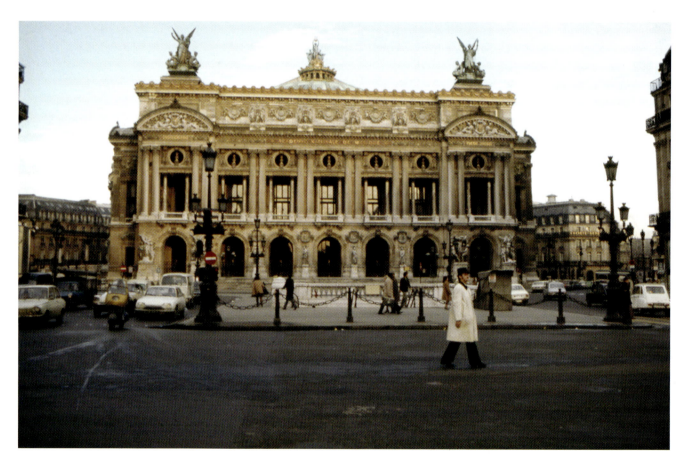

 16.3 J. L. CHARLES GARNIER. *Opera House.* Paris, France, 1861–1874. © Art Resource, NY.

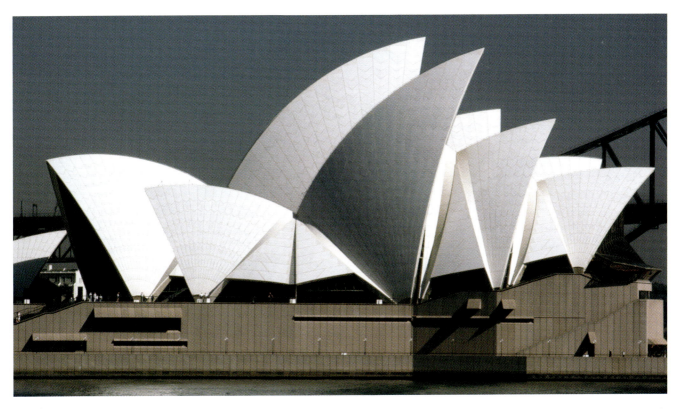

16.4   JOERN UTZON. *Opera House.* Reinforced concrete; highest shell 200' high. Sydney, Australia, 1959–1972. © Roger Ressmeyer / Corbis. See also the text accompanying Figure 3.16.

tated its form and that this form should enclose fluid, uninterrupted space (see the *Solomon R. Guggenheim Museum* in Figure 16.5). They also felt that architecture should express democratic ideals rather than simply imitate a Greek temple, as did so many government buildings, museums, libraries, and churches. With new building materials, such as reinforced concrete, architecture was freed to take practically any shape desired. This style of architecture, rooted in the work of Wright and incorporating flowing lines, was called "organic" architecture. Joern Utzon was influenced by this thinking and by the platform architecture of Mesoamerica.

> ### CONNECTION
> *Utzon was influenced by Mesoamerican architecture like the Palace at Palenque, Figure 11.8, page 308.*

Utzon's 1956 design for the *Opera House* was very controversial. Many expressed doubts about whether the technology necessary for its construction was sufficiently advanced. This

controversy delayed construction until 1959. While the building was under construction, the project incurred gross cost overruns, the government of Australia changed, and Utzon himself resigned in 1966. Fortunately, the project was not abandoned; a group of Australian architects persevered, and work was finally completed in 1972. The structure is a series of cascading vaults faced with gleaming ceramic tile, adding an element of jewel-like reflections to the fluid forms. Visually they suggest the billowing and unfurling of sails on top of a tall ship, and, in fact, their design blends with the many sailboats that are common in the Sydney Harbor. The inside of the *Opera House* is as exquisite as the outside. Window openings contain two laminated layers of amber glass, allowing quiet in the interior while giving spectacular views of the surrounding harbor. The concert halls, theaters, auditoriums, and recording studio are all lined with rich natural woods, making the interior acoustically sound.

The museum, like the opera house, flowered in Europe with the rise of the nouveau riche. To make them impressive, many museums were built in the Classical Greek style or modeled after Roman baths (see Figure 16.7). Twentieth-century architects chose other models, as did Frank Lloyd Wright when he designed the *Solomon R. Guggenheim Museum* in New York City (Figure 16.5), built between 1957 and 1959. With the flexibility and plasticity of reinforced concrete, Wright's "organic architecture" could enclose any kind of space, and here he used a spiral ramp, which opens up to a ninety-foot central well covered with a huge skylight. The viewer takes an elevator to the top and then walks down past individual bays with paintings, allowing closer focus on small groups of artworks. Overall, the space is very flowing.

There are critics of the *Guggenheim*'s design. Artwork can be seen either very close or from all the way across the central open well. There is no in-between vantage point, and some works suffer. Rather than wandering around or choosing their own course, viewers must see the works in the predetermined order. The exhibition space is good only for paintings on canvas, and even so, they seem to float or tilt when hung above a sloping ramp and against a curving wall.

Frank Gehry's *Walt Disney Concert Hall* (Figure 16.6), 2003, in Los Angeles, is the most recent entry among world-class music centers. Trained as a sculptor, Gehry creates designs that are irregular, colliding, sculptural, and perhaps even disorienting, since they have no symmetry or apparent central point. The building's structural systems are disguised under the curving stainless-steel surface. Gehry has said, "I approach each building as a sculptural object, a spatial container, a space with light and air, a response to context and appropriateness of feeling and spirit. To this container, this sculpture, the user brings his baggage, his program, and interacts with it to accommodate his needs. If he can't do that, I've failed" (*http://www.pritzkerprize.com/gehry.htm#. . .about%20Frank%20Gehry*).

Such architecture is called **Deconstructivist,** because of its many unique viewpoints that do not coalesce into a unified whole. It is also **Neo-Modernist,** with its emphasis on abstract form.

CONNECTION
For a view of the inside of the Solomon R. Guggenheim Museum, see Jenny Holzer's installation Untitled (Selected Writings) in Figure 12.29 (page 359).

CONNECTION
The British Museum (Figure 6.12, page 135) in London is one of many museums that have a facade inspired by the Parthenon from Classical Greece.

OTHER VISUAL AND PERFORMING ART ENVIRONMENTS

Art spaces may be combined with recreational or religious spaces, or spaces with other uses.

CONNECTION
Art was displayed in the building that served as a gateway to the Acropolis shrines in Athens (see Figure 9.32, page 250).

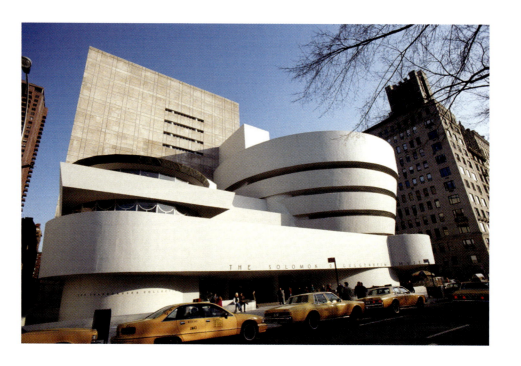

16.5   FRANK LLOYD WRIGHT. *Solomon R. Guggenheim Museum.* New York City, USA; design begun in 1943, structure completed in 1959. © Alan Schein / Corbis. See also the text accompanying Figure 6.13.

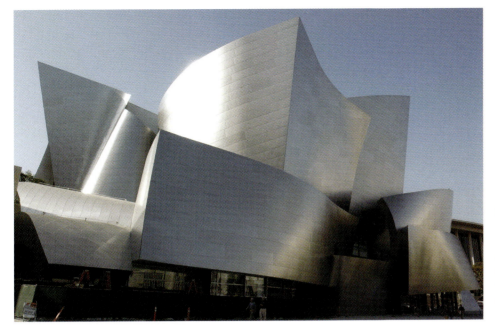

16.6   FRANK GEHRY. *Walt Disney Concert Hall,* Los Angeles, California. USA, 2003. Photo by Al Seib. © Lucy Nicholson / Reuters Newmedia Inc. / Corbis. See also the text accompanying Figure 4.3.

In the Roman Empire, many rulers spent public funds to build bathhouses, theaters, amphitheaters, circuses, arenas, and stadiums for the pleasure of their subjects and to adorn those structures with art. Later in this chapter, we will see the *Colosseum* in Rome, but now we will look at another form of recreational architecture that continues to be popular: the spa. By the third century CE, there were estimated to be over nine hundred bathhouses in the Eternal City, ranging from imperial baths to no-frills public baths. Everyone went to the baths

to improve their health and to socialize. Features included workout rooms, steam rooms, massage rooms, swimming pools, and warm, hot, and cold baths. Imperial baths in Rome boasted libraries, art galleries, theater performances, restaurants, bars, gymnasiums, shady walkways, public lectures, athletic contests, and so on. The ruins of baths are excavation sites where much ancient sculpture has been uncovered.

The *Baths of Caracalla* (Figure 16.7), built between 211 and 217 by the emperor of the same name, provided all the

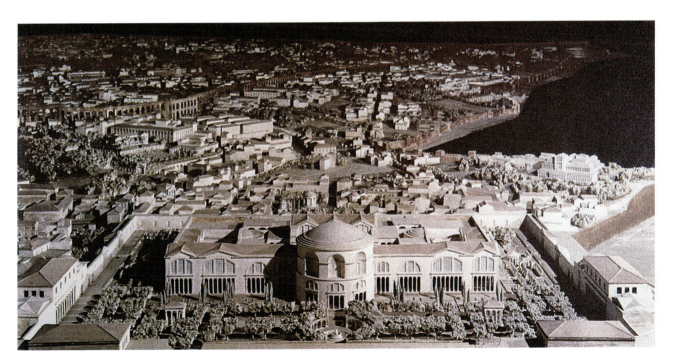

16.7   *Baths of Caracalla.* Reconstruction model.   Reconstruction in Museum of Roman Civilization, Rome.

services just mentioned for 1,600 clients. The baths, now ruins, covered fifty acres, were constructed in brick-faced concrete, and had walls 140 feet high that supported the huge vaulted ceiling. The interior was palatial, decorated lavishly with stucco ceilings, marble facing, mosaic floors, and colossal statuary. The water for the baths came from the aqueduct, another brilliant Roman invention. Inside the baths, furnaces heated not only water for the hot pools, but also air, which was circulated through hollow floors and walls throughout the complex to warm the rooms.

CONNECTION

In the sixteenth century, the Greek sculpture Laocoön and His Sons *(Figure 13.16, page 380) was discovered buried in the ruins of an imperial Roman bath.*

In the United States from the nineteenth century to today, the large city park has been the equivalent of the Roman baths for offering a variety of diversions, without the baths, of course. Everyone loves to picnic in a beautiful park, play a game of baseball or a round of golf, observe intriguing exotic animals at a zoo, attend an outdoor concert, or thrill to a wild roller coaster ride in an amusement park. These varied recreational environments are designed by engineers, architects, and landscape architects, who incorporate the land and flora with the structures. Their designs might be formal or informal.

Central Park (Figure 16.8) was built in the heart of the bustling city of New York, as a retreat from city life. Frederick Law Olmsted and Calvert Vaux designed the park, which is 2.5 miles north to south and one-half mile wide, to work with nature rather than reconstruct it. As a result, the park is considered an outstanding example of landscape architecture. It took a year to prepare the area by relocating hovels, hog farms, and a bone-boiling factory and by draining open sewers. Millions of flowers, trees, and shrubs were planted, water systems were incorporated, and trails, roads, and bridges were added within the natural rolling terrain of the site. The park today features all kinds of entertaining places and events:

- The Metropolitan Museum of Art
- Sheep Meadow, now used for free musical concerts
- Delacorte Shakespeare Theater (free)
- The Ramble (wilderness area trails)

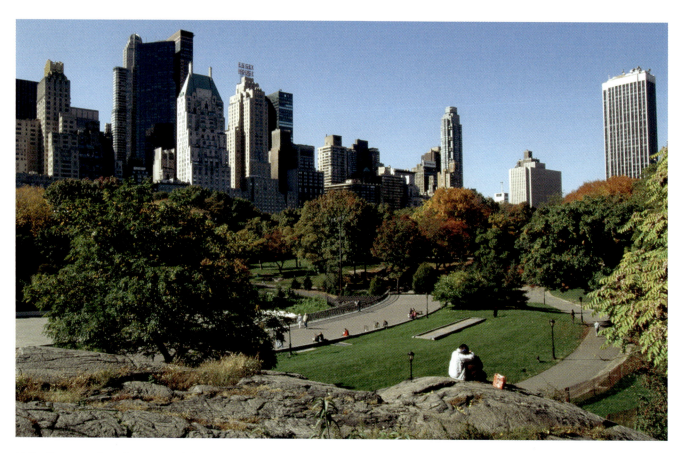

16.8 FREDERICK LAW OLMSTED and CALVERT VAUX. *Central Park,* New York City. USA, 1857–1887. © Michael S. Yamashita / Corbis.

- Zoo and the Children's Zoo

- Wollman Rink and Lasker Rink and Pool

- Chess and Checker Pavilion

- the Harlem Meer, a small lake with a boathouse

- Fort Fish and Fort Clinton, blockhouses from the Revolutionary War and the War of 1812

- hundreds of monuments and plaques honoring statesmen, writers, children, animals, birds, and military events

- tennis courts, baseball diamonds, football and soccer fields, children's playgrounds, a cafeteria, bike and bridle paths, and many gardens

In 1965, the park was declared a National Historic Landmark. This wonderful park is still the pride and joy of New Yorkers and a popular site for tourists from all over the world.

CONNECTION
The formal gardens of palaces like Versailles (Figure 5.4, page 105) were one inspiration for large urban parks in the United States.

The Hakone Open-Air Museum (Figure 16.9), opened in 1969, is a museum set in nature, located in the scenic Hakone National Park. The spectacular scenery of the Hakone Mountains is the gallery space for contemporary outdoor sculpture. Nature's art, which is forever changing with the seasons, is in breathtaking harmony with the art of human beings. The out-

door exhibition space has exquisitely manicured lawns, woods, and gardens that complement the many works displayed there. Indoors is the Main Gallery, with works by such celebrated sculptors as Brancusi, Boccioni, Miró, Calder, Dubuffet, Morie Ogiwara, and Kotaro Takamura. The Painting Gallery displays renowned twentieth-century Japanese and European artworks. The Picasso Pavilion is the world's first privately installed Picasso Museum.

Farther along on the park and recreation continuum we find gardens, wild animal parks, amusement parks, and theme parks. Even parklike cemeteries may contain art (see *Leonardo da Vinci's Last Supper* in Forest Lawn Cemetery, Figure 10.27, page 290). These parks are part of popular culture, but they are the "first cousins" of art parks. In addition, they are influential sites that are discussed frequently in relation to contemporary culture and theory, and they are powerful in the imaginations of many.

THE VISUAL ARTS WITHIN THE PERFORMING ARTS

ART AND THEATER

The visual arts have long been part of theater productions, especially in masks, puppetry, set design, costumes, and graphics. Theater has in turn influenced the visual arts, particularly Performance Art.

As mentioned, masks have been part of theater productions since the *Theater at Epidauros*. In some cultures, masks are used in performances that are partly entertainment and

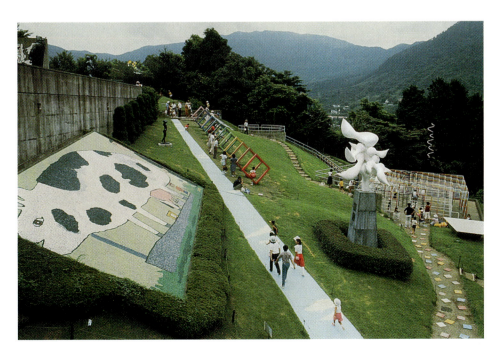

16.9 *The Hakone Open-Air Museum.* Hakone National Park, Japan, opened in 1969. © Courtesy Japan National Tourist Organization.

partly ritual; one example is the *Gu Mask* (Figure 16.10) of the Guro people of Ivory Coast in Africa. When worn in full masquerade, the *Gu Mask* embodies the female spirit as well as the Guro standard of ideal beauty and fashion. Both the *Gu Mask* and its male counterpart, called a *Zamble* mask, are often used in dance. This story-dance might mock or comment on gender relations, truly a universal source of material, and one utilized by entertainers worldwide. The masquerade performers and their bands perform at regional festivals, local community events, marriages, or funerals. Recently, they have also performed at hotels for tourists. The mask itself is finely carved and polished. Much like the naturalistic masks of the Dan and Baule peoples, the *Gu Mask* is a long flow of gentle curves. The high, bulging forehead extending below an elegant coif, the scarification of the face, and the filing of the teeth are all marks of female beauty among the Guro. For performances, brightly patterned cloth can be attached to the edges of the

mask. The excitement and spirit of the *Gu Mask* can be felt only when it is combined with the full costume and used with dance and music. (For an image of African masks being used in dance, see the *Kanaga Masked Dancers,* Figure 16.20).

The entire category of masks and masquerades is an example of how one culture's concepts and uses of art do not translate cleanly into those of another culture. The masquerade is an important African art form, performed in open spaces, with aspects of entertainment, art, music, drama, and, often, religion and ritual. Artists and community participate, and all are integral to the success of the event. However, Western art museums consider the mask itself to be art, and they retain it, rarely presenting the entire ritual, music, and performance.

CONNECTION
Ritual dances with masks have often had significant religious meaning. For example, see the discussion of the Kwakiutl Transformation Mask (Figure 9.13, page 235).

Akin to masks and costumes is puppetry, an art form that has existed for at least four thousand years. In Japan, an early form of puppetry was the "doll drama" called *Bunraku,* which was performed by traveling troupes. Today, puppeteers and puppet workshops continue to work in the old tradition (Figure 16.11). In the doll drama, the puppeteer was accompanied by a singer-narrator and a musician playing a three-stringed instrument called a *samisen.* The singer would describe the scenes, voice all the roles, and make any comments needed to enhance the drama. The style of singing was rooted in the Japanese kabuki theater (see Figure 16.2), and singers would achieve fame in their own right. The musical background would create the mood of the play as well as the tempo and would help punctuate the action and important moments of the story. The story themes came from previous Noh dramas, legends, and historical events, and generally dealt with human conflict concerning duty and desire, condemned love, and self-control.

The naturalistic puppets are one-half life-size and have articulated hands, heads, eyes, brows, and mouths. The male characters also have articulated legs, but the female puppets are dressed in long robes that make legs unnecessary. Originally, the puppets did not have movable parts; these were developed later as the craft was perfected. Three people operate the puppet: the master puppeteer, whose face we see, and two assistants, who are robed in black. The master wears elevated sandals so that he can be above the other two. He holds the puppet up and works the head and facial features with one hand while manipulating the doll's right hand with the other. The other assistants work the left hand and the feet. All the manipulations are done in full view of the audience on a long, narrow stage. All performers must be precisely synchronized,

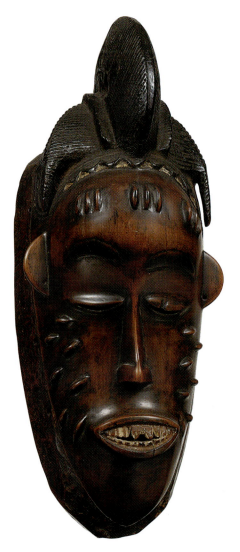

16.10 *Gu Mask.* Wood, 12¹/₂". Guro. Ivory Coast. The University of Iowa Museum of Art.

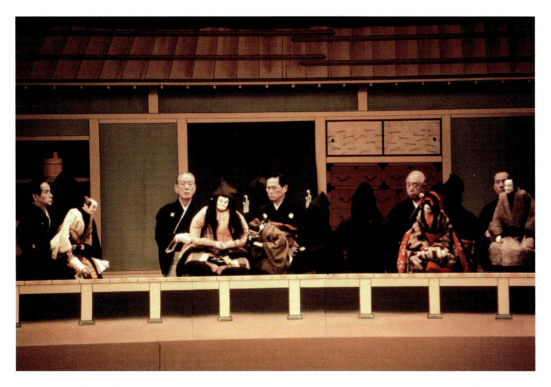

16.11 *Bunraku* performance on stage. Japan, c. twentieth century. See also the text accompanying Figure 5.23. © Michael S. Yamashita / Corbis.

an accomplishment requiring lengthy practice and discipline. It is no wonder that Japan recognizes artists and art forms such as Bunraku as national treasures.

Puppetry took a new form in the mid-1990s on the Broadway stage. Disney's *The Lion King* (Figure 16.12) deals with the rites of passage of a young lion king, as he struggles to find his place in life. One element that made the show so exciting was the unique combination of human-puppet characters, created and directed by Julie Taymor. Taymor's background ranges from Indonesian masked dance and Bunraku

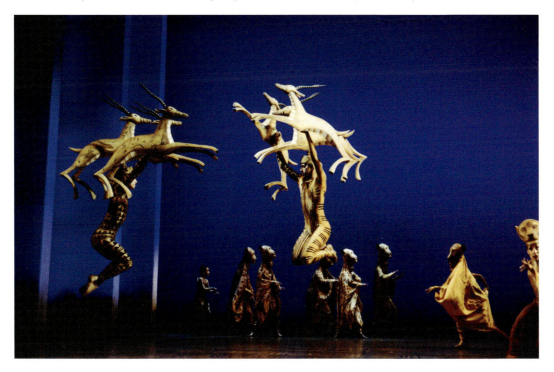

16.12 JULIE TAYMOR (designer and director). *A Scene from The Lion King.* New York City, USA, opened mid-1990s. © Robbie Jack / Corbis.

puppetry to Wagnerian and Stravinskyan opera. The audience saw the puppeteer-actors work the puppets, so both the story and the process of telling the story unfolded simultaneously. Because the story is about animals who endure humanlike experiences, the design of the characters was especially appropriate. In our example, warm gold tones and dark geometric markings unite the design of the antelope puppets and costumes of the dancers who carry them. The dancers perform high, graceful leaps, mimicking the animals' body movements.

Visual artists have produced graphics for the performing arts. Henri-Marie-Raymond de Toulouse-Lautrec lived in the cabaret and theater district of Montmartre, Paris, in the 1880s. There he became friends with the entertainers, street people, prostitutes, and other artists who frequented the area, and many of them became the focus of his work. In contrast to the traditional Western aesthetic, Toulouse-Lautrec preferred shallow space, decorative color, and the fluid contour line, as seen in Japanese prints.

CONNECTION

Toulouse-Lautrec was influenced by Japanese prints like Komurasaki of the Tamaya Teahouse (Figure 14.33, page 428).

Toulouse-Lautrec's work was seen everywhere in the streets, reaching an audience barred from attending the Paris galleries and salons. A favorite subject was *Jane Avril* (Figure 16.13), a singer and dancer at the famous cabaret Moulin Rouge. This famous poster from 1899 captures the provocative entertainer as she sings her song, inviting the public to come and see more. The artist caught Avril in costume and makeup, as if under theater lights, showing off her bright red hair and large plumed hat. Simple fluid shapes filled with bright flat colors silhouette Avril's graceful contour against a flat negative space that, in juxtaposition, becomes equally important in the composition. The coiling snake emphasizes her curves. The serpent imagery also suggests that she is a temptress, like Eve to Adam, enticing her audience to come to her sensuous performance. Her written name balances the negative space and at the same time visually supports her exaggerated back bend. Toulouse-Lautrec was one of the first to bring fine art to graphics and was a strong influence on graphic designers.

Set design is another area of significant overlap between the visual arts and performing arts. In 1958, U.S. artist Robert Rauschenberg, choreographer Merce Cunningham, and composer Morton Feldman created an innovative and provocative work entitled *Summerspace* (Figure 16.14), with John Cage as musical director, first performed at the American Dance Festival. Rauschenberg designed the set and costumes, Feldman

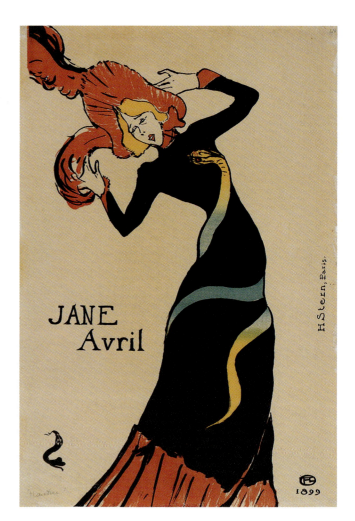

 16.13   HENRI DE TOULOUSE-LAUTREC. *Jane Avril.* Lithographic poster, 22" × 14". Paris, France, 1899. © Erich Lessing / Art Resource, NY. See also the text accompanying Figure 1.2.

composed the music, and Cunningham choreographed the movement. Although a collaboration, each component was designed to be performed simultaneously yet independent from one another, with all three parts using techniques of improvisation and chance.

In designing the choreography, Cunningham conceived of space as a continuum, without a focal point for the dancers, as was common in traditional dance. The dance space was handled more like an abstract painting in which all points in (pictorial) space are considered equally important. Cunningham was also influenced by Albert Einstein's theory of relativity, which posited that there are no fixed points in space. Rauschenberg based his set and costume design on Cunningham's choreography, on the dance that had no center point, but moved from all points on the stage. Rauschenberg turned to the French Impressionist **Pointillist** style and painted the sets and costumes with small dots (or points) in several colors.

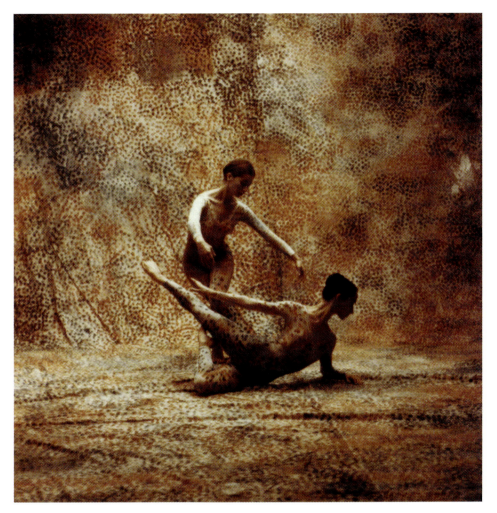

16.14 *Summerspace*. Music by Morton Feldman, choreography by Merce Cunningham, set and costumes by Robert Rauschenberg; John Cage, Musical Director of the Cunningham Dance Company. Premiered at the American Dance Festival at Connecticut College, New London, Connecticut. Dancers: Viola Farber (standing) and Carolyn Brown. Photo by Richard Rutledge.

Visually, the dancer's costumes were the same as the set and vice versa, giving each element equal importance and interest.

CONNECTION
Jackson Pollock's Lucifer (Figure 13.33, page 393) is an example of an abstract painting without a single, fixed focal point. For a Pointillist painting, see Georges Seurat's La Grande Jatte (Figure 14.29, page 424).

In recent years, the performing arts have had a great influence on the visual arts, especially in an area called *performance art*. Performance art is a visual art form that incorporates live action and mixed media and is presented before an audience. The first performances were artist Allan Kaprow's 1960s "Happenings," mixtures of traditional media with found and junk objects. These events involved all the senses and added chance in the artwork's process. No art objects of permanence and preciousness were created, only passing events of pure experience. Kaprow believed that art, like life, should be unstable, transitory, and unclear, a belief that was in opposition to much previous Western thought, which regarded an artwork as a pure, transcendent, universal object meant to endure. Kaprow felt that art should mesh with life, rather than interpret life experience.

For this new art form, Kaprow coordinated happenings by setting the scene in which improvisation could take place. For his happening entitled *Household*, Kaprow chose a dump area in Ithaca, New York, close to Cornell University. On a day in May at 11:00 A.M., the men participants built a tower of garbage, as the women participants built a nest of twigs and string, suggesting the traditional domain of each gender. From inside the nest, the women began screeching at the men. A

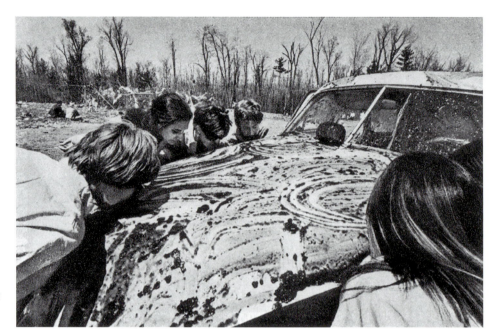

16.15 ALLAN KAPROW. *Household.* Performance "Happening." Commissioned by Cornell University, New York, May 1964. © 2004 Allan Kaprow. Used by permission of the J. Paul Getty Museum, Los Angeles. See also the text accompanying Figure 2.26.

wrecked car was brought, on which the men spread strawberry jam. The women left their nest and began licking the jam off the car (Figure 16.15) while the men destroyed the nest. The men returned to the car and began wiping the jam off the car with white bread, then eating it. While the men were busy, the women avenged the destruction of their nest by decimating the men's tower. The event continued with violence as the men demolished the car with sledgehammers and set it on fire. With the final and fierce destruction of the car, the tension between the sexes lessened. In silence, all participants watched the car burn, and then, without words, departed.

Indeed a bizarre and surreal enactment, the meaning of *Household* is as ambiguous as a dream. Kaprow welcomed individual interpretation, but offered no stock meaning to the work. *Household* also blurred the distinction between participants and audience; they were not clearly distinguished during the event. Kaprow would, however, likely agree that the process of the work as it *happened* was the important part of the work, and that its meaning was unclear, unstable, and passing.

Laurie Anderson's 1999 *Songs and Stories from Moby Dick* (Figure 16.16) represents one way that performance art has developed since Kaprow's time. *Moby Dick* is a lavish stage production supported by many designers, actors, musicians, and technicians. The work consists of projections, computer-generated art, narratives, songs, and voices based on Herman Melville's classic. Rather than being presented in a straight narrative, however, the elements are combined in a fragmented, almost cubist fashion. The work is intensely visual and aural. It combines biblical references, American mythol-

ogy, and multiple viewpoints. Anderson is known for her innovative use of technology in the arts. In this production, she portrays three characters and plays four instruments.

ART AND MUSIC

The visual arts and music also overlap, but in ways that are different from visual art and theater.

In the ancient city of Ur, chariots, sculpture, jewelry, elaborate headdresses, and a musical instrument were found in the royal tomb of Queen Puabi, dated c. 2685 BCE. One of the most remarkable pieces was the beautifully crafted *Lyre* made of wood, lapis lazuli, and gold and shell inlay (Figure 16.17). The lyre is a stringed instrument similar to a harp. The instrument's wooden sound box and body are composed of clean rectangles and subtle curves, with the instrument's function dictating its form. Decorative sculpture and scenes accent the front of the sound box yet do not detract from the precise lines of the instrument. The stunning head of a blue-bearded bull is made of gold and lapis lazuli, an imported semiprecious stone. The meaning of this image is unknown, but it is very likely connected to religious and ritual symbolism. Bearded bulls are a symbol of royalty. Although the bull's head is remarkably naturalistic, it also has highly stylized details, such as the outlined eyes and the patterned curls of the beard.

Beneath the bull's head are four scenes made of shell inlaid in bitumen. They may depict a fantastic banquet, or they may illustrate fables, something like Aesop's animal characters did

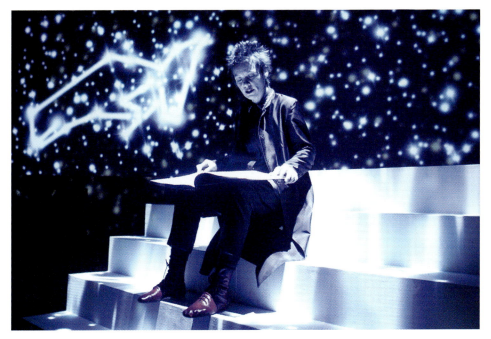

16.16 LAURIE ANDERSON. Scene from *Songs and Stories from Moby Dick*. Multimedia performance. USA, 1999. Canal Street Communications.

for the Greeks. Characters include a young man who may represent the legendary hero Gilgamesh, flanked by two human-headed bulls. Animal composite imagery was common in Near Eastern as well as Egyptian art. More whimsical, four-legged creatures are depicted standing upright on two feet, performing the menial tasks of servants. A lively dog with a dagger is bringing in a table, followed by a lion carrying a platter and a large jar. Below them is a donkey musician playing a lyre like the one it adorns.

CONNECTION
Lavish royal tombs from other cultures are illustrated in the Chapter 10 section on "Furnished Tombs."

CONNECTION
The human-headed bull may be a guardian figure like the Assyrian Lamassu sculpture (Figure 11.11, page 311).

The drum is nearly universal in human cultures. In Melanesia, there are three types of drums, created for males only: large slit drums, small hand drums, and the water drum. The slit drums are hollowed-out tree trunks with a long, narrow, vertical slit. Several feet tall, they stand upright on the ground and are struck with long poles. In contrast, the smaller

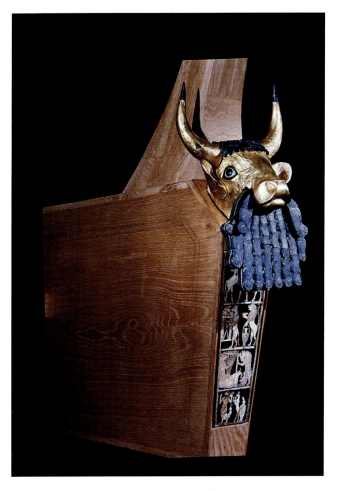

16.17 *Lyre*. Wood, gold and shell inlay, lapis lazuli, 5'5" high. Sound box from tomb of Queen Puabi. Ur (Iraq), c. 2685 BCE. University of Pennsylvania Museum.

Asmat Hand Drum (Figure 16.18) is carried in one hand, and the lizard skin head is struck with the other. Among the Asmat in Papua New Guinea, the hand drum was used in ceremonies for a boy's initiation, to placate ancestor spirits who died because of an enemy raid, and for magical rites. The slender, hourglass-shaped drums were usually decorated with ancestral and head-hunting symbolism, represented in the heads of the hornbill birds and stylized hands. The complex symbolism relates to the former head-hunting and cannibalistic traditions of the Asmat.

CONNECTION
For more information about Asmat culture and wood carvers, see Figure 14.17, page 413, Bisj Poles.

DANCE

Aspects of dance recall visual art. The North American Sioux *Open Circle Dance* (Figure 16.19) was part of the annual celebration of the springtime rebirth of nature. The dancer uses twenty-eight hoops made of wood or reeds, and each movement has a spiritual significance. The complicated manipulation of the hoops as the performer dances to a rapid rhythm creates visual images. The images connote the unity of all things in the universe, although they individually grow and change. Some parts of the dance recreate the image of an eagle soaring in flight. The eagle suggests that part of nature (including human beings) is not of this earth, but of the spiritual world in the heavens. Another configuration represents the caterpillar, which, during the dance, will become a graceful butterfly. Growth, change, and metamorphosis, all part of nature, are seen in the dance. The rigorous performance climaxes with the "Hoops of Many Hoops," in which the visual image relates that all things come together—the earth, sun, moon, light, all life, and the spirit of humans are all interconnected. It also symbolizes a hopeful Sioux prophecy for peace among all people. This dance, with its many hoops, is an elaborate variation of older forms of dance that has been developed because of the interest of tourists. Once again, entertainment and ritual mix.

For the Dogon people in Mali, the dance, costume, and the Kanaga mask are also interconnected (Figure 16.20). The dancers perform at public events, usually funerals (similar to the Guro masked dancers discussed earlier in this chapter). The performers are members of a male masked society called the *awa*, who, in their dance, tell their culture's story about how death entered the world. The dancers are costumed in vegetable fiber skirts that have been dyed red, because red can drive the dead person's spirit from its house. The masking and the color of the costume are believed to catch, manipulate, and rechannel vital forces that could pose potential danger to the community if unleashed. Awa initiates wear the Kanaga

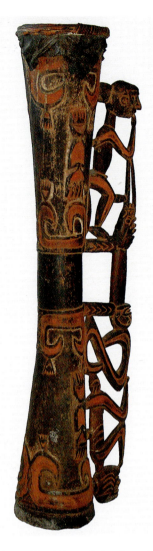

 16.18   *Asmat Hand Drum.* Painted wood, lizard skin, rattan, 45" high. Southwest Asmat coast, Indonesia, c. 1950. From the collection of Tobias Schneebaum, New York, N.Y. Photo by Tobias Schneebaum.

mask when the spirit of the deceased is believed to leave the body on the third day after death. The Kanaga masks, carved by the performers, have several interpretations, such as a bird in flight, a mythological crocodile, or a god in the act of creation. Through the interaction of mask, costume, and choreography, the Kanaga dancers express a vital force.

MUSIC AND DANCE IMAGERY

Artworks that depict music and dance can tell us about the musical forms of cultures now long lost, and about the social, political, and religious framework into which music fits.

In the Cycladic Islands off Greece, sculptures of male musicians were found buried in graves along with plank marble goddess figures. The musicians were of two kinds: harpists, who were seated holding their instruments on their laps (Figure 16.21), and woodwind players, who were depicted standing.

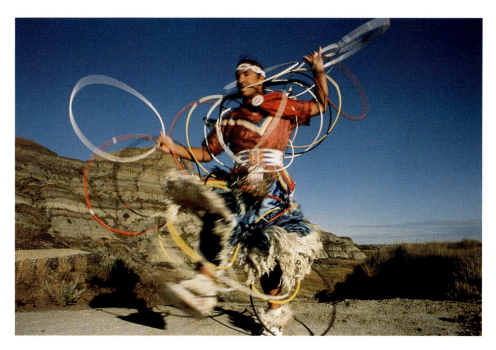

16.19 KEVIN LOCKE. Performing the *Open Circle Dance.* Sioux. USA, twentieth century. © 1995 Bruce Wendt Productions / Makoche Recording Company. Photo by Bruce Wendt Courtesy Makoche Recording Company.

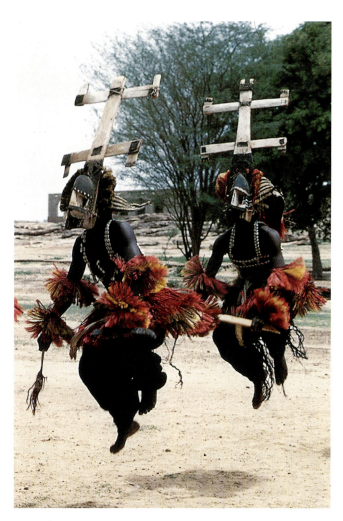

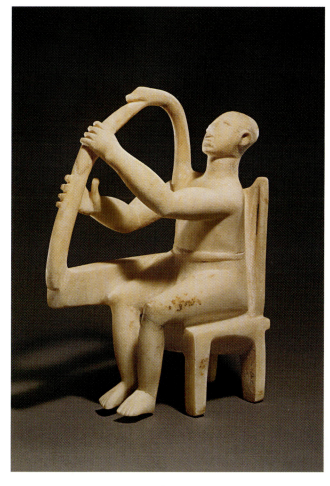

 16.20 *Kanaga Masked Dancers.* Dogon. Mali, twentieth century. Hutchison Library. See also the text accompanying Figure 2.23.

 16.21 *Harp Player.* Marble, approximately 14" × 3". Cycladic culture, c. 2500–1100 BCE. Metropolitan Museum of Art, New York, Rogers Fund, 1947. (47.100.1) Photograph © 1996 The Metropolitan Museum of Art.

The presence of both fertility goddesses and music makers in the grave suggests that life after death was seen as a positive and rewarding step.

Our *Harp Player,* from c. 2500–1100 BCE, is smoothly carved with clear, well-defined forms, like the fertility figures. Precise attention was given to the detailing of the hands and fingers, as we can see his thumb plucking the invisible strings. The upper torso is somewhat exaggerated, with elongated arms reaching across the harp. The figure's face and ears are simply stylized, and the head is a bit extended as well, perhaps indicating a cap, as traces of paint were found on the heads of some musician figures. The proportions of the musician figures appear standardized, with a fixed ratio of height to width, which may have been a reflection of the mathematical relationship of musical intervals. The *Harp Player* is better viewed in profile, rather than from the front. In this respect, the sculpture seems related to Egyptian sculpture, which indicated one viewpoint, as opposed to sculpture in the round, which would have many "correct" views.

CONNECTION

The Idol from Amorgos *(Figure 8.2, page 197) is the kind of goddess figure that was found with the Cycladic sculptures of male musicians. Like the* Harp Player, *the Egyptian sculpture* Menkaure and His Wife, Queen Khamerernebty *(Figure 11.1, page 302) is best seen from one point of view. Its formal depiction of royalty contrasts with the liveliness of the figures in* Musicians and Dancers.

An Egyptian wall painting of *Musicians and Dancers* (Figure 16.22), in the tomb of Nebamun, dated c. 1400 BCE, shows ancient forms of entertainment that were enjoyed by the living as well as the dead. It was traditional for living relatives to celebrate rituals and the anniversaries of the dead in their tombs, some of which were quite large and elaborate, consisting of many rooms. The many tomb frescoes depict a wide range of subject matter. In *Musicians and Dancers,* we see four finely dressed women seated very casually, with one playing an oboe-like instrument while the others clap along in rhythm. The cone on top of each woman's head was made of perfumed animal tallow, which would melt and run down their bodies, covering them with fragrant grease. To the right are barely clad dancers and stacked wine jars.

The painting style of this fresco is as relaxed as the seated figures that appear in it, which contrasts with depictions of high-ranking Egyptians. The ladies' hair is loose, the soles of their feet are shown, and two face the viewer head-on rather than in the typical Egyptian profile. The dancers are depicted smaller, indicating their lesser rank in the Egyptian social hierarchy. They are not rigid figures, but in lively movement, another unusual quality for standard Egyptian art. The whole scene gives the feeling of levity and pleasure meant both for the spirit of the deceased and for the living.

Centuries later in seventeenth-century Holland, Judith Leyster painted a young boy engrossed in playing his flute (Figure 16.23). Leyster was a prolific artist whose work was well known at the time, a rare accomplishment for a woman in a predominantly man's art world. *Boy Playing a Flute,* from 1630–1635, is considered her masterpiece. In the lyric painting, she captures the pride and the enthusiasm of the young musician as he glances at his audience, likely looking for their approval. The mellow tones of the painting suggest the soft tones of the flute. In the shallow space, the boy is balanced compositionally with the instruments hanging on the wall.

Holland at the time was predominantly middle class and Protestant, so music was not written for grand productions for the nobility or for elaborate rituals for the Catholic Church. Rather, music was mostly performed by ordinary people and enjoyed in their middle-class homes. Most surviving music notation from this time is in handwritten copies for home

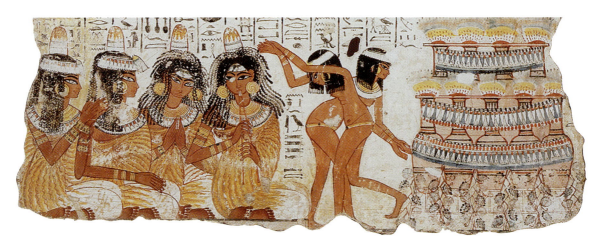

16.22 *Musicians and Dancers.* Fresco, 12" × 27". From the tomb of Nebamun, Thebes, Egypt, c. 1400 BCE. The British Museum, London.

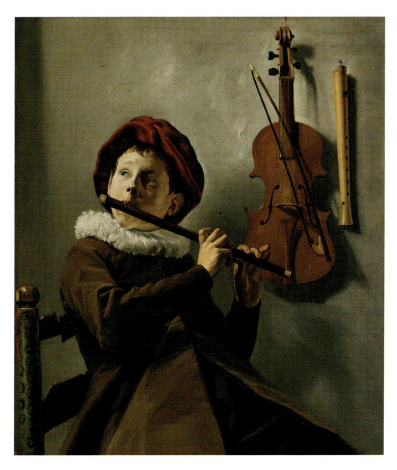

16.23 JUDITH LEYSTER. *Boy Playing a Flute.* Oil, 28¹/₂" × 24¹/₄". Netherlands, 1630–35. National Museum, Stockholm, Sweden. Source-Nationalmuseum, Stockholm.

use. Leyster's painting reflects this middle-class, self-reliant approach to music. The boy is an ordinary child, playing for his own pleasure and that of his family, in a home graced with several musical instruments.

THE TECHNOLOGY REVOLUTION IN ENTERTAINMENT

Technology has had an enormous impact on entertainment. In just a little more than one hundred years, we have seen the development of film, television, and digital imaging media. Despite their short history, these new media of entertainment are mainstays of popular culture. Video and film are also art media, and many artists have explored the many possibilities they contain. In this section, however, we will focus on examples that are aimed at a broad audience and that fit more closely into the category of entertainment.

CONNECTION
Nam June Paik's multi-imaged Megatron *(Figure 15.37, page 463) is a good example of art that refers to entertainment technologies.*

FILM AND TELEVISION

The first of the technological revolutions in entertainment was the motion picture, born of the marriage of photography and electricity. Early experiments in film soon led to elaborate productions with experienced actors. Film quickly became distinct from theater. The movable camera removed all boundaries from the staged space, and sequences could be shot on sound stages or anywhere in the world. Sound was added to the action in 1927, which made or broke many actors' careers.

CONNECTION
An example of Eadweard Muybridge's sequential images, which are early experiments to capture motion with photography, is Handspring, a flying pigeon interfering, June 26, 1885 *(Figure 13.19, page 383).*

Many films are considered classics, even works of art, in addition to their entertainment value. It is beyond the scope of this book to cover film history. However, we will look at *Gone with the Wind* (Figure 16.24). This famous film is an excellent example of the type of entertainment that came out of the MGM studios during the 1930s and 1940s. It is a glossy and expensive production, romantic and melodramatic, that essentially promotes conventional values. The film is replete with a lush musical score and symphonic accompaniment. This epic story of the Old South before and during the Civil War dealt with love and family conflict amid the hardships and horrors of war. Big-screen color played an important part in the magnificence of this motion picture, not only in depicting the grandeur and glory of the Old South, but also in conveying the mood of the film. The color red bombards the senses in the picture, underscoring the fiery spirit and burning desires of Scarlett, the blood of the dead soldiers, and the city of Richmond and Southern life in general going up in torrid flames. *Gone with the Wind* continues to be popular and has been recently restored and re-released.

CONNECTION

For more on the recently released version of Gone with the Wind, *and the controversy it sparked, see the section "Restoration" in Chapter 6.*

Another medium had so great an impact on the world that it would change it forever. Television in essence "shrank" the world as human beings could witness events from far-off places on the small screen right in their living rooms. Television became broadly popular in the 1950s. Most of the early television shows evolved from radio programs, such as the quiz show, talk show, travelogue, and "sitcom," or situation comedy. Eventually, television would rob radio of a great part of its audience. Television entertainment expanded to investigative reporting, political coverage, and world events. Educational programs were developed as well as specialty programming. Music videos are a current popular phenomenon, offering fans the opportunity to watch as well as listen to music. More recent trends include reality TV and makeover series. With satellite and cable hook-up, so much is available now that there is an overabundance of choice.

Nevertheless, no matter how many choices are offered in TV programming, the sitcom is one of the most popular of all, and the granddaddy (or better, "grandmama") of them all was *I Love Lucy* (Figure 16.25). Families and friends across the United States who had TV sets gathered every Monday night to watch the antics of Lucy, Ricky, Fred, and Ethel. Performed and taped before a live audience, this sitcom was number one among all the programming available at the time. In fact, more people watched the episode in which little Ricky was born than tuned in to the inauguration of President Dwight D. Eisenhower, which aired the same night in 1953. Although the scripts were undoubtedly effective, much of the humor was communicated through facial expression, gesture, and body language. Notice how the exaggerated facial expressions and tilted heads create the idea of a carefree trip. Still in syndication, *I Love Lucy* continues to be seen on TV and remains a popular favorite. In essence, it has become a video icon of American family humor.

Television and movies have borrowed from art, and vice versa. From 1995 through 2003, U.S. artist Matthew Barney

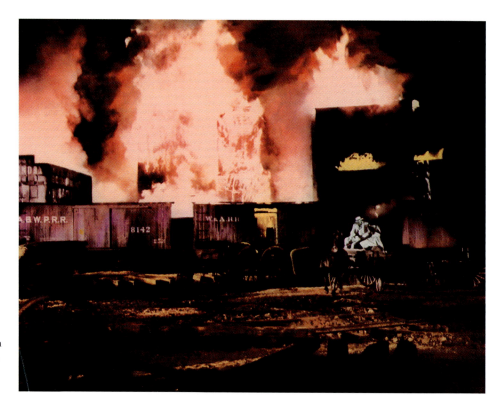

16.24 *Gone with the Wind.* MGM film, starring Clark Gable and Vivian Leigh. USA, 1939. Copyright Metro Goldwyn Mayer. See also the text accompanying Figure 6.20.

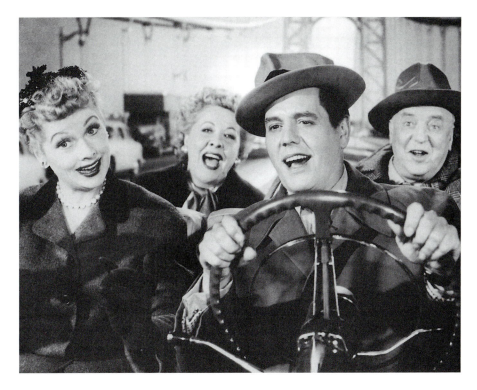

16.25 *I Love Lucy.* Television video, situation comedy (sitcom). USA, c. 1950s–1960s. CBS Entertainment, A Division of CBS, Inc. Images of Lucille & Desi Arnaz are licensed by Desilu, Too, LLC. See also the text accompanying Figure 6.18.

created the *Cremaster* cycle of films, filled with grand scenes from history, autobiography, bizarre creatures, bodily orifices, and so on. The ravishing imagery creates a presence rather than a narrative and promotes personal, free-associative meanings. Much of the films' content deals with gender identity, and many characters have mutant, ambiguous, or partially formed genitalia. Audiences are either repulsed or fascinated. All *Cremaster* films borrow from Hollywood types; for example, *Cremaster 1* references the Busby Berkeley musical extravaganza. Barney also creates individual artworks related to his films, such as *Cremaster 1: The Goodyear Chorus* (Figure 16.26), a color print in a self-lubricating frame, based on a film still.

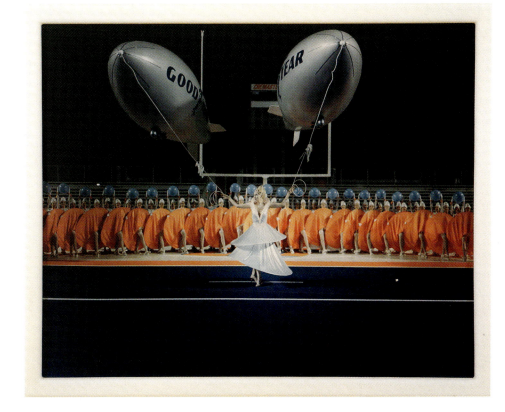

16.26 MATTHEW BARNEY. *Cremaster 1: The Goodyear Chorus.* Color print in self-lubricating plastic frame, 43³/₄" × 53³/₄". USA, 1995. Photo by Michael James O'Brien, Courtesy Barbara Gladstone Gallery. See also the text accompanying Figure 5.11.

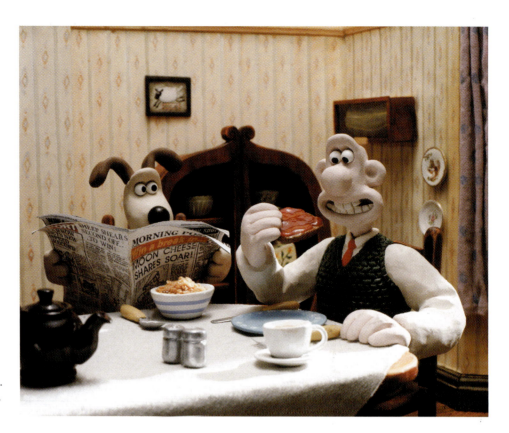

16.27 NICK PARK. *Wallace and Gromit eating breakfast.* Scene from *The Wrong Trousers.* Claymation film. © Aardman/Wallace & Gromit Ltd., 1993.

ANIMATION AND DIGITAL IMAGING

Cartoons have a long history in drawing, printmaking, and newspapers, where they entertain or promote political causes. More recently, cartoons have been made both for film and for television. The earliest form of animation grew out of flip books, in which a series of drawn images seem to move as book pages are rapidly flipped. Early animation features gained a wide following beginning in the 1930s. Animation is labor-intensive; as an indication, fourteen thousand drawings on average are required for a ten-minute animation sequence. Traditional animated images are drawn on transparent sheets, so that the foreground action figures, which move many times per second, can be separated from the background scenes that may remain constant for a while. The individual foreground scenes are then sandwiched with their appropriate background, and each is shot as a single frame of film. Disney and Warner Brothers were two pioneers in the industry, producing a number of animated features, but other studios and independent producers now exist.

Claymation, another relatively early form of animation, combines sculpture with film technology. Clay figures are sculpted and then moved in tiny increments, each of which is captured in a single film frame. *Gumby* was an early example of claymation, while *The Wrong Trousers* (Figure 16.27), featuring Wallace and Gromit, is a more recent production from the 1990s. *The Wrong Trousers* is remarkable for the quality of movement, its complex and charming character development,

and, visually, its rich colors, intricate patterns and textures, and overall detail. The fact that it is all clay in motion makes it more incredible.

Computer animation is a new form that has developed as a result of computer technology, which allows images to be converted to digital information. With computer animation, characters can be plotted as a series of points and vectors and made to move through mathematical computation. *Toy Story,* released by Disney in 1995, was the first full-length computer-generated film. The visual qualities of computer-generated animation are different from those of claymation and traditional animation, having a greater uniformity of line quality and form.

SPORTS AND SPORTS ARENAS

Art and architecture give visual form to sport activities, which helps to conceptualize the meaning of these activities beyond simply leisure or games. Sports often have political or religious implications, not only in long-past cultures, but also today; for example, sports commentators cast professional sports in terms of personalities and human drama, rather than simply describing the play-by-play.

SPORT SITES

The *Colosseum,* or the Flavian Amphitheater (Figure 16.28), was a Roman sports arena that also served a political agenda.

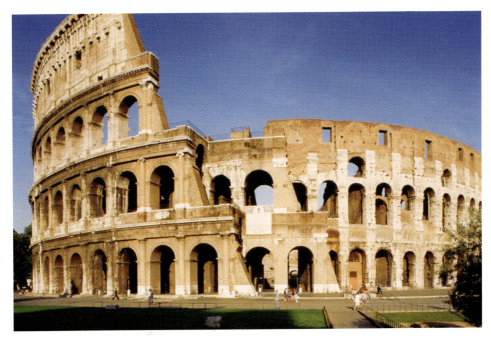

16.28 *Colosseum.* Rome, 70–82 CE. © Richard Glover / Corbis. See also Figure 6.1.

It was built between 70 and 82 CE by the emperors Vespasian, Titus, and Domitian of the Flavian dynasty, all of whom succeeded the infamous tyrant Nero, the last Juno-Claudian emperor. Their motivation was to return to the people what Nero had taken away, so the *Colosseum* was built on what had been Nero's artificial lake in his private park, where a colossal statue of the emperor stood. (Hence, the name *Colosseum* was given to the structure built next to the statue. After Nero's death, the statue was made over to represent Apollo.) With a stone foundation and concrete core walls covered with rich veneers of marble, tile, plaster, and bronze, the *Colosseum* was a feast for the eyes, evident in the drawing in Figure 16.29. It was built to enclose a huge space and house thousands of spectators in a brilliant environment. This structure, which evolved from the Greek theater (an amphitheater is two theaters put together), was the prototype for sports arenas that continue to be built. The stadium covered six acres and seated fifty thousand spectators, with standing room for thousands more. A complex design of ramps, arcades, barrel and groin vaults, halls, and passageways efficiently managed the flow of human traffic. The spectators were given numbered tickets to guide them to their arcade and then easily to their seats. Admission

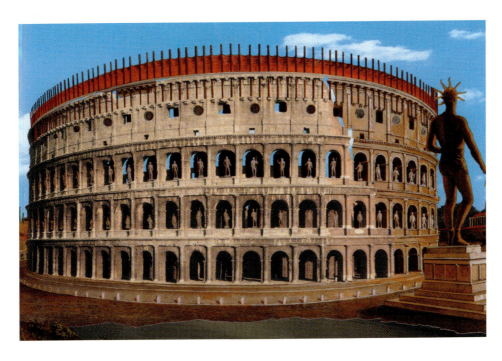

16.29 *Colosseum.* Restored interpretation, 1989. R. A. Staccioli. See also the text accompanying Figure 6.1.

was always free to all no matter what class; however, the seating was reserved by rank. The crowds were protected from the hot sun by a huge cloth canopy that was secured to 240 timber poles and was maneuvered by a special detachment of the navy. The center area originally had a wooden floor that was covered with sand for chariot races, hunting sports, and gladiatorial games, or filled with water to enact mock sea battles in which up to three thousand people participated. Later, Domitian added complex underground passages, rooms, and elevators, so that animals, scenery, and prisoners made dramatic entrances to the spectacles. The *Colosseum* was dedicated to blood sports. It is estimated that five thousand animals were put to death, not to mention the number of humans who perished in the gruesome games. Emperors continued to sponsor the games for four centuries, with the last production taking place in 523.

As outstanding as the interior was, the exterior equaled it. The 160-foot-high outer wall is encircled by four horizontal bands, with arched openings in the lower three. All arches are covered by lintels and flanked by Greek Classical columns—Doric on the first level, Ionic on the second, and Corinthian on the third. The uppermost horizontal band has no arches, but only a grid of columns and lintels. This harmonious arrangement of architectural elements not only unified the structure aesthetically, but also monumentally celebrated Greco-Roman architecture.

CONNECTION

See Chapter 3, Figure 3.5 (page 59), for a diagram of Greek columns, Figure 3.2 (page 57) for a diagram of post-and-lintel architecture, and Figure 3.8 (page 62) for arch construction.

On the North American continent, the Mayan culture developed a ball sport that was a form of ritualistic entertainment. One ball court is located in Chichén Itzá, Mexico (Figure 16.30), originating in the eleventh to thirteenth centuries. *The Great Ball Court* measures 567 feet by 228 feet, with walls 27 feet high. It is I-shaped, with two short, parallel areas at each end of a long alley. In the middle of the court, on each side, a stone ring is mounted near the top of the walls. The game was quite long and rigorous, lasting until one of the teams scored by striking the stone rings in the court's walls. To make the game even more challenging, the players could not touch the heavy ball with their hands. Much like a contemporary soccer game, the players had to use their heads and bodies to project the hard ball, which took much strength and skill. The Mayan people saw the ball game as a metaphor for the epic journey through the Underworld taken by the hero twins, the Sun and the Moon, with an underlying meaning about the conflict between good and evil and cycles of heavenly

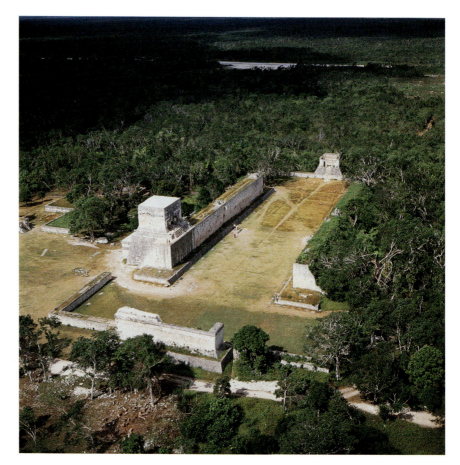

16.30 *The Great Ball Court.* Stone, 567' × 228', I-shaped. Maya-Toltec. Chichén Itzá, Mexico, eleventh–thirteenth centuries. Photograph © 1990 The Metropolitan Museum of Art, NY.

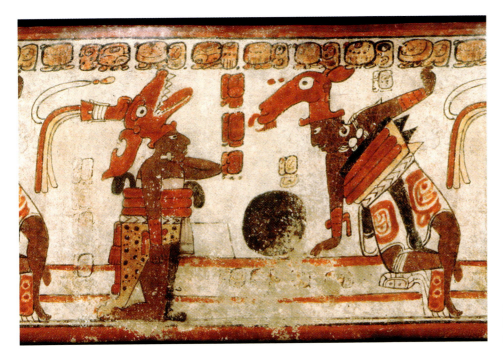

16.31 *Ball Players.* Vase painting. Maya. Mexico, eleventh–thirteenth centuries. © Justin Kerr K2022.

bodies. At the end of the game, one player (or perhaps one team) became a human sacrifice to the gods of the cosmos.

The ball court features the Temple of the Jaguar on the long east wall, and another temple at the far north end. Phenomenal decorative reliefs cover the walls in this court. One of the most astounding is of two teams of players in all their regalia facing one another. The first player on one of the teams has been decapitated, his body still kneeling in front of a large ball that is marked with a laughing skull. From the neck of the victim, serpentlike spurts of blood project profusely. Similar scenes are depicted in six other reliefs, which express the gravity of the game. The acoustics of the court are also phenomenal. A person standing on one temple at the far end of the court can hear a conversation taking place on the temple at the other end.

Ball courts existed at most major urban centers, both Mayan and those of other Mesoamerican peoples, with some variations in the designs. The game persisted for centuries and was likely played in remote areas even after the Spanish conquest. Many of the ball courts still stand.

SPORT IMAGERY

Our first image shows some of the very ballplayers who would have competed on Mayan ball courts. The vase painting *Ball Players* (Figure 16.31) shows two players, covered with elaborate dress and heavy padding. The padding is especially visible on the chest and knees. The game was played with a large, hard rubber ball, making the padding necessary for protection from blows. Patterns and insignia cover the players' clothing, and they are adorned with earrings and a large animal headdress. In usual Mayan fashion, the painting combines dark silhouette forms, strong outlines, and patterned areas, making the figure on this vase easily read. The figures, though stylized,

seem strong and large, yet bend and move with grace and suppleness. Their powerful forms and impressive regalia show that ballplayers enjoyed considerable status in Mayan society.

Also from Mexico comes the *Acrobat* (Figure 16.32), from the ancient village of Tlatilco located outside Mexico City. In

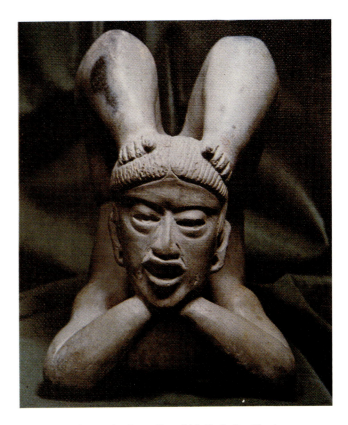

16.32 *Acrobat.* Light clay. 10" × 6¹/₂". Early Pre-Classic (1200–600 BCE). National Museum of Anthropology. Photo Constantino Reyes.

1940, archeologist and artist Miguel Covarrubias uncovered a large village with a residential complex and two hundred grave sites, all under a working brickyard. The graves were complete with burial offerings that included figurines of females, ballplayers, musicians, dancers, and acrobats. The female figures are likely fertility charms, and many were found in the graves. Bowls and long-necked jars were also among the items excavated. Clearly these artifacts indicate that these ancient peoples prepared for an afterlife full of entertainment.

The Tlatilco artists were accomplished sculptors. Looking at our *Acrobat,* from 1200–600 BCE, we see a somewhat naturalistic face framed with a stylized incised hair treatment. The smooth, contorted, and truncated body has detailed extremities, seen in the articulation of the feet and toes. The head is disproportionately large, with a concentrating, straining expression. The design and balance of the piece are seen in the bent arms and legs, which create diagonals that frame the face, and in the strong, horizontal curves at the eyes and mouth. The incised lines defining the toes parallel the lines of the hair.

From the Minoan culture on the island of Crete comes the wall painting *Bull Jumping* or *Toreador Fresco* (Figure 16.33), dating from c. 1550–1450 BCE. A dark-skinned man, doing a handstand on the back of a prancing bull, is caught in midair as he vaults over the animal. To the right of the bull is a light-skinned woman, who seems to be preparing to make her vault. Indicating gender with lighter or darker skin tones was common throughout ancient Mediterranean civilizations. On the left side is another figure holding the bull by the horns. The fresco is framed in decorative vertical and horizontal registers, one of which contains a pattern of overlapping oval shapes. The fresco is part of a group of murals that have bulls as the subject matter, located in a room in the east wing of the palace at Knossos.

This fresco may refer to an early Minoan legend dealing with the "Minotaur," a half-man and half-bull beast, who was born from the union of King Minos's wife and a sacred white bull. The Athenian hero Theseus killed the Minotaur, releasing Athenians from Minoan bondage. There were also early Greek legends telling of the sacrifice of young men and women to the Minotaur. Besides associations with the mythological creature, the bull symbolizes fertility and strength. Perhaps the dance of the bull jumpers alluded to the impact of divine forces on human lives and to how those forces are faced head-on; the contestants demonstrate their courage as they challenge the fury of the bull with every vault.

The style of Minoan art is distinctive. The overall forms are flowing, undulating, and floating, like the ocean that surrounds their islands. As we look at our fresco, we can see that the powerful bull, a beast of mass and strength, is expressed in graceful curves. He appears almost weightless as he leaps forward. The figures are also weightless, which suggests effortless movement, much like being suspended in water. The entire scene also seems effortless and fearless, like skilled acrobats performing a challenging circus act.

In our last example, we see an image of horseback riding, an activity that has been sport to some, work to others. Here it is presented as the privilege of the upper classes. In *Eight Riders*

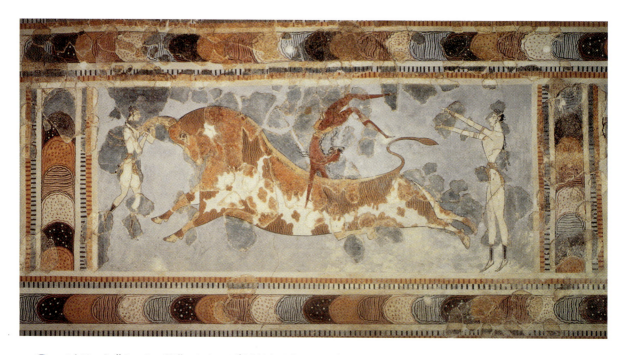

 16.33 *Bull Jumping.* Wall painting, 24¹/₂" high. Palace complex at Knossos, Crete, c. 1550–1450 BCE. © Scala / Art Resource, NY.

in Spring (Figure 16.34), artist Yan Zheo, son-in-law to the Chinese emperor, captured the pleasure of noblemen on an equestrian outing, accompanying in all likelihood their emperor, the figure in the center with the raised crop. The simple setting is divided by a balustrade, indicating the palace courtyard. The riders stand out in brightly colored garb in the foreground below.

The artist's style is a crisp and pristine rendering in a well-balanced composition, which is very much the heritage of the Tang painting tradition of the tenth century. The background, with landscaping and the courtyard enclosure in the upper half, is masterfully counterbalanced by the eight mounted figures in the lower half of the composition. The range of the intense colors worn by the figures is also counterbalanced by

the muted tones seen in the ornamental rock, the trees, and the sky and ground. All is in harmony in accordance with yin and yang philosophy, which was rooted in Chinese thought. This scroll of rich silk conveys human beings enjoying a pleasant moment with (and in a sense dominating) nature.

CONNECTION

Review the section "Class Activities and Lifestyles" in Chapter 14 for more images of upper-class leisure, such as Jean-Honoré Fragonard's The Swing *(Figure 14.25, page 420).*

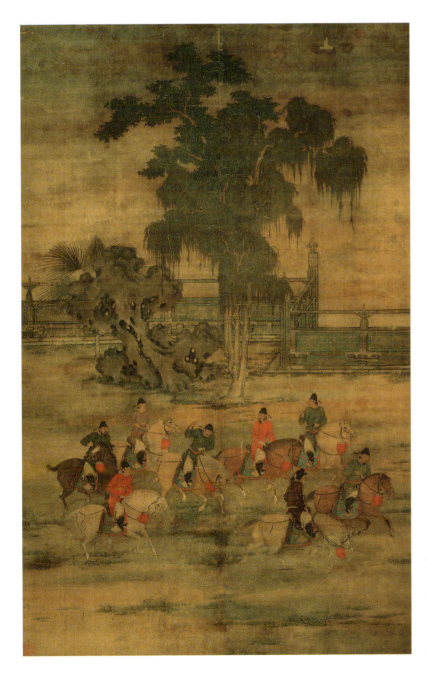

16.34   YAN ZHEO. *Eight Riders in Spring.* Hanging scroll, ink and colors on silk, 40$\frac{1}{8}$" wide. China, tenth century. National Palace Museum, Taiwan.

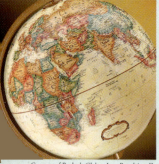

Courtesy of Replogle Globes, Inc., Broadview, IL.

At the end of World War II, the United States and the Soviet Union emerged as competing superpowers. The cold war (1950–1991) saw a massive arms buildup, pitting the United States and its Western European allies against the Soviet bloc, consisting of Russia, Eastern Europe, and central Asian states. The cold war was fought in major regional wars (the Korean War, the Vietnam War) as well as other conflicts in Latin America, Cuba, and Africa. In Latin America, dictatorships were common through the 1950s and 1960s; some were replaced later with democracies. The 1960s saw the founding of modern African states.

In addition to weapons of war, cold war competition centered around cultural superiority and superiority in technology. Abstract expressionist paintings were promoted in the United States as emphasizing individual self-expression over art made in service of the state, such as the social realism of the Soviet bloc and China. Technological competition was seen in the arms race and the race for space (moon landings, satellites. and space stations).

Communist China was the third major force in world politics, but communism itself underwent huge changes in this era. In 1975, China began a program of modernization to become a major manufacturer in goods and electronics. After 1991, the Soviet bloc disintegrated, and the

Below:
Map 10 The Global Cold War.

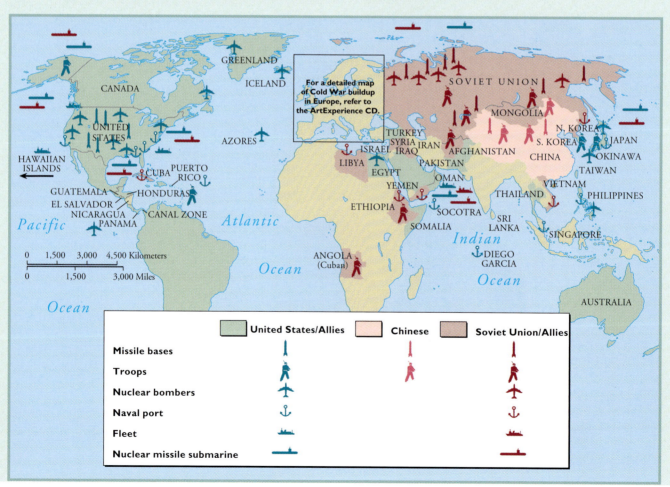

Communist system was discarded or modified. Several states in Eastern Europe, the Balkans, and central Asia became independent.

The Middle East has experienced intense unrest throughout this period. The Arab-Israeli conflict is ongoing. An Islamic revival and resistance to Western culture have resulted in the mixing of religion and civil government all over the region, for example, the fundamentalist revolution in Iran and the war in Kosovo. The independence of India (Hindu) and the creation of Pakistan (Moslem) produced

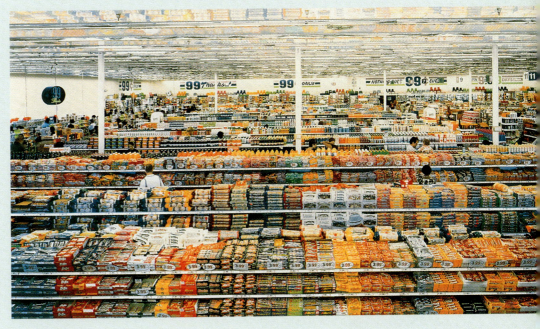
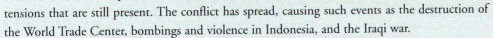

Above:
ANDREAS GURSKY. *99 Cent.* Chromogenic color print, 6'9¹/₂" × 11'. Germany, 1999. Courtesy Matthew Marks Gallery, New York, and Monika Spruth Galerie, Cologne. Copyright 2004 Andreas Gursky / VG Bild-Kunst / Artists Righs Society (ARS), NY. Cheap imports are one of the legacies of the global economy, as evident in this giant photograph.

tensions that are still present. The conflict has spread, causing such events as the destruction of the World Trade Center, bombings and violence in Indonesia, and the Iraqi war.

Our era has been described as the Post-Industrial Age, with a technologically intensive culture, global in scope. The trend toward globalism continues, with events in one part of the world often having profound effects everywhere. The technological revolution has created a need for governments to invest in education, communication systems, and transportation and has spurred the desire for open markets and international cooperation. Open trade agreements, such as the European Economic Community and the North American Free Trade Agreement (NAFTA), exist in many areas. The World Trade Organization (WTO), created in 1994, is an international organization that enforces trade treaties and laws. The global trade community has created opportunities as well as conflicts, economic hardships, and environmental problems.

Culture now can be and is exported globally. By 1980, anthropologists could find no group of people on the entire globe who did not listen to radio. Blockbuster exhibitions have brought the superstar phenomenon to art. The convergence of technologies (telephone, television, satellite communications, personal computers) means new possibilities for the future. People in industrial nations widely use digital technology for writing, information access, sound-mixing, video editing, and still image manipulation.

The global culture has brought changes to the natural world. AIDS and other new, quickspreading diseases have caused alarm. With global warming and destruction of rain forests and habitats, the earth's environment is changing.

	2500 BCE	Lyre
		Harp Player
Pipes and Chimes in Chinese tombs		
		Bull Jumping
	1400	Musicians and Dancers
	1000	Acrobat
	400	Polykleitos: Theater at Epidauros
Early museum— Alexandria		
	100	
Three orchestras/829 members. Han Dynasty		
	100 CE	Colosseum
Roman art placed in baths, temples, gardens, villas, and forums		
	200	Baths of Caracalla
Early theater in India based on Sanskrit epics		
	900	Yan Zheo: Eight Riders in Spring
First fully developed Chinese opera		
	1200	The Great Ball Court
Noh theater—Japan		Ball Players
Shakespeare, the Globe	1600	Leyster: Boy Playing a Flute
Pre-colonial Masquerades in Africa		
Bunraku and Kabuki theater—Japan		
	1700	
Beginnings of modern museums		
Opera at high point in Europe	1800	A Theatre in Edo
Peking Opera		Garnier: Opera House, Paris
Zoetrope— precursor to film		
Telegraph invented		
	1850	Olmsted and Vaux: Central Park
First art museums in West	1870	
Telephone lines installed in New England		

First film screenings	1900	Gu Mask
		Toulouse-Lautrec: Jane Avril
		Asmat Hand Drum
Hollywood— film capital	1920	
First commercial radio broadcast		
Beginning of global music culture		
		Gone with the Wind
	1940	Wright: Solomon R. Guggenheim Museum
Television broadcasting begins		
Cold war	1950	
Color television and color movies		
Korean War		
Space programs begin in U.S. and U.S.S.R.		I Love Lucy
End of European Colonies in Africa	1960	Utzon: Opera House, Sydney
		Hakone Open-Air Museum
		Feldman, Cunningham, and Rauschenberg: Summerspace
		Kaprow: Household
		Kanaga Masked Dancers
Vietnam War		
	1970	
Technological and Industrial Revolution—China	1980	
VCR and cable networks		
Operation Desert Storm	1990	Taymor: The Lion King
Digital video		Anderson: Scene from Songs and Stories from Moby Dick
Internet		Locke: Open Circle Dance
		Park: Wallace and Gromit eating breakfast
War on terrorism	2000	Barney: Cremaster 1: The Goodyear Chorus
		Gehry: Walt Disney Concert Hall

The art of entertainment covers a large range of diverse genres. One of the earliest established architectural forms in the West was the theater, with excellent acoustics and seating for thousands. This prototype would become the point of departure for the Roman amphitheater, which in turn would influence today's modern sports arena. In Japan, the type of performance dictated the theater design. Other "houses" for the arts include the art museum and the opera house. The visual arts, theater, music, recreation, and education are combined in some locations, such as Roman baths and large contemporary parks.

Artists contribute to the performing arts in several ways—for example, in mask design, theater sets, theater posters, and puppet making. Art and theater combined to create a new art medium in the 1960s called a "Happening," which later developed into Performance Art.

Artists have designed or decorated musical instruments since earliest history. Dancers have used visual imagery in their movements as part of their choreography. Also, artists have made images of musicians through the ages.

Both entertainment and art in the twentieth and twenty-first centuries have felt the impact of new technologies. The development of film dates from the late nineteenth century, but it has become an enormous cultural influence in our era. Television also affected both art and the entire world. Animation is another popular medium that relies heavily on the visual arts.

The visual arts have provided a framework for understanding the ritual or political meanings behind sports. Architects have designed sports structures, while artists have depicted athletes and athletic events.

FOOD FOR THOUGHT

As we observed the many forms of art and architecture that pertain to entertainment, we saw that some of those forms were traditional while others were unconventional and controversial. Some questions come to mind concerning the unconventional:

- Have the new technologies, such as television and the computer, changed the practice of the artist for better or worse?
- Has Western art come full circle? Has art begun to leave the museum and opera house and intermingle more with life, as it does in some non-Western cultures?
- Should art and life become more fluid, as U.S. artist Allan Kaprow believed?

Some performance art includes actual sexual intimacy and contains acts of violence. For example, in one famous performance, artist Chris Burden had himself shot as part of the artwork, while in others, artists may perform sexual acts. (See Jeff Koons' "Made in Heaven," Figure 8.17, page 207).

- How much should "life" be a part of art?

YOUR CD-ROM RESOURCES

- World History in Context
- Exploring Art Timeline
- Flashcards
- Food for Thought
- Companion Site
    Chapter 16 Quiz
    InfoTrac® College Edition Readings
    Artist Flashcards
    Online Study Guide

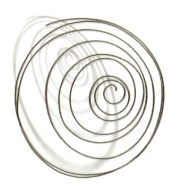

Postscript

WHERE DO YOU FIND ART AND HOW CAN YOU USE IT IN YOUR LIFE?

The overall purpose of this book has been to inquire into human creativity, and therefore our own creativity. We have seen that art is something that human beings have to do, through the ages, throughout the world. And what about you? Art is already part of your life. With a little effort, you can make it even more enriching for you. Here are some suggestions on how you may do that.

Seeing Original Artwork. One of the most thrilling ways to enjoy art is to see it in person! Nothing can describe the awesome feeling of standing in front of the *Great Pyramids* at Gizeh, or walking through the Mayan ruins at *Chichén Itzá,* or experiencing the space in the church of *St. Peter's* in Rome. If distant travel is not possible, you probably have many opportunities to see original artwork within a reasonable drive from your home. Here are some places to seek out art.

- **Museums and Galleries:** Almost all communities of any size support museums and galleries, ranging from modest to grand. Although local museums may not display the most famous "masterpieces," they contain works of real value that are rewarding to study and may surprise the first-time visitor. When you are in a city in the United States or abroad where a major museum or an archeological site is located, such as the Metropolitan in New York City or the tomb of Shi Huangdi in Shaanxi, China (Figure 10.9), make it a point to spend some time there.

- **Schools:** Student art is extraordinarily inventive, spontaneous, and expressive. Art exhibits can be found in the hallways and libraries of elementary and secondary schools, and the artwork is absolutely delightful and dazzling. On a professional or near-professional level, you can find art at most colleges and universities. Undergraduate and graduate student art is often high-quality, exciting work. Art department galleries show the work of faculty and professional artists both to enrich the art program and to expose the academic community to this art. These exhibits are often free and open to the public. Large universities sponsor major exhibitions, like the art of the Peruvian Moche at a University of California at Los Angeles gallery (Figure 10.12). A phone call to the school is all it takes to find out about the schedules of the exhibits.

- **Civic Buildings, Private Institutions, and Corporations:** Often, government buildings have been designed by accomplished architects, and the buildings are examples of fine works of architecture. In your area, post offices, courthouses, and the like may have distinctive designs as well as housing paintings, sculptures, and art treasures. Other places to look for art in your community are banks, libraries, and hospitals. Many of these institutions have their own collections to enhance their interiors. Often, libraries will have exhibition space available and will host artworks by local artists. Some hospitals collect art. For example, an impressive collection of contemporary artwork can be found in the University Hospitals of the University of Iowa in Iowa City. Many corporations have large art collections displayed in their corporate offices.

- **Public Art:** Since the 1930s, the United States has had a great tradition of art in public places. More recently, the Percent for the Arts Programs have incorporated art into all new government-funded buildings and in redevelopment areas where private investors are receiving tax abatements. You may be able to find excellent art in transportation centers, at bus stops, and along jogging paths, river walks, and historic trails.

- **Historic Homes, Mansions, and Palaces:** The homes of historic or celebrated people sometimes become museums for public viewing, such as *Monticello,* which was built by Thomas Jefferson. This house is full of art treasures and Jefferson's own amazing inventions. Also, the Palace of *Versailles* and the *Forbidden City* are now open to everyone, examples of magnificent opulence originally known to only a few. In the United States are several mansions formerly belonging to wealthy entrepreneurs who bequeathed their estates as museums. Every city and town has a chamber of commerce that can aid the visitor in finding these interesting sites.

- **Places of Worship:** Churches, temples, synagogues, and mosques are rich places to look for art. Besides their architectural designs, they likely are decorated with both old and contemporary artworks. A place of worship may have exquisite stained-glass windows, as seen in the twelfth-century *Chartres Cathedral* (Figure 9.39), fine paintings, sculptures, or elaborate tile work.

- **Parks:** Many parks are designed by landscape architects, so the gardens, walks, lakes, and so on are carefully planned. The *Boboli Gardens* in Florence, Italy, boast two museums. The well-known *Central Park* in New York City (Figure 16.8), planned in the nineteenth century, has an art museum, several theaters, a zoo, and many more features. It is also the home of several commemorative sculptures. The open-air park brings art and nature into one enjoyable and relaxing environment. Most community parks are free to the public or charge a small parking fee to help with maintenance.

- **Art Online:** Art is available in many forms on the Internet. Most museums and many galleries have Web sites where you can find information about current exhibitions and permanent collections. Commercial galleries also have Web sites focused on the sale of artwork. Artists have their own Web sites that feature their work. To find artists' Web sites, inquire at arts organizations or do a Web search on art resources or media art centers. They will likely have links to artists' pages or feature recent artists' projects.

Art in Everyday Life. The art in our everyday lives is art in the broadest sense of the word, consisting of aesthetic objects that surround us. You may be aware of some of this, but much is taken for granted. Your home is both aesthetic and functional and is on a continuum with the nineteenth-century Sioux *Tipis* (Figure 7.33) and Frank Lloyd Wright's *Fallingwater* (Figure 7.34). Your utensils, dishes, and furniture have aesthetic and design qualities, whether they were mass produced or made by an artist/craftsperson. Notice the quality of light in your room, or the ceramic bowl that holds your serving of soup. Make choices about the space you live in, and the shapes and colors with which you surround yourself. To enjoy art more, you have to take notice. Make a conscious effort to see it and observe it in your life and in your environment. You might be surprised at how often art is right in front of you!

Develop your own artistic expression. All human beings have the potential to be creative. One of the best ways to enjoy art is to make art, even if you are not an art student or if you question your skills. Studio classes are available for the taking and can be found at local art museums, schools, and community centers. If you would rather study art than make it, look for art history courses available at colleges and museums. If you would rather not take a formal course in studio work or art history, then try it on your own. Many fine artists and learned persons in the world are self-trained. Whatever you choose, have a great time!

Living with Art in Your Home. Start or continue your own collection of work you enjoy and like to look at. There are several resources from which to draw your collection, and the first is right in your home. Frame some work of your own or that of a family member. Children are prolific artists and will have several selections from which to choose. You can purchase art at a reasonable price from student exhibitions and art sales at art schools and departments. Students are usually enormously encouraged and gratified when their work is purchased.

Seek out artists in your area and make an appointment to see their work in their studios. Some artists are open to barter or to swapping services in place of a cash transaction.

Many museums have museum stores where reproductions of major works are sold at affordable prices. Sculpture replicas are also available. If you prefer original art, some museums have sales and rental galleries. Of course, galleries are another outlet where you can purchase original art.

Arts and Crafts Fairs are fun and great for purchasing artwork directly from the artists. The artists set up displays of their work and sell it directly to the public. They are usually happy to talk about their work. Many of the artists are working on the site, which makes these fairs all the more interesting and enjoyable.

Congratulations! You have finished this book. The authors wish you well as you personally continue your journey into the art world, which is inherently *your* world.

Pronunciation Guide for Proper Names of Persons and Places

(Note: For art terms, their pronunciations, and their definitions, see the Glossary)

A

Abakanowicz, Magdalena	ah-bah-kah-NOH-vich, mag-dah-LAY-nah
Abbot Suger	AB-ot SOO-zhayr
Achaemenid	ah-KEE-meh-nid
Akua'ba	ah-KOO-ah-bah
Allah	AL-luh
Ara Pacis Augustae	AY-rah PAH-chees oh-GUS-tie
Ariadne	ar-ee-AD-nee
Ashanti	eh-SHAN-tee
Ashurbanipal	AH-shure-BAH-nee-PAHL
Asoka	ah-SHOH-kuh or ah-SOH-kuh
Assyria	ah-SEER-ee-ah
Athens	ATH-enz

B

Babur	BAH-ber
Babylonia	bab-eh-LOH-nee-eh
Baule	bau-LAY
Benin	be-NEEN
Bernini, Gianlorenzo	bair-NEE-nee, jahn-loh-REN-zoh
Bisj Poles	bizh
Boccioni, Umberto	boh-CHOH-nee, oom-BAIR-toh
Bourgeois, Louise	boorzh-WAH, lweez
Brahma	BRAH-mah
Brancusi, Constantin	brahn-KOO-see, KOHN-stahn-teen
Bruegel, Jan	BROY-gul, YAHN
Bruegel, Pieter, the Elder	BROY-gul, PEE-ter
Buonarroti, Michelangelo	bwoh-nar-ROH-tee, mee-kay-LAN-jay-loh
Byzantium	bih-ZAN-tee-um

C

Caracalla	kar-eh-KAL-eh
Çatal Hüyük	chah-TAHL huh-YOOK
Chagall, Marc	shah-GAL, mark
Chartres	SHAR-tr'
Chichén Itzá	chee-CHEN eet-ZAH
Cicciolina	chee-choh-LEE-nah
Colleoni	co-lay-OH-nee
Colosseum	kah-leh-SEE-um
Constantinople	kon-stan-te-NOH-pel
Cuvilliès, François de	kyu-vee-YAY, fran-ZWAH duh
Cuzco	KOOS-koh
Cycladic	sik-LAD-ik

D

Dali, Salvador	dah-LEE or DAH-lee, sal-vah-DOHR
Daoism	DAU-izm
Darius	duh-RYE-us

D (continued)

Daumier, Honoré	DOH-mee-ay, on-ohr-AY
David, Jacques-Louis	dah-VEED, ZHAK loo-EE
Degas, Edgar	deh-GAH, ed-GAR
Delacroix, Eugène	del-uh-K(R)WA, oo-ZHEN
Dionysos	die-uh-NEE-sus
Dogon	DOH-gahn
Doryphoros	doh-RIFF-oh-rus
Dürer, Albrecht	DOO-ruhr, AL-brekt

E

Eisenstein, Sergei	EYE-zen-stine, sair-gay
Etruscan	eh-TRUSS-can
Euphrates River	yoo-FRAY-teez
Eyck, Jan van	IKE, yahn vahn

F

Fragonard, Jean-Honoré	frag-uh-NAR, zhan on-ohr-AY

G

Gabon	gah-BOHN
Garnier, Charles	gar-NYAY, sharl
Ghiberti, Lorenzo	ghee-BAYR-tee, loh-REN-zoh
Gislebertus	gheez-lay-BERT-oos
Gizeh	GHEE-zah
Gogh, Vincent van	go, vin-SENT van
Golub, Leon	GOL-ub, LEE-on
Goya, Francisco	GOY-yah, fran-SIS-koh
Grande Jatte	Grahn ZHOT
Grosz, George	GROHS, jorj
Grünewald, Matthias	GRU-nuh-valt, mah-TEE-as
Guanyin	gwahn-YEEN
Guernica	GWAR-nih-kah
Guggenheim	GOO-ghen-hime

H

Hakone	hah-koh-neh
Hammurabi	ham-uh-RAH-bee
Hanuman	hahn-oo-MAHN
Harappan	har-RAP-an
Hardouin-Mansart, Jules	ar-DWAN-man-sar, zhool
Hatshepsut	hat-SHEP-soot
Hesperides	hes-PER-i-deez
Hogarth, William	hoh-GARTH

I

Ikere	i-KEE-ree
Iktinos	EEK-tee-nos
Imhotep	im-HOH-tep
Inca	ING-kah
Ise	EE-say

K

Kabuki	kah-BOO-kee

Kachina	kah-CHEE-nah
Kahlo, Frida	KAH-lo, FREE-dah
Kandarya Mahadeva	gan-darh-ree-ah mah-hah-DAY-vuh
Kaprow, Allan	KAP-ro, al-un
Katsushika Hokusai	kat-s'-SHEE-kah HOH-k'-sye
Khufu	koo-foo
Kitagawa Utamaro	kee-tah-gah-wah oo-tah-mah-roh
Kollwitz, Käthe	KOHL-vits, KET-uh
Krishna	KRISH-nah
Kristallnacht	KRIS-tal-NAHCHT
Kusama, Yayoi	koo-SA-ma, yay-yoy-ee
Kwakiutl	kwah-kee-OOT-'l

L

Lange, Dorothea	lang, dor-uh-THEE-ah
Laocoön	lay-AH-koh-on
Lascaux	las-KOH
Le Brun, Charles	leh-BRUN, sharl
Le Corbusier	leh kor-byoo-see-AY
Le Nôtre, André	leh NOHTr', an DRAY
Le Vau, Louis	leh VOH, lwee
Léger, Fernand	lay-ZHAYR, fer-NAN
Leonardo da Vinci	lay-o-NAR-doh da VEEN-chee
Leyster, Judith	LIE-stur, YOO-dit
Lin, Maya Ying	lin, MY-ah yeeng
Lorenzetti, Ambrogio	loh-rent-SAYT-tee, am-BROH-joh

M

Ma Yuan	ma yoo-an
Mali	MAH-lee
Mamluk	MAM-look
Maori	MAH-oh-ree
Mao Zedong	mau zee-DONG
Marisol	mah-ree-SOL
Masaccio	muh-SAT-choh
Masjid-i-Shah	MUS-jid-i-shah
Maya	MAH-yah
Menkaure	men-KOW-ray
Mesopotamia	mess-oh-poh-TAME-ee-uh
Michelangelo	mee-kay-LAN-jay-loh
Millais, John Everett	mil-AY, jan EV-ruht
Minoan	mi-NO-en
Moche	MOH-chay
Moctezuma	MOCK-teh-SOO-mah
Mori, Mariko	moh-ree, mah-ree-koh
Mu Qi	moo kee *or* moo chee
Mughal	MUH-ghel
Munch, Edvard	mungk, ED-vard
Muybridge, Eadweard	MY-brij, ED-wurd

N

Nam June Paik	nahm joon pahk
Notre Dame du Haut	NOHTr' dahm doo OH

O

Odalisque	OHD-'l-isk
Olmec	AHL-meck
Orozco, José Clemente	oh-ROHS-coh, ho-SAY cleh-MEN-tay

P

Palenque	pah-LENG-kay
Palladio, Andrea	pul-LAY-dee-oh, an-DRAY-uh
Papua New Guinea	PAHP-uh-wah noo GHIN-ee
Père Lachaise	PAYR la-SHAYZ
Pericles	PER-i-kleez
Persepolis	per-SEP-uh-lis
Phoenician	fi-NISH-un
Polykleitos	pal-ee-KLIY-tos
Pompeii	pom-PAY
Poseidon	po-SYE-den
Potawatomi	PAHD-eh-WAHD-eh-mee
Protagoras	proh-TAG-eh-res

Q

Qin	chin
Quetzalcoatl	ket-SAHL-kwaht-'l
Quran	koo-RAN

R

Radha	RAD-uh
Ramayana	rah-MAH-yuh-nuh
Raphael	rah-fay-el
Rembrandt van Rijn	REM-brant van RIYN
Renoir, Pierre Auguste	ren-WAR, pee-AYR oh-GOOST
Riefenstahl, Leni	REE-fen-stahl, len-EE
Rivera, Diego	ree-VAY-ra, dee-AY-go
Ryoanji	ryoh-an-jee

S

Saarinen, Eero	SAR-uh-nen, EER-oh
Sacsahuaman	sack-say-hwua-MAHN
Safavids	suh-FAH-weedz
Safdie, Moshe	SAHF-dee, MOSH-eh
Sanchi	SAHN-chee
Sanzio, Raphael	SAHN-zee-oh, rah-fay-el
Seurat, Georges	sue-RAH, zhorzh
Shi Huangdi	SHI(r) HWANG-dee
Shiva Nataraja	SHIH-vah nah-tah-RAH-jah
Siddhartha Gautama	sid-AR-tha ghu-TAW-mah
Sioux	SOO
Siqueiros, David	see-KAYR-ohs
St. Lazare	SAHN lah-ZAR

T

Tenochtitlán	tah-NOHCH-tee-TLAHN
Teotihuacán	tay-oh-tee-hwah-KAHN
Tinguely, Jean	tan-GLEE, zhon
Tlaloc	TLAH-lohk
Tlingit	TLING-git
Toulouse-Lautrec, Henri de	too-LOOZ low-TREK, on-REE deh
Toussaint L'Ouverture, François	too-SAN loo-vur-TOOR, fran-ZWAH
Trajan	TRAY-jan
Tutankhamen	too-tahn-KAHM-un

U

Ukeles, Mierle Laderman   oo-KEL-leez, murl LAD-er-man
Utzon, Joern   UT-zone, YOHR-'n

V

van Rijn, Rembrandt   van RIYN, REM-brant
Velasquez, Diego   vay-LAS-kas, DYAY-go
Veracruz   ver-eh-KROOZ
Vermeer, Jan   ver-ME(U)R, yan
Verrocchio, Andrea del   vur-ROHK-kyoh, an-DRAY-uh del
Versailles   vair-SYE
Vesalius, Andreas   vih-SAY-lee-us, AN-dree-as

W

Warhol, Andy   WOR-hal, AN-dee
Wilke, Hannah   WILL-key, Han-nah
Willendorf   VILL-en-dorf

X

Xilonen   shi-LOH-nen

Y

Yahweh   YAH-wah
Yakshi   YAK-shee
Yoruba   YOH-roo-bah

Z

Zapotec   zah-peh-TEK
Zeus   zoos
Zhou   joe
Zimbabwe   zim-BAH-bway
Zoroaster   ZOR-oh-as-ter

Glossary

A

Abstract Art   An art style developed in Western cultures in the early twentieth century. Its imagery ranged from somewhat abstract to nonobjective forms. Its roots are accredited to Cubism.

abstracted texture   The treatment that artists give to the element of texture in their work that is a distortion, a simplification, or an exaggeration of an actual texture.

Abstraction   Visual imagery in art that does not copy reality. This might be achieved by simplifying, distorting, or exaggerating objects from nature, and it might resemble completely nonobjective forms.

academy   A teaching institution developed in various cultures to set strict standards and guidelines for artists. Some academies began in France and Japan in the seventeenth and eighteenth centuries.

accent   Special attention given to any element of a composition in order to attract the viewer's eye to it. This may be done by giving an element a brighter color, isolating it, or enlarging it in order to emphasize it. Any visual device may be used in an accent.

achromatic (ak-ruh-MAT-ik)   Without color, consisting only of grays, black, and white.

acropolis (ah-KRAH-pul-us)   The highest ground in an ancient Greek city; originally fortified and, later, the site of temples.

acrylic   A water-soluble, permanent synthetic paint that was developed in the 1960s.

actual shape   Clearly defined positive areas, not ambiguous.

actual space   Areas that exist in reality.

actual texture   Surface qualities that exist in reality and can be felt.

additive color system   Color that is created by mixing light rays. When the three primary colors (red, blue, and green) are mixed, a white light is produced. Cyan, yellow, and magenta are the secondary colors in this system.

adobe (ah-DOH-bee)   Sun-dried brick made of straw and clay.

aerial perspective   The blurring of forms, colors, and values as they recede into the background. This is sometimes referred to as *atmospheric perspective,* as receding forms in space take on the colors and tones of the natural atmosphere.

Aesthetics (es-THET-iks)   A branch of Western philosophies that is concerned with the meaning of beauty. The notion of what is beautiful is a cultural value and, therefore, has an enormous range of meaning.

afterimage   A phenomenon that occurs after staring at an area of color for a while, then glancing at a white ground. The eye will see the complementary color.

agora (AG-uh-ruh)   An open square surrounded by colonnades and porticos where markets and places of business were located in an ancient Greek or Roman city.

alla prima (ah-la PREE-mah)   A technique in painting in which pigment is laid directly on the surface without any underpainting.

ambient light   The light all around us in the world.

amphitheater (am[p]-feh-THEE-et-er)   An oval or circular arena surrounded by tiers of seats.

amulet (AM-yoo-let)   A charm worn to protect one from evil.

analogous colors   Colors that are close to each other on the color wheel.

Ancestor Dreaming   A system of spiritual beliefs for the Aboriginal people in Australia that accounts for creation and the cosmos.

animation   A series of drawings that vary slightly from one to the next, so that the figures within the drawings appear to move.

animism   The belief that all things in nature contain a spiritual force or soul.

anthropomorphic (an-threh-poh-MOHR-fick)   Giving human characteristics and attributes to a nonhuman being.

apotheosis (ah-poth-ee-OH-sus)   The raising of human beings to a divine level, or to be deified.

appliqué (ap-leh-KAY)   Designs made of cutout material joined (usually by sewing) to another piece of material.

apse (aps)   Vaulted, semicircular area at the end of a building; usually seen in churches, mosques, and Roman basilicas.

arabesque (ar-ah-BESK)   Intricate interlocking surface decorations usually of spiral forms, knots, and flora. There is no suggestion of human forms in the designs.

arcade   A line of arches placed side by side on piers or columns that may be freestanding or attached to a wall.

arch   A curved structure made of stone or brick that supports weight over an opening, such as a door or window.

architectural systems   Organized methods and principles that result in functional and durable buildings. These systems must endure the forces of gravity and weather as well as forces within the building itself.

architecture   The science and art of designing buildings and other structures that are both aesthetic and functional.

armature   The underlying framework on which clay, wax, or plaster is placed; used in making sculpture.

Art Nouveau (ar noo-VOH) A Western art movement in the early twentieth century that included art forms that were based on natural forms and could be mass-produced in the age of technology and industrialism.

artifact An object made by one or more human beings and usually categorized by time and culture.

ashlars Precisely cut, regularly shaped, and fitted stone used in masonry constructed without mortar.

assemblage (ah-sem-BLAHZH) Sculptures made from various found objects or prefabricated parts that are put together.

asymmetry Balance that is achieved in a composition by the careful placement of dissimilar objects of equal visual weight and attention.

atlantid (at-LAN-tid) *See* **caryatid.**

atlatl (AHT-[uh]-lat-[uh]l) A stick thrower, or a device that aids the throwing of a stick or spear.

atmospheric perspective *See* **aerial perspective.**

atrium (AY-tree-um) The entrance room with an open skylight in a Roman house. Also, the attached, open-colonnaded court at the entrance of a Christian basilica.

attic The uppermost story in a structure.

automatism (aw-TAHM-eh-tism) The expression of the unconscious mind, released from conscious control, usually in painting or drawing.

avant-garde (av-an[t]-GAR) Late-nineteenth- and twentieth-century Western artists who developed new concepts in their work.

avatar (av-uh-TAR) In Hinduism, the manifestation of a deity, or an aspect of a deity.

B

ba Part of the human soul, in ancient Egyptian beliefs, that resides in the heart or abdomen in life. *See also* **ka.**

balance Visual equilibrium in a composition; achieved by organizing the weight and attention of all elements in an artwork. Types of balance are *symmetrical, asymmetrical, radial,* and *crystallographic.*

baldacchino (bal-dah-KEE-no) A canopy placed over a throne or an altar, sometimes resting on columns.

balustrade (BAL-us-trade) A railing supported by short pillars.

bargeboards Boards that conceal roof timbers projecting over gables; often decorated.

Baroque style (bah-ROHK) Sculpture and art in seventeenth- and eighteenth-century Western cultures (specifically in Europe) characterized by exaggeration, overstatement, and a flair for artifice and the theatrical.

barque (bark) A small sailing ship.

barrel vault *See* **vaulting.**

bas relief (bah reh-LEEF) *See* **relief.**

base The lowest part of an Ionic or a Doric column.

basilica (beh-SIL-i-keh) A Roman colonnaded hall consisting of a nave and two side aisles, sometimes with an apse attached to the short ends; usually a place of business or government. The Christians adapted this plan for their worship space.

bay A division of interior space that is usually defined by architectural supports, such as columns or buttresses.

belfry A tower that houses a bell.

bestiary (BES-tee-air-ee) A type of medieval natural history book with actual and mythical animals, along with descriptions and moral and religious interpretations.

binder A liquid, glue, or wax that holds pigment particles together and dries to create a paint layer.

bitumen A natural, tar-like substance.

black figure style Greek pottery that has been decorated with dark figures placed on a lighter background of red clay.

bodhisattva (boh-dih-SAHT-vah) In Buddhist beliefs, those humans who have attained the level of Buddhahood but choose to postpone their achieving nirvana to remain on earth to help others.

bronze An alloy of copper and tin.

Buddhism An Asian religion with the belief that the rejection of personal desires will lead to nirvana.

bust A sculpture of a human being that includes only the head and shoulders.

buttressing A mass of brick or stone that supports a wall or an arch; a *flying buttress* is a buttress placed some distance from the structure it is supporting, and it is connected to the main structure with an arch.

C

calligraphy (keh-LIG-reh-fee) Handwriting that is considered exceptionally beautiful.

canon (KAN-on) A rule of proportion that meets the requirements of a specific cultural aesthetic.

cantilever (kant-el-EE-ver) A structure in architecture that extends or protrudes horizontally beyond its support.

capital Uppermost element on a column, serving as a transition from the shaft to the structures above.

cartouche (kar-TOOSH) An oblong oval or scroll shape that usually contains glyphs or a heraldic device.

caryatid (kar-ee-AYT-id) A supporting element, like a column, that is carved to represent a female figure. A male supporting figure is called an *atlantid.*

caste system In Hindu societies, the social system in which rank is determined by the family into which one is born.

catacombs (KAT-eh-kohmz) Subterranean chambers used for the burial of the dead.

cathedral (keh-THEE-drel) A church that is the official seat of a bishop.

cenotaph (SEN-uh-taff)   A coffinlike monument commemorating a person who has died, but is buried at a different location.

centaur (SEN-tar)   A half-man, half-horse creature, from fables.

ceramic   Pottery and objects made of clay.

chatra (CHAH-trah)   An umbrella-like disk on a pole surmounting a dome in Buddhist or Hindu architecture.

Chi-Rho (ki roh)   The initials of Christ's name in Greek.

chiaroscuro (kee-ar-eh-SK[Y]OOR-oh)   In a drawing, the use of various tones (black, white and grays) to create the illusion of volume.

chroma (KRO-ma)   Brightness or dullness of a hue, or intensity.

cili   An ancient symbol of wealth, fertility, and luck. It appears in the shape of a woman's head with a large, fanlike headdress radiating from it.

cire perdue (seer per-DOO)   *See* **lost wax.**

city-state   An autonomous political entity, consisting of a city and its surrounding territory.

Classical   The art of ancient Greece during the fifth century BCE, based on ideal proportion grounded in the human figure. The term also refers to a style that is clear and rational. Western art aesthetics are heavily influenced by Classical Greek art, seen in Roman, Romanesque, Renaissance, and Neoclassical styles.

Classical Baroque   The Baroque style that also contains classical characteristics, especially in architecture. *See* **Baroque style.**

claymation   A method of animation using clay figures in place of drawings.

clerestory (KLEER-stor-ee)   An area of wall that contains windows and that rises above roof areas that surround it.

cloisonné (kloiz-eh-NAY)   A method of fusing enamel in metal compartments with the application of heat.

coffer   A recessed panel in a ceiling, vault, or dome.

collaboration   Arrangement in which two or more artists work together on one artwork.

collage (kuh-LAZH)   A two-dimensional composition in which paper, cloth, or other materials are glued to a surface.

colonnade (kol-uh-NADE)   A row of columns that supports an entablature or arches.

color wheel   A circular arrangement of the hues of the spectrum.

column   A cylinder consisting of a base, shaft, and capital (top element) that usually supports a roof. However, freestanding columns sometimes function as monuments. *See* **Orders.**

complementary colors   Hues that are located directly opposite each other on the color wheel.

composition   The unified organization of the elements of an artwork in such a way that harmony and balance are achieved.

concentric   Spheres or circles having the same center.

conceptual   Artwork whose primary purpose is to convey an idea or a concept in any medium. Printed text is often included.

contained style   In a sculpture, all the forms are kept within the overall outer shape.

conté (KON-tee)   A hard wax crayon used for drawing. Traditional conté comes in browns, black, and white; more recently, it has been available in an array of colors.

contour line   The outline of a shape.

contrapposto (kon-trah-POS-toh)   A standing position in which the body weight rests on one leg, with the other leg posed forward, giving the human form an s-shaped curve.

cool colors   Generally, blues, greens, and purples.

corbel (KOR-bul)   Stones or bricks stacked so that each new layer projects beyond the layer below it; corbels can be arranged to create a corbeled arch or corbeled vault.

Corinthian (kuh-RIN-thee-en)   *See* **Orders.**

cornice (KOR-niss)   A projecting horizontal member that crowns a structure.

cosmos   A systematic, orderly, harmonious universe.

C-print   A non-archival color print made from a negative.

crayon   A small stick used as drawing material, with pigment held together by a wax binder.

cross-hatching   *See* **hatching.**

cross vault   *See* **vaulting.**

crystallographic balance (kris-teh-leh-GRAF-ik)   Visual equilibrium in which equal emphasis is given to all the elements in a two-dimensional composition so that there is the same visual weight wherever the viewer looks.

cubiculum (koo-BIK-yoo-lum); *pl.* **cubicula**   A small room that opens onto the atrium of a Roman house; or, a small room in a catacomb that serves as a mortuary chapel.

Cubism   An art movement that represents multiple viewpoints or facets on a two-dimensional picture plane. Analytical Cubism broke down forms, while Synthetic Cubism used collage and assemblage to represent parts of objects in order to visually play with illusions and reality.

cuneiform (kyoo-NAY-uh-form)   A system of writing with wedge-shaped characters, used in the ancient Near East.

curvilinear   Consisting of visual elements that are made up of or allude to curved lines.

D

daguerreotype (deh-GARE-[e]-o-type)   A photographic process invented in the nineteenth century for fixing an image on a silver-coated metal plate.

damascene (dam-eh-SEEN)   Ornamentation created on a metal surface, such as iron or steel, using wavy patterns or inlaid work of precious metals.

damask (DAM-esk)   An elaborately patterned fabric woven on a Jacquard loom.

dealer A person whose business is to buy artwork directly from the artist and then sell it, or take artwork on consignment.

deconstruction A method for analyzing works of art developed in the late twentieth century, in which artworks are treated as texts that can have a variety of meanings, based on the person who perceives them, emphasizing subjectivity.

Deconstructivist Architecture A contemporary architectural style in which building parts are disassembled and reassembled in an almost sculptural fashion, without regard to the function of the building.

decorative (space) Pictorial space in a two-dimensional work that remains true to the picture plane and shows very little depth.

dharma (DAR-muh) In Hinduism, the laws and duties intended to guide the behavior of people of various castes.

digital art Art that is made with the assistance of electronic devices, or intended to be displayed on a computer.

diptych (DIP-tik) A two-paneled painting, often hinged.

distortion The changing of an accepted perception of a form or object so that it may be barely or not at all recognizable.

dome A hemisphere used to cover an open interior space, made of an arch rotated 360 degrees on a vertical axis.

Doric *See* **Orders.**

drum A cylindrical stone that is stacked with others to create the shaft of a column.

drypoint An etching, which is a kind of printmaking, in which the design is scratched into the surface of a metal plate.

dymaxion A term invented by R. Buckminster Fuller by combining the words *dynamic, maximum,* and *tension,* to describe his view of architecture that is economical and does more with less.

dynasty A powerful group or family that rules a territory or nation for an extended period.

E

earthenware Ceramic ware made of slightly porous clay fired at a low temperature.

eave The edge of the roof that overhangs the wall.

eclectic Consisting of many varied elements.

effigy mound Ceremonial earthen mound, shaped like an animal, built by Native North American peoples.

egg tempera Paint created by grinding dry pigment into egg yolk, which is the binder.

elements (formal) That which makes up an artwork. The elements are line, value and light, color, shape, space, texture, volume and mass, time, and motion.

emphasis A device in art that draws the attention of the viewer to one or more focal points in an artwork.

enamel A glossy, often colorful surface, fused onto the surface of metal, glass, or pottery.

encaustic (en-KAH-stik) A paint medium in which dry pigments are mixed into heated beeswax.

engaged column A column partly embedded in a wall.

English Perpendicular Style *See* **Perpendicurlar Style.**

engraving The process of incising or scratching lines on a hard material, such as wood or a metal plate.

entablature (in-TAB-leh-chur) In classical Greek architecture, the part of the building that is above the capital of the supporting columns. It consists of three parts: the architrave, the frieze, and the pediment.

entasis (EN-teh-sis) An apparent swelling or bulging in the shaft of a Doric column.

Environmental art A form of art that surrounds and affects the viewer; it may be in an interior space or out in nature.

ephemeral arts Artworks that are fleeting or transitory and are not permanent. Examples include the masquerade from Africa, and twentieth-century Performance Art or a Happening.

Epicureanism (ep-i-kyoo-REE-en-izm) An ancient Greek philosophy that advocated intelligent pleasure-seeking in life, because death was the end to existence.

equestrian An artwork that depicts a figure mounted on a horse.

etching The creation of lines or areas on glass or a metal plate, using acid that eats into the exposed surface but leaves coated, protected areas unchanged. When etched plates are inked, they can be used in printmaking.

Eucharist (YOO-keh-rist) The Sacrament of Holy Communion in the Christian faith. The ritual involves the consecration of bread and wine into the sacrificial body and blood of Jesus Christ.

Expressionism A Western art movement of the mid-twentieth-century that focused on capturing the subjective feeling toward objective reality. The movement developed a bold, colorful, and vigorous style, especially in painting.

F

façade (feh-SAHD) The front facing of a building.

faience (fay-ANS) Earthenware or pottery decorated with highly colored designs.

Fauvism (FOH-vizm) An early-twentieth-century art movement in Europe led by Henri Matisse that focused on bright colors and patterns. The term comes from the French word *fauve,* meaning "wild beast."

fengshui (FUNG-shway) The science and art of arranging architecture and furnishings to allow for a good flow of energy. The term comes from the Chinese words for *wind* and *water.*

fetish An object that is empowered with magic that can heal and protect; also known as a *power figure.*

feudalism (FYOOD-el-izm)   An economic and political system in rural societies in which the land is owned and controlled by a few warrior-rulers, and the rest of the people work the land as peasants.

filigree (FIL-eh-gree)   Delicate ornamental work.

finial (FIN-ee-el)   A crowning ornament or knob.

flute, fluting   Narrow vertical channels carved from top to bottom into the shafts of columns.

Fluxus   A late-twentieth-century art movement that sought to create a kind of anti-art or non-art; art was conceived as an artist-initiated experience rather than an object.

flying buttress   *See* **buttressing.**

focal point   Main area of visual concentration in an artwork.

folk art   Traditional styles of art produced by common people.

form   The total appearance and organization of the physical and formal qualities of an artwork.

formal qualities   All that makes up the physical artwork, such as the formal elements (line, value and light, color, shape, space, texture, volume and mass, time, and motion), the medium, proportion, size, and subject matter.

formalism   A method for analyzing artworks based solely on their formal qualities.

forum   A central, open space surrounded by public buildings in ancient Roman cities.

found objects   Actual everyday objects, such as shoes, tools, and so on, that are incorporated into artworks.

freestanding sculpture   Sculpture in the round, intended to be seen from many viewpoints.

French Gothic   *See* **Gothic.**

French Impressionism   An art movement in early-twentieth-century France in which artists sought to capture the changing effects of light and color as the eye perceives them.

fresco   A painting made on plaster; in *true fresco,* or *buon fresco,* water-based pigments are painted directly on a wet lime plaster ground and bind with the plaster when dry; in *dry fresco,* or *fresco secco,* the paint is applied to dry plaster.

frieze (freez)   A decorative band in the central section of the entablature in classical Greek architecture, or a decorative band on a building.

frontal   Sculpture whose focal point or emphasis is placed on the front side of the piece.

futurists   *See* **Italian Futurists.**

G

gable   *See* **pediment.**

gallery   In Christian church architecture, an upper story over an aisle opening onto a nave. In secular architecture, a large room in which items of art are displayed.

gargoyle (GAR-goil)   A carving of a grotesque human figure or animal that is incorporated into a roof to function as a waterspout.

genre painting (ZHAH[n]-reh)   Paintings that contain subject matter of everyday life.

genres (ZHAH[n]-reh)   Various categories of paintings, as well as arts in general.

geodesic dome (jee-oh-DEES-ik)   A dome shape made of framework consisting of interlocking polygonal units, developed by R. Buckminster Fuller.

geometrical   Objects, lines, or shapes based on mathematical concepts, such as the circle, square, or rectangle.

gesture   A quickly sketched image that captures the essence of the form of the subject.

gild, gilding (gild)   Coating or layering a surface with gold, gold leaf (a very thin layer of gold), or a gold color.

glaze   In painting, a thin layer of glossy, transparent color applied on top of previously painted, dry areas of the painting; in ceramics, a hard, waterproof, often glossy coating fired onto the clay surface of pottery or sculpture.

glyph (glif)   A figure or character that has symbolic meaning and is most often carved in relief.

Gothic   The history, culture, and art of western Europe from the twelfth through the fourteenth centuries. Local variations include French Gothic and the English Perpendicular Style.

gouache (gwash)   Painting with opaque watercolors.

graffito; pl. **graffiti**   Writing or drawing written or painted on public walls.

Greek Revival   A style of architecture that visually echoes Greek Classical architecture. This style was popular in nineteenth-century Europe and United States.

grillwork   Metalwork, usually of iron, that adorns windows and doors while also protecting the building against intruders.

groin vault   *See* **vaulting.**

guilds (gilds)   Organizations of merchants, artisans, and craftsmen that developed in medieval Europe.

H

handscroll   An Asian horizontal painted scroll that is unrolled from the right to the left to view individual scenes and read text.

Happening   An art event that is planned by the artist and that may be performed spontaneously and solicit participation of its audience. This art form was invented by Allan Kaprow.

harmony   The quality of relating the visual elements of a composition through the repetition of similar characteristics. A pleasing visual interaction occurs through harmony.

hatching   The placing of lines side by side to create values and tones. Layers of hatched lines, rotated and overlapped, create cross-hatching.

Hellenistic   The culture that flourished around Greece, Macedonia, and some areas bordering the Mediterranean Sea from around 323 to 31 BCE.

hieratic (hi-uh-RAT-ik) A system of proportion of figures or subject matter in a work of art that gives emphasis to what or who is considered to be the most important; for example, the largest figure would be the most important or highest in rank.

hieroglyphic (hi-ro-GLIF-ik) Ancient picture writing, especially that used by the Egyptian culture.

hilt The handle of a sword, dagger, knife, or tool.

Hinduism A major religion developed in India whose basic beliefs encompass the cycle of reincarnation and the striving to achieve nirvana.

hip roof A roof with sloping ends and sides.

horizon line In linear perspective, a horizontal line that represents eye level.

hue The pure state of color that the eye sees in the spectrum.

Humanism A system of thought in which the efforts, values, and achievements of human beings are the focus.

hydria (HI-dree-ah) A Greek ceramic water jar, usually with two handles.

hypostyle hall (HI-puh-style) A large hall in which rows of columns support the roof.

I

ibex (EYE-beks) A wild goat with long, back-curving horns found in Eurasia and North Africa. This animal is found in prehistoric iconography.

icon A visual image, pictorial representation, or symbol that may have religious or political connotations.

iconoclasm (eye-KON-uh-klazm) The act of destroying religious images or opposing their veneration.

iconography (eye-keh-NOG-reh-fee) The study of visual images and symbols within their cultural and historical contexts.

idealism An artistic interpretation of the world as it should be according to respective cultural aesthetics. Generally, all flaws and imperfections found in nature are removed.

illumination A hand-painted manuscript that has been decorated with drawings or paintings.

imago mundi (im-AG-o MUN-dee) Image of the world.

imam (eye-MAM) A leader of collective worship in Islam.

impasto (im-PAHS-toe) Paint that has been thickly applied to the ground or surface of a painting.

implied line A drawn line having missing segments that are visually completed by the viewer.

impluvium (im-PLOO-vee-um) A small pool that collects rainwater; located in the atrium of a Roman house.

Impressionism A late-nineteenth-century painting style, originating in Western Europe, that attempts to capture subtle light qualities with small strokes of strong color.

incise To cut into a surface with a sharp instrument.

inlay To piece together or insert materials, such as ivory or colored wood, into a surface.

installation An art piece usually of mixed media that is designed for a specific space.

intaglio (in-TAH-lee-oh) A printmaking process in which lines are incised or etched into a metal plate, which is then inked and wiped so that the ink remains only in the incised lines.

intensity Brightness or dullness of a hue, or chroma.

intermedia The mixing and overlapping of any materials and/or disciplines in an artwork.

International style A style developed in the thirteenth and fourteenth centuries in Europe with characteristics of French Gothic and Sienese art. Later, in the twentieth century, a style of architecture based on simple geometric forms without adornment.

invented texture An imaginary surface quality created by the artist.

Ionic (eye-ON-ik) *See* **Orders.**

Islam The religion of Muslims as revealed to the prophet Mohammed and recorded in the Holy Koran, or Quran.

isometric projection A perspective system for rendering a three-dimensional object on a two-dimensional surface by drawing all horizontal edges at a 30-degree angle from a horizontal base. All the verticals are drawn perpendicularly from the horizontal base.

Italian Futurists Artists in Italy who, beginning in 1909, were influenced by Cubism and intrigued with light and movement. They were also fascinated with the sensation of speed and with the mechanics of the machine age, as well as the dangers of war.

iwan (EE-wan) A vaulted, recessed area that opens into a courtyard in Islamic architecture.

J

jamb (jam) The vertical side or post of a doorway.

Jihad (jee-HAHD) A holy war in the Islamic religion.

Judeo-Christian Characteristic of cultures whose roots are made up of both the Jewish and Christian traditions.

juxtapose To place contrasting elements, images, or ideas side by side.

K

ka Part of the spirit or soul of a human being in ancient Egyptian culture that resides in the mind in life. *See also* **ba.**

kachina (kuh-CHEE-nuh) A spirit doll of the Pueblo culture in North America.

kami (kah-mee) Spirits or deities in the Shinto religion, believed to dwell in nature and in charismatic people.

karma (KAR-muh) The consequences of the actions of this life, which influence the next reincarnation.

kitsch (kich) Works that are done in what is considered to be poor taste.

kiva (KEE-vuh)   An underground, circular ceremonial structure of the Pueblo culture in North America.

Koran (koo-RAN)   The sacred book of the Islamic religion; also *Quran.*

L

labret (LA-bret)   A mouth ornament.

labyrinth (LAB-eh-rinth)   A maze.

lacquer   A resinous varnish that adds a rich sheen to a surface.

lamassu (lah-MAH-soo)   A winged, human-headed bull, from Assyria.

laminated   Composed of layers of glued or fused material.

landscape   Art depicting natural land formations and scenes.

lapis lazuli (LAP-is LAHZ-eh-lee)   A semiprecious stone with a deep blue color.

lei (LAY-ee)   A Hawaiian necklace usually made of feathers or flowers.

limner (LIM-[n]er)   A painter or a draftsman.

line   An element in art with length but negligible width.

linear perspective   *See* **perspective.**

lintel (LINT-el)   In architecture, a horizontal member spanning an opening, and usually carrying weight from above.

lithography (lith-OG-reh-fee)   A form of printmaking, invented in the nineteenth century, based on the principle that water and oil do not mix.

lost wax [*cire perdue*]   A sculptural method in which a cast is made from a wax model by coating the model with an investment material that can be heated to high temperatures. The wax melts away, leaving a negative mold of the model, into which molten metal is poured or clay is pressed, leaving a positive form of the original wax model.

lotus   A water lily. In some cultures, the flower was thought to induce a state of contented forgetfulness.

low key   Any values or tones and colors that have a value level of middle gray or darker.

luau (LU-au)   A Hawaiian feast.

luminosity   The quality of radiating or reflecting light.

M

malagan or **malanggan** (mah-lah-gan *or* mah-lang-gan)   The carvings and ritual pieces created to honor the dead in Papua New Guinea; also, the festivals for which the carvings are made.

mana (MAH-na)   Supernatural power or influence that flows through some individuals or resides in some objects.

mandala (MUN-duh-luh)   A design with geometric elements that delineates deities, the universe, and wholeness in Hinduism or Buddhism.

masjid (MUS-jid)   Mosque.

masquerade (mas-ker-ADE)   A ceremony or a festive gathering in which masks and costumes are worn.

mass (volume)   An area of occupied space. *Mass* usually refers to a solid occupying a space, while *volume* may refer to either a solid mass or an open framework occupying a space.

Mass   The Roman Catholic Eucharistic ritual consisting of prayers, ceremonies, offerings, and the consecration of bread and wine.

mausoleum (maw-seh-LEE-um)   A stately tomb usually built above the ground.

medieval (meh-DEE-vel)   Of or like the period between ancient and modern times.

medium, media   Traditional and nontraditional materials used to make art, such as charcoal, paint, clay, bronze, video, or computers.

megalith (meg-ah-LITH)   A huge stone, especially one used in ancient or Neolithic monuments or tombs.

menorah (meh-NOR-eh)   A Jewish candelabrum with seven branches (a traditional symbol of Judaism) or with nine branches (used during the festival of Hanukah).

Mesoamerica (mes-oh-eh-MER-i-kah)   The Central American regions of Mexico, Guatemala, El Salvador, and Belize.

Mesolithic (mes-oh-LITH-ik)   The middle Stone Age, between the Paleolithic and Neolithic eras, marked by the earliest use of local and permanent food sources.

Middle Ages   A period between ancient and modern times, often used in reference to Europe from the fifth through the fourteenth centuries.

mihrab (MEE-rahb)   In a mosque, a niche in the wall that faces Mecca.

minaret   A prayer tower that is part of an Islamic mosque.

minbar (MIN-bar)   The pulpit for the imam, in an Islamic mosque.

Minimalism   A nonobjective art movement in the twentieth century in the United States in which artists reduced their images and objects to pure form. These images and forms were called primary structures.

mixed media   The mixing of art materials and forms in creating an artwork. *See* **intermedia.**

moai (moh-eye)   A large stone figure from the Easter Islands (Rapa Nui).

Modernism   A period of Western art, primarily in the twentieth century, during which innovation and self-critical practice were emphasized.

module, modular   A composition that incorporates modules, or distinct visual units or sections.

monochromatic   An artwork that contains the hue, tints, and shades of only one color.

monolith   A large, single block or column.

montage (mahn-TAHZH)   A composite picture created by combining several separate pictures or separate clips from movies or videos.

mortise and tenon (MORT-is and TEN-en)   A technique for joining pieces of wood. A *mortise* is a notch or a slot made in a piece of wood. A *tenon* is a projection made on a separate piece of wood to fit precisely into the mortise to create a joint.

mosaic (mo-ZAY-ik)   An image or decoration created by covering a surface with small pieces of variously colored material, such as metal, glass, or stone.

mosque (mosk)   An Islamic place of worship.

motif (mo-TEEF)   A repeated design or image in a composition that takes on visual significance.

mudra (MOO-druh)   A hand gesture with symbolic meaning in Hindu and Buddhist art.

muqarna or **mukarna** (moo-KAR-na)   Numerous niches and niche fragments, or hanging vaults, clustered in a honeycomb-like pattern, that appears in Islamic domes, arches, portals, and window openings.

mural   Images painted directly on a wall, or covering a wall.

Muslim   A follower of the Islamic religion.

N

nadir   The lowest point.

narrative   An artwork that relates a story.

natural pattern   Repeated elements that resemble each other, but are not exactly alike; the interval between elements may be irregular.

Naturalism   A style of art with imagery that resembles what we see in the world around us.

nave   The tall, center aisle of a church or a basilica, usually flanked with side aisles.

necropolis (neh-KROP-eh-lis)   The city of the dead.

negative space   Voids within an artwork.

Neolithic (nee-oh-LITH-ik)   A period of the Stone Age in which humans used polished stone tools and developed agriculture; the New Stone Age.

neophyte (nee-oh-FITE)   A new convert to a faith or a belief.

niche (nich)   A recess in a wall, usually designed to hold a decorative or votive object.

nirvana (nir-VAH-nah)   The ultimate release from the cycle of reincarnation in the Buddhist and Hindu faiths, achieved by the expulsion of individual passion, hatred, and delusion. The attainment of total peace.

nkisi n'kondi ([n]kee-see [n]kon-dee)   A carved power figure of the Kongo people from central Africa, used by a shaman to bestow good or inflict harm on someone.

nonobjective   Artwork that has no imagery that resembles the natural world.

O

obelisk (OB-eh-lisk)   A tall, four-sided monolith that is tapered at its apex into a pyramid form.

oblique projection   A three-dimensional object rendered two-dimensionally with the front and back sides parallel, and all receding lines positioned at forty-five degree angles.

obsidian (ob-SID-ee-en)   A dark, volcanic glass.

oculus (AH-kyoo-lus)   The round opening in the center of a dome.

odalisque (OH-deh-lisk)   A Turkish harem girl.

one-point perspective   A drawing in which all front-facing planes are shown as parallel to the picture plane, and all other planes recede to a single point.

onion dome   A pointed dome whose middle diameter swells outward, creating a smaller diameter at its base.

Op Art   A 1960s style of art that created unusual visual vibrations with contrasting colors or closely placed lines.

Orders   In Classical Greek architecture, an Order consists of a column with a base, a shaft, a capital, and an entablature that is decorated and proportioned to the Classical Greek canon. The Greek Orders are Doric, Ionic, and Corinthian, and the Roman variations are Tuscan, Roman Doric, and Composite.

Organic architecture   A style of American architecture developed by Louis Sullivan and Frank Lloyd Wright that incorporated flowing natural forms in its design.

organic shape   A shape that seems to be drawn from nature or that is like nature; not geometric.

orthogonals (or-THOG-eh-nelz)   The converging lines that meet at the vanishing point on the horizon line in linear perspective.

outsider art   The art produced by marginalized people within a culture, such as prisoners or the mentally ill.

P

pagan   A follower of a polytheistic religion, or an irreligious or a hedonistic person.

pagoda (peh-GO-deh)   A multistoried, Asian, towerlike temple with upward sweeping roofs over each story.

paint   Colored pigment ground with a binder, having a semi-liquid or paste consistency.

Paleolithic (pay-lee-oh-LITH-ik)   Old Stone Age, dating from 25,000 to 8000 BCE; the era of hunters and gatherers.

palmette (pal-MET)   Decorative drawing or relief sculpture in palm leaf shapes.

pan   To rotate a camera horizontally, to create a panorama effect or to follow a moving subject.

papyrus (peh-PI-rus)   A tall water plant, abundant around the Nile River, used for making an early form of paper.

parapet (PAR-eh-pet)   A low wall or railing.

parchment   Animal skin, usually of a goat or sheep, specially prepared to be used as paper.

pathos   The power to provoke compassion.

patriarch   The male head of a family or family line.

patron   A person who supports the artist and the arts.

pattern   In art, a repetition of any element in the composition.

pedestal (PED-es-tel)   The base of a column or colonnade in Classical architecture, or a base on which a sculpture or a vase may be placed.

pediment (PED-eh-ment)   A low, pitched gable resting on columns, a portico, a door, or a window.

pendentive (pen-DENT-iv)   The triangular concave sections that are created when a dome is supported by a base of arches.

Performance Art   Influenced by the "Happening," performance art consists of live-action events staged as artworks.

peristyle   A colonnade around the inside and/or the outside of a court or room.

Perpendicular Style   An English Gothic style of architecture that has strong vertical emphasis and dense ornamental vault ribs that serve only for decoration; also known as the "Tudor" style.

perspective   A system of rendering the illusion of three-dimensional depth on a flat, two-dimensional surface.

pharaoh (FA-ro)   Title of kings in ancient Egypt.

photojournalism   News reporting in which photographs are more important than the text.

photomontage   A composition of many photographs, or of one using many prints to create a new image.

photomural (fo-to-MYOOR-el)   A very large photograph installed as a mural.

piazza (pee-AHT-za)   An open court or plaza.

pictograph (PIK-to-graf)   A picture or picture-like symbol used in early writing to convey an idea or information.

picture plane   The flat, two-dimensional surface of a drawing, a print, or a painting.

pier   A solid stone or masonry support, not a column.

pigments   Colors in powder form, mixed with binders to create paint.

pilaster   A pier that projects somewhat from a wall. Also, a rectangular column that would be designed after one of the Classical Orders.

pillar   Any freestanding, column-like structure that does not conform to the Classical Orders. A pillar may or may not be cylindrical.

pinnacle   Usually a pointed or conical ornamentation that is placed on a spire or a buttress.

plan   A diagram showing the ground plan of a building.

Pointillism   An art movement in Europe in the early twentieth century in which artists applied daubs of pure pigment to a ground to create an image. The paint daubs appear to blend when viewed from a distance.

polyptych (POL-ip-tik)   Four or more separate panels, hinged together to create an artwork, often for an altar.

pommel   A knob that is attached to the hilt of a knife or sword.

Pop Art   An art movement in the mid-twentieth century that used popular commercial items as subject matter, including newspapers, comic strips, popular and political personalities, Campbell's soup cans, and Coca-Cola bottles. Usually created as satire, these artworks glorified the products of mass popular culture and elevated them to twentieth-century icons.

porcelain   High-fired, lightweight, white ceramic ware.

portal   An opening, a door, an entrance, or a gate.

portico (POR-ti-ko)   A porch or covered walkway, with columns on one side supporting the roof.

post and lintel   A method of construction that uses posts to support a crossbeam that can bear the weight of the roof.

Postimpressionism   The late-nineteenth-century movement in European painting that followed Impressionism, in which artists emphasized their subjective viewpoint or the formal qualities of the painting.

Postmodernism   The late-twentieth-century movement in art, based to some extent on deconstructivism and accommodating a wide range of styles.

power figure   A carved figure that is empowered with magic, which can heal and protect. *See* **fetish** and **nkisi n'kondi.**

Precisionism   An art movement in the United States in the first half of the twentieth century that was concerned with rendering human-made environments and the beauty of precise and perfect machine forms in a clear and concise manner. The style of painting was flat and decorative.

primary colors   In any medium, those colors that, when mixed, produce the largest range of new colors.

print   In printmaking, an image created by pressing an inked plate onto a surface; in photography, a photograph usually made from a negative.

proportion   The size relationship, or relative size, of parts of objects or imagery to a whole or to each other.

pueblo (PWEB-lo)   A type of communal housing built by Native Americans, primarily in the Southwest.

putto (POOT-toh); *pl.* **putti** (POOT-tee)   A young, plump, child-angel used as subject matter in Italian sculpture and painting.

pylon (PIE-lan)   A truncated pyramid form usually seen in Egyptian monumental gates.

Q

Quran (koo RAN)   Variation of *Koran.*

R

radial balance   Visual equilibrium achieved when all the elements in a composition radiate outward from a central point.

rampart (RAM-part) An earthen embankment, usually with a parapet, used as fortification for a castle or fort.

Realism A nineteenth-century Western style of art that depicts everyday life without idealism, nostalgia, or flattery.

rectilinear (rek-teh-LIN-ee-er) Consisting of straight lines set at 90-degree angles in a composition.

Reformation (ref-or-MAY-shun) A sixteenth-century European movement aimed at reforming the Catholic Church, but resulting in the establishment of the Protestant churches.

register A band that contains imagery or visual motifs; often, several registers are stacked one above the other to convey a narrative sequence.

relic A sacred fragment of an object, a deceased saint, or an ancestor.

relief Sculpture that is partly projecting from a flat surface. When the sculptural form is at least half round or more, it is called a *high relief;* when it is less, it is called a *low* or *bas relief.*

reliquary (REL-i-kwer-ee) A vessel or receptacle designed to house a holy relic.

Renaissance (ren-eh-SAHNZ) A rebirth of learning and the arts in the fourteenth through the seventeenth centuries in Europe, along with the revival and study of ancient Greek and Roman cultures.

render To depict or execute in an art form.

repetition Use of the same element over and over again in a composition; similar to pattern.

representational art Art that presents nature, people, and objects from the world in a recognizable form.

retable (reh-TAY-bel) An architectural wall or screen behind and above an altar. It is usually richly decorated with painting, sculpture, or carved ornamentation.

retablo (reh-TAH-blo) A small votive painting.

rhythm A form of repetitive beats that are usually seen in a composition as a pattern. This is accomplished by repeating one or more of the formal elements in the organization of a work.

ribbed vault *See* **vaulting.**

ridgepole The beam running the length of the building, located under the highest point of a gabled roof.

Rococo (ro-ko-KO) The style of art, architecture, music, and decorative arts from early-eighteenth-century Europe, made primarily for the upper class.

Romanticism An art movement in nineteenth-century Europe that focused on the intuitive, emotional, and picturesque, a spirit that was felt between human beings and nature. It rejected the carefully planned and rationalized compositions of the Renaissance and added a sense of mysticism to art.

roof comb A decorative architectural element that crowned Mayan temples and palaces.

rose window A large, circular, stained-glass window in a Gothic church, composed of many segments.

rotunda (ro-TUN-dah) A round building, hall, or room, usually roofed with a dome.

rubble Broken bits and pieces of brick and gravel that were used as fill in Roman architecture.

S

saltcellar A dish or a container designed to hold salt.

samisen (SAM-eh-sen) A Japanese guitar-like instrument with a long neck and three strings plucked with a spatula.

samurai (SAM-uh-rye) In feudal Japan, a member of the warrior class.

sanctuary A sacred or holy place in a church or temple.

sanskrit (SAN-skrit) The classic Indo-Aryan language from the fourth century BCE; still used in some Buddhist rituals.

sarcophagus (sar-KOF-eh-gus) A coffin.

sarsen A type of sandstone monolith found in ancient ruins, such as Stonehenge in England.

saturation The intensity or brightness of a color.

scale The size of an object or image that is measured by its relationship to other objects and images that are recognized for their normal or actual size.

scarification (skar-i-fi-KAY-shun) The cutting or scratching of the skin in various designs that will heal as permanent body decoration.

scrollwork An architectural ornamentation that echoes the form of a partially unrolled scroll. Ionic and Corinthian columns have scrollwork in their capitals.

secondary colors Colors that result when any two primary colors are mixed in a particular medium.

secular Of nonreligious matters.

seppuku (seh-POO-koo) A Japanese ritual of taking one's life.

serigraphy (seh-RIG-reh-fee) A printmaking technique in which ink is applied to a stencil that has been temporarily adhered to a stretched cloth. Also called silk screen.

shade The addition of black to a hue.

shah (shah) A title of the former rulers of Iran.

shaman (SHAH-men) A person, priest, or priestess who is empowered to use magic to cure and heal, imbue an object with magic, control spirits and commune with ancestors, and foretell the future.

shape A flat, two-dimensional element with a defined outline and usually without interior detail.

Shinto (SHIN-to) A major Japanese religion, with emphasis on ancestor and nature worship.

Shiva (SHIH-vah or SHEE-vah) Hindu god of destruction and reproduction.

shogun (SHO-gun) Any of the various hereditary leaders of Japan until 1867, who were the real rulers instead of the emperors.

shrine A receptacle for holy objects; a holy place or site; a site of the entombment of a saint; a place devoted to a deity or a holy person.

silk screen *See* **serigraphy.**

simulated texture Texture rendered in a composition to look like the actual or natural texture.

skeletal In architecture, relating to a framework of steel that is covered with a "skin" of glass or other light materials.

space An area in which objects or images can exist.

spandrel (SPAN-drel) The area between two arches or alongside one arch, or the space between the ribs of a vault.

spectrum The breakdown of white light into its components of red, orange, yellow, green, blue, indigo, and violet.

sphinx (sfinks) A figure made up of a human head and a lion's body, likely of Egyptian origin.

spire A pointed roof of a tower or steeple.

squinches The spatial areas created when a dome is placed on a square or a polygonal base.

stained glass Pieces of colored glass arranged to create an abstract composition or representational image.

stainless steel Steel alloyed with chromium, which is virtually rust-free and corrosion-free.

stele (STEE-lee); *pl.* **stelae** (STEE-leh) A stone slab or tablet that is carved with images and/or inscriptions usually in commemoration of a person or an event.

still life An assembled composition of objects set up by the artist to use as subject matter for an artwork.

stoa (STO-ah) A roofed colonnade in ancient Greek architecture that may or may not be attached to another structure.

Stoicism (STO-i-siz-em) Indifference to pleasure or pain.

stucco (STUK-oh) A plaster material that may be used for reliefs and architectural ornamentation, such as moldings and cornices. It is also a wall covering made of a thin layer of cement.

stupa (STOO-pah) A dome-shaped Buddhist shrine.

style Specific recognizable attributes and characteristics that are consistent and coherent in the artwork within a historical period, within a cultural tradition, or of an individual artist.

stylization The distortion of an image or a figure according to an artistic convention or canon.

subject matter The specific idea of an artwork.

subtractive color system Mixing of pigment to create a color.

subtractive method (sculpture) A technique in which a sculptural material, such as clay or wood, is carved away to produce a form.

sultan (SULT-n) A former ruler of Turkey, or a Muslim ruler.

support A surface upon which a two-dimensional artwork, such as a painting, is made.

Surrealism (ser-REE-el-izm) An art movement in early-twentieth-century Europe influenced by the work of Sigmund Freud. Fantastic and dreamlike imagery drawn from the subconscious was executed through automatic drawing similar to doodling.

suspension (bridge) A bridge in which the deck is suspended by ropes or cables that are attached to two piers.

sutra (SOO-trah) A documented sermon or a dialogue of the Buddha.

symbolic geometry The use of geometry to demarcate sacred alignments in nature; the use of geometric shapes in art and architecture to symbolize divine attributes.

symmetry Balance achieved by distributing equal weight evenly throughout a composition. If an imaginary line could be drawn vertically down an artwork that has symmetrical balance, one side would mirror the other.

sympathetic magic A form of ritual or prayer that is directed to an image or an object in order to bring about a desired result, such as a successful hunt.

syncretism (SIN-kreh-tizm) The blending of different religious beliefs and rituals.

T

tabernacle A sacred place that holds the Holy Eucharist in the Christian religion.

taboo Forbidden for general use; usually applied to sacred rituals, places, or objects.

tapestry A heavy fabric woven with designs or images, intended as a wall hanging or furniture covering.

tempera (TEM-per-ah) Painting with pigments mixed with size, casein, or egg yolk.

tensile strength (TEN-sil) The degree to which a material can withstand stretching, stress, or tension.

terra-cotta (TER-eh KOT-ah) A low-fired ceramic clay, such as that found in red-earth flowerpots.

tertiary colors (TUR-shee-er-ee) Colors that result from the mixing of one primary color and a neighboring secondary color.

tetrahedron (teh-trah-HEE-dren) A solid contained by four triangular plane faces.

thatch A roof covering made of straw or reeds.

three-dimensional Having or appearing to have height, length, and depth.

three-point perspective A drawing in which only one point of each volume is closest to the viewer, and all planes recede to one of three points.

tone *See* **value.**

tooth The surface texture of paper.

torana (TO-rah-nah) Gateway in the stone fence surrounding a stupa, located at the cardinal points.

torso   The trunk of the human body from the shoulders to the hips.

totem   The emblem or symbol of a family clan.

Tourist Art   Art that is based on a particular ethnic tradition, but is specifically created to sell to tourists.

tracery   The ornamentation of the upper part of a Gothic window. *Plate tracery* was carved through solid stone, while *bar tracery* was incorporated in the mullions of a window.

transept (TRAN-sept)   The crossing arm (space) that intersects the nave, forming a cross in a basilica or a church.

triptych (TRIP-tik)   A three-paneled painting.

triumphal arch   A freestanding Roman arch commemorating an important event.

trompe l'oeil (tromp-LOY)   Illusionistic painting that fools viewers into believing that they are seeing actual three-dimensional objects instead of their representation.

truss   Wooden or metal beams arranged in connected triangles to make a framework.

tufa (TOO-feh)   A porous rock formed from deposits of springs. The material can be easily carved when first exposed to air, then hardens with age.

two-dimensional   Having or appearing to have height and length, without significant depth.

two-point perspective   A drawing in which no planes are parallel to the picture plane, but all recede to one of two points on the horizon.

tympanum (TIM-peh-num)   In architecture, a half-circular space below an arch, and above a doorway or window.

U

ukiyo-e (oo-kee-yo-ay)   A kind of Japanese print or painting; literally, "pictures from the floating world."

unity   A quality achieved in an artwork when the artist organizes all the compositional elements so that they visually work together as a whole.

V

value   The relationship of lights and darks in a composition; sometimes referred to as *tone.*

Vanitas (VAH-nee-tas)   A style of Dutch painting in which the theme is the transitory nature of earthly things along with the inevitability of death.

variety   Opposing or contrasting visual elements in a composition that add interest without disturbing its unity.

vaulting   A system of masonry roofing or ceiling construction based on the principle of the arch. There are several types of vaults: The *barrel* vault is a single arch extended in depth from front to back, forming a tunnel-like structure; a *groin* or a *cross* vault is formed with two barrel vaults positioned at 90-degree angles so as to cross or intersect one another; a *ribbed* vault is a variation of the groin vaulting system in which arches diagonally cross over the groin vault forming skeletal ribs; a *dome* is formed by rotating arches on their vertical axis to form a hemispheric vault.

Veda (VAY-dah)   One of the four ancient books of Hinduism, with chants, hymns, and sacred formulas.

vellum (VEL-um)   A fine kind of parchment.

video; video art   Art made with recording cameras and displayed on monitors, and having moving imagery.

vignette (vin-YET)   A decorative design that might be used on a page of a book or in a drawing, print, or painting; the outer edges of the composition are softened or blurred.

visual texture   The rendering of illusionary texture on a surface or a ground. This texture may be simulated, abstracted, or invented.

volume   See **mass.**

voussoir (voo-SWAR)   Wedge-shaped stone used to build an arch or a vault.

W

walik   A horizontal sculpture used as part of malagan rituals.

warm colors   Generally, reds, oranges, and yellows.

woodcut   A kind of printmaking done by cutting away non-printing areas from the surface of a woodblock.

Y

Yakshi (yak-shee)   A lesser Hindu and Buddhist female divinity, associated with fertility and vegetation; the male counterpart is the Yaksha.

yin-yang   Ancient Chinese symbol of balance and harmony.

Z

Zen   A variation of Buddhism, practiced mostly in Japan, Vietnam, and Korea, that seeks intuitive illumination of the mind and spirit, primarily through meditation.

ziggurat (ZIG-oo-rat)   A terraced, flat-topped pyramid surmounted by a temple, from the ancient Near East.

Bibliography

Abbate, Francesco, ed. *Precolumbian Art of North America and Mexico.* Translated by Elizabeth Evans. London: Octopus Books, 1972.

Abbott, Helen, et al., eds. *The Spirit Within: Northwest Coast Native Art from the John H. Hauberg Collection.* New York: Rizzoli, 1995.

Abiodun, Rowland, Henry J. Drewal, and John Pemberton III, eds. *The Yoruba Artist: New Theoretical Perspectives on African Arts.* Washington, DC: Smithsonian Institution Press, 1994.

Adachi, Barbara. "Living National Treasures." *Japanese Encyclopedia.* Tokyo: Kodansha, 1983, pp. 60–61.

Adams, Laurie Schneider. *A History of Western Art.* New York: McGraw-Hill, 1997.

Albarn, Keith, Jenny Miall Smith, Stanford Steele, and Dinah Walker. *The Language of Pattern: An Inquiry Inspired by Islamic Decorations.* New York: Harper and Row, 1974.

Alva, Walter, and Christopher B. Donnan. *Royal Tombs of Sipan.* Los Angeles: The Fowler Museum of Cultural Heritage, University of California, Los Angeles, 1993.

American Film Institute. "Preservation." *American Film Institute.* http://afionline.org (accessed July 16, 1998).

Andah, Bassey W. "The Ibadan Experience to Date." In *Museums and Archeology in West Africa,* edited by Claude Daniel Ardouin. Washington, DC: Smithsonian Institution Press, 1997.

Anderson, Richard L. *Calliope's Sisters: A Comparative Study of Philosophies of Art.* Englewood Cliffs, NJ: Prentice Hall, 1990.

Ardouin, Claude Daniel, ed. *Museums and Archeology in West Africa.* Washington, DC: Smithsonian Institution Press, 1997.

Arnason, H. H. *History of Modern Art.* Englewood Cliffs, NJ: Prentice Hall, 1986.

Atkins, Robert. *Art Speak: A Guide to Contemporary Ideas, Movements, and Buzzwords, 1945 to the present.* New York: Abbeville Press, 1997.

Auping, Michael. *Jenny Holzer.* New York: Universe Publishing, 1992.

Baines, John, and Jaromir Malak. *Cultural Atlas of the World: Ancient Egypt.* New York: Facts on File, 1994.

Barrie, Dennis. "The Scene of the Crime." *Art Journal* 50, no. 3 (Fall 1991): 29–32.

Barrow, Terrence. *An Illustrated Guide to Maori Art.* Honolulu: University of Hawaii Press, 1984.

Barrow, Tui Terrence. *Maori Wood Sculpture of New Zealand.* Rutland, VT: Charles E. Tuttle, 1969.

Baumann, Felix, and Marianne Karabelnik, eds. *Degas Portraits.* London: Merrell Holberton, 1994.

Beaver, R. Pierce, et al., eds. *Eerdmans' Handbook to the World's Religions.* Grand Rapids, MI: William B. Eerdmans, 1982.

Beck, James, and Michael Daley. *Art Restoration: The Culture, the Business and the Scandal.* New York: W. W. Norton, 1993.

Becker, Carol. "Art Thrust into the Public Sphere." *Art Journal* 50, no. 3 (Fall 1991): 65–68.

Beckwith, John. *Early Medieval Art.* New York: Praeger, 1973.

Benton, Janetta Rebold. *The Medieval Menagerie: Animals in the Art of the Middle Ages.* New York: Abbeville Press, 1992.

Benton, Janetta Rebold, and DiYanni, Robert. *Arts and Culture: Volume II.* Upper Saddle River, NJ: Prentice Hall, 1998.

Bernadac, Marie-Laure. *Louise Bourgeois.* Paris: Flammarion, 1996.

Berrin, Kathleen, ed. *The Spirit of Ancient Peru: Treasures from the Museo Arqueológico Rafael Larco Herrera.* London: Thames and Hudson, 1997.

Bersson, Robert. *Worlds of Art.* Mountain View, CA: Mayfield, 1991.

Bertelli, Carlo. *Mosaics.* New York: W. H. Smith, 1989.

Bianchi, Emanuela. *Ara Pacis Augustae.* Rome, Italy: Fratelli Palombi Editori, 1994.

Blake, Nayland, Lawrence Rinder, and Amy Scholder, eds. *In a Different Light: Visual Culture, Sexual Identity, Queer Practice.* San Francisco: City Light Books, 1995.

Blier, Suzanne Preston. *The Royal Arts of Africa.* New York: Harry N. Abrams, 1998.

Bluemel, Carl. *Greek Sculptors at Work.* New York: Phaidon, 1969.

Blunden, Caroline, and Mark Elvin. *The Cultural Atlas of the World: China.* Alexandria, VA: Stonehenge Press, 1991.

Blunt, Wilfrid. *Isfahan, Pearl of Persia.* London: Elek Books, 1966.

Boardman, John. *Greek Art.* London: Thames and Hudson, 1996.

Boyd, Andrew. *Chinese Architecture and Town Planning 1500 B.C.–A.D. 1911.* London: Alec Tiranti, 1962.

Brainard, Shirl. *A Design Manual.* Upper Saddle River, NJ: Prentice Hall, 1998.

Brotherston, Gordon. *Painted Books from Mexico: Codices in UK Collections and the World They Represent.* London: The British Museum Press, 1995.

Brown, Kendall H., et al. *Light in Darkness: Women in Japanese Prints of the Early Shwa (1926–1945).* Los Angeles: Fisher Gallery, University of Southern California, 1996.

Buehler, Alfred, Terry Barrow, and Charles P. Mountford. *The Art of the South Sea Islands.* New York: Crown, 1962.

Burson, Nancy. *Faces.* Santa Fe, NM: Twin Palms, 1993.

Burton, Rosemary, and Richard Cavendish. *Wonders of the World.* Chicago: Rand McNally, 1991.

Bushnell, G. H. S. *Ancient Arts of the Americas.* New York: Praeger, 1965.

Cahill, James. *The Lyric Journey: Poetic Painting in China and Japan.* Cambridge, MA: Harvard University Press, 1966.

Cameron, Elisabeth L., with Doran H. Ross. *Isn't S/he a Doll? Play and Ritual in African Sculpture.* Los Angeles: UCLA Fowler Museum of Cultural History, 1996.

Canaday, John. *Mainstreams of Modern Art.* New York: Holt, Rinehart and Winston, 1959.

Cantrell, Jacqueline Phillips. *Ancient Mexico: Cultural Traditions in the Land of the Feathered Serpent.* Dubuque, IA: Kendall/Hunt, 1984.

Carpenter, T. H. *Art and Myth in Ancient Greece.* London: Thames and Hudson, 1991.

Caruana, Wally. *Aboriginal Art.* London: Thames and Hudson, 1993.

Casson, Lionel. *Ancient Egypt.* New York: Time-Life Books, 1971.

Caygill, Marjorie, and John Cherry. *A. W. Franks: Nineteenth Century Collecting and the British Museum.* London: The British Museum Press, 1997.

Center for African Art. *ART/artifact: African Art in Anthropology Collections.* New York: Prestel Verlag, 1989.

Chandra, Pramod. *The Sculpture of India 3000 BC–AD 1300.* Washington, DC: The National Gallery of Art, 1985.

Chicago, Judy. *Through the Flower: My Struggles as a Woman Artist.* Garden City, NY: Doubleday, 1975.

Chui, Hu. *The Forbidden City, Collection of Photographs.* Beijing: China Photographic Publishing House, 1995.

Clark, Kenneth. *Animals and Men: Their Relationship as Reflected in Western Art from Prehistory to the Present Day.* New York: William Morrow, 1977.

Clark, Kenneth. *The Nude: A Study in Ideal Form.* Princeton, NJ: Princeton University Press, 1956.

Clearwater, Bonnie. *Mark Rothko: Works on Paper.* New York: Hudson Hills Press, 1984. Distributed by Viking Penguin.

Cocke, Thomas. *900 Years: The Restorations of Westminster Abbey.* London: Harvey Miller, 1995.

Coe, Michael, Dean Snow, and Elizabeth Bensen. *The Cultural Atlas of the World: Ancient America.* Richmond, VA: Stonehenge Press, 1990.

Coe, Michael D. *The Maya.* New York: Thames and Hudson, 1982.

Collcutt, Martin, Marius Jansen, and Isao Kumakuro. *Cultural Atlas of the World: Japan.* Alexandria, VA: Stonehenge Press, 1991.

Collier's. *Photographic History of World War II.* New York: P. F. Collier and Son, 1946.

Collignon, Maxime. *Manual of Mythology in Relation to Greek Art.* New Rochelle, NY: Caratzas Brothers, 1982.

Colton, Joel. *Great Ages of Man: Twentieth Century.* New York: Time-Life Books, 1968.

Colvin, Howard. *Architecture and the After-life.* New Haven and London: Yale University Press, 1991.

Compassion and Protest: Recent Social and Political Art from the Eli Broad Family Foundation Collection. New York: Cross River Press, a Division of Abbeville Press, 1991.

Corbin, George A. *Native Arts of North America, Africa, and the South Pacific.* New York: Harper and Row, 1988.

Cotterell, Arthur. *The First Emperor of China.* New York: Holt, Rinehart and Winston, 1981.

Cowart, Jack, et al. *Georgia O'Keeffe: Art and Letters.* Washington, DC: The National Gallery of Art, 1987.

Craven, Roy C. *Indian Art: A Concise History.* London: Thames and Hudson, 1997.

Crimp, Douglas. "The Photographic Activity of Postmodernism." In *Postmodern Perspectives: Issues in Contemporary Art,* edited by Howard Risatti, 131–139. Englewood Cliffs, NJ: Prentice Hall, 1990.

Culbertson, Judi, and Tom Randall. *Permanent Parisians: An Illustrated Guide to the Cemeteries of Paris.* Chelsea, VT: Chelsea Green, 1986.

Cunningham, Lawrence S., and John J. Reich. *Culture and Values: A Survey of the Western Humanities, Volume II.* Fort Worth, TX: Harcourt Brace College Publishers, 1998.

Cuttler, Charles D. *Northern Painting from Pucelle to Bruegel: Fourteenth, Fifteenth and Sixteenth Centuries.* New York: Holt, Rinehart and Winston. 1968.

Davies, J. G. *Temples, Churches and Mosques: A Guide to the Appreciation of Religious Architecture.* New York: The Pilgrim Press, 1982.

Dawson, Barry, and John Gillow. *The Traditional Art of Indonesia.* London: Thames and Hudson, 1994.

de Franciscis, Alfonso. *Pompeii: Civilization and Art.* Naples, Italy: Edizioni Interdipress, 1997.

DeMott, Barbara. *Dogon Masks: A Structural Study in Form and Meaning.* Ann Arbor, MI: UMI Research Press, 1982.

Denyer, Susan. *African Traditional Architecture.* New York: Africana Publishing, 1978.

Derson, Denise. *What Life Was Like on the Banks of the Nile, Egypt 3050–30 BC.* Alexandria, VA: Time-Life Books, 1996.

Desai, Vishakha N., and Darielle Mason. *Gods, Guardians and Lovers: Temple Sculptures from North India A.D. 700–1200.* New York: The Asia Society Galleries; Ahmedabad: Mapin Publishing, 1993.

Dewald, Ernest T. *Italian Painting.* New York: Holt, Rinehart and Winston, 1965.

de Zegher, M. Catherine. *Inside the Visible: An Elliptical Traverse of 20th Century Art.* Cambridge: MIT Press, 1996.

Dickerson, Albert I., ed. *The Orozco Frescoes at Dartmouth.* Hanover, NH: The Trustees of Dartmouth College, 1962.

Drewal, Henry John, and John Pemberton III, with Rowland Abiodun. *Yoruba, Nine Centuries of African Art and Thought.* New York: Center for African Art, 1989.

Duiker, William J., and Jackson J. Spielvogel. *World History.* 4th ed. Belmont, CA: Thomson/Wadsworth, 2004.

Durand, Jorge, and Douglas S. Massey. *Miracles on the Border: Retablos of Mexican Migrants to the United States.* Tucson and London: University of Arizona Press, 1995.

Ebrey, Patricia Buckley. *Cambridge Illustrated History of China.* London: Cambridge University Press, 1996.

Edwards, Jim. *Precarious Links: Emily Jennings, Hung Liu, Celia Munoz.* San Antonio, TX: San Antonio Museum of Art, 1990.

Edwards, I. E. S. *The Treasures of Tutankhamun.* New York: Penguin Books, 1977.

Encyclopedia Americana. S.v. "Central Park," by Harry L. Coles; "China: Theater," by Chia-pao Wan; "Globe Theater," by Bernard Beckermen; "Japan: Doll Drama," by Donald Richie; "Disneyland and Disney World," "Epcot," "Palenque," by Pedro Armillas; "Zoological Gardens," by William Bridges. Danbury, CT: Grolier, 1986.

Encyclopedia Britannica Online. S.v. "Animal Behaviour: Behaviour of Animals in Groups." *http://www.eb.com:180/cgi-bin/g?DocF=macro/5000/62/94.html* (accessed May 19, 1998).

Etienne, Robert. *Pompeii: The Day a City Died.* New York: Harry N. Abrams, 1992.

Ezra, Kate. *Art of the Dogon.* New York: The Metropolitan Museum of Art, 1988.

Fagan, Brian M. *Rape of the Nile.* Kingston, RI: Moyer Bell, 1992.

Fagg, William. *Yoruba: Sculpture of West Africa.* New York: Alfred A. Knopf, 1982.

Feder, Norman. *American Indian Art.* New York: Harry N. Abrams, 1995.

Feest, Christian F. *Native Arts of North America.* New York: Oxford University Press, 1980.

Fichner-Rathus, Lois. *Understanding Art.* Englewood Cliffs, NJ: Prentice Hall, 1994.

Fiero, Gloria. *The Humanistic Tradition.* Madison, WI: WCB Brown and Benchmark, 1995.

Fiodorov, B., ed. *Architecture of the Russian North, 12th through 19th Centuries.* Leningrad: Aurora Art Publishers, 1976.

Fisher, Robert E. *Mystics and Mandalas: Bronzes and Paintings of Tibet and Nepal.* Redlands, CA: The University of Redlands, 1974.

Flaherty, Thomas H. *Incas: Lords of Gold and Glory.* Alexandria, VA: Time-Life Books, 1992.

———. *The American Indians: The Spirit World.* Alexandria, VA: Time-Life Books, 1992.

———. *The Mighty Chieftains.* Alexandria, VA: Time-Life Books, 1993.

Flaherty, Thomas H., ed. *Aztecs: Reign of Blood and Splendor.* Alexandria, VA: Time-Life Books, 1992.

Fleming, William. *Arts and Ideas.* 3rd ed. New York: Holt, Rinehart and Winston, 1970.

Frank Gehry: Pritzker Architect Prize Laureate 1989. http://www.pritzkerprize.com/gehry.htm (accessed April 13, 2004).

Frankfort, Henri. *The Art and Architecture of the Orient.* New Haven, CT: Yale University Press, 1970.

Furst, Peter T., and Jill L. Furst. *North American Indian Art.* New York: Rizzoli, 1982.

Gardner, Joseph L. *Mysteries of the Ancient Americas.* Pleasantville, NY: Reader's Digest, 1986.

Gardner, Paul. *Louise Bourgeois.* New York: Universe Publishing, 1994.

Getty, Adele. *Goddess, Mother of Living Nature.* London: Thames and Hudson, 1990.

Getz-Preziosi, Pat. *Early Cycladic Sculpture: An Introduction.* Malibu, CA: J. Paul Getty Museum, 1994.

Gilbert, Creighton. *History of Renaissance Art Throughout Europe.* New York: Harry N. Abrams, 1973.

Gillon, Werner. *A Short History of African Art.* New York: Penguin Books, 1991.

Goggin, Mary-Margaret. "'Decent' vs. 'Degenerate' Art: The National Socialist Case." *Art Journal* 50, no. 4 (Winter 1991): 84–93.

Goodman, Susan Tumarkin, ed. *Russian Jewish Artists in a Century of Change 1890–1990.* Munich: Prestel-Verlag, 1995.

Gowing, Lawrence. *Lucian Freud.* London: Thames and Hudson, 1982.

Graves, Eleanor. *Life Goes to War: A Picture History of World War II.* Boston, MA: Little, Brown, 1977.

Graze, Sue, Kathy Halbreich, and Roberta Smith. *Elizabeth Murray: Paintings and Drawings.* New York: Harry N. Abrams, in association with the Dallas Museum of Art and the MIT Committee on the Visual Arts, 1987.

Greenberg, Clement. "Avant-Garde and Kitsch." *Partisan Review* 6 (Fall 1939). Reprinted in Greenberg, *Art and Culture: Critical Essays.* Boston: Beacon Press, 1961.

Gregory, Richard L. *Eye and Brain: The Psychology of Seeing.* 5th ed. Princeton, NJ: Princeton University Press, 1997.

Grolier Encyclopedia. S.v. "Pacifism and Non-violent Movements," "Gandhi's Campaigns." 1996.

Grube, Ernst J. *The World of Islam.* New York: McGraw-Hill, 1977.

Gruzinski, Serge. *The Aztecs: Rise and Fall of an Empire.* New York: Harry N. Abrams, 1992.

"Guernica." www.web.org.uk/picasso/guernica.html (accessed March 15, 2004).

Guiart, Jean. *The Arts of the South Pacific.* New York: Golden Press, 1963.

Guilbaut, Serge. *How New York Stole the Idea of Modern Art: Abstract Expressionism, Freedom, and the Cold War.* Translated by Arthur Goldhammer. Chicago and London: University of Chicago Press, 1983.

Hadington, Evan. *Lines to the Mountain Gods.* New York: Random House, 1987.

Hanson, Allan, and Louise Hanson, eds. *Art and Identity in Oceania.* Honolulu, HI: University of Hawaii Press, 1990.

Harle, J. C. *The Art and Architecture of the Indian Subcontinent.* London: Penguin Books, 1986.

Harris, Ann Sutherland, and Linda Nochlin. *Women Artists 1550–1950.* New York: Alfred A. Knopf, 1984.

Hartt, Frederick. *History of Italian Renaissance Art: Painting, Sculpture, Architecture.* Englewood Cliffs, NJ: Prentice Hall, 1969.

Hawthorn, Audrey. *Kwakiutl Art.* Seattle and London: University of Washington Press, 1979.

Hay, John. *Masterpieces of Chinese Art.* Greenwich, CT: New York Graphic Society, 1974.

Heartney, Eleanor. "Pornography." *Art Journal* 50, no. 4 (Winter 1991): 16–19.

Helm, Mackinley. *Mexican Painters: Rivera, Orozco, Siqueiros, and Other Artists of the Social Realist School.* New York: Dover, 1941.

Hershey, Irwin. *Indonesian Primitive Art.* New York: Oxford Press, 1991.

Heusinger, Lutz. *Michelangelo.* Florence, Italy: Scala; New York: Riverside, 1989.

Hillier, J. *Japanese Colour Prints.* London: Phaidon, 1991.

Hoffman, Katherine. *Concepts of Identity: Historical and Contemporary Images and Portraits of Self and Family.* New York: HarperCollins, 1996.

Holm, Bill. *Northwest Coast Indian Art: An Analysis of Form.* Seattle: University of Washington Press, 1995.

Holt, Elizabeth Gilmore, ed. *Literary Sources of Art History: An Anthology of Texts from Theophilus to Goethe.* Princeton, NJ: Princeton University Press, 1947.

Holt, John Dominis. *The Art of Featherwork in Old Hawaii.* Honolulu: Topgallant, 1985.

Honour, Hugh, and John Fleming. *The Visual Arts: A History.* Englewood Cliffs, NJ: Prentice Hall, 1995.

hooks, bell. *Art on My Mind: Visual Politics.* New York: New Press, 1995.

Hopkins, Jerry. *Yoko Ono.* New York: Macmillan, 1986.

Howard, Jeremy. *Art Nouveau: International and National Styles in Europe.* Manchester, UK: Manchester University Press, 1996.

Hughes, Robert. *American Visions.* New York: Alfred A. Knopf, 1997.

Hulton, Paul, and Lawrence Smith. *Flowers in Art from East and West.* London: British Museum Publications, 1979.

Huntington, Susan L., and John C. Huntington. *Leaves from the Bodhi Tree.* Seattle: University of Washington Press, 1990.

Identity and Alterity: Figures of the Body 1895–1995. Edited by Manlio Brusatin and Jean Clair. Venice, Italy: Marsilio, 1995. Exhibition catalog of La Biennale di Venezia 46, esposizione internationale d'arte.

Indych, Anna. "Nuyorican Baroque: Pepón Osorio's *Chucherías.*" *Art Journal* 60, no. 1 (Spring 2001): 72–83.

Internet Medieval Sourcebook. www.fordham.edu/halsall/sbook.html (accessed March 30, 2004).

Ivory: An International History and Illustrated Survey. New York: Harry N. Abrams, 1987.

J. Paul Getty Museum Handbook of the Collections. Malibu, CA: J. Paul Getty Museum, 1991.

Janson, H. W. *History of Art.* New York: Harry N. Abrams, 1995.

Jellicoe, Geoffrey, and Susan Jellicoe. *The Landscape of Man.* London: Thames and Hudson, 1987.

Jonaitis, Aldona. *From the Land of the Totem Poles.* New York: American Museum of Natural History, 1988.

Jones, Alexander. *The Jerusalem Bible.* Garden City, NY: Doubleday, 1966.

Jones, Amelia, ed. *Sexual Politics: Judy Chicago's Dinner Party in Feminist Art History.* Berkeley: University of California Press, 1996.

Kaplan, Janet A. "*Give and Take* Conversations." *Art Journal* 61, no. 2 (Summer 2002): 68–97.

Kaprow, Allen. *Assemblage, Environments and Happenings.* New York: Harry N. Abrams, 1961.

Kessler, Adam T. *Empires Beyond the Great Wall: The Heritage of Genghis Khan.* Los Angeles: Natural History Museum of Los Angeles County, 1994.

Kettering, Alice McNeil. "Gentlemen in Satin: Masculine Ideals in Later Seventeenth-Century Dutch Portraiture." *Art Journal* 56, no. 2 (Summer 1997): 41–47.

Kienholz, Edward, and Nancy Reddin Kienholz. *Kienholz: A Retrospective.* New York: Whitney Museum of American Art, 1996.

Kirsh, Andrea. *Carrie Mae Weems.* Washington, DC: The National Museum of Women in the Arts, 1993.

Kitchen, K. A. *Pharaoh Triumphant: The Life and Times of Rameses II.* Cairo, Egypt: American University in Cairo Press, 1982.

Koons, Jeff. *The Jeff Koons Handbook.* New York: Rizzoli, 1992.

Kopper, Phillip. *The Smithsonian Book of North American Indians before the Coming of the Europeans.* Washington, DC: Smithsonian Books, 1986.

Kulka, Tomas. *Kitsch and Art.* University Park: Pennsylvania State University Press, 1996.

Kundera, Milan. *The Unbearable Lightness of Being.* Translated by Michael Henry Heim. New York: Harper and Row, 1984.

Kuroda, Taizo, Melinda Takeuchi, and Yuzo Yamane. *Worlds Seen and Imagined: Japanese Screens from the Idemitsu Museum of Art.* New York: The Asia Society Galleries; Abbeville Press, 1995.

Laude, Jean. *African Art of the Dogon.* New York: Viking Press, 1973.

Lauer, David A., and Stephen Pentak. *Design Basics.* Fort Worth, TX: Harcourt Brace College Publishers, 1995.

Lazzari, Margaret, and Clayton Lee. *Art and Design Fundamentals.* New York: Van Nostrand Reinhold, 1990.

Lee, Sherman E. *A History of Far Eastern Art.* New York: Harry N. Abrams, 1973.

Levenson, Jay A. *Circa 1492.* New Haven, CT: Yale University Press, 1991.

Levi, Peter. *The Cultural Atlas of the World: The Greek World.* Alexandria, VA: Stonehenge Press, 1992.

Lewis, Bernard. *Islam and the Arab World.* New York: Alfred A. Knopf, 1976.

Lewis, Phillip. "Tourist Art, Traditional Art and the Museum in Papua New Guinea." In *Art and Identity in Oceania,* edited by Allan Hanson and Louise Hanson. Honolulu: University of Hawaii Press, 1990.

Lincoln, Louise. *Assemblage of Spirits: Idea and Image in New Ireland.* New York: George Braziller, 1987.

Linker, Kate. *Love for Sale: The Words and Pictures of Barbara Kruger.* New York: Harry N. Abrams, 1990.

Lion King: The Broadway Musical ("Circles of Sound," by Lebe M, "New Visions for Pride Rock," by Eileen Blumenthal and Julie Taymor). *Stagebill,* 1998.

Lippard, Lucy R. *Mixed Blessings: New Art in a Multicultural America.* New York: Pantheon Books, 1990.

Lippard, Lucy. *The Pink Glass Swan: Selected Feminist Essays on Art.* New York: New Press, 1995.

Lossing, Benson J. *Mathew Brady's Illustrated History of the Civil War.* Washington, DC: Fair Fax Press; Barre Publishing, 1912.

Lowe, Sarah M. *Frida Kahlo.* New York: Universe Publishing, 1991.

Lundquist, John M. *The Temple: Meeting Place of Heaven and Earth.* London: Thames and Hudson, 1993.

Lyle, Emily, ed. *Sacred Architecture in the Traditions of India, China, Judaism and Islam.* Edinburgh: Edinburgh University Press, 1992.

Machida, Margo. "Out of Asia: Negotiating Asian Identities in America." In *Asia America: Identities in Contemporary Asian American Art.* New York: The Asia Society Galleries; New Press, 1994.

Mackenzie, Lynne. *Non-Western Art: A Brief Guide.* Upper Saddle River, NJ: Prentice Hall, 2001.

Malone, Maggie, and Hideko Takayama. "A Japanese Buying Spree: The Tycoon Who Spent $160 Million at Auctions." *Newsweek,* May 28, 1990, p. 75.

Mann, A. T. *Sacred Architecture.* Rockport, MA: Element, 1993.

Marcus, George E. "Middlebrow into Highbrow at the J. Paul Getty Trust." In *Looking High and Low,* edited by Brenda Jo Bright and Liza Bakewell. Tucson: University of Arizona Press, 1995.

Mariani, Valerio. *Michelangelo the Painter.* New York: Harry N. Abrams, 1964.

Matilsky, Barbara C. *Fragile Ecologies: Contemporary Artists' Interpretations and Solutions.* New York: Rizzoli, 1992.

Matt, Leonard von, Mario Moretti, and Guglielmo Maetzke. *The Art of the Etruscans.* New York: Harry N. Abrams, 1970.

McLanathan, Richard. *The American Tradition in the Arts.* New York: Harcourt Brace and World, 1968.

Mead, Sidney Moko. *Te Maori: Maori Art from New Zealand Collections.* New York: Harry N. Abrams, 1984.

Media Scape. New York: Solomon R. Guggenheim Museum, 1996.

Miller, Arthur G. *The Painted Tombs of Oaxaca, Mexico: Living with the Dead.* Cambridge: Cambridge University Press, 1995.

Miller, Kimberly J. "Battle for Iwo Jima." http://www.usmc.mil (accessed 1997).

Miller, Mary Ellen. *The Art of Mesoamerica from Olmec to Aztec.* New York: Thames and Hudson, 1986.

Mirzoeff, Nicholas, ed. *The Visual Culture Reader.* London and New York: Routledge, 1998.

Mitchell, W. J. T., ed. *Art and the Public Sphere.* Chicago and London: University of Chicago Press, 1992.

Monod-Bruhl, Odette. *Indian Temples.* London: Oxford University Press, 1951.

Morgan, William N. *Prehistoric Architecture in the Eastern United States.* Cambridge, MA: MIT Press, 1980.

Moynihan, Elizabeth B. *Paradise as a Garden in Persia and Mughal India.* London: Scolar Press, 1979.

Munroe, Alexandra. *Japanese Art After 1945: Scream Against the Sky.* New York: Harry N. Abrams, 1994.

Murray, Jocelyn. *The Cultural Atlas of the World: Africa.* Alexandria, VA: Stonehenge Press, 1992.

Murray, Peter, and Linda Murray. *The Art of the Renaissance.* New York: Praeger, 1963.

Nagle, Geraldine. *The Arts-World Themes.* Madison, WI: Brown and Benchmark, 1993.

Nemser, Cindy. *Art Talk: Conversations with 15 Women Artists.* New York: HarperCollins, 1995.

Newhall, Beaumont. *History of Photography from 1839 to the Present Day.* New York: Museum of Modern Art, 1964.

Newland, Amy, and Chris Uhlenbeck, eds. *Ukiyo-e to Shin Hanga: The Art of Japanese Woodblock Prints.* New York: Mallard Press, 1990.

Newton, Douglas. *New Guinea Art in the Collection of the Museum of Primitive Art.* New York: Publishers Printing–Admiral Press, 1967.

Nochlin, Linda. *Women, Art, and Power and Other Essays.* New York: Harper and Row, 1988.

Norwich, John Julius, ed. *Great Architecture of the World.* New York: Bonanza Books, 1979.

Nou, Jean-Louis, Amina Okada, and M. C. Joshi. *Taj Mahal.* New York: Abbeville Press, 1993.

Ocvirk, Otto G., Robert E. Stinson, Philip R. Wigg, Robert O. Bone, and David L. Clayton. *Art Fundamentals: Theory and Practice.* Madison, WI: Brown and Benchmark, 1998.

Of Sky and Earth: Art of the Early Southeastern Indians. Edited by Roy S. Dickens. Dalton, GA: Lee Printing Company, 1982. Published in conjunction with the exhibition shown at the High Museum of Art, Atlanta, GA.

O'Hara, Frank. *Robert Motherwell.* New York: Museum of Modern Art, 1965.

Ohashi, Haruzo. *The Japanese Garden: Islands of Serenity.* Tokyo: Graphic-sha, 1997.

Oliver, Douglas L. *The Pacific Islands.* Honolulu: University of Hawaii Press, 1989.

O'Neill, John P., ed. *Mexico: Thirty Centuries of Splendor.* New York: Metropolitan Museum of Art, 1990.

Pacific: A Companion to the Regenstein Halls of the Pacific. Edited by Ron Dorfman. Chicago: Field Museum of Natural History, 1991. Field Museum Centennial Collection.

Papanek, John L. *Mesopotamia: The Mighty Kings.* Alexandria, VA: Time-Life Books, 1995.

Papanek, John L., ed. *Africa's Glorious Legacy, Lost Civilizations.* Alexandria, VA: Time-Life Books, 1994.

———. *Ancient India, Land of Mystery.* Alexandria, VA: Time-Life Books, 1994.

Pasztory, Esther. *Aztec Art.* New York: Harry N. Abrams, 1983.

Pelrine, Diane M. *Affinities of Form: Arts of Africa, Oceania and the Americas from the Raymond and Laura Wielgus Collection.* Munich: Prestel-Verlag, 1996.

Pendlebury, J. D. S. *A Handbook to the Palace of Minos at Knossos.* London: Macmillan, 1935.

Penny, David W. *Art of the American Indian Frontier: The Chandler-Pohrt Collection.* The Detroit Institute of Art. Seattle: University of Washington Press, 1992.

Perani, Judith, and Fred T. Davidson. *The Visual Arts of Africa: Gender, Power and Life Cycle Rituals.* Upper Saddle River, NJ: Prentice Hall, 1998.

Perchuk, Andrew. "Hannah Wilke [exhibition at] Ronald Feldman Fine Arts." *Artforum* (April 1994): 93–94.

Phipps, Richard, and Richard Wink. *Invitation to the Gallery.* Dubuque, IA: Wm. C. Brown, 1987.

Pierson, William H., and Martha Davidson. *Arts of the United States: A Pictorial History.* New York: McGraw-Hill, 1960.

Preble, Duane, Sarah Preble, and Patrick L. Frank. *ArtForms.* Upper Saddle River, NJ: Prentice Hall, 1999.

Ragghianti, Carlo Ludovico, and Licia Ragghianti Collobi. *National Museum of Anthropology, Mexico City.* New York: Newsweek (Simon and Schuster), 1970.

Ramseyer, Urs. *The Art and Culture of Bali.* Singapore and Oxford: Oxford University Press, 1986.

Rawson, Jessica, ed. *The British Museum Book of Chinese Art.* London: Thames and Hudson, 1992.

Reilly, Maura. "The Drive to Describe: An Interview with Catherine Opie." *Art Journal* 60, no. 2 (Summer 2001) 83–95.

Rhodes, Colin. *Outsider Art, Spontaneous Alternatives.* World of Art. New York: Thames and Hudson, 2000.

Richter, Anne. *Arts and Crafts of Indonesia.* San Francisco: Chronicle Books, 1994.

Risatti, Howard, ed. *Postmodern Perspectives: Issues in Contemporary Art.* Englewood Cliffs, NJ: Prentice Hall, 1990.

Rochfort, Dennis. *Mexican Muralists.* New York: Universe Publishing, 1993.

Ross, Doran H. "Akua's Child and Other Relatives: New Mythologies for Old Dolls." In *Isn't S/he a Doll? Play and Ritual in African Sculpture,* by Elisabeth L. Cameron, 43–57. Los Angeles: UCLA Fowler Museum of Cultural History, 1996.

Rowland, Anna. *Bauhaus Source Book.* New York: Van Nostrand Reinhold, 1990.

Roy, Christopher. *Art and Life in Africa: Selections from the Stanley Collection, Exhibitions of 1985 and 1992.* Iowa City: University of Iowa Museum of Art, 1992.

Rubin, Barbara, Robert Carlton, and Arnold Rubin. *Forest Lawn: L.A. in Installments.* Santa Monica, CA: Westside Publications, 1979.

Santini, Loretta. *Pompeii and the Villa of the Mysteries.* Narni-Terni, Italy: Editrice Plurigraf, 1997.

Sasser, Elizabeth Skidmore. *The World of Spirits and Ancestors in the Art of Western Sub-Saharan Africa.* Lubbock: Texas Tech University Press, 1995.

Saunders, J. B. de C. M., and Charles O'Malley. *The Illustrations from the Works of Andreas Vesalius of Brussels.* New York: Dover, 1950.

Sayre, Henry M. *The Object of Performance: The American Avant-Garde since 1970.* Chicago: University of Chicago Press, 1989.

Schmitz, Carl A. *Oceanic Art: Myth, Man and Image in the South Seas.* New York: Harry N. Abrams, 1971.

Schwarz, Hans-Peter. *Media-Art-History.* Munich: Prestel-Verlag, 1997.

Seaford, Richard. *Pompeii.* New York: Summerfield Press, 1978.

Setton, Kenneth M., et al. *The Renaissance, Maker of Modern Man.* Washington, DC: National Geographic Society, 1970.

Sharer, Robert, and Sylvanus Morley. *The Ancient Maya.* Stanford, CA: Stanford University Press, 1994.

Sharp, Dennis. *A Visual History of Twentieth Century Architecture.* Greenwich, CT: New York Graphic Society, 1972.

Shearer, Alistair. *The Hindu Vision: Forms of the Formless.* London: Thames and Hudson, 1993.

Sickman, Lawrence, and Alexander Soper. *The Art and Architecture of China.* New Haven, CT: Yale University Press, 1971.

Silva, Anil de, Otto von Simons, and Roger Hinks. *Man Through Art, War and Peace.* Greenwich, CT: New York Graphic Society, 1964.

Simmons, David. *Whakairo Maori Tribal Art.* New York: Oxford University Press, 1985.

Simon, Joan, ed. *Bruce Nauman.* Minneapolis: Walker Art Center, 1994.

Sitwell, Sacheverell. *Great Palaces.* New York: Hamlyn, 1969.

Skinner, Charles Montgomery. *Myths and Legends of Our Own Land.* Philadelphia and London: J. B. Lippincott, 1924.

Skira, Albert. *Treasures of Asia: Chinese Painting.* Cleveland, OH: World, 1960.

Slatkin, Wendy. *Women Artists in History: From Antiquity to the Present.* Upper Saddle River, NJ: Prentice Hall, 1997.

Smith, Bradley, and Wan-go Wen. *China: A History in Art.* New York: Doubleday, 1979.

Snellgrove, David L., ed. *The Image of the Buddha.* Paris: UNESCO (United Nations Educational, Scientific and Cultural Organization); Tokyo: Kodansha, 1978.

Solomon-Godeau, Abigail. "The Other Side of Vertu: Alternative Masculinities in the Crucible of Revolution." *Art Journal* 56, no. 2 (Summer 1997): 55–61.

Sontag, Susan. *Against Interpretation and Other Essays.* New York: Farrar, Straus and Giroux, 1966.

Spayde, Jon. "Cultural Revolution." *Departures* (September/October 1995): 115–123, 154–157.

Sporre, Dennis J. *The Creative Impulse: An Introduction to the Arts.* Upper Saddle River, NJ: Prentice Hall, 1996.

Staccioli, R. A. *Ancient Rome: Monuments Past and Present.* Rome: Vision, 1989.

Staniszewski, Mary Anne. *Believing Is Seeing: Creating a Culture of Art.* New York: Penguin Books, 1995.

Stanley-Baker, Joan. *Japanese Art.* London: Thames and Hudson, 1984.

Sterling, Charles. *Still Life Painting: From Antiquity to the Twentieth Century.* 2nd ed. rev. New York: Harper and Row, 1980.

Stewart, Gloria. *Introduction to Sepik Art of Papua New Guinea.* Sydney, Australia: Garrick Press, 1972.

Stewart, Hilary. *Looking at Indian Art of the Northwest Coast.* Seattle: University of Washington Press, 1979.

Stierlin, Henri. *Art of the Aztecs and Its Origins.* Translated by Betty and Peter Ross. New York: Rizzoli, 1982.

Stierlin, Henri. *The Pharaohs, Master-Builders.* Paris: Terrail, 1992.

Stokstad, Marilyn. *Art History.* Upper Saddle River, NJ: Prentice Hall, 1995.

Stooss, Toni, and Thomas Kellein, eds. *Nam June Paik: Video Time–Video Space.* New York: Harry N. Abrams, 1993.

Stuart, Gene S., and George E. Stuart. *Lost Kingdoms of the Maya.* Washington, DC: National Geographic Society, 1993.

Sullivan, Michael. *Art and Artists of Twentieth-Century China.* Berkeley: University of California Press, 1996.

Sutton, Peter C. *The Age of Rubens.* Boston: Museum of Fine Arts, Boston: 1993.

Swann, Peter C. *Chinese Monumental Art.* New York: Viking, 1963.

Tadashi Kobayashi. *Ukiyo-e: An Introduction to Japanese Woodblock Prints.* Tokyo: Kodansha, 1992.

Tallman, Susan. "General Idea." *Arts Magazine* (May 1990): 21–22.

Tannahill, Reay. *Food in History.* New York: Stein and Day, 1973.

Tansey, Richard G., and Fred S. Kleiner. *Gardner's Art Through the Ages.* Fort Worth, TX: Harcourt Brace College Publishers, 1996.

Taylor, Pamela York. *Beasts, Birds and Blossoms in Thai Art.* Kuala Lumpur, Malaysia: Oxford University Press, 1994.

Taylor, Simon. "Janine Antoni at Sandra Gering." *Art in America* 80 (October 1992).

Tello, J. C. "Arte Antiguo Peruano." *Inca: Revista de Estudios Antropolico.* Vol. 2. Lima, Peru: Universidad de San Marcos de Lima, 1924.

Terrace, Edward L. B., and Henry G. Fisher. *Treasures of Egyptian Art from the Cairo Museum.* London: Thames and Hudson, 1970.

Thomas, Nicholas. *Oceanic Art.* London: Thames and Hudson, 1995.

Thucydides. *The Peloponnesian War.* Translated by Rex Warner. Baltimore: Penguin Books, 1954.

Time-Life Books. *Lost Civilizations: Anatolia—Cauldron of Cultures.* Richmond, VA: Time-Life Books, 1995.

Tom, Patricia Vettel. "Bad Boys: Bruce Davidson's Gang Photographs and Outlaw Masculinity." *Art Journal* 56, no. 2 (Summer 1997): 69–74.

Townsend, Richard F., ed. *The Ancient Americas: Art from Sacred Landscapes.* Chicago: Art Institute of Chicago, 1992.

Tregear, Mary. *Chinese Art.* London: Thames and Hudson, 1991.

Truettner, William H. *The Natural Man Observed: A Study of Catlin's Indian Gallery.* Washington, DC: Smithsonian Institution Press, 1979.

Turner, Jane, ed. *The Dictionary of Art.* New York: Grove, 1996.

Vercoutter, Jean. *The Search for Ancient Egypt.* New York: Harry N. Abrams, 1992.

Vickers, Michael, ed. *Pots and Pans.* Oxford: Oxford University Press, 1986.

Vogel, Susan. *Africa Explores: 20th Century African Art.* New York: Center for African Art, 1991.

Vogel, Susan Mullin. *African Art, Western Eyes.* New Haven and London: Yale University Press, 1997.

Von Blum, Paul. *The Art of Social Conscience.* New York: Universe Books, 1976.

von Hagen, Victor W. *The Desert Kingdoms of Peru.* London: Weidenfeld and Nicolson, 1965.

Vroege, Bas, and Hripsim Visser, eds. *Oppositions: Commitment and Cultural Identity in Contemporary Photography from Japan, Canada, Brazil, the Soviet Union and the Netherlands.* Rotterdam: Uitgeverij, 1990.

Wallach, Alan. *Exhibiting Contradiction: Essays on the Art Museum in the United States.* Amherst: University of Massachusetts Press, 1998.

Wallis, Brian, ed. *Hans Haacke: Unfinished Business.* New York: The New Museum of Contemporary Art; Cambridge: MIT Press, 1986.

Washburn, Dorothy, ed. *Hopi Kachina: Spirit of Life.* San Francisco: California Academy of Sciences, 1980. Distributed by the University of Washington Press.

Weibiao, Hu. *Scenes of the Great Wall.* Beijing: Wenjin Publishing House, 1994.

Weintraub, Linda, ed. *Art What Thou Eat: Images of Food in American Art.* Mount Kisco, NY: Moyer Bell, 1991.

Wescoat, James L., Jr., and Joachim Wolschke-Bulmahn. *Mughal Gardens: Sources, Places, Representations and Prospects.* Washington, DC: Dumbarton Oaks Research Library and Collection, 1996.

Wheat, Ellen Harkins. *Jacob Lawrence: American Painter.* Seattle: University of Washington Press, 1986.

Willett, Frank. *African Art.* New York: Thames and Hudson, 1993.

———. *Ife in the History of West African Sculpture.* New York: McGraw-Hill, 1967.

Willis, Deborah, ed. *Picturing Us: African American Identity in Photography.* New York: New Press, 1994.

Willis-Braithwaite, Deborah. *VanDerZee Photographer 1886–1983.* New York: Harry N. Abrams, 1993.

Wilson, David M., and Ole Klindt-Jensen. *Viking Art.* Minneapolis: University of Minnesota Press, 1980.

Wilson, Sir David M., ed. *The Collections of the British Museum.* Cambridge: Cambridge University Press, 1989.

Wingert, Paul S. *An Outline of Oceanic Art.* Cambridge, MA: University Prints, 1970.

———. *Art of the South Pacific.* New York: Columbia University Press, 1946.

Winkelmann-Rhein, Gertraude. *The Paintings and Drawings of Jan "Flower" Bruegel.* New York: Harry N. Abrams, 1968.

Witherspoon, Gary. *Language and Art of the Navajo Universe.* Ann Arbor: University of Michigan Press, 1977.

Wolff, Janet. *The Social Production of Art.* New York: New York University Press, 1984.

Yau, John. "Hung Liu [exhibition at] Nahan Contemporary." *Artforum* (March 1990):162.

Yenne, Bill, and Susan Garratt. *North American Indians.* China: Ottenheimer, 1994.

Yood, James. *Feasting: A Celebration of Food in Art.* New York: Universe Publishing, 1992.

Zarnecki, George. *Art of the Medieval World.* New York: Harry N. Abrams, 1975.

Zelanski, Paul, and Mary Pat Fisher. *Design Principles and Problems.* Fort Worth, TX: Harcourt Brace College Publishers, 1996.

Zelevansky, Lynn, et al. *Love Forever: Yayoi Kusama 1958–1968.* Los Angeles: Los Angeles County Museum of Art, 1998.

Zigrosser, Carl. *Prints and Drawings of Käthe Kollwitz.* New York: Dover, 1969.

Credits

Index